China's Changing Population

China's Changing Population

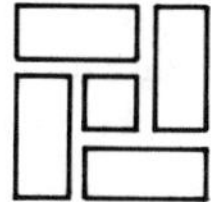

Judith Banister

Stanford University Press 1987
Stanford, California

Stanford University Press
Stanford, California

Printed in the United States of America

CIP data appear at the end of the book

For Kim, Adrian, and Dawn,
who made it possible
to combine productivity
and the fullness of life

Preface

THIS BOOK is an attempt to describe and explain the momentous population changes that have taken place in the People's Republic of China since its founding in 1949. The cut-off point for incorporating newly available information in the analysis was January 1985. More current data and sources would perhaps change some small details in the book, but would not substantially alter the assessments and conclusions reached here.

In writing this book for a broad audience, the author has excluded some of the detailed descriptions of demographic techniques used, assumptions made, and Sinological fine points dear to the hearts of China scholars and demographers. Where undocumented generalizations are made, they are based on some demographic sophistication and a decade of studying the population of the People's Republic of China. Therefore, though any given assertion might turn out to be incorrect, it is not frivolously made. Readers who may wish to delve more deeply into any particular topic addressed in this book are welcome to write the author in care of Stanford University Press.

The book was written over a period of six years while the author was simultaneously fulfilling other job requirements. Several times it was almost in final form, ready to be handed to the eager staff at Stanford Press, when the Chinese government and statistical organizations released thirty years' worth of crucial demographic data that had to be incorporated into the manuscript. The author wishes to thank the unparalleled editor of Stanford Press, J. G. Bell, for his unaccustomed patience in the face of these circumstances beyond our control. Also worthy of note are the editors who monitored and pored over the manuscript for longer than they would have preferred, John Feneron and Andrew L. Alden.

The research derives from the author's Ph.D. dissertation for Stanford University, and subsequent research was carried out at the China Branch of the U.S. Bureau of the Census, whose precious library collection and data files are a tribute to the work of the China Branch's resource specialist and translator Florence Yuan. Her thorough search for relevant source materials and highly skilled translation work were crucial to the success of this research effort. The author would also like to thank John Aird for allowing her full use of his research files.

The entire manuscript was typed by Andrea Miles, whose excellent and dedicated work was critical for the accuracy of the published book. She also generated most of the tables and graphs by computer. Beverly Honda typed part of an earlier draft. Previous drafts of all or some of the chapters were carefully and critically read by John Aird, Samuel Baum, Arthur Wolf, Eduardo Arriaga, Barbara Torrey, and Haitung King. Their insights helped eliminate many errors, misinterpretations, and confusions in the manuscript. Any problems that remain are the sole responsibility of the author.

Computer assistance was provided by Peter Johnson, Peter Way, Eduardo Arriaga, Victoria Ho, Frank Hobbs, and Jack Gibson. The author would also like to thank the East-West Population Institute in Hawaii and the U.S. Bureau of the Census in Washington, D.C., for permitting her to continue work on the book while carrying out her other duties as an employee. Neither organization bears any responsibility for the analysis or conclusions expressed in the book.

J.B.

Contents

Tables and Figures

TABLES

FIGURES

PEOPLE'S REPUBLIC OF
CHINA
Urumqi
XINJIANG
GANSU
AFGHANISTAN
PAKISTAN
QINGHAI
Xining
XIZANG
(TIBET)
INDIA
NEPAL
Lhasa
SICHUAN
BHUTAN
BANGLADESH
Kunming
YUNNAN
BURMA
BAY OF BENGAL
LAOS
THAILAND

SOVIET UNION
MONGOLIA
NEI MONGOL
HEILONGJIANG
Harbin
JILIN
Changchun
Shenyang
LIAONING
NORTH KOREA
SEA OF JAPAN
Hohhot
Huang He (Yellow River)
BEIJING
TIANJIN
SOUTH KOREA
JAPAN
Yinchuan
Taiyuan
Shijiazhuang
HEBEI
NINGXIA
SHANXI
Jinan
YELLOW SEA
Lanzhou
SHANDONG
Xian
Zhengzhou
JIANGSU
SHAANXI
HENAN
ANHUI
Nanjing
SHANGHAI
Hefei
HUBEI
Changjiang (Yangzi River)
Chengdu
Wuhan
Hangzhou
EAST CHINA SEA
ZHEJIANG
Nanchang
Changsha
HUNAN
JIANGXI
Fuzhou
Guiyang
FUJIAN
GUIZHOU
TAIWAN
GUANGDONG
GUANGXI
Guangzhou
Nanning
HONG KONG
VIETNAM
SOUTH CHINA SEA
Hainan
PHILIPPINES

China's Changing Population

1

Introduction

The people's republic of China (PRC) since its inception has set startling precedents in managing its great and burgeoning population. Some innovative policies have been relatively successful, such as the Chinese government's determination to minimize, control, and channel urbanization. Other pacesetting developments have been China's reduction of deaths from infectious disease, and its delivery of primary health care using paramedics, or "barefoot doctors," as the base of a rural cooperative health system. On the other hand, some population policies have been very unpopular, and a few have been repudiated or quietly reversed. For instance, the government's insistence that young adults put off marriage until age 23 or 25 in rural areas (and even later in the cities) was partly successful but met with much dissatisfaction until the policy was changed in 1981. Similarly, the policy of forcing urban-born city residents to move to rural or remote frontier areas had to be dropped in the late 1970's owing to widespread popular resistance.

But these innovations pale before the unprecedented control of fertility (which means actual births rather than fecundity, or potential to bear children) exercised by the PRC's government during the 1970's and early 1980's. China has instituted and sustained the world's first nationwide compulsory family planning program that has lasted more than a few years. During 1975–77, India tried a compulsory sterilization program that provoked popular outrage, helped topple the government of Indira Gandhi, and set back the struggle to control India's population growth. This traumatic experience prompted the generalization in the population field that compulsory family planning is more likely to bring down the government than the birth rate. But whereas India failed, China has succeeded so far in persuading some couples and forcing many others to use birth control techniques and drastically limit their fertility. If a massive backlash does not occur, then the world may learn that forced fertility control can rapidly reduce population growth and keep it at a low level, at least in a country that has a highly organized, authoritarian government reaching into local areas. Will the Chinese model of compulsory birth control prompt other countries to abandon the principle that each couple's acceptance of birth control must be completely voluntary? If government control of childbearing continues to work in China, then it is likely that more developing nations will opt for this path.

China's government is also the first in the world to attempt to popularize the ideal of a one-child family. Other governments, realizing that the concept of raising only one child is anathema to most couples, have been content to promote the two- or three-child family. In promoting this unpopular one-child policy, the Chinese government has recourse to compulsion to assure compliance. So far no other country has tried imposing such a stringent limit, but the idea of encouraging the one-child family is beginning to catch on elsewhere, for example in Bangladesh, where an Association for the Promotion of the One-Child Family was founded in 1981.[1]

Given the drastic nature of China's attempts to solve its population problems, one would suppose that these problems are uniquely grave. Indeed, in some ways China's population problems are more serious than those of most other developing nations. In the first place, the People's Republic of China is the world's most populous country: within its borders live over one-fifth of the world's people.* Of the total population in the world's less developed countries, almost one-third resides in China. Whatever population problems China has are magnified by its enormous size.

In the second place, China has been blessed with fertile lands and a history of many centuries of highly organized government. This combination favored population growth and resulted in extremely dense settlements on the arable land by the middle of the nineteenth century. Therefore, the PRC upon its founding in 1949 inherited a huge population densely packed in agricultural areas, and the new government needed to immediately increase agricultural production in order to guarantee that these people's basic needs would be met and to raise living standards.

* From the seventeenth century onward the island of Taiwan was settled by migrants from China and therefore was considered part of China. But since 1895 it has been politically separate from the mainland, and both have followed separate paths during the twentieth century. Taiwan was controlled and administered by Japan from 1895 to 1945, then given to the Nationalist Chinese government (Guomindang), which was battling the Communist armies for control of the Chinese mainland. The defeated Nationalists fled to Taiwan in 1949 and since then have maintained a separate government. Therefore, all data for Taiwan have been excluded from this study, even though both the government of the PRC and the government of Taiwan agree that Taiwan is part of China.

Some further historical background information is necessary for an understanding of demographic conditions in China as of 1949.

A Brief History of China's Population

The Chinese empire took a population count in 2 A.D. and others at irregular intervals thereafter. Table 1.1, which traces China's population over the last two millennia, is based on these census and registration counts, adjusted when necessary.[2] A striking feature of China's demographic history is that the population apparently fluctuated between 37 and 60 million for a thousand years, showing no consistent trend. The first recorded instance of sustained population growth (averaging an estimated 1.2 percent a year) took place in the last half of the eleventh century under the Song (Sung) Dynasty, but this trend was reversed by subsequent centuries of dynastic struggle, civil war, Mongol invasion, and bubonic plague. Then, starting from the early years of the Ming Dynasty in the late fourteenth century, China experienced six centuries of population growth. Only twice was this growth checked, once because of the fall of the Ming Dynasty in the early seventeenth century, and once during the Taiping Rebellion that hastened the decline of the Qing (Ch'ing) Dynasty in the late nineteenth century. In neither instance are population statistics adequate to document the temporary reversal. The period of most rapid population growth (1749–1851) saw more than a doubling of China's population in a century. Growth in this period averaged 0.9 percent per year. Population pressure on China's arable land became a matter of official concern during the Ming and Qing Dynasties, prompting several different dynastic efforts to increase food production and feed the growing population. The amount of land under cultivation multiplied about 4.5 times, high-yielding rice seeds were introduced from abroad, new food crops were imported from the Americas, grain storage was emphasized, and irrigation works were expanded.[3] The recognition of population problems and the adoption of policies designed to solve them began well before the twentieth century.

The century between 1851 and 1949 was one of societal breakdown, dynastic decline and collapse, imperialist penetration, armed invasion, and civil war. The recorded population grew from about 429.5 million in 1851 to 582.6 million in 1953, an annual average population growth rate of only 0.3 percent; in fact, as the 1953 census was very likely a more complete count than the 1851 population registration data, the growth rate was probably even lower.

To comprehend fully the profound demographic changes that have taken place in the PRC since 1949 would require an accurate picture of

TABLE 1.1
Historical Population Estimates, A.D. 2–1953

Date	Dynasty	Persons counted	Implied persons per household	Adjusted to current PRC boundaries (millions)
2	Han	59,594,978	4.9	
88	Han	43,356,367	5.8	
105	Han	53,256,229	5.8	
125	Han	49,690,789	5.2	
140	Han	49,150,220	5.1	
144	Han	49,730,550	5.0	
145	Han	49,524,183	5.0	
146	Han	47,566,772	5.1	
156	Han	56,486,856	5.3	
606	Sui	46,019,956	5.2	
705	Tang	37,140,000	6.0	
726	Tang	41,419,712	5.9	
732	Tang	45,431,265	5.8	
734	Tang	46,285,161	5.8	
740	Tang	48,143,609	5.7	
742	Tang	48,909,800	5.7	
754	Tang	52,880,488	5.8	
755	Tang	52,919,309	5.9	
1290	Yuan (Mongol)	58,834,711	4.5	
1291	Yuan	59,848,964	4.5	
1381	Ming	59,873,305	5.6	
1393	Ming	60,545,813	5.7	
1749	Qing	177,495,000		176.5
1776	Qing	268,238,000		267.0
1791	Qing	304,354,000		303.0
1811	Qing	358,610,000		357.0
1821	Qing	355,540,000		353.7
1831	Qing	395,821,000		393.8
1841	Qing	413,457,000		411.3
1851	Qing	431,896,000		429.5
1953	PRC	582,603,417		582.6

Date	Dynasty	Persons counted	Households counted	Recorded persons per household	Adjusted population (millions)
1014	Song	21,996,965	9,055,729	2.4	54.3
1029	Song	26,054,238	10,562,689	2.5	63.4
1048	Song	21,730,064	10,723,695	2.0	64.3
1065	Song	29,077,273	12,904,783	2.3	77.4
1075	Song	23,807,165	15,684,129	1.5	94.1
1086	Song	40,072,606	17,957,029	2.2	107.7
1094	Song	42,566,243	19,120,921	2.2	114.7
1103	Song	45,981,845	20,524,065	2.2	123.1
1193–95[a]	S. Song	27,845,085	12,302,873	2.3	122.3
	Jin	48,490,400	7,223,400	6.7	

China's marriage, fertility, mortality, and migration patterns in the several decades prior to 1949. Although no satisfactory benchmark data exist, we do have useful information from one large survey that provides an approximate demographic picture of rural China twenty years before the PRC was founded.

During 1929–31, interviewers gathered population data from farm households as part of a survey of land utilization in China.[4] The survey did not cover urban areas or rural families in nonagricultural occupations. The families surveyed thus were not a representative sample of the whole population of China, but detailed tabulations survive from 119 localities in 16 provinces, containing records of 46,601 rural agricultural families. A group of demographers at Princeton University who recently reanalyzed the data concluded that Chinese rural farm families in 1929–31 had early and universal marriage but only moderate levels of marital fertility.[5] The proportion of people who married was over 99 percent; the average age of women at their first marriage was 17.5 years and that of men was 21.3. Such a marriage pattern is found in many Asian populations.

The age-specific marital fertility pattern of these farm families followed a standard natural fertility pattern, indicating that they did not practice contraception. Yet the level of fertility was far below the number of births that are theoretically possible with early and universal marriage. The total fertility rate was estimated to be 5.5 children per woman and the crude birth rate 41 per thousand population, compared to the total fertility rate of 10.8 and the crude birth rate of 55 that have been seen in high-fertility populations. (Demographic terms such as "age-specific marital fertility pattern," "natural fertility," "total fertility rate," and "crude birth rate" are defined in the Glossary of Demographic Terms, Appendix B.) Was this moderate fertility level typical of China before 1949 or was it unusual in some way? The survey was taken in parts of China that were relatively calm and prosperous, not involved in active warfare, and rather firmly but recently under the control of the Guomindang (Kuomintang) government. Respondents were asked the number of children they had ever borne, so women were being asked about their fertility during the decline and fall of the Qing Dynasty, which ended in 1911, and the cha-

---

SOURCE OF TABLE 1.1: Durand (1960).

NOTE: Large-scale migration to Taiwan began in the sixteenth century. Taiwan's population is estimated to have been 1 million in 1749, rising gradually to 3 million in 1900. See Taeuber (1944). Taiwan's estimated population is deducted from Qing Dynasty counts above.

Population counts from the Song Dynasty must be adjusted, because only some males were counted, totaling two persons per household. Durand makes the adjustment by assuming 6.0 persons per household throughout the Song period, as shown in the table.

[a]In 1126 the Song Dynasty was pushed to the south by the victory of the Jin Dynasty in the north. The adjusted population total of 122.3 million for 1193–95 is an estimate for all China derived from the recorded counts reported here, with an adjusted population total of 73.8 million for the Southern Song.

otic warlord period that followed. It is possible that civil war, food shortages, and other dislocations during the years before 1929–31 depressed the fertility of these families. Fertility was probably even lower in places where active warfare or famine were prevalent prior to the survey. But fertility may have been higher in urban areas, among the nonagricultural population, or in more peaceful parts of China. For instance, it was calculated from a 1930 Japanese census that rural areas of Manchuria (then a part of the Japanese empire) had a crude birth rate of 47 per thousand population, and a vital registration experiment in a rural area of Jiangsu province recorded a high birth rate of 45 per thousand population during 1931–35.[6]

China's fertility level from the mid-nineteenth to the mid-twentieth century may have been on average somewhat higher or lower than that found in the 1929–31 survey. But a total fertility rate of 5–6 births per woman, corresponding to a crude birth rate just above 40 per thousand population, is a reasonable fertility estimate for traditional Chinese culture. Throughout Chinese history certain customs have kept fertility well below the theoretical maximum. A long period of breastfeeding depressed postpartum fecundity and delayed subsequent births. Sexual taboos lowered coital frequency. Long separations between spouses were considered acceptable. A ban on the remarriage of widows, when men as well as women tended to die young, caused many women to cease childbearing long before their fecundity declined.

Although the fertility of the Chinese farm families of 1929–31 was moderate in comparison to other non-contracepting populations, estimated mortality was very high. The Princeton group estimated that only about 52 percent of all male deaths and 56 percent of all female deaths were reported; after adjusting the raw data on deaths, they estimated that the expectation of life at birth was only 23.7 years for females and 24.6 years for males. The resulting crude death rate, 41.5 per thousand population, was slightly higher than the crude birth rate. Infant mortality, in particular, was extremely high: it was estimated that some 30 percent of all babies died in their first year.

The 1929–31 rural survey provides the best information available on China's demographic situation early in this century. At least among rural agricultural families, which constituted the great majority of China's families, marriage was universal and early, fertility was moderately high, and mortality at all ages was very high.

In 1982, China's government carried out a nationwide fertility survey that included asking women up to age 67 about the births they had had during their lives.[7] Their responses indicated that fertility was slightly depressed in China during the war years 1940–45, when the total fertility rates were in the range 5.0–5.3 births per woman. In the late 1940's, when the Japanese invasion had ended but civil war continued, the rates rebounded to 5.5–6.1 births per woman. These data are consistent with the notion that China's fertility stayed in the range 5–6 births per woman, at least during this century and possibly in other recent centuries.

After six centuries of almost uninterrupted population growth, China was the world's most populous nation. For several centuries, increasing population pressure had led to more intensive cultivation and the tilling of marginal lands.[8] As late as 1957, a year for which agricultural production data and total population data are available, China's per capita grain supply was good in comparison to most developing countries and approximately matched that of Japan.[9] China's food situation was not desperate.

However, the very success of Chinese agriculture in recent centuries had permitted high population density on the arable land. As the most productive land became fully utilized, it was no longer possible to expand the cultivated area enough to provide for the increasing population, as it had been since the fourteenth century. Furthermore, as China approached the limits of traditional agriculture, it became more and more difficult to increase yields through traditional methods. Expensive technological inputs like chemical fertilizer were required. Meanwhile China's population began to grow at an unprecedented rate during the 1950's. The historical relationship between population growth and increasing food production had weakened. No longer did more agricultural labor mean a corresponding increase in food production; instead, China's government discovered, raising food production to pace or overtake population growth became extraordinarily difficult.

International Perspectives on China's Population

While in some ways China's population problems may be unusually serious, in others they are wholly typical of those found in many other developing countries since the 1940's. Demographic and related socioeconomic changes in China have had strong parallels elsewhere, notwithstanding China's ancient civilization and its communist government.

During the decades after World War II, many poor countries of the world became independent of the colonial powers. China had never been fully colonized, but it had been humiliated and invaded, and its politics and foreign trade had been under foreign influence in the century before 1949. The success of the Chinese communist revolution coincided with similar attempts in many countries to throw off outside influences and chart their own course of development.

All of these new governments had the task of establishing their legitimacy. They had the powerful force of nationalism on their side, but in addition they needed to bring tangible benefits to their citizens to foster popular loyalty. Therefore, most developing countries' governments have promoted industrialization and expanded education as key long-term development aims. And in order to directly and quickly enhance the quality of life, they have tried to reduce death rates dramatically and improve the people's health. In the 1940's and 1950's, governments were aided in these endeavors by advances in public health and epidemic disease control, spraying of DDT for the control of malaria, the invention of antibiotics, and a host of new preventive and curative medical techniques. Another important factor in reducing mortality was that strong governments were able to suppress much of the internecine warfare and random violence that had been a constant threat to life. In many countries of Asia and Latin America, and in some countries of the Middle East and Africa, crude death rates dropped precipitously during the 1950's and the expectation of life at birth rose significantly.[10] By the period 1960–64, the developing world had achieved an estimated crude death rate of 20 per thousand population per year.[11] This was far below the crude death rate in those areas before World War II, which must have been well over 30 per thousand population. After an initial skepticism, population and health specialists accepted as genuine this mortality decline of unprecedented speed.

The same startling mortality decline happened in China. The cessation of civil war and the restoration of civil order combined with immunization programs, massive sanitation campaigns, and epidemic-control measures to produce better mortality conditions than had ever before been achieved in China.

In the 1950's it was not easy to foresee that this rapid and worldwide improvement in mortality would bring about explosive population growth rates in the developing world and result in a geometric increase in the world's population. This occurred because people did not immediately comprehend what had happened to mortality and because they found it difficult to change their fertility attitudes and practices instantaneously to adjust to the new mortality situation. By the early 1960's Asia's population was growing at 2.0 percent a year, Africa's at 2.3 percent, and Latin America's at 2.8 percent.[12] During the next decade, 1965–74, slight declines in crude birth rates in some developing regions were offset by continuing declines in crude death rates. The result was nearly steady or even rising rates of natural population increase.[13] The world had a high annual growth rate of 1.9–2.0 percent during the 1960–74 period, which if continued would double the world's population in 35 years.[14] Such rapid population growth neutralized many of the significant gains made by developing countries. For example, many countries achieved absolute increases of 15 or even 30 percent in agricultural production between the early 1960's and the early 1970's, but found that their production per capita fell, stayed constant, or rose only imperceptibly.[15] Continuing high fertility combined with declining infant and child mortality also resulted in very young populations with rapidly increasing numbers of children. Providing basic elementary education for all these children has proved an elusive goal in many countries; in some developing nations, educational costs are a greater proportion of the government budget than any other item. Now that large numbers of young people born in the 1950's and 1960's are reaching working and childbearing ages, many developing countries are experiencing rising unemployment, in spite of vigorous development efforts, and are trying to combat the surge of births that these young adults threaten to produce.

China also experienced rapid population growth during the 1950's, the 1960's, and the early 1970's. As elsewhere, continued high fertility and declining or low mortality underlay this phenomenon. In China as in other developing areas, rapid population growth strained the agricultural and other parts of the economy, thus dashing hopes for quick per capita economic gains. China has had to divert considerable resources to education of its youth during the last few decades, and the effort has met with some success. Now, however, unemployment and underemployment of young adults are causing dislocations in the economy at the same time the government is challenged with minimizing their fertility in order to control population growth in the next decade.

During the 1950's China and India, the world's two most populous countries, first came to realize the danger inherent in high population growth rates and established family planning programs. In the 1960's governments of some other developing nations were able to overcome strong pronatalist tendencies in their popular traditions and introduced programs to encourage family planning. But most governments were slow to grasp the serious problems that rapid population growth was causing in developing nations. Some governments in poor countries did not see a 2 or 3 percent annual population growth rate as a problem, and some still do not. When the United Nations hosted the World Population Conference in 1974, some developing countries scoffed at the idea that rapid population growth was causing them any problems, and China joined them for ideological reasons.[16] They blamed their economic difficulties on imperialism and exploitation. Nevertheless, many leaders of developing nations were made aware of the demographic changes they were experiencing. Since then, quite a few have introduced family planning programs. By 1982, eight years later, 39 developing countries with 78 percent of the population of developing areas had an explicit official policy to reduce their population growth rates, and 33 countries with another 16 percent of the developing world population officially supported family planning activities, ostensibly for nondemographic reasons.[17]

The official encouragement of family planning and the provision of birth control devices do not guarantee a decline in fertility, however. While it was relatively easy to reduce the high death rates in developing countries, traditional high birth rates have been resistant to change. Some countries that introduced family planning programs during the 1950's and 1960's still have not reported a significant fertility decline. A few small developing areas did greatly reduce their birth rates and natural population increase rates during the 1960's, in particular Taiwan, South Korea, Hong Kong, Singapore, Sri Lanka, Fiji, Mauritius, and some other islands. The most populous developing nations did not register rapid fertility reduction before 1970.

Modest fertility declines were achieved during the 1970's in both Indonesia and India, however.[18] Indonesia had had a total fertility rate of 5.6 births per woman in 1967–70, which declined to 5.2 in 1971–75 and further to 4.7 as of 1977–79. The country's crude birth rate dropped from 41 per thousand population in 1971 to 35 in 1980, but the natural increase rate did not change because the death rate declined from 18 to 12 during the same period. India had a birth rate decline from about 39 per thousand population in 1970 to 35 in 1980, but the death rate dropped by 4 per thousand population, leaving the natural increase rate unchanged as in Indonesia.

Some populous developing countries, including China, Thailand, Mexico, and Brazil, achieved significant reductions in their population growth rates during the 1970's.[19] Of these, the most pronounced drop was in the People's Republic of China. This book will describe and document the extraordinary fertility decline that has taken place there. It now appears that China is one of the first developing countries to reduce its annual population growth rate to below 1 percent and may be the first to reach a zero growth rate.

In outline, China's demographic transition is similar to that in many other parts of the developing world. Rapid mortality decline in the 1950's was followed by peak population growth rates for two or more decades, and now fertility declines have begun or are beginning in China and elsewhere. Therefore we can go a long way toward understanding China by investigating demographic changes in other areas. But China differs from most other developing areas in some important ways. For example, China's current fertility decline may be more rapid than in any other developing country, or at least any other populous and heavily rural one.

China's urbanization and internal migration patterns, too, have been distinctive. When demographic trends in the PRC diverge radically from those in most other countries, we must look for explanations in what sets China apart, such as its particular development path or socialist political system.

This book is an examination of demographic changes affecting the more than one-fifth of the world's people who live in China. The PRC is in the midst of a rapid demographic transition, the shift from the high fertility and mortality of the past to the low fertility and mortality of the future. Tracing the population changes in China is important if we wish to understand that country at all. Moreover, we cannot ignore China's lessons for other nations. If this most populous country can achieve advanced mortality and fertility conditions while still at a relatively early stage of economic development, perhaps there will be other countries choosing to adopt parts of the Chinese model and adapt these policies to their own national conditions. Finally, if we can ascertain China's demographic trends, we have added the largest missing piece to our knowledge of world population dynamics. That helps us assess the unprecedented global population changes of recent decades, decide the world's present position in its great demographic transition, and better predict its course during the next few decades.

2

The Quality of China's Population Data

A MAJOR transformation took place in the quality and availability of China's collected demographic data beginning in 1982. For over 30 years after 1949, the population statistics collected were seldom published. The field of demography was taboo, so that important demographic indicators were not measured, there were no representative sample surveys, and weak analyses of population matters were the norm. Now that some crucial demographic data from these three decades have finally been released, it is possible to conclude that some of the collected data were of high quality, while most were imperfect but still usable for analysis of population trends. In 1982, China conducted a census that was more comprehensive and carefully planned than the previous two, and began full release of the collected data as soon as feasible. The census was followed by China's first retrospective fertility survey that was reasonably representative of the country as a whole. Again, the collected statistics were published as fast as possible in some detail. Because the field of demography became respectable in China beginning in 1978, China's own demographers have recently been allowed to develop their demographic skills and have begun producing good analyses of the collected statistics.

Statistical Trends Since 1949

Prior to 1949, statistical data for China above the local level in almost any category were of questionable validity and frequently useless. For the first two years after the founding of the PRC, statistics remained undeveloped. Then in late 1952, the State Statistical Bureau (SSB) was established and began to build a modern statistical system in China on the Soviet model. Progress in the gathering of economic and population statistics was good during the First Five-Year Plan period, 1952–57.[1] The

SSB attempted to build a system of objective statistical reporting in order to monitor and support the growth of the planned economy. By 1957, the SSB had achieved centralized control over the quality and supply of important national statistics. But some serious problems remained. First, the SSB excluded statisticians trained before 1949 or educated in the West, exacerbating the critical shortage of competent statistical personnel. Second, the SSB followed a policy of suppressing almost all official data in the name of national security. Third, sampling methods were not applied and most collected statistics depended on reporting from all relevant units.

China's statistical system began to disintegrate in early 1958 and did not fully recover until over two decades later. Criticism of the SSB's work, requested by its Director in May 1957, soon was violently denounced in a thought-reform campaign, and further suggestions for improving China's statistics were silenced. The statistical system then became one of the many casualties of the Great Leap Forward, Mao Zedong's campaign to increase production in all sectors of the economy through frenzied escalation of physical labor demanded of the population. It was decided that politics should take command over the statistical reporting system, because figures collected by Communist Party cadres assisted by the masses of people would be more accurate than figures compiled by statistical workers. The result was gross exaggeration of production figures in 1958 and breakdown of much statistical reporting for several years. Inflated production and consumption statistics hid the disastrous consequences of the Great Leap Forward's economic policies, lulled national leaders into complacency, and resulted in fatal delays in implementing crisis relief efforts. Statistical operations at all levels were still seriously defective as of 1962.

After several years of economic crisis and famine, China's government once again tried to build an objective statistical system. In July 1961, professional statisticians were again appointed to head the SSB after a two-year hiatus.[2] The following 1981 report by the late Chinese economist Sun Yefang provides an unusually candid description of the short-lived statistical reforms of the early 1960's and the chaos that followed:

> In order to draw a lesson from this experience, which was paid for with a high price of blood, the Central Committee of the Chinese Communist Party and the State Council made "the decision on consolidating statistics work" in 1962 in accordance with the instructions of Comrade Liu Shaoqi and Comrade Zhou Enlai. It was required that a powerful, centralized, and unified statistics system be set up as quickly as possible. . . . Comrade Zhou Enlai even added one more point to the "decision": The party and government departments were forbidden to change statistical figures. In this way the statistics system of the whole country was soon

consolidated, the state statistics system and methods were better implemented, and the accuracy and speed in gathering statistical figures were substantially raised. Unfortunately, even on the eve of "the Great Cultural Revolution," Comrade Wang Sihua, then the head of the State Statistics Bureau, was being criticized. It was alleged that his carrying out the above-mentioned decision of the party Central Committee and the State Council was the implementing of "a revisionist" line and the "seizing of power from the party," and that he was "asserting his independence"! In those ten chaotic years nearly all statistics organs at different levels throughout the country were disbanded, the staff were transferred, and large quantities of materials were burned. The statistics work of the whole country was suspended for almost three years. It has not yet regained its strength. At present the strength of statistics departments at or above the county level throughout the country is only about 76 percent of that of 1965, and the strength of the State Statistics Bureau is less than that of 1976. The statistics bureaus of many cities and counties have not yet been reestablished. In some counties only two or three people are handling the statistics work of the whole county, and most people's communes in the countryside do not have full-time statistics workers. Therefore problems which exist in varying degrees such as inaccurate statistical figures, incomplete statistical content, unsound statistical methods, low level in statistical analysis, and statistical materials falling short of the demands of the state leadership and economic administration are even more difficult to solve.[3]

The Great Proletarian Cultural Revolution that began in 1966 was the most wrenching of a succession of struggles led by Mao Zedong to purify the thoughts and actions of China's people and rectify perceived errors in the direction the country's revolution had taken. Intellectuals and professionals, including statisticians, were politically suspect. Those treated least harshly were merely reassigned from their regular work to a physical labor job for a few years. But many were harassed, attacked, imprisoned, maimed, or murdered. After the death of Mao in late 1976 and the imprisonment of his leading supporters, the "gang of four," intellectual work was slowly revived and increased in status. Statisticians resumed their work and many new statistical personnel were trained, in an attempt to make up for lost decades of statistical development. In general, however, China's statisticians remain cautious about making any political errors in what they say or write, mindful of the decades of vilification to which they and their colleagues have been subjected. They are placed in an awkward role. The political leaders have recognized that statistical concepts and techniques from nonsocialist countries must be introduced, so that China can accurately monitor its progress or lack of progress toward the achievement of its ambitious development goals.[4] To learn the meaning of these concepts and how to measure and apply them, China's statisticians need to receive training from foreign statisticians and engage in joint research with their colleagues abroad. But China's government warns its skilled personnel in all the social sciences against working closely with foreigners, for fear of the contamination of China's elite by capitalist or democratic ideas.

In January 1984 a new national Statistics Law took effect, superseding the "Provisional Regulations for Statistical Work" that had been issued in 1963.[5] The content and emphasis of this law highlight the problems that continue to plague the gathering, reporting, and analysis of economic and social statistics in China. The 1984 Statistics Law strongly concentrates responsibility for the conduct of surveys and collection of all kinds of statistics in the hands of the State Statistical Bureau and its provincial branches. The SSB is ordered to modernize data gathering and data transmission, and to standardize nationwide all the definitions of statistical concepts and indices, the methods of computation, the category classifications, and the survey questionnaire designs. Local and provincial units, as well as other parts of the government, are subject to the supervision of the SSB if they need to conduct surveys and collect statistics, in order to avoid replication and duplication of effort, but especially to stop the previous proliferation of ill-conceived, poorly designed, nonrepresentative sample surveys that were useless for measuring what they were supposed to measure.

The Statistics Law also stresses that all statistical positions are to be filled by responsible and qualified people, and that if they need further training, professional study classes should be organized for them. The independence of statistical personnel is emphasized, and all political interference with the work of statisticians and the figures they report is now, for the first time, illegal. Cadres are expressly forbidden to falsify any statistics reported from their unit, a practice that has been common at the local level for decades according to press reports. Local officials are also prohibited from concealing statistics from higher level authorities, resisting the reporting requirements, or intentionally delaying the submission of data. As summarized in the Statistics Law, all government, business, and private organizations are required "to furnish statistical data without exaggeration, concealment, resistance, delay, falsification, or change."

There is one aspect of the Statistics Law that will continue to impede the open dissemination of collected statistics. While the law mandates regular publication of statistics, it also forbids the release of any data until political approval has been secured. In practice, the highest levels of China's government have had to give their explicit approval for the release of every national statistical figure in recent decades. The policy that every datum is a state secret until expressly declassified has stopped or greatly delayed the publication of most statistics. In the early 1980's, it appears that the government has been willing to approve the publication of whole categories of statistics, such as all data from the 1982 population census, thus expediting the dissemination of collected information. But the Statistics Law is stern in its prohibition of the release of any figure without formal approval, which continues to hamper the analytical work, writing, and publication of articles by China's statisticians. For instance, a PRC statistician puzzled by some anomalies in the collected statistics cannot confer with a foreign colleague about how best to resolve the discrepancies and discover the truth behind the problematic figures, if this would require carrying out calculations together on data not approved for release. A statistician who did so would be violating the following stipulations in the 1984 Statistics Law:

> Article 13. The State Statistical Bureau and the statistical organs of the people's governments of provinces, autonomous regions, and independent municipalities are to publish their statistics periodically in accordance with state regulations. Statistical data to be published by all areas, departments, and units must be checked and ratified by the statistical organs and the responsible statistical personnel . . . and the units must abide by the state-stipulated procedure of requesting approval.
>
> Article 14. Statistical data involving state secrets must be protected. . . .
>
> Article 25. Administrative disciplinary action is to be taken against those persons in positions of leadership and persons with direct responsibility when one of the following serious violations is committed: . . . 6. Publishing statistical data without verification and approval in violation of the stipulations of this law; and 7. Violating the stipulations of this law concerning the protection of secrets.

Population Statistics

Though the whole field of statistics was held in some contempt by Maoist leaders, China's government has almost always recognized the practical benefits of knowing how many people China had, who they were, where they were, how many people were entitled to grain or cloth rations, how many births and deaths there were each year, how fast the population was growing, and how fast urbanization was proceeding. In order to discover these basic demographic facts, population censuses were conducted in 1953, 1964, and 1982. More frequently collected statistics were also needed to monitor ongoing population trends. During the 1950's, a population registration system was gradually introduced to record the permanent residence location of people, as well as births and deaths among them.[6] Local political units were supposed to report their total population size and the total number of births and deaths from each calendar year early in the next year. Such data were to be compiled upward by county governments followed by provincial governments, then reported to the central government. At some point in the late 1950's or the 1960's, these cumulated reports became the basis for China's official figures on its population size and vital rates, but some estimation may always have been necessary to account for local units that did not report. The annual population reporting system has continued to the present. Most of these data, though not without error, can be used to analyze China's population trends, sometimes with adjustment and in some cases without adjustment. But population statistics were so ideologically loaded in the eyes of China's Communist leadership that they were largely unreported between 1959 and 1979.

The problem was that the orthodox Marxist ideology inherited by China's leadership insisted that rapid population growth would not interfere with swift increases in popular living standards under socialism.[7] This dogma was based on the texts of Marx and Engels vehemently denouncing the writings of Thomas Malthus, who had sounded the alarm that continuing population growth would eat up all the surplus that people could produce and keep them in poverty.[8] China's radical leaders inched toward the control of population growth out of obvious necessity, but they were reluctant to abandon the Marxist line on this emotionally charged subject. So they suppressed most statistics that did not show socialist production far outstripping population growth, and those few figures released were presented in the most favorable light possible.

During the first decade after the PRC was founded, there were economic and demographic successes to report, and any continuing economic problems could be attributed to conditions inherited from the past. Production had been so depressed by warfare and economic chaos prior to 1949 that the rehabilitation period through 1952 showed impressive gains. The government was proud of the genuine achievements through the end of the First Five-Year Plan in 1957, particularly the rapid industrialization and the sharp mortality decline taking place. Occasional bits of economic and demographic data were therefore released for domestic and foreign consumption. From the 1953 census results, the government published China's total population size, provincial and rural-urban population distribution, and some details on the age structure. Later, population totals with urban and rural components for 1949–56 and vital rates for selected years were given out. This period culminated in the 1959 publication of *Ten Great Years: Statistics of the Economic and Cultural Achievements of the People's Republic of China*. This small volume included some economic data, mostly in graphic form, and some demographic data, such as population totals by province and for major cities as of yearend 1957.

There followed more than a decade of almost complete statistical blackout on population statistics and most economic statistics. The probable reason for the decision to suppress the collected data was that they no longer documented success under socialism. In particular, China's death rate rose sharply and food production declined steeply during the Great Leap Forward crisis. After the worst was over, the national population growth rate was high, making the real economic gains less impressive on a per capita basis. China even hid the fact that it was taking a census in 1964, and only in 1972 was an undated list of provincial population totals published that was later confirmed to be from a 1964 census.

As the decade of the 1970's began, one province, one city, one rural people's commune after another began to record low mortality and rapidly declining fertility. As these successes became apparent to the central leadership, tidbits of demographic data from such model localities began to be selectively publicized. For some areas, scattered population figures from particular years in the 1960's were reported along with current data to show progress in controlling population growth. As the decade continued, the volume of published data slowly increased, and little by little the historical picture of demographic change as reflected in the official data began to take shape.

During these two decades, until after the 1976 death of Mao Zedong and arrest of the "gang of four," Marxist population orthodoxy was vociferously promoted and defended, even while the government tried to reduce population growth through the family planning program. Any scholar or official who dared mention population growth as a problem was in danger of censure. A highly publicized case was that of Ma Yinchu, President of Beijing University, whose writings on "The New Theory of Population" cost him his position in 1960 and made him the object of attack for a decade and a half. Finally in 1979, at age 98 shortly before his death, Ma received this official apology: "Facts over the past 20 years have proved that his views on the question of population are correct and that the criticisms directed against him are wrong."[9] For this whole period, China's few population specialists were refused access to official population data. Even though some continued to write articles about China's population, they were not allowed to publish their work, and many of these papers were destroyed during the Cultural Revolution of the late 1960's. A Chinese scholarly article described the period 1957 to 1978 as characterized by

> an upsurge of leftist ideology which identified the study of population with the propagation of the Malthusian theory of population. Those engaged in population studies were violently attacked and castigated, and many were even labeled rightists. Since then there has been neither a single individual who dared to tackle the study of population nor a single organization devoted to population research. The problems of tabulating the population increase and the ratio between popula-

tion increase and economic development were not even included in the agenda of state economic planning.[10]

Clinging to Marxist population dogma and suppressing both population statistics and population scholars, while at the same time strongly promoting the control of population growth, led to increasingly awkward official positions in the 1970's. Throughout the 1960's and 1970's, the size of China's population was not divulged from official sources. Whenever a rhetorical population total was called for in a public statement, a severely rounded outdated figure was used. This tactic appeared to be ideologically motivated. For instance, China's official yearend 1972 civilian population size was 867 million, but it was greatly underestimated in the following anti-Malthusian broadcast from 1973: "China's grain output has more than doubled in the past 24 years while population rose a little more than 50 percent. Grain output in 1972 was 240 million tons as against 110 million tons in 1949. The population in the same period topped 700 million compared with upward of 500 million."[11] Until mid-1979, official sources almost always referred to China's population as "800 million" or "over 800 million" or "nearly 800 million," though some sources continued to use "700 million." Meanwhile, the national totals compiled from registration reports but not published were close to or over 900 million people. The reasons for the systematic use of outdated totals are not altogether clear, but the following quotation indicates that the resulting confusion was intentional. In March 1979, Vice-Premier Li Xiannian was asked by a Japanese journalist to clarify the official statistics on China's population. Li answered, "We would like you to use the figure 'some 800 million.' Our population has not reached 1 billion."[12]

Soon thereafter, the veil of secrecy began to be lifted from demographic statistics. In June 1979, the government released its official figures on China's 1978 population size and natural population increase rate. The period since 1979 has been characterized by a rising flood of quantitative and qualitative information that threatens to swamp specialists in China's population. By 1981, not only current data but also retrospective data series were published. As of early 1982, enough of the details of the 1982 census pretests had been published to indicate that for the first time ever the Chinese government was planning to publish most of the results of a census. By late 1983, the government had released 54 tables of data from a 10 percent sample tabulation of census questionnaires, several complete series of historical population statistics, and most of the important results from a national fertility survey conducted in late 1982. Under present policy the release of population data is much more open than in former times but still not completely unrestricted. Statistics on some politically sensitive subjects either do not appear or are delayed for a long time. For instance, data on abortions and infant mortality, carefully gathered in the national fertility survey, were not released when other detailed figures on marriage and fertility were published from the survey.

Since 1978 China has set up 22 regional centers for demographic research and training and has begun to send students abroad for advanced demographic studies. Gradually, newly trained demographers and statisticians have begun to conduct small surveys and analyze the PRC's collected population data. However, as of this writing, Chinese demographers are not free to privately arrange and conduct joint research projects with foreign demographers without prior approval, and apparently they are not free to publish analyses that challenge established government policy.

China's 1982 census and national fertility survey ushered in a new era of great attention to the quality and completeness of collected population statistics. The census was meticulously planned and carried out. After decades of poorly designed "surveys" skewed toward progressive localities, the 1982 fertility survey was designed to be fully representative of the whole country. These massive population investigations were so conscientiously accomplished that they provide a standard by which to judge the previously collected population statistics. In this chapter the quality of China's population data on age structure, sex ratio, and total population size will be evaluated. Subsequent chapters will assess the quality of data on mortality, fertility, urbanization, and other topics.

Census Data on Age-Sex Structure

The PRC has taken three censuses, the latest being that of midyear 1982. The belated release of 1953 and 1964 census data by single year of age and sex, available for the first time in 1983, allows a more thorough analysis of these censuses than was ever before possible. At the end of 1983, age structure data also became available from a 10 percent sample of 1982 census questionnaires.

The analysis of age structure is greatly enhanced by accurate age reporting and impeded by age misreporting. The reporting of age in all three of China's censuses appears to have been extraordinarily accurate compared with age data from other countries. Figures 2.1 through 2.4 graph the recorded ages of males and females in successive censuses. Each cohort, those persons born in the same year, can be traced from the 1953 to the 1964 to the 1982 census to see if a surplus or dearth of persons at a particular age in 1953 is duplicated when the cohort was eleven years older in 1964 and another eighteen years older in 1982. If so, the aberration is probably genuine, resulting from fertility and mortality fluctuations in the past. If not, then age misreporting in one of the censuses is suspected.

In general, age misreporting was a very minor problem in all three censuses, but was slightly more pronounced in 1953 than in 1964 or 1982. For example, both sexes showed a preference for reporting age 18 in 1953 while avoiding ages 15, 16, and 17. In 1964 and 1982, no such heaping on age 18 is visible. Similarly, heaping on age one is apparent, and there is a slight preference for reporting age two as well, for both sexes in 1953 but not in the subsequent two censuses. This means that in 1953 some parents reported an infant as age one or two instead of its true age of less than twelve months. The likely cause of this error is the traditional Chinese custom of calling a baby age "one" at birth and age "two" at the next New Year. In 1953 most of the infants, and in 1964 and 1982 virtually all of the counted infants, were accurately recorded as age "less than one," a tribute to the elaborate procedures devised for enumerators to change an age as reported in the traditional manner into the corresponding age in complete years of life.

In the older ages there were small age misreporting problems in 1953. Males disproportionately reported their age as 55 or 60 and females chose to report age 60 or 70 to slight excess. In 1964 and 1982, even these mild tendencies to misreport age had been overcome.

The age reporting graphed in Figures 2.1 through 2.4 appears so accurate that the results of historical trends in fertility and infant mortality can be seen. For instance, there was a slight dearth of females ages 41 and 42 in 1953, seen again when the same cohorts were ages 52 and 53 in 1964. The deficit of males in the same cohorts can be seen in the age structure of both censuses but is less pronounced than for females.This comparison suggests that China had some reduction in fertility and rise in female infant mortality during the overthrow of the Qing Dynasty and founding of the Republic of China from midyear 1910 to midyear 1912. There is also a shortage of females ages 26 and 27 in 1953 reflected again in 1964 when the same cohorts were ages 37 and 38, and duplicated in 1982 at ages 55 and 56. The male deficit in those age groups parallels the female very closely in all three censuses, suggesting that there was not a surge of female infanticide or selective neglect of female infants but there was a decline in fertility from midyear 1925 to midyear 1927, a period of civil disturbances among warlords and the northern expedition of conquest by Chiang Kai-shek's army to unify China under his rule.

The single year of age data from the 1953 census graphed in Figures 2.1 and 2.3 are incomplete in that they add up to 567.4 million of the total census population of 582.6 million on the China mainland. Missing from the single year data are 8.4 million persons "indirectly surveyed" in remote areas, and 6.8 million persons in the military or living in military compounds, the latter group including 5.6 million males and 1.2 million females.[13] In the left half of Table 2.1, reported single year data from the

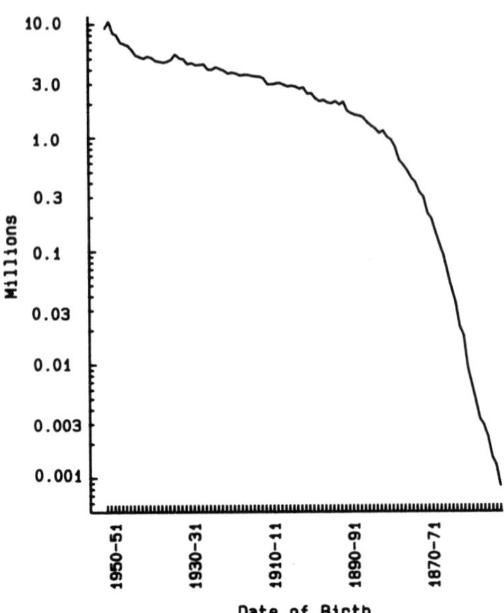

Fig. 2.1. Partial Data on Female Age Structure, 1953 Census. Data from State Council Population Office (1982): 37–39. Age is not available for the 1,175,471 women in the military or the 4.05 million women indirectly estimated. Therefore Fig. 2.1 does not represent the entire enumerated female population of 1953. To superimpose Fig. 2.1 on Fig. 2.2 would be to show too few females dying in the 1953–64 intercensal period. For those whose reported age is available, each point in the figure represents the absolute number of females reported at each single year of age.

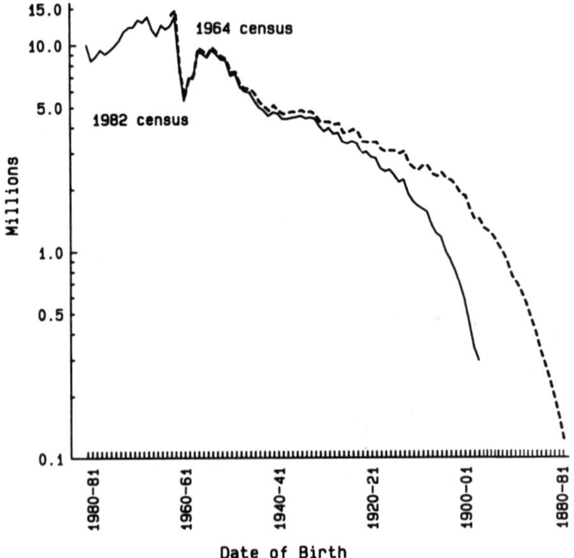

Fig. 2.2. Female Age Structure as Reported, 1964 and 1982 Censuses. Data from State Council Population Office (1982): 40–41; (1983): 264–73.

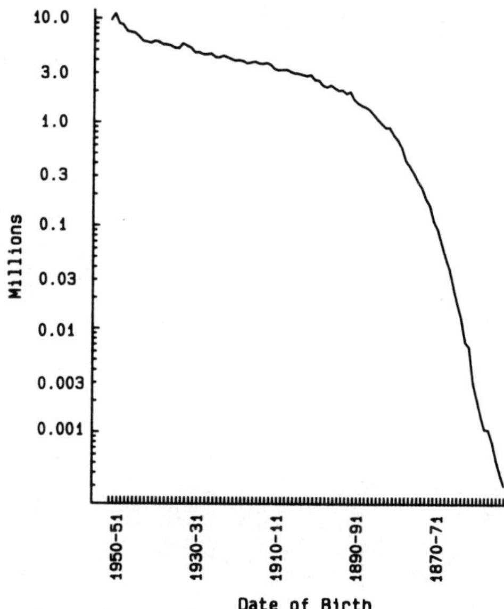

Fig. 2.3. Partial Data on Male Age Structure, 1953 Census. Data from State Council Population Office (1982): 37–39. Age is not available for the 5,583,711 men in the military or the 4.35 million men indirectly estimated. Therefore Fig. 2.3 does not represent the entire enumerated male population of 1953. To superimpose Fig. 2.3 on Fig. 2.4 would be to show too few males dying in the 1953–64 intercensal period. For those whose reported age is available, each point in the figure represents the absolute number of males reported at each single year of age.

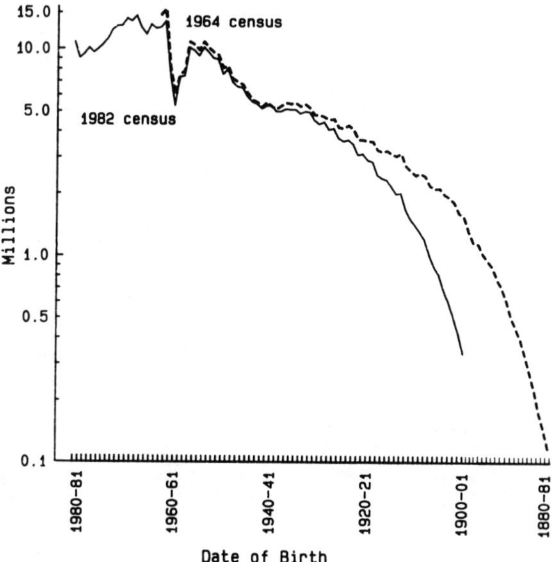

Fig. 2.4. Male Age Structure as Reported, 1964 and 1982 Censuses. Data from State Council Population Office (1982): 40–41; (1983): 264–73.

TABLE 2.1

Reconstructed Age-Sex Structure of the 1953 PRC Census

Age group	Reported partial data			Extrapolated to total count		
	Total	Males	Females	Total	Males	Females
0	18,981,848	9,716,971	9,264,877	19,341,000	9,901,000	9,440,000
0–4	89,275,126	46,104,886	43,170,240	90,886,000	46,937,000	43,949,000
5–9	62,775,537	33,264,941	29,510,596	63,965,000	33,895,000	30,070,000
10–14	53,790,234	29,082,491	24,707,743	54,394,000	29,409,000	24,985,000
15–19	51,726,787	27,072,984	24,653,803	53,069,000	28,072,000	24,997,000
20–24	46,324,595	23,718,199	22,606,396	48,007,000	24,887,000	23,120,000
25–29	42,316,003	21,711,735	20,604,268	45,186,000	23,972,000	21,214,000
30–34	38,086,610	19,595,040	18,491,570	40,044,000	21,194,000	18,850,000
35–39	36,281,374	18,778,517	17,502,857	37,390,000	19,483,000	17,907,000
40–44	31,654,941	16,454,333	15,200,608	32,289,000	16,800,000	15,489,000
45–49	28,760,397	14,676,352	14,084,045	29,315,000	14,977,000	14,338,000
50–54	24,356,677	12,435,470	11,921,207	24,681,000	12,601,000	12,080,000
55–59	20,560,034	10,398,207	10,161,827	21,053,000	10,648,000	10,405,000
60–64	16,500,186	8,006,104	8,494,082	16,813,000	8,158,000	8,655,000
65–69	11,775,245	5,400,767	6,374,478	11,998,000	5,503,000	6,495,000
70–74	7,815,815	3,308,199	4,507,616	7,964,000	3,371,000	4,593,000
75–79	3,592,488	1,368,411	2,224,077	3,660,000	1,394,000	2,266,000
80±	1,854,709	593,171	1,261,538	1,889,000	604,000	1,285,000
TOTAL	567,446,758	291,969,807	275,476,951	582,603,000	301,905,000	280,698,000

SOURCES: The partial data were derived from the 1953 census age structure by single years of age reported in State Council Population Office (1982): 37–39. The total 1953 census count was reported in Communique on 1953 Census (1954): 1. The extrapolated figures for the total number of males and females were calculated from the sex ratio of the directly enumerated population, as reported in the same communique. The age-sex structure of the total count was derived from the following sources. (1) Sex ratios by age from the 1953 census that agree with the partial data for nonmilitary ages but differ for military age groups, as reported in Tai Shih-kuang (1956): 21. (2) The percentages of the total 1953 census population in overlapping 10-year age groups as reported in Ch'en Ta (1957): 23; and T'ien Feng-t'iao (1959): 462. For a compilation and analysis of these data and sources, see Aird (1961): 65–77. The percentages do not agree with the partial data reported in 1982. (3) The percentages of the total 1953 census population in each 5-year age group by sex, as displayed in a population pyramid reported in T'ien Feng-t'iao (1959): 463. John S. Aird has measured this somewhat fuzzy pyramid to estimate the range of possible values in each 5-year age-sex group; all the estimates of age-sex groups above fall within the permissible ranges.

TABLE 2.2

Comparison of the Age-Sex Structures of the 1953 Destabilized Model and the 1953 Census

Age group in 1953	Percent of total population, 1953		Percent of male population, 1953		Percent of female population, 1953		Sex ratio, 1953		Enumerated survivors, 1964	
	Model	Census	Model	Census	Model	Census	Model	Census	Sex ratio	Age group
0	3.7%	3.3%	3.7%	3.3%	3.8%	3.4%	106.9	104.9	108.2	(11)
0–4	15.6	15.6	15.6	15.5	15.7	15.7	108.0	106.8	109.3	(11–15)
5–9	11.4	11.0	11.5	11.2	11.4	10.7	109.3	112.7	108.1	(16–20)
10–14	10.1	9.3	10.1	9.7	10.1	8.9	108.3	117.7	109.6	(21–25)
15–19	9.2	9.1	9.1	9.3	9.2	8.9	107.7	112.3	113.6	(26–30)
20–24	8.4	8.2	8.4	8.2	8.3	8.2	108.9	107.6	111.9	(31–35)
25–29	7.5	7.8	7.6	7.9	7.5	7.6	110.6	113.0	109.7	(36–40)
30–34	6.8	6.9	7.0	7.0	6.7	6.7	112.8	112.4	106.6	(41–45)
35–39	6.2	6.4	6.4	6.5	6.0	6.4	115.4	108.8	103.3	(46–50)
40–44	5.5	5.5	5.7	5.6	5.4	5.5	116.2	108.5	98.7	(51–55)
45–49	4.9	5.0	5.0	5.0	4.8	5.1	114.5	104.5	89.6	(56–60)
50–54	4.2	4.2	4.3	4.2	4.2	4.3	111.6	104.3	84.0	(61–65)
55–59	3.5	3.6	3.5	3.5	3.5	3.7	107.4	102.3	76.5	(66–70)
60–64	2.6	2.9	2.5	2.7	2.8	3.1	100.5	94.3	66.7	(71–75)
65–69	1.9	2.1	1.7	1.8	2.0	2.3	95.8	84.7	55.8	(76–80)
70–74	1.2	1.4	1.1	1.1	1.3	1.6	91.3	73.4	45.2	(81–85)
75–79	0.6	0.6	0.5	0.5	0.7	0.8	70.8	61.5	36.9	(86–90)
80±	0.3	0.3	0.1	0.2	0.4	0.5	34.8	47.0	43.6	(91±)
TOTAL	—	—	—	—	—	—	108.8	107.6	104.5	(11±)

SOURCES: Table 2.1 for 1953 age-sex structure; destabilized model 1953 age structure derived from mortality and fertility patterns in Barclay et al. (1976); 1964 census data, State Council Population Office (1982): 40–42.

NOTE: The destabilized model 1953 age structure was derived at the U.S. Bureau of the Census as follows. A stable population was created for 1949, the year the PRC was founded, using fertility and mortality patterns from China's rural agricultural families as of 1929–31, with a total fertility rate of 5.5, male e_o (life expectancy at birth) 27.4 years, female e_o 26.7 years. The population was destabilized to 1953 with rapid mortality decline to male e_o 38.3 years and female e_o 38.1 years and with a total fertility rate after 1949 estimated at 6.2.

1953 census have been grouped into five-year age groups. The right half of the table is an upward adjustment of the grouped single year data to the total count, using independently reported statistics from the 1950's on the complete census age-sex structure. It is not clear how the full age-sex distribution of the 1953 census was derived by the three demographers who reported it in the 1950's. Statisticians of China's State Statistical Bureau who worked on the 1953 census report that the military never provided its census age data to the SSB. Either the demographers guessed the military age structure or they had some sources of information on the age and sex distribution of the military.

As an aid in determining whether the age-sex structure derived from China's 1953 census is plausible, a reconstruction of the expected age-sex pattern can be compared with that enumerated. The model age structure summarized in Table 2.2 was created from the patterns of fertility by age of women and of mortality by age and sex found in the 1929–31 survey of rural agricultural households.[14] A stable population (one assuming constant fertility and mortality) was created for 1949, the year the People's Republic of China was founded, with a total fertility rate of 5.5 births per woman and an expectation of life at birth of 27.4 years for males and 26.7 years for females, slightly better mortality conditions than estimated from 1929–31 data. The 1949 hypothetical stable population was projected to 1953 assuming a "baby boom" total fertility rate of 6.2 births per woman and rapidly improving mortality. In general, the enumerated population of the 1953 census is close to the model age-sex structure derived from China's 1929–31 patterns of fertility and mortality, with some exceptions because real-life trends did not accord with this theoretical construct. For example, a deficit of people ages 5–9 and 10–14 in comparison to the "expected" proportion of the population in those ages is correct while the model is wrong. These cohorts were born during the period from midyear 1938 to midyear 1948, the years of the Japanese invasion and occupation of China, World War II, and civil war following Japan's defeat. Fertility apparently dropped below the stable level of 5.5 births per woman assumed in the reconstruction, producing smaller cohorts of both sexes. In addition, the dearth of females in those age groups is more extreme than for males, suggesting either female infanticide and selective neglect of female babies in the war years, or undercounting of females ages 5–14 in the 1953 census.

Except for this plausible shortage of persons ages 5–9 and 10–14, the rest of the male age structure is reasonably close to the "expected" 1953 age structure. The enumerated female age structure, however, has a somewhat higher proportion of the population than expected in ages 35–74,

TABLE 2.3
Age-Sex Structure of the 1964 Census

Age group	Percent of total population	Total	Males	Females	Sex ratio
0	4.1%	28,483,827	14,509,500	13,974,327	103.8
1	4.4	30,248,104	15,515,387	14,732,717	105.3
2	2.2	15,569,154	8,025,093	7,544,061	106.4
3	1.7	11,535,264	5,961,473	5,573,791	107.0
4	2.1	14,305,607	7,450,438	6,855,169	108.7
0–4	14.4	100,141,956	51,461,891	48,680,065	105.7
5–9	13.6	94,177,434	49,283,349	44,894,085	109.8
10–14	12.4	86,351,645	45,005,259	41,346,386	108.8
15–19	8.9	62,115,488	32,356,349	29,759,139	108.7
20–24	7.3	50,820,751	26,483,045	24,337,706	108.8
25–29	7.3	50,395,408	26,798,450	23,596,958	113.6
30–34	6.7	46,706,090	24,719,798	21,986,292	112.4
35–39	5.9	41,169,912	21,591,224	19,578,688	110.3
40–44	5.1	35,645,215	18,438,348	17,206,867	107.2
45–49	4.4	30,852,836	15,710,681	15,142,155	103.8
50–54	3.8	26,505,382	13,292,133	13,213,249	100.6
55–59	3.2	22,568,247	10,749,195	11,819,052	90.9
60–64	2.5	17,671,454	8,125,730	9,545,724	85.1
65–69	1.7	11,635,116	5,109,214	6,525,902	78.3
70–74	1.1	7,378,249	3,002,343	4,375,906	68.6
75–79	0.5	3,757,366	1,377,689	2,379,677	57.9
80±	0.3	1,812,603	566,631	1,245,972	45.5
Age unknown	0.7	4,876,607	2,445,682	2,430,925	100.6
TOTAL	—	694,581,759	356,517,011	338,064,748	105.5

SOURCE: State Council Population Office (1982): 40–42.

even after an adjustment is made to eliminate the deficit at ages 5–14. This discrepancy suggests that female mortality in the middle and older ages prior to 1953 was slightly better than assumed in the model. Once again it is plausible that the census is correct and the model is inappropriate for part of the age structure. Therefore, for males, females, and both sexes combined, the enumerated 1953 census age structure is reasonable, given the history of prior decades and the expected levels and patterns of fertility and mortality.

The single year data from the 1964 census were compiled into five-year age groups for Table 2.3. Comparing the percent of the population in each age group with the 1953 census results indicates that, as enumerated, China had a younger population in 1964 than in 1953. That is, the proportion of the population under age 15 was 40.4 percent in 1964 compared to 35.9 percent in 1953, and in almost every older age group the 1964 census found a smaller percent of the population than in the same age group in 1953. The bulge in the ages 0–14 was caused by higher fertility and lower infant and early childhood mortality for most of the fifteen years prior to 1964 than for the fifteen-year period leading up to the 1953 census.

The counts of males and females at each age from successive censuses can be analyzed to detect possible undercounts or overcounts of persons in particular age-sex groups. For instance, if a particular age group appeared to lose few or no members through death from the first census to the second, perhaps that group was undercounted in the first census or overcounted in the second. If on the other hand far fewer survivors were counted in the second census than expected, the group may have been undercounted in the latter census or overcounted in the first. For China, cohorts can be compared from the 1953 and 1964 censuses, once the available 1953 age data are adjusted to comprise the total population as in Table 2.1. Figure 2.5 graphs the five-year age groups of females from both censuses. It would be preferable to use complete data by single years of age from both censuses, but the results are misleading because too many people, including the military and the population "indirectly surveyed," are missing from the 1953 single year data. Because Figure 2.5 approximates the total enumerated population of females by age group in the 1953 and 1964 censuses, the vertical space between the curves represents persons deceased by cohort group in the intercensal period, slightly distorted by a one-year displacement in the data points. In general, the female pattern appears plausible, with fewer people dying in youth and young adult years, and progressively more dying at higher ages. There are no visible anomalies, such as the lines crossing or touching at particular ages, or a wide gap between the lines in one age group but not in nearby ones.

Another way to detect census undercounts or overcounts of either sex at particular ages is to calculate survival ratios for each age group from the first census to the second. These are compared with model life tables and any deviations from a reasonable mortality pattern in the intercensal period are evidence of error in the count of one census or the other. The application of this technique to China's 1953 and 1964 censuses is possible but is complicated by the need for a ten-year rather than eleven-year intercensal period, and by a famine intervening for several years, which violates any assumption of a constant or smoothly shifting mortality pattern, level, or trend. Table 2.4 shows the levels of mortality implied by the survival ratios, a higher number meaning better mortality conditions. One would normally expect to see the same mortality level at all ages,

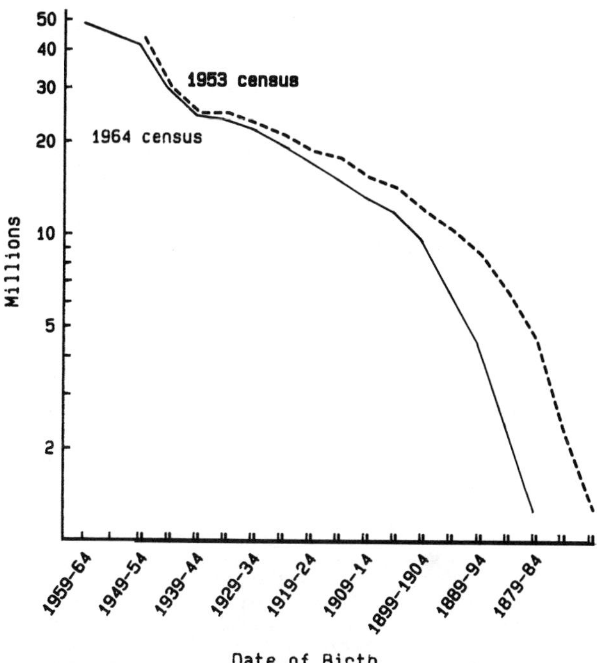

Fig. 2.5. Female Population by Five-Year Age Groups, 1953 and 1964 Censuses. Data from Tables 2.1 and 2.3. The dates of birth specified on the x axis refer to five-year age groups counted in the 1964 census. There is a one-year displacement for the 1953 five-year cohorts, who were born in 1948–53, 1943–48, and so on.

such as level 10 in the Coale-Demeny West series, if the census counts were accurate and if the actual mortality pattern in China between 1953 and 1964 closely resembled that in the model. Instead the approximate pattern seen is an improving mortality level from younger to older children, with the best mortality level (level 14 of the Coale-Demeny West model) experienced by the cohorts who were ages 10–19 in 1953 maturing to ages 21–30 in 1964. West model level 14, if it had been applicable to all ages in China during 1953–64, would have implied an expectation of life at birth of 52.5 years for females, far higher than China's pre-1949 life expectancy. But older cohorts appear to have experienced generally worsening mortality levels the higher their age group. Those women already ages 60–69 in 1953 recorded very poor survival chances equivalent to a West model level 6–7 life table, which would pertain to a West model life table with a life expectancy of only 32.5–35.0 years. A search for a Coale-Demeny or United Nations family of model life tables

TABLE 2.4
Intercensal Survival Ratios for Males and Females by Age Group, 1953–64

	Males			Females		
Age group in 1953	Estimated 1953 total (thousands)	10-year survival ratio	Equivalent West model life table	Estimated 1953 total (thousands)	10-year survival ratio	Equivalent West model life table
0–4	46,937	.90638	11	43,949	.88739	9–10
5–9	33,895	.91519	4	30,070	.95017	11
10–14	29,409	.90346	4–5	24,985	.96334	14–15
15–19	28,072	.96171	17	24,997	.95155	14
20–24	24,887	.96264	18	23,120	.92970	12
25–29	23,972	.89299	10	21,214	.91697	12
30–34	21,194	.84575	7–8	18,850	.88724	10
35–39	19,483	.81843	7–8	17,907	.85686	8
40–44	16,800	.77230	7	15,489	.83955	8
45–49	14,977	.71232	6	14,338	.81528	9
50–54	12,601	.62267	5	12,080	.75147	9
55–59	10,648	.49456	3–4	10,405	.63100	7
60–64	8,158	.38344	3–4	8,655	.50419	6–7
65–69	5,503	.27808	4	6,495	.37519	6–7

SOURCES: Census data, see Tables 2.1 and 2.2; model life table levels, Coale & Demeny (1966): 2–25.

NOTE: The intercensal period was 11 years. Five-year cohorts from 1953 were compared to the surviving cohorts 11 years older in 1964. The difference, that is the implied absolute number of deaths to the cohort between 1953 and 1964, was multiplied by 10/11 to approximate the losses to the cohorts in 10 of the 11 intercensal years. The resulting 10-year survival ratios are estimates of average survival probabilities for 1953–64 applicable to the 1953 cohorts. This technique introduces a slight bias because the eleventh single-year age group does not have the average survival chances of the standard age groups surviving for 10 years. Consequently, the survival chances estimated for the youngest group in 1953 are slightly too high, and those for all older groups are slightly too low. The Coale-Demeny West model life tables were used in preference to others, because other patterns of mortality produce similar results or erratic results. The U.N. Far Eastern and South Asian models were tested with meaningless results. See U.N. Population Division (1981): 118–201, 278–81.

more suitable to China's 1953–64 mortality experience found none with an age pattern of mortality like China's in this period.

The usual response of demographers to the above results would be to try to adjust one or both of the censuses for undercounting at some or all ages in order to come up with the same mortality level at all ages. But the relative smoothness of the observed pattern and the cataclysmic mortality changes in the short eleven-year intercensal period dictate caution in assuming major errors in the censuses. The observed deviations from a model mortality pattern for females shown in Table 2.4 may be genuine. In the first place, since the few life tables we do have for China do not match any set of model life tables, we should not expect the 1953–64 mortality pattern to fit a model either. Second, when a country is experiencing rapid mortality improvement as China was during 1953–57, those causes of death most successfully overcome may in the short run benefit some age groups far more than others. Perhaps teenagers and young adults were the greatest beneficiaries at first. Third, there was famine in China during 1959–61 and it was very widespread. We have no model life tables applicable to deaths during famine. It is thought that infants, young children, and the elderly are the worst victims of famine, while young adults are least likely to perish from such conditions. The intercensal pattern of deaths seen for females in Table 2.4 could approximate a famine life table for the cohort groups traced from 1953 to 1964.

Though the general pattern is reasonable, some undercounting of females ages 10–19 may have occurred in 1953, thus exaggerating the survival chances of these cohorts. The better mortality level for women who began the period ages 45–54 than those age 35–44 also appears suspect. Nevertheless, it is possible that women in the older childbearing ages were more vulnerable to excess famine mortality than women just beyond childbearing age. Therefore, no errors in the female age structure data from the first two censuses can be pinpointed with certainty.

The age structure statistics for males are a little more problematic. Figure 2.6 graphs the male population counted in both censuses, with military males included in the 1953 age distribution as derived in Table 2.1 from reported 1950's sources. Whether the 1964 military population of 3.36 million is fully or partially included in the reported single-year age structure from that census is not clear. Statisticians who worked on the 1964 census maintain that the military never released its 1964 census age structure to the SSB. Yet, Table 2.3 shows that the ages of only 2.4 million males from the census are "unknown." That is not enough to account for the military men, who might have been 3.0 million of the military total, plus the male share of the remaining unknown ages, which would be expected to be at least 0.7 million of the other 1.5 million people with unknown age above the military total. One possibility is that the military is entirely in the "age unknown" category, but someone mistakenly broke down those with unknown age almost evenly between the sexes. This would imply that the reported census totals by sex and census sex ratio do not accurately reflect China's 1964 census data. Another possibility is that someone estimated the 1964 military age structure and included those estimates in the reported single-year age structure. It is clear from the graph that men age 20–24 were undercounted in both censuses. The points defining intercensal deaths are too far apart for those age 20–24 in 1964 and too close together for those 20–24 in 1953. No other errors are apparent from the graph. Table 2.4 displays the mortality levels implied by male intercensal survival ratios. If the observed female pattern is correct, then we would expect a male pattern something like it, character-

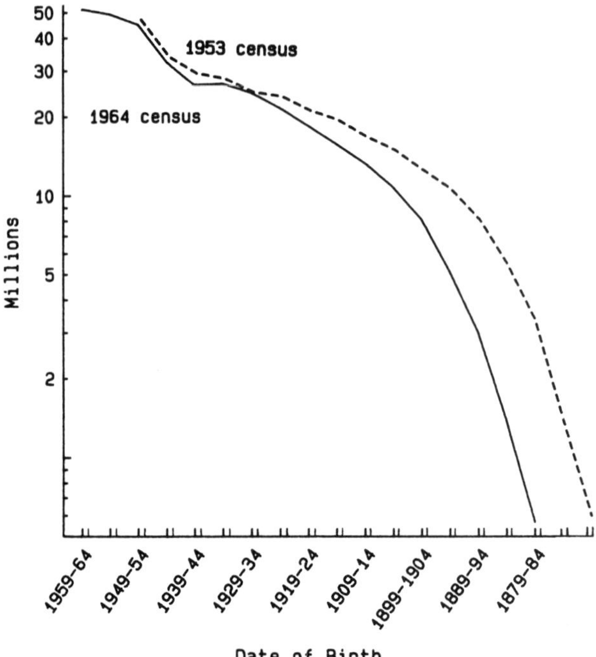

Fig. 2.6. Male Population by Five-Year Age Groups, 1953 and 1964 Censuses. Data from Tables 2.1 and 2.3. See note on Fig. 2.5.

ized by an improving mortality level peaking at level 14 or so in the teen and young adult years with declining mortality levels at older ages. This pattern is apparent for men 25–29 and older in 1953, and for the youngest age group. But the implied mortality level is far too low to be correct for those age 5–14 in 1953, and is too high for those who began the period age 15–24. One possible explanation for these anomalies is that males age 15–24 were undercounted in 1953 and males 16–25, survivors of those 5–14 in the first census, were undercounted in 1964.

Beginning at age 25–29 in 1953 and at all higher ages, men experienced worse intercensal mortality levels than women, with the model mortality level again dropping with increasing age. The strikingly bad mortality picture for older males is even more severe than would be expected from all the trends discussed for women, yet the pattern is reasonable. Much worse mortality for males than females at older ages was also observed in Taiwan, Hong Kong, Singapore, and South Korea until the early 1970's.[15] In all these places the apparent cause was a strong sex difference in tuberculosis mortality interacting with related causes of death at older ages. China would be expected to fit this "Far Eastern" pattern of mortality in the 1953–64 period. As discussed in subsequent chapters, tuberculosis was thought by government officials to be the country's leading cause of death in 1957. By the 1970's, however, China probably paralleled other East Asian areas in overcoming tuberculosis enough to minimize excess male mortality from that cause at older ages.

Intercensal comparisons from 1953 and 1964 cannot be used to test the age structure data for children from the later census, because children under age 11 in 1964 were born after the 1953 census. But the 1982 census age structure can be compared with that from the 1964 census to test the completeness of the counts at each age from the two censuses, including children in 1964. As shown in Figures 2.2 and 2.4, the single-year age data from 1964 and 1982 are remarkably parallel, confirming that the extraordinary shifts in cohort size among children in 1964 were genuine. Very large numbers of children were counted in ages 6–12, indicating high fertility and relatively low infant and early childhood mortality from midyear 1951 to midyear 1958. There was a fertility peak from midyear 1954 to midyear 1955, and a slight dip in births from midyear 1955 to midyear 1956 (coinciding with the collectivization of agriculture), rising to another peak in births during midyear 1957 to midyear 1958. This was immediately followed by a mortality and fertility crisis of four years' duration that dwarfed all the previous crises of the twentieth century in its effects on the population's age structure. Fertility plunged and deaths of infants and young children increased sharply, leaving all the cohorts born from midyear 1958 to midyear 1962 decimated in size. After the crisis, there was an unprecedented surge in the level of fertility in the period from mid-1962 to mid-1964. These extreme fluctuations in fertility and mortality during 1957–64 will be visible in China's age structure for more than half a century as the tiny and the huge cohorts age.

Table 2.5 summarizes China's midyear 1982 age structure as extrapolated from a 10 percent sample of census questionnaires tabulated by computer. The military is not included in this tabulation, so that the male age structure is distorted, particularly in the 15–19 and 20–24 age groups. Between 1964 and 1982, a notable shift took place in China's age structure. The proportion of the population age 0–14 dropped from 40.4 percent to 33.5 percent because of a sharp fertility decline during the 1970's. The population pyramid in Figure 2.7 shows the cutback in cohort sizes that began about the middle of 1971 and continued until a year before the census.

Eighteen-year survival ratios for the period 1964–82 can be calculated

TABLE 2.5

Age-Sex Structure of the 1982 PRC Census Sample

Age group	Percent of total population	Total	Males	Females	Sex ratio
0	2.06%	20,810,080	10,782,120	10,027,960	107.52
1	1.72	17,379,630	9,017,280	8,362,350	107.83
2	1.81	18,274,230	9,462,880	8,811,350	107.39
3	1.95	19,623,660	10,131,280	9,492,380	106.73
4	1.85	18,629,040	9,598,780	9,030,260	106.30
5	1.93	19,421,340	10,013,440	9,407,900	106.44
6	2.03	20,415,990	10,521,120	9,894,870	106.33
7	2.16	21,775,320	11,221,080	10,554,240	106.32
8	2.38	24,030,680	12,368,520	11,662,160	106.06
9	2.49	25,088,300	12,916,540	12,171,760	106.12
0–4	9.39	94,716,640	48,992,340	45,724,300	107.15
5–9	10.98	110,731,630	57,040,700	53,690,930	106.24
10–14	13.07	131,802,210	67,861,520	63,940,690	106.13
15–19	12.43	125,312,480	63,747,990	61,564,490	103.55
20–24	7.37	74,312,110	37,855,290	36,456,820	103.84
25–29	9.18	92,591,020	47,781,440	44,809,580	106.63
30–34	7.24	72,957,770	37,906,430	35,051,340	108.15
35–39	5.38	54,203,370	28,545,980	25,657,390	111.26
40–44	4.80	48,381,030	25,792,360	22,588,670	114.18
45–49	4.70	47,364,000	25,046,990	22,317,010	112.23
50–54	4.05	40,850,780	21,560,990	19,289,790	111.77
55–59	3.36	33,909,310	17,499,710	16,409,600	106.64
60–64	2.72	27,382,530	13,714,630	13,667,900	100.34
65–69	2.11	21,267,130	10,175,000	11,092,130	91.73
70–74	1.42	14,348,950	6,439,050	7,909,900	81.40
75–79	0.85	8,608,540	3,497,630	5,110,910	68.43
80±	.50	5,050,950	1,763,720	3,287,230	53.65
Total from 10% sample	99.57%	1,003,790,450	515,221,770	488,568,680	105.46
Military as reported	0.42	4,238,210	4,129,390	108,820	—
Total population as reported	100.00%	1,008,175,288	519,433,369	488,741,919	106.28

SOURCES: State Council Population Office (1982): 1–5, 14–15; State Council Population Office (1983): 264–73.

NOTE: The military and total population figures are from the complete count. The population extrapolated from the 10 percent sample tabulation does not exactly equal the civilian population count.

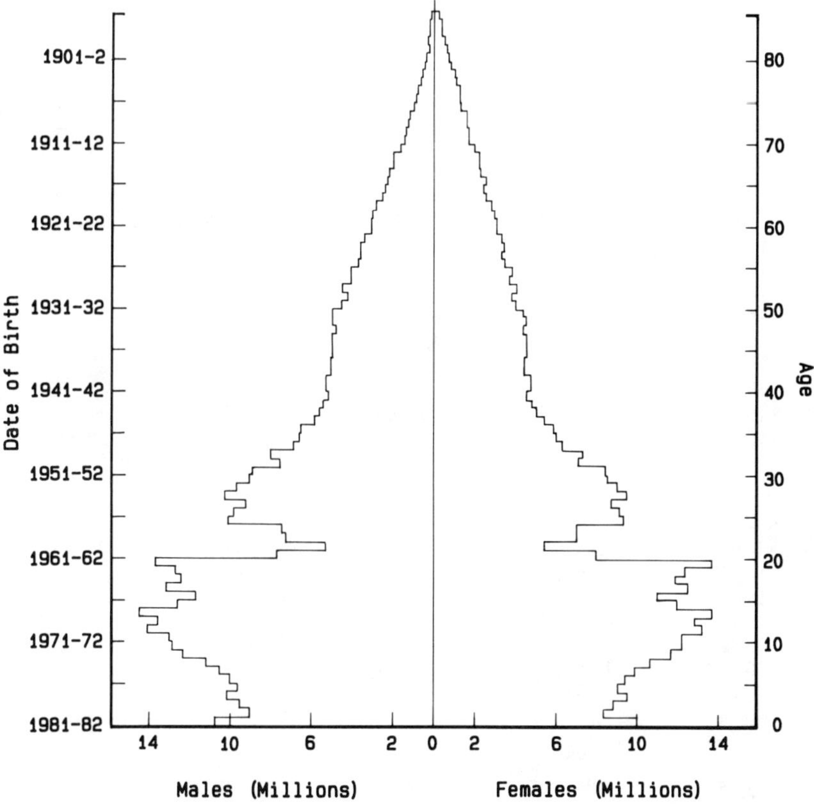

Fig. 2.7. Reported Age-Sex Structure from the 10 Percent Sample of 1982 Census Questionnaires. Data from State Council Population Office (1983): 264–73. Military personnel are missing from the reported 1982 age structure.

for male and female cohorts to detect peculiarities that might be attributable to undercounts or overcounts at specific ages in either census. Table 2.6 shows the survival ratios for 5-year age groups, and in Appendix Tables A.1 and A.2 the survival ratios by single year of age are presented. At first glance, the 18-year survival record of females appears too favorable to be true, with 95 percent of girls 0–4 surviving to age 18–22, with 97 percent of the 5–9 cohort living to age 23–27, with 98 percent of those girls 10–14 still alive at ages 28–32, and so forth. But as will be shown in Chapter 4, these 18-year survival ratios are consistent with mortality data from a mortality survey applicable to the midpoint of the intercensal period, and the levels are plausible. There is no obvious problem with the survival record of the 5-year cohorts of females from the 1964 census to the 1982 census, suggesting that females were not differ-

TABLE 2.6
Intercensal Survival Ratios for Males and Females by Age Group, 1964–82

1964		1982		
Age group	Census total	Age group	10% sample total	18-year survival ratio
		MALES		
0–4	51,461,891	18–22	46,693,460	.90734[a]
5–9	49,283,349	23–27	46,725,190	.94809[a]
10–14	45,005,259	28–32	43,038,250	.95629[a]
15–19	32,356,349	33–37	31,421,290	.97110[b]
20–24	26,483,045	38–42	26,224,620	.99024[b]
25–29	26,798,450	43–47	25,232,060	.94155[c]
30–34[c]	24,719,798	48–52	23,297,070	.94245[c]
35–39	21,591,224	53–57	19,163,390	.88755
40–44	18,438,348	58–62	15,446,520	.83774
45–49	15,710,681	63–67	11,304,830	.71956
50–54	13,292,133	68–72	7,916,800	.59560
55–59	10,749,195	73–77	4,612,140	.42907
		FEMALES		
0–4	48,680,065	18–22	46,367,010	.95248
5–9	44,894,085	23–27	43,496,020	.96886
10–14	41,346,386	28–32	40,331,560	.97546
15–19	29,759,139	33–37	28,543,070	.95914
20–24	24,337,706	38–42	23,114,910	.94976
25–29	23,596,958	43–47	22,282,090	.94428
30–34	21,986,292	48–52	20,695,890	.94131
35–39	19,578,688	53–57	17,575,120	.89767
40–44	17,206,867	58–62	15,012,830	.87249
45–49	15,142,155	63–67	11,921,010	.78727
50–54	13,213,249	68–72	9,131,430	.69108
55–59	11,819,052	73–77	6,296,270	.53272

SOURCES: State Council Population Office (1982): 40–42; State Council Population Office (1983): 264–73.

[a]Military omitted in 1982 sample.

[b]Undercount in 1964.

[c]Anomaly of higher survivorship than the preceding cohort possibly owing to overcount of 49- and 52-year-old men (as well as women) in 1982.

entially undercounted or overcounted at any age. The single-year survival pattern for females shown in Appendix Table A.1 does include some anomalies, however. The survival ratio of girls at ages 2 and 4 in 1964, cohorts that were ages 20 and 22 in 1982, is greater than 1.0, which cannot be correct. Possible explanations include an undercount of girls ages 2 and 4 in 1964, an overcount of women ages 20 and 22 in 1982, or age heaping on ages 20 and 22 in 1982. Minor fluctuations in the survival ratios from one age to another are visible for females in Appendix Table A.1, and in most cases very slight age preference is as likely an explanation as a differential undercount or overcount in one census at a certain age. In general, the 18-year survival ratios are surprisingly regular, indicating very good age reporting and comparable completeness of the female count at almost every age in the 1964 and 1982 censuses. In particular, for women above age 50 in 1964, the survival ratios decline monotonically at every single higher age, suggesting no problem with age exaggeration, age heaping, undercounting, or overcounting of older women in either census. The analysis of all three censuses presented here has concluded that the count of females in China's 1953, 1964, and 1982 censuses was of approximately the same degree of completeness and that there is no clear evidence of age-specific undercounts or overcounts among females.

Data on male survival from the 1964 to the 1982 census display more anomalies and obvious errors than the female statistics. In Table 2.6, the very low 18-year survival ratio from ages 0–4 in 1964 to ages 18–22 in 1982 is incorrect. Military men are missing from the age structure in the later census, particularly at ages 18–22 judging from aberrant reported sex ratios in those ages, resulting in a greatly distorted survival ratio. The survival ratios for 1964 boys ages 5–9 and 10–14 are also underestimated because some military males are missing from the 1982 age structure at ages 23–32.

The 1964 census undercount of men ages 20–24, visible in Figure 2.6, also shows up in Table 2.6 as a spuriously high 99 percent survival ratio for the 18-year period 1964–82. Another error in one of the male census age structures is indicated by the survival ratio of 1964 men ages 30–34 being slightly higher than that of the men 25–29, when the older survival ratio should be slightly lower based on a China male life table of the mid-1970's. The source of the error is unclear, but a look at the single-year survival ratios in Appendix Table A.2 suggests that the survival ratios from age 31 in 1964 to age 49 in 1982 and from age 34 to 52 are unexpectedly high compared to those for nearby ages, not only for men but for women as well. There may have been a small overcount of both sexes at ages 49 and 52 in the 1982 census, and there appears to have been some avoidance of age 51 and preference for reporting age 52 by both sexes.

At ages 35–39 and in higher ages as of 1964, the survival ratios for men decline regularly with increasing age as expected, and in all the higher age groups shown in Table 2.6 female survival ratios are higher than male, a pattern found in most countries. Perusal of the single-year survival ratios for men in Appendix Table A.2 shows steadily declining survival ratios above age 42 in 1964 at almost every single age, indicating high quality of age reporting in both censuses and comparable completeness of the count at different ages. Therefore, there is no clear evidence of undercounts or overcounts of men at any age in the 1982 census, with the possible exception of an overcount at ages 49 and 52. Perhaps the 1982 census undercounted men within the ages 15–25, as may have happened in 1953 and 1964, but the nonreporting of military ages makes it difficult to test for this possibility.

Data on China's Sex Ratio

How many women are there in China and how many men, at each age and in the population as a whole? The first firm data on the sex ratio of the population came from the 1953 census, which recorded a sex ratio of 107.56 males per hundred females in the population directly counted.[16] Table 2.2 shows that in several age groups, the enumerated sex ratio was in the high range of 112–13, and in one age group 118 males per hundred females were recorded. Normally, demographers consider such high recorded sex ratios an indication of severe undercounting of females relative to males, a common problem where females are not valued as much as males. For example, the best analysis of the early data released from China's 1953 census concluded that females were badly undercounted and that the actual sex ratio of the population was much lower than recorded.[17] However, we now have enough information to reassess this conclusion. The Princeton reanalysis of China's 1929–31 population data estimated that female expectation of life at birth was lower than that for males, and that females experienced worse mortality than males in many age groups.[18] Based on this mortality pattern, Table 2.2 lists China's expected 1953 sex ratios by age, along with the recorded 1953 sex ratios.

A startling result derived from this exercise is that the projected 1953 sex ratio of 108.8 is even higher than the recorded sex ratio. In fact, it is quite possible that China's true sex ratio in 1953 was higher than the recorded ratio of 107.6 males per hundred females, perhaps as high as 108.1 if only males were undercounted. We have more convincing evidence of male undercounts than female undercounts in the 1953 census. Actual sex ratios at ages 15–19 and 20–24, the ages at which men were apparently undercounted as analyzed in the previous section, were probably 113 or higher, rather than 112.3 and 107.6 as shown in Table 2.2. This estimate and the high sex ratios recorded for ages 5–9 through 30–34 indicate that females had worse survival chances than males in infancy, childhood, and probably early adulthood in the war-torn decades prior to 1949. The mortality differential in favor of males at young ages was even more pronounced than that estimated for 1929–31, since the actual sex ratios were far higher than those expected from the model population reconstruction. At ages 35–39 and older, sex ratios were lower than expected, and declined with advancing age as expected, indicating that female adult mortality chances were relatively better than indicated in the 1929–31 data and better than male survival chances at ages above 30. China's high population sex ratio of the 1950's is predicted, given the historical evidence on male and female mortality differentials, though the male survival advantage was concentrated at younger ages than estimated from 1929–31 data.

The 1964 census reported a population sex ratio of 105.5 males per hundred females, considerably lower than the enumerated population of 1953. Once again it is likely that the actual sex ratio was higher, at least 105.8 and possibly over 106, since teenage and young adult males were underreported in the age structure while no female undercount can be pinpointed with confidence. In fact, if the whole military population is missing from the reported 1964 census age structure, and the "age unknown" category was actually about 80 percent male, then the 1964 census sex ratio was approximately 106.3 males per hundred females.

As shown in Table 2.2, the recorded decline in the population sex ratio from 1953 to 1964 was caused in large part by a sharp drop in the sex ratio of the survivors from every 1953 group ages 25–29 and above. This means that in the intercensal period, female adult survival chances were better than male at least for age groups older than the twenties, continuing a historical pattern that had been seen in the 1953 census data. Because of age-selective male undercounts in both censuses, it is not clear whether actual sex ratios increased or decreased as the 1953 age groups 5–9 through 20–24 aged to 1964. But the 1953 single-year cohorts from age zero through age five all experienced a rising sex ratio as they aged from 1953 to 1964, indicating that male survival chances were better than female after infancy at least through age 16, also continuing the historical pattern. A look at the 1964 sex ratios of all the cohorts born after the 1953 census also reveals a slight male survival advantage throughout childhood, except that the male infant mortality rate was higher than the female rate, which reduced the sex ratio of babies below the sex ratio at birth. Even though boys retained a slight survival advantage over girls until 1964, the gap was narrowed in comparison to the fifteen years before 1953. This is suggested by the sex ratios of the age groups 0–4 through 10–14 in the 1964 census (see Table 2.3), which were lower than the sex ratios of the same age groups in 1953 (Table 2.2). From this evidence we can tentatively conclude that female infanticide and severe neglect of little girls diminished in the early Communist period.

After China's population sex ratio declined from 1953 to 1964, it reportedly rose slightly to 106.3 as of the 1982 census.[19] Part or all of this apparent rise may be spurious, if the male population was more completely enumerated in 1982 than in 1964 or if the 1964 "age unknown" category included the military. From 1964 to 1982 there was a rising sex ratio in two parts of the age structure. First, in every 5-year age group ages 35–39 and above, the 1982 census recorded a higher sex ratio than did the 1953 or the 1964 censuses. There are several reasons for this shift. China has engaged in no major wars since the Korean War, so excess male mortality from warfare has largely ceased. In addition, China's vastly improved mortality conditions since the 1964 census have resulted in far fewer people of either sex dying at any age. This means that the normal high sex ratio at birth, discussed below, is retained into adulthood, and that the cohorts from the 1953 census with very high sex ratios have retained their surplus of males through middle age. Finally, although male mortality in the middle and older ages has remained worse than female, the disparity may have narrowed from earlier decades, especially in comparison to the excess male mortality of the 1953–64 period.

Second, children enumerated at ages 0–2 in 1982 had a higher sex ratio (107.6) than in 1953 (105.7) or 1964 (105.0). This shift is attributable to the introduction of China's one-child limit in many parts of the country and two-child limit elsewhere. Many couples, determined to have a son, have killed their infant daughters, either outright or by severe neglect, so that they could try again for a son. This phenomenon is discussed more fully in Chapter 7. It is also possible that part of the high 1982 sex ratio at ages 0–2 is spurious, caused by selective undercounting of female infants and young children.

As for the sex ratio at birth in China, very few data have been reported. Tianjin Municipality recorded a sex ratio at birth of 106 boys per hundred girls in 1963 and 105 in 1976.[20] These data appear to be accurate. In comparison, relatively complete data for other oriental populations usually show a sex ratio at birth in the range 105.0–107.2 in any particular year, if the number of recorded births is large enough to smooth out random fluctuations. In Singapore in almost all years since 1961, the sex ratio at birth has been in the range 105.0–106.2. Hong Kong's sex ratio at birth has been between 105.8 and 107.2 from 1956 to 1974. Japan has had a sex ratio at birth of 105.3–107.1 in different years, and Taiwan's sex ratio at birth during 1969–73 was 105.9–106.9.[21] Therefore, for population projections for the PRC let us assume a sex ratio at birth of 106.0, which is at the center of the usual range for Chinese and other oriental populations.

Beijing Municipality in 1980 reported data on the sex ratio at birth from its records. The broadcast claimed that Beijing newborns had a sex ratio at birth of 109.4 in 1950, 104.3 in 1957, 106.8 in 1961, 107.4 in 1978, 108.7 in 1979, and 108.6 in the first half of 1980.[22] The data for 1957, 1961, and 1978 are close to reasonable, given that annual fluctuations could account for a sex ratio at birth just below 105 or just above

107, but the sex ratios at birth recorded for 1950, 1979, and 1980 appear too high and may reflect slight underregistration of female births. In China, wherever the recorded sex ratio at birth is outside the range 105–107 it is prudent to consider sex-selective underregistration of births as a possible explanation.

Data on Total Population Size

Table 2.7 lists China's official national population totals as reported, alongside an alternate series derived from the computer reconstruction of China's demographic trends presented in this book. Official figures usually refer to the population at the end of each calendar year, except for the census counts that refer to the exact midpoint of the year. Where do these yearend population totals come from? Since 1954, China has maintained a permanent population registration system at local levels that attempts to register each person in the country at one location, that person's officially designated permanent place of residence. At the end of each calendar year, rural production brigades and urban public security offices are required to report the size of their registered population to higher levels. Counties and municipalities compile the figures from their subunits and report the totals upward, where they are compiled at prefectural and provincial levels, and finally at the national level.[23]

This is how the system is supposed to work, but in actual practice it is not quite so smooth. Probably only since the early 1970's has the reality approached that description, and even then the State Statistical Bureau has had to make some estimates to fill in missing pieces of local data. In the late 1960's and most prior years, the permanent population registration and reporting system may have been so incomplete and uneven that national or provincial statistical personnel had to estimate all or part of their totals. In particular, in the 1950's the permanent population registration system was only beginning to be set up, and at first it did not cover the entire population. All the national population totals for the 1950's, except the census total, were probably based on incomplete local reports supplemented by estimates. The estimates for years prior to the 1953 census are extrapolations backward from the census total. The Great Leap Forward caused such confusion in population reporting that the official national total for yearend 1960 is a somewhat arbitrary 10.00 million less than the estimate for the previous yearend. National population totals for the Cultural Revolution years of the late 1960's should also be used with caution because some estimates may have been substituted for areas that could not report when their regular political apparatus was under attack.

As of the early 1980's China's permanent population registration and

TABLE 2.7
Comparison of Official Data and Reconstruction of the Size and Sex Structure of the PRC Population, 1949–84
(In thousands)

Date (mid-year and yearend)	Official size and sex structure				Reconstructed size and sex structure	
	Civilians	Military (derived)	Total population	Sex ratio	Total population	Sex ratio
1949			536,360		559,545	
1949			541,670	108.2	561,338	
1950			546,820		563,253	
1950			551,960	108.1	565,169	
1951			557,480		567,659	
1951			563,000	108.0	570,150	
1952			568,910		574,991	
1952			574,820	107.9	579,832	
1953			582,603	107.6	584,191	108.1
1953			587,960	107.6	589,458	
1954					594,725	108.1
1954			602,660	107.6	600,727	
1955					606,730	108.0
1955			614,650	107.3	612,933	
1956					619,136	107.9
1956			628,280	107.4	626,175	
1957					633,215	107.8
1957			646,530	107.3	639,959	
1958					646,703	107.7
1958			659,940	107.5	650,526	
1959					654,349	107.6
1959			672,070	108.0	652,505	
1960					650,661	107.1
1960			662,070	107.4	647,665	
1961					644,670	106.4
1961			658,590	105.9	648,986	
1962					653,302	106.0
1962			672,950	105.3	663,775	
1963					674,249	106.0
1963			691,720	105.6	685,157	
1964	691,220	(3,362)	694,582	105.5	696,065	105.9
1964			704,990	105.2	705,806	
1965					715,546	105.9
1965			725,380	104.9	725,725	
1966					735,904	105.9
1966	742,060	(3,360)	745,420	105.1	745,612	
1967					755,320	105.9
1967	760,320	(3,360)	763,680	105.0	765,736	
1968					776,153	105.9
1968	781,980	(3,360)	785,340	105.0	787,397	

TABLE 2.7 *(continued)*

Date (mid-year and yearend)	Official size and sex structure				Reconstructed size and sex structure	
	Civilians	Military (derived)	Total population	Sex ratio	Total population	Sex ratio
1969					798,641	105.9
1969	803,350	(3,360)	806,710	104.8	809,522	
1970					820,403	105.9
1970	825,420	(4,500)	829,920	105.9	831,429	
1971					842,456	105.9
1971	847,790	(4,500)	852,290	105.8	852,947	
1972					863,439	106.0
1972	867,270	(4,500)	871,770	105.8	873,229	
1973					883,020	106.0
1973	887,610	(4,500)	892,110	105.9	892,169	
1974					901,318	106.0
1974	904,090	(4,500)	908,590	105.9	909,608	
1975					917,899	106.0
1975	919,700	(4,500)	924,200	106.0	925,285	
1976					932,671	106.0
1976	932,670	(4,500)	937,170	106.2	939,385	
1977					946,100	106.0
1977	945,240	(4,500)	949,740	106.2	952,433	
1978					958,766	106.1
1978	958,090	(4,500)	962,590	106.2	965,276	
1979					971,786	106.1
1979	970,920	(4,500)	975,420	106.0	977,582	
1980					983,379	106.1
1980	982,550	(4,500)	987,050	106.0	989,142	
1981					994,905	106.2
1981	996,220	(4,500)	1,000,720	106.1	1,001,540	
1982	1,003,937	4,238	1,008,175	106.3	1,008,175	106.3
1982			1,015,410	106.3	1,014,318	
1983					1,020,461	106.3
1983			1,024,950	106.5	1,025,869	
1984					1,031,278	106.4

SOURCES: Official yearend figures, Statistical Yearbook of China 1984 (1984): 81 (these data include the military and are broken down by sex); all other official figures, Aird (1985b); computer reconstruction, by the author at the China Branch, Center for International Research, U.S. Bureau of the Census.

reporting system should be rather complete as such systems go, because of the strong attempt of the government to link food rationing and the legal right to be somewhere with being registered. An overcount of the population is theoretically possible, if people have powerful incentives to register their presence somewhere and to register the existence of their children, but also to delay or avoid reporting deaths because the family will lose benefits. It is also possible that some persons who have moved or who reside in two places during the year are double-counted by the registers. Indeed, in preparation for the 1964 census, government officials attempted to update the permanent population registers, discovered double-counting and deceased persons still on the books, and estimated that the population registers just prior to the census had produced a 0.85 percent net overcount of the population. This explains the slow growth of the official population totals from yearend 1963, before the checkup of registers, to the midyear 1964 census count tied to the adjusted population registers. Smaller net overcounts were estimated from a pretest of the 1982 census in the permanent population registers of Wuxi Municipality and Wuxi county, Jiangsu province.[24]

At the same time that some people are double-counted or remain listed in the registers after death, other people are not counted for years by the registration system. In part this is because China's registration apparatus is a rather draconian system for controlling people's lives, and anyone who does not fit neatly into the government's definition of where and how he or she should live may avoid being registered or may be refused registration. It is easy to run afoul of China's permanent registration system. For example, if someone wishes to move from her village, officialdom says no, and she moves anyhow, her name may be stricken from the registers in her place of origin because she is gone, yet she may not be able to get official permission to be at her new location. Or someone may be born and raised in a city, but the government may assign him to a rural area, transferring his permanent registration to the assigned destination as a means of forcing him out of the city. If he then does not leave the city, or goes but soon returns, he may not become or remain officially registered in the rural locality yet may be unable to renew his urban registration. Other categories of people who might not be legally registered anywhere are those living on the margins of polite society, those who wish to evade the police, persons in hilly areas tilling land on their own instead of being part of an established village, nomads resisting permanent settlement, or some members of minority groups who are not happy with the way they are being governed.

From the late 1970's on, the most serious undercount in China's population registration system is probably the systematic underregistration of young children. There is a tendency for local cadres to refuse legal registration to children born in excess of birth targets in the family planning program.[25] For example, the leadership of one village in Fujian province adopted a policy that all households that did not comply with the birth control guidelines could not register additional children.[26] As of 1981, a village in Hebei province had among its one hundred households eight children who had never been registered.[27] Even children born completely in accordance with government restrictions may remain unregistered for months or years, thus contributing to a constant undercount in the population registers of infants and toddlers. One father in early 1982 complained to a newspaper as follows:

> I am a teacher at the Teachers' School of Hegang Mining Bureau in Heilongjiang province. Last May, my wife gave birth to our first child, a boy. In order to have him registered, I went from one place to another no less than 20 times, and still have not succeeded. . . . There are two families above us in the same building whose situation is similar. Their children are already one year old and still not registered.[28]

Couples who do bear a child outside the government's plan may themselves decide not to try to register the child, through fear of political or economic reprisals.[29]

Another cause of underregistration is that each locality is responsible for supplying food, shelter, education, and other minimum essentials of life to its entire registered population. Urban areas try to minimize the number of people for whom they are responsible, but so do rural areas. China's local and national governments often treat permanent registration of a person with its attendant benefits as a privilege and not a basic human right. They sometimes refuse people permanent registration or delay their registration. It may be common for persons to spend short or long periods in an unofficial status after losing their registration in one place and before regaining it there or gaining it at another place. For example, one Chinese source discusses the problem of newly established municipalities that have very high sex ratios because of the in-migration of working men. The municipalities try to prevent wives and children from coming to live with their husbands, but some do, with the potential result that they become official non-persons, no longer registered anywhere and not included in China's total population count:

> According to my survey of Nanshan mine in Maanshan Municipality, conducted by the end of 1979, the number of female workers from the countryside amounted to only 13 percent of the total number of workers. Because of the fairly large difference between urban and rural areas which still exists, and the large population and scarcity of land in the suburbs, 150 families from the countryside have for a long time stayed in the mining site and thus become unregistered households without grain ration. This has caused many social problems. According to the statistics of the relevant departments in Zhuzhou in 1978, more than 4,600 dependents from the countryside were staying in the city and unwilling to leave.[30]

The foregoing factors suggest the possibility that the annual population total for China derived from local reports of the registered population could be an undercount rather than an overcount. Rechecks of the registers tend to estimate a net overcount because it is much easier to detect duplications in the existing registers than to detect persons or whole households missing from the registers.

Before the 1982 census, during 1981 and early 1982, there was a nationwide attempt to update and correct the permanent population registers. The plan was to use the household registration list as the basis for the census count. The discovery of accumulated errors in the population registers, and the planned link between the registers and the census count, were reflected in this May 1981 report from Fujian province:

> All prefectures, cities, and counties must bend their efforts to straightening out the household records and conducting a census field test. . . . At present, Fujian province must emphasize the following work: 1. Diligently rectify the household records in order to lay a good foundation for census taking. This must be done according to the demands of the "Household Registration Regulations of the PRC" and the relevant documents of the State Council and of the Fujian Provincial People's Government. Household registration is an important system of administrative control by the state. However, during the ten years of catastrophe household control was disrupted. The household registration regulations were not followed carefully. Some household records exist where the occupant is dead or gone, and some people are not registered where they do reside. There are some serious discrepancies between the household registration records and the actual numbers and locations of people. Cleaning up the household records must be done well to solve this problem and thoroughly correct these mistakes. This work is to be completed within this year.[31]

The original design of China's 1982 census linked the count so closely to the permanent population registration system that unregistered persons and households might have been systematically excluded, and people would have been counted where the government insisted they be registered rather than where they actually resided.[32] But this census benefited from more planning and pretesting than had previous censuses.[33] By late 1981, as a result of experience with pretests and in response to the suggestions of United Nations advisers, China had modified the census design to count persons where they lived rather than where they were registered and to count persons "whose residence registration status is to be settled."[34] These modifications would be expected to result in a more complete population count nationwide and in a more realistic count of local populations.

At midyear 1982 the census counted 1,008,175,288 persons. The permanent registration system had reported a yearend 1981 population total of 996,220,000 excluding the military. If the military population of 4,238,000 as counted in the census were added, China's yearend 1981 total population based primarily on reporting from the permanent registration system would have been 1,000,460,000. If it is assumed that the population was growing at about 1.455 percent annually as estimated by the census, then the registered population of yearend 1981 would have grown to about 1,007,740,000 by midyear 1982. This comparison shows that the permanent population registration system and the 1982 census were in almost total agreement as to the size of China's population. One possible and plausible conclusion from this evidence is that both the permanent registration system and the census counted approximately 100 percent of the population, and any differences between the two systems cancelled each other out. For instance, perhaps the overcounting of some migrants and elderly persons by the registration system was roughly matched by the undercounting of other migrants, infants, and young children. The census was at least partly successful in excluding the dead people, getting rid of double-counting, and recording the existence of children not previously registered. While the census improved on the registration system by removing compensating errors, the resulting total turned out to be the same. Another key difference between the registers and the census was one of location. The registration system might have regularly reported the existence of people at their government-approved locations, while the census more realistically reported them at their actual residences, but to the extent that the two systems counted the same people once and only once in different locations, the total population counts would be expected to agree.

The hypothesis that the registration system and the 1982 census both accurately counted China's population has not been conclusively proved. It is possible that agreement between the two systems reflects their high degree of mutual interdependence rather than an amazing level of accuracy in both systems. Perhaps the two ways of counting China's population systematically overcount the true population size by several percent, or undercount it by several percent. But since there is no independent evidence of either alternative hypothesis, it is simplest to use the 1982 census count as the population size of China at that date. Besides, analysis of the single-year age structure from the 1982 census reveals no glaring undercounts or overcounts specific to any age-sex groups, and shows remarkable consistency with the age structures reported from the two previous censuses. Any systemic undercount or overcount by the registers and the 1982 census would have to be assumed universally applicable to all age groups in all three censuses, and an explanation would have to be devised to account for this type of error.

The reconstructed population series presented in Table 2.7 uses the 1982 census total without adjustment, and all the totals for other years are consistent with that decision. For most purposes, one could arbitrarily choose to utilize the official population series or the reconstructed one, since they are not very different. But for precise work, it is preferable to use the reconstructed series because it overcomes some weaknesses in the official series. First, the reconstructed series includes an adjustment for the apparent undercount of men within the age range 15–25 in both the 1953 and 1964 censuses. No similar undercount is assumed for the 1982 census, because the nonreporting of the military age structure has masked the evidence supporting or contradicting any such undercount. Second, the reconstructed series of population totals is consistent with a reconstruction of China's birth, death, and natural increase rates that agrees with the available evidence on fertility, mortality, population growth, and age structure. In contrast, the official series of population totals does not agree with China's official series of vital rates. Third, the official series includes some troubling arbitrary components, such as the sudden shift from an assumed military total of 3.36 million in 1969 to 4.50 million in 1970, accompanied by an abrupt rise in the official sex ratio. The reconstructed series estimates more realistic and gradual transitions in population size to replace such lurching adjustments.

Some differences between the official and the reconstructed series of population totals require explanation. The official totals for 1949 are very likely too low, because the government underestimated the mortality of the early 1950's and overestimated population growth, and because the official 1949–52 totals are estimated backwards from the official 1953 count unadjusted for the apparent male undercount. The reconstructed series more realistically assumes rapidly falling mortality and a rapidly rising population growth rate in the early 1950's, and is consistent with the adjusted 1953 total. For the years 1954 through 1963, China's official population totals are higher than the reconstructed series. But the official series has the problem of a sharp discontinuity between the high totals of the late 1950's and the low census count of 1964, necessitating somewhat arbitrary downward adjustments from yearend 1959 to yearend 1961 and from yearend 1963 to midyear 1964 that contradict the official vital rates for those years. The reconstructed series models higher mortality and slower growth in the 1950's, very high death rates for the Great Leap Forward to account for the population decline, and no inconsistency between the yearend 1963 and midyear 1964 totals. The reconstructed series, if more accurate than the official series, implies that the official totals of the 1950's and early 1960's were inflated by double-counting and retention of dead persons in the registers, and by overestimation of population size whenever an estimate substituted for data, which probably happened every year in one part of the country or another. After 1964, the official and reconstructed series follow each other closely, but the reconstructed series has the advantage of being consistent with the best available information on fertility, mortality, and age structure, while the official totals include minor anomalies and are inconsistent with the official vital rates.

Conclusion

After 30 years of suppressing China's population data, the government seems to have overcome its obsession with secrecy on this important subject. The wealth of population statistics released in the early 1980's has made possible a detailed reassessment of the quality of the data. The permanent population registration system seems to have a tendency to overcount some parts of the population while undercounting others, but the 1982 census total agrees almost perfectly with the total from the registers. Analysis of reported age-sex structures from the three censuses has shown the excellent quality of age reporting, the high but plausible sex ratios, and a possible tendency to undercount men 15–25 but no other age-sex groups in the population. In the 1980's China's statistical system is improving in important ways, particularly through training in modern statistical techniques and a vast improvement in census and survey design.

3

Health and Morbidity

WHEN the People's Republic of China was founded in 1949, its people had just been through decades of war that had added to the already high levels of mortality and chronic ill health. Sanitary conditions in cities and villages were very poor. Water supplies were polluted, and the application of untreated night soil (human excrement) to crops as fertilizer spread epidemic and parasitic diseases. Control of endemic and epidemic diseases was minimal or nonexistent in most localities; immunization programs for the major killer diseases had reached only a tiny proportion of the population. Table 3.1 shows some of the major causes of death in China as recorded in the 1929–31 survey of rural agricultural families. Table 3.2 lists China's major diseases at the time the PRC was founded.

Curative medical care was hardly available. According to one Chinese source in early 1950, investigations in rural areas had shown that approximately 80 percent of patients could not receive proper medical treatment.[1] Traditional practitioners and healers of various kinds provided what treatment there was, if the patient could afford it, and a small number of Western-style hospitals and missionary clinics had begun to introduce Western medicine to China. But most Chinese had no access to effective medical care.

Rapid Mortality Decline in the 1950's

Into this dismal situation came a government determined to improve the health conditions of the Chinese people. Yet China was a poor country, and the government's top priorities were items such as national defense in a hostile world and the rapid development of a heavy industrial base. During 1949–50, only 1.0 percent of total government expenditure was allocated to health care, and from 1950 to 1956 the government

TABLE 3.1
Crude Male and Female Death Rates by Cause, Rural Survey, 1929–31
(Deaths per 100,000)

Cause of death	Males	Females	Cause of death	Males	Females
Smallpox	205	209	Tetanus	27	15
Typhoid	198	194	Scarlet fever	29	27
Dysentery	196	236	Typhus	15	12
Tuberculosis	178	184	Plague	10	6
Cholera	168	159	Leprosy	9	6
Measles	126	118	Accidents, suicide	122	76
Diphtheria	67	62	Other	1,003	1,139
Pneumonia	57	23	Unknown	182	209
Skin disease	48	38	TOTAL	2,671	2,760
Malaria	30	45			

SOURCE: Notestein & Chiao (1937): 393.

NOTE: These data are from a survey of rural farm families in 22 Chinese provinces. Since deaths were significantly underreported in this survey, it is likely that the rates for each cause of death were also underreported. See Barclay et al. (1976).

TABLE 3.2
Leading Health Problems in China before 1949

INFECTIOUS	PARASITIC
Anthrax	Amebic dysentery
Bacterial dysentery	Ancylostomiasis (hookworm)
Brucellosis	Ascariasis
Chicken pox	Clonorchiasis
Cholera	Enterobiasis (pinworm)
Dengue fever	Fasciolopsiasis
Diphtheria	Filariasis
Epidemic meningitis	Kala-azar (visceral leishmaniasis)
Gonorrhea	Malaria
Japanese B encephalitis	Paragonimiasis
Leprosy	Ringworm
Leptospirosis (rice fever)	Schistosomiasis
Measles	Taeniasis
Mumps	Tapeworm
Pertussis (whooping cough)	OTHER
Plague	Chronic bronchitis
Poliomyelitis	Diabetes
Rabies	Encephalomyelitis
Relapsing fever	Fluorosis
Scarlet fever	Glaucoma
Smallpox	Goiter
Syphilis	Influenza
Tahyna fever (encephalitis)	Kashin-Beck disease
Tetanus	Keshan disease
Trachoma	Malnutrition
Tuberculosis	Nephritis
Typhoid, paratyphoid	Opium addiction
Typhus	Pneumonia
Viral hemorrhagic fever	Rheumatic fever
Viral hepatitis	Rickets

SOURCE: King & Locke (1983).

never budgeted more than 2.6 percent of expenditures to health.[2] Because of the serious dearth of funds, medical facilities, and trained personnel, it was not feasible to provide immediate high-quality medical care to the entire population. Therefore the government emphasized cheap mass programs for the prevention of disease as the only workable health strategy for the country as a whole. County governments were responsible for carrying out public health programs, almost always on the basis of "self-reliance" without national government funding. They had to charge a fee for each health service or devise local taxation and community funding mechanisms to pay for public health measures.[3] Much of the work involved in carrying out these programs was unpaid volunteer labor; citizens were expected to contribute their time because they were the direct beneficiaries of the public health work.

In 1952, the first "patriotic public health campaign" was launched nationwide to emphasize the importance of environmental sanitation to people's health: "Within six months great piles of rubbish which had lain around for years were cleared away; innumerable filthy ditches were cleaned up; and flies, mosquitoes, and rats [were] eradicated in many cities and villages."[4] The patriotic public health campaigns have been carried out at least twice a year, for one week in the fall and one week in the spring, throughout most of China almost every year since 1952. The aims during the 1950's were to clean up trash and filth where pests could breed and to physically kill flies, rats, mosquitoes, fleas, lice, and bedbugs. Attempts were made to clean up water supplies. Health workers stressed the building of latrines, and launched educational campaigns to teach peasants how to compost night soil to kill parasites and other disease organisms before putting it on the crops. China cannot afford to forgo the use of human waste as fertilizer, because it has been and still is absolutely essential to the maintenance of soil fertility while chemical fertilizers remain in short supply.

Environmental sanitation work can be effective in minimizing the spread of infectious and parasitic diseases, if a clean environment is maintained year round, but in addition many of the diseases listed in the tables require a more specialized attack. The spread of many infectious diseases can be slowed or stopped by monitoring outbreaks, imposing quarantine in areas where outbreaks occur, isolating infected persons, rapidly treating patients, and selectively immunizing persons who have risk of exposure. For these purposes the PRC established epidemic-control stations at the county level during the 1950's. Table 3.3 shows the increase in both generalized and specialized epidemic stations between 1947 and 1958. The number of generalized epidemic-control stations grew slowly between 1950 and 1955, multiplied fourfold between 1955 and 1957, and

TABLE 3.3
Public Health and Epidemiology Centers in China, 1947–58

Year	Epidemic control centers	Specialized centers[a]
1947	—	7
1950	61	30
1952	147	188
1955	315	287
1957	1,411	626
1958	1,420	667

SOURCE: Chien & Kochergin (1959): 36.
[a]Specialized centers for the fight against such diseases as malaria, plague, kala-azar, schistosomiasis, and brucellosis.

increased slowly in 1958. By 1957 there were 1,411 of these stations among China's 2,097 counties. In addition, in the 1950's there was a steady increase in the number of centers designed to attack those diseases endemic to particular areas.

Certain particularly widespread or dread diseases were singled out for eradication during the 1950's. In 1950 the government decided to stamp out plague and set up a number of anti-plague centers. In 1956 recorded plague cases were only 0.1 percent of the number in 1950,[5] partly because plague came under better control during the 1950's but also because 1950 happened to be a plague epidemic year while 1956 was not. It is possible that plague recurred periodically in subsequent years, but if it did, it was probably better controlled than in 1950 or before.

Typhus was attacked early in the 1950's. Because it is carried by fleas, lice, or mites, the incidence of typhus was reduced through environmental sanitation and epidemic control. By 1953, the number of cases recorded was down to 29 percent of the 1951 number and by 1958 to 5 percent of that in 1951.[6]

In the early 1950's the new government was particularly eager to wipe out any afflictions that resulted from societal decadence or breakdown under previous regimes. Therefore, it mounted vigorous campaigns to wipe out opium addiction and venereal disease. In February 1950 the government strictly prohibited opium drugs and, after three years of intense effort, claimed to have completely eliminated the cultivation, production, importation, and sale of opium and other narcotic drugs.[7]

As of 1949, venereal disease prevalence was high in some localities. It was reportedly unknown in China before 1504, and was presumably introduced by contact with Europeans. Syphilis appeared in port cities and in rural areas through which armies passed; in some urban areas investigated in 1949, 5 percent of the population had syphilis.[8] When infected women became pregnant, their babies were born with congenital syphilis, which can produce retardation and physical deformities. Ten percent of the babies born during 1949 at the Beijing Medical College had congenital syphilis.[9] In many minority-group areas, over 10 percent of the population had syphilis.[10] Some of the minority groups had very high prevalences of both syphilis and gonorrhea, probably owing in part to customs allowing varied premarital or extramarital sexual relations. In some groups of the far northwest 40 to 70 percent suffered from venereal disease.[11] Among some nomadic Mongol groups in Inner Mongolia tested for syphilis in 1952, up to 50 percent of the population had infectious or congenital syphilis.[12] The infected minority groups had been declining in population during recent centuries, in part due to warfare and famine, but also because syphilis increases infant and adult mortality and reduces fertility through subfecundity and increased fetal loss, while gonorrhea can cause sterility.

Soon after 1949, in some cities such as Shanghai, all inhabitants were given a blood test for syphilis, and those found to have the disease were given penicillin injections. The eradication campaign was linked with an attempt to eliminate prostitution. In other cities and in Han (nonminority) rural areas, an intensive education campaign and search for venereal disease sufferers was conducted during the early 1950's. In some minority-group areas, the population was universally tested for venereal disease and those infected received penicillin injections.[13] China used imported penicillin until 1954, but since then has produced its own.

As a result of this intensive effort, in China's major cities and in Han rural areas there were very few new cases of early stage syphilis after 1952, and cases of congenital syphilis declined to a small number. The effort to eradicate syphilis from minority-group areas went on throughout the 1950's until by 1959 it was basically under control in Inner Mongolia and most other minority areas except Tibet and Ningxia. Follow-up mass examinations during the 1960's detected almost no recurrences or new cases of syphilis. Gonorrhea is more difficult to detect than syphilis, so there may still be some gonorrhea in China, though most cases were probably cured at the same time as syphilis with penicillin.[14] One visitor was told of some continuing ill effects of venereal disease in Inner Mongolia as of 1979.[15]

Another loathsome disease that the government attacked during the 1950's was leprosy. Provincial delegates to a national disease-prevention conference in 1951 reported that leprosy was found in every province of China, and that a total of about 1.2 million Chinese suffered from its most visible forms.[16] The PRC started a campaign to educate the public about leprosy and to find and treat the lepers. Those with non-contagious leprosy were treated in outpatient clinics, and contagious lepers were moved to leprosaria alone or to leprosy villages with their families. By 1959 China had established 151 leprosy prevention and control centers, built or expanded 56 large leprosaria, and set up 703 specialized leprosy villages. Patients far from these centers were treated by mobile medical teams. Though leprosy could not easily be cured, efforts began during the 1950's to prevent new infections.[17] Despite all the efforts, only a small proportion of China's leprosy patients received treatment by 1960, and only modest progress was made in controlling the disease.[18]

Subsequent work on leprosy control was not described in the public media until 1981, when it was reported that lepers were still separated into leprosy villages.[19] China's Second National Leprosy Prevention and Treatment Work Conference, held in 1981, described progress in curing the disease as follows: "At the beginning of liberation there were approximately 500,000 lepers in China; 250,000 were cured and about 200,000 are still under treatment at present."[20]

Some contagious diseases were tackled during the 1950's, mainly through vaccination programs or epidemic-control measures combined with selective inoculations. In a three-year period, the PRC nearly eradicated smallpox throughout its enormous population. The mass vaccination program began during 1950, and by the end of 1952, it was reported, 512 million had been vaccinated in a population of about 580 million persons.[21] By 1959, the disease had been eradicated throughout the country except for some frontier and minority-group areas.[22] The last outbreak of smallpox in China was in Yunnan province in 1960, almost twenty years before it was finally wiped out worldwide.[23]

It appears that there was no other vaccination program that covered the whole population during the 1950's. Diphtheria, for example, was a nationwide health problem, but preventive immunizations during the 1950's focused on urban areas. From fewer than 2 million diphtheria vaccinations given during 1951, the number increased annually until 11.5 million children were immunized in 1957.[24] This was a good start, but during the 1950's the program probably had little effect on diphtheria in rural areas.

China also attempted to control tuberculosis during the 1950's, but again primarily through detection and vaccination in urban areas. Tuberculosis was extremely widespread in China until recently but was more prevalent in urban than in rural areas. During 1950–56 surveys discovered that 70–80 percent of Shanghai children aged 10–14 in the central city districts had been infected with tuberculosis, while 50 percent of this group in the Shanghai suburbs had contracted the disease.[25] Privileged groups had not been spared. For instance, 60 percent of all applicants for student visas to study abroad in 1946 were found to be suffering from tuberculosis.[26] Though most prevalent in densely crowded cities, tuberculosis was also found among minority nationalities in remote areas. A doctor who inspected health conditions in China's northwestern provinces during 1951 wrote that "according to reports from various localities, tuberculosis is also very common, and it is learned that the national minorities in Sinkiang show a very low resistance and succumb easily to this disease."[27]

Tuberculosis was clearly a major public health hazard. The government began in 1950 administering tuberculosis tests to children in Shanghai and Beijing and inoculating with BCG (bacillus Calmette-Guérin) vaccine all those children not already infected.[28] The program spread to other major cities. By the end of 1958, 10.5 million Chinese children had been inoculated, primarily in urban areas.[29] By then China was producing its own BCG vaccine and anti-tuberculosis drugs. But even in China's most advanced urban areas, success against tuberculosis was not complete by the late 1950's. Tuberculosis mortality in Beijing during 1956 was still 28 percent of the 1949 level.[30] Experimental work for the control of tuberculosis in rural areas had only begun in 1956.[31] Epidemiological work remained weak during the 1950's, and as of 1958 it was reported that "tuberculosis ranks first in our country as the cause of death at present."[32]

Cholera was a serious epidemic disease and a significant cause of death in China prior to 1950, as shown in Table 3.1. It appears that there was no mass inoculation program against cholera during the 1950's, and yet the PRC claimed not to have a single case of cholera during 1950–57.[33] If that report is accurate, this happy result was due partly to luck and partly to intensive environmental sanitation work.

The PRC found it impossible to eliminate most of the previously prevalent diseases during the 1950's, but officials proudly reported that mortality from many diseases had been significantly reduced. Many persons still contracted the diseases, but far fewer died from them. In 1950, for example, 9 percent of those who contracted measles died; in 1958 the proportion was down to 2 percent.[34] Similarly, of those who got scarlet fever, 18 percent died in 1950 and 1 percent died in 1958. Recorded mortality from dysentery was 4 percent in 1950 and less than 0.5 percent in 1958.

As the decade progressed, the government periodically targeted additional diseases for a concerted attack. Malaria was one of these that was apparently not a high priority for eradication during the early 1950's. The government set up 49 specialized anti-malaria centers by 1956 but made no claims of success in combatting the disease.[35] Malaria was very widespread in the southernmost provinces, where all species of malaria vectors were present. More than half the population in hilly regions of these provinces, and 10 to 50 percent in plains areas, had the disease.[36] Though less prevalent in the rest of China, malaria was found almost everywhere. In 1956 China launched a nationwide anti-malaria campaign. The main emphasis was on treating victims with anti-malarial drugs and draining and filling ditches to eliminate mosquitoes. Success was slow because of the enormity of the task, and because funds and insecticides were scarce. As of 1959, an estimated 30 million persons still suffered from malaria in China.[37]

Also in 1956, the PRC began a major effort to eradicate kala-azar, a disease of the spleen and liver prevalent in north China. A nationwide survey in 1951 had found 530,000 infected persons, predominantly children. Dogs were a chief reservoir of human infection, and the disease was spread by sandflies. During the 1950's the government campaigned to eliminate dogs in urban areas and minimize their numbers in rural areas. The success of this policy, along with insecticide spraying and the development of an effective drug, helped control kala-azar, reducing the number of infected persons to no more than 10,000 at the end of 1958.[38]

The major health campaign launched in the second half of the 1950's was a concerted attack on parasitic diseases, which debilitated large proportions of China's population and were sometimes fatal. One of the most serious was schistosomiasis; therefore the government committee set up in 1955 to direct the assault on parasitic diseases was called the Nine-Person Subcommittee on Schistosomiasis.[39] This disease, also called snail fever, is caused by a blood fluke that attacks the liver, intestines, pituitary gland, lung, and brain and can cause fever, bodily swelling, liver cirrhosis, endocrine disturbance, and death. A necessary intermediate host in the life cycle of the fluke is a snail, which is found in wet areas of the Changjiang (Yangtze) River basin in southern China. It was estimated that in 1949 there were 100 million people living in parts of twelve provinces where the snail was found, and well over 10 million people were infected with schistosomiasis.[40] The struggle against schistosomiasis included an attempt to eliminate snails in waterways through mass projects to drain the water, turn over the earth, kill each snail found, and return water to the waterway. Persons suffering from schistosomiasis were treated en masse by health workers using rather toxic but effective drugs. During

1956 many areas were cleared of snails and 400,000 persons were treated.[41] During 1958 one million children were reportedly treated for schistosomiasis.[42] But thereafter, schistosomiasis control work slowed down. As of the end of the 1950's, the long struggle to control schistosomiasis had only begun. Similarly, several reports in 1959 described the high prevalence of other parasitic diseases such as hookworm, filariasis, ascariasis, paragonimiasis, and enterobiasis, but reported almost no success in controlling them.[43]

Another major emphasis in public health programs of the 1950's was setting up maternal and child health clinics. There was an obvious need to tackle China's inordinately high infant and maternal mortality. To this end, counties and cities set up maternal and child health stations; as of 1958, it was reported, 4,315 stations had been established.[44] Though there was undoubtedly a pronounced urban bias in the locations of these stations, they had a powerful effect reaching into the countryside. Their purpose was not to provide direct obstetric care to women in childbirth—this was impossible given a lack of medical personnel and the enormous numbers of births taking place—but rather to retrain traditional midwives, who attended a large but unknown proportion of births in China. The "old method of delivery" included the midwife biting the umbilical cord or cutting it with a non-sterile instrument, then placing dung or a piece of cloth over the cut. Unsanitary techniques caused tetanus in newborns and puerperal fever in mothers. The maternal and child health clinics began immediately in 1950 to retrain 44,000 traditional midwives in modern midwifery. By the end of 1958, according to one source, 774,983 midwives had been retrained.[45] This program surely had a pronounced effect in reducing both infant and maternal mortality throughout most of the country.

In sum, between 1949 and 1958 the PRC developed a powerful public health system that emphasized prevention of ill health and early death through environmental sanitation, extermination of pests, immunization, mass screening, treatment for targeted diseases, and retraining midwives. But there was no general system of curative medical care in China's vast countryside in the 1950's. By 1957 the PRC had only 74,000 trained doctors of modern medicine and about 261,000 auxiliary medical workers such as nurses, pharmacists, or doctor's assistants, a number totally inadequate for a population of over 625 million.[46] In reality, those few modern medical personnel were concentrated in urban areas, where less than 20 percent of the population lived. Even within the urban populations, full access to medical care was limited to government and Communist Party personnel and workers in state-owned factories, whose medical expenses were paid entirely by the state health budget.[47] The majority of China's urban inhabitants during the 1950's were near a medical facility but probably could not afford to utilize it.

Rural areas during the 1950's were served by practitioners of traditional medicine, China's ancient herbal and acupuncture system, who reportedly numbered 487,000 as of 1955.[48] Not much changed in rural areas during the 1950's regarding access to medical care. To visit a traditional practitioner and fill a traditional medicine prescription cost money, and the expense was probably enough to preclude a visit to the traditional doctor every time someone fell ill. Modern medical care and medicines were not available to most peasants.

The Great Leap Famine

By the late 1950's, leaders of the PRC had discovered to their chagrin that while socialism had reduced disease and mortality as hoped, it had not released the people's productive forces enough to ensure that food production grew significantly faster than population. The situation China faced in the 1950's was that the country's industrious farmers were already wresting yields from the soil that were fairly high for traditional agricultural techniques. If China wished to increase crop yields rapidly, it would be necessary to extend irrigation and flood control, develop high-yielding seed strains, add chemical fertilizer, use pesticides or other pest-control techniques, and incorporate the kinds of machines that contribute to increased yield. Because China could not quickly supply its farmers with all these improvements, the leadership searched for organizational changes that could bring about the desired results without more modern inputs. A crash program of agricultural collectivization was implemented in 1955 and 1956, but the immediate results were disappointing. The Chinese leaders then turned to a still more radical expedient, the attempt to substitute increased physical labor by the peasants for all the agricultural inputs in short supply.

The Great Leap Forward was launched in 1958. Rational economic planning collapsed under the expansive demands of the government, and statistical reporting began to reflect wishful thinking rather than true production. A recently revealed report originally written in October 1959 states that in the fall of 1958, when the peasants were required to produce backyard steel, they were unable to harvest their crops, with the result that serious food shortages began in early 1959.[49] Three years of poor yields followed. Food grain production in 1960 was reported to be 26.4 percent less than that of 1957, a shortfall that caused famine in

1960 and 1961.[50] Hunger was so widespread that it was impossible to feed persons in deficit areas with grain shipped from surplus areas. The government even launched a program to find and popularize food substitutes, such as corncobs and marshwater plankton, to mix with the scarce food in 1961 and fill people's stomachs.*

Meanwhile, the general health of the population deteriorated. Malnutrition and starvation became more widespread each year. Public health work was neglected as the populace and local leaders became unwilling to divert scarce resources to anything but survival. A severe shortage of medicines developed, the quality of modern medicines deteriorated, and land used to grow medicinal herbs was diverted to growing grain.[51] The incidence of malaria, after some reduction during 1956–58, rose again for the three years 1959–61.[52] Anti-parasite work was given low priority or abandoned altogether. There were outbreaks of disease owing to the population's weakened condition from famine.[53] For instance, after the government had proudly proclaimed that cholera was eliminated, a cholera plague began in Guangdong in March 1962 and spread in southern China in subsequent months.[54]

By 1963 the country had barely time to restore agricultural production and the population's caloric intake. Malnutrition and rickets were still diseases of high incidence.[55] From fragmentary information it appears that the preventive public health system was not yet restored to its 1957 level of coverage and efficiency.

In the first half of the 1960's China resumed the attack on some of the nation's health problems. For example, household spraying of insecticides and the use of insecticides on rice fields reduced mosquito populations in some areas, and a steady drop in the incidence of malaria was reported.[56] China was producing almost all of its own anti-malarial drugs by 1965. Even so, as of 1965, China had only begun mass treatment to cure those persons who already had contracted malaria. The results of pilot studies on how best to cure the various strains of malaria were only then being evaluated. We do not know when, or even if, China achieved nationwide control of malaria. Many localities reported eradicating malaria during 1962–66, but some other areas did not begin malaria-control work until the end of the 1960's.

* A campaign to find food substitutes was reported from Shenyang in Liaoning province in 1961 (Lampton 1977: 130). A prisoner in northern China reported that in late 1960 the government required that prisoners supplement their starvation rations with wild plants they had foraged, and tested paper pulp as a potential food substitute with disastrous results. Various food substitutes were tried out on prisoners starting in December 1960. By early 1961 the prisoners had managed to survive on ground corncobs mixed with flour for bread, and this food substitute was reportedly popularized (Bao Ruo-wang 1973: 170–216).

Work also continued on those infectious diseases that were still problematic during the early 1960's. China began attacking measles and poliomyelitis with vaccines in 1960. By 1963 some 6 million (mostly urban) children had received measles vaccine and 50 million children had received live polio vaccine in liquid or chewable form. Such coverage should have reduced mortality and morbidity from these diseases, especially polio. As of 1963 four infectious diseases still had high incidence rates with significant mortality among children: measles, hepatitis, pertussis, and dysentery.[57]

Barefoot Doctors and Cooperative Medical Care

After the mid-1960's China developed and expanded a new system of rural health maintenance that resulted in greatly improved health and mortality conditions in the countryside by the mid-1970's. This program has received worldwide recognition for providing primary health care to the populous rural areas. In 1965 Mao Zedong made a famous speech in which he derided China's health establishment for its extreme urban bias.[58] He charged that 90 percent of the doctors, 70 percent of the auxiliary health workers, and 80 percent of all health expenditures were concentrated in urban areas at the level of county seat and above. He ordered a shift of emphasis in the entire health system toward the countryside. During the early years of the Cultural Revolution, political chaos prevented implementation of this directive, except that the rotation of medical workers in mobile medical teams from urban to rural areas continued. Starting late in 1968, however, city and county hospitals and urban doctors visiting the countryside began training "barefoot doctors" to serve as the primary-care physicians in rural areas. The barefoot doctor was usually a village resident chosen by the locality to receive a short medical course, at first only six weeks to six months long, which emphasized first aid, disease prevention, management of common illnesses, eclectic use of Western and Chinese medical techniques and drugs, and family planning services. The barefoot doctor often worked part-time as an agricultural or rural industrial worker and was usually paid by the production team, that is the collectivized village, in work points rather than cash wages.

Barefoot doctors received minimal training and returned to work in their villages rapidly after 1968. Much of the improvement in China's health and mortality conditions since about 1968 may be attributable to the preventive and curative work of the barefoot doctors. For the first time, the vast majority of China's people had access to at least a minimally trained paramedic able to provide some curative medical care.

But the development of paramedics in the villages would not have had much effect in itself had there not been a support system developed to complement their work. Paramedics supplied with acupuncture needles and a few herbal and antibiotic drugs cannot by themselves substantially improve the health and mortality of the several hundred or one thousand persons each of them serves. Their work is effective because, first, each barefoot doctor is backed up by midwives and local health workers, often volunteers, who carry out much of the screening work, immunization, routine checking, and maintenance of health records in the small health station, sometimes just a bare room with a dirt floor, located in each village or group of villages.

Second, the barefoot doctors have often worked as part of a cooperative medical system set up by the production brigade to serve its members. The cooperative medical system was popularized at the end of the 1960's and during the early 1970's, at the same time the barefoot doctors were being trained. Because the national and provincial governments in China give very little financial support to rural medical care, most medical costs have been borne by the individual, the family, or the rural collective. Members of a production brigade could choose to have or not to have a cooperative medical plan; if they did not set up this system, then each family had to pay for each visit to the barefoot doctor, each drug used, and each visit to a commune or county hospital. In brigades that had a cooperative medical plan, each member paid a small fee such as one or two yuan per year to join, and the brigade welfare fund also heavily subsidized the cooperative health service from brigade income. Cooperative health plans differed in the extent to which they covered catastrophic or hospital medical costs; it depended on how well off the brigade was. Usually costs were controlled by the requirement that when anyone got sick, except for serious emergencies, the patient must first see the barefoot doctor, who would refer the patient to the commune or county hospital if the ailment was too complex for a paramedic to handle. This system rationed access to the few fully trained doctors who worked at the commune clinic or hospital, who then dealt with only the more difficult cases. Such a system, if and when it worked as designed, could be an inexpensive way to provide basic health care for both simple and moderately complex medical problems.

Morbidity in China Today

Although the PRC has achieved a relatively advanced mortality situation for a developing country, its people must still contend with a variety of chronic and acute health problems that, while not usually fatal, can be very debilitating. China continues to work to bring these diseases under control.

There is some indication that tuberculosis is more of a problem in rural areas than in cities and in the inland than in the east coast provinces. A pediatrician visiting China in 1973 made the following report:

For example, we visited a children's hospital in Peking and were shown a ward for tuberculous children. We saw about 40 children with the usual complications of primary tuberculosis, including cases of miliary tuberculosis, bone disease and tuberculous meningitis, such as were commonly seen in this country twenty years ago in special centers for childhood tuberculosis. We were told, however, that less than 5 percent of these children had come from Peking, that nearly all had come from the countryside. Considering the types of cases we saw, there is probably considerable tuberculosis disease in both adults and children in the countryside, advice to the contrary notwithstanding.[59]

In December 1976 a "conference on exchanging experience in prevention and treatment of tuberculosis in southwest and northwest China" was held in Kunming, Yunnan. In October 1977 at a follow-up conference in Xining, Qinghai, it was reported that during 1977 progress had been made in surveying, preventing, and treating tuberculosis in these inland provinces: Xinjiang, Gansu, Ningxia, Shaanxi, Sichuan, Guizhou, Yunnan, Tibet, and Qinghai.

Although China has made great progress in control of tuberculosis since the late 1950's, nationwide prevention and treatment programs are sporadic. A 1980 report stated that there were still several million tuberculosis patients in China, one-quarter of them infectious, and that at least 80 percent of the counties had not carried out proper prevention and treatment work.[60] The report's author noted that while China spends annually over 10 million yuan on BCG vaccines to prevent tuberculosis, in rural areas only 20 percent of the vaccinations are effective because vaccines are of poor quality or the method of vaccination is improper. This report highlights a general problem with China's vaccination programs: the quality of some Chinese vaccines may be poor when they leave the factory, but even if they are of good quality, slow transportation and a near-absence of refrigeration may cause them to deteriorate before they can be used. A nationwide pulmonary tuberculosis survey apparently conducted in 1979 and 1980 found that China had about 6.63 million people with active tuberculosis, or 0.7 percent of the population, and another 1.66 million, or 0.2 percent, under observation because of tuberculosis bacilli in their sputum. The survey showed that "more rural people suffer from the disease than urban people" and that incidence rose with age.[61]

Most other infectious diseases are now under fairly good control in China. Smallpox, syphilis, kala-azar, and perhaps gonorrhea have been greatly reduced in prevalence or eliminated. Plague is reported under control. Some diseases that were still common in the mid-1960's have been reduced in incidence through immunization and other epidemic-control measures. China's Minister of Public Health in 1979 claimed marked success in preventing diphtheria, pertussis, poliomyelitis, measles, and acute encephalitis.[62] The incidence of polio dropped from 0.07 per thousand population in 1963 to 0.01 per thousand, according to a 1980 estimate based on information from 3,000 epidemic-prevention stations.[63] Guangdong was one province that reported dramatic improvements with these diseases: "In the province, comparing 1975 with 1965, the incidence of poliomyelitis fell by 93.6 percent, that of epidemic encephalitis (Japanese B) by 79.4 percent, and that of measles by 72.5 percent."[64] In early 1982, the Minister of Public Health, Qian Xinzhong, summed up China's health successes during the late 1970's as follows:

> Health work in China has developed smoothly since the end of the Cultural Revolution in 1976. From 1977 to 1980, the incidence of malaria dropped by 35 percent; measles, 59 percent; epidemic meningitis, 60 percent; epidemic encephalitis, 53 percent; diphtheria, 69 percent; and pertussis, 59 percent. Schistosomiasis has been basically wiped out in 244 of 347 affected counties and cities in 12 provinces, municipalities, and autonomous regions.[65]

Though great strides have indeed been made, many infectious diseases and at least three deficiency diseases still cause frequent illness and occasional death. Typhoid fever has been reduced in incidence but not eliminated: Shanghai reported about 600 cases in 1975.[66] Another cholera outbreak was reported during the Cultural Revolution of the late 1960's.[67]

As of 1979, major remaining communicable diseases in the PRC were infectious intestinal diseases such as hepatitis, diarrhea, and dysentery, and infectious respiratory diseases including influenza.[68] A national conference was held in August 1981 to coordinate the fight against infectious intestinal diseases.[69] Although one locality, Chengdu Municipality in Sichuan province, reported success in greatly reducing hepatitis incidence and slightly reducing dysentery incidence in early 1981, parts of Beijing Municipality and other areas reported rising incidence of hepatitis and dysentery at the same time.[70] The conference urged stronger sanitation controls over food and drink;[71] but national regulations governing the quality and safety of food and drugs had been introduced on a trial basis just three years before, in 1978. Only in February 1981 did the government set up the Chinese National Committee for Sanitation Standards in the Ministry of Health to monitor sanitation practices and enforce standards throughout the country; and it was not until July 1983 that experimental implementation of a national Trial Food Sanitation Law began.[72]

It is likely that infectious intestinal diseases will not be controlled quickly, because providing pure food and water nationwide will be a herculean task. Hepatitis, for example, remains stubbornly hard to control in the environmental context of the PRC. Hepatitis was the most important viral disease under discussion at most sites visited by the American Tropical Medicine Delegation in 1979.[73] It is still common throughout China, often in severe form; patients are hospitalized and treated for a month or longer, when they can afford such care. It also appears in children during times of malnutrition.[74] Hepatitis may be spread by water supplies and food contaminated with human waste, and there may be a serious problem with the transmission of hepatitis by non-sterile needles used for all kinds of injections and for acupuncture treatments. Rarely do visitors to China see steam sterilization devices, even in clinics.

Another communicable disease that remains widespread is leptospirosis, a severe pulmonary disease, which is prevalent in at least ten provinces.[75] China is developing and testing a vaccine as part of a major public health campaign to control this disease. Because leptospirosis is spread by animals such as rats and pigs, control of rodent populations and good management of animal manure are the preventive measures required.

Trachoma (viral conjunctivitis) is not a fatal disease, but it can lead to blindness and is thought to be the most prevalent and disabling infectious disease in China. As of 1958 it was estimated that half of China's population was infected.[76] Research on trachoma was carried out in the PRC during the late 1950's and early 1960's, with results that helped improve trachoma control programs throughout the world. Recent data are not available, but indications as of 1970 were that the disease was not under control.[77]

The deficiency diseases and conditions of greatest concern today in the PRC are anemia, rickets, and goiter. Whenever an area experiences serious crop shortfalls, malnutrition in the children is very soon accompanied by rickets and anemia.[78] In China, as elsewhere, these are diseases exacerbated by hunger. But they are also prevalent when food supply is not a problem. For instance, a 1979 survey of seven-year-olds in urban parts of Beijing Municipality concluded that a "considerable proportion" of the children had anemia.[79] A national conference on rickets held in 1980 reported that of 110,000 children age 3 and under surveyed in 21 provinces and municipalities, fully one-third had rickets.[80] The conference suggested adding vitamin D to foods, educating the population on the need for regular sunshine, and working to alleviate the severe smog problem in some localities so that sunshine can get through.

Endemic goiter has been widespread in many inland areas of China where iodine is lacking in the soil. Goiter causes an unsightly swelling of the thyroid gland in the front of the neck, along with other sometimes serious complications. In the late 1970's, sixteen provinces of northern China conducted a survey and found that there were 861 iodine-deficient counties in which over 160 million people were affected by goiter.[81] Thereafter, iodized salt was popularized in 600 of these counties, causing a dramatic reduction in goiter incidence. It was reported in late 1980 that there were still 8.04 million goiter patients in northern China. At that time, southern China was reportedly far behind the north in the prevention and treatment of endemic goiter.[82]

Since the late 1970's China has waged a concerted campaign against diseases endemic to certain regions. A 1982–85 work plan for preventing and treating endemic diseases was in effect for northern China, but work in southern China appears to have low priority.[83] In addition to the anti-goiter campaign, regulations for preventing and treating fluoride poisoning in areas of excessive natural environmental flouride were approved in late 1981.[84] The most spectacular success has been the control of Keshan disease, a cardiac muscle disease endemic to a wide belt across China from the northeast to the southwest. Research in the late 1970's confirmed that low selenium content in food grains was associated with the Keshan disease belt.[85] A selenium supplement was used as a preventative and cure for Keshan disease with marked success, particularly in the most affected province of Heilongjiang.[86]

Another disease targeted for attention in the 1980's is diabetes. In 1980 the first national survey of the prevalence and distribution of diabetes found that it affected 0.61 percent of the total surveyed population.[87] Diabetes prevalence was associated with adult obesity, was about the same in males and females, increased sharply after age 40, and peaked between ages 60 and 70.

Parasitic diseases still debilitate large numbers of people in China. Recent estimates have indicated 20 million cases of clonorchiasis and 2–3 million of paragonimiasis in the PRC, and ascariasis and hookworm infections remain common, particularly among children.[88] This continuing scourge of parasitic disease results from inadequate treatment of human feces, which contaminate food and water supplies. Partial success has been achieved in the fight against some of the parasitic diseases. Filariasis was successfully attacked by supplying infected populations with medicated salt.[89] The campaign against schistosomiasis continues after some setbacks during the 1960's. Constant vigilance in this work is required, because localities and populations have periodically been reinfected in areas declared free of snail fever. As of 1978 there were an estimated 2.5 million persons afflicted with schistosomiasis, compared to about 10 million during the 1950's; and by 1982 some 1.0 million of the remaining patients were pronounced cured.[90]

The PRC has reportedly made further progress against malaria since the Cultural Revolution, and the disease has been brought under control in many parts of the country.[91] Pockets of malaria remain, especially in some mountainous areas of the south. China emphasizes environmental alterations for killing mosquito larvae and thus controlling mosquito populations. Three different insecticides are used for household spraying to kill malarial mosquitoes, but there is danger of resurgence of malaria as mosquitoes become resistant to DDT and other sprays, as has happened in other Asian countries since the early 1970's. Occasional outbreaks in China have recently been reported; for example, Shanghai Municipality had about 5,000 new cases of malaria during 1975 in its rural counties and had another resurgence during 1979.[92] China reported a total of 3.1 million cases of malaria in 1978.[93] While some provinces, such as Zhejiang, reported steady declines in malaria through 1980, others (including Jiangsu, Shandong, Henan, Anhui, and Hubei) experienced a resurgence in 1980 and 1981.[94]

Another massive health problem tackled during the 1970's was gynecological diseases. Once large numbers of female barefoot doctors had been trained, it was possible to carry out mass screening of adult women. The female barefoot doctors, working with midwives and female health aides, began in the early 1970's to check almost all women in a given locality for long-standing gynecological problems such as vaginal infections and prolapsed uterus. At first they found that very high proportions of those being examined for the first time had some gynecological problem needing medical attention. The introduction of gynecological care was intentionally coupled with education and training in birth control techniques. This program was probably unprecedented in human history in terms of the number of women who were given a gynecological checkup and treatment and family planning assistance in a few years' time. For instance, between 1970 and 1975, a reported 14 million married women in Jiangsu province, 90 percent of the total number of married woman, received at least one gynecological checkup, including a Pap smear to detect cervical cancer.[95]

China continues to have some health problems that are barely dealt with. One is dental care, which still has low priority. Surveys of children reportedly find that more than half of them have cavities.[96] Another is occupational diseases and accidents. Visitors to China during the 1970's noticed the lack of safety standards in most factories.[97] As a result, industrial workers in the PRC probably experience excessive work-related accidents. They also contract lung diseases from breathing industrial pollutants and particulate matter such as coal dust and cotton fibers, heightened cancer rates in some industries, and other occupational diseases.

China has only begun to attack these problems. Occasional improvements are reported; for example, in 1979 the PRC claimed to have overhauled some coal-mining equipment and eliminated some dangers in coal mine shafts, thus reducing accidents.[98] But in general China runs into the same contradiction found in other industrial or industrializing countries: Safety and occupational health rules are often neglected or ignored because it is cheaper and easier to produce without regard for worker health. Workers in China do not have the right to organize to press demands for occupational safety. Glaring safety and health violations are apparent in every kind of enterprise, whether owned by the state or by a collective. Even newly constructed factories largely ignore requirements for health and safety, according to one broadcast:

> The harmful effect of dust and noxious substances on workers' health is currently a serious problem for factories, mines, and other enterprises. . . . The state has promulgated a series of relevant regulations, rules, and measures. However, in a recent visit to Shandong, this reporter discovered that the leadership of a number of places, departments, factories, mines, and other enterprises still do not well understand the significance of preventing dust and noxious substances and preventing and treating occupational diseases. . . . During the period of construction, many factories, mines, and other enterprises only pay attention to production and rarely consider safety and facilities to prevent dust and noxious substances. . . .
>
> According to a survey conducted by Qingdao municipality, more than 400 newly built, expanded, and rebuilt production and construction projects were approved by the relevant local departments in 1975–77, but only 12 percent met public health requirements for the design of industrial enterprises. In addition, more than 900 other projects were either not approved or built secretly, and almost all of these lack facilities for safety and for the prevention of dust and noxious substances.[99]

Part of the problem has been government neglect; that is, the necessary equipment and funds are often not available for controlling hazardous substances and emissions in the workplace. As of 1979 the government had not defined maximum permissible levels of dangerous substances in factory air, and examination programs for detecting occupational diseases were inadequate. A beginning was made in January 1980 with a trial program to control factory noise levels.[100]

A related problem is industrial pollution of China's air and water. During the 1970's the government became aware of the country's serious pollution problems, partly because China participated in the United Nations Conference on the Human Environment held in Stockholm in 1972. Since then, the media have occasionally discussed pollution problems and highlighted local attempts to clean up air and water pollution. For instance, Daqing oilfield in Heilongjiang, China's largest oilfield, began to tackle its massive pollution problem in 1973. By 1980 it was reported that all of Daqing's oily water discharged in crude-oil production was treated daily and that other measures were succeeding in cleaning up spilled oil all over the huge complex.[101] Another report stated that discharge of oil, heavy metals, and other industrial wastes into the sea had polluted Liaoning's coastal waters, but at the same time claimed success in treating ballast water from oil tankers in a special processing pond.[102]

In July 1979 China held its first national meeting on air-pollution control. Conference participants stressed the seriousness of air pollution in China's cities and suggested that other cities follow the lead of Shenyang in Liaoning province. Shenyang has emphasized shifting from coal to gas for factory use, heating, and domestic uses and has thereby cut back on its black smoke problems.[103] However, China's urban air pollution remains excessive. An American newspaper in July 1981 reported some examples: "A delegation from the [U.S.] Environmental Protection Agency visited China last year . . . and took tests on a street corner in Peking [Beijing]. It showed the air contamination was six times the alert level of Washington, D.C. The measuring device literally broke down when they tried to use it in the industrial city of Wuhan."[104]

Water pollution also remains serious. Lakes and rivers in or near cities are often seriously polluted by sewage and industrial effluents.[105] In rural areas, water is polluted by livestock and by agricultural activities. In some places the fish catch from fresh water aquaculture has declined owing to water pollution. For example, Anhui province reported in 1979 that "although the province has 8 million *mu* [1.3 million acres] of water surface suitable for fish feeding, because of water pollution the catch in 1976 was only one-tenth of [that in] 1963."[106]

In late 1979 the Chinese government passed a trial law on environmental protection that emphasized controlling the "three industrial wastes"—waste gases, liquids, and solids.[107] Since then some factories have been fined for repeated violations,[108] but government efforts to prevent or clean up pollution meet vigorous resistance from industrial management in China, as in the West, and the health bureaucracy must contend with the industrial bureaucracy when attempting to enforce pollution standards. In the words of an official of China's Ministry of Public Health: "With industrial development, the environmental pollution problem will become very serious. We must do something to prevent it from getting worse. . . . Of course the Ministry of Health wants high standards and the Ministry of Industry, low standards. You can spend less money on low standards."[109]

By the late 1970's China could afford to turn its attention to health problems characteristic of developed countries. As most of the infectious diseases associated with high mortality in traditional populations had come under reasonable control, China embarked in the late 1970's and the 1980's on an effort to ascertain and address the remaining causes of death and ill health. China also turned its attention to widespread conditions that, though not deadly, caused considerable illness, deformity, and human misery. The results of these efforts have been, first, a relatively advanced mortality situation and, second, much improved health for China's people. But although progress has been impressive, further improvement of China's morbidity and mortality conditions depends on constant vigilance in monitoring disease and keeping up public health work. As soon as local or national officials relax their support of public-health programs, deterioration of health and resurgence of disease occur. For example, political struggle among China's top leaders after Mao's death caused neglect of sanitation work, resulting in outbreaks of hepatitis and meningitis.[110]

China's Medical System Today

China's medical system at the beginning of the 1980's can be described as follows. As of 1980 the nation had 1,982,000 hospital beds; this was an average of one bed per 500 persons in the entire population, but hospitals were heavily concentrated in urban areas serving primarily the urban and suburban population. As of yearend 1980, the PRC had 447,000 senior doctors of Western medicine, 444,000 medical orderlies or junior doctors of Western medicine, and 466,000 nurses. These personnel worked primarily in hospitals located in cities, towns, and county seats, and they also helped staff those hospitals set up to serve one or several rural people's communes.

In addition to Western-style medical personnel, China in 1980 had 262,000 doctors of traditional Chinese medicine. Though some of them worked in urban areas, most worked in county and commune hospitals serving the rural population. A comparison with data from the 1950's shows that the number of traditional doctors declined from 487,000 in 1955 to 262,000 in 1980. At the same time, the number of Western-style senior medical doctors rose from 74,000 in 1957 to 447,000 in 1980, according to official reports. This shift sums up China's movement away from primary reliance on traditional medicine toward primary reliance on Western medicine, supplemented by traditional practices when they appear efficacious.[111]

As of 1979 the PRC had 1,575,000 barefoot doctors.[112] These paramedics were serving a population of about 790 million in rural areas, for an average of one barefoot doctor per 500 rural people. But they were not evenly distributed throughout the countryside. Wealthy production brigades could afford to support several, while poor brigades might have one barefoot doctor or none.

The number of barefoot doctors had not increased rapidly for some years. One million barefoot doctors had been minimally trained in the crash program between 1968 and 1970. Then the total number increased more slowly to 1.3 million in 1973.[113] During the late 1970's, the earlier policy of increasing the numbers of barefoot doctors was replaced by a policy stressing further training of existing barefoot doctors and improving the quality of their diagnoses and treatments. Barefoot doctors, meanwhile, have demanded better conditions of work, better training, better pay, less overwork, and a title more commensurate with their upgraded medical skills, such as "country doctor."[114] Some technically qualified barefoot doctors have abandoned their practices in favor of more lucrative work, while others have been unable to pass newly established tests for minimal medical competence and have been dismissed. The total number of barefoot doctors reportedly peaked at 1.76 million in 1977 and declined to 1.46 million in 1981.[115] These figures were not broken down by sex; however, as of 1975 one-third of the barefoot doctors were female.[116] The barefoot doctors were assisted by about 3.8 million part-time health aides and midwives, predominantly women.[117]

At least until the early 1980's, rural medical workers have usually, but not always, worked as part of a cooperative medical service. This system was popularized during 1968, and by 1971 it was claimed that 76 percent of China's rural production brigades had established a cooperative medical service.[118] This proportion fluctuated during the 1970's; the highest nationwide figure ever reported was for 1977, when it was claimed that over 90 percent of China's production brigades had a cooperative medical service and a health station staffed by barefoot doctors.[119] As of 1979 it was reported that about 80 percent of China's rural production brigades had a cooperative medical system and that the proportion was 90 percent in richer rural localities but only 50 percent in poorer areas.[120] These fluctuations resulted from the continued necessity for local self-reliance in health care.

Some effort was made to provide medical benefits to those persons, families, villages, brigades, or even whole provinces that could least afford to pay for medical care. The national government sent to poor areas mobile medical teams of professionals whose salaries were paid from public funds, subsidized training of barefoot doctors, and provided paramedics with free contraceptive supplies. County governments supported anti-epidemic projects and maternal and child health programs to some extent. Richer brigades in a commune sometimes helped to support medical care in the commune's poorer brigades through joint management of the cooperative medical service. But, as a general rule, each production brigade in the PRC was essentially on its own in financially supporting a cooperative medical service or other forms of subsidized medical care.

A poor production brigade with few or no brigade-owned industries had no source of funds for subsidizing a cooperative medical service. Poor families could not afford to pay the small annual fee of one to three yuan per person for joining a cooperative health system, nor could they afford the "nominal" fees charged for seeing the barefoot doctor or receiving medication. Such sums are not small for families living at subsistence level. If the poorest production brigades did not have a cooperative medical service, and if the villagers had to do without medical care or pay for services rendered every time they saw a medical worker, mortality and morbidity were likely to be much worse in them than in wealthier brigades. Even when poor brigades could staff a health station with a barefoot doctor and could nominally offer a cooperative health service, the services provided have not matched those of richer brigades. The poorer brigades tended to have fewer and more marginally trained barefoot doctors, a more rigid referral system to minimize referrals to the commune clinic or county hospital, fewer modern drugs and herbal medicines, and much less coverage for chronic or major diseases.[121]

During good agricultural years, cooperative medical services tended to have relatively healthy financial status, but after a poor harvest the medical plan, because of a rise in disease due to poor nutrition and a shortfall in membership fees, tended to run out of money and disband, leaving brigade members to their own devices just when their need was greatest. Guangdong province, for example, had small grain harvests in 1972 and 1975. As a result, during 1973 and 1976 the proportion of production brigades in the province offering a cooperative medical service dropped.[122] Increases in grain production, in turn, have often been followed by increases in the numbers of cooperative health programs.

What is the current state of China's medical and public health system? A balanced assessment is difficult to make, because in recent years the Chinese media have given conflicting evaluations. On the one hand, there are glowing accounts of progress in upgrading the training of barefoot doctors, expanding coverage of cooperative medical services, further control of endemic and epidemic diseases, the first attempts to prevent the sale of contaminated food, and vigorous public sanitation campaigns. But on the other hand, the media have been unusually candid for several years about poor public health conditions, outbreaks of disease, incompetent medical care, and the dismantling of cooperative medical service in some areas.[123] This may simply mean that they are now freer to address problems that were always there but were off limits for public discussion, or it may mean that there has been increasing complacency and neglect of public-health work since the mid-1970's in some areas.

During the late 1970's and early 1980's, China began giving more decision-making power to industrial and production-team management and more incentives to workers in rural and urban areas in order to increase the quantity and efficiency of production. This change in policy aroused concern among national and provincial leaders that greater local economic autonomy was resulting in abandonment of the cooperative medical system and neglect of public sanitation work. For example, Guangdong province reported that during 1979 cooperative medical services in some of its rural areas were totally or partially suspended.[124] The main problem seems to have been financial and was concentrated in poorer areas.[125] Zhejiang province reported that 87 percent of its production brigades operated cooperative medical services in 1977 and that there were 82,000 barefoot doctors throughout the province. But during 1978 and 1979, both the proportion of brigades maintaining a cooperative medical service and the number of barefoot doctors fell.[126] The lack of medical care was worst in mountainous areas of the province, suggesting that here, too, financial factors were the problem and that the poorest areas are becoming increasingly unable or unwilling to fund public health and medical services. This weakening of the cooperative medical system in rural areas has continued. One county reported, "Owing to the discontinuance of cooperative medicine after the adoption of the agricultural responsibility system, public health and disease-prevention work are not being taken care of by anyone, and epidemics of some diseases have erupted."[127]

Very little information has been published on rural health services in the early 1980's. An optimistic assessment of the confused situation was given by the Minister of Public Health in 1982:

> With regard to medical treatment in rural villages, Cui Yueli said that with the extension and perfection of the system of responsibility of agricultural production, the medical and public health organizations of production brigades have taken on many forms to suit the locality so as to mobilize the positiveness of all sectors. As a result, the 610,000 brigade public health centers and the 1.3 million barefoot doctor teams are stabilized and developed so that the rural villages all over the country are basically provided with medicine and drugs and have persons to do the work of prevention, control, and planned parenthood.[128]

The impression gleaned from official sources is that the government made no plan for the smooth continuation of public health work under the new system of agricultural organization, and to fill this vacuum makeshift solutions have proliferated from one locality to another. A new system seems to be slowly emerging, in which barefoot doctors and other medical personnel may set up a private medical practice but at the same time are under contract to work for the brigade clinic.[129] It is not clear to what extent cooperative medical services have been superseded by a fee-for-service system with no medical insurance component, which would be detrimental to those who develop serious health problems. Yunnan province, following 1983 national guidelines on "the reform of brigade health organizations," has abandoned the cooperative medical system in all but a small number of economically well-off brigades.[130] China's new model of rural medical care as applied in Yunnan combines the charging of fees for all services, including visits to a barefoot doctor, medicines, inoculations, and hospital stays, with a brigade subsidy that pays for the brigade clinic building and guarantees remuneration to the barefoot doctors.

In urban areas, providing basic medical services does not appear to be a problem, but mediocre public sanitation and continuing pollution still plague urban dwellers, along with crowding and traffic noise. A 1979 report described the urban sanitation situation as follows:

> Thanks to the measures taken by the party Central Committee and many provinces, municipalities, and prefectures to step up the patriotic health campaign, since 1978 many cities have to varying degrees improved hygienic conditions. But viewing the situation as a whole, the hygienic conditions in most cities are still not quite ideal. In some cities, they are no better than in the 1950's. Environmental hygiene has become a very serious problem in some localities where filthy water and piles of dirt and garbage are scattered all over the place. Under the threat of the three industrial wastes—waste water, slag, and gas—beautiful rivers have been turned into filthy mires, posing a direct threat to the people's health.[131]

Vulnerability to Mortality and Morbidity

In a year when harvests throughout China are neither unusually good nor unusually poor, food production increases about as fast as the population does, and people have about their usual amount of food to eat. That is to say, urban populations get enough calories and their nutritional level is fairly good, advanced rural and suburban populations have enough calories and barely enough protein and other nutrients, and the people of poor rural areas that are chronically short of food experience chronic malnutrition. The government attempts to supplement the grain supplies of hungry areas with extra grain from elsewhere, which means the people do not starve but neither do they have enough calories for vigorous activity or enough protein, fat, vitamins, and minerals for proper growth.

However, very few years have fully fit that norm. Some years there has been such political chaos that the transport system, the timely supply of tools and materials, and food distribution systems may have been affected. The early years of the Cultural Revolution might have seen such disruptions. In addition, during most years China has experienced serious local droughts, floods, or attacks of crop pests that have wiped out or badly diminished yields in some areas. What has happened to the people who lost their food crops to these natural disasters?

In theory, China's government guarantees to all its people all the time a basic minimum processed grain allotment of 150 kilograms per year, which works out to about 1,350 calories a day per person unless supplemented by other foods, an absolute minimum subsistence allocation.[132] When everything is working according to design, grain is quickly transported to grain-deficit disaster areas out of stored grain supplies or from areas with surpluses or from grain bought on the international market if necessary. The people in the agricultural disaster areas probably would not directly starve to death, but they might be more vulnerable to disease in their malnourished condition, and local mortality conditions could temporarily worsen, especially if the rural cooperative medical system was suspended for financial reasons.

We have minimal information on several natural disasters in agriculture during the 1970's. Sichuan province, for instance, was seriously deficient in grain in 1976, which reportedly caused local famines with people fleeing the famine areas. The railroads could not move enough grain into the province from the other areas of China. Emergency grain was moved by boat up the Changjiang (Yangtze) River, a process that probably took too long.[133] It is likely that mortality conditions deteriorated temporarily in the localities affected by the famine.

Xizang (Tibet) is a food-deficient province in normal years, but in addition, owing to serious natural calamities in 1979, there was a large decrease in agricultural production and animal husbandry was adversely affected.[134] At the same time, relief work was already being directed to chronically poor families in material difficulties, and the provincial leadership reported in January 1980 that countermeasures were expanded to deal with the food production shortfall and that "losses were kept to a minimum."[135]

In 1980 agricultural disasters in China covered a large number of provinces. Xinjiang province made the following announcement in January 1981:

> Natural disasters in our region were very serious last year. Thirty-seven counties and municipalities in eleven prefectures were hit by heavy snows, hailstorms, mountain torrents, drought, windstorms, plant diseases, insect pests, and other natural disasters. These natural disasters caused grave damage to the region's agri-

cultural and animal husbandry production. As a result, people in the disaster areas have encountered grave difficulties in livelihood.[136]

The same report stated that the national government allocated relief funds "in good time" for grain, clothing, and blankets, and that relief work was carried out adequately.

In the summer of 1980, the Changjiang River flooded after torrential rains, cresting at its highest level in 26 years, and inundating heavily populated rural areas in Hubei and Anhui provinces. Chinese officials reported that 550 people died in the floods and about 41,000 people were injured. The homes and crops of millions of persons were destroyed, and as of April 1981, as many as 20 million were said to be living on minimum government-supplied grain rations.

However, the worst agricultural disaster of 1980 was a devastating drought in northern China affecting parts of Gansu, Ningxia, Inner Mongolia, Shaanxi, Shanxi, Liaoning, and most seriously, Hebei provinces. Over 100 million people faced food shortages.[137] For the first time the PRC asked for international food relief, partly because stored grain supplies appeared to be running short. It was reported that, although people did not starve to death outright, disaster victims subsisted on emergency rations of only 1,200 to 1,500 calories a day and malnutrition was serious. It is noteworthy that China did a good job of minimizing the human effects of the natural disasters. According to an international relief official, "There is malnutrition, and some of it is serious and getting more serious. There are diseases growing out of it. But there is food to guarantee survival, and the Chinese are handling the bulk of the problems themselves with varying degrees of effectiveness."[138]

These events serve as a reminder that China's system of food supply and distribution is still precarious; the people can never be certain that hunger and malnutrition will not reappear. The PRC has to assure its self-sufficiency in food production and supply, because given its great size, there is no way that the world market or international relief supplies can make up for a serious failure in its grain production. The 1980 grain shortfall that caused so much hunger and dislocation was a drop of less than 5 percent from the 1979 record crop of 332 million metric tons to 321 million tons. In fact more grain was reportedly produced in 1980 than in 1978 or any previous year, but China is living so close to the line that one bad year in agriculture is one too many. If the PRC experiences another series of three poor crop years as during the Great Leap Forward, famine will accompany it and death rates will rise once again.

China is also subject to earthquakes. Though the PRC has made headlines by accurately predicting when earthquakes would hit in a particular locality, seismologists did not predict the sudden and devastating Tangshan earthquake in Hebei province in 1976. Almost immediately, 242,000 people were killed and 164,000 seriously injured in this populous industrial area, and the city of Tangshan was completely flattened.[139] From the available reports it appears that China organized an enormous relief effort in a short time and thus was able to prevent many further deaths from disease, hunger, and exposure.

From these and other reports of natural disasters in the 1970's and 1980, we can assess how the PRC handles calamities. Once a flood, drought, or earthquake has happened, the government is quick to respond and tries to move relief workers, food, medical personnel, and medical supplies to the stricken area. It is hampered in this effort by a weak transportation system; indeed, many of the casualties may result from transport bottlenecks.

Although China does an admirable job of coping with natural disasters after they occur, the government does not do so well with preventive measures. For example, until the rebuilding of Tangshan began, the government had apparently never promoted earthquake-resistant construction in seismic areas. So many people died in Tangshan, it seems, because they were asleep in houses constructed of heavy materials, which immediately collapsed on their heads. Another way China could prevent deaths from natural disasters is to strengthen agricultural production and augment its system of grain storage. For 30 years China's agricultural system was plagued with problems of low incentives for production and limited storage capacity. The current leadership is trying to remedy this situation by changing the economic conditions under which peasants work, with outstanding results for agricultural production. It is important that China produce and store enough food to easily withstand a poor agricultural year, because it is certain that there will be occasional poor harvests.

To safeguard China's gains in mortality and health requires constant vigilance in promoting agricultural production, moving grain quickly to deficit areas, preserving public order, maintaining preventive public health work, and minimizing the spread of epidemics. If all goes well, slow improvement in mortality and more rapid improvement in the population's health status can be anticipated as the PRC attacks its major causes of death and the many remaining health problems of its people.

4

Mortality

DURING the last three decades, as China has attacked one cause of death after another, the mortality level of the population has undergone a profound transformation. As in many other developing countries, China's mortality transition took place most spectacularly during the 1950's, with subsequent gains being more gradual and modest. Therefore, a careful look at mortality data for the 1950's should tell us much about the historic shift from China's traditional very high mortality to the relatively low mortality of today.

Mortality Change in the 1950's

Keeping in mind trends in China's health system during the 1950's, let us explore China's reported mortality data for that decade. Official and semiofficial sources have reported the national crude death rate estimates presented in Table 4.1. One Chinese source estimated the death rate before the founding of the PRC in October 1949 as around 28 per thousand population. An earlier official estimate was that "during the period of Kuomintang control, the population death rate [in China] was 25 for every thousand."[1] Because there was no nationwide vital registration system at that time, these estimates are probably based on a variety of surveys conducted in different localities during this century, such as those compiled in Table 4.2. But careful analysis has demonstrated that deaths in the farmers survey of 1929–31, for example, were seriously underreported—a crude death rate of 27 per thousand population calculated from the data as reported corresponded to an actual death rate estimated at over 40 per thousand.[2] Similarly, the other surveys in Table 4.2 probably also tended to undercount deaths; the surveys in four provinces in 1924–25, in Ding county 1931–36, and in Chenggong county 1940–44

TABLE 4.1
Reported Crude Death Rates in the PRC, 1949–57
(Deaths per 1,000 population)

Year	Source (1)	(2)	(3)	(4)	(5)	(6)
1949					20.0	20.0
1950		18	18	18.0	18.0	18.0
1951					17.0	17.8
1952	18		17		17.0	17.0
1953	17				14.0	14.0
1954	13	14			13.2	13.2
1955	12.4				12.3	12.3
1956	11.4				11.4	11.4
1957	11.0	10.8	10.8	10.8	10.8	10.8

SOURCES: (1) Chandrasekhar (1959); (2) Zhu Zhengzhi (1980); (3) Liu Zheng (1980b; 1981a); (4) Ling (1981); (5) Zhang Huaiyu et al. (1981); (6) Statistical Yearbook of China 1983.

NOTE: Three of the sources provide estimates of China's death rate "prior to liberation"; Zhu Zhengzhi, "around 28"; Liu Zheng, "nearly 30"; and Ling, "about 25."

TABLE 4.2
Reported Crude Male and Female Birth and Death Rates in China, 1920's–1940's

Area and date	Crude birth rate	Crude death rate: Males	Crude death rate: Females	Infant mortality rate: Males	Infant mortality rate: Females
Four provinces, 1924–25	42.2	27.9		129.4	
Rural areas in 22 provinces, 1929–31					
All areas	38.3	26.7	27.6	160	152
North China	37.4	22.1	26.2	152	159
South China	39.0	31.0	28.9	166	147
Xiaoxi, Jiangyin county, Jiangsu, 1931–35	45.1	38.3	39.2	220.7	263.6
1931–32	48.3	44.0	41.4	184.8	223.8
1932–33	44.1	35.2	37.2	201.2	284.8
1933–34	40.0	49.3	55.0	378.5	402.4
1934–35	48.0	24.8	22.8	153.8	154.5
Ding county (Ting Hsien), Hebei					
1931	37.1	33.7		—	
1933	40.1	27.2		199.0	
1934	27.4	27.2		163.1	
1935	25.9	29.1		185.2	
1936	25.1	20.4		145.0	
1st Special Health Area, Beijing, 1920's–30's	19.9 (1926–31)	18.5 (1926–31)		138.6 (1934)	113.1 (1934)
Chenggong county, Yunnan, Feb. 1940–June 1944	24.9	26.3	23.1	212.1	211.1

SOURCE: King & Locke (1983): 378–79.

NOTE: Crude birth and death rates are per 1,000 population; infant mortality rates are per 1,000 live births. Figures centered in the male-female columns represent the combined rate for the two sexes.

all gave suspiciously low death rates, in contrast to the relatively complete death rates reported for Xiaoxi in 1931–35. The high and volatile death rates of this locality provide a more appropriate model for China's pre-1949 mortality level and pattern than any of the other surveys cited in Table 4.2. It is likely that the crude death rate was close to 40 per thousand population in 1930 and stayed that high or higher during most of the 1930's and 1940's, in part because of active warfare between Japan and China and between the Communist and Nationalist armies. It is fair to conclude that the last half of the 1940's may have witnessed some mortality gains where hostilities had subsided, but that no major improvement in China's mortality level would be expected by 1949. Several other scholars concur in this conclusion.[3] As of 1948–49, China's crude death rate was probably high, around 35 per thousand population or above. The death rates of 25–30 reported in Table 4.1 underestimate the mortality of the pre-1949 period, thereby also underestimating the great gains that have been made since that time.

Similarly, every crude death rate officially or semiofficially reported by the PRC for any year in the 1950's is likely to be far below the actual crude death rate at the time. China could not have achieved a crude death rate of 18 in 1950. Warfare had just ceased in many parts of the country and recovery from its ravages was just beginning. A tumultuous land-reform struggle was in progress, and public health work was barely launched. There was as yet no patriotic public health campaign. There were very few epidemic-control centers, maternal and child health stations, or specialized disease-prevention centers. There was a plague epidemic in 1950, plus high mortality from typhus, measles, scarlet fever, and dysentery, according to scattered hints in press reports. As of 1950 China had not begun to prevent or cure tuberculosis, diphtheria, malaria, kala-azar, typhoid, poliomyelitis, or parasitic diseases. The one big public health success in that year was a widespread smallpox vaccination campaign, which no doubt began to reduce mortality from smallpox. A crude death rate as low as 18 is a relatively advanced death rate by historical standards, yet mortality conditions in China were still backward in the first year after the Red Army victory. It is most likely that in the year 1950 the PRC had a crude death rate of about 30 per thousand population or above.

All other reported crude death rates for China in the 1950's are also far too low for conditions at the time. As another example, let us look closely at the year 1957. China reported that it had achieved in that year the very advanced death rate (for a developing country) of 10.8 per thousand, corresponding to an expectation of life at birth of 57 years.[4]

This is an unrealistic claim. Of course, the PRC made great strides in mortality reduction during the 1950's. As of 1957, the patriotic public health campaigns had reduced the level of filth and the number of disease-carrying pests. A large proportion of China's midwives had received instruction in modern midwifery. There were many epidemic-control stations monitoring infectious diseases and specialized centers attacking particular diseases. Smallpox was almost eradicated. Death rates from many infectious diseases—plague, typhus, syphilis, measles, scarlet fever, dysentery, and kala-azar—were far below their 1950 levels. Yet underlying health conditions in China remained poor. The populace was still afflicted with typhoid, tuberculosis, diphtheria, malaria, poliomyelitis, and many other infectious diseases with high cause-specific mortality. Contamination of water, soil, and food was also a problem. China in 1957 had over one-fifth of the world's people in its sphere of responsibility, yet it had a very tiny health budget, severe shortages of all kinds of pharmaceuticals, very little available curative medical care, a bare beginning on immunizing the rural populace, continuing occasional outbreaks of infectious disease, and a massive burden of parasitic diseases debilitating most of the population. This population might have achieved a crude death rate below 20 per thousand by 1957, but not nearly so low as the official death rate of 10.8.

What was the source of China's reported crude death rates for the years 1950 through 1957? China began setting up a vital registration system after 1954. The regulations for reporting of births and deaths were promulgated in 1955. But it appears that the vital registration system never attained nationwide coverage during the 1950's. If the system of death registration was used as a basis for any of the estimated death rates for 1955 through 1957, the rates were derived from only those localities that had set up the system, which would tend to be more advanced or more urbanized locations.

It is likely that the reported death rates are based on sample surveys for some years. China took several surveys of vital rates during 1951–54. One major survey was the source of the reported crude death rate of 17 for 1951 and 1952. This was an unrepresentative survey based on a population of 30 million people, a disproportionate number of whom lived in cities and towns.[5]

Let us review the figures. The reported 1949 and 1950 death rates are obviously unsubstantiated estimates, since there were no data for those years except perhaps in a few cities. The death rates reported for 1951 and 1952 are based on the skewed survey just described. The figures for 1955–57 are probably based on an incomplete registration system biased toward urban and advanced rural areas. All of these were affected by significant underreporting or underregistration of deaths.

Estimates of infant mortality for the 1950's and before were also too low. During the 1950's three Chinese sources estimated that before 1949 or "during the period of Guomindang control" the national infant mortality rate was approximately 200 deaths in the first year of life per thousand live births.[6] Two Soviet publications in 1958 claimed that China's 1955 infant mortality rate was down to 74.3 deaths per thousand live births.[7] China's Minister of Public Health reported an infant mortality rate of 77 for 1956, and the *Chinese Journal of Pediatrics* reported a rate of approximately 70 for about 1958.[8] Similar claims for the 1950's are still being released; for instance, a 1981 paper reported that in 1957 China had an infant mortality rate of 71.[9] The basis for these claims is unknown.

Complete reporting of infant mortality, in China and everywhere else, is usually very hard to achieve. For instance, pre-1949 infant mortality rates shown in Table 4.2 appear in most cases to be unrealistically low. The Princeton reanalysis of Chinese farmers survey data from 1929–31 indicated that almost half of the infant deaths were unreported and estimated the infant mortality rate at about 300, rather than the much lower reported rates of 160 for males and 152 for females.[10] Because these data were from rural farm families only, it is possible that other groups in the population such as city dwellers had lower infant mortality, and that the national infant mortality rate for 1929–31 was below 300. Given the lack of significant improvement in conditions that affect infant mortality during the 1930's and 1940's, it is unlikely that China attained an infant mortality rate of 200 before 1949.

There is no doubt that China made great progress in the reduction of infant mortality during the 1950's. Training midwives probably had the greatest impact in reducing neonatal tetanus and other infections associated with non-sterile childbirth conditions. Relatively stable nutritional conditions for mothers during the mid-1950's probably helped them in nursing their babies, almost all of whom were breastfed. The emphasis on environmental sanitation and control of pests beginning in 1952 no doubt reduced the incidence of fatal diseases among infants. Epidemic-control measures were also instrumental in lowering infant mortality.

But as of the late 1950's there were still many conditions that contributed to high infant mortality. Almost all births in the country were at home rather than in hospitals or clinics, except in advanced urban areas. Midwives could handle a normal birth but had essentially no emergency backup in cases of complications, which usually affect 5–10 percent of all births. For example, almost everywhere it was impossible to carry out a cesarean section or provide oxygen or blood transfusions to mothers and infants in distress during childbirth. If a woman could not properly nurse her baby, there was little or no safe infant formula. Respiratory and intestinal diseases continued to be serious problems for infants. Many contagious diseases continued to cause infant death, especially in rural areas. For example, pneumonia epidemics in 1953 and 1958 raised fatality rates among infants in northern China.[11] Under these conditions, it is very unlikely that China could have achieved the officially estimated infant mortality rates of 70–77 for the years 1955–58.

Somewhat more realistic infant mortality rates were reported from a peasant household survey taken in 1954 and 1955. For rural areas, the survey derived an infant mortality rate of 138.52 for 1954 and 109.66 for 1955. The 1954 figure was based on results from fourteen provinces and the 1955 figure on 24 provinces, but the report cautioned that "in both cases registration is incomplete."[12] The actual rural infant mortality rate was probably considerably higher. Similarly, urban areas underreported their infant mortality during the 1950's. Nine cities already recorded relatively low infant mortality rates in the range of 44–87 for the year 1952, declining to 25–44 in 1956. China estimated overall urban infant mortality rates of 47 for 1954 and 32 in 1957. Considering the health problems that continued to affect even urban areas in China, these estimates are probably too low.

It is clear, nevertheless, that the PRC attained very rapid mortality decline during the 1950's. It is probable that the pre-1949 crude death rate and infant mortality rate were approximately halved by 1957. This is a monumental achievement for such a huge population. China was similar to most other developing countries during the 1950's in that it achieved significant mortality control through cheap public health measures, but the reduction of mortality in the PRC was steeper and more far-reaching than in most other countries, in part because China started with a worse mortality situation.

How can we explain this extraordinary mortality decline? First, the cessation of warfare and the maintenance of public order were powerful factors. For almost a century the Chinese had been victimized by foreign invasion, civil war, feuds between local warlords and clans, and constant banditry. These calamities, which caused catastrophic mortality, largely ended with the establishment of the PRC.

Second, the redistribution of agricultural land and the gradual nationalization of business and commercial assets during the 1950's greatly diminished the extremes of wealth and poverty in China. Though the average per capita wealth and income were not much increased by 1957, China's national income was more evenly distributed than ever before. Therefore, the poorest part of the population had a better chance to provide for their own basic subsistence needs than before the 1950's. This

TABLE 4.3
Reported Crude Death Rates in the PRC, 1957–83
(Deaths per 1,000 population)

Year	Sources (1)	Sources (2)	Year	Sources (1)	Sources (2)
1957	10.80	10.80	1973[b]	7.08	7.04
1958	11.98	11.98	1974[b]	7.38	7.34
1959	14.50	14.59[a]	1975[b]	7.36	7.32
1960	25.43	25.43	1976	7.29	7.25
1961	14.38	14.24	1977	6.91	6.87
1962	10.08	10.02	1978	6.29	6.25
1963	10.10	10.04			6.27[c]
1964	11.56	11.50	1979	6.20	6.21
1965	9.55	9.50			6.29[d]
1966	8.87	8.83			6.24[e]
1967	8.47	8.43	1980	—	6.2[f]
1968	8.25	8.21			6.34[g]
1969	8.06	8.03	1981	—	6.36[h]
1970	7.64	7.60	1982	—	6.60[i]
1971	7.34	7.32	1983	—	7.08[j]
1972	7.65	7.61			

SOURCES: (1) Zhang Huaiyu et al. (1981): 83; (2) Statistical Yearbook of China 1983 (1983): 105, except as noted.
[a]Also Tian Xueyuan (1981): 39, 41.
[b]7.30 for the 3-year period 1973–75, according to unadjusted survey data in Banister & Preston (1981a): 99.
[c]Wu Zhongguan et al. (1980): 28.
[d]"In the Coming Years China's Population Should Not Have Negative Growth," GMRB, 13 Apr. 1980: 3.
[e]Li Chengrui (1982a): 15–16.
[f]"From 36 to 68," BR 24, no. 27 (6 July 1981): 4.
[g]Li Muzhen (1982): 3.
[h]Also Communique on 1982 Census: K3.
[i]Also Statistical Abstract of China 1983 (1983): 13.
[j]Communique on 1983 Economic Plan (1984): K14.

change alone surely had a major impact on the mortality of China's poorest people.

Third, the government set up a system of state purchase, storage, and distribution of grain. During the period 1950–57, whenever local areas experienced crop failures but national grain production was adequate, the government reportedly tried to move grain to the affected areas. Given the abysmal state of China's transportation, communication, and food-storage systems, it was and still is probably impossible for the government to make up for all local shortfalls by moving grain. Even so, the distribution of food grain as part of China's disaster relief program in the 1950's helped to minimize local famine mortality.

Fourth, preventive public health measures resulted in rapid reduction in mortality from infectious diseases and filth. The PRC, therefore, achieved very rapid mortality decline through cessation of warfare, maintenance of public order, redistribution of agricultural land, movement of grain to deficit areas, and a massive preventive public health system. Unfortunately, these successes could not guarantee that mortality would not rise again. After 1957 China entered the Great Leap Forward, which was accompanied by a dramatic and temporary reversal of its earlier mortality decline.

What happened to China's mortality level during this period of food shortages and diminished public health work? Official mortality data, presented in Table 4.3, show a slight rise in the crude death rate in 1958, a somewhat sharper increase in 1959, a sudden peak famine death rate of 25.4 per thousand population in 1960, recovery in 1961 back to the 1959 level, and full recovery from the famine in 1962. We do not have province-by-province data, but some provinces were much harder hit than others, for example Gansu, which recorded a peak death rate of 41 per thousand population in 1960.[13]

Assuming that without the Great Leap Forward's policies and experiences China would have maintained its claimed 1957 death rate of 10.8 during the years 1958–61, the official data imply that those four years saw 15 million excess deaths attributable to the Great Leap Forward in combination with poor weather conditions. The computer reconstruction of China's population trends utilized in this book, which assumes underreporting of deaths in 1957 as well as in all the famine years, results in an estimated 30 million excess deaths during 1958–61.

The official figures may actually underestimate China's mortality during the crisis years. At that time the death registration system was inadequate to record all deaths even in ordinary years. But during a famine, vital registration systems have a tendency to be neglected. Deaths among a destitute population engaged in a fight for survival are not likely to be properly registered.

Post-Famine Mortality

Once the famine was over, health conditions and mortality returned to previous levels within a couple of years, according to official mortality data and according to the adjusted mortality estimates given in this book. Since then mortality has stayed relatively low and improvements in health have been impressive. Table 4.3 lists the PRC's reported crude death rates since the 1950's, and Table 4.4 gives the reported or estimated expectation of life at birth for some years. The most problematic rates in this

TABLE 4.4
Reported Male and Female Life Expectancy, 1957–81
(In years)

Year	Total	Males	Females
1957	57[a]	—	—
1973–75	(65.81–66.20)[b]	63.62[c]	66.31[c]
1975	68.25[d]	67.17[e]	69.32[e]
1978	68.28[f]	66.95[f]	69.55[f]
1979	Over 70[g]	68[h]	70[h]
1981	67.88[i]	66.43[i]	69.35[i]

SOURCES:
[a]Liu Zheng (1980b): 2.
[b]Life tables calculated by Judith Banister, Victoria Ho, and Frank Hobbs based on Cancer Epidemiology Survey data.
[c]Rong et al. (1981): 25–26. [d]Song & Li (1980): 63.
[e]Liaoning Provincial Statistical System (1982): 75.
[f]Liaoning Provincial Statistical System (1982): 75; also Ling (1981): 128, 131, and "Woguo renkou pingjun shoming yanchang" (The life expectancy of China's population has been prolonged), JFRB, 15 Feb. 1981: 2.
[g]Zhu Zhengzhi (1980); also "Average Life Expectancy Passes 70 Years in China," JPRS 76642 (17 Oct. 1980): 48.
[h]"Measures to Improve Population Quality Outlined," JPRS 77665 (25 Mar. 1981): 4.
[i]Jiang, Zhang & Zhu (1984): 15–17.

series are the reported death rates of 10 per thousand for 1962 and 1963. As the year 1961 was reportedly a bad crop year and followed two other poor crop years, people were still starving or malnourished and vulnerable to disease throughout 1961 and at least until the first crops of 1962 were harvested. This implies excessive mortality in the first half of 1962, with considerable improvement in the last half of the year. The proposition that malnutrition was still serious in 1962 is supported by a local study in Jiangxi province that measured indices of chronic and acute malnutrition among children in March 1962. The study team documented a significant reduction in the proportion of malnourished children between March 1962 and March 1964.[14] Though the official death rates of 10 per thousand population for 1962 and 1963 are probably too low in absolute terms, the concept of a two-year trough in the death rate after a famine is consistent with experience elsewhere, because the most vulnerable members of the population had already died in the famine. It is reasonable to assume that there was some mortality improvement between 1962 and 1963, though the official death rates do not indicate any. The official death rate for 1964 of 11.6 is a more reasonable level for the time than the reported 1962 and 1963 death rates. It is possible that death registration in the areas where the system worked was conscientiously improved just before 1964 so that in 1964 for the first time there was relatively complete reporting of deaths. A more plausible explanation is that the official 1964 death rate comes not from the weak death registration system but from 1964 census data. The census asked a question on deaths in the first half of 1964, from which an annual death rate for 1964 could be extrapolated.[15]

After 1965 the political system dissolved into the chaos known as the Cultural Revolution, and the statistical record-keeping and reporting system was again under attack, as it had been during the Great Leap Forward. It is likely that some provinces did not compile and report province-wide demographic data for the years 1966 through 1969 or so; therefore, any numbers now reported as the official death rates for those years may be educated guesses based on incomplete data. The neatly and gradually declining death rates after 1965 may represent no more than the national government's interpolation of death rates between the beginning and end of the Cultural Revolution. These official death rates are probably lower than the true death rates, and there is no guarantee that even the hypothesized trend is correct. It is just as possible that mortality either rose temporarily and then returned to the 1965 level or remained approximately steady for most of the Cultural Revolution. The number of excess deaths directly attributable to persecution, atrocities, mass murders, and armed conflicts during those years has been estimated from a minimum of 34,300 deaths, blamed personally on the top leaders, to an upper estimate of 400,000 excess deaths nationwide, including 67,000 in Guangxi province alone and 40,000 in Guangdong province alone.[16] Even the larger number, though horrifying, would not noticeably increase the crude death rate for those four years, because China's huge population already had 7 or 8 million deaths a year without the added atrocities. If the crude death rate rose during 1966–69, it would have to be attributed to indirect effects of administrative breakdown, such as neglected public health and epidemic work, disruption of curative medical care, and the spread of disease by young people traveling around the country.

Starting around 1969 or 1970, the first beneficial effects of the massive deployment of barefoot doctors in rural areas should have been evident in conditions affecting rural mortality. The rapid spread of the cooperative medical system must have regularized access to simple primary medical care for most of China's people. Once this medical system was functioning by around 1971 or 1972, a rise in life expectancy and decline in death rate would be expected. It is therefore reasonable to suppose that China's death rate, which probably stayed at or above 10 per thousand population throughout the 1960's, dipped and stayed below about 10 from the early 1970's on.

In all years prior to 1973–75 the PRC's data on crude death rates, infant mortality rates, expectation of life at birth, and causes of death were nonexistent, useless, or, at best, underestimates of actual mortality. But finally, China conducted what is perhaps the largest mortality survey ever taken anywhere, and derived imperfect but usable statistics on mortality for the survey reference years 1973–75.

China's Mortality Level, 1973–75

In 1980, for the first time, age-specific mortality data became available from China's Cancer Epidemiology Survey, a nationwide survey of deaths by age and causes of deaths. The collected data as reported are shown in Table 4.5.[17] The primary purpose of this survey was to determine causes of death throughout China, with an emphasis on cancer mortality. The survey was conducted by health personnel. The data on China's 1976 age structure, shown in the second column of Table 4.5, were taken from household registration lists and were to be verified by household surveys of approximately 10 percent of the 842 million "study population," then extrapolated to the whole study population. In contrast, the age-specific death data presented in the fourth column apparently came from a 100 percent sample of all the deaths detected in the whole study population for three successive years, in most cases 1973, 1974, and 1975.[18] This means that survey personnel filled out a cause-of-death card for each of the 18.4 million deaths in an unprecedented attempt to discover China's age pattern of mortality and exact ranking of the major causes of death.

For each production brigade in rural areas and each residential committee in urban areas, survey workers searched permanent population registration records and, where available, any records of who died during 1973–75. They inquired about additional unregistered deaths in some places, and they were required to document in the survey at least as many deaths as had been reported by the local unit for each of the three years. For each death, survey workers attempted to record the name of the deceased, sex, dates of birth and death, age at death, major illness prior to death, cause of death, and basis of the diagnosis. Because most of this information was not written down in easily usable form in rural areas, survey workers called meetings of local officials, health workers, and knowledgeable village elders to help fill in some of the details. Then they visited the family of the deceased, if the cause-of-death card was not already complete, to get further information that might help pin down the cause of death. The work went on in most provinces throughout 1976, but a few provinces did not complete the work for several years. Death data from those provinces might refer to 1974–76 or 1975–77, but these data were simply lumped with data from 1973–75 to produce the death totals by age listed in Table 4.5.

TABLE 4.5
Age-Specific Death Rates for China, 1973–75, from the Cancer Epidemiology Survey

Age group	Study population: Number (thousands)	Study population: Percent of population	Average annual deaths (thousands)	Death rate (per thousand)
0–4	104,413	12.41%	1,422	13.62
5–9	113,808	13.52	251	2.21
10–14	103,941	12.35	95	0.92
15–19	78,425	9.32	81	1.03
20–24	77,000	9.15	112	1.45
25–29	63,154	7.50	104	1.65
30–34	50,067	5.95	102	2.04
35–39	46,595	5.54	133	2.85
40–44	42,981	5.11	168	3.91
45–49	38,390	4.56	221	5.76
50–54	32,896	3.91	291	8.85
55–59	27,610	3.28	375	13.58
60–64	23,285	2.77	512	21.99
65–69	16,936	2.01	559	33.01
70–74	11,739	1.39	653	55.63
75–79	6,444	0.77	485	75.26
80±	3,986	0.47	579	145.26
TOTAL	841,670	100.01%	6,143	7.30

SOURCE: Frederick P. Li (1980).
NOTE: The survey covered 842 million of a total population of 900 million at the midpoint of the survey reference years 1973–75.

These data were intended to provide nationwide figures for causes of death and age-specific mortality. Indeed, a major attempt was made to include information from at least some part of every county or county-level unit in China. This goal was achieved, except for about 35 counties in Tibet and Sichuan.[19] Even so, the survey's data probably were not fully representative of the PRC's total population. The "study population" comprised 841.67 million persons estimated (for most provinces) at the midpoint of the period 1973–75. This study population was 93 percent of a midyear 1974 population total of just over 900 million persons. The study apparently excluded military personnel and their dependents, nomads, people in inaccessible areas of the country, members of some minority groups, and people in the poorest and least developed localities where death registration was probably weak.[20] It is likely that mortality conditions were on average considerably worse among the excluded 7 percent than among the included 93 percent.

A life table is a tool for understanding the mortality experience of a large group from birth until all have died, showing the ages at which they died. It is often based on age-at-death data from one point in time, and so

TABLE 4.6
Unadjusted Life Table for China, 1973–75, from the Cancer Epidemiology Survey
(N = 842,000,000)

Age group	Probability of dying during age interval q_x	Age-specific death rate m_x	Survivors entering age interval l_x	Person-years lived during age interval L_x	Life expectancy (years) e_x
0	0.04817	0.05013	100,000	96,098	66.20
1–4	0.01701	0.00430	95,183	376,634	68.54
5–9	0.01099	0.00221	93,563	465,245	65.70
10–14	0.00459	0.00092	92,535	461,612	61.40
15–19	0.00514	0.00103	92,110	459,368	56.67
20–24	0.00722	0.00145	91,637	456,530	51.95
25–29	0.00822	0.00165	90,975	453,006	47.31
30–34	0.01015	0.00204	90,227	448,848	42.69
35–39	0.01415	0.00285	89,312	443,400	38.10
40–44	0.01936	0.00391	88,048	435,979	33.61
45–49	0.02839	0.00576	86,343	425,588	29.22
50–54	0.04329	0.00885	83,892	410,380	25.00
55–59	0.06567	0.01358	80,260	388,123	21.02
60–64	0.10422	0.02199	74,989	355,408	17.32
65–69	0.15247	0.03301	67,174	310,265	14.05
70–74	0.24419	0.05563	56,932	249,905	11.13
75–79	0.31671	0.07526	43,030	181,079	8.91
80±	1.00000	0.14526	29,402	202,408	6.88

SOURCE: Constructed by the author, with computer assistance from Frank Hobbs, based on the unadjusted data in Table 4.5.

NOTE: A Coale-Demeny West model life table Level 19 was used for estimating $m_x$values for age 0 and 1–4 from the reported data for ages 0–4. Use of the West Level 20 pattern of deaths under age 5 is equally plausible, and would raise the infant mortality rate from 48 to 50, but leave the life expectancy at birth unchanged. The m_x column is age-specific mortality rates derived from Table 4.5. The rest of the table is based on information in the m_x column. The q_x column shows the probability of dying between the beginning of that age interval and the end of it. The l_x column shows the number of persons still alive at the exact age out of 100,000 born theoretically at the same time. The e_x column gives the life expectancy at that age—if you live to that exact age, as a statistical average, how many years of life are you likely to have left?

indicates the pattern of deaths in that population as of that time. Table 4.6, for example, gives a life table based on the Cancer Epidemiology Survey data in Table 4.5. This life table is not adjusted for underreporting of deaths, for age misreporting such as the use of traditional age reckoning, or for the error introduced by the fact that the death column in Table 4.5 refers to 1973–75 while the age structure column refers to 1976. Some of these discrepancies can be adjusted for, while some cannot. Because separate mortality data for ages 0 and 1–4 were not given, the reported data for ages 0–4 were arbitrarily subdivided into the two components using a West model 19 life table, derived from many populations with relatively complete mortality data.[21] The mortality data as reported result in an estimated crude death rate of 7.3 per thousand population for

1973–75. The unadjusted life table shows an expectation of life at birth of approximately 66.2 years for males and females combined, and an infant mortality rate of about 48 per thousand.

An expectation of life at birth of 66 years is quite high compared to most developing countries. It is reasonable to ask whether the survey recorded essentially all of the deaths in a representative fashion or whether significant underreporting of deaths produced a deceptive picture of China's success in mortality control as of 1973-75. Several demographic techniques were used in a study by Banister and Preston to evaluate the completeness of death reporting.[22] The study concluded that the completeness of adult death reporting in the "study population" area of the PRC for 1973–75 fell between 80 and 90 percent. This adjustment resulted in the following estimates for 1973–75: an expectation of life at birth of 62.4–64.4 years, a crude death rate of 8.1–9.1, and an infant mortality rate of about 53–60 per thousand live births. An adjusted life

TABLE 4.7
Adjusted Life Table for China, 1973–75, from the Cancer Epidemiology Survey
(N = 842,000,000)

Age group	Probability of dying during age interval q_x	Age-specific death rate m_x	Survivors entering age interval l_x	Person-years lived during age interval L_x	Life expectancy (years) e_x
0	0.05629	0.05898	100,000	95,440	63.43
1–4	0.01998	0.00506	94,371	372,714	66.20
5–9	0.01292	0.00260	92,485	459,438	63.52
10–14	0.00539	0.00108	91,290	455,223	59.32
15–19	0.00603	0.00121	90,799	452,624	54.63
20–24	0.00851	0.00171	90,251	449,334	49.95
25–29	0.00965	0.00194	89,483	445,254	45.35
30–34	0.01193	0.00240	88,619	440,451	40.77
35–39	0.01661	0.00335	87,562	434,172	36.23
40–44	0.02274	0.00460	86,107	425,641	31.80
45–49	0.03333	0.00678	84,149	413,733	27.49
50–54	0.05073	0.01041	81,344	396,404	23.35
55–59	0.07683	0.01598	77,218	371,256	19.46
60–64	0.12149	0.02587	71,285	334,773	15.87
65–69	0.17701	0.03884	62,624	285,408	12.72
70–74	0.28123	0.06545	51,539	221,459	9.92
75–79	0.36247	0.08854	37,045	151,654	7.82
80±	1.00000	0.17089	23,617	138,200	5.85

SOURCE: Table 4.5; Banister & Preston (1981a).

NOTE: For the definitions of q_x, m_x, etc., see the note to Table 4.6. The Banister-Preston analysis of the mortality data suggests that some 80–90% of the deaths occurring after the age of about 5 are reported. There are no data with which to assess the completeness of the reporting of deaths below age 5, which is probably less complete than for adults. This "best guess" life table is based on the assumption that 85% of "adult" deaths are reported among the study population, and the optimistic assumption that infant and child deaths are also 85% reported.

table for 1973–75 based on the assumption of 85 percent completeness of death reporting at all ages is given in Table 4.7.

As shown in Table 4.4, a Chinese source claimed an expectation of life at birth of 57 years in 1957, which should be taken as an underestimate of mortality at that time. Similarly, Table 4.4 indicates that unadjusted data from the cancer survey give a life expectancy of 65–66 years in 1973–75, and that other official and semiofficial sources have claimed a life expectancy of 68 years in 1975, of 68 years in 1978, and around or above 70 years in 1979. The 1975 and 1978 estimates are based on age-specific mortality data from sample areas of China.[23] The 1975 sample, in comparison to cancer survey data referring to about the same time, shows either that underreporting of deaths was worse or that the sample area selected had unusually advanced mortality conditions. The 1975 sample area claims lower mortality rates at every age than the cancer survey.[24] For any of the years 1973, 1974, or 1975 it would be wiser to rely on the data from the Cancer Epidemiology Survey, suitably adjusted for underreporting, than to rely on the less representative data from the 1975 sample area. The 1978 claim of a national life expectancy of 68 years was also "based on partial statistics."[25] It is likely that the 1978 sample area was also biased toward areas with unusually favorable mortality conditions and that there was some underreporting of deaths in those areas as well.

As this book was in the final stages of preparation, life tables based on death reporting in the 1982 census were released. They show a 1981 expectation of life at birth of 67.9 years for China's population, composed of life expectancies of 66.4 years for males and 69.4 years for females. It has not yet been possible to test these mortality data for completeness of reporting. The 1981 life tables are included in the Appendix without adjustment for underreporting. The deaths detected by the 1982 census give a 1981 crude death rate of only 6.36 deaths per thousand population, even lower than the death rate of 6.60 estimated by a vital rate survey for 1982 (see Table 4.3). As will be discussed in the final section of this chapter, these death rates are very likely underestimates for 1981 and 1982, and the estimated life expectancies from the census probably exaggerate China's actual expectation of life at birth for 1981.

Table 4.8 compares China's expectation of life at birth for 1973–75 as estimated here with that of other countries at the time. The developed countries, of course, had achieved a significantly higher expectation of life than China, as had several Asian and Latin American countries. Sri Lanka and Chile had about the same life expectancies as the PRC as of the early 1970's. But it is clear that a large proportion of the world's developing countries had estimated expectations of life at birth lower than China's during the 1970's. This enormous group of nations included al-

TABLE 4.8
Estimated Life Expectancy in 48 Selected Countries, Early 1970's
(In years)

Country	Date	Life expectancy	Country	Date	Life expectancy
Sweden	1975	74.7	Peru	1970–75	54.6
Japan	1974	73.7	Guatemala	1970–75	54.6
United States	1974	72.1	Algeria	1970–75	54.0
Hong Kong	1971	71.2	Kenya	1970–75	53.3
China, Taiwan	1975	70	Libya	1970–75	53.0
Romania	1973–75	69.6	Egypt	1970–75	52.4
USSR	1971–72	69.0	Burma	1970–75	50.1
Uruguay	1970–75	68.7	India	1970–75	49.4
Singapore	1970–75	68.6	Pakistan	1970–75	49.3
Costa Rica	1972–74	68.4	Bolivia	1970–75	48.8
Peninsular Malaysia	1974	67.7	Tanzania	1970–75	48.1
			Indonesia	1970–75	47.6
South Korea	1970	65	Bangladesh	1974	46.2
Venezuela	1970–75	64.8	Ghana	1970–75	45.9
PRC	1973–75	61.7–64.4	Saudi Arabia	1970–75	45.4
Sri Lanka	1970–72	64	Nigeria	1970–75	45.0
Chile	1970–75	62.6	Nepal	1970–75	43.6
Brazil	1970–75	61.5	Mozambique	1970–75	43.5
North Korea	1970–75	60.7	Zaire	1970–75	43.5
Colombia	1970–75	59.9	Sudan	1970–75	43.4
Turkey	1970–75	58.9	Chad	1970–75	41.3
Philippines	1970–75	58.5	Mali	1970–75	41.0
Thailand	1970–75	58.1	Somalia	1970–75	41.0
Syria	1970–75	55.7	Ethiopia	1970–75	38.6
Tunisia	1970–75	55			

SOURCES: Demographic Yearbook Historical Supplement (1979): 542–63, except Taiwan and Sri Lanka, World Population 1977 (1978), and PRC, Banister & Preston (1981a): 104.

NOTE: The overall ranges in the developed parts of the West and the USSR are as follows.

North America	1972–74	72.1–72.9
Western Europe	1972–75	68.7–74.7
Eastern Europe, USSR	1971–76	68.0–71.6

most all of Africa, the Middle East, and South Asia, as well as many countries in Latin America. It is noteworthy that China had achieved much greater success in mortality control than India and Indonesia, the other populous developing countries of Asia.

China's crude death rate calculated from unadjusted cancer survey data was 7.3. As Table 4.3 shows, the crude death rate for 1973–75 based on the yearend vital reporting system was also about 7.3. The cancer survey was linked to death registration records, and except for better reporting of infant mortality in the cancer survey, it appears that the survey did not improve on the completeness of the regular reporting system. It may therefore be inferred that the regular reporting system underregistered deaths by about the same margin as did the cancer survey, and that the actual crude death rate for 1973–75 was around 8.1 to 9.1. If the level of underregistration of deaths was constant, it can be estimated that the death rate declined to about 6.9–7.9 in 1979 and 1980.

In early 1981 several Chinese scholars published an analysis of mortality data from the cancer survey presented separately by sex and province for 24 of China's 29 provinces. Because the missing five provinces have 24 percent of the Chinese population, these data are not fully representative of the whole country. Life tables for the 24 provinces as a group, presented in Appendix Table A.3, indicate an expectation of life at birth of 63.5 years for males and 65.9 years for females. The longer life expectancy for women than men is a switch from the 1930 pattern, discussed in Chapter 2. The table indicates that women in the peak childbearing ages 25–34 had slightly higher probability of dying than men of the same ages, but for almost all other ages the probability of dying was higher for males than females. According to our previous analysis of the cancer survey, adult death reporting in these life tables should be assumed to be 80–90 percent complete. Based on the assumption of 85 percent completeness of death reporting at all ages, Table A.4 in the Appendix presents life tables for China separately by sex. For the 24 provinces on which these life tables are based, the table gives an expectation of life at birth of about 61 years for males and 63 years for females in 1973–75.

Table 4.9 lists the life expectancies for these same 24 provinces as derived from the cancer survey alongside life expectancies for 10 provinces from 1982 census data. Some interesting results are apparent. In all these provinces, for 1973–75 and 1981, life expectancy was reportedly higher for females than males, the pattern commonly found elsewhere in the world, although in Guizhou the difference was very small, reminiscent of China's traditional mortality pattern. Also, absent any adjustments for underreporting of deaths, these data suggest that life expectancy among China's provinces is roughly uniform and relatively high, in the range 59–73 years. Some uniformity is plausible in view of the efforts to bring the benefits of public order, preventive health work, and basic medical care to all the people. But the lack of variation between provinces is so pronounced as to invite suspicion, as are the high life expectancies claimed for the poorest and most remote provinces. As the most extreme example, it is hard to believe that Xizang (Tibet) in 1973–75 had achieved a life expectancy of 59.5 years for males and 63.2 years for females, higher even than in Sichuan. Because the introduction of environmental sanitation measures and preventive medical care to Tibet had been delayed until the early 1970's, by 1973–75 the expectation of life in Tibet was probably not much greater than the 43.6 years estimated for neighboring Nepal.[26] It is more likely that in 1973–75, life expectancies at

TABLE 4.9
Reported Male and Female Life Expectancy by Province, 1973–75 and 1981
(In years)

Province	1973–75 Males	1973–75 Females	1981 Males	1981 Females
Shanghai	69.24	74.84	70.76	75.37
Tianjin	69.93	71.96	70.11	72.15
Heilongjiang	69.25	71.53	—	—
Liaoning	68.64	70.78	69.84	72.10
Beijing	68.34	70.77	70.61	73.56
Hebei	67.11	70.17	—	—
Zhejiang	66.44	70.52	—	—
Guangdong	—	—	68.65	73.91
Fujian	65.23	69.37	66.47	70.95
Jiangsu	65.10	69.34	—	—
Henan	65.06	68.82	68.00	71.58
Shanxi	65.33	68.00	—	—
Nei Mongol	65.25	67.31	—	—
Jilin	65.00	66.73	—	—
Anhui	64.50	66.88	—	—
Shaanxi	63.96	65.18	—	—
Jiangxi	62.06	64.34	—	—
Hunan	61.39	63.63	—	—
Xinjiang	61.77	63.29	—	—
Gansu	—	—	65.38	66.85
Ningxia	61.86	62.66	65.14	66.81
Xizang	59.47	63.22	—	—
Qinghai	60.55	62.04	—	—
Yunnan	59.80	61.35	—	—
Sichuan	59.16	61.08	—	—
Guizhou	59.03	59.48	61.72	62.21
National	63.62	66.31	66.43	69.35

SOURCES: *1973–75*, data for 24 provinces in Rong et al. (1981): Tables 3, 4; *1981*, data for 10 provinces in Jiang, Zhang & Zhu (1984): Table 6. Analogous data for the provinces of Shandong, Hubei, and Guangxi are unavailable.

NOTE: The data have not been adjusted for the underreporting of deaths or for the misreporting of some infant deaths as deaths to children age 1 or 2.

birth by province ranged from a low of around 45–50 years in Xizang to a high of 65–70 years in some advanced municipalities. This is a wider range than reported and, for most provinces, a less advanced mortality level than claimed. We can hypothesize that death reporting in the cancer survey was, in general, least complete in the provinces with the worst mortality conditions; this would mean that the actual range of variation between provinces was greater than the survey data indicate.

Underreporting of deaths aside, comparison of 1973–75 and 1981 life tables shows that life expectancy for China increased by 3 years for both males and females. Very slight improvements were registered in those provinces and province-level municipalities that had already achieved high life expectancies by the early 1970's. Greater improvement was reported in the most backward provinces. For instance, while Tianjin Municipality calculated almost no change in life expectancy for either sex during the interval, Ningxia reported an increase from 62 years to 65 years for males, and from 63 to 67 years for females, while Guizhou claimed an increase in life expectancy from 59 years to 62 years for both sexes.

China's Pattern of Mortality

An important shift over many decades in China was the widening differential between male and female expectation of life. In 1929–31 expectation of life at birth was 0.9 years higher for males than females among the rural farmers surveyed.[27] But by the mid-1970's China reported that female life expectancy was about 2.7 years higher than male life expectancy (see Table 4.4). Some advanced urban areas report greater differentials. Beijing Municipality, for example, claimed a difference of 2.8 years, Hangzhou 3.4 years, Wuhan 4 years, and Shanghai Municipality 4.7 years in 1979.[28]

Is the 1973–75 pattern of mortality as shown in Tables 4.5 to 4.7 a plausible one, or does this pattern contain anomalies and obvious errors? To test the plausibility of the PRC's reported mortality pattern, we can compare it with patterns of mortality in other countries and regions.[29] An important characteristic of China's reported progression of deaths by age is that its pattern does not fit any of the four families of model life tables compiled by Ansley Coale and Paul Demeny in 1966 and widely used in the field of demography. For example, in Table 4.10 China's age-specific death rates, corrected for 15 percent underreporting, are matched with a "West" model life table at comparable life expectancies at age 10. The West model is a composite set of life tables based on the mortality experience of most countries with relatively complete data. The Chinese data show much lower mortality in the age groups 15–34 than the West model, which suggests that China by 1973–75 had achieved a lower prevalence of respiratory tuberculosis than "West" populations would have at similar levels of mortality, an achievement all the more striking when China's 1929–31 pattern of high tuberculosis mortality is kept in mind.[30] Mortality at ages 0–4 is very close to that in the "West" standard, but mortality at ages 5–9 is almost twice as high. The only one of China's 1973–75 age-specific mortality rates that appears questionable in comparison to the "West" pattern is that for ages 5–9. But that mortality rate is exactly the same as in Coale and Demeny's "North" model life table level 19, which has the same expectation of life at age 10 as China after correction for 15 percent underreporting. Therefore, in comparison to

TABLE 4.10
Percentage Differences in the Age-Specific Death Rates of PRC and Other Life Tables

Age group	PRC, 1973–75[a] (deaths per 1,000 population)	PRC, Percentage difference from: West Level 19[b]	South Asia[c]	Taiwan, 1960[d]
0–4	16.02	0	−51	+26
5–9	2.60	+73	+9	+143
10–14	1.08	−7	+4	+37
15–19	1.21	−34	−10	−14
20–24	1.71	−33	+6	−23
25–29	1.94	−31	+2	−10
30–34	2.40	−26	+1	−12
35–39	3.35	−16	+7	−4
40–44	4.60	−12	+3	−6
45–49	6.78	−6	+3	−2
50–54	10.41	0	−1	−2
55–59	15.98	+4	−3	−4
60–64	25.87	+10	−2	+1
65–69	38.84	+6	−4	−6
70–74	65.45	+12	+6	+1
75–79	88.54	−4	−3	−13
80±	170.89	−10	+8	−12

SOURCE: Banister & Preston (1981a): 106.

NOTE: For comparison, the model life table levels and the Taiwan life table year were chosen to match as close as possible the PRC expectation of life at age 10, e_{10}, of 59.32 years from Table 4.7.

[a]Corrected for 15 percent incompleteness.

[b]$e_0 = 63.12$; $e_{10} = 58.63$ (Coale & Demeny [1966]: 20).

[c]$e_0 = 59.00$; $e_{10} = 59.51$ (U.N. Population Division [1981]).

[d]$e_0 = 64.34$; $e_{10} = 58.76$ (Preston et al. [1972]: 712–14).

these model life tables, there are no anomalies in the 1973–75 Chinese mortality pattern.

Comparison with life tables from other developing countries and regions reinforces this conclusion. The United Nations Population Division prepared new model life tables after an exhaustive appraisal and synthesis of mortality patterns in developing countries. One of their three regional patterns, the "South Asian" pattern, pertains to India, Bangladesh (Matlab), Iran, and Tunisia. As shown in Table 4.10, it is remarkably similar at age 10 and above to the age pattern of mortality recorded in China. The average of the positive or negative deviation between Chinese and "South Asian" patterns above age 10 is only 5 percent; for the "West" pattern the average is 16 percent. The South Asian pattern also matches closely the relatively high mortality at age 5–9 of China. However, it contains mortality rates at age 0–4 that are double those in China when life expectancies at age 10 are equal. China appears to have made much better progress against mortality below age 5 than would be expected on the basis of this homology. It is of course possible that Chinese data are especially deficient at very young ages; we have no way at present of knowing the quality of data at these young ages. If the cancer survey missed deaths below age 5 to a much greater degree than adult deaths, mortality for China age 0–4 would be higher than shown in Table 4.10, and China would fit the South Asian mortality pattern even more closely. At the same time, it is believable that China has achieved mortality below age 5 that is unusually low for developing countries, because of its emphasis on providing maternal and child health services, retraining midwives, sanitation work, and immunization of young children.

The final column of Table 4.10 indicates that the pattern of mortality in China is similar to that in Taiwan at ages 15 and above, though the fit is not nearly as close as between China and the South Asian pattern. At the same assumed mortality level, the China mainland had higher age-specific mortality in ages 0–14 than did Taiwan. Why China by 1973–75 had a mortality pattern much closer to that of South Asia than to Taiwan's or to the United Nation's "Far East" pattern (Hong Kong, Singapore, and South Korea) is a question for further research.

Infant Mortality in China Since the 1950's

This section presents the reported infant mortality rates available for areas the size of a county or larger in China after the 1950's. First the urban and rural components will be assessed separately, then the national infant mortality will be discussed.

Infant mortality rates in urban areas of China, which are listed in Table 4.11, are in general seriously underreported. The only exception to this generalization in the table is Beijing city proper and perhaps Beijing Municipality as a whole, which includes nine suburban counties. Beijing city has the most advanced medical facilities and public health system of any city in China. It is the seat of government and the showplace of the nation. One would expect that in recent years the Beijing city districts might have been able to achieve an infant mortality rate not too much higher than those in the world's most advanced urban areas, which reported infant mortality rates of 8–10 per thousand live births during the late 1970's. Beijing city claimed an infant mortality rate of about 10 for the years 1976–78 and for 1980, which seems too low even for Beijing. The higher figure of 12.8 for 1979 may represent somewhat more complete reporting of both neonatal (up to 1 month) and postneonatal (1 month to 1 year) deaths. A neonatal mortality rate of 8.1 was barely possible anywhere in the world as of 1979, and an infant mortality rate of 12.8 was at the very low end of world experience as of that time. Beijing city's reported neonatal, postneonatal, and infant mortality rates for 1979 represent the low end of a plausible range for any place in China as of 1979. Perhaps the city actually achieved these levels in 1979, or there may still have been some underregistration of infant deaths.

Beijing Municipality as a whole reported a neonatal mortality rate of 10–12, a postneonatal rate of 5–7, and an infant mortality rate of 17 for 1978 and 1979. For 1981 the municipality claimed an infant mortality rate of only 15 (see Table 4.15). Infant mortality rates of 17 for 1978–79 and 15 for 1981 are at the extreme low end of the range of possible infant mortality rates for Beijing Municipality or for any municipality in China as of those dates. With this yardstick in mind, let us look at reported data for other urban areas of China.

Shanghai city has a serious problem with underregistration of neonatal mortality. The data reported for 1972 were absurd. Table 4.11 indicates that Shanghai was recording a neonatal mortality rate of only 3.2 when the lowest neonatal mortality rate anywhere in the developed world was 8.7. By about 1975, Shanghai city seems to have made some improvement in the recording of infant mortality. The reported rates of 11.9 by about 1974 and 11.1 by 1979 can be considered just possible in one of China's most advanced cities at the time, but probably some infant deaths still went unrecorded. The 1978 claim of a neonatal mortality rate of 6.4, whether it applied to the whole municipality or just to the city districts, is too low to be correct. The world's most advanced developed areas had neonatal mortality rates that year no lower than 5.5, and in most developed areas they were far higher—even Beijing city claimed a higher rate that year. From the 1982 census (as shown in Table 4.15), Shanghai Municipality derived a 1981 infant mortality rate of 17, about the lowest possible rate for a municipality in China.

Other urban areas of China show the same tendency to underestimate infant mortality. Tianjin Municipality in 1978 could not have achieved an infant mortality rate of 13, far below that of Beijing Municipality. Tianjin's claimed 1981 infant mortality rate of 18 from census data is more plausible. The claim by Nanjing of an infant mortality rate of 11 in 1973 is just as unreliable as Shanghai's rates during the early 1970's. Dalian in 1980 claimed an infant mortality rate below 10, even lower than the suspiciously low claim made by Beijing city for that year.

Now let us look at the data in Table 4.11 that claim to represent China's overall urban infant mortality rates for the 1970's. A 1977 survey reported infant mortality rates of 11–20 for urban areas in twelve provinces during the previous three years. Given the relative backwardness of most Chinese cities in comparison to the city districts by Beijing and Shanghai, which might possibly have achieved infant mortality rates be-

TABLE 4.11

Reported and Estimated Infant Mortality Rates in Urban Areas, 1957–81

(Deaths per 1,000 live births)

Location and date	Neonatal mortality: Reported rate	Neonatal mortality: Source	Estimated postneonatal mortality rate	Infant mortality: Reported rate	Infant mortality: Source
Beijing city proper					
1960	14.2	1	(15.6)	29.78; 29.8	1;2
1961	14.3	1	(21.3)	35.64	1
1962	11.3	1	(10.4)	21.72	1
1963	12.4	1,3,4	(9.9)	22.28; 22.3	1;3,5
1964	11.3	1	(16.6)	27.90	1
1972				15	6
1973	6.1	1	(5.5)	11.6; 11.63	5,7;1
1974	6.6	1	(5.9)	12.53	1
1975	7.9	1	(4.5)	12.4	1
1976	5.2	1	(5.2)	10.4	1
1977	6.5	1	(3.6)	10.1	1
1978	7.35; 7.4	8,9; 1,5	(2.9)	10.3	1,5
1979	8.09	8,9	(4.7)	12.8	10
1980				10.4	11
Beijing Municipality					
1965				30	12
1972?				"Under 20"	12
1978	12.21	9	(4.90)	17.11	9
1979	10.08	8,9	(6.89)	16.97	9
1980				14.8	11
Shanghai, International Peace Maternity Hospital area					
1962–71				27	13
1971				19	13
Shanghai city proper					
1970				Male, 9.81; female, 7.64	14
1972	(3.2)	15	(9.4)	(12.6)	15
1972				8.7	16,17,18
1974?				11.85	19
1979				Male, 12.85; female, 9.26	14
Shanghai (Municipality?)					
(1977)	10.5	20			
1978	6.4	20			
Shanghai suburbs, 1972				"Well over 20"	18
Tianjin Municipality, 1978				13.0	21
Nanjing city proper, Jiangsu, 1973				11	22
Dalian city, Liaoning, 1980				"Less than 10"	23
"Cities" of 12 provinces and province level municipalities, 1974–76 (1977 survey)				11–20	5,24
General urban (variously characterized)					
1957				Male (34.2); female (34.9)	25
1975				Male (10.2); female (9.7)	25
1978				"About 12"; 12	26, 27; 28
1981?				13	29

low 15 by 1974–76, these cities surely had infant mortality rates above that. The range 11–20 seems to be too low for urban infant mortality rates in 1974–76, even in the twelve most advanced provinces, and definitely does not represent nationwide urban infant mortality rates of the mid-1970's.

A 1981 paper presented data purporting to represent all the urban areas of China in 1975 and 1978, though the author hinted that these data may be based on a very small number of cities. Table 4.11 lists infant mortality rates of 10.2 for males and 9.7 for females, directly calculable from the data presented, which are clearly impossible for urban China in 1975.[31] Some developed countries had achieved such low urban infant mortality rates in 1975: Japan, 9.7; Netherlands, 10.5; Norway, 10.6.[32] But no city in a developing country had attained such low rates in 1975: Hong Kong, for example, reported a 1975 infant mortality rate of 14.9 (16.4 for males, 13.3 for females), and Singapore's reported 1975 rate was 13.9 (16.0 for males, 11.6 for females).[33] Even Beijing city proper reported a 1975 rate of 12.4. These data that produce an infant mortality rate of 10 for urban China in 1975 are obviously defective.

The same paper reported that the PRC had a 1978 urban infant mortality rate of about 12, a figure the World Health Organization also reported without even questioning it; but that figure could not have any basis in reality. Possibly Beijing or Shanghai city districts could have come

SOURCES OF TABLE 4.11: (1) Ling (1981): Table 2. (2) Data from the Beijing Health Department. "Peking Children's Hospital," SCMP, no. 2752 (5 June 1962): 18. (3) Chu Fu-t'ang. "Pa-nien lai wo-kuo erh-k'o kung-tso te chin-chan" (China's progress in pediatrics during the last eight years), CJP 13, no. 5 (6 Oct. 1964): 342. (4) Minkowski (1973): 219. (5) Xue Xinbing (1979): 193–96. (6) DeBakey (1974): 19. (7) "Initial Success Noted in P.R.C.'s Planned Population Growth," FBIS 166 (26 Aug. 1974): E4. (8) "Benshi huifu zhuchanshi ban bing jian xinshenger qiangjiu zhongxin" (This municipality restores training of midwives and establishes newborn rescue centers), BJRB, 5 Oct. 1980: 1. (9) "Survey Produces Statistics on Population, Birth Rate in Beijing," FBIS 191 (30 Sept. 1980): R1-R2. Also in SWB-WER, no. W1103 (8 Oct. 1980): 1.

(10) Qian (1980): L5. (11) Wu Yafang. "Shehui zhuyi wei yinger jiankang chengzhang tigong youyue tiaojian" (Socialism offers superior conditions for the healthy growth of infants), BJRB, 26 May 1981: 1. (12) Wray (1973). (13) Faundes & Luukkainen (1972): 171. (14) Shanghai Public Health and Epidemic Prevention Station, Vital Statistics Group. "Yijiuqijiu nian Shanghai shiqu jumin wanquan shoumingbiao de chubu fenxi" (A preliminary analysis of the 1979 complete life table of the city of Shanghai), RKYJ, no. 3 (July 1981): 38. (15) Calculated from data on the first quarter of 1972 by Lamm & Sidel (1973): 252–58. For a fuller analysis of these data, see Banister (1977a): 289–90; or Banister (1977b): 156–57. (16) Wegman (1973): 64. (17) Lythcott (1973): 143. (18) Arena (1974): 23. (19) "Child Health Care in New China," CMJ, new series, no. 1 (1975): 91; cited in Lampton (1977): 16.

(20) Er Bao. "Benshi ertong baojian shiye pengbo fazhan" (Child health work in Shanghai is developing vigorously), WHB, 16 May 1979: 2. (21) Reported by Tianjin Municipal Health Department. Lyle et al. (n.d.). (22) Enderton (1975): 45. (23) Liaoning Provincial Statistical System (1982): 75. (24) "Medical Care for Children," SWB-WER, no. W1036 (20 June 1979): 1–2. (25) Ling (1981): Table 3. For calculation procedure, see text note 31, Chapter 4. (26) Ling (1981): 127–28. (27) "Woguo renkou pingjun shouming bi jiefang qian yanchang jin yibei," (The life expectancy of China's population has practically doubled since before Liberation), WHB, 15 Feb. 1981: 1. (28) WHO Health Statistics Report (1979): 4. (29) Zhu Minzhi (1981).

NOTE: Figures and information in parentheses are derived from other reported information.

close to an actual rate of 12 in 1978, but China's urban areas as a whole could not. Similarly, the 1981 claim that China's cities had attained an infant mortality rate of 13 is probably based on underregistered data from atypical cities and is likely to be far below the actual level.

There are several possible reasons why China's urban areas so badly underestimate their infant mortality rates. First, whenever Chinese traditional age reporting is used, an infant's death may be registered as having happened to a child age 1 or 2. This would reduce the numerator of the infant mortality rate while the denominator—the number of births that year—would be unaffected.

A second and probably much more important source of underreporting is that the parents of an infant who dies in the first week of life would have a tendency to report neither the birth of the baby nor its death. Therefore the component of infant mortality that consists of early neonatal deaths tends to be underreported. According to registration regulations, it is the parents' responsibility to register the birth of a baby, and its death if that happens, at their neighborhood public-security office after the mother comes home from the hospital. But if the baby dies, their incentive to register the birth and death of the child is lessened. This problem could be reduced if the city required parents to register a child's birth, or its birth and death, before the mother left the hospital. For any births that take place at home, the birth attendant should be responsible for registering the birth and early neonatal death, should that occur.

A survey was conducted in Shanghai in 1973 to detect unreported infant deaths in 1972. The survey found that half the neonatal deaths had been omitted. Reasons for the unreported infant deaths were given as follows:

> In 62 percent of the cases, the families for various reasons were reluctant to carry out the procedures of reporting the birth and the death. In 34 percent of the cases, medical units had failed to fill out the birth and death certificates for the family members, and 4 percent of the cases were for other reasons. The medical units were not sufficiently aware of the requirement that certificates of birth and death must be filled out simultaneously and be given to the family of the infant who died soon after birth. They thought that the birth and the death would cancel each other. Some of the units do not know the concrete method of and the requirement for reporting the death of a newborn infant. Some of them are unclear about the definition of neonatal mortality, or do not have the same definition, and have treated these cases as stillbirth.[34]

Another problem with urban infant death registration is the urban rationing system. In at least some urban areas, parents have an incentive to register births if they can afford to buy the extra food and cloth rations to which they are then entitled. But if the infant dies, the parents might postpone or avoid registering its death to prolong the extra rations. If infant deaths are not reported, the permanent population registers retain the names of those who died in infancy as if they are still alive. If the death registration is only postponed for months or years, the death of an infant would be recorded as the death of an older child. In either case, the result is underregistration of infant mortality. In general, with the possible exception of Beijing data for some years, all the Chinese urban infant mortality rates listed in Table 4.11 appear to be underestimates.

China's rural infant mortality data, listed in Table 4.12, are as bad as or worse than the urban data, though there are some exceptions. So far the only rural area that has reported apparently complete infant mortality data is the relatively prosperous suburban county of Shuangliu, part of Chengdu Municipality in Sichuan province. A retrospective survey in 1979 found an infant mortality rate there of 71.93 deaths per thousand live births during 1974–77. It should be noted that such complete reporting of infant deaths was due to the use of a mortality survey, not the regular annual death reporting system. This datum can be used as a yardstick by which to judge the reported infant mortality rates of other suburban or rural areas of China.

Rudong county in Jiangsu province is one of China's leading counties in terms of medical and public health work. It also began recording neonatal and postneonatal mortality data in 1965 or before. As of 1973 this model county recorded a neonatal mortality rate of 20, a postneonatal rate of 14, and an infant mortality rate of 34. More recently reported data for Rudong county are somewhat contradictory; from the table it appears that Rudong county recorded a rate somewhere in the range of 20–30 for about 1975, and perhaps as low as 19 for 1976. On the assumption that Rudong county is much more advanced than Shuangliu county in prenatal, childbirth, and infant-health work, Rudong might have achieved an infant mortality rate well below 70 by the mid-1970's. But the claim of a rate of 30 by that time suggests significant underreporting of infant deaths. The more recent claim of an infant mortality rate of 19 for 1976 appears far too low by comparison.

Any suburban or rural area of the PRC that claims a neonatal or infant mortality rate for the 1970's far below that of the model county of Rudong is surely underreporting its infant mortality. For example, Helong county in Jilin province reported rates of 9.6 in 1974 and 9.2 in 1976, lower even than urban infant mortality rates in the world's most advanced countries and less than half of Rudong county's rates during those years (Table 4.12). Even if they are taken to be neonatal mortality rates, the figures are still far too low to be correct. In 1978 Maigaiti county in the far northwestern province of Xinjiang reported an infant mortality rate of under 20. This

TABLE 4.12

Reported and Estimated Infant Mortality Rates in Rural Areas, 1957–81

(Deaths per 1,000 live births)

Location and date	Rate	Source
Shuangliu county, Sichuan, 1974–77	71.93	1
Rudong county, Jiangsu		
1965[a]	46.6; 46.98	2; 3
1973[a]	33.89	3
1974–76[b]	29.6	2
1976	19.3	4
Helong county, Jilin		
1974	9.6	5
1976	9.2	6
Markit (Maigaiti) county, Xinjiang, 1978?	"Under 20/1,000"	7
Jiangsu province, 1974?	33.9	8
Inner Mongolia (Nei Mongol), 1977?	"About 0.5%" (5/1,000)	9
Yanbian Korean Autonomous Prefecture, Jilin, 1973	"6%" (60/1,000) "6 per thousand"	10 11
Tibet (Xizang), 1980?	"Survival rate has risen to 800 per thousand"	12
PRC rural (variously characterized)		
1957	Male (72.1), female (72.9)	13
1975	Male (20.3), female (19.5)	13
1974–76, "countryside" in 12 province-level units[b]	30	2, 14
1978	20–30	15
"Rural areas of China"	20	16
"Remote mountains of China"	30	16
1981 ("at present")	24	17
Experimental rural area in 19 provinces, child health care experiment[c]		18
Pre-experiment, ca. 1977	23.99	
End of experiment, ca. 1981	18.22	

SOURCES:

(1) Shuangliu County Retrospective Infant and Child Mortality Investigation, 1979; data released to H. Yuan Tien, 1979. (2) Xue Xinbing (1979): 193–96. (3) Rudong County Woman and Child Health Care Station, "Barefoot Doctors Active in Rural Child Health Care," CMJ, no. 10 (Oct. 1974): 601. (4) "Kiangsu," SWB-WER, no. W933 (15 June 1977): 1. (5) "Mother and Child Care in Rural China," SPRCP, no. 6299 (15 Mar. 1977): 61–62. (6) "Child Health Care," PR 20, no. 42 (14 Oct. 1977): 31–32. (7) "Sinkiang," SWB-WER, no. W1003 (25 Oct. 1978): 1. (8) "Child Health Care in New China," CMJ, new series, no. 1 (1975): 91; cited in Lampton (1977): 16. (9) "Inner Mongolia," SWB-WER, no. W939 (27 July 1977): 1. Also in FBIS 135 (14 July 1977): K4.

(10) "Children's Health," FBIS 109 (5 June 1974): E6. (11) Yin Ming (1977): 90. (12) Qian (1980): L5. (13) Ling (1981): Table 3; for calculation procedure, see text note 32, Chapter 4. (14) "Medical Care for Children," SWB-WER, no. W1036 (20 June 1979): 1–2. (15) Ling (1981): 127–28; "Woguo renkou pingjun shouming bi jiefang qian yanchang jin yibei" (The life expectancy of China's population has practically doubled since before Liberation), WHB, 15 Feb. 1981: 1. (16) WHO Health Statistics Report (1979): 4. (17) Zhu Miuzhi (1981). (18) Zhao Beibei (1981): 1.

[a]Source 3 puts the neonatal mortality rate at 22.41 in 1965 and 19.75 in 1973. The estimated postneonatal rates for those years are (24.57) and (14.14), respectively.

[b]Period covered by a 1977 survey.

[c]Source 18 puts the neonatal mortality rate at 15.26 before the experiment and 11.34 at the end of the experiment. The estimated postneonatal mortality rates are (8.73) and (6.88).

claim should be rejected. Severe underregistration of infant deaths is likely there. As for the 1975 claim that one of China's most advanced provinces, Jiangsu, achieved the low rate of 33.9, this datum probably incorporates unrealistically low infant mortality rates reported from Nanjing and other cities in Jiangsu. Besides, Rudong county, which is Jiangsu's model county, reported an infant mortality rate for around the same time only slightly lower than the rate reported for Jiangsu as a whole. It is likely that most rural areas in Jiangsu had considerably worse infant mortality than Rudong county; therefore, Jiangsu's claim should be considered an underestimate.

Inner Mongolia (Nei Mongol) in mid-1977 broadcast the startling claim that it had reduced its infant mortality rate to 5 per thousand live births. According to the broadcast, its rate "plummeted from 38 percent in the initial period after liberation to about 0.5 percent." No place in the world has yet achieved an infant mortality rate of 5, nor of course has Inner Mongolia. The likelihood in this case is either that infant deaths are hardly recorded at all there or that someone made a gross miscalculation, such as misplacing the decimal point. If Nei Mongol had claimed a rate of 50, that might not be far from a reasonable estimate.

The misplacing of a decimal point is not unknown in official or semi-official sources. For example, the Yanbian Korean Autonomous Prefecture reported that its infant mortality rate had declined from "20 percent" (200 per thousand) before 1949 to "6 percent" (60 per thousand) in 1973. A rate of 60 is not impossible for a large section of Jilin province in 1973. But another publication extolling the progress of China's minority groups under socialism reported that by 1973 infant mortality in the Yanbian Korean Autonomous Prefecture "had declined to 6 per thousand."

Because the Chinese government does not make sure that its trained demographers analyze such demographic reports before publication or give them authority to delete or qualify such claims, official reports are riddled with absurd infant mortality rates such as those just described. These meaningless numbers come either from gross underregistration of infant deaths or from miscalculations based on inadequate data or even from casual misplacements of decimal points. They should not be taken seriously.

The highest infant mortality rate reported for any part of China in recent years is the indirect estimate of 200 per thousand live births for Tibet. Because Tibet began to institute preventive public health work only in 1973, and only in the mid-1970's began retraining midwives in modern midwifery, it is plausible that it continues to have a high infant mortality rate.[35] If conditions in adjacent Nepal are illustrative of those in Tibet, it may be customary for births to be unattended by anyone except relatives, which makes it more difficult to reduce infant mortality. As of the early 1970's Nepal's high mountain regions had an infant mortality rate of 188 according to Nepal Fertility Survey data; it is likely that Tibet's rate during the early 1970's was roughly comparable.[36] However, the indirectly reported rate of 200 for Tibet in about 1980 is probably a guess based on very weak data or none at all. It is possible that the infant mortality rate was actually lower than that as of 1980. Incidentally, an infant mortality rate of 200 is not consistent with a claimed life expectancy in Tibet of over 60 years.

In light of the foregoing discussion, let us look at the claimed infant mortality rates for rural China shown in Table 4.12. One author presented life tables supposedly applicable to rural China from which can be derived a 1975 infant mortality rate of 20 per thousand live births, which is even lower than Rudong county's rate that year. This number could apply to rural China only if almost all rural areas had infant mortality as low as that of the model county of Rudong, which is impossible. Similarly, the reported 1978 infant mortality range of 20–30 for rural areas of the PRC is a serious underestimation. If correct, rural China would have been comparable to rural parts of Israel, Peninsular Malaysia, Bulgaria, Hungary, or Poland.[37] Although China's improvements in infant mortality have been impressive, the PRC's 1978 rural infant mortality rate was probably not as low as in rural areas of eastern Europe, for instance.

The best estimates of China's national infant mortality rate for the mid-1970's are those that can be derived from the cancer survey, which is the most representative mortality survey yet taken for China. Breakdown of the reported death rate for ages 0–4 from that survey gives an absolute minimum infant mortality rate of 48, using only the most optimistic plausible assumptions (see Table 4.6). Other plausible patterns for deaths under age 5, based on a "West" model 20 life table or on "East" model life tables, would produce higher infant mortality estimates for 1973–75. Most important, if there was any underreporting of infant deaths in the survey population, then China's actual infant mortality rate for 1973–75 was higher than 48–50 per thousand. Cancer survey life tables reported separately by sex based on data from 24 of the 29 provinces gave an infant mortality rate of 49 for males and 43 for females. Correction for apparent Chinese age reporting of infant deaths can raise the infant mortality rates as high as 63 for males and 56 for females, as shown in Table 4.13 and Appendix Table A.3.

China's 1982 census and 1982 fertility survey gave us further information which may help us estimate China's infant mortality rate up to that date. The census asked women how many live births they had had and

TABLE 4.13
Reported and Adjusted Infant Mortality Rates in the PRC, 1973–80
(Deaths per 1,000 live births)

Category	Rate	Source
1973–75		
PRC "study population" of 842,000,000 assuming no underreporting	48–50	1
PRC "study population," 24 provinces		
As reported	Male, 48.9; female, 42.8	2
Corrected for ages as reported	Male, 62.9; female, 55.8	3
Corrected for ages as reported and for 85% completeness	Male, 73.5; female, 65.3	4
PRC total population from adjusted cancer survey data	53–63	5
1980	20	6

SOURCES: (1) Tables 4.5, 4.6 (also Banister & Preston 1981a). (2) Rong et al. (1981): 25–26. (3) Appendix Table A.3. (4) Appendix Table A.4. (5) Banister & Preston (1981a). (6) State Statistical Bureau, "Woguo renmin shenghuo you xianzhu gaishan" (The standard of living of China's people has improved significantly), ZGQNB, 13 Aug. 1981: 1; "Improvements in Living Standards Since the Founding of the People's Republic," CR 30, no. 11 (Nov. 1981): 57.

how many of those children were still surviving at census time. Table 4.14 uses an indirect demographic technique with these statistics to estimate the infant mortality rate at different points in time. The technique assumes that younger women have lost children in recent years, while older women have experienced child deaths at earlier dates. Of the several variants of this technique, the one designed by Griffith Feeney gives the most plausible results for China. The results in Table 4.14 show a decline in the infant mortality rate from 80 per thousand live births in late 1968 to 68 at the end of 1971 to 57 in late 1974—the last figure being fairly consistent with cancer survey results for the same period, as discussed above. The results according to the Feeney method show China's infant mortality rate falling to a low point at the beginning of 1979 at 45 infant deaths per thousand live births.

By late 1980, according to use of the Feeney method, China's infant mortality rate had risen to 53 deaths per thousand live births. Caution is required in interpreting this latest estimate because it may be biased. The estimate of 53 is based on the proportion dead of children born to women aged 20–24. Sometimes the infant mortality rate estimated from this age group is higher than the rate for the whole population, because the experiences of the youngest married women are somewhat atypical. In 1982, fewer than half the women aged 20–24 had borne a child. The infant mortality experience of their children would not be fully representative of all China, for women who bear children before age 25 are disproportionately rural and of minority nationalities. Urban women marry and

TABLE 4.14

Indirect Estimation of Infant Mortality for China, 1968–80

Age of woman	Total women	Children ever born: Total	Children ever born: Number per woman	Children surviving: Total	Children surviving: Number surviving per woman	Proportion dead	Estimated infant mortality rate[a]	Reference date of infant mortality estimate[b]
20–24	36,378,430	15,292,480	0.420	14,342,800	0.394	0.062	53	1980.8
25–29	44,744,640	71,271,910	1.593	66,731,380	1.491	0.064	45	1979.1
30–34	34,995,810	96,684,880	2.763	89,393,640	2.554	0.075	48	1977.2
35–39	25,605,300	97,357,860	3.802	87,864,560	3.431	0.098	57	1974.8
40–44	22,540,230	104,670,870	4.644	91,780,400	4.072	0.123	68	1971.9
45–49	22,272,080	119,535,340	5.367	100,789,590	4.525	0.157	80	1968.7

SOURCES: State Council Population Office (1983): 438–39; Griffith Feeney, "Estimating Infant Mortality Trends from Child Survivorship Data," PS 34, no. 1 (Mar. 1980): 109–28; Feeney, "Addendum to Estimating Infant Mortality Trends from Child Survivorship Data," Apr. 1982, unpublished; Feeney, "Mortality Estimation from Child Survivorship Data: A Review," in Thomas M. McDevitt, ed., *The Survey Under Difficult Conditions*, forthcoming.

NOTE: The Feeney infant mortality technique was used to derive estimates of infant mortality from 1982 census data on children ever born and children surviving by age of mother.

[a] Per 1,000 births.

[b] The decimal place refers to tenths of a year. For example, 1980.8 means about Oct. 19, 1980. But since this is an indirect estimation procedure, the reference date cannot be so exact.

TABLE 4.15
Reported Male and Female Infant Mortality Rates in the PRC and Selected Provinces, 1981
(Deaths per 1,000 live births)

Category	Males	Females	Both sexes
Beijing Municipality	15.50	14.21	14.88
Shanghai Municipality	18.95	15.17	17.11
Tianjin Municipality	18.70	17.09	17.93
Guangdong province	18.36	17.79	18.09
Henan province	19.30	20.00	19.62
Liaoning province	12.10	18.23	19.72
Fujian province	21.00	19.96	20.50
Gansu province	37.64	33.64	35.70
Ningxia Hui Autonomous Region	60.82	49.97	55.55
Guizhou province	65.72	59.95	62.92
PRC	35.56	33.72	34.68

SOURCE: Jiang et al. (1984): Table 6.

bear children later than rural women, and Han Chinese women delay their first and subsequent births in comparison to the minorities. Infant mortality rates are reported to be much higher in rural areas, and it is likely that minority group infant mortality rates are higher than Han rates, so the extent of the rise in infant mortality estimated in Table 4.14 may be exaggerated by selectivity bias.

Infant mortality rates for 1981 can be derived directly from the census questions on deaths and births in the household in calendar year 1981. These are presented in Table 4.15 for the country as a whole and for ten of the provinces. A wide range of infant mortality rates is reported, from 15 infant deaths per thousand live births in Beijing Municipality to 63 in Guizhou province. Minor anomalies are obvious, such as a male infant mortality rate for Liaoning province that is well below the claimed rates for the three province-level municipalities. The Liaoning figure is surely underreported. But the most surprising result in Table 4.15 is that the female infant mortality rate is reported to be below that for male infants. This relationship is what would be expected in the absence of female infanticide, a problem widely reported in China's media to be increasing under China's one-child-per-couple family planning program. It is clear that couples who killed a newborn female infant in 1981 did not report this event to census enumerators in 1982. Therefore, the male infant mortality rate given in Table 4.15 may be considered slightly underreported, while the actual female infant mortality rate must be estimated by adding assumed infanticide deaths to the rate given in the table.

Births reported from the census for calendar year 1981 had an implausibly high sex ratio at birth of 108.47 male per hundred female births.[38] If the actual sex ratio at birth is assumed to be 106.0, as discussed in Chapter 2, then at least 230,000 female births in 1981 were unreported. Some of them may simply be nonreporting of the births of little girls still alive at census time. If the extreme assumption were made that all the unreported female births for 1981 were victims of infanticide, this would add 23 infanticide deaths per thousand live births to the female infant mortality rate shown in Table 4.15, resulting in as high an estimate as 57 female infant deaths per thousand live births. Caution is required when trying to adjust for any female infanticide, however, because the actual sex ratio at birth might be somewhat higher or lower than 106.0, and some or even most of the little girls whose births were not reported might have survived.

The nationwide fertility survey of 1982 achieved about the same completeness of reporting of infant deaths as did the census. Compared to the census-based estimate for 1981 of 35 infant deaths per thousand live births for both sexes combined, the fertility survey reported an infant mortality rate of 35 for 1980 and 1981 averaged together.[39] The infant mortality rate from this source has not been reported separately by sex.

The preceding evidence clarifies that any claim of an infant mortality rate for China of 30 or less for any year is contradicted by China's best data sources and must be rejected. For 1973–75, the minimum infant mortality estimate than can be defended is 48 from the cancer survey, if no adjustment is made for underreporting. Similarly, for 1981 the census-based figure of 35 is the minimum possible infant mortality rate. The actual infant mortality rate was very likely higher than the documented rate at both dates.

Causes of Death

Table 4.16 lists the leading causes of death in the PRC based on the cancer survey. It is important to keep in mind that if the survey missed 10–20 percent of the adult deaths and possibly more of the deaths of young children, then all the death rates listed by cause of death are probably too low, and if deaths due to certain causes are better recorded than deaths due to other causes, the ranking of causes of death may be not quite correct.

It is clear from the table that great changes took place in the pattern of leading causes of death between 1929–31 and 1973–75. Around one-third of the reported deaths in 1929–31 had been caused by infectious diseases, as shown in Table 3.1. In 1973–75 only 7 percent of the reported deaths were due to infectious diseases, and this category was the

TABLE 4.16
The Eight Leading Causes of Death in the PRC by Sex, 1973–75
(Yearly deaths per 100,000 population)

Cause of death	Males		Females		Both sexes	
	Number of deaths	Percent of male deaths	Number of deaths	Percent of female deaths	Number of deaths	Percent of all deaths
Circulatory diseases	143.50	19.25%	166.30	23.29%	154.65	21.17%
Respiratory diseases	95.03	12.74	95.13	13.32	95.08	13.02
Cancer	84.35	11.31	63.12	8.85	73.99	10.13
Accidents, injury	66.32	8.89	47.17	6.61	56.96	7.80
Digestive diseases	58.71	7.87	48.79	6.83	53.86	7.38
Infectious diseases	51.82	6.95	51.02	7.15	51.43	7.04
Perinatal diseases	41.23	5.53	33.41	4.68	37.40	5.12
Tuberculosis	37.21	4.95	32.55	4.56	34.93	4.78
TOTAL	578.17	77.49%	537.49	75.29%	558.30	76.44%

SOURCE: Derived from Li Bing & Li Junyao (1980): Table 4.

sixth leading cause of death. By 1978, according to reports compiled from local areas, the leading causes of death among diseases classified in China as infectious or communicable were dysentery, measles, meningitis, encephalitis B, diphtheria, viral hepatitis, hemorrhagic fever, and pertussis, but the numbers of deaths due to each of these diseases had become rather small.[40] A notable shift had also taken place between 1957 and 1973–75. Tuberculosis, reported as the leading cause of death in 1957, by the mid-1970's had become the eighth leading cause of death.

By the mid-1970's China's pattern of causes of death was similar to that of developed countries, in that cardiovascular disease was by far the leading cause of death and cancer had risen to third. Among cardiovascular diseases, the most prevalent in China are hypertension and stroke, followed by coronary heart disease.[41] The PRC has organized a cardiovascular community control program in several pilot areas, in order to develop a workable program for prevention, detection, and cure of cardiovascular disease. The hope is that by the end of the century, such a program will be operating effectively in most parts of the PRC.[42] Meanwhile, research and public education on the causes and prevention of cardiovascular diseases will be emphasized.

It appears that cancer receives much more attention from China's government and health specialists than either cardiovascular or respiratory disease, though these categories of disease cause far more deaths. Using results of the cancer survey, the Ministry of Public Health published an *Atlas of Cancer Mortality in the PRC*, which maps the prevalence of different kinds of cancer by geographical area, as well as a very detailed report on incidence of each type of malignancy by sex and locality.[43]

Stomach cancer was the leading cause of cancer death for both sexes, accounting for 23 percent of all cancer deaths.[44] For males the second ranking cause was esophageal cancer; for females cervical cancer ranked second. Cancers of the esophagus, liver, and nasopharynx have high incidence in certain geographical areas, where cancer registries have now been established. The search is on for the causes and cures of these geographically localized cancers.

Despite a relatively advanced pattern of mortality, dominated by cardiovascular disease and cancer instead of infectious diseases and tuberculosis, important vestiges of China's historical mortality picture remain. Digestive disease, possibly caused or exacerbated by intestinal parasites, contaminated water and food, and dysentery and diarrheal diseases, is still a leading cause of death. Respiratory diseases still rank second. It is not clear what respiratory diseases are the worst killers. Chronic bronchitis seems to be the main respiratory problem, aside from respiratory tuberculosis. As of 1978 chronic bronchitis was mentioned in many localities as a major disease of great public health concern.[45] Possible causes of chronic bronchitis are the use of coal and wood fires inside homes without ventilation, heavy smog in industrial areas, tobacco smoking, and the lack of safety precautions in industries, such as textiles, coal mining, and chemicals, with dangerous airborne particles. Other respiratory killers are pneumonia, tracheitis, emphysema, influenza, and asthma.

The common causes of death in China vary markedly by age, as shown in Table 4.17. Circulatory disorders (including stroke, atherosclerosis, and other cardiovascular diseases) begin to cause a substantial proportion of the deaths in the 15–34 age group; by ages 35–54 they account for 20 percent of all deaths. In ages 55–74, circulatory diseases cause 32 percent of the deaths, and the proportion rises to 37 percent for those 75 and older. Circulatory disease would need to be tackled on a massive scale if a great reduction in deaths of middle-aged persons is contemplated.

Respiratory disease is the leading cause of death in children below age 15. It is not much of a problem in the young adult ages, but in ages 55–74, respiratory disease causes 11 percent of all deaths, and at ages 75-plus it is the second leading cause of death.

Cancer begins to be a problem in ages 15–34, and in ages 35–54 it is the leading cause of death, followed closely by circulatory disease. In ages 55–74 cancer still causes 16 percent of all deaths, but in the oldest group it is not one of the top three causes of death. In every five-year age group, males have a higher cancer death rate than females, and the male rates increase much faster with age than do those of females.[46] By age 65–69 the male rate is 1.6 times the female rate.

TABLE 4.17

The Leading Causes of Death by Age Group, 1973–75

(Percent of total deaths in 3 years)

Age group and cause of death	Percent of deaths
Ages 0–14	
Respiratory diseases	19.43%
Neonatal complications	17.81
Infectious diseases	16.03
Accidents, injury	12.33
Digestive diseases	6.94
Other circulatory diseases[a]	1.82
Nutritional, metabolic problems	1.60
Tuberculosis	1.26
Congenital deformities	1.04
Urinary diseases	0.83
Percent of total	79.09%
Ages 15–34	
Accidents, injury	25.71%
Tuberculosis	9.87
Other circulatory diseases[a]	8.05
Cancer	7.88
Infectious diseases	6.56
Digestive diseases	5.69
Pregnancy, childbirth	3.77
Urinary diseases	2.34
Mental problems	1.67
Nervous-system diseases	1.52
Percent of total	73.06%
Ages 35–54	
Cancer	21.58%
Circulatory diseases	19.57
Tuberculosis	10.27
Digestive diseases	9.06
Accidents, injury	8.42
Respiratory diseases	5.01
Infectious diseases	3.07
Urinary diseases	1.83
Percent of total	78.81%
Ages 55–74	
Circulatory diseases	32.24%
Cancer	16.09
Respiratory diseases	11.29
Digestive diseases	7.45
Tuberculosis	5.85
Accidents, injury	3.09
Infectious diseases	2.60
Urinary diseases	1.72
Percent of total	80.33%
Ages 75 and over	
Circulatory diseases	36.98%
Respiratory diseases	15.68
Digestive diseases	7.29
Cancer	5.96
Infectious diseases	4.10
Tuberculosis	2.43
Urinary diseases	1.91
Accidents, injury	0.68
Percent of total	75.03%

SOURCE: Cancer Investigation Report (1980): Table 2-2. Translated by Florence Yuan.

NOTE: "Disease" is used for convenience to cover all problems in the respiratory, circulatory, etc., systems that lead to death.

[a] "Other circulatory" is one sub-category of cardiovascular diseases. It does not include all circulatory diseases (stroke and heart attack, for example).

Tuberculosis today ranks highest as a cause of death in the ages 15–54. Among older age groups it causes a smaller and smaller proportion of the deaths.

Digestive disease causes a rather even proportion of the deaths in all age groups, between 6 and 9 percent. This suggests that deaths from digestive diseases may be due to environmental factors that affect all age groups equally.

At the life expectancy China had attained by 1973–75, the hierarchy of leading causes of death and the causes of death by age were similar to what is seen in other populations with the same level of mortality.[47] It is typical for the leading cause of death to be cardiovascular disease, with respiratory disease second. But normally, under the age of 15 digestive and neonatal problems each cause more deaths than respiratory disease, while in China respiratory disease causes a greater proportion than usual of child deaths. It is normal for men to have a slightly higher cancer death rate than women, but China's excess of male over female cancer mortality at older ages is extreme. In general, cancer survey data appear plausible in relation to other international experience.

Reconstruction of Mortality Trends

China's mortality trends can now be reconstructed with some confidence because of the wealth of demographic data available only since 1982. As shown already, survival ratios by cohort from one census to the next are plausible, except for those male cohorts undercounted or not reported by the military in the late teens and early twenties. Therefore, China's three censuses can be assumed about equally complete in their coverage of the population, which gives us fairly reliable intercensal population growth figures for 1953–64 and 1964–82. Regarding birth rates, China took a national retrospective fertility survey in late 1982 which for the first time gave believable age-specific and total fertility rate estimates for each year from 1940 through 1981. Using these data essentially without adjustment in combination with China's age structure from the censuses yields the number of births in China each year. International migration for China is so negligible that China's population can be considered a closed one. Therefore, for each of the two intercensal periods, subtracting the absolute population growth from the absolute number of births gives us the total number of deaths for 1953–64 and for 1964–82. The overall level of mortality is a residual figure fully determined by the other fairly firm data.

The given total number of deaths during each intercensal period must be allocated by age group in the population. This estimation task is greatly aided by the excellent age reporting in all the censuses and by the apparent equal completeness of coverage of the population at most ages for both sexes in all the censuses. Each age-sex cohort in the 1953 census is diminished by that number of deaths needed to reduce the surviving cohort to its 1964 size. The attempt to reconstruct each succeeding census age structure from the previous one constrains the choice of age patterns of mortality in the interim.

The foregoing logical process leaves only one question unanswered. In each intercensal period, how many of the given total number of deaths happened in each intercensal year? This arbitrary estimation process is assisted by the falling or rising trends in the official death rates. One could assume that even though the official death rates are too low in every or almost every year, the trend shown in the official rates reflects the underlying reality. For most periods this assumption is used for the mortality reconstruction shown here.

Table 4.18 presents the annual mortality estimates used to generate each successive census population from the previous one. These death rates produce the right number of deaths for 1953–64 and 1964–82, given the census counts and the fertility survey age-specific fertility rates as reported. All these data are consistent with the reconstructed total population sizes given in Table 2.7.

Comparison with Tables 4.1 and 4.3 shows that the reconstructed death rates are considerably higher than the official ones. For most years 1953–61 only about 54–60 percent of the deaths were reported, while in the 1960's through the early 1980's the death reporting system was more complete, registering 79–92 percent of the deaths in most years. It is striking that apparently no attempt to obtain complete reporting of deaths has yet succeeded in China. The Cancer Epidemiology Survey gave the same crude death rate as the regular reporting system and achieved about 80–90 percent completeness of death coverage. The 1982 census asked about deaths in 1981 and derived a crude death rate not much higher than that from vital registration. Though it is not yet clear what proportion of actual mortality was incorporated into the census life tables, it is likely that coverage remained incomplete. In an attempt to obtain more complete reporting of births and deaths than obtained by vital registration, the State Statistical Bureau instituted an annual vital events survey that interviewed residents of randomly selected geographical units in January 1983 and again in January 1984, asking about births and deaths in the previous calendar year. Death rates calculated from these surveys have been higher than from the census or vital registration, suggesting greater completeness. Though no independent evidence is available to estimate the percent of deaths missed by this technique, again a fair assessment is that deaths remain underreported.

China has laws requiring that deaths be reported, and yet usually 10–20 percent of them are not. It appears that at least in the countryside it is possible for family and neighbors to know of a death and even for a funeral and burial or cremation to take place without the official recording of the death. In Table 4.19, an attempt is made to determine the age groups in the population whose deaths are not fully reported. Survival

TABLE 4.18

Reconstructed Crude Death Rates, Life Expectancy, and Infant Mortality Rates by Sex, 1953–84

Year	Crude death rate (per 1,000 population)	Life expectancy (years from birth)			Infant mortality rate (per 1,000 live births)		
		Males	Females	Both sexes	Males	Females	Both sexes
1953	25.8	39.8	40.8	40.3	179.3	169.5	174.6
1954	24.2	41.7	43.1	42.4	167.1	161.3	164.3
1955	22.3	43.8	45.5	44.6	154.7	153.0	153.8
1956	20.1	46.1	48.1	47.0	142.0	144.5	143.2
1957	18.1	48.4	50.9	49.5	129.0	135.9	132.4
1958	20.7	44.9	46.9	45.8	144.5	148.1	146.3
1959	22.1	41.8	43.3	42.5	159.6	160.1	159.9
1960	44.6	24.3	25.3	24.6	283.2	284.9	284.0
1961	23.0	36.2	41.6	38.4	186.9	179.6	183.4
1962	14.0	51.3	54.8	53.0	92.3	84.4	88.5
1963	13.8	53.2	56.7	54.9	90.8	83.1	87.1
1964	12.5	55.5	58.7	57.1	89.4	81.7	85.6
1965	11.6	56.3	59.3	57.8	87.2	81.5	84.4
1966	11.1	57.2	59.9	58.6	85.0	81.3	83.2
1967	10.5	58.2	60.6	59.4	82.9	81.0	82.0
1968	10.1	59.2	61.3	60.3	80.7	80.8	80.7
1969	9.9	59.8	61.9	60.8	75.5	75.6	75.6
1970	9.5	60.3	62.5	61.4	70.3	70.4	70.4
1971	9.2	60.8	63.1	62.0	65.1	65.2	65.2
1972	8.9	61.4	63.7	62.6	59.9	59.9	59.9
1973	8.6	61.8	64.0	63.0	56.1	56.3	56.2
1974	8.3	62.3	64.4	63.4	52.2	52.6	52.4
1975	8.1	62.7	64.8	63.8	48.4	48.9	48.6
1976	7.8	63.2	65.2	64.2	44.5	45.2	44.9
1977	7.7	63.7	65.6	64.6	40.7	41.5	41.0
1978	7.5	64.1	66.0	65.1	36.8	37.7	37.2
1979	7.6	64.3	65.7	65.0	36.3	42.7	39.4
1980	7.7	64.4	65.3	64.9	35.8	47.7	41.6
1981	7.7	64.5	65.0	64.8	35.3	52.6	43.7
1982	7.9	64.7	64.7	64.7	34.9	57.5	45.9
1983	8.0	64.8	64.4	64.6	34.4	62.4	48.0
1984	8.0	64.9	64.1	64.6	33.9	67.2	50.1

SOURCE: Computer reconstruction by the author at the China Branch, Center for International Research, U.S. Bureau of the Census.

NOTE: This reconstruction modeled the female infant mortality rate rising after 1978 in a successful attempt to project the slightly high sex ratios of young children counted in the 1982 census. There is, however, no independent proof that female infanticide caused a statistically significant number of female infant deaths.

TABLE 4.19
Comparison of Official and Cancer Epidemiology Survey Data on Female Survival Ratios, 1964–82

Age group in 1964	18-year survival ratio: From censuses	From cancer survey: Corrected but not adjusted	From cancer survey: Adjusted (85% complete assumed)	Cohort's ages in 1982	Completeness of death reporting (percent)
0–4	.95248	.96582	.95959	18–22	<85%
5–9	.96886	.97755	.97361	23–27	<85
10–14	.97546	.97615	.97196	28–32	Almost 100
15–19	.95914	.96973	.96444	33–37	<85
20–24	.94976	.96140	.95471	38–42	<85
25–29	.94428	.95006	.94151	43–47	85–100
30–34	.94131	.93259	.92122	48–52	—[a]
35–39	.89767	.90568	.89009	53–57	85–100
40–44	.87249	.86318	.84129	58–62	—[a]
45–49	.78727	.79799	.76733	63–67	85–100
50–54	.69108	.70522	.66410	68–72	85–100
55–59	.53272	.58118	.53002	73–77	85

SOURCES: Census survival ratios were calculated directly from the 1964 and 1982 census single-year age structures. Cancer survey survival ratios were interpolated from 15-year and 20-year survival ratios calculated from the female life tables assuming 100% completeness and 85% completeness of death reporting, Appendix Tables A.3 and A.4.
[a]Too many deaths recorded.

ratios for the 18-year intercensal period 1964–82 are calculated from the female age structures in the two censuses. These are compared with 18-year survival ratios calculated from the female cancer survey life tables applicable to the midpoint of the intercensal period. The following results are only tentative and suggestive, because the assumptions underlying this comparison may not be completely met. Completeness estimates for each cohort are attributed to their age at the midpoint of the intercensal period 1964–82; the midpoint coincides with the reference dates of the cancer survey. Table 4.19 indicates that death reporting for females in the cancer survey was less than 85 percent complete for most cohorts from birth up to about the early thirties, close to 100 percent complete from the early thirties to the early sixties, and only 85 percent complete in the late sixties. Because the cancer survey retrospectively gathered further information on deaths that had already been registered in the years 1973–75, we can assume that the pattern of omissions found in the cancer survey is also applicable to the death registration system. It cannot be determined whether omissions in the reporting of male deaths parallel the female pattern, because male intercensal survival ratios are distorted by missing males in the age structures.

Perhaps this age pattern of omitted deaths can provide clues for determining why some deaths are not reported. Deaths appear fully reported for people in the prime working ages, which may indicate that their work units have a part in initiating and carrying through on the registration of the deaths. But in the ages where the reporting of deaths may depend entirely on family initiative, 15 percent or more of the deaths apparently are never formally registered. Local cadres do not seem to overcome family reluctance and report the deaths for them. One possibility is that families wish to keep receiving the rations of the deceased, and another hypothesis is that some families wish to bury their dead and avoid cremation favored by the authorities. Once a family has neglected to register a death, family respondents to census or survey questions may continue to hide the death. Also, some underreporting of deaths is due to the perception that a baby who dies never really lived, that it is stillborn or that its birth and death cancel each other. Another source of underreporting may be people who live alone with no family to report their deaths, or people who die away from their residence location.

The reconstruction of population trends in Table 4.18 estimates that China's death rate had already dropped to about 26 by 1953, probably from a much higher death rate in 1949. A life expectancy of around 40 years had been attained by 1953, and the infant mortality rate, though far below the 1929–31 level estimated at close to 300, was still around 175 infant deaths per thousand live births. Mortality improved until 1957, when a life expectancy close to 50 years, a death rate about 18, and an infant mortality rate of around 130 were achieved.

The Great Leap Forward brought about a sharp temporary reversal of the earlier mortality decline. The disruptive policies of the Great Leap caused the death rate to rise in 1958 and 1959, until it peaked at a very high level estimated at 45 deaths per thousand population in the peak famine year of 1960. A very high infant mortality rate is also modeled in the reconstruction for 1960. High infant mortality during these years is implied by the small number of survivors counted in the 1964 census from the birth cohorts as generated by nationwide fertility survey data. Mortality dropped off steeply in 1961 and by 1962 the death rate and infant mortality rate seem to have improved beyond the 1957 levels. China's own official mortality data suggest that there were 15 million excess deaths during the four years 1958–61, above what would have been expected from a smooth death rate trend between 1957 and 1962. The reconstruction in Table 4.18 results in an estimated 30 million excess deaths in the four-year crisis period.

The reconstruction models a gradual decline in China's crude death rate from 14 in 1962 to a low of about 7.5 in 1978. A life expectancy of about 63 years was achieved by 1974, consistent with Cancer Epidemiology Survey data adjusted for incompleteness by Banister and Preston. China is estimated to have achieved a peak expectation of life at birth of 65 years in 1978, with about a two-year advantage for females.

Using reported age-specific fertility rates from China's 1982 retrospective fertility survey to generate annual births, then choosing infant mortality estimates to allow enough survivors of the birth cohorts as counted in the 1964 and 1982 censuses, results in the series of low infant mortality rates for 1962–82 shown in Table 4.18. These infant mortality estimates are below the Feeney estimates of Table 4.14 in most years, which suggests that either the Feeney and other similar techniques overestimate China's infant mortality or the fertility survey underreported births. Assuming the fertility survey to be correct gives a low infant mortality rate of only 37 in 1978.

With the advent of the one-child family planning policy, a rise in female infanticide and selective neglect began to be reported. This is reflected in a slowly rising sex ratio in the 1982 census cohorts born after midyear 1978. The reconstruction assumes a continuing sex ratio at birth of 106.0, slow improvement in male infant mortality, and a rise in the female infant mortality rate that generates the sex ratios of each single-year cohort ages 0 through 3 counted in the 1982 census. The hypothesized levels and trends in infant mortality should be viewed as informed speculation until further evidence on infant mortality is available. The rising mortality among young females assumed in the reconstruction reduces the estimated female expectation of life at birth by two years.

Therefore, a fair estimate is that China's population had a life expectancy of around 65 years in the early 1980's, rather than 68–70 years as officially reported, and a crude death rate of 8 rather than the official figures of 6–7. Infant mortality is estimated to be around 50 in 1984, with the female rate far higher than the male, compared to official claims of an infant mortality rate of about 20–35 in the early 1980's depending on the source.

Conclusion

Until the 1980's the study of mortality in China was an exercise in frustration. It was clear that reported death rates from the 1950's were far too low, but there was no convincing evidence with which to adjust the official figures. Similarly, claimed death rates and infant mortality rates for the 1970's were suspiciously low, and reported expectation of life appeared too high, but one could only voice skepticism that was then labeled as unfounded.

Cancer Epidemiology Survey data finally released in 1980 gave us the first usable life tables for the People's Republic of China, and demographic techniques gave an estimate of 80–90 percent completeness of death reporting. Then in 1983, the sudden availability of single-year age structures from the three censuses and annual fertility rates from the 1982 fertility survey, all data of high quality, made it possible for the first time to reconstruct with confidence the levels of mortality for 1953–64 and 1964–82, showing severe underreporting of deaths in the first intercensal period and moderate underreporting of deaths in the second period. More realistic infant mortality data from the cancer survey, the 1982 census, and the 1982 fertility survey set the minimum infant mortality estimates for 1973–75 and 1981 and superseded the implausibly low official infant mortality rates. Indirect techniques used on 1982 census data gave higher estimates of infant mortality.

Based on consideration of all the population data at our disposal, a reconstruction of China's demographic trends was created for 1953–84. The mortality estimates in that reconstruction are fairly robust for each intercensal period because the level of mortality is determined by fertility survey data in combination with successive census counts. Annual mortality estimates are less certain but unlikely to be far wrong, because they are based on trends in official death rates, single-year age structure data from the 1964 and 1982 censuses, and cancer survey life tables suitably adjusted, as well as other fragmentary mortality data. The mortality estimates presented in Table 4.18 are preferred to official data because they are consistent with census and fertility survey data, and because they adjust for the persistent underreporting of deaths in China.

5

The Setting for Fertility Decline

THE PROFOUND mortality decline and improvements in health experienced by the people of China initiated a period of rapid population growth, which is typical of developing countries today during their demographic transition. To curb such traumatic population growth, fertility must come under control as well as mortality. But there is no guarantee that this will happen in any particular country. Because of the influence of tradition, many developing countries are having great difficulty achieving a reduction in fertility sufficient to offset the reduction in mortality. For millennia most human societies have had social customs, family relationships, and economic systems supportive of high fertility. At least some aspects of this traditional milieu must change in order to allow or encourage low fertility.

Fertility decline began in China's cities during the mid-1960's, but the birth rate remained high in rural China until after 1970. During the 1970's very rapid fertility decline took place in rural as well as urban areas. China's level of fertility at the end of the decade was approximately one-half of what it had been in 1970.[1] Most of the fertility transition was probably due to the determined government effort to reduce fertility through its family planning program. In addition, some of the deep societal changes engineered by the government may have contributed to spontaneous fertility decline or created the context in which the family planning program could succeed. This chapter is devoted to an exploration of the social and economic milieu in which rapid fertility decline took place. The next two chapters describe the particulars of the government's program.

Household Structure

China continues to maintain the traditional family system that has always encouraged moderately high fertility. A young woman in China is almost certain to marry soon after she reaches the eligible age. It is customary for her to marry a young man from another village. She moves into her husband's village, and possibly into his parents' household, for life. She is no longer part of her own family of birth, and her household work and outside income rarely if ever go to support her own parents. Rather, the considerable contribution she makes of unpaid and paid work is likely to benefit her husband's parents for the rest of their lives. In sharp contrast, a young man brings his wife into his household of birth, or he and his wife set up a household near his parents. Therefore, by raising a daughter a couple derives very little benefit after she marries. But by raising a son a couple is likely to get his financial support for life plus that of his wife, not to mention valuable intangibles such as status in the community, emotional satisfaction, closeness with grandchildren, and long-term relationships within a big family. The system of patrilocal marriage combined with patrilineal descent was the main reason in the past for China's strong preference for sons, and because it endures, the eagerness to bear sons and unhappiness at the birth of a daughter continue today.

Based on this system, the most prosperous and successful families in rural China today are still those with several married sons. The government promotes low fertility and the equal valuation of daughters and sons, yet, ironically, when China's media pick out a rural family as an example of the success of rural economic policies, they usually choose a large extended family with two or more grown sons. After all, it is these families that have succeeded economically. For example, in late 1979 a Chinese journal described a large extended family with many grown sons, implying that their prosperity was somehow typical of rural farm families. The article was entitled "How a Farm Family Gets Its Income."

> At 60 Feng Maoru is patriarch of a big family. He and his wife and three of their five sons live . . . in their village in the Wugui brigade in western Sichuan's Xindu county. Two other sons are working elsewhere and the two daughters are married and live with their husbands' families.
>
> As the youngest son spends most of his time at the middle school he attends in the county town, the three full-time workers at home are the two remaining sons and a daughter-in-law. The latter, being a whiz at rice transplanting, is a good work-point earner. Feng Shifu, 25, works for the bee farm run by the commune brigade. His brother Feng Shigui, 27, works as carpenter in one of the brigade's sideline units. Since these sons are skilled men and contribute a lot to the brigade's collective income, they get extra pay in addition to the work points they earn.

> Last year the family earned 13,020 work points, the equivalent of 1,240 yuan. With the two sons' extra pay of 108 yuan and bonuses of 40 yuan their total income from collective work came to 1,388. On top of this is their income from family sideline production . . . [for a] total 1978 income of 1,798.
>
> Expenditures . . . added up to 1,281 yuan, leaving a surplus of 517 yuan, part of which was put into the bank, for there were few other necessary expenses. . . . In addition to the family savings, the old couple have a savings account of their own. The two sons working outside send them 300 to 400 yuan a year for their own expenses, but the couple prefers to bank it with the aim of using it for the weddings of the younger sons.[2]

In China's rural villages, the contrast between such families with many sons and the lot of most other families is not lost on the peasants.

This strong preference for sons naturally affects fertility. Because approximately half of all births are daughters, if couples desire a certain number of sons they will on average require twice as many children in order to get the desired number of sons. But the effects of son preference on the fertility of particular couples depends on the order of male and female births, and so varies greatly from couple to couple. For example, if a couple bears a son first, will that couple be willing to stop at one child? In the Chinese context, couples usually will choose to cease childbearing after the birth of one son only if they are convinced that he has a very good chance of living well into adulthood. Given the current infant and child mortality levels in the PRC, which mean that the loss of a child is more than a remote possibility, stopping at one son is a little risky, and it is safer to bear two. This calculation would vary greatly by locality. In advanced urban areas that have low childhood mortality, the birth of one son might be enough, but in poor rural areas, the chances are that the son might die before reaching productive age, in which case it is wiser to bear two sons in hopes that at least one will survive. Therefore, if a family bears two sons and no daughters, it is economically rational for them to stop at two births.[3]

However, if the first child is a daughter, her parents will very likely not choose to stop childbearing after one child. If the first two children are daughters, the answer is the same. Until a couple bears at least one healthy son, it is unlikely that they will voluntarily cease childbearing. Even then, it is important that the son have good survival chances, or the couple might be tempted to try for a second son as a form of insurance.

Some important changes have happened in China to reduce the pronatalist effects of this system. First, the reduction of infant and child mortality to today's moderate levels makes it more likely that a son is going to live for a long time. Second, the age at marriage for women has risen greatly, so daughters contribute their household labor and earned income to their family of birth until they marry in their early or mid-twenties.

Therefore daughters are not such an economic liability as they were in the past.

Third, the relative worth of daughters may have grown by evolution in the system of financial exchange between the families of the betrothed at the time of marriage. Most parts of China used to have a system in which the groom's family paid the bride's family a high bride price at marriage, but in turn the bride's family provided her with a dowry that was sometimes of greater value than the bride price. This has been characterized as an "indirect dowry system."[4] When the dowry was substantial in comparison to the bride price, the main beneficiary would be the household of the groom and his parents, not that of the bride, because much of the wealth exchanged at the time of marriage would end up in the household of the groom's family. Such a system would only reinforce the preference for sons rather than daughters.* Interviews with refugees from Guangdong province during the early 1970's suggest that the traditional bride price has stayed high or increased while the dowry has been reduced to a token amount of money or goods.[5] Parents of girls can and do refuse permission for their daughter to marry unless the prospective groom's family pays the large bride price, which averages about a year's income for the groom's household. Some sources attribute the phenomenon of the high bride price to "low production levels and poor living standards," and other sources blame it on the "gang of four."[6] The government strenuously opposes the custom of paying a bride price, because it seems equivalent to buying and selling a woman like a piece of property. But the bride price has increased in relation to family income while the dowry has declined in importance, possibly because young women are now much more valuable to a household than they ever were in the past. They are likely to live much longer after their marriage and to contribute substantial income in addition to household services. Where there is a system of high bride price combined with small dowry, it enhances the perceived value of daughters to their own parents and reduces the apparent advantage of having sons rather than daughters.

Fourth, the government began about 1975 to promote the practice of the groom moving in with the bride's family—a custom termed matrilocal or, more technically, uxorilocal marriage—if the bride has no

* In the past, many poor families could not afford to raise a daughter and then provide her with a dowry at marriage. Similarly, poor families with a son feared they could not accumulate the bride price and pay for the wedding ceremony so the son could marry. A solution to this dilemma was that parents of a daughter would sell her cheaply or give her away at birth or when she was still young, to be raised as the future wife of the son in the receiving household. High costs at the time of marriage were avoided by both families. This practice, which was widespread in some parts of China, has been illegal since 1950 and appears to have ceased in the PRC. See Wolf & Huang (1980).

brothers. For instance, a *People's Daily* article extolled one county's campaign to popularize matrilocal marriage.[7] This county in Hebei province claimed that its drive had been somewhat successful, that couples with no sons had begun to show greater willingness to cease childbearing, and that the more flexible living arrangements had reduced the burden of unsupported older people in the county. Another county in the same province reported in 1975: "There are more than 2,000 couples throughout the county with husbands settled in the families of their wives, accounting for 25 percent of the families which have only daughters. This new practice has promoted the popularization of planned parenthood."[8] This policy could set up a struggle between the bride's and groom's parents over which household the couple will join. Precedent favors the groom's family, and if the young woman's family insists that a son-in-law move in with them, she may have trouble finding a willing husband. So far the practice of matrilocal marriage does not appear to have caught on, but it does happen occasionally with the encouragement of some political leaders and Communist Party members. If the PRC can develop a flexible system in which matrilocal marriage is as acceptable as patrilocal marriage, then parents of daughters would be less desperate to bear a son, and reduced fertility could result.[9]

Fifth, the Chinese government has attempted to provide some old-age support so that couples do not have to have sons to provide for them in their old age. A chief reason behind the desire for sons is that parents hope to reside with their children and grandchildren when they grow old rather than live in loneliness and poverty. The government understands this concern and has tried to mitigate it in order to reduce the national fertility level. In urban areas persons employed by national or local governments and those working in state factories or retail outlets for a long time are guaranteed a pension when they retire. They should not need sons to support them. But the government budget has not been large enough to provide social security to all the elderly. In other urban families and in all rural areas, the government depends on grown children, primarily sons, to support their parents so that the government does not have to. Collective organizations in the countryside give very little support to old people. Through their small welfare funds they try to provide the "five guarantees"—minimum provision of food, clothing, shelter, medical care, and burial—to aged persons who have no children to support them. But poor villages can do very little to provide for old people who have no sons to care for them, and almost no village can guarantee regular support during periods of economic crisis or poor harvests.[10] To the extent that China has been able to establish a floor under poverty in old age, social security has helped to weaken pronatalist tendencies in the society, but the system's weakness is one of the most powerful factors promoting high fertility today.[11]

In 1979 the government began to urge counties and communes to set up social-security systems that guarantee old-age support. Shanghai Municipality led in this innovation. By the end of 1979 almost half the communes in the municipality's suburban counties, those in the "more developed rural areas" of Shanghai, provided pensions for persons in poor health age 65 and above.[12] Retirement apparently is not automatic at 65 but comes when the person can no longer work for income. There appears to be no financial criterion to qualify for the pensions in Shanghai communes. The pension is around ten yuan per month, a small sum but reportedly enough to guarantee an average rural living standard.

Since 1979 other localities have experimented with instituting various forms of old-age security.[13] Relatively wealthy suburban and rural areas can afford it, but average and poorer areas evidently cannot. Thus the more prosperous rural areas have this powerful option for encouraging low fertility, while poorer areas cannot yet offer enough old-age security to obviate the need for sons.

A 1978 conference of Chinese population specialists summed up the effect of son preference on fertility as follows:

> All comrades pointed out that there are still some obstacles to promoting planned parenthood. Especially in our rural areas, there still exist such old-fashioned ideas as "attaching importance to men while looking down upon women" and "more sons, more happiness." In the final analysis, such old ideas and practices were the result of economic factors. Therefore, we must step up ideological education, propagate scientific knowledge of birth control and change existing habits and customs, along with adopting the necessary economic measures to do an even better job in social welfare work.[14]

As of the early 1980's pension schemes for the elderly outside the state sector of the economy appear to be rare. Where they exist, the income they provide is usually very low.[15] The outlook for a viable nationwide old-age security system is bleak: collective welfare schemes are being weakened by a decline in the collective financial resources of production brigades and communes as households take responsibility for agricultural production and retain most of their earnings under the new "production responsibility system in agriculture," introduced to increase production incentives for farm families. Meanwhile, the government cannot afford to take over the huge task of caring for the aged and shows little willingness to divert resources for this use. Instead, the legal responsibility of children to care for their aged parents has been reaffirmed. This only reinforces the desire of couples to have children, especially sons.

China's common housing pattern, in which older people live in the same family compound or very near their children and grandchildren, also promotes high fertility by subjecting young couples to constant pressure to have children. Older Chinese tend to have more traditional ideas than those born or raised after 1949; they often encourage their sons and daughters-in-law to bear them many grandchildren. For instance, on a visit to the PRC in 1971, I spoke with a young woman leader in one of the model rural areas. She said that she and her husband were very modern in their attitudes, but they lived with his parents, who clung to traditional customs and insisted that they be followed within the household. This is not an easy situation. Old people in China are usually loved and respected, and they generally expect their children to listen to and follow their advice. Grown children tend to go along with their elders rather than cause family disharmony. After all, they are living together in close quarters; life can get unpleasant if the old want to have their way and the young defy them.

How is this problem dealt with? On the one hand the government encourages young people to respect their parents and elders to the extent that this is needed to promote social stability. But at the same time it constantly promotes policies, such as controlled and low fertility, that overturn traditional customs. This dilemma is resolved by using political meetings to push the new values, and by sending those dedicated to the new values to the homes of recalcitrant persons to persuade them to change their minds. Older people who urge their children to bear many children are the targets of much political pressure to conform to the new policies.

In general, though the traditional family system has been modified to some extent by government policies and demographic changes, it still promotes fertility. For example, when peasants are asked why they are reluctant to stop childbearing with a very small number of children, or before they have a son, they respond that it is very important to continue the ancestral line, that they need a son to care for them in their old age, and that "everything would be finished" if the death of their child or children left them childless.[16]

Pronatalist Economic Influences

It is not only patrilocal, extended-family households that promote continued high fertility in China; several important aspects of the economy play a supportive role. For example, China is still a poor country. The history of fertility declines in other countries suggests that a major rise in a nation's per capita income coincides with and supports fertility reduction. Countries that continue to have low per capita income usually also continue to have high fertility. There is some confusion in the calculation of China's per capita income or per capita gross national product, but reasonable approximations can be derived. One Chinese source reported a per capita gross national product of U.S. $208 in 1978 and around $240 in 1979.[17] These figures, if correct, would place China not among the very poorest of countries but just above that group and below most developing countries. Another source reported that China had a national income of 337 billion yuan in 1979, which using official population totals for the PRC yields a 1979 per capita income of 349 yuan.[18] The actual purchasing power of this sum is far beyond what is implied by the equivalent value of $233 annual per capita income at the 1980 exchange rate of 1.5 yuan to the dollar. Nevertheless, these data still placed China low among the developing countries in terms of per capita income, at least until the early 1980's. According to this criterion, the PRC's economic development is still at an early stage and the country is poor on a per capita basis. Spontaneous fertility decline is unlikely to happen under such economic conditions, though it is not impossible. Recent historical studies have indicated that there is no particular level of development required before fertility can begin to fall; China may be one of the rare cases in which fertility decline begins at a low level of economic development.[19]

Another aspect of economic development that usually accompanies and supports fertility decline is a shift of the bulk of the working population from agricultural to nonagricultural employment. One reason is that agricultural work by women is more compatible with pregnancy, childbearing, and child rearing than is work in factories or offices. A second reason is that labor-intensive agricultural production on family farms requires many laborers in the family. This encourages high fertility because children can begin being productive in agriculture at an early age and because a farm family without enough laborers can be in serious economic trouble. When agriculture is mechanized and more productive, fewer laborers are needed and they must be more skilled, which requires that children receive more education and training before they go to work. Raising children becomes more expensive, and they consume more before contributing to family income. Therefore, once the proportion of the population in agriculture declines significantly, the average family has more economic incentives to control fertility.

However, farming is still by far the most common occupation in China. Based on the 1982 census, 69 percent of China's employed population is engaged in farming, including 64 percent of working men and 75 percent of working women.[20] The large proportion of the population working in labor-intensive agriculture and living in agricultural families would be expected to exert a pronatalist influence.

Particular economic policies of the government sometimes encourage high fertility, even while the government promotes low fertility through the family planning program. For instance, under China's collective agricultural system from the late 1950's to the end of the 1970's, rural income from agricultural labor was seldom paid directly and explicitly to the person whose labor earned the income. Rather, work points earned by any member of a household were recorded under the name of the head of that household, who is usually the oldest man of the household still active in field work. To some extent it did not matter who in the household got the income, because peasants were usually paid mostly in kind—grain—and the grain was stored in the household for the whole family's use. But the fact that income from the collective accrued to the extended family household meant that men and women from 15 to 50 or so, except for the designated household head, had little independence in deciding how they would use their incomes. This strengthened their dependence on the family decision-making structure on all important matters, including economic considerations in deciding whether to have another child.[21] Chinese rural economic policies have in general reinforced the dependence of the individual on the household, in turn setting the scene for family members to intervene in marriage and fertility decisions.[22]

For decades, many localities supplied grain rations or private agricultural plots or land for housing on a per capita basis.[23] It was administratively easier, for example, to divide the land available for private plots by the total population of the production team or village, with each family's allotment based on the number of family members. But this technique promoted high fertility, it is now thought, because with each new child families could get more land. Only since 1979 has the national government tried to stop this incentive by encouraging localities not to award land in response to a couple's second or higher order birth.

Similarly, many of China's villages during the last two decades have distributed all or most of the grain they produced on the basis of need (so-called "basic grain") rather than the work contributed by the family to grow that grain ("work-point grain"). In some places, households with many children normally received enough distributed grain to get them through the year, while households with few or no children ran out of the grain that had been distributed in kind and were forced to buy the rest of the grain they needed at high prices.[24] In addition, rations of cooking oil, sugar, meat, or other items in scarce supply were allocated on a per capita basis.[25] It is now thought that supplying food to a family according to its size, regardless of its ability to pay at the time, has promoted high fertility in the countryside. During the 1970's steps were taken to counteract this pronatalist policy. In the first part of the decade, some localities refused to issue more grain, other rationed foods, or additional land to families in which a couple bore a fourth or higher order child. This forced the family to buy any needed increments of grain with precious cash in the free market.[26] But on the whole, the custom of distributing most grain to families on the basis of need apparently persisted at least to the end of 1978; a November 1978 broadcast noted that this custom "encourages having more children and is also detrimental to the principles of 'to each according to his work' and 'more pay for more work' and cannot arouse the peasants' enthusiasm."[27]

In 1979 a number of provinces began issuing trial regulations aimed at changing pronatalist aspects of the grain distribution system. Hunan announced that "when agriculture and forestry farms and vegetable-growing communes and brigades, which consume grain provided by the state, decide on the amount of grain to be supplied according to the size of the population, they must ensure that families with fewer children do not receive less grain and that those with more children do not receive more grain."[28] In the same broadcast the Hunan provincial authorities stated that the grain ration for the third or higher order child in urban or rural areas was to be charged at a high price. Also in 1979, Sichuan and Anhui provinces stipulated that an only child was to receive an adult grain ration, and Anhui's regulations stated, "we must implement the method of allocating fixed amounts of basic grain rations on the basis of each individual's contributions."[29] This probably meant that if a family had not earned enough work points to pay for the needed grain, they were not supposed to get it.

One by one, other provinces attempted to steer grain rations toward the one-child family and away from the several-child family. Several provinces announced that hardship payments and relief grain would not be given to families with more children than are allowed, regardless of need or circumstances.[30] The effect of such a restriction on a poor locality or on any locality after a bad crop year, to the extent it was actually carried out, could be devastating, resulting in unnecessary malnutrition and starvation and perhaps out-migration. It is still not clear whether the regulations work in practice. One refugee from Guangdong province suggested that they might not: "It is easy for someone in Beijing to say that a third child must be denied full rations, but few cadres can bring themselves to do anything that might harm some handsome little baby next door. Few are that heartless."[31]

Women's Role and Fertility

The economic and social factors still exerting a pronatalist influence in China would in most countries be enough to keep fertility as high as or almost as high as traditional levels. But some powerful political, social, and economic changes have made rapid fertility decline possible in China despite its poverty and traditional household structure. Perhaps one of the most important of these changes is the transformation in the lives and roles of women. Recent demographic research suggests that the status of women has a strong effect on fertility.[32]

Before 1949 the typical life situation of a Chinese woman was consistent with and supportive of moderately high fertility. She had no independence or rights: she was essentially owned by her parents until her early marriage, then owned by her husband and his family. Almost all important decisions in her life were made by someone else. She was severely limited in her freedom of physical movement, and in a large minority of cases was actually crippled by the custom of binding her feet as a child, which broke the bones and made walking painful and difficult throughout her life. She had very low status in the household of her birth, where she generally learned to be subservient. When she first moved into her husband's family, she might be treated as a despised outsider until she earned a measure of acceptance by producing sons. If she lived long enough, which was in doubt given the high mortality level, upon the marriage of her son she could increase her status in the household by bossing around her new daughter-in-law.

Her role in the economy was also conducive to high fertility. She was almost totally economically dependent, because she had no rights of inheritance or ownership, even of the fruits of her own labor. The usual situation was that she worked hard, but her work consisted of unpaid, unrecognized household and agricultural production. This pattern of women's work is typically found to be consistent with high fertility.

Before 1949 there were sporadic attempts to free women from the worst of these traditional constraints. Some successes were achieved, in particular in urban elite families and in the Communist base areas. The most modernized women were not subjected to footbinding, received some education, and began working in factories and other non-traditional jobs. But the vast majority of China's women were hardly affected by these trends.

The Communist Party has always been ideologically opposed to the traditional oppression of women. Soon after the PRC was founded in 1949, the party set out to transform the societal role of women into a modern one, not in order to reduce fertility but to promote socialist development of society and the economy. The Marriage Law of 1950 proclaimed full equality between husbands and wives, gave property rights and rights of inheritance to females, forbade arranged marriages and child marriage, permitted divorce, gave women some rights to custody of their children after divorce, forbade polygamy and concubinage, legalized the remarriage of widows, and set minimum marriage ages for males and females.[33] During the early 1950's the Communist Party and the Women's Federation of China tried vigorously to implement the main provisions of the Marriage Law in the villages. They encountered stiff resistance, far more than they expected. According to the following official sources, tens of thousands of people died in struggles over the Marriage Law. For instance, the law was promulgated in May 1950, and in September 1951 the press reported:

> There are still frequent occurrences of such illegal acts as interference with people's freedom to marry, and the violation of the rights of women, often reaching the serious state of the persecution of the lives of women, so that in various parts of the country many women had been murdered or forced into suicide as the result of marriage complications. According to incomplete statistical data . . . , more than 10,000 thus lost their lives in the Central-South region during the past one-year perod; 1,245 also died similarly in Shantung province during the same period.[34]

Chinese propaganda correctly pointed out that murder and forced suicide of women happened frequently under the traditional marriage system, and therefore at first the abruptness of the Marriage Law campaign was not blamed for the wave of marriage-related deaths of females. Thus one report in 1953, after stating that more than 70,000 women and men had died as a result of marriage problems in a year's time, claimed that this epidemic "is one of the most serious evil consequences brought about by the arbitrary and compulsory feudal marriage system."[35]

The violence connected with traditional marriage had apparently been acutely exacerbated by the bitterness of the early Marriage Law campaign. During the middle months of 1953 the government made one more attempt to completely implement the provisions of the Marriage Law and when that did not succeed retreated to a more gradualist approach. It began emphasizing family harmony rather than struggle, and turned to the use of education, propaganda, and concrete changes in women's economic role to bring about compliance with the spirit and the letter of the Marriage Law.

In spite of this initial violent setback, the lives of women in China have undergone great change since 1949. Footbinding is a thing of the past, though visitors to China still see older women whose feet were irreversibly damaged when they were young. Marital abuses such as child marriage and concubinage are now rare or nonexistent, according to refugee accounts.[36] A mixed system for choosing marriage partners has evolved: there is the occasional fully arranged marriage and the occasional marriage by free choice, but most marriages involve informal go-betweens and formal introductions of the prospective partners, both of whom have a veto over the proposed match, as do both sets of parents.[37]

Once married, young couples are presumably much less subject to the arbitrary authority of the husband's parents because the ownership of land and other production facilities was taken away from families and given to the collective. Because the male head of household has less economic power over household members than he had in the past, his power in other aspects of life is also less. Even under the production responsibility system the production team retains technical ownership of the land with authority to reallocate parcels of land to couples who wish to set up their own household and farm separately.

Women have become less subject to abuse by their husbands than in the past. Government propaganda has encouraged their equal participation in household decisions and in the wider society for over 35 years now, and the climate of opinion about the proper role of women has become more liberal. Today when a husband beats his wife, refuses to let her work outside the home, insists that she keep having babies until she has a son, or oppresses her in other ways counter to government policy, she is likely to have the active support of several community organizations and some political leaders as she tries to reform her husband's behavior. But her power in relation to her husband under such circumstances has been limited by the severe restrictions on divorce in force since about 1953. If she, with the help of her community, could not stop abuses by her husband, she has often been forced by the law to stay with him and live with the abuses. Divorce might have become more available now that the Marriage Law of 1981 allows divorce when there is "complete alienation of mutual affection, and when mediation has failed."[38]

The greater degree of communication, equality, and reciprocity between spouses in China by the 1970's may have facilitated the adoption of joint fertility control. Research from other countries suggests that reducing fertility in a society requires some sharing of decision-making power between husband and wife.[39]

Very gradually, the economic role of some women has developed in ways conducive to fertility decline. As of 1982, 36 million urban women and 16 million rural women were employed in nonagricultural jobs.[40] Their work is needed to support their families, yet it is incompatible with high fertility because their free time is so limited and the costs of child care are so high.

But the vast majority of working women live in rural areas and are engaged in agricultural occupations, 163 million as of 1982, and there is no inherent contradiction between agricultural work and continuing high fertility.[41] In Chinese agriculture, women have traditionally been and are still treated as a reserve labor force. It is deemed important to provide men with income-generating work for as much of the year as possible, and women work whenever there is more work to be done, particularly in peak agricultural seasons. But the PRC has tried to transform working conditions for women in agriculture, partly in order to liberate them from feudal oppression and partly to encourage low fertility. The government's goal is to have women employed and working in agriculture for as much of the year as possible and on a full-time basis. The more hours per day and days per year that women work outside the home, the fewer hours and days they have to devote to bearing and rearing children.

The PRC has emphasized increased labor as a cheap and feasible way to raise agricultural production. But many localities have reported in the press that if women are very unequally treated in the agricultural labor force, they stay home. For example, under the system of collective agriculture, if all the work points a woman earned were credited under the name of the designated household head and not even recorded in her name, her enthusiasm for work was dampened. Similarly, if she worked for eight hours in the fields and if, as was typical, she earned only one-half to four-fifths of the work points of a man doing the same job, she was discouraged and inclined to work less.[42] China has a policy of equal pay for equal work, but male village leaders, probably in most localities, have successfully maintained a pay differential by reserving highly paid jobs and tasks for men, by undervaluing women's skills and output while overvaluing men's contributions to production, or simply by setting limits on women's earnings. The press has reported periodically that as soon as women are given control over their own earnings and paid as much as men, or even almost as much as men, many more women enter production and they work much harder and longer than before.

In each locality in China, as it becomes possible for women to earn a good income from their work in agriculture or in other jobs outside the home, the cost in lost income of taking time to bear and raise a child rises, and fertility tends to decline.

As China's women work more outside the home, there is in particular one remaining inequality between men and women that encourages low fertility: the unshared burden of household work. The available information suggests that to this day, practically all the men of China leave the household tasks to women. Chinese women, rural and urban, are far more overworked than men because they carry a double burden all the time.[43] They are expected to work and earn outside the home just like men, but in addition they still do almost all the housework, shopping, cooking, cleaning, clothes washing, sewing, fuel gathering, vegetable growing, and child care, with almost no help from the men of the family and few modern conveniences. And of course it is women who bear the children and breastfeed their babies for a year in the cities and longer in rural areas, tasks that take additional time. The double burden is imposed on women because men are reluctant to do their share of household tasks, and women have few sanctions they can use to persuade or compel their husbands to share housework equally. For example, a woman in the PRC cannot get a divorce just because her husband refuses to do household tasks, and she cannot get effective community support to persuade her husband to do half the household work because the vast majority of local leaders are men who do not see women's double burden as a problem.

The double burden of women may be a major factor behind fertility declines during economic and social development in patriarchal societies; however, research on women and fertility has not focused on this factor as a fertility determinant. In the case of the PRC, the overwork of women owing to this double burden appears to have a powerful antinatalist effect. If women, even when they have only one or two children, work nonstop from 5 a.m. to 10 p.m. every day of the year, they will think twice before adding another.[44]

Industrialization and Urban Life

As a country industrializes, its fertility tends to decline. Workers in the modern sector and their families gradually adopt a set of modern attitudes, which usually includes a preference for fewer children. China's industrial output has grown by about 13 percent annually since the early 1950's. Whereas in the 1930's industrial output accounted for only about 10 percent of China's gross national product, by 1975 that share had reached 55 percent.[45] Meanwhile, the modern-sector work force has increased. In 1957 there were 35 million nonagricultural workers in China, of whom 28 million worked in "material production" and 7 million in services such as education, government, health, and finance. In 1978 there were 89 million, of whom 68 million worked in material production and 21 million in services. The proportion of the total population engaged in nonagricultural work rose from 5.4 percent in 1957 to 9.3 percent in 1978. These modern-sector workers and their families would be expected by now to have spontaneously adopted a low fertility pattern, especially since 77 percent of these workers in 1978 were employed in the state-owned sector, which pays pensions after retirement.[46]

This long-term increase in the nonagricultural work force was paralleled by an even greater increase in its female component, a process that has encouraged urban fertility decline. A 1980 article in *Zhongguo funü* (Women of China) implied that women should not be treated as a reserve army of labor, to be laid off during a period of high unemployment, because that would contribute to a new rise in urban fertility:

At the present, the employment problem of our country is rather acute, and most of those who are waiting for employment are young women. For this reason, there are some who have suggested that we let a large number of women return to their homes. I really cannot agree with this idea. I believe that the people who uphold this view . . . fail to realize that more numerous and more difficult social problems [than unemployment] would arise if women returned to their homes. I believe that to let more women, especially young women, participate in social labor is also a means of controlling population growth. Conditions in many countries of the world show that the higher the rate of women in employment, the lower the natural population increase rate. . . . China has had a somewhat similar situation. In 1966 there were 8.26 million women workers and employees in enterprises under the state ownership and collective ownership systems, and the urban natural increase rate was 15.9 per thousand. In 1978 the number of women workers and employees increased to 30 million, while the urban natural increase rate was down to 8.8 per thousand. This indicates that following the rise in their economic and social status and their cultural level as they participate in social labor, women will more willingly practice planned parenthood, and thereby the growth of the population will be effectively controlled.[47]

Patterns of life in the city and suburbs also promote lower fertility. City couples have many incentives to limit themselves to one or two children and few to bear more children. First, the cost of raising a child is high in urban areas. According to one source, "it has been estimated that to rear a child from birth to age 16 requires 1,600 yuan in rural areas, 4,800 yuan in small and middle-sized cities, and 6,900 yuan in large urban centers."[48] Therefore, even though incomes are higher in urban than rural areas, the costs of raising a large family in the city are prohibitive.

Second, in urban areas both spouses commonly work full-time six days a week. They have little free time to spend with their children, and child care during working hours is often a problem. If they do not have a grandparent near at hand to care for young children, the parents must pay a child-care-center fee for each child, which can amount to as much as a third of the income of a working adult.

A third factor keeping fertility low in urban areas is a severe shortage of housing space. For instance, in 1966 residential living space in the urban districts of China's 192 municipalities was only 4.5 square meters per person (a space about 7 feet square), probably less than it had been in the early 1950's because of an influx of migrants from the countryside as well as high urban natural population increase.[49] But continuing population growth without commensurate housing construction reduced per capita residential living space to 3.6 square meters (slightly more than 6 by 6 feet) by 1976. It is common for an entire family to live in one or two small rooms and share a toilet and kitchen facilities with several other families. For example, a visitor to a worker's apartment complex in Shanghai described living conditions as follows:

> We were dismayed by the very confining living areas. The structure of a Worker's New Residential Area living quarters is very much like a rooming house. Each wing is shared by four families who share a common kitchen. Two of the families share one bedroom. A family of three share one room, the size of approximately 12 feet by 8 feet. The two beds, one double and one single, took up almost one-third of the room. The families in the wing are not related. There is no separate living room.[50]

Such crowding discourages high fertility because there is no place to put additional children, and it is most unlikely that a family will be allocated more housing space because it has increased in number.

Fourth, the government has tighter control over the lives of urban dwellers than of village residents. The majority of the urban labor force is employed by the state, and public and worker housing, amenities, hospitals, schools, and markets are owned by the state.[51] Therefore, if the government demands that urban dwellers marry late and bear only one or two children, that demand can be enforced. The national government, through the city government and state-owned enterprises, can effectively reward low fertility and penalize high fertility if desired by adjusting people's income or access to services on the basis of their compliance with government family planning policy.

Fifth, beginning in the early 1960's, China had a policy of minimizing urban unemployment by attempting to permanently transfer high-school graduates to rural areas if they could not be immediately employed in their city. However, urban parents were allowed to keep one or two of their children in the city. This policy encouraged urban couples to bear only one or two children, but it was discontinued at the end of the 1970's.

Finally, China's urban medical system is supportive of fertility control because all birth control techniques are readily available and relatively safe. Urban hospitals are experienced at providing abortions, intrauterine devices, and sterilizations, so a person can expect a safe operation. In contrast, delivery of family planning services in rural areas varies greatly in quality.

In response to these influences, spontaneous fertility decline appears to have begun in some cities even before an effective family planning program was in place. For example, the recorded crude birth rate in Shanghai's city districts declined from 46 per thousand population in 1957 to 23 per thousand in 1963.[52] And when the family planning program was actively promoted during the mid-1960's, it succeeded most in urban and contiguous suburban areas, because socioeconomic conditions in cities also promoted lower fertility. For instance, Beijing Municipality and Xian Municipality reported rapid fertility decline between 1963 and 1965–66, and it appears that the municipalities of Shanghai, Nanjing, Suzhou, Yangzhou, Hangzhou, Zhengzhou, Guangzhou, and Wuhan achieved most of their fertility declines before the renewed family planning drive of the early 1970's.[53] Urban life in China, especially in the big cities, seems to be conducive to low fertility.

Education

Another factor that may be contributing to a decline in fertility in China is the growing number of the educated. Mass formal education of both husbands and wives might be expected to prompt them to challenge traditional values and traditional authority structures within the family, giving them wider horizons, and making it more likely that they can effectively carry out family planning measures.[54] Studies in other countries have shown that the educational level of the wife is a particularly important factor in determining her fertility.[55] For some countries there seems to be a threshold below which the wife's education has little or no impact on fertility, but at higher levels education correlates with reduced fertility. At what level of education the threshold occurs depends on cultural and other factors;[56] however, in many developing countries, including several in Asia, even one to six years of education for females measurably reduces the total number of children they bear, and seven or more years of education further reduces their completed fertility.[57] This effect holds even after the comparison is controlled to allow for urban-rural residence and other factors likely to affect fertility.

The example of Taiwan may be relevant to the mainland Chinese experience. In 1966, before Taiwan's family planning program had had a strong effect on fertility, there was almost no difference in fertility between illiterate women and those who were barely literate or had only a few years of education.[58] But primary-school graduates had lower age-specific fertility at most ages than women with less education; moreover, women who had graduated from junior high school had much lower fertility at all ages than women with less education. (Some of this difference may be accounted for by whether women live in urban or rural areas, however.) In Taiwan some of the effect of education on fertility seems to be through raising the age at marriage. For the PRC we might expect similarly that basic literacy or a few years of education would not affect women's fertility much, but if women have graduated from primary school or especially junior high school, their fertility might be lower independent of family planning programs.

We have few reliable data on educational attainment of today's adults in the PRC. Interviews with refugees indicate that both males and females who reached elementary school age after 1949 attained much higher levels of education than earlier cohorts.[59] The 1964 and 1982 censuses asked respondents about the "level" of formal education or equivalent informal education attained, such as primary level or university level, but did not ask the number of years of education completed. A comparison of the results documents the considerable progress in the interim.[60] As of the 1964 census, 28.3 percent of the total population had received some primary school instruction but no advanced education; this category increased to 35.4 percent of the population in 1982. In 1964, only 4.7 percent of the whole population had attained junior middle school level, and this multiplied to 17.8 percent in 1982. Those who had attended senior middle school but no higher level constituted 1.3 percent of the population in 1964 and 6.6 percent of the 1982 population. Adults who had begun or finished college were 0.4 percent of the total population in 1964 and 0.6 percent in 1982.

Based on the 10 percent sample tabulation of 1982 census questionnaires, Table 5.1 shows the levels of education reportedly reached by men and women in each age group, and the proportion who are illiterate or semiliterate. The most important finding is that women of all ages are as a group far less educated and literate than men. For the cohorts aged 45 and above who were children before 1949, the vast majority of the women are illiterate, rising from 74 percent illiterate at ages 45–49 to 95 percent at ages 60 and above. In contrast, over half the men in the ages 45–59 received some education either before or after the founding of the PRC. Illiteracy falls off at younger ages for both sexes, but in the peak childbearing ages 25–29 through 35–39, well over a third of the women are illiterate, while over a third more say they have reached only a primary level of education. About 15 or 20 percent report attaining junior middle school level, and less than 10 percent have reached senior middle school.

For men and women in their teens and twenties, the improvement in educational level has been great. Illiterates are only 6 percent of men ages 20–24 and 4 percent at ages 15–19. While 23 percent of women remain illiterate at ages 20–24, this is far better than the situation among the older cohorts, and the proportion illiterate drops to 15 percent in the age group 15–19. The rest have had at least some elementary education, and the increased attainment of junior or senior middle school level is impressive for young adult women and even more striking for the men.

Some data have been reported on enrollments of schools in China. Primary school enrollment reportedly increased from 24 million in 1949 to 64 million in 1957, to 116 million in 1965, to 127 million in 1972, to 146 million in the years 1977 through 1980.[61] China has claimed that the proportion of children of primary school age that are enrolled in school has increased from 25 percent in 1949 to 85 percent in 1965 to 94–96 percent during 1977–79. But these figures are somewhat inflated, partly because some drop out after the beginning of the school year. Many who

TABLE 5.1
Literacy and Educational Level of the PRC Population by Sex and Age Group, 1982
(Percent of the age-sex group)

Age group	Illiterate and semiliterate	Elementary level	Junior secondary level	Senior secondary level	Higher educational level
		MALE			
6±	—	44.85%	24.55%	8.97%	0.98%
12±	19.17%	—	—	—	—
6–9	—	59.29	—	—	—
10–14	—	78.06	16.01	0.09	—
15–19	4.25	25.88	51.95	17.22	0.70
20–24	5.71	21.21	39.95	31.90	1.24
25–29	9.56	34.65	38.15	16.58	1.06
30–34	13.24	48.57	30.12	7.00	1.07
35–39	14.20	48.55	28.04	7.27	1.94
40–44	22.43	47.18	19.32	7.98	3.09
45–49	32.33	45.75	14.44	5.08	2.40
50–54	40.59	41.54	12.79	3.62	1.46
55–59	47.39	38.65	10.12	2.80	1.03
60±	60.89	31.03	5.95	1.55	0.58
		FEMALE			
6±	—	34.76%	15.24%	5.89%	0.36%
12±	45.27%	—	—	—	—
6–9	—	52.36	—	—	—
10–14	—	71.79	13.23	0.06	—
15–19	14.74	30.65	41.19	13.16	0.26
20–24	23.27	25.04	26.67	24.51	0.52
25–29	36.18	32.31	21.16	9.80	0.56
30–34	40.38	39.69	15.78	3.68	0.46
35–39	43.45	37.05	14.34	4.30	0.85
40–44	57.47	28.47	9.04	3.85	1.17
45–49	74.49	18.99	4.03	1.76	0.73
50–54	85.18	11.31	2.18	0.95	0.38
55–59	89.75	8.05	1.39	0.60	0.20
60±	95.46	3.66	0.54	0.26	0.09

SOURCE: State Council Population Office (1983): 312–17. The data in this table refer to the civilian population.

enroll in elementary school never graduate; this is particularly true of girls, who are sometimes kept at home by their parents to care for their younger siblings.[62] School enrollment figures for 1982 were reported by sex, as shown in Table 5.2. Boys predominate even in primary schools, constituting 56 percent of the students. In middle schools nationwide only 39 percent of the enrolled students are girls, and the proportion female drops to only 26 percent of students enrolled in higher education.

Some fragmentary results from the 1982 nationwide fertility survey indicate that illiteracy and low educational level of women are associated

TABLE 5.2
School Enrollment by Sex, 1982
(Thousands of students)

Type of school	Total students	Males	Females	Females as percent of total
Primary schools	139,720	(78,721)	60,999	43.7%
Regular secondary schools	45,285	(27,511)	17,774	39.2
Agricultural and vocational middle schools	704	(432)	272	38.6
Specialized secondary schools	1,039	(679)	360	34.6
Institutions of higher learning	1,154	(852)	302	26.2
TOTAL	187,902	(108,195)	79,707	42.4%

SOURCE: Statistical Yearbook of China 1983 (1983): 511–18.

with high fertility, while each successive level of educational attainment correlates with lower fertility. One report from the survey compared the completed fertility of women age 50 who had attained different educational levels:

> Educational level had a marked effect on the fertility of women. Take the women age 50 as an example. The average number of children ever born to illiterate women was 5.86; to women with an elementary school level of education, 4.80; to women with a junior secondary school level of education, 3.74; to women with a senior secondary school level of education, 2.85; and to women with a college level of education, 2.05 children.[63]

Part of this differential can be explained by the strong urban bias among women who attend middle school or university. The only published compilation from the survey that attempted to control for the effect of urban or rural residence on fertility and derive the effect of educational level on fertility is shown in Table 5.3. The authors grouped together women ages 35, 40, and 45, most of whom had largely completed their fertility. At each level of education, urban women had had fewer births than rural women, as expected. Within the rural or the urban sectors, educational level of women was inversely correlated with fertility.*

* Several biases remain in Table 5.3. Other factors affecting fertility should also be controlled for, such as minority group status. The choice of ages for the women is too wide a spread, and introduces a spurious correlation because women age 35 have been affected by an insistent family planning program during their most fecund years, and they also have received more education. This makes it appear that their lower fertility is caused by higher educational attainment when it might have been caused by the family planning program. Women age 45, on the other hand, had completed some or all of their childbearing before they were influenced by the family planning program, and also received less education.

TABLE 5.3
Fertility of Women Ages 35, 40, and 45 by Educational Level and Rural-Urban Residence, 1982 Fertility Survey

Category	Illiterate	Level of schooling				Total
		Primary	Junior middle	Senior middle	Higher and technical school	
Rural						
Number of women	7,935	4,029	772	115	9	12,860
Number of children ever born	37,934	16,086	2,716	365	20	57,121
Number ever born per woman	4.78	3.99	3.52	3.17	2.22	4.44
Urban						
Number of women	391	1,071	701	427	115	2,705
Number of children ever born	1,554	3,365	1,821	942	221	7,903
Number ever born per woman	3.97	3.14	2.60	2.21	1.92	2.92
Totals						
Number of women	8,326	5,100	1,473	542	124	15,565
Number of children ever born	39,488	19,451	4,537	1,307	241	65,024
Number ever born per woman	4.74	3.81	3.08	2.41	1.94	4.18

SOURCE: Zhao Jianmin and Sun Jinghua, "Education and Fertility of Women at Child-bearing Age," in China Population Information Centre, *Analysis on China's One-per-Thousand-Population Fertility Sampling Survey*, Beijing (1984): 87.

In both sectors, there was almost a one-child difference between the fertility of illiterate women and that of women with an elementary level of education. Therefore China's strong emphasis on the provision of primary education in the last several decades may have contributed to its fertility decline. The attainment of a junior middle school level of education correlates with a further drop in fertility averaging about half a child per woman in rural or urban areas, and higher levels of education mean even fewer children.

China supports a wide variety of schools and literacy classes in its effort to wipe out illiteracy and provide universal basic education for adults as well as children. As of 1978 there were 8 million children in kindergarten, 146 million in primary school (of whom 45 percent were girls), 65 million in middle school (41 percent female), and 850,000 in college (24 percent of them women).[64] In addition there were 530,000 students in secondary technical schools, 68 million adults enrolled in spare-time primary and middle schools, and 550,000 adults in spare-time colleges. All together, about 290 million persons, 30 percent of the PRC's 1978 population, were enrolled in some kind of educational class.

Extrapolating from studies in other countries suggests the hypothesis that mass enrollment of children in schools, achieved during the 1960's and 1970's in much of China, tends to depress fertility among the parents of these cohorts of children as each child becomes more expensive to raise. In the first place, tuition is charged for preschools, elementary schools, and secondary schools. Second, during school hours the children are not working to augment the family's food production or income. Therefore, children being educated are consumers for many years before they begin to be producers. In theory, this long period when children are a drain on family resources encourages couples to limit the number of children they bear.

Popular education gives parents the chance to raise the ability and achievement of each of their children. Based on observations outside of China, it is hypothesized that there is for most of the world's families a trade-off between "quality" and quantity of children.[65] If a couple has many children, each one receives fewer health benefits, possibly less food, less parental attention, and fewer opportunities for personal growth and enrichment. As long as mortality is high, it makes no sense to lavish too much care on each child, because chances are that some will be sickly or will die young. But as soon as infant and child mortality have declined as far as they have in China, it becomes rational for parents to produce fewer children and invest more in each, according to this theory. Educational opportunity for the children can speed this shift; therefore, it is possible that China's striking mortality reduction and its speedy provision of mass primary education have worked together to encourage the rapid decline in fertility.

Restrictions on Geographical Mobility from Rural Areas

In many developing countries, rural families and rural political leaders have little incentive to control fertility in the villages, because they can deal with their rapid natural population increase by sending their excess population to the city, to developing frontier areas, or abroad. In fact, families are encouraged by this out-migration pattern to continue their high fertility in hopes of having one or more children who go to a city or abroad, get good jobs, and send remittances home to their family.

In the PRC, restrictions on geographical mobility are severe. For over 35 years there has been very little legal emigration. People are not allowed to travel freely within the country. In particular, village residents cannot easily move to cities in search of a job, because they cannot ride on public transport without travel papers, they do not qualify for food rations in the city, they cannot find a place to live there, and they are likely to be physically ousted from the city by the local police if discovered. Also, arable lands in China have been so crowded for so long that there remain no large, easily cultivated frontier areas suitable for the spontaneous resettlement of surplus population from densely populated areas.

By and large, Chinese villages cannot export their own natural population increase. Any child born in a village is going to have to be provided with food, education, housing, health care, and employment throughout his or her life from that village's land, resources, and economy, the only general exception being the more or less balanced exchange of women between villages at marriage. For example, from interviews with refugees regarding the Guangdong province villages from which they came, Parish and Whyte reported in 1978 that "in the countryside, 90 percent of the young males are still in their home villages, frequently living with or next door to their parents. This contrasts with Taiwan, where over half of the young village males have left to seek urban jobs."[66] In addition to providing for their native-born population, villages after 1968 were forced to absorb an additional population of persons born and raised in urban areas. Government policy was to relocate surplus population from the cities, usually to the villages of the same province. A village's arable land can hardly ever be expanded to provide for new residents, so the villagers must control their own fertility if they hope to minimize increases in the village's population density and the pressure on their arable land.

The lack of geographical mobility in China helps give village residents and especially their leaders the incentive to control village fertility. But they could not respond to this incentive if Chinese villages were not highly organized, because the locus of fertility decision-making is the couple and their household. If couples all over the village do not simultaneously control their fertility, then it would be self-defeating for some to unilaterally stop at one or two children while everyone else was bearing four or more. The net effect would be little or no improvement in the village's per capita income over time, but a further shift of village income toward the prolific families with many sons and a possible decline in the real income of the small families with one or no sons. The PRC, however, has such a high degree of organization in the villages that it can educate, persuade, or force most of the village couples to simultaneously limit their childbearing.

The testimony of one former villager shows that a local government can indeed enlighten villagers about the negative consequences of population growth in the village and persuade them to limit their fertility: "No one opposed the movement—they have received their lesson. Before, the brigade population was only 600, but now it is 1,400-plus. So there has been an increase of over 100 percent in recent years, and everybody understands the need. The economic difficulties of actual life persuade them." Reports from refugees indicate that villages with the greatest population pressure on the arable land had had lower fertility in the years prior to 1973 and were having greater success in family planning at that time than were less densely populated villages.[67] In 1981 a county in Shaanxi province indicated that the people in 21 of its communes were more amenable to government calls for very low fertility because these communes were located in the flat, wet region of the county and had high population density, small land area, ample labor supply, and good economic, cultural, medical, and public health conditions. The people of seventeen communes in hilly regions were more resistant because they had a large land area, greater difficulty in cultivation of crops, and more backward economic, educational, medical, and public health conditions.[68] In China, because out-migration is blocked, the only way densely populated villages can expect to ease their overpopulation in the future is to control their own fertility today.

In sum, rapid decline in fertility did not begin in most rural areas of the PRC until the government began pursuing a determined family planning program in the early 1970's. Without the government goal of reducing fertility and a widespread family planning program to further it, rural fertility likely would have remained high during the 1970's. Only a strong program could have overcome the pronatalist effects of China's poor economic development, the large proportion of its population working in agriculture, its traditional family system, and the economic policies supportive of high fertility in rural areas. But in many other countries, a national family planning program vigorously promoted by the government would have been less successful in reducing fertility and would have encountered much greater popular indifference or resistance. In China, the context within which the program operates has contributed greatly to its success.

In the first place, the Chinese people, wherever they reside, have shown themselves more open to fertility control than many other ethnic, religious, or cultural groups in the world. Some qualities of Chinese culture seem to have promoted fertility decline in Taiwan, Hong Kong, and Singapore as well as in the PRC. Secondly, the tight political links from the central government to the villages in the PRC have ensured thorough penetration of the country by the family planning program. Finally, the profound socioeconomic changes that have taken place have contributed greatly to China's surprisingly rapid fertility decline. The women of China have been liberated from their traditional oppression enough to be recognized for their role in agricultural and other types of production rather than only for generating sons. The provision of some primary or secondary education to more than half the women who reached childbearing ages in the 1970's contributed to their lower fertility. Infant and childhood mortality and morbidity have declined to such an extent that parents have reason to believe that their children will survive to adulthood. Low mortality and the widespread provision of elementary education have allowed parents the option of raising fewer and better educated children. Finally, the lack of geographical mobility has forced villages to face the consequences of their own natural population increase. The high level of village organization has not only made it possible for villagers to respond collectively to this threat to their welfare, but also has facilitated the government program of mandatory fertility control applicable simultaneously to all families in the village.

6

Late Marriage and Birth Planning

THE DEVELOPED countries of today achieved their transition to low fertility without any government efforts to promote fertility decline. Mortality improved gradually over decades or even centuries, and usually, after a time lag, fertility also declined slowly. The rates of natural population increase that these countries experienced during their demographic transitions tripled or quadrupled their populations, but many of the excess people from European countries migrated to the colonies of the New World or to other sparsely inhabited areas.

However, today's developing countries cannot rely on slow natural processes to complete their demographic transitions, for their situation differs greatly from the past. The declines in mortality that once took a century or more were compressed within a decade or two, and as a result, developing countries since the 1950's have had unprecedentedly high rates of natural population growth. The strains of such rapid growth cannot be tolerated for very many decades. Nor can the developing countries export the problem through massive emigration, since most of the world's empty lands are populated now, and most countries that might take the excess population strictly limit immigration. Therefore, they must actively encourage fertility control in order to bring about the required rapid decline in population growth.

China's First Family Planning Drive

China has been one of the world's leading countries in the attempt to bring about a steep fertility decline to balance its earlier steep mortality decline. Already in 1956, the government recognized that rapid population growth was threatening its economic development plans.[1] Shortly thereafter, the press began cautiously promoting a rise in the marriage

age and the adoption of birth control as two effective means of reducing fertility. But government leaders at the time were naive about demographic processes. Some of them thought that if they told the people to limit their fertility, the people would instantly do so and a stationary population size could be achieved immediately. Mao Zedong even made a 1957 speech in which he reportedly advocated holding the population at 600 million for a long time.[2] Most of the leaders did not understand the concept of demographic momentum: a population will continue growing long after replacement level fertility is achieved because the young age structure will produce huge cohorts in the childbearing ages for decades. When instantaneous fertility control and population stabilization were not achieved, the government in 1958 abandoned its fledgling family planning effort and simultaneously launched the Great Leap Forward, which it hoped would once and for all solve the problem of frustratingly slow per capita economic growth.

During 1955–58 China made a beginning in the mass production and distribution of contraceptives.[3] According to official figures, the PRC produced 45 million condoms during 1957, as well as almost 2 million tubes of spermicidal jelly. A few cities and provinces reported large increases in sales of contraceptives in 1956, 1957, and early 1958. But during the first fertility-reduction campaign the only available modern contraceptives were diaphragms, unlubricated condoms, and contraceptive jellies and foams, all of which were often of inferior quality. Intrauterine devices, some imported and some made in China, were tested and sold in a few cities but apparently were not otherwise available to the general public. Contraceptive use in China during the 1950's remained low, partly because demand for birth control was not great, and partly because contraceptives, where available at all, were limited in variety, poor in quality, and prohibitive in price. As of February 1958 it was stated in the Chinese press that the supply of contraceptives then available was enough to meet the needs of only about 2.2 percent of all couples in the childbearing ages.[4] There was some experimentation with traditional birth control remedies, but this attempt was abandoned when large proportions of the women testing the formulas became sick or pregnant. It is unlikely that this first birth control campaign had any major effect in reducing China's fertility, except perhaps in a few large cities.

The lack of success in the first birth-planning effort was attributed to poor local leadership and to traditional reluctance to discuss sexual matters in public:

> Judging from the reports handed in, the main obstacle blocking the progress of birth control stemmed primarily from the lack of understanding of the important meaning of this program and the benefits of birth control to home and country on

the part of leadership cadres in some places as well as their disbelief in the possibility of extensively propagating birth control, with the result that this topic had not been put on the agenda. Although many of the masses, including cadres, felt the need for controlling births, they thought that matters concerning both sexes should not be brought up for discussion in public. They therefore would not talk about contraceptives and birth control. Nor would they learn skills and buy devices. This tendency must be reversed.[5]

The first campaign served a useful purpose in showing the leadership how difficult and complex fertility reduction would be. It became apparent that a national and provincial apparatus was required to promote birth control and conduct the campaign, that popular resistance was deep, and that new birth control techniques were needed, such as a birth control pill, because many people disliked the inconvenience of the barrier methods of contraception.

Another positive result that evolved from the dynamics of the first campaign was that by the time it ended, most laws blocking birth control had been repealed. In 1957 both abortion and sterilization were legalized. The importation and sale of contraceptives had been legalized earlier. By the 1960's the legal and regulatory system had been adjusted to allow all the necessary birth control techniques for a successful family planning drive. This may not seem significant at first glance, but many countries, even when they are trying to reduce their birth rates, continue to forbid or restrict the use of abortion, sterilization, or the pill. Such legal hindrances can cripple a birth-planning program.

Another benefit of the first campaign was that it encouraged research into better birth control methods. The most immediate result was that Chinese doctors developed the vacuum aspiration abortion method. Results of this early research were reported in late 1958.[6] This innovation has since spread around the world, revolutionizing abortion practices and paving the way for legalized abortion by making it medically safer in most countries for a woman to have an abortion than to carry the pregnancy to term.

During the spring of 1958 birth control propaganda suddenly ceased: the Great Leap Forward had begun, and the premises on which it was based were incompatible with concerns about overpopulation or rapid population growth. The leaders felt that massive application of labor power in rural areas would free the forces of production once and for all and that the unlimited expansion of agriculture and industry would obviate fears of population growth outstripping production. Press and radio reports stopped encouraging birth control and began talking about the need for more people in China to carry out the labor-intensive work of development.[7]

Three poor harvests later, the Great Leap Forward's formula for speedy economic development had been discredited. The famine of 1959–61 had convinced the leadership that the pressure of the large and rapidly growing population on the food production system was serious. As soon as the country showed signs of agricultural recovery in the beginning of 1962, the leaders launched a second campaign to promote birth control. Factories that had made contraceptives before 1958 resumed production in 1962 to meet the anticipated demand.

The Second Family Planning Drive

A renewed family planning campaign was visible in the Chinese media from early 1962 until mid-1966. Later marriage was heavily emphasized in this propaganda, to the point that young people were warned of dire health consequences if they married before their middle twenties.[8] Young men were told that too much sex too early would dissipate their vital body fluids and cause numerous physical ills. Young women were warned of the dangers of early and frequent childbearing to their own health and that of their children.

In addition to encouraging late marriage, the press campaign promoted the ideal of a two-child family with the two births spaced three to five years apart. A greater variety of birth control methods was encouraged including, for the first time, intrauterine contraceptive devices. The press also tried to popularize vasectomy, against strong resistance by Chinese men. The ease and safety of the new suction abortion technique was explained in a few newspaper and magazine articles. In 1963 a crash effort to raise the quantity and quality of available contraceptives apparently succeeded in meeting the effective demand, at least in the cities, and no more complaints of supply problems were publicized after 1963. Meanwhile, medical research continued on the improvement of sterilization and abortion techniques as well as the development of a birth control pill suitable for Chinese women.[9]

In 1964 the State Council set up the first national Family Planning Office to direct and coordinate the family planning program.[10] Some provinces and municipalities set up guidance committees to coordinate their propaganda work and the supply of contraceptives.

The family planning program of the 1960's was targeted with great intensity to big cities and to some smaller urban and suburban localities, where modern medical systems were in place and could supply needed birth control supplies or operations.[11] Conditions were more conducive to fertility decline in cities than in the countryside, in part because city governments had the power, by threatening loss of a job or privileges, to forbid students, apprentices, factory workers, and government personnel to marry before their mid-twenties or to bear more than the permitted number of children. Rapid fertility decline reportedly took place in many cities during 1962–66.

Evidence from a 1965 survey of refugees from China suggests that rural resistance to fertility control was softened during the campaign, perhaps by the newspaper and magazine propaganda.[12] However, until after the Cultural Revolution of 1966–69 the rural network of contraceptive supply and medical skill for birth control operations was too weak to meet the latent demand generated by more receptive attitudes toward birth control. Besides, in many villages, local family planning campaigns did not begin until the late 1960's or the early 1970's. The fertility control network that now pervades China was established first in the cities during the early 1960's, later in suburbs and towns, and last in the countryside.

The Cultural Revolution

The Cultural Revolution was a bitter struggle among the leadership concerning the direction of China's development. For a few years the Communist Party was so badly divided and disorganized that in many locations the party could not have been very effective in promoting late marriage and birth control. The media concentrated almost completely on political verbiage and the unfolding of internecine struggles. Family planning was rarely mentioned.

Press reports indicate that in cities, once the pressure to postpone marriages eased, there ensued a wave of earlier marriages. Some urban and suburban localities have reported data showing a slight increase in the crude birth rate during about 1968 and 1969. A temporary increase in a local birth rate could result from a wave of marriages and first births after a period of postponing them. Whenever family planning was brought up in broadcasts and newspaper articles, it was to decry this early marriage trend and to encourage late marriage. Birth control within marriage was given little publicity.

Very little is known about the family planning program during the Cultural Revolution years. Press reports suggest that the birth control program lost momentum, and even that the progress made in fertility reduction before 1966 was lost, but this impression may be faulty. While the press was focusing on events in a few advanced urban areas, the rest of the country was expanding its rural medical system and, along with it, a delivery system for modern birth control methods in rural areas. By the end of the 1960's more and more rural localities were able to satisfy any existing demand for contraceptives. The story of the family planning program during the Cultural Revolution has not yet been told, but there may have been some provinces or localities that continued actively promoting fertility control during most of the late 1960's. If so, these areas had a head start when the national family planning program resumed in the early 1970's.

By 1970 the family planning program had laid a great deal of groundwork. First, a large segment of the adult population had been exposed to public and media discussion of the taboo subjects of sex and birth control, and most adults had at least heard of some birth control technique.[13] Second, China had repealed all legal barriers to the use of birth control techniques. Third, the PRC had carried out a decade and a half of research and development on the vacuum aspiration abortion technique, several different intrauterine devices, and low-dose birth control pills more suitable for China's women than imported ones. Fourth, factories had been built and workers trained to produce all needed contraceptive devices. By 1970 this birth control industry was poised to meet the demands of over a fifth of the world's population, a monumental achievement. Sixth, some urban areas had already achieved substantial fertility decline. Seventh, China had begun a crash program to train and deploy a million barefoot doctors and millions of health aides and midwives, with one of their primary tasks the encouragement of birth control and the convenient distribution of birth control supplies. Eighth, China's leaders had learned firsthand about the determined and sustained effort needed to accomplish fertility decline. Over the previous fifteen years they had seen the destructive consequences of rapid population growth on the PRC's attempt to develop a modern economy and high living standard. No matter how divided the leadership was on most other questions, it proved united in determination to reduce the birth rate and population growth rate as fast as possible.

Late Marriage

Until 1981 the fertility control program had two equally important components, promoting late marriage and promoting fertility control within marriage. In a society without contraception, early marriage usually means that a woman begins childbearing earlier, continues childbearing longer, and bears more children than she would if she married at a later age. China's traditional pattern included early marriage for females and childbearing beginning before age 20. Starting in early 1957, the family planning program promoted late marriage as a way to reduce fertility. Before that, late marriage was encouraged for nondemographic reasons such as the desire to liberate women from family bondage.

China's first Marriage Law, adopted in 1950, stated that the minimum legal marriage ages were 18 for females and 20 for males. But during the entire three decades that this law was in force these limits were frequently either ignored or superseded by other, usually higher, minimum marriage ages enforced in different localities. At first, during the early attempt to enforce all the law's provisions, popular resistance to the Marriage Law included widespread refusal to postpone marriage until the legal ages, which after all were much higher than the customary ages at which teenagers began marrying. Without a comprehensive marriage registration system in place, the law was unenforceable in any case.

After much social upheaval the government backed down on enforcement of the Marriage Law, shifting instead to a slow educational process. Presumably this means it also relaxed attempts to enforce the minimum marriage ages. One indication of this relaxation was a court decision in 1953 stating that individuals could legally marry when they reached the marriage age according to Chinese traditional reckoning.[14] So, for example, when a girl turned "18" and a boy turned "20" by the traditional calendar, she was really only 16 or 17 and he only 18 or 19. It is unclear how geographically widespread was this interpretation of the Marriage Law, but it is likely that people continued marrying even earlier than the 1953 legal decision allowed, as a system of required marriage registration had not yet been set up in many areas.

Very little information has been released on the establishment of an enforceable system of marriage registration. Some cities, as they set up their permanent population registration and rationing systems in the 1950's or 1960's, probably included a marriage registration system. In rural areas the people's communes may have been authorized to set up marriage registration when they were instituted during 1958, but the chaos of the Great Leap Forward could have postponed attempts to start a meaningful system.

Many places may have seen stronger enforcement of minimum marriage ages during the first half of the 1960's. But by that time the regulations on minimum marriage ages had begun to differ by locality. Big cities like Shanghai, if they had registration systems in place by the beginning of the second family planning campaign in 1962, could require people to wait until much later than the legal ages of 18 and 20 before marrying. In urban areas, employers could enforce late marriage among their employees even in the absence of effective marriage registration. Press reports during 1962–66 spoke of the desirability of women waiting till age 25 and men till age 30 to marry, or ages 23–27 and 25–29 respectively, or other combinations.[15] Cities, urban neighborhoods, towns, and factory complexes were supposed to encourage marriage ages as high as was feasible in their unit, which might mean effective minimum marriage ages of 23 and 25 in one city and 25 and 28 in another. But more in keeping with their actual situation, rural authorities attempted to impose much lower legal ages, such as 18 and 20 or 20 and 22.

During the 1970's the target minimum marriage ages continued to vary by locality. Many rural areas settled on the attempt to postpone marriages until women were 23 and men 25, but some areas probably continued to allow the subterfuge of Chinese age reckoning. Minority group areas were always technically exempt from the minimum ages in the Marriage Law, and they could and did set lower ones. Urban areas, on the other hand, instituted high ages of 25 and 28, or a combined age of 50 for the two prospective partners, or other combinations.

Not only did China institute a crazy quilt of target minimum marriage ages, but enforcement varied substantially from place to place. First, some areas and not others had functioning systems of marriage registration. Second, the target ages were applied with various degrees of flexibility. Large cities in particular set high minimums and enforced them strictly, with little regard for unnecessary personal hardships. For example, in such a city, if a man of 30 and a woman of 22 were betrothed, or a woman of 28 and a man of 25, they might be forced to wait years to marry through rigid application of the city's target minimums. Compliance could be enforced, because housing could not be obtained without legal marriage, both members of a defiant couple could be demoted or harassed at work, and so forth. Some big cities claimed great success in preventing marriages of people younger than the high ages set by the regulations. For example, in 1980 Tianjin Municipality claimed that since 1963, "the actual average marriage age in the municipal districts has been 27 full years of age, and in the rural areas 25 full years of age, which are higher than the deferred marriage ages stipulated."[16] On the other hand, many rural areas had target ages but used them only as guidelines, frequently allowing younger persons to marry. For example, in interviews with Hong Kong refugees from Guangdong province in the early 1970's, William Parish and Martin Whyte discovered that while minimum marriage ages in rural areas were supposed to be 23 for women and 25 for men, in actuality the *average* marriage ages were about 21 and 25 respectively.[17] The rural guidelines were compromised or ignored in a variety of ways. Some areas did not register marriages or report marriage ages; for example, most marriages in Tibet went unregistered. A survey of Guizhou province in 1977 indicated that unions without legal registration made up two-fifths of all marriages.[18] But regardless of how completely marriages were registered, the age data were unreliable. There was such pressure not to marry below the target ages that a great deal of falsification of ages at marriage went on. Perhaps the most common tactic was for a couple to have a customary marriage ceremony and begin their married lives when they were ready, ignoring registration altogether or postponing it until they reached the target ages. As one Chinese report described it,

> It is difficult for a portion of the young people, especially rural youths, to accept the deferred marriage age. Yet the local officials refuse to let them register for marriage. They therefore often resort to adopting the traditional folk ways of inviting guests and bowing three times in front of the portrait of Chairman Mao and consider themselves married. Although they have not gone through the legal procedure, they have the recognition of their parents and neighbors. Thus, *de facto* marriages have materialized. They are not favorable to family planning and have negative social consequences.[19]

In short, at least until 1981 the marriage registration data did not accurately reflect levels and trends in age at marriage, and no other data were available for determining marriage ages.

During the late 1970's some localities measured their success in fostering late marriage by calculating a "late marriage rate," which was simply the proportion of all persons marrying during the year that had reached the target minimum ages. As of 1977 or 1978, Guangdong province claimed a 75 percent late marriage rate, Jiangsu province an 88.5 percent rate, and Hebei province a 93 percent rate, and model counties and cities also claimed rates above 90 percent. Similar figures continued to be reported through 1980.[20] That different areas used different target ages to calculate their late marriage rates is suggested by the fact that Shanghai, China's most advanced urban area, reported a 1978 rate of 90 percent in the city proper and 80 percent in its suburban counties. These rates would have been higher than those of Jiangsu and Hebei provinces if all localities were calculating from the same target ages. It appears that late marriage rates should not be used for comparative purposes because they are based on different target ages, and that no particular figure should be taken literally because it might comprise noncomparable data from different subunits of a province. Furthermore, in some provinces falsified ages and delayed registration of marriages may have inflated the late marriage rates. Notwithstanding these likely biases in reported late marriage rates, by the late 1970's many provinces had succeeded in pushing marriage ages up into the mid-twenties from the far earlier ages typical in 1930, about age 17.5 for women and 21.3 for men on average.[21]

The information available on the timing of this rise in marriage ages from 1930 to the late 1970's suggests that the increase may have occurred throughout that period.[22] Already in 1950, the average age at first marriage for women had risen to 18.7 years, as shown in Table 6.1 and Figure

TABLE 6.1
Women's Average Age at First Marriage in Urban and Rural Areas of the PRC, 1950–81

Year	Urban	Rural	National	Year	Urban	Rural	National
1950	19.7	18.5	18.7	1966	22.5	19.4	19.8
1951	19.7	18.5	18.7	1967	22.5	19.5	20.0
1952	20.1	18.7	19.0	1968	22.4	19.7	20.1
1953	20.2	18.7	19.0	1969	22.4	20.0	20.3
1954	20.4	18.8	19.1	1970	22.3	19.9	20.2
1955	20.5	18.8	19.1	1971	22.8	19.9	20.3
1956	20.7	18.8	19.2	1972	23.3	20.3	20.6
1957	20.5	18.9	19.2	1973	23.6	20.6	21.0
1958	20.7	18.8	19.1	1974	23.9	20.9	21.4
1959	20.7	19.0	19.3	1975	24.3	21.3	21.7
1960	21.1	19.3	19.6	1976	24.7	21.8	22.3
1961	21.2	19.4	19.7	1977	25.1	22.0	22.5
1962	21.2	19.3	19.6	1978	25.2	22.3	22.8
1963	21.1	19.3	19.5	1979	25.5	22.6	23.1
1964	21.7	19.2	19.5	1980	25.3	22.5	23.0
1965	22.1	19.3	19.7	1981	24.8	22.3	22.8

SOURCES: Fertility Survey (1984): 174–82; author's computer reconstruction of the age structure of women by year.

NOTE: Based on annual first marriage rate data by single years of age from China's nationwide 1982 retrospective fertility survey applied to the annual reconstructed single-year age structure of women. The calculation assumes that marriages to women at each age are distributed evenly throughout the year of age, so that the average age at marriage for women who marry at age 19 before they reach age 20 is age 19.5. "Urban" is defined as the nonagricultural permanent resident population of cities and towns; "rural" covers all the rest of the population.

6.1. A slow increase in mean marriage age has continued almost unabated for the last three decades. Women's average age at first marriage rose gradually to 19.2 years in 1956–7, then increased during the Great Leap Forward to 19.7 years in 1961. After a slight decline in the early 1960's, mean marriage age rose quickly during the Cultural Revolution to 20.3 years in 1969. Women in the 1970's, under pressure from the family planning program to marry late, increased their mean age at first marriage from 20.3 years in 1971 to 23.1 years in 1979, a very steep rise.

In 1950, the urban nonagricultural population of women married on average 1.2 years later than the rest of China's women, as seen in Table 6.1 and Figure 6.2. Through 1958, while rural women increased their marriage ages only slightly, the age at marriage for urban women rose from 19.7 years in 1950 to 20.7 in 1958, resulting in a 2-year differential between the mean marriage ages of urban and rural women. Women in both sectors married on average half a year older in 1962 than they had in 1958. Though the disruption of the Great Leap Forward may have contributed to delayed marriage, other changes of a more permanent nature must have caused much of the increase because it was never reversed

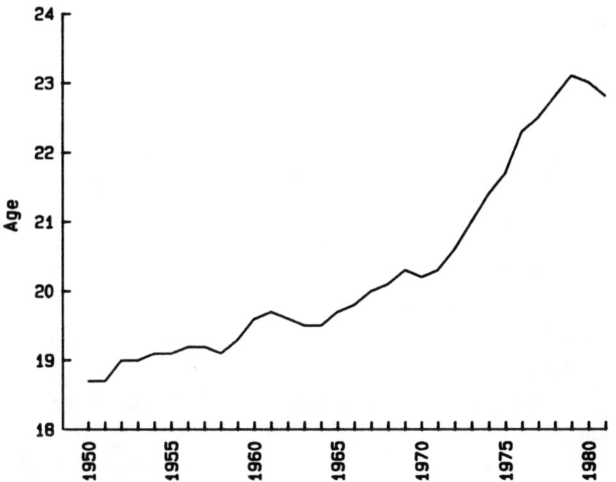

Fig. 6.1. Average Age at First Marriage for Women, 1950–81. Data from Table 6.1.

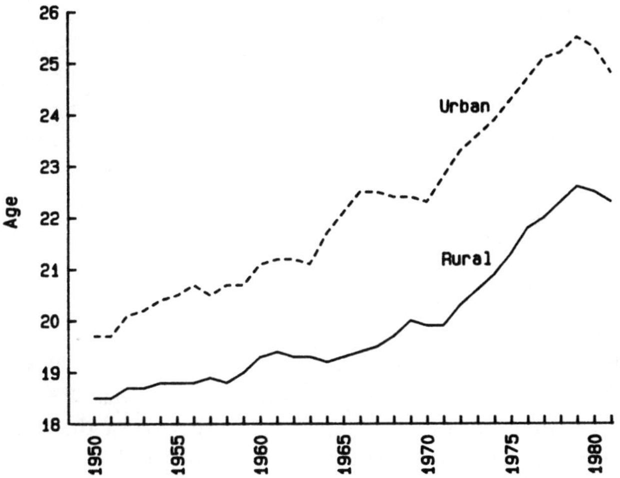

Fig. 6.2. Average Age at First Marriage for Urban and Rural Women, 1950–81. Data from Table 6.1.

thereafter. In the early 1960's, average marriage ages vacillated for rural women from 1960 through 1965, then in 1967 began a steady rise that continued through the Cultural Revolution years to 1969. Meanwhile, marriage ages for urban women held steady during 1960–63, then increased sharply in 1964 and 1965 under the late marriage campaign that most affected urban areas. As the Cultural Revolution began in 1966, the pressure to marry later was eased in urban areas, and the mean age at first marriage for urban nonfarm women declined slightly from 1966 through 1970. The urban-rural difference in women's first marriage ages had risen from 2 years in 1962 to 3 years in 1967, but then declined to 2.4 years in 1969 because rural marriage ages slowly rose while urban marriage ages dropped a little.

During the late marriage campaign of the 1970's, urban women were affected earlier and more than rural women. A sharp increase in urban marriage ages began in 1971 and continued to 1979, totaling a 3.2-year rise in mean age at first marriage for women. Average rural marriage age began rising in 1972 and peaked in 1979 having increased 2.7 years in comparison to 1971. As of 1979 the urban-rural differential in women's first marriage ages was once again almost 3 years.

The sharp rise in marriage ages of women during the 1970's had a strong temporary depressing effect on crude birth rates. Postponing marriages and first births each year lowers the number of births each year, all else being equal, until the marriage age stabilizes at a higher level. In addition, the large cohorts of babies born during the 1950's began to reach marriageable age in the late 1960's and early 1970's. As long as their marriages were postponed, the birth rate was doubly depressed. Taking the cohort of 1953 as an example, this group became age 20 in 1973, and in former times most of the women would already have been married. But if their marriages were postponed until they became age 22, for example, then this cohort would have begun marrying in large numbers in 1975, and their first births would have begun in 1976. If city women of the 1953 cohort did not begin marrying until age 25, then their first births would have begun in 1979. Therefore, the success of the late-marriage policy during the 1970's contributed to the rapid decline in the birth rate through the middle of the decade. But a rising birth rate would be expected in the late 1970's unless counteracted by great and continuing reductions in the number of births per woman and a postponement of births after marriage. The late 1970's did witness a surge of marriages as the huge 1950's cohorts reached the minimum ages. One city district of Beijing, for example, reported a fivefold increase in couples registering for marriage between 1976 and 1979; in the last year of that period alone, the number doubled.[23]

In late 1980 a dramatic reversal of the late-marriage policy was announced. A new law drafted to supersede the 1950 Marriage Law stipulated: "A marriage can be contracted only after the man has reached 22 full years of age and the woman 20 full years of age. Those who are applying for marriage in accordance with this law shall be allowed to register and shall be issued marriage certificates."[24] The phrase "full years of age" means that no longer would traditional age reckoning be acceptable for determining legal marriage age. The State Council in Beijing clarified the intent of the law, so contradictory to actual practice for the previous two decades, as follows:

> In dealing with problems concerning family and marriage, all localities must act strictly in accordance with the relevant regulations. Problems must be handled according to the law whenever the law is available and the law must be enforced strictly whenever it is enforced, and the law should never be changed at will. During a certain period in the past, some localities have made some provisional regulations of their own concerning the legal age for marriage and the procedures for marriage registration. From the day that the new marriage law comes into force, all regulations that do not conform to the marriage law will become invalid.[25]

When the new Marriage Law took effect in January 1981, in most localities the legal minimum marriage ages for each sex were suddenly lower by as much as several years. Suddenly many young adults became eligible for legal marriage who had been ineligible the month before. The discontinuity was far more pronounced in urban areas. In Beijing, for example, the minimum legal marriage ages fell by five years; the number of young people eligible for marriage in 1981 was estimated to be three times the 1980 number.[26] In Shanghai Municipality, the number of young adults entering marriage age increased from over 150,000 in 1980 to over 700,000 in 1981.[27]

Why did the Chinese government make this abrupt change? Several important considerations seem to have entered into the decision. First, China's post-Mao government vehemently criticized the "gang of four" for weakening the legal system, for governing by autocratic decree, and for victimizing the people by unrestrained, arbitrary authority. During 1979 and 1980 the government devised a new system of laws for China of which the new Marriage Law was a part. Their purpose was to codify the laws, to standardize the laws and their enforcement nationwide, and to instill in the people a new respect for the law. To be consistent with these goals, the legal minimum marriage ages had to be uniform, reasonable, enforceable, and perceived by the public as fair. None of these standards was met during the 1970's, when minimum ages were unrealistically high, variable, and unevenly enforced.

Second, keeping minimum marriage ages high for rural areas made little sense because they were ineffective. Legal minimum ages of 23 and 25 invited noncompliance and disrespect for the laws and regulations. Mass evasion in turn made it impossible to maintain an accurate system of marriage registration. To encourage registration and foster respect for the Marriage Law, it was necessary to lower the minimum marriage ages to something realistic in the rural context.

Third, the government would not have retreated on such a strongly backed policy as the late-marriage drive unless it was faced with a popular backlash against the extremes in the policy. The source of effective opposition was probably in urban areas, where the enforced minimum ages were so high and so rigidly applied that they caused popular discontent. The post-Mao government, in order to defend its legitimacy, adjusted its policies to minimize the sources of that discontent. The new minimum marriage ages got rid of the problem of unfairly high minimum ages applicable only to urban youth.

Fourth, the late-marriage regulations were causing social problems, personal hardships, and occasional crimes. Historically, when girls married in their late teens, they had little time after puberty to engage in premarital intercourse and risk pregnancy. But during the 1970's, particularly in urban areas, young men and women might fall in love and become betrothed years before they were allowed to marry. It was unrealistic to suppose that all such couples would postpone sexual relations until the bureaucracy let them marry. A 1981 article admitted, "Studies show that because of restriction on marriage the number of instances of couples living together before marriage, illegitimate children, and abortions by unmarried mothers has increased."[28] This article also highlighted the tragic case of a young couple near Beijing who were betrothed but forbidden to marry for three years until they reached the local minimum marriage ages. Their premarital sexual relationship provoked such family violence and hostility toward their love that they committed suicide. Some Beijing delegates to the National People's Congress alluded in their speeches to the notion that young adults not allowed to marry and settle down in a normal manner were contributing disproportionately to urban crime and socially unacceptable behavior.[29] Another possible negative effect of enforcing late marriage ages was that some urban women postponed their births until their thirties, when there would be an expected increase in complications and birth defects. The press has apparently never admitted that late marriage, combined with the policy of promoting long intervals between births, had physically harmful consequences for urban women and their babies. But the 1981 reduction of the minimum marriage age for females to 20 may have been a tacit admission that the healthiest age for childbearing, for both mother and baby, is the twenties.

Fifth, some demographers argued that the late-marriage policy was no longer necessary in pursuit of China's fertility goals. Once a population adopts contraception, they reasoned, age at marriage is no longer a crucial determinant of couples' completed fertility. This idea was presented at the National People's Congress by the vice chairman of its standing committee, when discussing the proposed minimum marriage ages of 20 and 22:

> Some people in urban areas considered the age limit too low and in contradiction with policy of promoting late marriage and birth planning. Here a clarification is in order. The age limit set by the law prohibits people from marrying before the legal age; it does not say that every man and woman must be married at the legal age. Although child bearing is related to marriage, it may be delayed in spite of marriage. . . . As long as birth planning is promoted effectively, population growth can be controlled. If birth planning is not promoted, more children will be born to a couple even if they marry very late. In a number of economically developed countries, the legal marriage age is set fairly low. In several West European countries, for instance, the legal age is 15 or 16 for a woman and 16, 18, or 21 for a man. There has been no large population growth; instead, there have been signs of decline in past years.[30]

Marriage data from 1981 indicate that young people took full advantage of the change in the marriage ages. In some urban localities, for example, the number of marriages in January 1981 was five times the number recorded for January 1980.[31] During the first half of 1981, the number of newlyweds in Liaoning province reportedly tripled in comparison to the same period in 1980, and the late marriage rate in Liaoning's cities was half that of the year before.[32] Nationwide, it was estimated that 6,730,000 marriages took place during the first six months of 1981, as compared with 3,260,000 in the first half of 1980.[33] Given the weaknesses in the marriage registration and reporting system, these figures should be treated with caution; even so, there is no doubt that the year 1981 saw a great surge of marriages.

Table 6.1 and the corresponding figures show that the female average age at first marriage began dropping in 1980, especially in urban areas, because the new Marriage Law was publicly debated and then passed in 1980, and people were anticipating its impact and acting on it before the technical implementation date. Average marriage age continued dropping in 1981, more sharply in urban than rural areas. In 1980 and 1981, there was almost no increase in the first marriage rates of women over age 27, but the proportion of women at each age 19–27 marrying for the first time increased greatly in 1980, then shot up again at ages 19–23 in 1981.[34] Nationwide, in 1981 alone, 10 percent of the women age 19 got married, and 17 percent of the women age 20 entered marriage for the first time, as did 16 percent of women age 21, 21 percent of women age 22, 20 percent of women age 23, 16 percent of women age 24, and 11 percent of women age 25. The increase in first marriage rates was most dramatic at ages 20-24 for urban nonagricultural women and at age 20 for rural women.

In lowering marriage ages, the government did not intend to abandon its encouragement of late marriage, only to eliminate compulsory late marriage. The *People's Daily* was very explicit that there would be no exceptions made, that no units could forbid students or persons in special categories from marrying if they had reached the new legal minimum marriage ages: "This means that those who are engaged in special occupations requiring that they get married late should be persuaded to do so, rather than compelled by administrative orders."[35] But voluntary postponement of marriage was encouraged after the new Marriage Law took effect. The law itself states, "Late marriage and late births should be encouraged," and many officials and publications echoed that statement, including the head of the Women's Federation and the magazine *China Youth News*.[36] Beijing Municipality, too, promoted late marriage while publicizing the new Marriage Law:

> The new Marriage Law sets the marriage age at 22 years for men and 20 for women, compared with 27 and 25 previously. Though late marriage is still encouraged, increasing numbers of young people are registering for marriage licenses. A city-wide public education campaign begun January 1 is in full swing throughout the rural and urban areas of the Beijing Municipality to drive home to the young people that the age for marriage may be different from the age for starting a family and [to] encourage them to get married at an appropriately later age.[37]

Several other municipalities and provinces reiterated their support for late marriage while announcing that they would not tolerate administrative orders compelling people to marry later than the new legal ages.

Since the minimum legal marriage ages became low enough to be perceived as fairly reasonable by the public, the government has been trying to build a nationwide system of marriage registration that succeeds in registering all marriages when they happen and with accurate information on the ages of the newlyweds. In November 1980, before the Marriage Law went into effect, the Civil Affairs Ministry promulgated new regulations on the required method of marriage registration.[38] Perhaps the low age requirements have contributed to more complete and accurate marriage registration. On the other hand, since local cadres may perceive that marriage has become a less crucial matter among their many pressing work priorities, they may neglect marriage registration as unimportant. In minority-group areas, however, relatively complete and accurate marriage registration will probably be a long time coming, the main reason being that in some minority areas the minimum ages are still unrealistically high. Both the 1950 and the 1981 Marriage Laws allowed minority areas to set their own lower minimum marriage ages. But all minority provinces that have announced their new legal ages, namely Xinjiang, Tibet, and Ningxia, have set ages 18 for females and 20 for males as the legal minimums. Perhaps the national government is unwilling to let the autonomous regions set their minimum marriage ages any lower than 18 and 20. But according to a November 1980 article in the magazine *Women of China*, "In the mountainous and border areas especially, even the original marriage ages of 20 for males and 18 for females have been impossible to attain."[39] Where this is true, we can expect falsification of marriage ages, avoidance of marriage registration, and early *de facto* marriages to continue.

It appears that the government as of early 1981 genuinely intended to substitute voluntarism for compulsion in determining marriage ages. But the popular repudiation of late marriage, symbolized by the headlong rush to marry when finally allowed, triggered a strong reaction in government leaders. Some provincial and local governments have since then developed new ways, or dredged up old ones, to persuade or force women in particular to wait until their mid-twenties to marry. Some localities award paid leaves at the time of marriage if the woman has reached age 23 and longer paid leaves if she is older.[40] At least one province has defined "late marriage" ages since the advent of the new Marriage Law as 23 for women and 25 for men in rural areas, and 24 and 26 in urban areas.[41] Creeping coercion is once again forcing many young couples to postpone their marriages to these ages. In late 1981 the first exception to the new lower minimums was announced: "In some professions, due to the specific nature of the job, it is necessary to raise the marriage age. For example, for service personnel in the civil aviation system and students in higher educational institutes, their marriages should be handled according to regulations relevant to them."[42] Since then, several provinces have begun to require unmarried persons to sign contracts to defer their marriages until the administratively set late marriage ages. While the signing of such contracts is ostensibly voluntary, in fact young adults are forced to sign as a condition of economic survival for themselves and their families, because they must sign the late marriage contract at the same time they sign the agreement with the production team giving them use of a contract plot of land for growing food.[43] It remains to be seen how successful the government will be in reversing its reversal of the late-marriage policy.

Along with the continued promotion of late marriage is a new emphasis on "late birth," which means that no matter what the age at marriage, couples should be persuaded or required to postpone their first birth until the woman is 24 or 25.[44] This idea is contrary to historical and current custom in China. Surveys conducted around 1980 indicated that, owing to premarital pregnancy and high frequency of intercourse just after marriage, 65 percent of women who married became pregnant within three months after marriage, and by one year after marriage, less than 15 percent were still not pregnant.[45] The same provinces that require young people to sign contracts to marry late also require newlyweds to sign contracts stating that they will defer their first child until the birth would qualify as a "late birth."

What are the likely trends in age at marriage during the 1980's? It is likely that mean ages at marriage will remain in the early twenties for women and the mid-twenties for men in rural areas. The continuation of very high bride prices in the villages forces men to wait to marry until their families can afford it. But the early 1980's may have seen a widening in the customary several-year rural age differential between husbands and wives because of a temporary marriage squeeze. During 1981 women age 20–23 in rural areas suddenly became legally eligible for marriage, but because they were born during the years 1958–61 they were members of deficit cohorts. Men about four years older than these women were members of huge cohorts born during 1954–57. Therefore, many rural men may have been well over the minimum marriage age in 1981 but could not marry, both because of high bride prices and because of a dearth of women in the customary age range. These men will search for spouses among the bigger cohorts of women younger than 20. The situation should have eased considerably in 1983 and thereafter, as the large cohorts of women born in 1963 and subsequent years reach marriage age while the deficit cohorts of men born during the Great Leap Forward reach marriage age.

In urban and suburban areas, mean ages at marriage are likely to drop below the artificially high ages enforced during the 1970's, but they will probably remain higher than in rural areas, because urban life is conducive to later marriage. One of the key problems is a critical dearth of housing for newly married couples. Men who cannot supply a living space for their wives have difficulty getting married. In addition, the educations and careers of urban people encourage voluntary postponement of marriage until it fits into their busy lives. The marriage squeeze outlined above was probably exacerbated by in-migration of young men to urban areas, creating a dearth of eligible brides in many cities and towns. In the short run, these difficulties may widen the age gap between marriage partners. Finally, the wrenching dislocations that blocked the marriages of so many urban men and women during the 1970's may make it impossible for many of them ever to marry, because they have already passed the prime marriage ages.

Family Planning in China, 1969–78

The decade 1969–78 was a remarkable period in the history of China's fertility and family planning. In these years the proportion of married couples of reproductive age who practiced contraception became the majority. Though some of this transformation can be attributed to changes in the status and role of women and to other antinatalist trends discussed in the last chapter, much of the credit goes to the PRC's pervasive and insistent family planning program, developed with considerable innovation and at great speed during the 1970's.

Most details of the family planning program were suppressed during the early 1970's. Specific information about demographic targets, organization, program implementation, contraceptive supply, motivational work, funding, problems encountered, and the solutions devised have not been and may never be described to the world. This reticence about the most important period in the evolution of the family planning program makes it difficult for other countries to learn from the PRC's experience in devising their own programs. Two reasons underlie the secrecy. First, the government during that period typically withheld information about failures or moderate successes and publicized only success stories to the world. From 1969 through 1973 or so, the only big success stories were some cities and a few suburban communes. Family planning information from all other places was suppressed while demographic data from the few model localities were released and publicized again and again. Gradually, more places achieved outstanding success in fertility decline and joined the list, but even for model localities the government reported only the spectacular results of the family planning program, with very few specifics about how they were achieved.

The second reason was political. Some time early in the 1970's a strong element of compulsion was incorporated into the family planning program, thus setting it apart from every other family planning program in the world. China's leaders were naturally reluctant to publicize this ethically objectionable aspect of the program, particularly the dominant radical faction that associated family planning in any developing country except China with attempted genocide by imperialist countries. While China was accusing the United States and the Soviet Union of forcing family planning on developing countries, China was doing just that to its own people. The clash between the line China's representatives were ritually promoting and the policies they were implementing at home could only be muted by non-information and misinformation. For example, at the World Population Conference in August 1974, the representatives of China accused the "superpowers" of forcing family planning on the governments and people of the Third World:

> The superpowers raise the false alarm of a "population explosion" and paint a depressing picture of the future of mankind. . . . The pessimistic views spread by the superpowers are utterly groundless and are being propagated with ulterior motives. . . . Any international technical cooperation and assistance in population matters must follow the principles of complete voluntariness of the parties concerned, strict respect for state sovereignty, absence of any strings attached, and promotion of the self-reliance of the recipient countries. We are firmly opposed to the superpowers intervening by any means in the population policy of other countries on the pretext of what they call "population explosion" or "overpopulation." We are firmly opposed to the attempt of some international organizations to infringe on the sovereignty of recipient countries by conditioning aid on restricting their population growth rate.[46]

While thus standing "firmly together with the Third World countries and all oppressed nations and oppressed people, strengthening unity with them in waging the common struggle" against forced fertility control by the superpowers, the PRC ordered the United Nations not to distribute two papers on its family planning program especially prepared by UN personnel for use at the conference.[47] To deflect international criticism of its methods, the Chinese government withheld information on its family planning program until spectacular successes had been achieved. After that, international observers, if they chose to, could rationalize that the important end of sharply reduced population growth already achieved by China justified whatever means China used to attain it.

In spite of the lack of detailed reported information, a few highlights of the family planning program in the early 1970's can be discerned. A crucial decision was made in about 1971 that henceforth married couples of reproductive age throughout China would receive IUD (intrauterine device) insertions, vasectomies, tubal ligations, induced abortions, pills, and barrier methods of contraception without charge.[48] In addition, those who accepted sterilization, abortion, or IUD insertion were supposed to receive pay or work points for the period of recovery, which might be several weeks. The payments could be viewed as a financial incentive to adopt contraception or simply as fair compensation for lost work time. These financial arrangements mean that the considerable costs of the family planning program during the 1970's and since have been shared by collective units at the local level and by government organizations nationwide. The national government shoulders the burden of producing and distributing all the birth-control supplies for China's great population. The state also reimburses hospitals, clinics, and paramedics for each contraceptive operation and pays all state employees during their recovery.

Governments of most poor countries would not consider taking on such an expense: international or bilateral aid agencies usually supply the free contraceptives, or users are expected to pay for birth control themselves. The fact that the Chinese government met this expense in spite of its severe budget constraints indicates the seriousness with which its leaders viewed rapid population growth in the early 1970's. As costs have risen, the government's financial support for birth control has continued to be large. As an example, in 1977 the government of Guangdong province spent 4 or 5 million yuan to procure contraceptive supplies and to reimburse hospitals and clinics for operations.[49] If Guangdong (with 6 percent of the national population) was typical, then the nation in 1977 spent about 70–85 million yuan (at the formal exchange rate, equivalent to about 45–55 million dollars). This sum probably underestimates the costs of contraceptive research, development, production, and distribution, plus the full costs of birth control operations. This total also does not include all the costs of salaries and work-point payments to family planning personnel, motivational and publicity work, training family planning workers, and paying recipients of birth control operations. Our knowledge of these matters must rely on guesswork until China releases a national budget for its family planning program.

The current family planning program was launched in some places and accelerated in others in response to a State Council directive in 1971.[50] As an appendage added in 1973, China's five-year plan for 1971–75 included demographic targets, apparently not expressed in terms such as the number of accepters of each birth control method, or the proportion of couples practicing contraception; instead the plan set target population increase rates of 10 per thousand for urban areas and 15 per thousand for rural areas.[51] One of the first major tasks addressed by government at all levels during the early 1970's was to gather vital rate data for some year between 1969 and 1973, or for all those years, to serve as baseline data from which subsequent progress could be measured. Thereafter, annual data began to be compiled on births, deaths, and natural population increase in order to monitor progress toward the targets set in the plan, but because of the lack of explicit family planning targets the compilation of data bearing more directly on the family planning program was neglected. Local areas sometimes gathered data on current use or recent acceptance of different types of contraceptives, but these data were not and apparently still are not systematically compiled for the whole country. Gradually, provinces began compiling data on the number of IUD insertions, induced abortions, vasectomies, and tubal ligations—the "four contraceptive operations"—carried out each year, based on requests for reimbursement by medical units.

Throughout most of the 1969–78 period, the PRC tried to popularize the two-child family with slogans such as "one is not too few, two is good, three is too many."[52] Most cities strongly discouraged couples from having more than two children. Women were not allowed to marry until around age 25. As custom dictated, they had their first birth soon after marriage, but they were then urged or required to wait three or four years for a second birth, after which tubal ligation was strongly encouraged. National policy was summed up in the succinct phrase "wan, xi, shao" ("later, longer, fewer"), that is, later marriage and childbearing, longer spacing between births, and fewer children.[53]

For rural areas, national policy was a little looser during the early 1970's. The government tried, with partial success, to get rural residents to postpone marriage until age 23 for women. Lengthy spacing between births was also promoted, but the degree of success has not been documented. The birth of a third child was tolerated during the first half of the decade in most villages, but local cadres attempted to block the birth of fourth or higher order children.

During the latter half of the 1970's the PRC began to abandon its previous policy of setting different targets and expectations for urban and rural areas. Ignoring the very different conditions in cities and in villages, which give rise to different requirements for offspring, it began in 1977 to implement the policy that henceforth all couples must stop at two children.[54]

The success of such a policy depends on a large and reliable organization to carry it out. During the early 1970's the PRC established a family planning network that reached from the central government down to most villages, at least most Han Chinese villages. (Minorities had always been and were still technically exempt from the family planning program.) The "Planned Birth Leading Group" of the State Council, which had ceased to function sometime during the Cultural Revolution, was revived in 1973 with the job of drafting national policy for family planning.[55] This group was composed of representatives from relevant government ministries and mass organizations. Every province, prefecture, municipality, county, and people's commune in China, with the exception of those serving minority populations, was supposed to have set up its own planned-birth committee by 1974. The political importance attached to these planned-birth committees is reflected in their composition: representatives of women's organizations and medical units are in the groups, but the leading members are the top political leaders and Communist Party leaders of the locality. Their tasks are to coordinate family planning propaganda, to ensure the supply of contraceptives, and above all to see that the people in their political unit follow orders to stop bearing children at a certain parity.

Public statements of the 1970's indicate a shift during the decade away from reliance on health and family planning workers as the primary motivators for late marriage and birth control because by themselves they could not force compliance. Press reports stated that the family planning program was highly successful only when the Communist Party gave it high priority and the Party Secretary personally took command of implementing it.[56] With the party in command, economic and political pressure could be brought to bear on recalcitrant couples.

Within each people's commune and city district, planned-birth committees operate in the villages and neighborhoods. They consist largely of female cadres, barefoot doctors, midwives, and other family planning motivational workers, and their job is to actually implement the family planning instructions handed down from higher authorities. They hold meetings of the married women or couples in their unit to transmit the latest policies.[57] They visit households regularly to promote family planning and deliver contraceptives. They focus the efforts of many political and medical personnel on persuading each recalcitrant couple to postpone, to space, and especially to limit childbearing. China's family planning network is enormous, and its leaders from Beijing down to the people's commune level are paid a government salary. At local levels most motivational and technical workers are volunteers or are expected to carry out family planning work as part of their duties as a medical worker, women's leader, or production team cadre.

Much of the success of the family planning program can be attributed to the huge number of people who carry it out. The local motivational workers are not in it for the money, as they are not paid commissions for their successes. Rather, they are educated about the importance of fertility control to their country's progress. Many pursue their tasks with dedication and almost missionary zeal. Their compensations for their difficult work are not monetary but are still considerable. One is that they become important figures in their village or neighborhood. Another is the opportunity to interject themselves into the private relationship of the couples whose fertility they are charged with controlling. Their efforts to control other people's reproductive behavior are backed up by the power of higher political authorities, so they can dominate a very important aspect of their neighbors' lives with some impunity. A third compensation is that they are praised for their successes; they are told that their work is bringing about a better standard of living for China's people in the near future and that "family planning is honorable and difficult work."[58] Patriotic zeal and pride in their work are powerful rewards for China's family planning workers.

The family planning program is closely linked with the health network. Doctors, midwives, nurses, barefoot doctors, and health aides are charged with distributing contraceptive devices and drugs, and with providing safe sterilizations, abortions, and IUD insertions. They are supposed to follow up with patients who have had a birth control operation or are using contraceptives. In addition, medical workers are supposed to encourage birth control as one of their professional tasks.

During the years after 1968, the training of barefoot doctors, health aides, and "red medical workers," as well as the further training of midwives, doctors, and nurses, included a strong component of technical contraceptive knowledge. One of the few things barefoot doctors were immediately trained to do was provide some birth control information and advice as well as some forms of birth control. They could dispense condoms, contraceptive jelly, and diaphragms. Where the newly produced birth control pills or monthly steroid injections were available, barefoot doctors supported by health aides dispensed them. Sometimes barefoot doctors or even health aides have been trained to insert IUD's in village clinics or homes and to provide early abortions using an electric or hand-operated suction abortion machine designed and produced in China.[59] Sterilizations are usually done in hospitals by doctors, or in villages by mobile medical teams, but gradually some barefoot doctors have been trained to perform them.[60]

To make all these birth control operations available everywhere frequently means that a barefoot doctor or other medical worker will do IUD insertions, abortions, and sterilizations outside a hospital setting. The government strongly promotes immediate availability of these operations so that anyone who has just been "persuaded" to accept one can receive it before reconsidering the decision. But there is a cost in safety: the media frequently mention the need to improve the quality of birth control operations. There has clearly been a problem of botched sterilizations, abortions, and IUD insertions. It is likely that this problem is worst in poor, rural, mountainous, or pastoral areas. Gansu province, for instance, noted that women suffering from sequelae of sterilization operations would be financially assisted by the state.[61] Such complications tend to become known among relatives and neighbors of the victim and encourage resistance to birth control operations. As the director of the National Family Planning Commission stated in 1980, "Mishaps in birth control techniques and methods have also had widespread repercussions."[62]

Birth Control Techniques

As the decade progressed, some localities reported high proportions of couples of reproductive age practicing contraception, and sometimes they revealed the contraceptive mix used in that place. The most systematic variations in patterns of contraceptive use are those among urban, suburban, and rural areas, according to family planning statistics that have been released to date. Table 6.2 shows the contraceptive mix in urban compared to rural areas as of 1982.

In urban and suburban areas, birth control pills tend to be used by over 15 percent and in some places by over 30 percent of married women who practice birth control. By 1982, it was reported, 19 percent of women using a contraceptive in urban areas relied on the pill, compared to only 6 percent in rural areas. Chinese birth control pills are reported to be of high quality by international standards and have a low estrogen dose suitable to oriental women.[63] Experimental pill use began in China in about 1965, testing of the low-dose variety continued during the late 1960's, and large-scale promotion of the low-dose pill began in 1969. As of 1972 China had substantial unused capacity for producing birth control pills, and this is still the case, so there has been no problem in manufacturing enough for the whole country; however, occasional local shortages are reported, probably owing to distribution problems.[64] In both 1972 and 1979, the PRC apparently produced enough birth control pills to supply at least 9 million women, and as of 1982 about 9.7 million women in China were using oral contraceptives.[65] There is no evidence of a substantial increase in pill use during the 1970's. The lack of any major increase may reflect the fact that many urban areas in 1972 were already rather saturated with contraceptive use while rural areas, where contraceptive use expanded rapidly during the decade, do not use the pill much.

TABLE 6.2
Contraceptive Mix in Urban and Rural Areas, 1982
(Percent of women ages 15–49 practicing birth control)

Method	National average	Urban	Rural
Intrauterine device	50.16%	38.86%	52.45%
Tubal ligation	25.39	20.30	26.42
Male sterilization	10.00	2.77	11.47
Oral pill	8.44	18.99	6.30
Condom	2.00	9.68	0.45
Other	4.01	9.41	2.92

SOURCE: Qiu et al. (1984): 139–40.

NOTE: "Urban" is defined as the nonagricultural permanent resident population of cities and towns; "rural" covers all the rest of the population.

Similarly, barrier methods of contraception (almost exclusively condoms, with some diaphragms and vaginal suppositories) and "other" methods (including abstinence, rhythm, lactation, and withdrawal), all backed up by abortion, appear to be much more heavily used in urban than suburban areas, and much more in turn in suburban than rural areas. Table 6.2 shows that in 1982 less than half a percent of rural contraceptive users relied on condoms, in contrast to 10 percent of urban couples practicing birth control. Chinese-made condoms, of thick rubber and unlubricated, are not well accepted by users. The United Nations Fund for Population Activities has supplied equipment to make high-quality condoms, which should have become available in 1983 and which may raise the popularity of condoms.[66]

Tubal ligation is frequently used in urban and suburban areas, accounting for up to 40 percent of contraceptive use in some cities. In the early 1970's rural areas apparently could not provide tubal ligation because of a dearth of trained personnel, hospitals, and equipment, but by the late 1970's those areas that could offer the operation and that encouraged its use provided it to 30 or 40 percent of birth control users. In other counties that remained unable to provide it, tubal ligation continued to account for less than 5 percent of total contraceptive use. By 1980, perhaps as few as one-third of the people's commune hospitals in China were equipped to provide female sterilization.[67] Other areas relied on mobile medical teams or transporting women some distance to be sterilized. As shown in Table 6.2, of those married women practicing contraception, 20 percent in urban areas and 26 percent in rural areas had been sterilized by 1982. As of 1972 tubal ligation was done via an abdominal incision under local or acupuncture anesthesia.[68] This still seems to be the technique of choice, though China is experimenting with mini-laparotomy and other recently devised variations.[69]

Few data are available on the age of women who undergo contraceptive sterilization in China. The older they are, the fewer births are averted by the operation.[70] Data from two brigades in a suburban commune of Beijing Municipality prior to October 1979 indicate that almost half the 131 women sterilized had been sterilized at age 30–34, a fourth had been 25–29, over a fifth had been 35–39, and less than 5 percent had been 40 or older.[71] Two production brigades near Chengdu city in Sichuan had prior to late 1979 given tubal ligations to women mostly age 25–29. These fragmentary data also show that one-third of the women who received a tubal ligation had two children, one-third three children, and the rest had more children. What little we know suggests the hypothesis that in the PRC during the 1970's, women who were sterilized were in their late twenties or thirties with two or three living children. Table 6.3 shows

TABLE 6.3
Contraceptive Mix by Age Group, 1982
(Percent of women practicing birth control)

Method	15–19	20–24	25–29	30–34	35–39	40–44	45–49
Intrauterine device	65.89%	71.87%	60.94%	48.08%	41.93%	43.69%	44.11%
Tubal ligation	1.55	5.26	15.33	29.57	34.94	30.02	24.17
Male sterilization	0.39	1.26	5.58	9.85	12.43	13.16	15.97
Oral pill	20.16	13.22	11.73	8.31	6.65	6.42	4.75
Condom	1.55	1.73	2.15	1.67	1.72	2.36	2.59
Other	10.47	6.65	4.26	2.51	2.33	4.35	8.40

SOURCE: Qiu et al. (1984): 139.

NOTE: Two figures were incorrectly transcribed in the English source. The errors have been corrected here from the Chinese original.

that as of 1982, about 15 percent of women practicing birth control at age 25–29 and about 30 percent at age 30–34 had been sterilized. Of those controlling births in the 35–39 age group, 35 percent had had a tubal ligation. Therefore, female sterilization in China is a powerful tool for averting the several more conceptions those young women might otherwise have experienced.

Male sterilization has not been as popular as female sterilization in most parts of China, particularly in most urban areas reporting. In Tianjin Municipality, for example, there were only 175 vasectomies in 1978 compared to 3,593 tubal ligations.[72] Other municipalities have reported that between 2 and 10 percent of couples practicing contraception depend on vasectomy. As shown in Table 6.2, male sterilization accounted for only 3 percent of urban couples practicing contraception in 1982, but 11 percent of rural couples using birth control. It has been more common in some rural areas (20 percent of couples using birth control in Xinghui county, Guangdong) but almost completely absent in others (1 percent in Hengxian county, Guangxi).[73] As with female sterilization, male sterilization has been almost totally unavailable in some localities while it is available and strongly encouraged in others. Vasectomy is often provided by hospitals or mobile medical teams.

In some parts of the PRC, men reject vasectomy because they associate it with castration and insist that if anyone in the couple is going to be sterilized it will be the wife. The most populous province of Sichuan, however, has emphasized male sterilization over most other birth control techniques in both urban and rural areas. In this province alone, more than 10 million vasectomies were reportedly performed between 1970 and 1980 in a population of just under a hundred million.[74] The usual male sterilization procedure everywhere in China is outpatient vasectomy, but in 1979 Sichuan reported that 50,000 men had been sterilized since 1972 by spermatic duct injection, a nonsurgical method that is about 91 percent effective, and Sichuan also developed a "visual clamping method" of nonsurgical male sterilization.[75]

The demographic effect of male sterilization depends on the age of the wife at the time her husband has a vasectomy. Very few data are available. One production brigade in Sichuan reported that one-third of the wives were age 25–29, one-third were 30–34, and 16 percent were 35–39 when their husbands were sterilized.[76] More than half of these couples had three living children, and 35 percent had four or more. In this brigade and one other reporting from Sichuan, vasectomy was used prior to late 1979 to stop a couple's fertility after three or more births.

The intrauterine device was, at least through 1982, the main birth control technique used in China's rural areas. During the 1970's, those few counties that released data on their contraceptive mix reported IUD's in 40 to 90 percent of those practicing birth control. Whole provinces reported that 50–60 percent of couples using birth control used the IUD.[77] It appears that IUD's are a more prevalent contraceptive in rural than suburban areas, and in suburban than urban areas. For instance, 1978 data from Tianjin showed that among those using contraceptives, 68 percent in the counties used an IUD, compared to 37 percent in suburban areas and 16 percent in urban areas.[78] During the early 1980's the IUD continued to be strongly promoted in China's rural areas.[79] Table 6.2 shows that as of 1982, of women practicing contraception, 52 percent in rural and 39 percent in urban China used an IUD.

As of the early 1970's China produced six types of IUD, most of which were designed in China.[80] Because all had some major problem such as high expulsion rates, excessive bleeding, high pregnancy rates, or high rates of ectopic pregnancy, it appears that most of these were discontinued or are now used only on a small scale. Two modifications were in wide use as of 1980.[81] The most used IUD was a single ring of tightly coiled stainless steel wire; 11 million were produced in 1979. Within a year of insertion, users have about a 2 percent pregnancy rate, and over 5 percent expel it. For most women who tolerate it well, it is reportedly left in place for up to 15 years.[82] The intertwined-ring device, of which about 1.2 million were produced annually, has problems with a high rate of removal and expulsion. The United Nations Fund for Population Activities has provided a factory for producing plastic and copper IUD's up to international quality standards, which should enhance their acceptability in China.

Fragmentary data indicate that Chinese women use the IUD only after the birth of their first child; it is appropriate to wait until then because

IUD's usually do not work without problems in nulliparous women.[83] As shown in Table 6.3, as of 1982 the IUD was the leading birth control technique for every age group of married women in the reproductive ages, but was especially heavily used by women under age 30. Before the one-child limit became a reality, the IUD was used for spacing of births. It also was and still is used by many women who have borne all the children that government policy says they may bear, which now is usually one child. These women may be avoiding sterilization for themselves or their husbands by electing to continue IUD use instead.

At least until the 1980's the availability and use of induced abortion also varied greatly between city and countryside. Cities reported many abortions: In Shanghai Municipality in 1972 there were 80,000 abortions and 110,000 births, Tianjin Municipal hospitals reported 70,505 abortions in 1978 and 108,235 births, and Chengdu Municipality in Sichuan had between 26,000 and 52,000 abortions for every year 1971 to 1979 and in most of these years reported more abortions than live births.[84] These data probably exaggerated the use of abortion in municipalities because women from outside the municipality may have come to city hospitals for an abortion if this service was unavailable in their communes. Though the reported data are very sparse, during the 1970's the population outside municipalities seems to have resorted to abortion less frequently than municipal women. The few rural localities reporting abortion data had about three or four times as many births as abortions in the mid-1970's.[85]

Therefore, there have been great differences between contraceptive use patterns in urban and rural areas. As of 1982, the urban population made heavy use of IUD's, tubal ligation, birth control pills, condoms, abortion, and some other less effective methods of birth control. Most rural areas relied very heavily on intrauterine devices and tubal ligation. The other main geographical difference was that Sichuan province utilized male sterilization in its family planning program to a far greater extent than the other provinces.

Statistics and Trends

Trends in the use of different birth control techniques are difficult to document because the government did not systematically compile local data on patterns of contraceptive use, at least not until after March 1980 when it began to standardize reporting of statistics on family planning service.[86] Even those data it has have hardly been reported.

An important long-term trend must have been a marked increase in the absolute number of IUD users from the early 1960's through the early

1980's. Table 6.4 lists the reported number of IUD insertions annually in China for 1971 through 1982. These data were based on the reports of local medical units, which were reimbursed for each IUD insertion and IUD removal they claimed to have performed. The number of insertions increased rapidly to 1973, then leveled out at about 11–14 million per year through 1982, peaking at 17 million in 1975. Data are not available on how long these IUD's were retained by the women who received them. Some are expelled within a year, some are removed during the first year of use after unpleasant side effects, some are removed to allow the women to bear another child or to switch to another form of birth control, and some fail to prevent pregnancy while in place. Table 6.4 indicates that during 1972–75 there were 9–12 times as many IUD insertions as there were legal IUD removals each year. The number of reported removals of IUD's nationwide increased until there were one-fifth as many IUD's removed as inserted in 1978. In 1981–82 there were one-seventh as many legal removals as IUD insertions. These figures do not count the unknown number of illegal removals of intrauterine devices, a practice first reported in the media in 1978 and discussed in Chapter 7. Table 6.5 presents data from Tianjin Municipality that show one removal for about every three insertions in 1978. The proportion of devices legally removed appears higher in urban and suburban Tianjin than in the rural areas. China's nationwide fertility survey of 1982 found that 50.2 percent of the 118 million married women of reproductive age practicing birth control, that is about 59 million women, were using the IUD.[87]

Sterilization was, until 1983, the second leading birth control technique in China. Table 6.6 lists reported data on the 54 million male and female sterilizations recorded in the PRC during the years 1971 through 1982. During each of those years tubal ligations outnumbered vasectomies, the total number of female sterilizations being almost twice the figure for male sterilizations. By 1982, according to the nationwide fertility survey, there were about 30 million married women of reproductive age who were sterilized, constituting 25.4 percent of couples practicing birth control, and another 12 million whose husbands had been sterilized, making up 10.0 percent of birth control use.[88] Such widespread use of sterilization meant that about two-fifths of the contraceptively sterilized couples in the world at that time were in China.[89] These figures compared with Table 6.6 suggest that there was serious overreporting of the number of vasectomies during 1971–82, possibly in Sichuan province which claimed most of them, or that a significant proportion of the vasectomies had been given to men whose wives were already in their forties at the time their husbands were sterilized.

In January 1983, the government began implementing a policy of re-

TABLE 6.4
Reported IUD Insertions and Removals in the PRC, 1971–82

Year	Insertions	Removals	Year	Insertions	Removals
1971	6,172,889	—	1977	12,974,313	1,941,880
1972	9,220,297	853,625	1978	10,962,517	2,087,420
1973	13,949,569	1,126,756	1979	13,472,392	2,288,670
1974	12,579,886	1,352,787	1980	11,491,871	2,403,408
1975	16,743,693	1,702,213	1981	10,344,537	1,513,376
1976	11,626,510	1,812,590	1982	14,069,161	2,056,671
			TOTAL	143,607,635	19,139,396

SOURCE: Public Health Yearbook of China 1983 (1984): 69.

TABLE 6.5
Reported IUD Insertions and Removals in Tianjin Municipality, 1978

Category	Insertions	Removals
Urban	8,823	3,678
Suburban	8,774	3,459
County	25,081	7,325
Municipal hospitals[a]	2,855	1,356
TOTAL	45,533	15,818

SOURCE: Lyle (1980): 559.

[a]Municipal hospitals serve the entire municipality, and data are not available on the residence of the patients.

TABLE 6.6
Reported Male and Female Sterilizations in the PRC, 1971–82

Year	Males	Females	Both sexes
1971	1,223,480	1,744,644	2,968,124
1972	1,715,822	2,087,160	3,802,982
1973	1,933,210	2,955,617	4,888,827
1974	1,445,251	2,275,741	3,720,992
1975	2,652,653	3,280,042	5,932,695
1976	1,495,540	2,707,849	4,203,389
1977	2,616,876	2,776,448	5,393,324
1978	767,542	2,511,413	3,278,955
1979	1,673,947	5,289,518	6,963,465
1980	1,363,508	3,842,006	5,205,514
1981	649,476	1,555,971	2,205,447
1982	1,230,967	3,925,927	5,156,894
TOTAL	18,768,272	34,952,336	53,720,608

SOURCE: Public Health Yearbook of China 1983 (1984): 69.

quired sterilization for couples with two or more children, an escalation that is discussed more fully in Chapter 7. As a result, 3.58 million sterilizations were reported nationwide during that month alone, equivalent to more than 1.5 times as many sterilizations as had been carried out in the whole year of 1981. From the beginning of 1983 through August that year, more than 10 million sterilizations were performed in China, according to the Director of the State Family Planning Commission.[90]

Statistics from the fertility survey show that as of 1982 the vast majority of birth control users in China, 85.6 percent, were using a long-term or permanent method that did not require constant motivation to control births or frequent attention to details of use. The main other method was the birth control pill. The use of oral contraceptives appears to have increased very rapidly during the early 1970's only to level off in the absolute number of users nationwide, hence probably declining as a proportion of all those using contraceptives during the latter part of the decade to 8.4 percent in 1982.

Trends in condom use were probably similar during the 1970's. The number of users was probably already high by 1970 or 1971, since condoms are used most in urban and suburban areas where contraception was well established, but the number very likely grew only slowly during the decade, as contraceptive use rapidly increased in rural areas where condoms are not much used. It is likely that the proportion of condom users among those who practiced birth control declined during the decade. As of 1979 China produced enough condoms to supply about 7 million couples, but according to the fertility survey, only 2.0 percent of those practicing birth control, about 2.4 million couples, used the condoms in 1982.[91] Other birth control methods including abstinence, rhythm, withdrawal, monthly steroid injections, diaphragm, contraceptive jellies and foams, and breastfeeding were used by 4.0 percent of those practicing contraception in 1982.

The pattern of contraceptive use in China as of 1982 had parallels elsewhere. For example, at about the same time, half the couples practicing birth control in Taiwan were using the IUD, the same proportion as in the PRC. In South Korea, 37 percent of those controlling fertility used sterilization, compared to 35 percent in China.[92] Therefore, in comparison to other developing countries with high contraceptive prevalence rates, there was nothing particularly striking about the contraceptive mix used in China in 1982.

The fertility survey found that 69.46 percent of the estimated 170 million married women ages 15–49 were practicing birth control in 1982. However, this figure may exaggerate actual contraceptive use because the survey questions conveyed the expectation that the respondent was practicing family planning. The interview began, "How are you? In order to do a better job of family planning work, the state very much needs to learn about the marital status and childbirth of women. We are here to do a survey. Please help us do a good job." After some questions about age and marital status, the interviewer asked, "What contraceptive method are you using?" It would have been difficult to answer "None" to this question, and any woman who did was then asked, "Why aren't you practicing contraception?" Respondents who wanted to please the interviewer might have reported a technique of birth control they had last used, such as an IUD that had been expelled but not replaced, or might have claimed to be using one of the undetectable techniques, such as withdrawal or rhythm.[93]

Even allowing for some overreporting of birth control practice, fertility survey results imply that by the early 1980's a large majority of married couples in China were consciously limiting their fertility, and most couples not currently involved in having a baby were using some form of modern birth control. In 1982, in addition to the 118 million women practicing contraception, the survey classified 31 million women as not using birth control for government-approved reasons; for example, some were pregnant with a first child or trying to conceive a first baby, others were in the immediate postpartum period, and some couples were subfecund or sterile. From the official perspective, "the number of women who should practice contraception but have not adopted any constitutes 12.22 percent of the married women of reproductive age, and totals about 21 million persons" as of 1982.[94] China's high contraceptive use rate of 1982 is similar to levels attained in other parts of East Asia. Hong Kong reported 72 percent of married women ages 15–49 practicing birth control in 1977, and of married women ages 15–44, the following proportions were reported using contraception: South Korea, 55 percent in 1979; Japan, 68 percent in 1974; Taiwan, 70 percent in 1981; and Singapore, 71 percent in 1978.[95]

Data on nationwide abortion trends in China for the years 1971 through 1982 are shown in Table 6.7. The annual number of reported abortions rose from 4 million in 1971 to 5 million in 1972 and remained under 5.5 million through 1978, if the initially reported high figures for 1976 were incorrect. As the total number of births declined in the PRC during the early part of the decade, the ratio of abortions to births rose. From 1973 through 1976 China had about one-fifth as many abortions as live births. Thereafter, the trend was an increasing number of abortions and a rising abortion-to-birth ratio. There has been a sharp escalation in the annual number of abortions since the advent of the one-child program and required abortion for subsequent pregnancies, discussed in

TABLE 6.7
Reported Abortions and Estimated Annual Abortion Ratios in the PRC, 1971–82
(Number of induced abortions per 1,000 live births)

Year	Reported number of abortions	Estimated number of births	Ratio of abortions: 1,000 births
1971	3,910,110	29,376,010	133
1972	4,813,542	28,017,808	172
1973	5,110,405	26,361,110	194
1974	4,984,564	25,306,168	197
1975	5,084,260	22,756,465	223
1976	4,742,946	21,502,102	221
	6,570,000		306
	7,370,000		343
1977	5,229,569	19,902,503	263
1978	5,391,204	19,875,290	271
1979	7,856,587	20,766,030	378
1980	9,527,644	17,334,732	550
1981	8,696,945	20,932,674	415
1982	12,419,663	21,260,043	584
TOTAL	77,767,439	273,390,935	284

SOURCES: *Number of induced abortions*, Public Health Yearbook of China 1983 (1984): 69, for the entire period; Zhang Lizhong (1980): 35–36, and Chen Pi-chao (1981): Table 4, for 1971–77; Cai Shangzhong (1982): 238, for 1971–78. These sources agree for all years except 1976. The low figure for that year is the Public Health Yearbook's, the high one is from Cai, and the one in between is from Zhang. *Number of births*, author's computer reconstruction; see Chapters 8 and 10 and Table 10.1 for the basis of the reconstructed birth series.

NOTE: The total abortion figures for the whole period are based on the figure of 4.7 million abortions in 1976.

Chapter 7. There were 7.9 million abortions reported in 1979. In 1982 there were 12.4 million, almost three-fifths as many abortions as births.

Let us assess these abortion statistics. In most countries the number of legally approved abortions is a fraction of the actual number performed because abortion is illegal, highly restricted, or disapproved of by custom or religious belief. Therefore abortions tend to be underreported. But in the PRC abortions are not only legal, they are free for married women, encouraged by the government, and rewarded by paid leave for the recipient of the abortion. Those who have abortions therefore have an incentive to report them, and the medical facilities that provide abortions also have reason to report them to be reimbursed by the government. Any underreporting of abortions in China is mostly due to slippage in the statistical reporting system. The one category of women who might get an illegal and unreported abortion is unmarried women. An unmarried woman can get a legal abortion, but she might be required to pay for it, and as soon as she requests it her family, neighbors, and work unit are informed, and she is thereafter likely to be harassed about her premarital sexual relationship.[96] Confidentiality and personal privacy are not honored in the PRC in these matters; therefore, an unmarried woman might have strong incentives to get a clandestine abortion. It is also possible that there is some overreporting of abortions in China because medical units might want more reimbursement from the government. Because the direction of any net error in the abortion data is not clear, let us assume that the reported number of abortions is approximately correct.

In many countries the early years of rapid fertility decline were characterized by heavy use of legal or illegal abortion before modern contraceptives became widely available. This may have happened in urban areas of China during the 1950's and 1960's; but by the early 1970's, when rural couples were adopting birth control in great numbers, they had access to at least one modern contraceptive technique, so they probably did not need to rely almost exclusively on abortion for birth control.

Abortion use in the PRC so far does not follow the pattern that was common in Eastern Europe in the 1950's and 1960's and is still the case in the Soviet Union, in which few contraceptive techniques are available to couples and these are not very effective or are poor in quality; thus couples frequently conceive when they do not mean to and then resort to abortion. A common pattern in some communist countries has been to have at least as many abortions as live births, and in some countries to have two or three times as many abortions as births.[97]

Who gets abortions in China? For the most part, family planning workers and official sources have implied that most abortions are given to married women in cases of contraceptive failure. However, some sources indicate that many women who get abortions did not use contraceptives beforehand. For example, one report from Beijing Municipality stated: "According to a study of 2,000 abortions carried out in the municipal women's hospital, 78 percent of them were performed on persons who either had not practiced contraception or had not been persistent in practicing contraception."[98] Another report on a district of Beijing city proper stated that "over half of those who had abortions last year in the Xuanwu district had no knowledge of family planning."[99] The nationwide fertility survey found that, of married women who had an abortion during 1979–82, almost half had not been practicing birth control before they conceived, and the rest blamed method failure.[100] Many of these couples who use no contraceptives or use them halfheartedly probably would like to have more children but have been told not to by local authorities.

Some of the women who get abortions in China are unmarried. For example, one hospital in Tianjin reported that 9 percent of the abortions performed there in 1977 were for unmarried women; this proportion rose to 14 percent in 1978 and 16 percent in the first half of 1979.[101] Part of the reason for the occurrence of premarital pregnancy was, of course, forced late marriage. But another problem was the basic puritanism of Chinese culture. During the 1950's and 1960's the family planning program openly publicized details of sexuality and birth control, which was so offensive to popular mores that when the program resumed after the Cultural Revolution, instruction in family planning was confined to married couples, and unmarried persons were not given access to information on human sexuality or contraceptive techniques.[102] Contraceptives were made easily available to married couples free of charge but not offered to unmarried people. Now in China, as in so many other countries both developed and developing, the problem of premarital pregnancy is finally receiving some attention. A few premarital counseling centers have been set up, and the occasional human physiology or "family life" course is being taught in some high schools.[103]

In conclusion, China's population was transformed from one largely without contraception to one saturated with birth control practice in one decade. By 1970 the PRC had achieved high contraceptive use and low fertility only in the cities and some relatively advanced suburban and rural areas. Thereafter, a rising age at marriage helped rapidly reduce birth rates in both urban and rural areas. The 1970's also witnessed the historic shift in rural China to a population in which the great majority of couples use some form of birth control. These couples do not rely on traditional or inefficient forms of birth control such as folk medicines, withdrawal, or the rhythm method; by far the leading birth control techniques are the intrauterine device, sterilization, and induced abortion, all modern and effective methods. The heavy emphasis on effective techniques contributes to the success of China's family planning program. Other factors behind the achievement of low fertility are the large number of family planning workers, the strong motivational component of the program, and the ready accessibility of birth control techniques to married couples. Finally, the pervasive organizational structure of the birth control campaign and the fact that the government insists on contraceptive practice ensures that few couples in China can remain completely outside the family planning network.

7

The One-Child Family Campaign

By 1978 the PRC's family planning program had achieved remarkable success in birth control use and the limitation of fertility. A majority of the couples in China were practicing contraception, most using effective modern methods. Married couples were for the most part confining themselves to raising two or three children. Governments in most developing countries might have been content with such success, deciding simply to try to achieve replacement level fertility (an average of just over two births per woman) in a few years and then hold to that level in the succeeding decades.

But the Chinese government was just at that time discovering the existence and usefulness of the field of demography. During 1978 and thereafter, some of China's emerging statisticians and demographers began briefing top government leaders on the demographic momentum built into the current age structure of the population. They demonstrated that owing to a huge bulge in China's age structure at the young adult ages, the population would continue growing at over 1 percent annually for decades even if replacement fertility was maintained. A new understanding of demographic reality was expressed in public statements such as the following:

Reducing our country's natural population growth rate to zero by the year 2000 is the goal put forward by the State in accordance with Marxist population theory and with the reality of the development of our country's population and economy. . . . According to estimates of departments concerned, if a couple in our country has two children, we cannot basically change the situation in which our population growth is far from meeting the needs of economic development by the end of this century. Really to solve this problem, the only way is vigorously to preach that a couple should have one child.[1]

Deputy Qian Xinzhong, Minister of Public Health, in an analysis, said: "Every year in China some 10 million couples of young men and women will reach marriageable age and they will marry and have children. At the existing rate of population growth, China will have a population of 1,300 million by the end of the century. If the population is to grow to such a size, we will be compelled to devote a considerable amount of financial and material resources to feeding the newly increased populace. That will inevitably slow down the four modernizations. We plan to lower the country's natural rate of population growth to around 5 per thousand by 1985. . . . This means that on the average each couple as of now can have only one child."[2]

The response of China's leaders, when they were informed about the likely prospect of continued population growth, was swift and might be seen as an overreaction. They were determined to raise living standards in China as fast as possible, and the prospect of continuing population growth eating up hard-won production increases was totally unacceptable to them. Therefore, before they had thoroughly considered all the consequences, they decided that the one-child family would be promoted with determination throughout China. The new catch phrase was to be "One is best, at most two, never a third."[3] China's leaders continue to exaggerate the negative effects of population growth in order to justify measures taken against couples of reproductive age, as in this 1982 statement: "If we were not most firmly determined to take resolute, appropriate and effective measures to practice family planning and to bring population growth under control, the consequences would be too dreadful to contemplate."[4]

Rewards and Penalties

The decision to promote the one-child family in both urban and rural areas was apparently taken in the summer or fall of 1978 by the Central Committee of the Chinese Communist Party.[5] The new policy was formally announced in January 1979: "Women who give birth to one child only will be publicly praised; those who give birth to three or more will suffer economic sanctions."[6] Model regulations, which have not been released, were communicated to provincial leaders, who were empowered to formulate detailed provincial policies that might differ slightly depending on the anticipated public reaction to the one-child campaign in that province.

Realizing that the idea of stopping at one child per couple would be unpopular, the government announced financial incentives to encourage this practice and devised the "single-child certificate." Couples with one child who sign a pledge stating that they will have no more children receive the single-child certificate entitling them to economic benefits. (In general there are no rewards given to persons who decide not to marry at all or who marry but have no children, even though the zero-parity option makes a greater contribution to reducing the nation's fertility than the one-parity alternative. The way the one-child campaign is set up assumes that everyone will choose to marry and that everyone will choose to have at least one child.) In urban areas, the rewards for signing the one-child pledge are supposed to include a monthly cash payment while the child is growing up, preference in housing allocation and job assignments, free medical care for the child, priority for kindergarten and school enrollment, and free schooling for the child. In rural areas the promised benefits are more vague, because the rural collectives, which were still in place when the policy was announced, could not afford to pay such expensive benefits for their members. Rural couples who signed the one-child pledge were supposed to receive extra work points while the child is growing up, a private plot of land as large as that of other families with more children, and a larger proportion of the team's collectively produced grain than would normally have been allowed for the age of the child. The rapid introduction of the production responsibility system in agriculture made these rewards meaningless, and since 1979 some rural areas have devised new economic incentives for stopping at one child.

In early 1979 when this policy was announced, couples were still supposedly allowed to have two births, with no rewards and no penalties, but a third or higher order birth was to be followed by harsh penalties. In urban areas, couples bearing a third child were supposed to have their salaries reduced for all the years that this child was growing up, were to be allocated no additional housing space for the family, and were charged full fees for the child's birth, subsequent medical care, and schooling. All this could make a higher order child quite expensive in urban areas. In rural areas work points were supposed to be reduced for all the years the child was growing up, the family's private plot was to be no larger than for smaller families, the child was to be allocated no grain ration, the child was barred from participation in the cooperative medical system, the child's schooling fees had to be paid by the couple, and large families in financial difficulties were supposed to get no welfare assistance. As some of these penalties became obsolete, new ones were devised to replace them.

When the one-child policy was launched, with all these associated rewards and punishments, China's top policymakers were probably only dimly aware of its many consequences. The program might, for example, exacerbate the already glaring differentials in living standards between urban and rural families, and between advantaged and disadvantaged families. Many city couples were already choosing to stop at one child, and many more were indifferent enough about having a second child that they would opt for the financial rewards of stopping at one. But not that many were still having third or higher order births, so the rewards promised to the one-child couples in cities and towns could not be paid for by the corresponding penalties exacted from urban parents bearing three or more children. The considerable benefits given to urban one-child couples have had to be paid for somehow, perhaps by raising the prices of factory products to consumers or diverting municipal funds to pay the rewards. Urban couples, already well off compared to those in rural areas, have received more financial gain from stopping at one child than have rural couples.

Similarly, it was already the more advantaged couples throughout China who were adopting very low fertility and the less advantaged who chose to continue high fertility. Couples choosing one child would tend to be educated, both employed in salaried jobs, eligible for pensions, and already at relatively high living standards. Couples choosing to have three or more children would tend to be poor, illiterate or minimally educated, ineligible for any kind of pension, scraping by at a subsistence level, and very much in need of the labor and income that children could provide. To give financial rewards to advantaged couples and take income away from disadvantaged couples would further widen income disparities in Chinese society.

Given the antinatalist influences of urban life combined with the more genuine rewards and punishments that could be brought to bear in urban areas, in contrast to the more nebulous and variable rewards and sanctions possible in the rural economy, it was likely that urban couples would more readily stop at one child than rural couples. In the extreme, poor villages which have no surplus beyond subsistence grain have no income to be taken away from the prolific couples and given to the one-child couples. The financial constraint faced by local leaders in poor rural areas as they tried to pressure couples to limit childbearing was emphasized in late 1981: "The work is very difficult. In some areas, they are not able to afford the awards and are not able to mete out the penalties. They do not know what to do."[7]

The One-Child Pledge

As of February 1978 the Chinese government was pursuing the goal of reducing the population growth rate to 1 percent in the year 1980.[8] The corresponding goal of a natural increase rate of 10 per thousand population could be achieved only by reducing China's fertility below replacement level, which in turn required considerable success in the one-child campaign. The success of each local and each larger political unit in the one-child drive was measured by its "single-child certificate acceptance rate"; that is, the percentage of couples eligible to sign the one-child pledge (with one child and with the wife of childbearing age) who had signed it.[9]

Table 7.1 documents the progress of the claimed rates for populous geographical units. In January 1979, soon after the one-child campaign was launched, China's leaders set the modest goal that 20 percent of urban couples and 5 percent of rural couples be persuaded to sign the one-child pledge.[10] But by year's end several provinces reported that around 70 percent of couples with one child had signed the pledge. A nationwide acceptance rate of 29 percent was claimed only one year after the one-child campaign had begun. China's vice-premier in charge of family planning then announced a very ambitious target in early February 1980: "We'll try to attain the goal that 95 percent of married couples in the cities and 90 percent in the countryside will have only one child in due course."[11]

In 1980 and 1981, some model localities claimed that over 90 percent of the couples with one child had signed the pledge, and several provinces claimed rates of around 80 percent, as shown in Table 7.1. Other provinces, such as Guangdong, Zhejiang, Nei Mongol, and Gansu, reported more modest success. In February 1981, a national single-child certificate acceptance rate of 57 percent was announced; that is, of the estimated 20 million married couples of reproductive age with one child, over 11 million reportedly had signed the pledge.[12] The number of couples having signed the pledge increased to 14 million by September 1982, or 42 percent of the 33 million couples of childbearing age with one child; these figures are more reliable than the earlier data on the number of couples with one child because the 33 million figure is based on the 1982 nationwide fertility survey.[13] An additional 2.3 million couples signed the pledge during January 1983, and the State Family Planning Commission reported that by the end of 1983, 25 million couples, 72 percent of the 34 million couples with one child, had signed.[14]

If the signing of the one-child pledge signifies that a couple is determined to raise only one child, whether or not the government can deliver all the rewards it has promised them, then the program is a spectacular success: the total fertility rate will shortly drop below two births per woman, if it has not already, and China will have no trouble holding its population growth rate to around 1 percent a year or below during the coming decades. But the true meaning of a couple's signature on the "one-child pledge" is far from obvious, and what the couple will actually do about their future fertility (unless one of them has been sterilized) is even more uncertain.

Much has changed in the PRC in the short time since the one-child

TABLE 7.1

Single-Child Certificate Acceptance Rates in the PRC and Selected Localities, 1979–83

(Percentage of childbearing-age couples with one child)

Category	1979	1980	1981	1982	1983
National total	29%[a]		57%[b]	42%[c]	72%[a]
Urban				78[c]	
Rural				31[c]	
Northeast				57[c]	
Heilongjiang province		79[a]			
Harbin Municipality	96[a]				
Liaoning province	68[a]				91[a]
Jilin province			77[a]		
North				45[c]	
Beijing Municipality		79[a]	83[d]		94[d]
City		90[a]	93[d]		
Counties		58[a]	63[d]		
Tianjin Municipality	52[a]		83[b],85[a]	87[c]	
City	80[a]				
Counties	30[a]				
Inner Mongolia (Nei Mongol)			34[c],38[a]		
East				50[c]	
Shanghai Municipality		67[d],75[a]	80[d],86[a]	92[c],95[a]	98,99[e]
City	90[a]	82[a]			
Counties	75[a]	61[a]			
Jiangsu province	64,68[e]		76[b],74[c] 79[a]		90[a]
Suzhou Municipality			95[b]		
Zhejiang province			41[a]		
Fujian province, Fuzhou Municipality			60[d]		
Shandong province		77[d],80+[a]	85[a]	87[c]	89[d]
Yantai prefecture		96[d]			
Taian prefecture					96[d]
Central South				25[c]	
Henan province		26[a]			
Guangdong province		45[d]			
Guangzhou Municipality			55[c]		
Guangxi province					26[a]
Southwest				45[c]	
Sichuan province	72[a]	79[d],80[a]	81[b]	81,83[e]	86,88,89[e]
Chongqing Municipality		91[d]			
Chengdu Municipality		70[d]			
Northwest				27[c]	
Shaanxi province		80[a]			
Gansu province		26[a]			
Qinghai province				35[a]	
Ningxia province		8[a]			
Yinchuan Municipality					58[d]
Military families on posts				99[a]	
Military families off posts				96[a]	

SOURCES: All sources on file at the China Branch, Center for International Research, U.S. Bureau of the Census. Some of these figures appear in Chen Pi-chao & Kols (1982): 604.

NOTE: "Urban" is defined as the nonagricultural permanent resident population of cities and towns; "rural" covers all the rest of the population.

[a]By yearend. [b]By March. [c]By September. [d]By midyear.

[e]By yearend. Two or more figures appeared in different sources in each case.

campaign was launched. The announced reward systems for stopping at one child were implemented in late 1979 or during 1980. The punishment systems apparently took longer; for example, Shanghai Municipality instituted rewards as of September 1979 and at the same time announced that starting on March 1, 1980, all couples bearing a third or higher order child would be penalized.[15] The time lag allowed the completion of pregnancies already well into the second or third trimesters when the policy was announced, but in order to avoid the penalties, couples would have had to abort pregnancies of less than 4 months gestation if the birth would bring a couple's third or higher order child.

In urban areas, as the single-child certificate acceptance rate has risen very high, "preferential treatment" for the single-child couples has become less meaningful. If almost all couples sign the one-child pledge, and there is still a shortage of housing space, nursery and kindergarten places, good schools, and jobs in the state sector, then those with "preferential treatment" still do not get a good job or a better apartment. In rural areas, the rewards for signing the one-child pledge were not great to begin with, but they became less effective in many ordinary rural areas with the introduction of the "responsibility system" in agriculture.

Agricultural production in the PRC has been sluggish, partly because farmers were given little incentive to produce more grain and other agricultural products. They could work hard and produce more or work less hard and produce less and either way get about the same low return. In an attempt to increase production incentives in agriculture, the government began at the end of 1978 to experiment with giving production teams, equivalent to a village or part of a village, more control of what would be grown and how it would be grown. In mid-1979 agricultural taxes were reduced and the government-paid prices for agricultural products were raised in an effort to spur production. Since 1979 there has been a big push to diversify China's agricultural economy. While attempting to keep up grain production, the PRC has promoted sideline production of all kinds, including forestry, animal husbandry, fisheries, supplementary foods, and cash crops. At the same time the national government has promoted the partial dismantling of collective controls on household production and income. Teams were ordered to give back private plots that they had taken from households, and in some provinces private plots were expanded to 15 percent of the team's land.[16] Meanwhile, the rest of the team's land has been allocated to small work groups or to households to work, like a tenant farming arrangement. The household, for instance, contracts to work a piece of land and pay the team and the state a certain quantity of product after the harvest. The rest of the product can be sold at a higher price to the state or at the rural free market or can be consumed by the household.

Many different kinds of such "production responsibility systems" are in effect.[17] Almost all of them retain the private plot, and if the same size of private plot is allocated to all households regardless of the number of members, then it could be argued that very small families are benefiting and large ones are being penalized. But when all the team land is contracted out to households, then the small private plot is less important. All the land allocated to the household is being used like a private plot, in that the household gets much of the benefit of its product, once "rent" is paid to the team and taxes to the state. Also, a much greater proportion of the family's income now comes from raising pigs, chickens, fruit trees, oilseeds, vegetables, and other agricultural products for sale, and from trading, services, household handicrafts, and small industrial production. In most teams, work points have entirely lost their function and are no longer calculated at all, and where people are still being paid in work points, they now constitute a much smaller proportion of the household's income.[18] Therefore, work-point bonuses or penalties mean much less to a household under the responsibility system than they would have before. Similarly, the denial of grain rations to third or higher order children is irrelevant to households able to grow surplus grain for their own use.

By 1982, half the production teams (villages) in China had adopted the system of fixing farm output quotas for each household and assigning households full responsibility for task completion.[19] The average and poorer agricultural areas led the way in abandoning collective production almost completely.[20] There, households are being allowed to earn all they can in any way they can. In these areas fertility has probably stayed the highest. Now, under the production responsibility system in agriculture, rural households in China need more labor to work their fields, to gather fuel, and to do sideline production for profit. Households with few members are finding that they do not have enough labor power to work the land allocated to them and do all the other income-earning tasks they are now allowed to do.[21] In some areas, the more laborers the family has the more land it will be allocated by the team to work.[22] Therefore, particularly in poorer agricultural areas, there is an incentive for each household to have several children to help with the work, an incentive that might outweigh whatever penalties the collective is able to muster. The genuine need for children in rural households is reinforced by the very slow pace of farm mechanization in China today and the concentration of machinery in advanced agricultural areas. As the desire of rural couples for more children was reinforced by the production responsibility system, the government escalated its use of coercion as the only way to ensure the success of the one-child campaign.

When China first set up its system of economic rewards and penalties, some foreign and Chinese observers likened it to systems of financial incentives for low fertility and financial disincentives for high fertility now found in many other countries. Indeed, at first couples in China were under the illusion that they could still choose to bear two children and receive no rewards or penalties, and that they could even choose to bear three or more children if they paid the financial penalties.[23] They rapidly discovered that this was not the case. During 1979 through 1981 urban governments moved to forbid all second or higher order births. By 1982 most provincial governments were trying to do the same in rural areas as well. For example, Jilin province announced in October 1979 that parents of all babies born outside the local government's birth plan each year would be penalized. Because the second child would no longer be officially authorized except in rare cases, this proclamation amounts to penalizing almost all second order births. In another example, "Tianjin Municipality in mid-1981 made explicit its economic penalties for the birth of a second child."[24]

As of late 1980 the State Council was strongly discouraging the birth of a second child anywhere in China. In September the Central Committee of the Chinese Communist Party issued an "open letter" urging couples to stop childbearing after one child, ignoring the chasm between life in urban areas and life in the countryside that tends to lead to different levels of fertility: "The State Council has issued a call to the people of the whole country, encouraging each couple to have only one child. This [program] is an important measure which concerns the speed and future of the four modernizations and the health and happiness of the future generations. It is a measure that conforms to the immediate and longer-term interests of the whole people."[25]

The transition from the originally announced incentive-disincentive system to a far more coercive system was completed in most parts of the country by 1982. This transition was effected through rapidly expanding penalties for the birth of a second or higher parity child. From 1979 to 1982 any second or higher order births that happened in spite of government pressure were met with escalating punishments designed to impoverish the offending couple for at least fourteen years if not for life. This repression continued to mount, until in mid-1982 official statements clarified that local government leaders must not permit a couple to have a second or third birth and then impose the stated economic sanctions. Rather, local officials must prevent conceptions of second and higher order children, and when that fails they are required to see to it that women have abortions:

After some units discovered second and higher order pregnancies which were not in the plan, the leadership did not actively carry out ideological education, and did not mobilize them to take remedial action, but let them take their own course. After the child was born, they then imposed economic sanctions. They felt that by doing it this way, they had followed the regulations and also avoided contradictions. Thus, neither side was offended. When second and higher order pregnancies are discovered in a unit, whether the leadership of the unit actively carries out ideological education or passively relies on penalties to solve the contradiction . . . indicates whether or not the leadership has a strong sense of responsibility and has the correct view of the work. . . . If ideological education is not carried out, and if we simply rely upon economic sanctions, the only result will be that those who have an excessive number of births will be punished. However, population growth will not really be controlled.[26]

In late 1981 the national government decided that under extraordinary individual circumstances, the birth of a second child might be allowed, but under no circumstances would a third.[27]

What is becoming increasingly apparent is that the PRC abandoned the policy of rewarding one-child couples, neutrality toward two-child couples, and allowing but taxing multiparous couples before that policy even got off the ground. Now the policy is to require most couples to stop at one child and to unleash government repression on those couples trying to have two or more children without official permission.

Coercion

Official and semiofficial statements from the PRC usually proclaim that the family planning program is entirely voluntary and that couples are persuaded but not forced to adopt birth control measures. Several examples follow, extending from 1973 to 1983. In 1973 an official Chinese delegation to a meeting of the United Nations Economic Commission for Asia and the Far East said:

China's work on birth control is carried out under the principle of voluntariness on the part of the masses with state guidance. The government and social organizations at all levels mobilize the masses to practice planned childbirth voluntarily through widespread propaganda and education.[28]

The Chinese spokesman at the 1974 World Population Conference stated:

Our birth planning is not merely birth control, as some people understand it to be; it comprises different measures for different circumstances. In densely populated areas, late marriage and birth control are encouraged on the basis of voluntariness, while active treatment is given in cases of sterility. In national minority areas and other sparsely populated areas, appropriate measures are taken to facilitate population growth, while birth control advice and help are given to those parents who have too many children and desire birth control.[29]

In 1978, Kang Keqing, leader of China's Women's Federation, said:

> Our Women's Federation Organization should work hand in hand with the departments concerned and, in accordance with provisions in the constitution, encourage and promote family planning, do patient and meticulous ideological and educational work and strive to raise the consciousness of the masses in family planning. We oppose coercion and authoritarianism.[30]

The chairman of the Chinese Communist Party, Hua Guofeng, in 1980 gave a speech to the National People's Congress in which he said:

> It is very common for one couple to have only one child in the developed countries. But for people in our rural areas, it is truly an important matter of transforming social customs and traditions. In our effort to achieve this, we rely chiefly on publicizing and implementing the policies of the Party and government and on ideological and political work, not on compulsion and arbitrary orders. . . . However, we must not shut our eyes to the fact that, for diverse reasons, cases of compulsion or even violations of the law and discipline have occurred in this work in some places. We must firmly put an end to this.[31]

China's official line on the question of coercion was stated in the authoritative *People's Daily* in late 1980:

> Positively and prudently formulate a law on planned parenthood. Planned parenthood concerns the vital interests of each household. We must patiently and meticulously conduct ideological and educational work and persuade the people. We oppose coercion or issuing orders or employing force or punishment, methods which are divorced from the masses.[32]

A 1980 editorial in China's *Southern Daily* protested that the implementation of rules requiring birth control use and limitation of fertility did not constitute coercion:

> The "Guangdong Provincial Family Planning Regulations" were formulated and approved by the standing committee of the provincial people's congress. They have the function of law. Practice has also shown that the spirit of the "Regulations" is correct, and that they conform to the basic interests of the broad masses. Now, there are some people who interpret our executing the "Regulations" as coercion. This is completely wrong.[33]

In 1981, China was represented by Li Xiuzhen, Director of the Birth Planning Leading Group of China's State Council at the International Conference on Family Planning in the 1980's in Jakarta. She asserted in her speech that "Family planning in China has always adhered to the principle of state guidance and voluntary participation."[34] Even after a distinct nationwide escalation of compulsory fertility control in the beginning of 1983, Chinese government representatives continued to maintain that the program is voluntary:

A spokesman of the State Family Planning Commission told Xinhua today that it is China's consistent policy to encourage people to practice birth control voluntarily. The Chinese Government has never resorted to compulsory means to force sterilization among people. He said in an interview that there were individual cases of using compulsory measures due to the simple working method of local cadres and staff members. But the government will take prompt measures to stop them, whenever it discovers such cases, he stressed. The spokesman was commenting on slanders spread by certain foreign newspapers and individuals that the Chinese Government adopts compulsory measures in family planning.[35]

Special note should be taken of the tendency in these official policy statements to use words like "voluntary," "willingly," "encourage," "desire," "persuade," and "educate," all words meant to imply that the people of China are not coerced into practicing birth control. Many observers from outside China when describing the family planning program echo these words because they believe, or want to believe, these official statements. For example, one writer said: "In the course of educating and motivating eligible couples, cadres exert some form of 'pressure' on them to make them conform to practices designed to help meet planned birth targets. Such 'pressure' must persuade, rather than coerce."[36] This quotation was in an article entitled "Information, Education, Motivation: Persuasion, Not Coercion." Another visitor to China suggested that since freedom of choice is a relative concept, we outsiders are not competent to judge whether family planning is voluntary there:

Many people I have talked with since my return are horrified by what they call lack of freedom in China. . . . As we talked with Chinese individuals, I sensed that they feel they do have freedom in their terms—a new expanding freedom which they have earned by their own hard work. . . . They have achieved for themselves a freedom of adequate food, health care, housing, permanent jobs, a chance to plan families and the comfort of knowing they will be taken care of in their old age. . . . All people are involved in solving local problems and implementing accepted goals. It may not be "freedom" in our terms, but in today's complicated world, we should commend the progress that has been made to ensure a stable productive life for each person in a country that contains at least one-fifth of all humanity. In a world where the cancer of exploding population on a finite globe is our greatest long-term danger, we might take a lesson from the Chinese and understand that our own future freedom may well depend on following their lead in birth planning.[37]

It is not only one-time visitors to China who echo the claim that China has a voluntary family planning program; some scholars who write extensively on family planning in China and know in detail of the coercive practices in the program continue to defend it as voluntary. For example:

Obviously, the Chinese government cannot force the people to practice birth control. Therefore the idea behind the birth planning policy is to combine state guidance (education and persuasion as opposed to administrative orders) with the voluntary cooperation of the people. However, the government can and will see that its wishes are carried out.[38]

China's population-planning programs rest on the dual principle of state guidance and mass voluntarism. At the grass-roots level, mass discussions are held to educate people on the importance of fertility restraint and to establish the timing of childbearing among women involved. By this process, each woman can exercise her social right to have a child or two.[39]

It is illuminating to list those aspects of the family planning program that are truly voluntary, that is, in any internationally accepted sense of the word. In some places in China, particularly cities and suburbs, there are more than just one or two methods of birth control available, and as far as we know couples in those places at least until 1983 were given some choice as to which contraceptive technique they preferred to use. It is possible that some urban couples are still given a choice of method. Another real choice couples can make is whether they wish to have no children or one child—the government is content with either of those decisions. Couples also may choose whether or not to postpone the birth of their first child through contraception. However, this last choice may now be gone in those local units whose quota of births for recent years has been smaller than the number of newlywed couples, a common situation with the rapidly increasing numbers of marriages every year since the mid-1970's. In some such localities newlywed couples are now being required to postpone the birth of their one authorized child.

From the perspective of some Chinese couples the family planning program is entirely voluntary because they want only one child or no children anyway. Such couples would tend to be urban and well educated, with both partners employed full-time in acceptable jobs and at least one of them eligible for a pension, probably a very busy couple living in a crowded housing space. If they already meant to stop at one child, then no coercion is applied to them. Similarly, if a couple would be happy with either two children or one, and the educational and motivational work of the family planning program persuades them that it would be patriotic and socially responsible of them to choose to stop at one child, which they do readily and cheerfully, then this couple is experiencing only the voluntary aspects of the family planning program. Another like couple attracted by the rewards promised for stopping at one child, who voluntarily sign the one-child pledge and then receive all the benefits as promised, can be considered voluntary acceptors of family planning.

But except for those categories of couples, married couples in China do not experience a voluntary program; they are instead subject to the world's first national compulsory family planning program. The policy of compulsory family planning developed rapidly during the 1970's in China, but this trend may not have been supported by all members of the leadership. It is even possible that Mao Zedong and some members of his radical faction, later represented by the "gang of four," opposed forced family planning. After Mao's death and the arrest of the "gang of four," China's subsequent leadership tended to blame all national problems on the legacy of the "gang of four," so all accusations such as the following should be analyzed with some skepticism. Even so, the post-Mao leadership hinted that the "gang of four" interfered with the rise of coercion in the family planning program:

> The [planned parenthood] meeting [in Shanghai] maintained that planned parenthood work was subjected to serious interference and sabotage by the gang of four. We must penetratingly expose and criticize the gang of four, thoroughly eliminate their pernicious influence, and clearly distinguish between the right and wrong ideology and line. We must create strong public opinion so that everyone promotes planned parenthood.
>
> There are many reasons why our province [Yunnan] has failed to promote planned parenthood work. However, the main reason is that the gang of four's remnant poison in planned parenthood work has not been eliminated.
>
> Planned parenthood work, like other work, also suffered from interference and sabotage by Lin Piao and the "gang of four." Lin Piao, the "gang of four," and their followers incited anarchism in marriage and childbirth. They talked such nonsense as "planned parenthood is a feminine triviality." They attacked the attention paid by party committees to planned parenthood as "forgetting the key link and the line" and "ignoring proper business." They slandered those who advocated "late marriage, longer intervals between children, and fewer children" as "controlling, restricting, and repressing."[40]

If compulsory birth control did not sit well with the radicals, it was probably because of the Marxist ideological line that equates pressure for birth control with capitalist, colonial, or superpower exploitation of Third World couples. These accusations do not prove that the radical faction had qualms about coercive family planning and tried to prevent it, but if they are true, then it follows that the usually more moderate faction now led by Deng Xiaoping is primarily responsible for the compulsory and coercive nature of China's family planning program.

How can the Chinese government vociferously maintain that it runs a voluntary family planning program when there is abundant evidence, some of which will be presented here, that the program is compulsory in tone and coercive in methods for the great majority of childbearing-age couples? In the first place, the protestations of voluntarism are primarily a ritual acted out for the benefit of the international community. People in China who are subjected to the program know that they have almost no choice in the matter, but people outside China depend for much of their information on statements by the PRC government about what it is doing or trying to do. The national government argues that it encourages but does not require compliance, and that any instances of compulsion or coercion are attributable to local cadres exceeding their instructions. This formula happens to fit the requirements of those international organizations that want to help China in the field of family planning, but whose charters forbid their support of compulsory programs.

It will be demonstrated here that the compulsory nature of China's family planning program is nationally mandated and that local cadres are required by the central government and the Chinese Communist Party to coerce the people into compliance. Cadres who are unwilling to compel people to practice birth control face public reprimands and economic sanctions from all levels of the administrative hierarchy above them. National government instructions to the local cadres, transmitted down through the chain of administration, are that the local leaders and family planning workers must secure compliance by all the couples of childbearing age in their area. This end is of primary importance, and the means to attain it are allowed to vary depending on local conditions, just so long as the desired result is achieved. Official instructions in the media to the local cadres argue that if they did their jobs right, all couples would be persuaded to cooperate fully with the national birth control guidelines, and no compulsion would be needed. Therefore, local cadres are saddled with conflicting and incompatible instructions. On the one hand they are ordered to succeed fully in meeting the family planning targets transmitted from higher authorities, and to use whatever means are necessary to get this result. On the other hand, they are told not to use "coercion and commandism" in their work. If couples resist the persuasive attempts of the cadres, as they often do, then cadres must ignore the "don't coerce" instruction in order to meet the more insistent demand, "you must fully succeed."

China's compulsory family planning program is designed by the national government and the Central Committee of the Chinese Communist Party. The documents resulting from the national meetings are usually classified and transmitted directly to provincial governments. The provincial authorities are responsible for transmitting national orders to all lower levels and seeing that they are carried out. The instructions are passed down via meetings, telephone conferences, or the media, and the central government origin of the demands is made very clear:

> Wang Kangjiu stressed that family planning work in Beijing should abide by the guidelines of the 1982 Central Document No. 11 and the recent central directive.[41]

The CPC [Communist Party of China] Central Committee and State Council have seriously studied the situation in all aspects and have formulated the birth policy of universally advocating that a couple have only one child, strictly controlling the birth of a second, and resolutely stopping the birth of a third. This is correct and farsighted. We must unswervingly and resolutely carry out this policy.[42]

The Guangdong Provincial CPC Committee and People's Government held a telephone conference yesterday evening, calling on all localities in the province to seriously implement the CPC Central Committee directive on continuously and firmly grasping planned parenthood work and to whip up a high tide in carrying out this work in May and June.

Lin Ruo, secretary of the Guangdong Provincial CPC Committee, spoke at the conference. He said: Planned parenthood work should not be slackened in the slightest. No matter how busy they are with other work, party committees at all levels must not waver in carrying out planned parenthood work. This year's task for planned parenthood work must be accomplished without fail.[43]

The coercion of cadres by the national and provincial governments is the means by which their cooperation is assured. In the first place, ever since the early 1970's, cadres at all levels of the government and party hierarchy have been required to "take the lead" in family planning if they wished to keep their position. The September 1980 "open letter" from the Central Committee of the Chinese Communist Party exhorted members of the Party and Communist Youth League to take the lead in stopping at one child. Cadres have been forced to delay their marriages, and to be among the first in their unit to practice family planning, sign a one-child pledge, abort any pregnancy not previously included in the local birth plan, or get sterilized. Once the cadres have been forced by higher government authority to cease childbearing well before they have their desired number of children, they are more likely to insist that other people be subjected to the same restrictions. Apparently the people know that they will be required to follow the cadres' example, as in the 1983 case of Hebei county where all couples with two children in cadre families were required to have one partner sterilized:

At the time of mobilization and making preparations at the county, commune, and brigade level, leadership cadres at all levels were asked to take the lead. The "three-first and three-following-behind" and the "four contracts" were achieved. The "three-first and three-following-behind" means that in undergoing sterilization, the leadership cadres take the first step before the cadres in general, the county organizations before the local communes, and the cadres and party members before the commune masses. Tan Shiying, chairman, and Liu Hui, vice chairman of the standing committee of the county people's congress, and vice-mayor Xie Zhijun have between them seven children who belong to the category for sterilization. They all successively took the lead to undergo the surgery. Communes and brigades followed. The masses said, "When the leadership takes the lead, it is the same as a silent command."[44]

Cadres who refuse to take the lead face severe penalties. They may be heavily fined, demoted, or fired from their jobs, in addition to being subjected to a forced abortion or forced sterilization anyhow.[45] Provincial regulations and instructions often include stipulations like: "As for those cadres, particularly the leading cadres, who do not practice family planning, it is necessary to investigate their cases thoroughly and to handle them severely,"[46] and: "After several efforts at persuasion, cadres, staff members and workers who still stubbornly refuse to give birth according to plans and whose offenses are serious and are very bad influences shall be given severe disciplinary or administrative punishment in addition to economic sanctions."[47]

Because many cadres were reluctant to force the people under their jurisdiction to severely limit their fertility,[48] the national government in the early 1980's required local cadres to include family planning work in a "cadre job responsibility system." Cadres at all levels have to sign contracts with the next higher level guaranteeing that their assigned family planning targets will be met. In the case of local level cadres, if there are births in their unit outside the official plan, their salaries are reduced, but if compliance is great the cadres get a salary bonus. For example, one brigade announced in 1981: "Cadres will be awarded 100 yuan if their units attain the planned parenthood quotas. Otherwise, 10 yuan penalty will be imposed on them for every birth not covered by the plan."[49] There are many variations of this punitive policy, sometimes involving the assignment of one cadre to fewer than 20 households with the job of ensuring complete adherence to the one-child policy in those households or suffering financial penalties for even one couple who successfully resist.[50] The family planning job responsibility system ensures that cadres at the local level will not dilute the national compulsory family planning program when it is implemented at the local level. In addition there is in some areas a "birth control operations responsibility system" whose main purpose is to improve the quality of the operations, but that apparently also deducts part of the salary of medical personnel who refuse to perform birth control operations required by the state.[51]

All married couples in the PRC are legally required by the state to practice contraception unless they are explicitly exempted from this requirement, which for almost all couples happens only temporarily while they conceive and bear a baby allowed in the government's plan. The Marriage Law in effect since January 1981 states in Article 2, "Family planning shall be put into practice." And in Article 12, "Both husband and wife shall have the duty to practice family planning."[52] The only exception allowed for in the law is that some couples who are members of small minority groups or minority groups located in very sparsely populated areas may be allowed not to use birth control. Members of the larger minority groups and those in densely populated areas have since 1980 encountered increasing insistence that they practice contraception.[53] In December 1982, China adopted a new Constitution that reiterated the obligation of married couples to use birth control in "Article 49: Both husband and wife have the duty to practice family planning."[54]

Therefore, the first element of coercion in China's family planning program is the requirement that all married couples must accept family planning. Couples who resist this requirement for whatever reason—religious belief, moral objection, the desire to have a child soon, the wish to have another child before subfecundity sets in, the desire to have a son or daughter when the first child is of the other sex, or the preference to have many children—may be subjected to harsh treatment by local cadres charged with carrying out official policy. For instance, in late 1978 a national newspaper reported: "Some localities popularizing birth control have dispatched 'militia propaganda teams' to those households that did not practice birth control to 'propagandize' and exercise control over their food, drinking water, and workpoints. These local laws have caused great dissatisfaction among the people."[55]

In China today, not to accept contraception requires courage, because penalties can be harsh. To refuse to control fertility or to encourage others to refuse is sometimes treated as a crime against the state. As one official said in 1978, "We must expose and deal resolute blows at class enemies who sabotage planned parenthood."[56] Most married people of reproductive age in China must control their fertility to avoid being guilty of an ideological offense in the eyes of the government.[57] Those who would rather not practice birth control find that they must do so, or at least pretend to, in order to avoid political reprisals. Therefore it is not surprising that a very high proportion of married couples in China practices family planning.

In 1983, official statements clarified that required birth control use is national and provincial, as well as local, policy. For instance, the province of Ningxia emphasized, "During family planning propaganda month, Ningxia extensively mobilized the masses and achieved very good results. This enabled people to realize that the practice of family planning is state policy and that it is imperative."[58] A speech by the Director of China's State Family Planning Commission in February 1983 cited the new Constitution and resolutions by the Twelfth Communist Party Congress and the Fifth National People's Congress to prove that birth control use is the law, or, as he put it, "that family planning must be understood as the implementation of party discipline and state law."[59]

The major propaganda purpose of the first "family planning propaganda month" in January 1983 was to inform couples that the law, in the form of the new Constitution passed the previous month, required them to practice family planning starting immediately.[60] Provincial governments emphasized that their laws and regulations enforcing birth control derived legitimacy from the national Constitution's requirement that every couple practice family planning. Courts and police could be used to guarantee compliance. Throughout 1983 and thereafter, detailed rules about who must practice what form of birth control proliferated at the provincial level, with the "protection of the law" behind each rule.[61] For example, the following justification was given for enforcing Sichuan province's body of family planning regulations during 1983:

> In short, the basic problem in planned parenthood work lies in legislation. Through legislation, it can be made even more explicit to the broad body of cadres and masses that implementing planned parenthood is not an expedient measure but that it is a principle stipulated by the laws of the nation and that it is a legal duty that the citizens must bear to the state. Because the laws of the nation have a relative stability, legislative organs have the right of interpretation and the judicial departments have the right of enforcement, sound growth of planned parenthood work can be effectively assured.[62]

There were national family planning propaganda months in January 1983 and January 1984, and some provinces conducted an extra period of intense family planning activity in the summer or fall of 1983. The name of these campaigns is misleading, because the emphasis was on immediate action in enforcing family planning "technical measures," rather than on persuading and educating people. The phrase "technical measures" is a euphemism for required sterilization, abortion, and IUD insertion. Cadres were ordered to promptly carry out these birth control operations during the "action stage" of family planning month.[63] The concentration on enforcing the adoption of these birth control measures in the first nationwide family planning propaganda month was given the sanction of the national leadership in the speech referred to here: "Recently, [Secretary-General of the Chinese Communist Party] Comrade Hu Yaobang pointed out that the work of population control should 'rely first on political mobilization, second on law and third on technical measures.'"[64]

In many broadcasts and newspaper articles, local cadres were warned that "ideological education" was not enough during the propaganda months, because this was not the main purpose of the campaigns, rather "the aim of doing well in ideological education is to carry out contraceptive and birth control measures."[65] Therefore, the cadres' success in propaganda month work was judged by the numbers of different kinds of birth control operations that were carried out in their units. "Earnest implementation of the technical measures for family planning is the main criterion for judging our achievements in the propaganda month campaign."[66]

The second element of coercion in the family planning program, after the requirement that all couples of childbearing age practice birth control, is that the national government sets a limit on the number of children couples may have. Currently it is attempting to enforce a limit of one apparently healthy living child per couple for all but some minorities and some Han couples in certain rare and rigidly defined situations. (Couples who have twins or triplets at the first birth are supposed to be neither rewarded nor penalized.) By the time of the first family planning propaganda month, January 1983, national government and Communist Party orders to all levels of the hierarchy below them were as follows:

> The responsible person said that the "Directive on Further Doing Well in Family Planning Work" issued by the CCP Central Committee and the State Council clearly stipulates that "state cadres, workers and employees, and urban residents, except for special cases which have been given approval, are to have only one child per couple. In the rural areas, one child per couple is to be universally promoted. Some of the masses, who truly have difficulties and request to have a second child, may be scheduled to have a second one according to plan after approval. Under no circumstances is a third child allowed."[67]

China's Premier Zhao Ziyang, in a June 1983 Report on the Work of the Government, said that "We must persistently advocate late marriage and one child per couple, strictly control second births, prevent additional births *by all means* [emphasis added], earnestly carry out effective birth control measures and firmly protect infant girls and their mothers."[68] These directives make clear that the compulsory cessation of childbearing after one child, or in exceptional cases two children, is China's national government policy. (Beginning in 1984 there was a slight easing of the one-child policy to allow more second births. This will be discussed in Chapter 10.)

If a couple's first child dies or is handicapped, the government will usually allow a second birth. In other cases of "extra" children the government inflicts harsh political, administrative, economic, and social penalties on the parents. It is interesting that in all other countries of the world the term "unwanted" birth means a birth unwanted by the parents; in China such a birth is one unwanted by the government, though perhaps very much wanted by the parents. Similarly, an "unplanned" birth everywhere else in the world means that the couple did not plan to conceive but nevertheless proceeded with the birth. In the PRC the press uses "unplanned births" to mean those not permitted in the government's plan, even if the couple did plan the birth.[69] To the government the desires and plans of couples regarding the number and spacing of their offspring do not count if these aspirations do not fit neatly into its official plan.

In order to enforce the universal one-child limit, local governments in many parts of China seem to have simply required every couple with one child to sign the one-child pledge. Constant official harassment is inflicted on any family that resists. For example, as reported by the *Washington Post* correspondent in Beijing as of early 1980:

> After months of gradually stronger birth control warnings, Chinese authorities have begun to use intense social and bureaucratic coercion to ensure that every Chinese baby born the rest of this century is an only child.
>
> Reports from foreigners and Chinese in both rural and urban areas say neighbors have been enlisted to visit nightly the homes of recalcitrant couples until they agree to sign a "one family, one child" pledge.
>
> A foreign researcher who has been living for the last month in a commune headquarters in southern Hebei Province said, "People are going and knocking on doors every night and arguing with people who don't take the pledge." Commune officials assigned to pursue the campaign are told "you must not be afraid of being beaten."
>
> A commune official said that 92 percent of the couples in that area with one child or less had taken the "one family, one child" pledge. "But what are you going to do about those who don't sign?" the researcher asked.
>
> "Everybody is going to sign the pledge," the official said.[70]

In Heilongjiang it was reported from an urban area in 1982 that couples were required to apply for a single-child certificate before they could register their first child.[71] Fujian province in early 1983 announced that all workers, staff, and cadres must apply for a single-child certificate or they would have their income reduced.[72] Under the cadre job responsibility system in some localities, cadres can receive a bonus only if all couples with one child sign a single-child pledge.[73]

It appears that it is this kind of universal requirement to sign the pledge which has produced single-child certificate acceptance rates of 70 to 99 percent in Sichuan, Jiangsu, Shandong, Shanghai, and other places, as shown in Table 7.1. But, one might ask, how can the local governments in these provinces succeed in forcing universal signatures? Perhaps the people have really been persuaded that the one-child limit is best for the country and themselves, and therefore they have all voluntarily signed the pledge. This is unlikely for several reasons. For example, the Birth Planning Leading Group in 1978 commissioned surveys to find out what proportion of couples were receptive to signing a one-child pledge. The response was described in the following December 1979 official speech:

The investigation shows that among the 16,768 women of childbearing age questioned in Shanghai, about 60 percent of those in the city districts are willing to have only one child. In the suburbs near the city, it is about 19 percent. In the suburbs farther away, it is only 1.9 percent. In Fuzhou Municipality of Fujian Province, it is 18.5 percent. Among the 3,719 couples of childbearing age questioned in factories, on the streets, and in government offices in Changsha and Shaoyang Municipalities in Hunan Province, it is 34.6 percent. A survey carried out in Hebei shows 11.35 percent in cities, and 11.4 percent in rural areas. Based on model surveys, we projected in January [1979] the population growth, and suggested that the targeted one-child rate for cities be set at 20 percent, and that for rural areas at 5 percent for 1980. Thereafter, the rate would be raised gradually to reach 80 percent in cities and 50 percent in rural areas by 1985.[74]

A propaganda campaign could increase somewhat the percentage of couples freely volunteering to stop childbearing after one child, but not from these low rates in rural areas as of 1978 to, say, 75 percent in 1979 or 1980. The difference between the suggestive survey results of 1978 and the later reported high pledge rates, after some allowance for the motivational effect of an educational campaign, is a rough measure of the enormous number of married couples in China who have been compelled to sign the one-child pledge against their will.

Universal required signatures on one-child pledges are supported by the government, while universal forced signatures in other realms have been scathingly denounced as "bogus democracy." For example, in October 1979 the *People's Daily* reported on a people's commune whose leaders forced all members to sign statements that they did not want their private plots of land back from the collective. A newspaper reporter went to investigate:

My firsthand investigation turned out to be just the opposite from the situation stated by the commune and cadres. Over 90 percent of the commune members preferred to cultivate their own private plots. I then asked them why they had put their thumbprints on those "signed documents" to "consent" to collective farming. Some commune members replied: "It was a trap set by the cadres; I was just compelled to take what's given in silence like a dumb person tasting bitter herbs!". . . We can once again discern the grave consequences of the pernicious influence of the ultra-"Left" line of Lin Biao and the "gang of four," and we are now certain that although the problem is seen at the grassroots level, its roots lay with the upper level.[75]

China's national government always disclaims any responsibility for the frequent occurrence of coercive practices in the birth control program, blaming them instead on the local cadres. But in fact the local cadres are required to succeed in reducing the birth rate, reducing the natural population increase rate, reporting a high single-child certificate acceptance rate and a high contraceptive prevalence rate. When the people resist, local cadres must either fail in their assigned high-priority tasks, coerce the people into compliance, or falsify the data they report upward. When the local cadres report failure, they are publicly criticized and admonished to stop wavering in their determination to succeed. Always speaking in euphemisms, the media urge the local cadres to achieve the ends no matter what the means required.[76] Indeed, when it comes to family planning program abuses, the reporter's conclusion applies here too: the roots of coercion originate from the top.

A nationwide policy of forced signatures on fertility-limitation contracts has become evident with the advent and spread of the "double-contract" system in agriculture. When the production responsibility system took hold throughout the nation, peasants began ignoring the economic penalties for bearing more than one or two children. They realized that under a system of family farming, more sons could mean greater income for the family in spite of the stipulated penalties for higher fertility.

To counteract this tendency, some localities devised a system whereby any peasant families who tilled land contracted out to them by the collective were required to sign a contract stating that they would bear no children during that production year. A couple who bore a child was declared to have violated the family planning and agricultural double contract with the collective. Harsh economic penalties followed, including sharp reductions in family land allotments or even the withdrawal of the entire allotment. This punitive system was so successful in controlling fertility that provincial and national governments have promoted or required its spread. As the double-contract system has become standard in many provinces, they have reported success in curbing births above one per couple.[77] Double contracts have become very widespread. For instance, as of early 1983, Liaoning province announced that "More than 70 percent of the production teams in Liaoning have established a family planning responsibility system together with the production responsibility system."[78] At the same time Shandong reported:

> The responsibility system in farm production which emerged in recent years is now followed by the adoption of a "double-contracting" system, whereby a peasant is required to sign two contracts with the production team, one for grain output and the other for family planning.
>
> As an economic incentive for family planning, this system has been instituted in 70 percent of the counties in Shandong. Other counties are following suit. . . .
>
> A commune member is awarded and accorded preferential treatment if he fulfills his contracted responsibility in both farm production and family planning. He who fails will be penalized according to the contracts. Those who refuse to comply with family planning are not entitled to sign contracts for farm production.[79]

The compulsory nature of China's family planning program is manifested in several main techniques: forced abortion, required IUD insertion, forced IUD retention, and forced sterilization. How widespread these practices are has obviously not been documented and publicized by the government, because to acknowledge that the instances were not confined to isolated cases would implicate the national and provincial governments as well. But indications are that these abusive techniques are widely practiced.

The required insertion of intrauterine devices appears to have been widespread during the late 1970's and early 1980's. It became explicit national policy in late 1982 with this order from the State Family Planning Commission: "Women of childbearing age with one child must be fitted with IUD's."[80] Usually in rural areas, IUD insertion would not be required by the authorities until after a couple had borne one child, but in late 1980 Tianjin Municipality reported that in some places an IUD was a precondition for legal marriage: "In some communes and brigades, stipulations have been set that a planned parenthood deposit must first be made, that a single-child certificate must be applied for, or that an IUD must be inserted before marriage registration would be carried out. Otherwise, marriage registration would be refused."[81]

Once the IUD is in place, it appears, couples cannot choose when to have it removed, go to a barefoot doctor or regular doctor, request the removal, and automatically have the request honored. They may resort to trying to remove it themselves or hiring an illegal IUD-removal specialist. Guangdong province in 1981 reported to a visiting delegation that strings were no longer attached to IUD's, a decision made to prevent removal of IUD's by the couples themselves.[82] The lack of a string makes removal more difficult and potentially dangerous for the woman.

China's press has documented numerous instances of women going to illegal practitioners. One "criminal element," a former barefoot doctor, reportedly followed around a county's planned parenthood operating team in 1978, offering to remove IUD's that had just been inserted. He did a brisk business but was caught and sentenced to two years' imprisonment because, as a result of his services, "a group of women gave birth to unplanned children, thus seriously disrupting planned parenthood work."[83] Since then similar reports have increased. The government is alarmed by this wave of "unplanned" IUD removals because it threatens the success of the one-child-per-couple program, and because some women die from resulting infections. The Ministry of Justice in 1981 authorized severe criminal punishment for those who illegally remove IUD's, and in some localities women who have an IUD in place are subjected to monthly X-rays or quarterly physical examinations to ensure that their IUD's have not fallen out or been removed.[84] As of 1983, Fujian province reported that illegal removal of IUD's in the rural areas was "extremely serious," and a county in Sichuan noted that "Since 1980, there have been more than 10,000 childbearing [age] women in the county who have stealthily removed their IUD's."[85]

When a woman gets pregnant outside the state's birth plan, after an illegal IUD removal or in other circumstances, it is likely that local cadres will attempt to "mobilize" her to have an abortion. In many urban areas and some rural areas, family planning workers reportedly keep monthly records of women's menstrual periods so they can detect when anyone gets pregnant. As soon as a pregnancy is detected and confirmed, if the pregnancy is not the first birth to a married woman or is not in the current government-authorized birth plan, family planning workers start suggesting that the woman volunteer to have an abortion. If that does not work, then they attempt to insist on an abortion. Couples are forced by government policy to resort to "trickery" in order to maintain a second or higher order pregnancy.[86] A woman might lie to the family planning workers about her menstrual periods until the pregnancy is halfway through, but then she would be vulnerable to political and economic reprisals by the government. In those rural areas where record-keeping on each woman is not so extensive, a couple wanting an "extra" baby might hide the pregnancy as long as possible and then refuse to submit to an abortion. For pregnant women in the PRC today, the continual official harassment throughout their pregnancies must be physically and emotionally draining. One article describes the official harassment process this way:

> [Mao Yuanying], former deputy director of the Xiangtan county people's armed forces department, has been dismissed from his post and downgraded for refusal to practice planned parenthood. [Mao] has three daughters. The organization frequently urged him and his wife to undergo sterilization, but he refused. In June this year, when his wife was found to be pregnant for the fourth time, the county people's armed forces, Xiangtan military subdistrict and the planned parenthood office sent people to Shaoshan on seven occasions to mobilize her to have her pregnancy artificially terminated. [Mao] had the gall to say to the comrades who had come to carry out mobilization work, "My mind is made up; I want this child." The comrades of the military sub-district, the CCP [Chinese Communist Party] committee of the county people's armed forces department and the planned parenthood leadership groups at all levels conducted education for him dozens of times but he turned a deaf ear. Eventually the fourth child was born.[87]

Some of the provincial governments appear to be unconcerned with the detrimental effects that forced abortion has on women. All that seems to matter, if the press is any guide, is keeping down the number of births each year in the province through any means. In China's press, induced abortions are euphemistically termed "remedial measures." As one example, in July 1979 Guangdong province urged local officials to increase the number of abortions in order to keep down the total birth rate for the whole year, because the number of births which had already taken place in the first half of the year was considered too many:

> At present, we must shift our work emphasis to women who are pregnant, particularly to women who have more than one child. We must seriously advise them and take remedial measures. . . . We must do our best to mobilize and persuade those who already have one child and are expecting a second child to have only one child and not to give birth to the second child. . . . We must mobilize those who have unplanned pregnancies to adopt effective remedial measures to solve the problem. All units and departments must go into immediate action and do well in mobilization, persuasion, and education work. We must especially get a serious grasp of the crucial period of July, August, and September.[88]

Pregnant women whose births were expected before the end of 1979 would already have been over three months pregnant by the time of that announcement, and by the end of September would be at least six months pregnant. The "remedial measures" suggested, therefore, would mean second or third trimester abortions, which are more dangerous to the health of the women than first trimester abortions. Yet Guangdong province officials announced on November 9, 1979, that because "the provincial birth rate from January to September rose by 1.53 per thousand compared with the corresponding period of last year," leaders "at all levels must attach a high degree of importance to this situation, adopt resolute and effective measures, and strive to ensure that the birth rate does not rise this year, or shows a slight decline."[89] This instruction implies that local leaders should require abortions of women who were seven or eight months pregnant, a policy that continued in the following years. Guangdong family planning authorities reported that 80 percent of the 624,000 abortions performed in 1982 were carried out "by order," and that one-third of the terminations were in the sixth month of pregnancy or later.[90] Then in November 1983, the Guangdong Provincial Family Planning Commission mandated very late abortions by instructing that in the last two months of the year "all authorities concerned in Guangdong Province should take remedial measures to cope with pregnancy cases beyond the limits of quotas . . . so as to fulfill this year's target of population control and to win an overall victory in this year's family planning work."[91]

Guangdong is not the only province that has emphasized late abortion as a primary means of limiting the number of births. Shandong province in August 1979 ordered local officials to take "[r]emedial measures . . . to deal with unwanted pregnancies, a condition which should not be considered absolute, so that the natural population growth of our province can be lowered to 8/1,000 this year."[92] Jiangxi province in May 1980 ordered local leaders to "resolutely terminate" all pregnancies "in excess of the plan" for 1980. In September 1981 the Yunnan Provincial Family Planning Office encouraged local leaders "to concentrate the technical forces and to adopt remedial measures before the fall harvest and during the winter months to strictly control excessive numbers of births." Family planning workers in Fujian province were ordered to strictly control births outside the 1982 plan by taking remedial measures against "unplanned pregnancies" in May and June of that year.[93] The implementation of "remedial measures" reached its logical extreme in Huiyang prefecture of Guangdong province in May-July 1981 as pregnant women were rounded up, bound, herded into vehicles, and transported to hospitals where they were subjected to mass forced abortions, according to an investigative report by a pro-Communist periodical in Hong Kong. Guangdong's leaders subsequently chose Huiyang as the province's model prefecture in family planning work and instructed other leaders to learn from Huiyang![94] Though national authorities are eager to divorce themselves from all responsibility for these instances of coercion, they are ultimately at fault because they insist on the achievement of a low natural population increase rate by any means. Once again, "although the problem is seen at the grassroots level, its roots lay with the upper level."

The negative effects of periodic forced abortion campaigns have been explicitly recognized in some 1982 and 1983 reports, such as this one from a Shandong province model county in family planning:

> In previous years when we carried out family planning work we used to do a crash job. Several times a year we would bring the work to a high tide and perform a number of abortions. Although some results were achieved, the situation in our county shows that three disadvantages resulted from only emphasizing crash jobs and not doing regular work well. First, it tied up so much of the energy of the leadership at all levels that it affected the performance of other work. Second, during these high tide periods, operations were concentrated in a short period of time. This exceeded the technical and material capabilities of the hospitals and put a great deal of pressure on them. Furthermore, the operations tended to be done crudely and mishaps occurred. Third, it affected our relations with the masses. When time is pressing and effort is focused, and when ideological work cannot catch up with the progress of events, it is easy for punishments on a large scale, for coercion, and for antagonism on the part of the masses to occur.[95]

During 1983 the media also noted potential harmful effects on women of abortions late in pregnancy and emphasized the need for preventing late abortions by detecting pregnancies early and carrying out required abortions promptly.[96] However, a municipality in Liaoning was praised as a model for its 1982 performance because "Women with unplanned pregnancies were subjected to remedial operations . . . and no time limit was set on the pregnancies."[97]

In preparation for the family planning propaganda months of 1983 and 1984, the national leadership ordered that "Women with unplanned pregnancies must adopt remedial measures as soon as possible."[98] Provincial governments echoed the required abortion policy.[99] However, the government expects that its policy of required sterilization will reduce the incidence of "repeated unplanned pregnancies and repeated use of remedial measures" accompanied by "violent methods."[100] Several 1983 reports emphasized that sterilization will reduce "the necessity for taking remedial measures" and therefore will protect women's health.[101] The authorities prefer the finality of sterilization. The head of the Hainan Regional Communist Party Committee expressed this view:

> In the past we were busy performing induced abortions every year. This could only bring about a temporary solution but it cannot effect a permanent cure. In the current upsurge of family planning work, we should concentrate on performing sterilizations.[102]

Pressure on couples to have the wife or husband sterilized escalated during the 1970's. At first forced sterilization was directed at still-fecund couples who already had many children. By 1980 couples bearing a third child, especially if they were cadres, were sometimes subjected to required sterilization, as in this instance: "A couple in Guizhou have been subjected to severe disciplinary action for having a third child in defiance of the state guidelines. According to the *Guizhou Daily*, the wife, Wen Jifang, who had been deputy head of a county people's court in the province, was stripped of the court post as a disciplinary measure. Her husband, Lu Yutang, deputy head of the public prosecutor's office in the same county, was ordered to be sterilized."[103] In the early 1980's before it became national policy, some areas tried to require couples to be sterilized after the birth of a second child. For instance Guangdong province, in its drive to stop all third and higher order births, stipulated in 1981 that "all couples who have had two or more children must be mobilized to undergo sterilization."[104] Needless to say, there are many couples in China who do not wish to be sterilized after the birth of two children. There have been reports that in some rural areas, sterilization teams are sent to a village to "mobilize" all eligible couples to have one partner sterilized. "Eligible" is defined by the state. Sometimes when it is rumored that a sterilization team is coming to a village, "eligible" people flee. One county in Sichuan reported that until 1983 sterilization had been performed on whoever was caught.[105] A county official in Hunan complained in late 1979:

> When certain comrades in the rural areas are mobilized to carry out sterilization measures, they run off to the urban office, factory, mine, or unit where their

spouses work. Their communes and brigades then send telegrams, make phone calls, and dispatch people to the units concerned to contact the responsible comrades and request them to assist in conducting ideological education for those comrades and mobilize them to return to their production teams for sterilization measures. Some units are very cooperative in doing this. However, the leading comrades of other units do not concern themselves with it. . . . As a result, sterilization measures cannot be carried out on these comrades. According to investigations, there are over 800 persons who should be sterilized on the 82 communes of Hengyang County.[106]

This source and others like it emphasize the importance of conducting sterilizations on the spot, as soon as either member of the couple has been "convinced" after intensive indoctrination to submit to sterilization.[107] In other countries like the United States, it has been realized that sterilization conducted immediately after a person has been persuaded to be sterilized is by its very nature a coercive procedure, because the person does not have time to reflect upon that decision. Once performed, the sterilization operation must be assumed irreversible, particularly in a country where official permission would be required for any attempt to reverse the sterility caused by the procedure.

The Hunan report is not an isolated instance. In early 1980 a foreign correspondent reported, "Officials have complained that in Henan Province many men are hiding to avoid required sterilization operations."[108] A Hong Kong Communist magazine documented serious abuses in southern Fujian province in early 1980. All women who had borne two children and were still potentially fecund were reportedly required to be sterilized in some localities. Some were physically bound and dragged to commune clinics for tubal ligations, and families were threatened with complete cutoff of grain rations and loss of all their property if they resisted, according to this report.[109]

China's forced sterilization policy has been escalated by setting province-level sterilization quotas—the targeted number of sterilizations to be performed that year in the province—and then allocating part of the quota to each subunit, which is then expected to perform that many sterilization operations. This happened, for instance, in Guizhou province in 1978.[110] If voluntary sterilizations do not meet this target, then the unit would be strongly tempted to resort to compulsory sterilization.

The policy of required sterilization would be ethically questionable even if all operations were carried out by skilled doctors under sterile conditions without physical side effects. To compound the insult, China has continual problems with the low quality of sterilization operations. The press rarely mentions the particular side effects, which could include infection, loss of sexual function, or even death. Press reports do imply that some provinces have increased the number of sterilizations regardless of shortages of technically trained personnel and appropriate medical supplies, for instance in this 1978 report on the conclusions of a conference in Yunnan: "The public health departments must vigorously strengthen technical guidance for planned parenthood and constantly improve the quality of sterilization techniques to guarantee the safety and health of the women undergoing such operations. Departments and units concerned must improve the quality of instruments and medicine used in sterilizations. Meanwhile, they must deliver such instruments and medicine according to plans."[111]

The policy of required sterilization, which had been sporadic and unevenly implemented around China, became national in scope during the first family planning propaganda month, January 1983, and thereafter. The national leadership made this decision and ordered provincial governments to carry it out, as revealed by the Vice Governor of Guangdong province quoting from the national directive:

> The technical policy of birth control is formulated by the State Family Planning Commission with the approval of the leadership of the Party Central. Its principal content is: "Those women who have already given birth to one child must be fitted with IUD's, and couples who already have two children must undergo sterilization by either the husband or the wife. Women with unplanned pregnancies must adopt remedial measures as soon as possible." This is based on the directives of the CCP Central Committee and the State Council and on the summation of family planning practice for many years.[112]

A circular was issued in early December 1982 by the highest national party and government departments and ministries concerned with family planning. It stated: "Permanent birth control measures are to be carried out among those who already have two children."[113]

Beginning in November 1982, provincial governments echoed the national directives in provincial newspapers and radio broadcasts, ordering that "one of the spouses in married couples of childbearing age who have two or more children must undergo a permanent type of birth control measure."[114] During the January 1983 propaganda month, sterilization was emphasized.[115] As the year progressed, the focus of family planning work shifted even more toward required sterilization. For example, Hebei province reported in April: "By summing up the experiences and lessons of the propaganda month activities, all areas have started this year to take sterilization as the main task. All couples of childbearing age who already have two or more children will be sterilized except for special cases."[116] Guangdong province reported that a May 1983 provincial meeting "decided that the focal point of family planning work for the province at present must be placed on compulsory sterilization for either party, husband or wife, of those couples who already have two children."[117] In November of that year, the provinces of Henan and Ningxia announced that in the winter and spring they would emphasize the sterilization of all those who "should" be sterilized.[118] This policy continued in 1984. For instance, an April conference of planned parenthood directors in Guangdong vowed to "continue to focus on ligations. Ligation measures should be implemented for all those for whom such measures are appropriate and who have not yet undergone them."[119]

Based on family planning service statistics and permanent population registration data, probably supplemented by census and fertility survey data, the provinces estimated at the end of 1982 or in early 1983 the number of couples "eligible" for sterilization. In most provinces this figure would have included all Han Chinese couples with two or more living children if the woman was under age 40, plus some different formula for eligible minority group couples. Apparently, this number was then used as the province's sterilization target for 1983, if it was thought that the hospitals and mobile medical teams could carry out that many sterilizations in a year. Otherwise the total number of required sterilizations was targeted over two or more years. Provincial leaders divided up the 1983 provincial sterilization quota into quotas for the various prefectures, counties, and municipalities, and these subunits were ordered to carry out the targeted number of sterilizations for 1983. Tianjin Municipality in December 1982 set the goal that over 70 percent of the married women of reproductive age in its rural areas would be sterilized by sometime in 1983.[120] Shaanxi province reported in late January 1983 that one of its counties had in one month sterilized half of "those who should undergo sterilization," and another county more than half.[121] Guangdong province decided in early 1983 that the 5.2 million couples of childbearing age with two or more children were to be sterilized. Of these, 2.5 million were sterilized by October 1983, and 2.7 million more sterilizations were targeted for completion in three years. By late that year, 32 counties in Guangdong reportedly had "overfulfilled their annual ligation quotas."[122] Hebei province targeted 2.06 million sterilizations for 1983, and decided that by the end of 1984 the task of sterilizing "all the couples of childbearing age who should undergo sterilization" would be basically accomplished.[123] By the end of May 1983, Hebei had carried out 1.77 million sterilizations, representing 86 percent of the year's quota. Then provincial government pressure was increased on the "leading comrades in quite a number of units" who "still fail to attach sufficient importance to this work." These leaders were admonished that "certain people who should have these operations have not yet done so."[124]

Nationwide, as discussed in the previous chapter, 3.58 million sterilizations were carried out during the first family planning propaganda month of January 1983. In February, the national health journal of the Ministry of Public Health noted that "based on investigation, there are still more than 17 million couples in the country who need to undergo sterilization."[125] Since 10 million sterilizations were performed in China from the beginning of 1983 to early August, there were an additional 11 million sterilizations targeted for completion during that year and the immediately succeeding years. No figure is yet available on the number of sterilizations carried out nationwide after August 1983. In June 1984, by which time a large proportion of the targeted required sterilizations had presumably been implemented, the national government belatedly reversed its policy and said:

> Surgical quotas will not be handed down from the upper levels to the lower levels. The number of operations must be scheduled based on seeking truth from facts to avoid the negative results of overconcentration. Sterilization is to be promoted based on the willingness of couples of childbearing age with two or more children, but it must not be carried out indiscriminately and must take individual circumstances into consideration.[126]

However, this emphasis on voluntarism should be assessed with caution. China has always claimed that all the required sterilizations are voluntary.

Some parts of China have encouraged or required sterilization for couples with only one child. Already in early 1979, sterilization after the birth of one child was being promoted as "the Party's policy" in the capital of Gansu province: "The Lanchow Municipal Planned Parenthood Committee recently held a rally to cite 43 comrades who have actively implemented the party's policy on planned parenthood, taken the lead to break away from old traditions and habits and were sterilized after producing only one child. All of the 43 comrades were awarded 100 yuan."[127] In 1983, a national health journal praised the example of one village that implemented special rewards for sterilization after the birth of one daughter.[128]

Even those who strongly support compulsory family planning have sometimes voiced reservations about the wisdom of required sterilization after one birth. For example, at the September 1980 National People's Congress, a deputy from Jiangxi province included in his speech the following comments:

> So long as we make things clear to the masses, everyone will consciously practice birth control. Of course, we must also combine propaganda and education with mandatory systems. If we just conduct publicity without taking strong measures, the natural population growth rate will also not drop. . . . We must not use the same contraceptive techniques in every case. So long as something effective has been done, we should not insist on ligation as the only means. In some areas, female comrades are now subjected to ligation after one child. This is not good. So

TABLE 7.2
Contraceptive Mix in the PRC, 1982–83

	September 1982		Yearend 1983	
Method	Millions of couples	Percent of users	Millions of couples	Percent of users
IUD	59.2	50.16%	50.8	41.0%
Tubal ligation	30.0	25.39	46.4	37.4
Vasectomy	11.8	10.00	16.0	12.9
Oral pill	10.0	8.44	6.3	5.1
Condom	2.4	2.00	2.6	2.1
Other	4.7	4.01	1.9	1.5
TOTAL	118	100.00%	124	100.0%

SOURCES: Table 6.2; Yu Wang & Xiao (1984): 9; Shen Guoxiang (1984): 6.

NOTE: For both dates, the only figures reported were the total number of couples practicing contraception (118 million and 124 million, respectively) and the percentage using each method. The estimated numbers of couples using each method are derived figures.

long as they do not want any more children, it is all right. Why must they be subjected to "an operation?"[129]

Sichuan province's model county in family planning, Shifang county, emphasized sterilization throughout the 1970's. By the end of 1980, it reported, 96 percent of the couples with two or more children had been sterilized. At that point the county decided to "no longer stress sterilization of couples with only one child," noting that there is no guarantee that a sterilization can be reversed.[130]

Beginning in 1983, forced sterilization after one child has been used to punish women who get pregnant again without authorization. For example, Hebei province announced: "If a woman becomes pregnant outside the plan, she must take remedial measures, and at the same time one of the couple must undergo ligation or vasectomy."[131]

As a result of China's required sterilization program, during 1983 there was a great increase in the total number of married women of reproductive age who themselves were sterilized or whose husbands were sterilized. Table 7.2 compares contraceptive use nationwide based on the fertility survey of September 1982 with official figures from yearend 1983 whose statistical origin was not reported. During the short intervening period of one year and three months, the astounding number of 21 million people became contraceptively sterilized, including about 16.4 million married women in the reproductive ages and approximately 4.2 million men.

Ethical Problems of the Family Planning Program

In sum, the PRC's family planning program makes extensive use of compulsory family planning, compulsory limitation of the total number of children to one child, required signing of double contracts and pledges to stop at one child, forced sterilization, compulsory IUD acceptance, forced IUD retention, and forced abortion. There are many officials and scholars in China, and many observers abroad, who would defend all these means as justifiable and good because the end to which they are directed is absolutely critical. There is a genuine ethical dilemma here. Let us examine both sides of this question to show how difficult it is.

In defense of the family planning program, one might argue that China is in a desperate situation that requires a desperate solution. For several decades before 1978, food production barely increased as fast as population growth in China, and the standard of living for most of the people was hardly better than before. The economic liberalization of the late 1970's and early 1980's has improved the situation, but further increases in production of food and other essentials will be difficult to attain, given China's unfavorable balance between population and resources. It is urgent that as much of the future production increases as possible go to raising popular living standards rather than just feeding more people. Without compulsory family planning, China's population might continue to grow at a rate averaging 1.5–2.0 percent a year for the next twenty years, but with compulsory fertility limitation that rate may be kept around 1.0 percent. This might mean the difference between economic stagnation on a per capita basis for the next two decades and rising living standards. China's people presumably want a rise in living standards, but for that, it is argued, a price must be exacted in the form of sacrifices from the generation of young adults reaching childbearing age between the mid-1970's and the end of the century. Compulsion is necessary because it is in each couple's genuine self-interest to have many children while letting somebody else limit fertility for the good of society. Only if everyone is forced to stop at one child will anyone be convinced to do so; then all will benefit when economic development can overtake population growth.

In opposition to the compulsory and coercive elements of China's family planning program, one might argue that forced family planning is repugnant to the great majority of the people of the world and the governments of the world, as well as to the millions subjected to coercion in China. The end cannot justify the means. China's government should simply continue improving the supply of all birth control techniques and continue its skillful educational and motivational work, but should abandon all forms of compulsion and allow couples to bear the number of children they think appropriate at a time suitable to them. The people of China are not stupid, nor are they insensitive to the needs of the wider society. With some education in simple demographic principles and a full choice of birth control techniques, both of which the government has shown itself remarkably capable of delivering, the vast majority of married couples of reproductive age will make responsible choices concerning number and spacing of their children, taking into account their personal and family needs, their community's needs, and their country's needs. China's government is not so wise that it can be depended on to make all the right economic and demographic choices for the people now or in the future. After all, it made a devastating series of mistakes of economic and demographic policy from 1949 right up to the late 1970's, partly because it imposed unpopular policies on the people, blocking their freedom of choice as well as all free public discussion of policy options.

Continuing this line of argument, the people of China can and should be allowed complete voluntarism in family planning, even if it means that the population growth rate is over 1.5 percent annually for the next two decades. This phenomenon is a natural and temporary result of the current age structure, and there is no justification for panic. China's situation is not nearly as desperate as it appears to the current leadership. Great progress has been made on many fronts since 1949, not least the provision of family planning services nationwide and a raised popular consciousness of the societal implications of personal fertility decisions. Voluntary family planning would get rid of the embarrassing contradictions between the government's verbal support for women's rights and its systematic violation of their reproductive freedom, between the government's claims that family planning is voluntary and the facts that prove otherwise, and between the government's policies of increasing freedom of economic decision-making and ever-decreasing freedom of fertility decision-making. Full voluntarism in family planning would also get rid of an unpopular government policy that causes dissatisfaction and resistance to the government today.

Whether the government decides to continue or discontinue the coercive aspects of its family planning program is an important consideration for any other government or any international organization that wants to help China in the population field. Such organizations are partly constrained to operate within the guidelines laid down by their constituents. For example, international meetings and forums sponsored by the United Nations frequently reiterate the internationally accepted standard that all use of birth control should be voluntary. The UN World Population Conference in 1974 adopted the World Population Plan of Action, which recommended that all countries "[r]espect and ensure, regardless of their over-all demographic goals, the right of persons to determine, in a free, informed and responsible manner, the number and spacing of their children."[132] The PRC concurred in the almost unanimous adoption of this Plan of Action. In July 1981 a UN Symposium on Population and Human

Rights emphasized, "Both compulsory use of abortion and its unqualified prohibition would be serious violations of human rights." Also that year a UN conference of the world's least developed countries adopted a Program of Action that called for "upholding and promoting the voluntary nature of population control measures."[133] The 1984 International Population Conference restated the right of persons to determine their own fertility, and again China agreed to the document.

China's family planning program is in violation of these oft-stated principles. China is also the most populous member country of the UN and as such has some claim to its population-related support and funding. The United Nations Fund for Population Activities has contributed to China's 1982 census, demographic training and research, contraceptive production, and training of family planning personnel since 1980. In this context, the Fund has some hard decisions to make about what types of financial aid to China's population programs are consistent with internationally accepted ethical principles. Foreign governments and voluntary family planning organizations face similar choices when considering verbal support for or financial assistance to China's family planning program. Only if and when an organization or government explicitly endorses compulsory family planning can it wholeheartedly approve the PRC's family planning program without violating its own principles. Finally, journalists and scholars who research, write about, and speak about the demography of China have a moral and ethical obligation not to gloss over the compulsory and coercive qualities in China's family planning program, so that their audiences can reach an informed judgment.[134]

This discussion has not included all the ethical questions inherent in China's family planning program. For example, the current push for the one-child family appears at first glance to be totally fair: every couple is allowed one and no more than one child, if the government has its way. But to impose the same limit on rural couples as on urban couples is discriminatory. Whereas an only child in an urban setting is very likely to survive and prosper, a rural child is subjected to more risks. Infant and childhood mortality are much higher in the countryside; therefore, the death of a rural couple's child before adulthood is a much greater possibility than the death of an only child in an urban area. Besides, the long-term welfare of rural couples is much more dependent on raising children than is the case for urban couples. To be childless in old age, or to be dependent on one child who turns out to be unwilling or incapable of supporting his or her parents, is more likely to be catastrophic for rural than for urban families. Rural families, then, are forced to take more risks with less guarantee that they will reap their fair share of the benefits. Therefore, the universal one-child limit is an unfair policy that discriminates against the rural population of China.

Another equally serious fault of the one-child policy is the government's arbitrary and intentional designation of two classes of children born in the 1970's and thereafter. The privileged class consists of children in one-child families; the low class consists of all children who have siblings, with the worst discrimination reserved for the higher parity children. All sorts of benefits are by policy given preferentially to the only child: free medical care, immunizations, priority in schooling, free schooling, extra food, extra clothing, first in line for everything. The only child, who did not earn these benefits, may risk the psychological hazards of being born to unjust privilege. Similarly, children with siblings are systematically denied free medical care, and some are effectively denied even the right to receive medical care, because by government policy higher parity children may not belong to cooperative medical services in the countryside.[135] Children with siblings are by policy last in line for everything—education, medical care, food, clothing, housing—which in China means that the government intentionally denies them some of the essentials of life. Children with siblings, through no fault of their own, are made to feel unworthy. They may grow to resent the unfair treatment they have received, become alienated from identifying with socialist China, and tend toward antisocial activities in the future.

Some Chinese teachers and parents have perceived this danger. In August 1981, after the one-child policy had been in effect for two years, the Beijing *Worker's Daily* printed two letters from readers deploring the discriminatory treatment against children of multi-child families, and the editorial comment, after an obligatory statement in support of the one-child policy, agreed with the letters:

Comrade Editor: . . . In recent years, we have seen some harm done to the feelings of young children by the so-called "distinction" in treatment. The single child is given priority receiving injections in hospitals. The other children are pushed back even though they had been waiting in line ahead of the only child. In kindergartens, children of one-child families receive sweets twice a day, whereas the other children get some only once a day, or twice a day at half the amount. In student enrollment, children of one-child families are given priority regardless of the quality of their earlier school performance. . . . These kinds of manmade contradictions are not only harmful to the unity among the children, they are also harmful to the pure and beautiful souls of the children. They induce the only child to acquire a sense of superiority and hurt the self-esteem of the other children. . . . We are appealing here that everyone refrain from making these "distinctions" noticeable to the children.

Comrade Editor: . . . In some units, a special status has been artificially created for the single child. This policy encourages the children of one-child families to acquire an improper attitude, as if they were a head taller than the others. The incentives for having a single child are directed toward the parents, not toward the children. When the children are born, they should have equal social status in new

China. Shades of inequality must not be painted upon their young souls. The control of population growth and the encouragement to have only one child are great plans of the state for the four modernizations. But doing well in child education to enable children to grow up intellectually and physically healthy is an even more important matter relating to the future and the fate of our country. We implore all relevant departments not to inflict unfavorable effects upon the pure souls of the children.[136]

A disturbing increase in female infanticide has come as a direct result of China's imposition of rigid fertility limits irrespective of the sex of a couple's child or children. The practice of killing or abandoning baby girls was common before 1949, but appeared to be in abeyance for the next three decades as most people had all the children they wanted and had reasonable assurance that the minimum subsistence needs of their large families would be met.[137] But at the end of the 1970's and in the early 1980's, the government severely restricted the number of children allowed per family. Some couples appear to have made the desperate decision that if they have to stop at three children, or two, or one, there absolutely must be at least one surviving son.

The phenomenon of rising female infanticide was first reported in the Chinese press in 1981 and was said to have occurred "after the extensive promotion of one child per couple."[138] Because infanticide is illegal, it is not directly reported and its extent must be inferred indirectly from other data. There is great room for error in such estimates. For instance, 1981 births reported to 1982 census enumerators had a sex ratio of 108.5 boys per hundred girls. If the actual sex ratio at birth was 106.0, then the births of about 232,000 girls were not reported. Some of the girls may have still been alive at census time, and their births were unreported because the respondents forgot the births of children less valued or were suppressing information about female births for some reason. Some of the missing girls were probably victims of infanticide. The 1982 fertility survey got a sex ratio of 107.8 for 1981 births, but in this case, the sex ratio of reported first and second parity births combined was 106.0, as one would expect. All the unreported female births were those of third and higher parity, equivalent to a total of about 173,000 girls whose births were unreported, if the sex ratio of 106.0 is assumed to hold at higher parities as should be the case.[139] Again there are several possible reasons for the underreporting, one of which is infanticide. The fertility survey thus indirectly suggests that as of 1981 most infanticide was the killing of infant girls of third or higher parity.

It is possible that as the one-child limit has been more effectively enforced, infanticide of firstborn and secondborn girls has become more pronounced, but no evidence is available. Anecdotal accounts in the press suggest that firstborn girls are drowned or abandoned to allow another authorized pregnancy that might be a boy.[140] According to press reports, infanticide seems to be almost nonexistent in some places while happening all the time in other places. The problem appears serious in Anhui province. The census reported a 1981 sex ratio at birth of 112.5 boys per hundred girls, and some counties reported figures as high as 130.7. It was reported that "the principal cause of the disproportion in the sex ratio at birth was infanticide," especially in Anhui's rural areas. In one county, 59 percent of the infant deaths were thought to be infanticide.[141] Abnormally high sex ratios among infants have been reported in some urban as well as rural areas in several provinces, and infanticide is always assumed to be the cause.[142]

The increasing female infanticide was an unintended result of the government's rigid fertility limitation policies. Official response at first was to absolve the government of any responsibility, to blame lingering feudal attitudes, and to punish these criminal acts without questioning the underlying causes of the resurgence of infanticide. In late 1984, however, there were hints that the government might allow some couples with female children to have another pregnancy and birth, in an attempt to head off some of the infanticide. Some areas have instituted extra awards and preferences for families with an only daughter.[143]

A final ethical question regarding China's family planning program has to do with medical research and, in particular, birth control research. China has in recent decades conducted massive clinical trials of vacuum aspiration abortion techniques, steroid contraceptives, intrauterine devices, a male birth control drug call gossypol, abortifacient medications, and numerous other traditional and modern birth control drugs. International ethical standards require that human subjects in medical research have the option of refusal to participate, and may participate only after they have been educated about the research and have given their informed consent. International practice also dictates that medicines of unknown effect be tried out first on animals, and only after the medicines are judged non-lethal and without crippling side effects are they tested on humans. Recent discussions with medical researchers have suggested that in China the ethics of medical research on humans is barely discussed, the concept of informed consent appears largely unknown, and human clinical trials appear to come first before animal experiments. Therefore, any agency that aspires to work with the PRC conducting biomedical research on Chinese subjects should ensure that internationally accepted standards on human experimentation be followed.

"Eugenics"

Until the mid-1970's China's government had little knowledge of and showed little concern with the number of handicapped individuals in the country or the frequency and types of birth defects. But during the late 1970's, as the government first attempted to limit married couples to two children and then to one child, it began to concern itself with what it calls eugenics. What this word means to government leaders is that, since couples are allowed only one child, it is important that their child be healthy and without any physical or mental defects of hereditary or environmental origin: "At present, we advocate one child for every couple. How to ensure that the one and only child born to a couple is healthy and intelligent has become a common concern. Therefore, spreading the knowledge of eugenics and adopting practical measures to improve the hereditary qualities of our children has assumed a more pressing significance."[144]

Under the one-child program, if a couple's first child is defective or sickly, the couple may apply for an exception to the one-child limit, which they are supposed to be granted if their political unit has been allocated a large enough quota of births in its birth plan. The government therefore wants to prevent the births of handicapped persons so that it does not have to allow couples to have a second child: "The advocacy of eugenics plays an important role in the control of the population. If a couple gives birth to a deformed or retarded child, they are bound to demand a second child. This would not only increase the proportion of the population who are of inferior quality, but it would also increase the birth rate."[145]

This concern has in turn led to a wider exploration of the extent and causes of birth defects. Because knowledge of the causes of birth defects is still in its infancy in China, government and scholarly statements on the subject are sometimes rather superficial, as if a few simple measures could prevent all birth defects: "In order that the response to the Party Central Committee's call for each couple to have only one child can be carried out in practice, we should conduct a vigorous study on the science of eugenics, reduce or even eradicate congenital diseases among the babies, and improve the quality of our population."[146]

With this impetus, the government has attempted to ascertain how many defective persons there are in China. A 1980 article stated, "According to surveys, at the present there are between four and five million retarded persons in the country."[147] Another source later in 1980 ventured an estimate of the number of Chinese suffering from congenital defects: "Because we have long ignored the question of the quality of population, various congenital and hereditary diseases are quite serious in our country. A pressing current matter is to push forward the research into preventive eugenics. Wu Min, a geneticist and professor of the Chinese Institute of Medical Science, is the scholar who first proposed redressing the case concerning eugenics. According to his estimate, our country now has over 10 million people suffering from various congenital defects at a minimum."[148]

An occasional article suggests that the incidence of birth defects in China is increasing.[149] However, this supposed increase may be spurious. Until the 1970's the detection, recording, and classification of birth defects in China appears to have been nonexistent except in some city hospitals. Therefore, any reported rise in birth defects may reflect nothing more than better reporting of birth defects. What has probably happened in the last few decades is that certain kinds of birth defects have decreased greatly in incidence, such as those caused by diseases in the mother (like syphilis) or by conditions during pregnancy (such as opium addiction or severe malnutrition in the mother), or those congenital defects found most commonly in infants born to mothers under age 20 or over age 35 (such as Down's syndrome) now that childbearing at these ages has diminished sharply.

At the same time other kinds of birth defects could have increased in incidence, such as those caused by marriage between close relatives. China's historical taboo on marriages between persons with the same surname seems to have weakened in recent decades.[150] Meanwhile, the government has hampered the work of matchmakers whose job it is to introduce potential marriage partners from different villages, and it has exacerbated the problem of finding a mate outside one's own village by blocking most geographical movement out of rural localities. Therefore, it would not be surprising if China has had an increase in marriages of close relatives from within the same village. However, China apparently has not collected data over time on the incidence of marriage between close relatives. The discovery that certain rural areas, particularly remote mountain villages or small minority groups, now have high rates of marriage between close relatives does not necessarily mean that this phenomenon is new; perhaps it was always common. Chinese researchers are now discovering and documenting the negative health effects of this practice:

> Medical scientists believe that the custom of marriage between close relatives still prevailing in our country today is a major factor causing certain congenital diseases. Geneticists say that genetically speaking, marriage between first cousins, whether they have the same family name or not, may bring hereditary diseases to their offspring. In some remote, economically and culturally backward border regions and remote mountainous districts, various cases of congenital deformity and intellectual retardation are as high as 1 to 2 percent. This situation is closely

related to marriage between close relatives. The scientific workers of the Institute of Genetics of the Chinese Academy of Sciences recently conducted a survey of the marriages of the Hui, Dongxiang and Baoan nationalities in Linxia Hui Autonomous Prefecture, Gansu, and found that the rate of marriage between close relatives is as high as about 10 percent.[151]

Certain aspects of China's industrialization and modernization processes are thought to have caused increases in congenital defects. Some medical personnel have suggested that there has been an increase in birth defects due to serious air and water pollution, increasing use of pesticides and other chemicals, and the ingestion of certain antibiotics and other medicines in early pregnancy.[152]

It is not clear whether China today has a higher or lower proportion of its population handicapped than in the past. On the one hand, many debilitating diseases that once caused blindness, deafness, physical deformity, or mental deterioration have been eliminated or greatly reduced. The increased availability of first aid and medical treatment might also mean that fewer accidental injuries today result in permanent deformities. But on the other hand, probably a higher proportion of babies born with obvious birth defects have been allowed to live in recent years. Before 1949 a clearly defective baby would likely have died through passive or active infanticide. In addition, it is thought that more hereditary diseases are now being transmitted to subsequent generations as carriers more often live to reproductive age.

The PRC has begun to try to minimize birth defects. In order to rapidly diminish and eventually wipe out congenital defects caused by marriage between close relatives, the Marriage Law of 1981 forbids marriage "where the man and woman are lineal relatives by blood or collateral relatives by blood up to the third degree of relationship."[153] Previously such marriages were not illegal.

Also, in a few places, the government has set up premarital counseling centers in which a complete family health history is taken for each prospective spouse, and those individuals with potential hereditary diseases or infectious diseases are persuaded not to marry or are forbidden by law to marry.[154] The new Marriage Law prohibits the marriage of lepers. It has also been suggested that mentally retarded persons should be forbidden to procreate, and Jilin province in late 1983 enacted a strict policy to this effect.[155] The latest and most comprehensive list of contraindications to marriage was published in January 1981: "Premarital examination is, by means of clarification and examination, to uncover diseases which make it unsuitable for a couple to marry, such as leprosy and mental disorder, or diseases which make it inadvisable to marry for the time being, such as acute infectious diseases, tuberculosis, and serious heart, liver, and kidney disease."[156]

It may be presumed that the list of official medical grounds for forbidding marriage will expand. Yet universal marriage has been China's tradition. Perhaps anyone who suspected that he or she was a carrier of a hereditary disease might avoid mentioning the possibility, lie about it, or avoid any premarital health examination that was not compulsory, in order to be able to marry. Besides, only a few medically advanced localities have a premarital counseling service. Such elaborate screening before marriage is not likely to become commonplace for some time, especially in rural areas, because it is expensive, time-consuming, and requires medical expertise to detect potential hereditary defects or incurable infectious diseases.

Several doctors have also published suggestions that China emphasize early prenatal care in order to teach women not to ingest teratogenic substances in the most vulnerable first three months of pregnancy.[157] X-raying the fetus is also to be avoided, they suggest. But comprehensive prenatal care from the beginning of all pregnancies is a long way off in China, as in most countries. And since many birth defects have no known cause, preventing them is still impossible. Good prenatal care from early pregnancy is worth pursuing for the benefit of both mother and baby, and many birth defects can thereby be prevented, but such care can by no means ensure that every infant will be healthy.

Finally, the technique of amniocentesis has been introduced in a few cities to detect fetuses with chromosomal and metabolic defects, so that these fetuses can be aborted.[158] Amniocentesis and chromosome analysis are expensive and delicate processes that require modern medical equipment, skilled doctors, trained geneticists, and competent laboratory analysis of the amniotic fluid. The vast majority of women in China do not yet have access to this service and will not in the near future, so China's ability to identify and abort fetuses with chromosome and metabolic defects is slight at the moment. There is also a serious cultural obstacle to nationwide introduction of this technology: prenatal chromosomal analysis detects the sex of the fetus, and most Chinese couples want their first and only child to be a boy. For example, it was reported that Anshan Municipality of Liaoning province successfully experimented with a technique for determining the sex of the fetus. But once they knew the sex of the fetus, 30 couples decided to abort it; of these fetuses, 29 were female.[159]

In the extreme, if all pregnant women in the PRC today had easy access to amniocentesis and chromosomal analysis, they would use the resulting information predominantly to abort healthy female fetuses, not fetuses with chromosome defects. The national sex ratio at birth would suddenly become very high. Although the immediate decrease in births might be an attractive prospect to the government, an extreme shortage of female marriage partners would follow in twenty years. Careful studies of the sex ratio at birth for all births to women who had received an amniocentesis are in order to see if even in advanced municipalities female fetuses are being selectively aborted. If selective destruction of female fetuses is occurring now or happens as amniocentesis is made available in county or township hospitals, then China's government will have a difficult decision to make. Either amniocentesis must be restricted to prevent a very abnormal sex ratio at birth, thus allowing the birth of babies with chromosome defects, or the one-child limit must be modified in some way such as allowing all couples to have a son.

The last several chapters have focused on the factors that have affected China's fertility levels and trends, including the role of women, age at marriage, infant and childhood mortality, economic arrangements, availability of birth control methods, and most important, government family planning policies. Now it is time to take a close look at the data on fertility.

8

Fertility

CHINA, like other countries undergoing demographic transition, experienced a lag between the remarkable mortality decline of the 1950's and the subsequent fertility decline. As mortality fell, Chinese parents were more likely to achieve their desired number of living children, perhaps for the first time in history. The joys of bearing children who lived instead of died and of raising relatively healthy children were only slowly tempered by the realization that the costs of raising all those children were becoming too great for families and local communities to bear, and that rapid population growth was dislocating the community economy and the national economy. In China's case the adjustment to this situation came very fast, in the course of one decade. The speed of China's national fertility decline during the 1970's was similar to the speed of its mortality decline of the 1950's.

Table 8.1 shows the PRC's "official" crude birth rates, crude death rates, and natural population increase rates as reported for each year. It was only in 1981 that a complete historical series was published, one that included the official figures on the sharp mortality increase and fertility decline of the Great Leap Forward crisis, 1958–61. In 1983, the State Statistical Bureau published the revised official series also given in Table 8.1. Very minor adjustments have been made in the official vital rates for 1951 and 1961–79. No explanation was given. It is possible that the small changes reflect an attempt to shift vital events from the year they were registered to the year they occurred.

The right column of Table 8.1 is annual natural population increase rates for China derived from the official series of yearend population totals, assuming zero net international migration for the country as a whole. This assumption is reasonable because the actual numbers of emigrants and immigrants are so small compared to the size of the total

TABLE 8.1

Reported Vital Rates and Implied Rates of Natural Increase in the PRC, 1949–83

(Rates per 1,000 population)

Year	Originally reported rates			Revised SSB series			Rate of natural increase implied by official population totals
	Crude birth rate	Crude death rate	Rate of natural increase	Crude birth rate	Crude death rate	Rate of natural increase	
Pre-1949	38[a]	28[a]	10[a]	—	—	—	—
	35[b]	25[c]	(10)	—	—	—	—
1949	36.00	20.00	16.00	36.00	20.00	16.00	—
		25[d]					
1950	37.00	18.00	19.00	37.00	18.00	19.00	18.82
1951	37.00	17.00	20.00	37.80	17.80	20.00	19.80
1952	37.00	17.00	20.00	37.00	17.00	20.00	20.78
	37[e]	18[e]	19[e]				
1953	37.00	14.00	23.00	37.00	14.00	23.00	22.55
	37[e]	17[e]	20[e]				
1954	37.97	13.18	24.79	37.97	13.18	24.79	24.69
		14[f]					
1955	32.60	12.28	20.32	32.60	12.28	20.32	19.70
	35[e]	12.4[e]	22.6[e]				
1956	31.90	11.40	20.50	31.90	11.40	20.50	21.93
1957	34.03[g]	10.80[g]	23.23[g]	34.03	10.80	23.23	28.63
1958	29.22	11.98	17.24	29.22	11.98	17.24	20.53
1959	24.78[h]	14.50[h]	10.28[h]	24.78	14.59	10.19	18.21
	24.78[i]	(14.59)	10.19[i]				
1960	20.86	25.43	−4.57	20.86	25.43	−4.57	−14.99
1961	18.13[h]	14.38[h]	3.75[h]	18.02	14.24	3.78	−5.27
1962	37.22	10.08	27.14	37.01	10.02	26.99	21.57
1963	43.60	10.10	33.50	43.37	10.04	33.33	27.51
1964	39.34	11.56	27.78	39.14	11.50	27.64	19.11
1965	38.06	9.55	28.51	37.88	9.50	28.38	28.51
1966	35.21	8.87	26.34	35.05	8.83	26.22	27.25
1967	34.12	8.47	25.65	33.96	8.43	25.53	24.20
1968	35.75	8.25	27.50	35.59	8.21	27.38	27.97
1969	34.25	8.06	26.19	34.11	8.03	26.08	26.85
1970	33.59	7.64	25.95	33.43	7.60	25.83	28.36
1971	30.74	7.34	23.40	30.65	7.32	23.33	26.60
	30.3[f]	(6.9)	23.4[f]				
1972	29.92	7.65	22.27	29.77	7.61	22.16	22.60
1973	28.07	7.08	20.99	27.93	7.04	20.89	23.06
1974	24.95	7.38	17.57	24.82	7.34	17.48	18.30
1975	23.13	7.36	15.77	23.01	7.32	15.69	17.03
1976	20.01	7.29[j]	12.72[j]	19.91	7.25	12.66	13.94
1977	19.03	6.91	12.12	18.93	6.87	12.06	13.32
1978	18.34	6.29	12.05	18.25	6.25	12.00	13.44
1979	17.90	6.20	11.70	17.82	6.21	11.61	13.24
	17.90[k]	6.24[k]	11.66[l]				
1980	16.98[m]	6.34[m]	10.64[n]	—	—	—	11.85
1981	17.64[o]	6.19[o]	11.45[o]	20.91	6.36	14.55	13.75
	18[p]		11.2[q]				
	17.6[r]		"<12"[s]				
	20.91[t]	6.36[t]	14.55[t]				
1982	21.09[u]	6.60[u]	14.49[u]	21.09	6.60	14.49	14.57
			13.5[v]				
			12.42[w]				
1983	18.62[x]	7.08[x]	11.54[x]				

population. It is immediately obvious that the natural increase rates derived from China's official population totals agree neither with the original series nor with the revised series of official natural increase rates. This means that there is error somewhere, either in the series of population totals or in the series of vital rates. We know that part of the error comes from consistent underreporting of deaths, as discussed in earlier chapters. It is also now clear that births have been underreported almost every year.

For many years, observers could only speculate that China's birth rates were underreported.[1] Then in September 1982, the State Family Planning Commission carried out a nationwide retrospective fertility survey of apparent high quality. They used as a sampling frame the address codes of the 1982 census, and randomly selected 815 rural production brigades and urban resident committees as sample units with probability proportional to population.[2] This type of sample selection was a vast improvement over China's earlier surveys that gathered data from unrepresentative, relatively advanced units. The sample population in the 1982 survey was just over 1 million people. Within the sample population, all women ages 15–67 were interviewed about their marital and fertility histories.

The resulting fertility estimates are presented in Table 8.2. For recent years, the age-specific fertility rates are based on the responses of large numbers of women covering all the age groups. For earlier years, fertility for some age groups had to be estimated or extrapolated from other data.

SOURCES OF TABLE 8.1: Unless otherwise noted, the first rows of the originally reported vital rates are from Zhang Huaiyu et al. (1981), and these data are confirmed by the other available sources. Where other sources disagree a separate row of figures follows and the sources are given below. The State Statistical Bureau series is from Statistical Yearbook of China 1983 (1983): 105.

[a]Zhu Zhengzhi (1980); Liu Zheng (1980b).
[b]Ling (1981).
[c]*Ibid.*; Encyclopedic Yearbook of China (1980): 625–26.
[d]Wang Weizhi (1982b): 20.
[e]Chandrasekhar (1959): 50.
[f]Zhu Zhengzhi (1980).
[g]Li Chengrui (1982a): 15–16; Ling (1981).
[h]Yang Deqing (1982): 128–29.
[i]Tian Xueyuan (1981): 41.
[j]Liu Zheng (1980b); Li Chengrui (1982a): 15–16.
[k]Li Chengrui (1982a): 15–16.
[l]*Ibid.*; Wang Weizhi (1982a): 41.
[m]Li Muzhen (1982): 3.
[n]*Ibid.*, "Birthrate Called Bigger Challenge Than Quadrupling," CD, 2 Dec. 1982: 3.
[o]Hu Huanyong & Zhang Shanyu, *Shijie renkou dili* (Population geography), Shanghai, 1982: 392.
[p]"Speech by Head of Chinese Delegation at Third Asian and Pacific Population Conference," mimeo, Colombo, Sri Lanka, Sept. 1982: 5.
[q]Cheng Hsiang (1982): 84.
[r]Li Chengrui (1982b): 36.
[s]"Population," SWB-WER, no. W1172 (17 Feb. 1982): 1.
[t]Communique on 1982 Census (1982): K3.
[u]Communique on 1982 Economic Plan (1983): K16.
[v]"Zhonghua renmin gongheguo 1983-nian guomin jingji he shehui fazhan jihua" (The 1983 national economic and social development plan of the PRC), RMRB, 20 Dec. 1982: 2.
[w]Based on the yearend cumulative reporting system. Circular on Sample Vital Rate Survey (1983): 822.
[x]Communique on 1983 Economic Plan (1984): K14.

NOTE: The implied natural increase rate is calculated from official yearend population totals assuming zero net international migration. Values in parentheses are derived from other statistics given in the table.

TABLE 8.2

Total and Age-Specific Fertility Rates in the PRC, 1940–81

Year	Total fertility rate	Age-specific fertility rates 15–19	20–24	25–29	30–34	35–39	40–44	45–49	Average age of child-bearing
1940	5.251	.079	.235	.239	.209	.173	.101	.014	30.0
1941	5.317	.079	.237	.241	.213	.177	.102	.015	30.0
1942	5.001	.076	.229	.223	.198	.165	.095	.014	30.0
1943	5.300	.077	.232	.241	.214	.178	.103	.015	30.1
1944	5.187	.072	.226	.235	.212	.176	.102	.015	30.2
1945	5.295	.075	.237	.239	.213	.177	.103	.015	30.1
1946	5.514	.075	.251	.248	.221	.186	.107	.015	30.1
1947	5.840	.078	.260	.266	.232	.200	.114	.016	30.2
1948	5.509	.077	.245	.248	.219	.188	.109	.015	30.2
1949	6.139	.090	.275	.275	.242	.209	.120	.017	30.1
1950	5.813	.087	.264	.259	.226	.194	.114	.019	30.0
1951	5.699	.090	.260	.259	.219	.186	.109	.017	29.9
1952	6.472	.104	.295	.296	.260	.205	.118	.018	29.8
1953	6.049	.096	.276	.287	.242	.192	.102	.016	29.8
1954	6.278	.099	.286	.298	.251	.200	.105	.016	29.7
1955	6.261	.090	.294	.299	.245	.197	.109	.018	29.9
1956	5.854	.078	.269	.286	.238	.184	.101	.015	29.8
1957	6.405	.083	.302	.310	.270	.201	.100	.014	29.7
1958	5.679	.075	.262	.271	.240	.182	.093	.012	29.8
1959	4.303	.046	.196	.222	.188	.136	.065	.008	29.8
1960	4.015	.040	.185	.205	.169	.137	.062	.006	29.9
1961	3.287	.035	.165	.175	.143	.094	.041	.005	29.3
1962	6.023	.058	.288	.324	.269	.186	.071	.010	29.5
1963	7.502	.080	.348	.374	.326	.254	.108	.012	29.8
1964	6.176	.070	.295	.309	.261	.193	.096	.011	29.7
1965	6.076	.058	.289	.311	.256	.196	.092	.012	29.8
1966	6.259	.056	.299	.322	.264	.205	.094	.011	29.9
1967	5.313	.043	.256	.287	.226	.165	.079	.007	29.8
1968	6.448	.053	.307	.346	.281	.199	.094	.010	29.8
1969	5.723	.046	.275	.310	.240	.179	.085	.010	29.8
1970	5.812	.045	.284	.313	.248	.179	.084	.010	29.8
1971	5.442	.040	.270	.303	.231	.162	.075	.008	29.6
1972	4.984	.032	.244	.285	.213	.148	.068	.007	29.7
1973	4.539	.028	.228	.271	.192	.126	.055	.007	29.5
1974	4.170	.024	.219	.259	.171	.105	.049	.006	29.2
1975	3.571	.020	.195	.230	.140	.086	.039	.005	29[a]
1976	3.235	.016	.179	.226	.118	.071	.032	.004	28.8
1977	2.844	.012	.161	.211	.102	.056	.023	.004	28.5
1978	2.716	.012	.153	.214	.096	.045	.020	.004	28.2
1979	2.745	.012	.161	.220	.096	.041	.018	.002	28[a]
1980	2.238	.010	.142	.190	.064	.027	.011	.003	27.4
1981	2.631	.015	.182	.213	.071	.031	.013	.002	27.2

SOURCE: Chen Shengli, "Fertility of Women During the 42-Year Period from 1940 to 1981," in China Population Information Centre, *Analysis on China's National One-per-Thousand-Population Fertility Sampling Survey*, Beijing (1984): 56–57.

NOTE: Age-specific fertility rates were calculated from figures on the breakdown of the total fertility rate by age group given in the source.

[a]Chen provides only rounded figures for this year.

The women age 67 at the time of the survey were age 25 in 1940 and 35 in 1950. The fertility of older women in those and the intervening years is estimated rather than reported.

Age-specific and total fertility rates from the fertility survey appear to be extraordinarily complete. When annual numbers of births are estimated from the single-year age-specific fertility rates reported in the fertility survey for the years 1953–81, and a plausible mortality schedule is applied to the births, the number of children counted at each age in the 1964 and 1982 censuses is produced very closely. In addition, adding up the age-specific fertility of women from the beginning of their childbearing until the 1982 census, based on the fertility survey, produces almost exactly the same number of children ever born that women of different ages reported in the census.[3] This level of consistency is remarkable and suggests low levels of error in reporting of births from the fertility survey. Nevertheless, some underreporting of births is still possible. For instance, if women neglected to report certain categories of births in both the fertility survey and the census, such as some high order births or infants dying soon after birth, then consistency of reporting does not prove completeness. Also, if fertility was higher than reported in the survey, the number of surviving children counted at each age in the censuses could still be replicated if infant and child mortality was higher than had been assumed.

Figure 8.1 graphs the age-specific fertility rates estimated from the fertility survey for selected years. Comparing China's overall fertility level and pattern for the years 1955 and 1970 shows very few differences. In both years women had a broad peak fertility pattern and high total fertility rate, suggesting little conscious fertility control. But by 1970 the age at marriage for women had risen enough to postpone the onset of childbearing by about a year, and some fertility control above age 35 was apparent. Births had become somewhat more concentrated in the peak childbearing ages 22–34.

The change from 1970 to 1981 is striking. Fertility dropped in half. Childbearing began much later because of the rise in marriage age, and peaked very sharply at age 25. Almost all fertility was concentrated in the age range 20–33, and by 1981 strong control of fertility was visible in the late twenties and all higher childbearing ages. China's fertility pattern by age of women in the early 1980's is very similar to that of Japan in recent decades.

Four decades of annual total fertility rates based on retrospective reporting in the 1982 fertility survey are shown in Figure 8.2. As estimated from the survey, the rate was slightly depressed during the second world war, in the range 5.0–5.3 births per woman, below the rate of 5.5 esti-

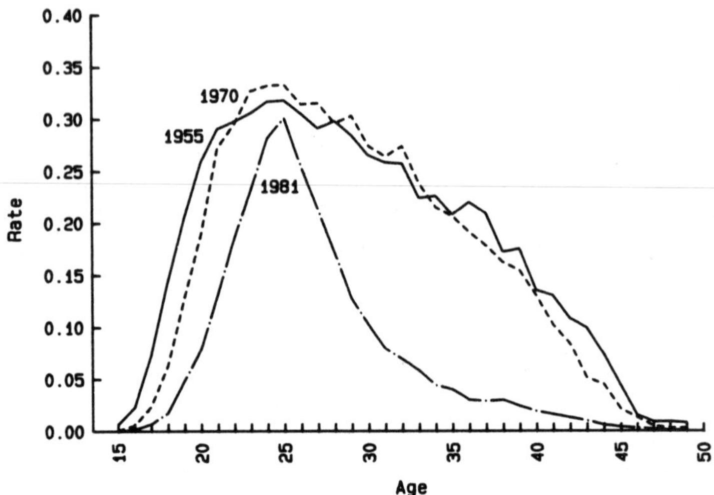

Fig. 8.1. Age-Specific Fertility Rates, 1955, 1970, and 1981. Data from Fertility Survey (1984): 159–61, 171.

Fig. 8.2. Annual Total Fertility Rates, 1940–81. Data from Table 8.2.

mated for China in 1929–31 by the Princeton reanalysis discussed in Chapter 1. We saw this wartime fertility deficit reflected in the 1953 census age structure as well. Fertility began rising in the late 1940's, and was near or above 6 births per woman during the years 1952–57, higher fertility than had been customary in the decades prior to 1949. There are several likely reasons for the increase in fertility in the 1950's. In the first place, the coming of peace after decades of warfare normally produces a postwar baby boom of several years duration. Secondly, the land reform of 1950–51 redistributed land to landless peasants and tenant farmers, perhaps triggering the idea that they needed more family laborers to work the land and that they would be able to feed more children from their newly acquired land. Finally, by the mid-1950's mortality and health had improved to such an extent that one would expect an increase in the fecundity of the population.

Birth rates based on the retrospective fertility survey as well as official birth rates for 1958 through 1961 show an extraordinary drop in fertility attributable to the famine of that period. From the experience of a few countries with good statistical data collected during a famine, for instance the Netherlands during World War II, we know that it is possible for a crude birth rate to drop to half its usual level nine months after a famine strikes, then recover quickly nine months after food supplies are restored.[4] By analogy, it is not impossible for China's birth rate to have fallen from 43 per thousand population in 1957 to 22 in 1961, rates implied by the fertility survey, followed by a sharp rebound to the prefamine level. It is likely that the birth rate dipped because of the low caloric intake of China's population during the Great Leap Forward and that the reduced fertility came nine months after widespread and serious food shortages. If fertility began dropping in 1958, as shown by both fertility survey and official data, this means that already in early 1958 as the Great Leap was beginning, the food supply was disrupted. The steep drop in fertility in 1959 indicates that famine was widespread during 1958,*

* There is some discrepancy between China's grain production statistics and the apparent timing of the famine. After attempts to correct the originally inflated 1958 figures on grain production, the adjusted figures still show adequate grain production in 1958. Yet famine seems to have hit that year. Either the revised 1958 grain figures are too high, or severe disruptions of food storage and distribution separated people from their basic food supply that year. The harvest of 1959 was unusually poor, thus a serious drop in the birth rate is expected by late 1960. The worst food production year was 1960, which extended the famine fertility through 1961. Then 1961, reportedly the third bad crop year in a row, should have continued to cause subfecundity in a population already debilitated by hunger for two or three years. Nevertheless, there was a sharp fertility rebound in 1962, doubling the total fertility rate at least one year earlier than would be expected on the basis of grain production statistics. Such a rebound was possible only if the supply and distribution of food improved considerably during 1961 as the government imported grain and tried to ensure minimum supplies in famine areas.

and the continuing fertility decline through 1961 shows that starvation spread during 1959 and 1960.[5]

After a sharp fertility rebound in 1962, there was an abnormally high fertility peak in 1963. The fertility survey estimated a total fertility rate of 7.5 births per woman, corresponding to a crude birth rate of about 50 births per thousand population. This post-famine baby boom followed a surge of marriages in 1962, so there was an unusual concentration of first births in 1963. In addition, couples married in earlier years may have had a birth in 1963 to make up for some of the subfecundity, postponed childbearing, stillbirths, and excess infant and child deaths of the famine years. The 1963 peak in births indicates that by sometime in 1962 enough food had reached the population to restore full fecundity. However, it is estimated that per capita grain availability in 1962 was only slightly better than it had been in 1959, a poor crop year that had been followed by continued famine fertility in 1960.[6] Perhaps in 1962 the government ensured that the available food was more equitably distributed across the population than had been the case in 1959.

China's fertility remained high in the Cultural Revolution period of the late 1960's. As seen in Figure 8.2, there appear to be annual fertility fluctuations with high points in 1966 and 1968, followed by troughs in 1967 and 1969. However, these variations are probably an artifact of the calculation procedure from lunar to solar years and should be ignored, as demonstrated by Coale.[7] The total fertility rate was about 5.9 or 6.0 births per woman during those years, if the peaks and valleys are smoothed, just barely below the high fertility of 1952–57 and 1964–65. So, except for the temporarily low fertility of the famine years, China's population had experienced very little fertility change by 1970.

The country began a sustained fertility decline after 1970. There was a steep drop in the total fertility rate from 5.8 births per woman in 1970 to 2.8 in 1977, as seen in Table 8.2 and Figure 8.2. China had a strong family planning program during those years, but in addition, it appears from this very rapid fertility transition that the Chinese people did not vigorously resist the shift from bearing six children to bearing only three per couple. In 1978 and 1979, fertility leveled out at a total fertility rate of 2.7. Only after the one-child program began in 1979 was another fertility decline experienced in 1980, to 2.2 births per woman. The crude birth rate meanwhile declined from 37 births per thousand population in 1970 to only 21 in 1977, stayed 21 through 1979, and dropped to 18 in 1980, based on the fertility survey.

Table 8.3 gives the annual birth rates implied when the age-specific fertility rates from the fertility survey are applied to China's changing age structure. These are compared to the official birth rates for each year.

TABLE 8.3
Comparison of Official and Fertility Survey Birth Rates, 1949–81
(Rates per 1,000 population)

Year	Birth rate: Official	Birth rate: Implied by Fertility Survey	Completeness of reporting (percent)	Year	Birth rate: Official	Birth rate: Implied by Fertility Survey	Completeness of reporting (percent)
1949	36	44	82%	1966	35	40	88%
1950	37	42	88	1967	34	34	100
1951	37–38	41	90–92	1968	36	41	87
1952	37	46	80	1969	34	36	94–95
1953	37	42	88	1970	33–34	37	90–91
1954	38	43	87	1971	31	35	88
1955	33	43	76	1972	30	32	92
1956	32	40	80	1973	28	30	94
1957	34	43	79	1974	25	28	88–89
1958	29	38	77	1975	23	25	93
1959	25	29	87	1976	20	23	86–87
1960	21	27	78	1977	19	21	90
1961	18	22	80–81	1978	18	21	88
1962	37	41	90–91	1979	18	21	83–84
1963	43–44	50	87–88	1980	17	18	96
1964	39	40	97–98	1981	18, 21[a]	21	86, 102[a]
1965	38	39	97–98				

SOURCES: Tables 8.1 and 10.1.
[a]The vital statistics registration system reported 86% of the 1981 births that were estimated by the Fertility Survey; the 1982 census reported more 1981 births than the Fertility Survey.

There are large annual fluctuations in the completeness estimates. These are probably incorrect, caused partly by delayed registration of births and partly by a problem converting the lunar to the solar calendar in the fertility survey.[8] After smoothing the peaks and valleys in the completeness estimates, the following picture emerges. The official birth rates for the early 1950's were around 87 percent of the actual birth rates. Births were about 80 percent reported in the late 1950's. Because the official birth rates for the 1950's are all far too low, they should now be superseded by birth rates derived from the fertility survey of 1982. Two main reasons underlie the low reported 1950's birth rates. First, the vital rate survey that provided a crude birth rate estimate of 37 for the early 1950's was too heavily urban to be representative of all China, and it probably also missed births in the surveyed areas.[9] Second, some birth rates for the mid-1950's seem to have been based on the system of birth registration, which was just being set up during 1954–56. The registration system, which may have been nationwide but more likely covered only some areas, seems to have routinely missed about 20 percent of the births even before the Great Leap Forward. Urban birth reporting was relatively complete during the 1950's; it was areas outside cities and towns that underreported their fertility in that decade. For example, one source reported that in 1957 the birth rate was 44.48 in the cities but in all other areas combined was only 32.81.[10] The latter figure is clearly deficient for the rural population, who in the absence of contraception probably had a birth rate over 40 per thousand population.

The completeness of birth reporting stayed around 80 percent through the famine years of the Great Leap Forward, continuing the deficient system of birth registration characteristic of the mid-1950's. Then, as shown in Table 8.3, a much greater proportion of the births, around 90 percent or above, began to be recorded in the vital registration system starting in 1962. The post-famine fertility rebound must have been accompanied by greater efforts to get births registered. Perhaps there were also changes such as an expanded rationing system or increased availability of primary education that motivated parents to register the births and presence of their children. Completeness of reporting rose in the early 1960's and peaked at about 95 percent in the mid-1960's and late 1960's, but then birth registration deteriorated in the 1970's. Just over 90 percent of the births were reported in the first half of the decade, and just under 90 percent in the latter half.

From Table 8.3 it is clear that China's vital registration system has never achieved complete reporting of births. Worse, birth reporting deteriorated in the 1970's as compared with the 1960's. Let us explore the sources of the underregistration of births.

At the end of each year, local administrative units such as the production brigade in rural areas and the neighborhoods in urban areas report their total number of births and deaths during the year and their total population size at year's end, and perhaps also their local vital rates. Higher administrative levels then compile the data to produce county or municipal vital rates, then provincial vital rates, and from these the national birth and death rates are calculated.

If all localities recorded and reported these data, and if vital registration everywhere were virtually complete, then the nationally compiled vital rates would be close to correct. But neither of these conditions is fulfilled. In the first place, as late as 1978 and perhaps since then as well, some localities had not instituted regular birth and death reporting. In some provinces these areas were ignored, and the crude birth and death rates of the rest of the province were assumed to apply to the nonreporting areas. This technique causes the most distortion when the nonreporting areas are numerous and differ greatly in fertility and mortality from the reporting areas. For example, at least one and probably several provinces with substantial minorities used only Han Chinese data to derive their 1978 provincial natural increase rates. The resulting errors in most cases would be to underreport fertility and mortality and probably natural population increase, because those areas not reporting would tend to be poor and backward with higher fertility and mortality than elsewhere. That China's government does not get vital statistics from all places is indicated by a comment from an official to a foreign group. In November 1979 members of a United States government delegation visiting the State Statistical Bureau in Beijing were told that the bureau prepares annual estimates of China's crude birth and death rates and natural population increase rate (as presented in Table 8.1) on the basis of incomplete reports.[11]

The second major source of error in official vital rates is underreporting of births by some areas that do send in annual reports. In these areas such underreporting of births may be completely unintentional, a result of poor record-keeping, unattended births, systematic forgetting of the birth event when a baby dies, a casual system of responsibility for birth reporting, or neglect of birth recording in remote areas. These problems are common in developing countries.

During the 1970's a new cause of underreporting of births became prominent. As the national government each year put increasing pressure on provincial governments to lower birth rates and natural population increase rates, provincial leaders in turn passed the pressure down to prefectural, county, and municipal governments. These governments informed local cadres that they must meet the targets, and increasing coercion was meted out to the populace to attain the low targets. Another predictable result was that at all levels, birth reporting became ever more tainted by falsification.

This problem begins with the people. It is they who are ordered not to have another child, and who so often want another child. If a couple can get away with conceiving and bearing a child, they will seek to minimize the repression that ensues. In many areas the birth is well known to the authorities by the time it happens, and the "excess" birth is duly recorded and followed by economic and political penalties, but some births are successfully concealed. The mother may go elsewhere for half the pregnancy to bear the child, an occurrence reported with increasing frequency during the 1970's in the press. She may live and work outside a compact village, feign a long illness, or collude with a sympathetic midwife or barefoot doctor. When a forbidden birth has been successfully concealed, it is unlikely that the family would then report its occurrence.

Village and neighborhood officials would also be tempted to underreport births. Their job effectiveness is measured in substantial part by their ability to enforce low fertility. Very ambitious goals for number of births, natural population increase, single-child certificate acceptance rate, acceptance of contraception, and number of "excess" births are regularly foisted upon local officials. Demands that local leaders deem unreasonable may demoralize them and foster cynicism. A tempting solution would be to minimize by a variety of easily concealed techniques the number of births reported to have occurred in the unit. Once this practice has occurred, however, it might be necessary to continue the falsification in subsequent years. Fudging fertility data can happen at any point in the chain of reporting from local to national level. One foreign scholar, for example, who intensively gathered fertility data from a model people's commune in 1981 discovered that one of the commune's twenty brigades reported more higher order births during a recent year than the entire commune reported for the same year.[12]

How could authorities get away with falsifying data, we might ask. In the PRC it has apparently been easy.[13] The annual statistical reporting system is still so rudimentary that there is often no independent check on population data or other kinds of data reported from local levels up the chain of command. Falsifying figures can continue for years without being detected, according to Chinese press reports. During the late 1970's some of China's political leaders and statisticians began to realize how much falsified information was reported to the national government. At first the press discussed cases of tampering with agricultural or production data without suggesting that population data too might be suspect. Finally during 1980, a scholarly article from China mentioned gingerly in passing that intentional falsification of population data under the pressure of official targets was possible:

> Experiences in planning work in the past 30 years have told us that in drafting whatever plans, there must be left some room to spare, and that they must not be drawn too tightly. This is the way with economic plans, and population plans should not be an exception. In the past, we have taken many a bitter pill of setting our targets too high. The "high target" of population control, same as the "high target" of economic construction, has few advantages, but many problems. It could give rise to bad practices of using coercion, of hiding reports on births, etc.[14]

In December 1980 China's leading official newspaper tackled a taboo subject by admitting that alteration of statistics, including fertility data, was continuing in the era after the 1976 arrest of the "gang of four." The article strongly condemned this practice, showed that there was no check on the accuracy of official reported data, and claimed that anyone who exposes intentional misreporting is in political trouble:

> At the present, the problem of falsification still exists to a varied extent in some important statistics; for example, in order to show the "success" of planned par-

enthood, fewer number of births are reported, thus creating an inaccuracy in the natural population increase rates. . . .

In most instances, those who have practiced . . . falsification are not the statistical departments and the statistical clerks, but are, often, the leadership of some units. They adopt various tricks to change statistical figures at will without any legal restraint. Some of them have not only received no punishment, but are given advancement and put in important positions. As time passes, being secure in the knowledge that one has strong backing, such practices become common. When someone exposes a case and reports to the court, it refuses to accept the case. When a case is reported to a higher authority, usually no one is sent down directly to conduct an investigation. Often the reports are sent back to the units, and many of them ended up in the hands of those being reported on, or their associates. The persons who have exposed and reported the cases are inflicted with retaliation.[15]

The simple substitution of a set of invented numbers for locally collected birth data is comparatively risky and detectable. There are other ways to falsify local population data without appearing to do so. Rural collective units or urban police stations could simply neglect birth registration on the excuse that they have other more pressing duties. Local officials could refuse to register a higher order child beyond the small number of births allowed to each couple, or they could harass household members so much when they attempt to report births that all "illegal" births in the locality go unregistered. For example, if village leaders are penalizing a couple for having a fourth child by stopping all food distributions and cotton rations for that child, as was done in some villages in Guangdong by 1973, there would be little incentive to register those higher order births in the brigade records.[16] As late as 1980 one locality reported that no babies born there would be registered in the local permanent registers during the first hundred days of life.[17] Such delay in registering newborns could easily be accompanied by failure to report all the births. In particular, if a baby died before being registered, there might be no incentive to report either its birth or its death. In late 1981, a delegate to the Hebei Provincial People's Congress lamented: "Dingma brigade in Duqiao commune of Jing county has more than one hundred households. Among them are eight children who have never been registered. Thus, to see how well family planning work has been carried out, it is not enough to look at the reports alone. Rather, it is necessary to go down to the basic level and find out about the situation."[18]

China does have standard rules for the registration and reporting of births, but they have not been enforced nationwide. Each area in practice has wide latitude in the births it chooses to report or not to report. The almost total lack of verification of reported figures perpetuates this variable quality in birth reporting.

Therefore, widespread intentional underreporting of births may have begun during the early 1970's as national and provincial fertility targets became more stringent. The practice apparently continued in the latter half of the decade. Under the cadre job responsibility system in the 1980's, local and higher level authorities have a strong financial incentive to avoid reporting any unauthorized birth that they are unable to prevent. It must be assumed that falsification of birth reporting is continuing. Occasional instances are detected, such as the intentional underreporting of 1982 and 1983 births by a commune and township government in Hunan province.[19] Manipulation of birth figures, in combination with underreporting of vital events due to continuing weakness in the statistical system, has resulted in substantial underreporting of the birth rate and natural population increase rate in some localities and some provinces. In consequence the national birth rate and natural increase rate derived from provincial reports have been significantly underestimated.

Because it is now clear that official birth rates from the birth registration system have always been and still are incomplete, they should no longer be used to represent China's actual birth rates. In their place, annual total fertility rates from the 1982 retrospective fertility survey can be assumed close to complete for the years 1940 through 1981. Crude birth rates for each year derived from these data and the census age structures, as shown in Table 8.3, should now supersede all official birth rates derived from birth registration.

The fertility survey verified that a remarkable fertility decline took place in China during the 1970's. It also documented the shifting parity distribution of births. In 1970, about 21 percent of births in China were the mothers' first births, 17 percent were second parity births, and 62 percent of all births were third and higher order. By 1977, first births constituted 31 percent of births, second births 25 percent, and third or higher parity 45 percent. Under the one-child program there has been a sharp rise in the proportion of births that are first parity. In 1981, as estimated from the fertility survey, 47 percent of all births were the first child, 25 percent were second parity, and only 28 percent were third or higher order births.[20] The 1982 census asked respondents about all 1981 births, and the parity figures are in close agreement with the fertility survey. The census recorded that of 1981 births, 47 percent were firstborn, 26 percent were secondborn, and 27 percent were third or higher parity.[21] It is likely that since 1981, the firstborn percentage has risen much further, and the percentage of third or higher order births has declined precipitously.

China's total fertility rate rose from 2.238 births per woman in 1980 to 2.631 in 1981, according to the fertility survey. As shown in Table 8.4, the rise in fertility was due primarily to a surge of first births that fol-

TABLE 8.4
Total Fertility Rates in Urban and Rural Areas by Birth Order, 1980 and 1981

	Total fertility rate	Total fertility rate broken down by birth order				
		First births	Second births	Third births	Fourth births	Fifth births and beyond
Urban						
1980	1.147	0.833	0.261	0.038	0.010	0.004
1981	1.390	1.196	0.162	0.024	0.007	0.001
Rural						
1980	2.480	0.893	0.630	0.389	0.237	0.335
1981	2.910	1.177	0.728	0.403	0.236	0.366
National total						
1980	2.238	0.869	0.564	0.325	0.200	0.277
1981	2.631	1.162	0.624	0.337	0.195	0.307

SOURCE: Xiao Wencheng et al. (1984): 62.
NOTE: In the tables in this chapter, unless otherwise noted, "urban" is defined as the nonagricultural permanent resident population in cities and towns, and "rural" covers all the rest of the population.

lowed implementation of the new Marriage Law and the surge of marriages. The crude birth rate increased from 18 in 1980 to 21 in 1981, the latter figure based on the census as well as the fertility survey.

China took the census at midyear 1982 and asked all households to report the number of births and deaths during calendar year 1981. Citizens were exhorted to report all births and deaths even if they had not been officially reported before, and even if a birth was contrary to official policy. The preparations and publicity paid off: more complete reporting of births and deaths was obtained from the census than had been gleaned from the regular reporting system. The death rate of 6.36 was slightly more complete than the 1981 registration figure of 6.19, and the 1981 birth rate from the census, 20.91, was 3 births per thousand population higher than the figure of 17.64 obtained from regular birth reporting.

Although the census improved reporting of births and deaths over the vital registration system, it is possible that fertility was still underreported even in the census. There was a tendency for parents to conceal the 1981 birth of a child that violated local fertility limits, and at the same time to conceal the existence of the child in the count. For instance, in one census pretest a family carefully avoided reporting the 1981 birth of their third child, who had never been legally registered and was easy to leave out of their census questionnaire.[22] This deception was uncovered when a neighbor revealed the facts, but in the census itself some such intentional underreporting of births may have remained undetected. It is likely that some local cadres tolerated or encouraged parents to keep "excess" children off the official records, including the census, so that their own regular underreporting of births would go undetected.[23]

In addition to the possible exclusion of some higher order 1981 births from the census, there was apparently selective underreporting of female births. The 10.8 million boys and 9.9 million girls reported by the census as having been born during 1981 would mean a sex ratio at birth of 108.5 boys per hundred girls.[24] As discussed in Chapter 2, the sex ratio at birth of such a large oriental sample should be about 106 and should not be outside the range 105–107. If the actual sex ratio in 1981 was the expected 106, then at least 232,000 female births were not reported in the census; the most conservative deficit is 137,000 if a high but theoretically possible sex ratio of 107 is assumed.

Like the census, the fertility survey seems to have underreported female 1981 births. The sex ratio of reported 1981 births was 107.8 boys per hundred girls, too high to be correct. But no sex-selective underreporting of births can be detected for firstborn and secondborn children. Their combined sex ratio was 106.0 boys per hundred girls, just what would be expected based on other populations. All the differential underreporting of female births happened with babies of third and higher parity, with an implausible sex ratio at birth of 112.6 as reported.[25] If it is assumed that these births also had an actual sex ratio of 106.0, unreported female higher order births for 1981 would be about 173,000 when extrapolated from the survey population to the total population.

After the census and fertility survey achieved much better birth reporting than the vital registration system, government statisticians designed a substitute for the annual reporting system. Beginning in January 1983, and each January thereafter, a nationally representative vital rate survey has been taken. The survey each year is supposed to be based on interviews conducted in selected sample households, asking the respondents details on any births or deaths among household members during the previous calendar year.[26] The January 1983 survey was described as "a sample survey of 556,188 people drawn at random from 3,503 production teams (residence groups) in 1,057 people's communes (streets) of 312 counties (cities) of 29 provinces, municipalities, and autonomous regions."[27] The January 1984 survey was "a sample survey of 661,455 people drawn at random from 4,166 production teams (residence groups) in 371 counties (or cities) in 29 provinces, municipalities, and autonomous regions."[28] We know that the national official vital rates for 1982 and 1983 were derived from these surveys rather than from the regular yearend reporting system.

Results of the surveys for 1982 and 1983 are given in Table 8.1. Death reporting seems to be more complete than had been the case from the vital registration system or the census. The completeness of birth reporting from the annual surveys is unknown. The January 1983 survey gave a birth rate of 21.1 for 1982, almost the same as the census had reported for 1981. The vital rate survey taken in January 1984 documented a drop in the birth rate to 18.6 and a national total fertility rate of only 2.07 births per woman for 1983.[29]

Urban and Rural Fertility

The nationwide fertility survey of 1982 produced separate estimates of age-specific and total fertility rates for China's urban and rural areas. In this survey, the "urban" population was narrowly defined as those persons living in cities and towns who were consuming commercial grain rations as of the survey date and therefore were called "nonagricultural." In 1982 this group comprised only 14.6 percent of China's total population and were the most economically urbanized of the total population living in urban areas, a factor that should be kept in mind when analyzing their fertility.[30]

Table 8.5 gives the estimated total fertility rates of urban and rural women for each year 1950–81.[31] Based on retrospective reporting by women classified urban and rural in 1982, the procedure assumes no migration between urban and rural areas during these three decades. This assumption is not correct, as will be discussed in Chapter 9, but it is close enough to correct because of China's very moderate degree of urbanization over this period. Throughout the 1950's, the fertility of urban

TABLE 8.5
Total Fertility Rates in Urban and Rural Areas, 1950–81

Year	Urban	Rural	National total	Year	Urban	Rural	National total
1950	5.001	5.963	5.813	1966	3.104	6.958	6.259
1951	4.719	5.904	5.699	1967	2.905	5.847	5.313
1952	5.521	6.667	6.472	1968	3.872	7.025	6.448
1953	5.402	6.183	6.049	1969	3.299	6.263	5.723
1954	5.723	6.390	6.278	1970	3.267	6.379	5.812
1955	5.665	6.391	6.261	1971	2.882	6.011	5.442
1956	5.333	5.974	5.854	1972	2.637	5.503	4.984
1957	5.943	6.504	6.405	1973	2.387	5.008	4.539
1958	5.253	5.775	5.679	1974	1.982	4.642	4.170
1959	4.172	4.323	4.303	1975	1.782	3.951	3.571
1960	4.057	3.996	4.015	1976	1.608	3.582	3.235
1961	2.982	3.349	3.287	1977	1.574	3.116	2.844
1962	4.789	6.303	6.023	1978	1.551	2.968	2.716
1963	6.207	7.784	7.502	1979	1.373	3.045	2.745
1964	4.395	6.567	6.176	1980	1.147	2.480	2.238
1965	3.749	6.597	6.076	1981	1.390	2.910	2.631

SOURCES: Xiao Wencheng et al. (1984): 59; Fertility Survey (1984): 159–73.

women was high, a total fertility rate of 5–6 births per woman in most years, but that of rural women was even higher, 6 or more births per woman. The difference was caused by later marriage among urban women and perhaps some conscious fertility control using simple methods of contraception (withdrawal, abstinence) and abortion.

The Great Leap Forward famine had a temporary devastating effect on the fertility of women at all ages in both urban and rural areas. Both rural and urban fertility began dropping in 1958 and declined to 3 births per woman in 1961. These data indicate that the women of cities and towns were not shielded to any significant degree from the effects of famine through food imports or domestic procurement and movement of food.

Beginning in the early 1960's, the differential between urban and rural fertility widened, and it has stayed wide ever since as measured by the total fertility rate. The post-famine fertility rebound was not nearly as high in urban as rural areas, partly because the post-famine surge of marriages in rural areas was far more pronounced than among the urban nonagricultural population. China's family planning program of 1962–66 concentrated on requiring urban women to marry late, space births, and limit the number of births, and the program appears to have had prompt and dramatic effect. Urban marriage age was rising sharply from 1963 to 1966, as discussed in Chapter 6, thus depressing marriage frequency each year and helping to reduce the total fertility rate and birth rate. While rural fertility in the 1960's after the Great Leap was even higher than it had been in the 1950's, urban fertility dropped steeply during 1964–66 and reached a low of only 3 births per woman in 1966–67.

During the Cultural Revolution of the late 1960's rural fertility remained high. By 1970 the rural population still had a total fertility rate of 6.4 births per woman. Essentially no conscious fertility control was evident among rural women, except as the result of slightly later age at marriage.

In the Cultural Revolution years, urban marriage age ceased rising and there was a surge of marriages during 1967–69 that contributed to a slight fertility increase in 1968–70. During the late 1960's urban fertility was already highly controlled. Marriage averaged three years later for urban than rural women. Urban fertility peaked sharply at ages 24–27 followed by strong control of births at all higher ages.

After 1970 urban and rural fertility declined rapidly. Urban nonagricultural women reduced their fertility to below replacement level in 1974, and urban fertility continued dropping to 1.1 births per woman in 1980. In 1981, the frequency of second, third, fourth, and higher order births declined further in urban areas, as shown in Table 8.4, but a concentration of first births following the new Marriage Law raised the 1981 total fertility rate.

Rural women experienced steep fertility decline after 1970. Their total fertility rate fell from 6.4 in 1970 to only 3.1 in 1977, then held steady at 3 births per woman through 1979. Fertility was reduced further to 2.5 births per woman in 1980. As shown in Table 8.4, the 1981 fertility increase in rural areas was mostly due to a concentration of first births, but there was also some increase in second and higher order births, partly in response to the spread of the agricultural production responsibility system.

In broad outline, China's fertility transition has followed a classic model of the demographic transition in which urban fertility starts lower, begins dropping earlier, and stays lower than rural fertility as both are declining. China's steep urban fertility decline came a decade before the same phenomenon among the rural population. In the Chinese case, both the urban and the rural fertility transitions were speeded by government pressure and regulations mandating late marriage and limitation of the number of children per couple.

The State Statistical Bureau and other sources have published a partial series of official vital rates for "cities" and "counties" as shown in Table 8.6. These categories do not correspond to the urban-rural distinction used in the fertility survey. The "city" columns seem to include all births and deaths reported for the whole population living inside the boundaries of cities, both nonagricultural and agricultural households, and seem to exclude vital events in towns. The "county" category appears to include towns and rural areas, in other words every place outside city boundaries. These figures are probably based on vital registration for most years.

These data show city death rates lower than county death rates for all years, and show city birth rates dropping sharply during the 1960's while county birth rates stayed high. According to these figures, city birth rates continued their decline in the early 1970's but began a slow rise after that, while county birth rates declined through 1980 and then rose. The city natural increase rate dropped lower than that of the counties in 1964 and stayed lower thereafter.

These broad generalizations are probably correct, but for drawing finer distinctions or judging true levels of birth, death, or natural increase rates for cities or counties, these statistics are weak, incorrect, or misleading. One problem is that there are no figures for the Cultural Revolution years, when reporting from the vital registration system apparently broke down. Another difficulty is that for 1959–61 and for 1966 the figures are internally inconsistent. For these years, the official city, county, and national birth rates taken together imply that a certain percent of the population is in the city category, but a different percent is implied by calculating from the death rates, and a third percent is implied by the set of three

TABLE 8.6

Reported Crude Birth, Death, and Natural Increase Rates for Cities and Counties, 1952–82

	Originally reported figures					
	Cities			Counties		
Year	CBR	CDR	NIR	CBR	CDR	NIR
1952	—	—	27.9	—	—	19.1
1953	—	—	—	—	—	—
1954	42.45	8.07	34.38	37.51	13.71	23.80
1955	—	—	31.4	—	—	19.1
1956	—	—	—	—	—	—
1957	44.48	8.47	36.01	32.81	11.07	21.74
1958	—	—	—	—	—	—
1959	—	—	18.5	—	—	9.2
1960	—	—	—	—	—	—
1961	—	—	—	—	—	—
1962	35.93	8.39	27.59	37.43	10.37	27.06
1963	45.00	7.19	37.81	43.38	10.55	32.83
1964	33.02	7.42	25.60	40.27	12.17	28.10
1965	27.6	5.9	21.7	39.5	10.0	29.5
1966	21.70	5.80	15.90	36.71	9.47	27.24
1971	21.92	5.52	16.40	31.86	7.57	24.29
1972	20.10	5.5	(14.6)	31.19	7.9	(23.3)
1973	18.09	5.16	12.93	29.36	7.33	22.03
1974	15.08	5.44	9.64	26.23	7.63	18.60
1975	15.25	5.6	9.6	24.17	7.6	16.6
1976	13.64	6.9	(6.7)	20.85	7.4	(13.5)
1977	13.93	5.76	8.17	19.70	7.06	12.64
1978	14.1	5.3	8.8	18.9	6.4	12.5
1979	13.9	5.1	8.8	18.5	6.4	12.1
1980	14.17	5.48	8.69	17.41	6.47	10.94
1981	—	—	—	—	—	—
1982	—	—	—	—	—	—

SOURCES: *Originally reported figures*, Liu Zheng (1980b): 6, 8, except as follows: 1952, 1955, 1959, 1975, 1979 NIR's, Tian Xueyuan (1981): 46; 1965, all data, Statistical Yearbook of China 1981 (1982): 89; 1972, 1975, 1976, 1979 CDR's, World Bank (1983): Vol. 3, Annex H, 86; 1978 CBR's, CDR's, World Bank *ibid.*, also Statistical Yearbook of China 1981 (1982): 89; 1978 NIR's, Statistical Yearbook 1981: 89, also Li Muzhen (1982): 4; 1980, all data, Li Muzhen (1982): 4. *SSB revised series*, Statistical Yearbook of China 1983 (1983): 105.

NOTE: "Cities" is not defined in the sources. These city data appear to be based on the births, deaths, and total population registered within the boundaries of around 200 cities. Vital events for towns appear to be included in the "county" data. Values in parentheses are derived from other statistics given in the table.

SSB revised series						
Cities			Counties			Implied "city" percent of total population[a]
CBR	CDR	NIR	CBR	CDR	NIR	
—	—	—	—	—	—	10%[b]
—	—	—	—	—	—	—
42.45	8.07	34.38	37.51	13.71	23.80	9
40.67	9.30	31.37	31.74	12.60	19.14	10
37.87	7.43	30.44	31.24	11.84	19.40	10
44.48	8.47	36.01	32.81	11.07	21.74	10
33.55	9.22	24.33	28.41	12.50	15.91	16
29.43	10.92	18.51	23.78	14.61	9.17	1–18
28.03	13.77	14.26	19.35	28.58	−9.23	17–21
21.63	11.39	10.24	16.99	14.58	2.41	11–22
35.46	8.28	27.18	37.27	10.32	26.95	15[c]
44.50	7.13	37.37	43.19	10.49	32.70	14
32.17	7.27	24.90	40.27	12.17	28.10	14
26.59	5.69	20.90	39.53	10.06	29.47	13
20.85	5.59	15.26	36.71	9.47	27.24	9–16
21.30	5.35	15.95	31.86	7.57	24.29	11
19.30	5.29	14.01	31.19	7.93	23.26	12
17.35	4.96	12.39	29.36	7.33	22.03	12
14.50	5.24	9.26	26.23	7.63	18.60	12
14.71	5.39	9.32	24.17	7.59	16.58	12
13.12	6.60	6.52	20.85	7.35	13.50	12
13.38	5.51	7.87	19.70	7.06	12.64	12
13.56	5.12	8.44	18.91	6.42	12.49	12
13.67	5.07	8.60	18.43	6.39	12.04	13
—	—	—	—	—	—	13[b]
16.45	5.14	11.31	21.55	6.53	15.02	13
18.24	5.28	12.96	21.97	7.00	14.97	24

[a]Weighting the reported city and county vital rates to derive the reported national vital rates implies that a certain percent of the population is in cities and the remaining percent in counties, if the reported vital rates are internally consistent. As a check for consistency, the city proportion of the population based on the set of city, county, and national birth rates for each year was verified by independently deriving the city proportion from the death rates and the rates of natural increase. But reported rates for the years 1959–61 and 1966 are problematic because they do not show a consistent proportion of the population in cities. For example, for the year 1959 the birth rates from the SSB revised series imply a city population of 18% of the total, the death rates imply 1%, and the natural increase rates imply 11%.

[b]Derived from the originally reported rates.

[c]The reported data as rounded imply a city population of 14–17%, but internally consistent assumptions about the next digits in the official rates allow those figures to converge on 15%.

natural increase rates. There is also a sharp discontinuity between 1981 and 1982. The 1981 figures continue to use the definition of "city" population used previously for this series, but the 1982 figures refer to a population slightly larger than the total urban population as counted in the 1982 census.

The biggest difficulty with the series in Table 8.6, however, is simply that the figures reflect China's usual underregistration of deaths and births. None of the birth or death rates can be assumed 100 percent complete, and some of the figures are far less complete than others, making internal comparisons within the series tricky and sometimes wrong.

By the early 1980's, urban fertility per woman was far lower than rural fertility, but there was some convergence in the crude birth rates and natural increase rates. This was partly due to differences in age structure. Women in the peak childbearing ages 20–34 constituted 11.1 percent of the 1982 rural population and 13.5 percent of the urban population based on the census.[32] In addition, a result of the Marriage Law effective at the beginning of 1981 was to concentrate the marriages and first births of many cohorts of urban young adults into very few years. The effect was less pronounced in rural areas.

The Fertility of Han and Minority Groups

The people of Han nationality constitute 93 percent of China's population, and members of the 55 minority groups total 7 percent. Until recently, the minorities were explicitly exempt from the family planning program, because of historical population trends among the minorities, Marxist ideology, and practical political considerations. Many of the minority groups were thought to have experienced population decline during the last several centuries. These small population groups were vulnerable to Han oppression, famines, revolts and suppression of revolts, generally high mortality, and high prevalence of venereal disease. The Chinese Communist variant of Marxist ideology said that the minority peoples would flourish under the People's Republic, thereby making up for former population decline by rapid increases in their number. Rapid population growth of each minority group was seen by the leaders as an indication that the benevolent care of the PRC government had finally reduced their high mortality and freed them from fertility-inhibiting venereal diseases. In addition, the minority groups tended to be so suspicious of any Chinese government, since Chinese governments are primarily Han governments, that further irritants were not needed. Had the PRC government included the minorities in its family planning program, the charge of attempted genocide would have been heard, and China's leaders were very sensitive to this accusation because they were accusing the superpowers of trying to wipe out Third World people with birth control programs.

Though the minorities were excluded from the compulsory family planning program, they were encouraged to marry later, and were supplied with birth control methods upon request. The 1982 fertility survey measured the differences between Han and minority fertility in rural areas as of 1981. The mean age at first marriage for women was younger among the minorities, age 20.5 years, than among the rural Han, who averaged 22.4 years in 1981. The 1981 rural total fertility rate was 2.76 births per Han woman and 5.05 births per minority woman. Rural Han women had 91 births per thousand women in the childbearing ages in 1981, while the general fertility rate of the rural minorities was 141 births per thousand reproductive-age women. The difference between rural Han and minority fertility is even wider than these figures suggest, because 12 percent of the women in the sample survey units representing minority groups were Han women whose lower fertility biased the minority estimates.[33] China's post-Mao government had already decided to vigorously promote family planning among the minority groups, as judged from numerous articles in the media arguing that this must be done, and fertility survey results added evidence for this argument. But there has been some flexibility in the policy, so that different minority groups can be treated differently: "While the Chinese Government encourages family planning in areas inhabited by the minority nationalities, the specific family planning policies for them are different from those for the majority Han nationality. The local governments in those areas may work out rules according to local conditions."[34]

The earliest reports of any limitations on the fertility of minority couples were in 1981. That year Fujian province reported, "In minority nationality areas, it is permissible to give birth to 3 or 4 children."[35] As of late 1982 and early 1983, the largest minority groups, those with 3 million members or more, came under modified versions of the family planning program in which some groups were "requested" not to have more than four children, some were limited to two or three children, and others to only one child if they lived close by Han Chinese families, to get rid of the jealousy and friction felt by Han couples limited to one child when minority couples could have more. The minority groups affected at that time were the Zhuang concentrated in Guangxi province, the Tibetans, the Uygur of Xinjiang, the Mongols in the north, the Manchu in the northeast, the Yi and Miao in the southwest, and the Hui scattered in many provinces.[36] It was argued in early 1983 that the minorities in cities should be subject to the same birth requirements and quotas as Han couples.[37]

During 1983, family planning policies toward minority groups became more restrictive. Gradually it was argued that only the smaller groups should be exempt. In April, one source suggested that lenient population policies should be continued for nationalities of fewer than 100,000 people if they live in sparsely populated areas, while another stated that minority groups of fewer than 10,000 should be exempt.[38] China's Sixth Five-Year Plan published in June 1983 stated: "Family planning must also be implemented in the areas where minority nationalities live in compact communities, and each area should work out a program for family planning that takes into account its economic, natural and population conditions."[39]

In October 1983 it was reported that 80 percent of the peasants and herdsmen in Tibet were practicing family planning. New regulations were promulgated that allowed Tibetan workers employed by the government to have two children at most, restricted Tibetan peasants and herdsmen in densely populated areas to a maximum of three children, and allowed unlimited fertility to those in sparsely populated areas.[40] Qinghai province announced at the same time that minorities in agricultural areas were subjected to the one-child program like the Han, while people in the minority nationality pastoral regions were allowed to have two children and strictly limited to three.[41] Also in October 1983, the government of the minority areas of Hainan Island in Guangdong province issued regulations restricting minority urban residents to one child and applying all the required IUD insertion and required sterilization policies to them. In addition the regulations stated:

> Li, Miao, and Hui couples in rural areas are still allowed to have two children. Certain people in real difficulty who request to have a third must get the approval of the family planning departments at and above the county-level. No one may have a fourth child in any circumstances. Women of child-bearing age with one or two children must insert an IUD. One member of those couples of child-bearing age who have had three or more children should undergo contraceptive surgery, unless they are physically unable to have more children.
>
> The regulations stress: Minority-nationality cadres and masses who violate the family planning regulations must be punished like the Hans.[42]

One month later, the Hainan Li-Miao Autonomous Prefecture announced that it had succeeded in its sterilization work by completing 43,606 sterilization operations, thus overfulfilling its annual sterilization quota by 9 percent.[43] Because of the swift extension of compulsory family size limitation to the minority groups, rapid reduction in the fertility of China's minority people is expected.

Provincial Variation in Fertility

Just as the fertility levels of Han and minority groups, as well as urban and rural areas, have differed over the decades, so have those of the various provinces. A common problem in the study of huge countries like China is the tendency to deal only in the aggregate, ignoring the variety and complexity of subnational experience. Yet better understanding of the regional and even the national picture can be derived from a look below the surface.

In the latter half of the 1980's, many analyses of demographic conditions and trends in particular provinces are expected to be produced, because in 1987 China will for the first time publish 29 provincial volumes of demographic data compilations, one volume per province. Each volume will include 1982 census data on the province plus data from myriad other sources to trace long-term trends in fertility, mortality, migration, urbanization, labor force, and other demographic variables. These volumes will be rich sources of data with which to work, but users of the compilations who are unaware of the variable quality of the figures may assume they are of high and equal accuracy. Such an assumption could easily lead to misinterpretations of demographic levels and false conclusions on demographic trends. This chapter includes a brief look at the demography of each of China's provinces, with a focus on fertility levels and trends, in order to report and assess the data already available, but also to provide a sound basis for the more extensive provincial demographic analyses that scholars will subsequently carry out.

For the three decades before the 1982 census, the quality of fertility data from individual provinces differed so greatly that provincial comparisons are risky. While only 80–90 percent of births for the whole country were reported in most years, some provinces in some years may have reported close to 100 percent of their births while other provinces might have detected only 70 percent. The census, however, appears to have achieved relatively complete reporting of 1981 births nationwide. We can proceed on the hypothesis that the census detected almost all the births in each of the provinces too, without serious variation in completeness from province to province, until data become available with which to test this hypothesis.

Table 8.7 presents 1982 census data on total fertility rates, parity distribution of births, and crude vital rates by province for 1981. The provinces are arranged according to the level of their total fertility rates, from the lowest to the highest, which range from 1.3 births per woman for the province-level municipality of Shanghai to 4.4 births per woman in the southwestern province of Guizhou. Very high proportions of births in

TABLE 8.7
Reported Provincial Total Fertility Rates, Crude Vital Rates, and Births by Parity, 1981

Province	Total fertility rate	Births as percentage of all births: First births	Second births	Remaining births	Crude birth rate[a]	Rate of natural increase[a]
Shanghai	1.316	87%	12%	1%	16.1	9.7
Beijing	1.589	85	12	3	17.6	11.8
Tianjin	1.645	79	16	5	18.6	12.5
Liaoning	1.773	71	19	9	18.5	13.2
Jilin	1.842	60	25	15	17.7	12.4
Zhejiang	1.982	54	27	19	17.9	11.7
Heilongjiang	2.062	54	27	19	19.8	14.8
Jiangsu	2.076	61	26	13	18.5	12.4
Shandong	2.104	61	25	15	18.8	12.6
Shanxi	2.385	48	28	24	20.3	13.8
Shaanxi	2.394	50	26	24	20.4	13.3
Sichuan	2.434	57	24	19	18.0	10.9
Hubei	2.445	50	28	22	20.2	12.8
Nei Mongol	2.621	44	26	29	23.1	17.3
Hebei	2.650	52	28	20	24.0	17.9
Henan	2.651	45	28	28	20.6	14.6
Fujian	2.717	41	30	29	22.1	16.2
Gansu	2.728	43	25	32	20.1	14.4
Jiangxi	2.790	37	28	35	20.4	13.9
Anhui	2.799	37	29	34	18.7	13.5
Hunan	2.833	43	31	26	21.1	14.1
Guangdong	3.283	37	28	35	25.0	19.5
Yunnan	3.814	28	23	48	25.4	16.8
Xinjiang	3.883	27	18	55	29.1	20.7
Qinghai	3.927	27	20	54	26.7	19.2
Guangxi	4.103	31	24	45	27.3	21.6
Ningxia	4.120	30	21	49	29.7	23.6
Guizhou	4.355	24	20	56	27.9	19.4
Tibet	—	—	—	—	31.1	21.1

SOURCES: "Third National Census (IV): Birthrate of Women of Child-Bearing Age," BR 27, no. 11 (12 Mar. 1984): 23; State Council Population Office (1982): 22.
[a]Per 1,000 population.

the three province-level municipalities were first births and tiny proportions were third and higher order births. In contrast, first births in nine provinces constituted less than 40 percent of the births, and in six provinces, 45 percent or more of the births were third or higher order. Most of China's provinces in 1981 had crude birth rates in the range 18–25, very low for regions in a developing country. The highest reported birth rates were in the range 29–31, which if complete suggests that considerable fertility control was being practiced in these provinces as well as all the other provinces of China. Provincial natural increase rates from census data ranged from 10 to 24 per thousand population, largely because of provincial variations in birth rates, but also because recorded crude death rates ranged from 5 to 10. The actual 1981 natural increase rates for some provinces may have been lower than recorded by the census if deaths were underreported in these provinces.

As will be shown in the provincial analyses, some provinces managed to obtain virtually complete reporting of births from their annual yearend reporting system for 1981, while other provinces originally reported only 75–85 percent of the 1981 births their populations later reported in the census. Unfortunately, reported provincial birth rates for 1982 and after are based on this same faulty registration system, perhaps exacerbated by the ever-greater incentives for cadres to underreport births. For example, when official provincial birth rates for 1982 are weighted by the provincial populations, the resulting national birth rate is 18.6 per thousand population, 88 percent of the official 1982 national birth rate of 21.1 derived from the January 1983 national vital rate survey. Deaths are also less completely reported by the provinces, whose 1982 yearend reports add to a national death rate of 6.2, than by the vital rate survey that derived a death rate of 6.6 for 1982. If the annual survey of population change reported provincial as well as national vital rates, it would be possible to discover which provinces are seriously underreporting their fertility each year.

The provinces will be considered roughly in order from those with the lowest to those with the highest total fertility rates as of 1981, based on census data. The provinces that reported the lowest fertility in 1982 were the three advanced municipalities that have been accorded the status of provinces: Shanghai, Beijing, and Tianjin. This would be expected, because these three are proportionally the most urban provinces, and urban life in China is conducive to low fertility.

Shanghai

Shanghai Municipality claimed an approximately steady population size for one and a half decades: 10.82 million in the 1964 census, 10.68 million in a 1972 census, and 10.98 million at yearend 1978.[44] The city districts held close to half the population (5.5–5.8 million) during the 1970's, the rest living in ten suburban counties. This claimed stability of Shanghai's population through 1978 was achieved by severely restricting in-migration, forcing large numbers of young adults to migrate out of the municipality (1.08 million educated youths during 1968–77),[45] and reducing the municipal natural population increase rate.

The city districts of Shanghai claimed the earliest fertility transition in all of China, with the birth rate reportedly dropping to half its 1957 level

TABLE 8.8
Reported Crude Birth, Death, and Natural Increase Rates for Shanghai Municipality, 1950–83
(Rates per 1,000 population)

Year	Crude birth rate	Crude death rate	Rate of natural increase
		CITY DISTRICTS	
1950	22.1	7.7, 20	14.4
1951		19.1	
1952	37.7, 38.0	8.3, 8.8, 12.4	(25.6), 29.4
1953	40.4	9.9	(30.5)
1954	40, 52.6	7.1, 7.6	(32), 45.5, 45.62
1955	41.4, 42	8.1	(33.3), 34
1956	38, 40.3	6.7	31, (33.6)
1957	45.7, 45.8	5.9	39.9
1962	23.5	5.2	18.3
1963	23.1		
1964	(13.7)		
1965	10.4	4.3	6.1
1970	8.1	5.3	2.8
1971	6.93	(5.5)	1.4, 2
1972	6.49	(3.9)	2.6
1973	6		
1974	6.24	6.0	0.24
1975	6.6	6.2	0.4
1976	6.6	6.4	0.2
1977	7.2	7.0	0.2
1978	7.41	6.7	0.7
1979	8.0	6.3	1.68
1980	8.92	6.84	2.08
1981	13.6	6.7	6.9
1982	17.4	6.6	10.8
		SUBURBAN COUNTIES	
1950	26.4	7.9	18.5
1952	48.2	11.9	36.3
1957	47.8	7.4	40.4
1962	30.1	10.4	19.7
1963	41		
1964	(about 30)		
1965	26.5	7.7	18.8
1970	21.0	4.6	16.4
1971	18.05	(4.87)	13.18
1972	15.66		
1973	15.9		
1974	12.44	5.63	6.81
1975	12.5	5.8	6.7
1976	14.1	5.9	8.2
1977	14.5	6.0	8.5
1978	15.3	5.8	9.5

TABLE 8.8 (continued)

Year	Crude birth rate	Crude death rate	Rate of natural increase
1979	16.94	5.87	11.07
1980	14.94	6.09	8.85
1981	20.3	6.1	14.2
1982	19.8	5.9	13.9
	MUNICIPALITY		
1950	24.2	8.5	15.7
1952	39.1	8.8	30.3
1954	52.2, 52.6	7.1	45.5
1957	45.6	6.0	39.6
1961	22.4		
1962	26.3	7.3	19.0
1963	30.3	(7)	23.29
1964	20.6		
1965	17.0	5.7	11.3
1970	13.9	5.0	8.94
1971	11.7, 12.08	5.20	6.88, 7.1
1972	9.7, 10.75, 12.7	5.2, 5.6	5.2, 5.95, 7.5
1973			4.8
1974	9.19	5.83	3.36
1975	9.43	6.0	3.42
1976	10.24	6.1	4.10
1977	10.81	6.5	4.31
1978	11.1, 11.31	6.2	5.07, 5.1, 5.7
1979	12.34	6.1	6.23
1980	11.79	6.48	5.31
1981	12.95, 16.14[a], 16.79	6.44[a], 6.5	9.70[a], 10.34
1982	18.15, 18.50, 18.8	6.30	12.20, 12.23
1983	14.99, 15.4	6.9	8.11, 8.5

SOURCES: All sources for this table and the analogous ones that follow are on file at the China Branch, Center for International Research, U.S. Bureau of the Census. In this and all subsequent tables, figures in parenthesis are derived from other reported figures.

NOTE: When vital statistics are reported for the 1950's, it is rarely clear whether the data refer to the city districts alone or include the suburban counties that were annexed to form the municipality in the late 1950's.

[a]Based on 1982 census questions referring to calendar year 1981.

by 1963. A further steep drop was registered for 1964 and 1965 during the family planning campaign of the early 1960's. (See Table 8.8.) By 1965 the city of Shanghai had essentially completed its fertility transition, according to the available figures. Throughout the 1970's the city proper claimed the incredibly low birth rate of 6–8 per thousand population, slightly less than the lowest birth rates recorded in any cities outside China.

The suburban counties of Shanghai reported high birth rates during the 1950's and again in 1963 after the Great Leap years, followed by a sharp drop in the birth rate in 1964 and 1965. The decline continued to a low of 12.4 per thousand population in 1974, then the suburban birth rate began to rise.

Combined statistics for the whole municipality show a low birth rate of 22.4 in 1961, the fertility nadir of the Great Leap Forward economic depression, and a moderate post-famine birth peak in 1963, followed by a very steep drop in fertility in 1964. Further fertility decline was reportedly achieved through 1974, after which the municipal birth rate began slowly rising.

Shanghai's rapidly shifting birth rates of these decades appear peculiar at first glance, yet the trends are plausible in broad outline. The city of Shanghai has the urban characteristics that could cause spontaneous fertility decline before a vigorous family planning program, and this trend was reported by 1963. Furthermore the family planning program of the 1960's was targeted toward cities and their suburbs, and was most effective there in supplying modern birth control techniques. As of 1971 it was reported that 70 percent of Shanghai Municipality's married women of reproductive age practiced contraception, half of them protected by sterilization and most of the rest using other reliable methods. Such contraceptive saturation of the married population could cause a low municipal birth rate by 1971.

By the end of the 1970's Shanghai had achieved a very low level of fertility, according to a survey taken there. As of 1979 the total fertility rate in the city districts was reported to be 0.83 and in the suburban counties 1.46 births per woman, for a 1979 municipal rate of 1.1 births per woman, far below replacement level fertility.[46] Contributing to the low birth rate and total fertility rate was a high and rising age at marriage. According to the 1979 fertility survey, women's average age at first marriage rose steadily from the early 1950's to the late 1970's. By 1975–79 city women married at age 26.8 years on average and suburban women at an average age of 24.2. Another factor contributing to the low birth rates from the early 1970's at least through 1977 was a temporary reduction in the number of people in their late teens and twenties because a significant proportion of this age group was sent out of the city, part to the Shanghai suburbs and the rest outside the municipality.

Shanghai's birth rate rose in the second half of the 1970's with the first births of the large cohorts born in the 1950's. They began marrying earlier in the suburbs than in the city proper. In 1978 many of those who had been sent out of Shanghai began to return home, marry, and start families. The sudden drop in Shanghai's minimum marriage ages due to the 1981 Marriage Law caused a surge of marriages in the city proper and the suburbs. The resulting births, beginning in the fourth quarter of 1981, caused a sharp increase in the municipal birth rate. The peak of first births to these newly married couples occurred in 1982 and 1983. Some observers predict that Shanghai will continue to have high numbers of marriages and first births until the end of the 1980's.[47] The higher rate of natural population increase in the early 1980's combined with some continuing in-migration raised the size of Shanghai's permanently registered population to 11.94 million at yearend 1983, of whom 6.39 million lived in the city districts.[48]

Beijing

Beijing Municipality's reported population rose slightly from 7.57 million in the 1964 census to 7.89 million in 1972 to 8.50 million as of yearend 1978.[49] The explosive population growth normally seen in the capital cities of developing countries was prevented in Beijing by the same techniques used in Shanghai. Many educated youths were sent out of the municipality after 1968, and in-migration was relatively well controlled until 1979, when 120,000 persons reportedly moved into the municipality.[50] Many of these in-migrants may have been educated youths born and raised in Beijing. Since 1978 the PRC has relaxed the policy of sending urban school graduates to rural areas against their will and preventing them from returning to the cities. Partly through in-migration, Beijing's population rose to 9.23 million at midyear 1982, of whom 5.60 million lived in the urban districts.

Beijing city districts reported high birth rates and relatively low death rates, with high natural population increase, during the 1950's. (See Table 8.9.) After the Great Leap Forward decline in the birth rate and rise in the death rate, the city reverted to a high birth rate of 40 per thousand population in 1963. But a remarkable drop in the city birth rate is claimed for 1964 and 1965, down to only 16 in 1965. These data, if true, would mean that Beijing city telescoped almost its entire fertility transition into a two-year period. An alternate explanation for these figures is that the intense family planning campaign of 1962-66 caused not only genuine fertility decline but also avoidance of birth reporting in the city districts. A more gradual birth rate decline was reported in the following decade. Meanwhile, the suburban counties reported birth rates that fell to 32 per thousand in 1965. The whole municipality claimed to have achieved a birth rate of 23 in 1965 and 18 in 1972, dropping to a low of 9 per thousand population in 1976, and rising thereafter. Age-specific fertility data for the year 1975 suggest that the city districts of Beijing then had a total fertility rate of 1.2 births per woman, and the suburban counties had reached approximately replacement level fertility at 2.2 births per woman.[51]

As in Shanghai, Beijing's depressed birth rates of the mid-1970's were due not only to control of fertility within marriage but also to other factors. The mass deportation of young adults produced a more favorable age structure for a low birth rate in city districts. Refusal to allow young adults to marry until the woman became about age 25 and the man about age 28 (with somewhat lower minimum marriage ages in the suburbs) held down the municipal birth rate until the late 1970's, when large cohorts born in the early 1950's began to marry. Some of Beijing's deported

TABLE 8.9
Reported Crude Birth, Death, and Natural Increase Rates for Beijing, 1949–83
(Rates per 1,000 population)

Year	Crude birth rate	Crude death rate	Rate of natural increase
	URBAN DISTRICTS		
1949	18.7, 19.40	11.90, 14.1	4.6, 7.50
1950	37	13.7, 14	23
1951		12.7, 15.25	
1952	34.44, 35.0	9.3, 10.89	23.55, (25.7)
1953	39.6	9.3	(30.3)
1954	43.1	7.7	(35.4)
1955	40.6, 43.2	8.1, 9.6	(31.0), (35.1)
1956	39.3	6.7, 7.6	(31.7), (32.6)
1957	42.0	7.1	33.91, (34.9)
1959	30.70	9.66	21.04
1962	34.36		
1963	39.94		
1964	23.75		
1965	16.04		
1971	12.24, 15		
1972	about 14		
1976	6.33		
1977	7.21		
1978	9.73	4.80	4.93
1979	10.44	(4.6)	5.8
1980	13.41, 13.42	4.85	8.57
	NINE SUBURBAN COUNTIES		
1962	38.15		
1963	48.2		
1964	39.52		
1965	32.42		
1971	20–21, 26.04		
1976	12.24		
1977	13.79		
1978	16.72, 16.73	7.69	9.04
1979	17.83		
1980	18.44, 18.46	8.23	10.21

TABLE 8.9 (continued)

Year	Crude birth rate	Crude death rate	Rate of natural increase
	MUNICIPALITY		
1963	43.41	8.11	35.30
1965	23	6.7	16.3
1969	20.68, 22.36	7.39	14.97, 16
1971	18.8	6.4	12.4
1972	17.8	6.1	11.7
1973			9.7
1975	9.93	6.54	3.39
1976	9.06	6.53	2.53
1977	10.23	6.21	4.02
1978	12.92, 12.95	6.12, 6.19	6.4, 6.76
1979	13.69, 13.71, 13.72	5.94, 6	7.5, 7.71, 7.78
1980	15.56, 15.57	6.30	9.26, 9.27
1981	16, 17.55[a]	5.78[a]	11.77[a]
1982	20.04	5.68	14.36
1983	15.63	5.49	10.14

SOURCES: See Table 8.8.
[a]Based on 1982 census questions referring to calendar year 1981.

youth also began returning in 1979, with the possibility that they too would marry and settle there. A 1980 report documented almost a doubling of marriages in Beijing from 69,000 in 1977 to 130,000 in 1979. "From 1977," it stated, "the city birth rate began to go up and the trend is expected to continue for the next fifteen years."[52] The number of marriages in the municipality rose to 190,000 in 1981.[53] A great increase in the number of first births followed the surge of marriages and caused a peak in the birth rate and natural increase rate in 1982.

But marital fertility is very low in Beijing. By early 1981, of couples with one child, 93 percent in the city districts and 63 percent in the counties had received a single-child certificate.[54] As shown in Table 8.7, Beijing Municipality already had the low total fertility rate of 1.6 births per woman in 1981, and 85 percent of the births were first births. This proportion increased to 89 percent in 1982 and 91 percent in 1983.[55] There was a great increase in the number of sterilizations performed in the municipality in the first three months of 1983 compared to all of 1982.[56] It appears that fertility has remained under tight governmental control in Beijing.

Tianjin

The 1964 census counted 4.28 million people in Tianjin Municipality. In 1973 Tianjin expanded to its current boundaries by incorporating

TABLE 8.10
Reported Crude Birth, Death, and Natural Increase Rates for Tianjin Municipality, 1949–82
(Rates per 1,000 population)

	Urban districts		Counties	Municipality (current boundaries)[a]		
Year	Crude birth rate	Crude death rate	Crude birth rate	Crude birth rate	Crude death rate	Rate of natural increase
1949	15	10.49				
1950	40					
1951–1963	35–45	6.5				
1967	14.52					
1968	20.91					
1974				13.99	6.22	7.77
1975				13.88	6.59	7.29
1976				12.75	10.04	2.71
1977				13.06	6.30	6.76
1978	13.52		18.92	15.42	6.26	9.16
1979	10.02		18.24	(14.61)	(5.95)	8.64
						8.66
1980	12.16		14.23	13.26	6.03	7.23
				13.29	6.04	7.25
1981				(18.0)	(6.1)	11.94
				18.60[b]	6.10[b]	12.50[b]
1982				20.07	5.64	14.43

SOURCES: Sources of all the rates are on file at the China Branch, Center for International Research, U.S. Bureau of the Census. Most of the figures for 1949–78 are from Lyle (1980): 566–67.
[a]For the boundary changes, see Banister (1977b): 211–12.
[b]Based on 1982 census questions referring to calendar year 1981.

nearby counties. The midyear 1982 census counted a municipal population of 7.76 million, of whom 5.14 million lived in the urban districts.

Birth rate estimates for the urban area are too low for 1949 but plausible for the 1950's. (See Table 8.10.) Tianjin city claimed a drop from high fertility in 1963 to remarkably low fertility in 1967, similar to Beijing's reported fertility decline of the mid-1960's. Tianjin's low official birth rate for 1967 may result partly from postponement or avoidance of birth reporting. Even so, the long-term decline in the city's birth rate appears to have come primarily in the mid-1960's and to a lesser extent in the early 1970's. The lowest birth rate was reported in 1979, after which the urban districts recorded a rising birth rate for the same reasons as Beijing and Shanghai.

From 1974 through 1981 Tianjin Municipality reported a crude death rate of 6.0–6.6, which is reasonable for a progressive municipality in the 1970's. The unusual 1976 death rate was due to deaths from the nearby devastating Tangshan earthquake. For the years 1974 through 1980 the municipality reported a crude birth rate rather steady in the narrow range 12.8–14.6, except for a slightly higher birth rate in 1978, thought to be due to some couples replacing children killed in the earthquake.[57]

During the years 1974–80, with the exception of the earthquake year, Tianjin's recorded natural increase rate stayed between 7 and 9 per thousand population. This and the low birth rates during those years were achieved through late marriage, contraception, and abortion. In 1978, 95 percent of men and 95 percent of women getting married in the municipality reportedly were 25 or older. The 1978 contraceptive prevalence rate was 80.6 percent of all married women of reproductive age.[58]

The birth rate began rising in 1980 in Tianjin urban districts and in the whole municipality as of 1981. This rise reflected age structure shifts and the 1981 drop in the minimum marriage ages. Fertility per couple is low in Tianjin. In 1981, a reported 79 percent of births in the municipality were first children, as shown in Table 8.7, and first births were 94 percent of all reported births in 1983.[59] As of September 1982, it was announced, 87 percent of couples with one child had received single-child certificates.[60] Because of a bulge in Tianjin's age structure in the young childbearing ages and a concentration of marriages after the beginning of 1981, the birth rate of the early 1980's was fairly high even if couples had only one child. When these temporary phenomena pass in China's three leading municipalities, their crude birth rates are expected to be quite low.

China's most urbanized provinces are, after the three province-level municipalities, the three northeastern provinces. As of the 1953 census Liaoning's population was about 42 percent urban, Heilongjiang's approximately 31 percent urban, and Jilin's about 29 percent urban. These provinces remain far more urban than other provinces. According to the 1982 census the urban proportion of the population of Liaoning was 42.4 percent, Heilongjiang 40.5 percent, and Jilin 39.6 percent.[61] As of 1981, these provinces had lower fertility than almost all other provinces, partly because of their more urbanized populations.

Liaoning

Liaoning is China's second most industrialized province after Shanghai. Much of its total population of 35.7 million (as counted in the 1982 census) is concentrated in a huge agglomeration of cities in its central plain area. Liaoning's industrial, urban, and suburban character suggests that this province has the background conditions for doing unusually well in family planning and fertility control.

In the 1950's and 1960's, Liaoning reported very high natural population increase rates: 35.76 per thousand population in 1954, 32.22 in

1957, and 29.12 in 1965.[62] Such high natural increase, if correct, would have resulted from high fertility combined with lower mortality than found in many other provinces. But it is possible that mortality was seriously underreported in Liaoning in those decades.

A provincial official who reported some vital rate data and family planning information to a visiting delegation in 1973 stated that large-scale family planning efforts had begun in 1963. By 1971, he reported, the province's collected population data showed a natural increase rate of 19 per thousand population, and this was reduced to 18 per thousand for the year 1972, calculated from a crude birth rate of 24 and a crude death rate of 6.[63] The death rate, though perhaps subject to some underregistration, is within the range expected for one of China's most urbanized and industrialized provinces. A crude birth rate of 24 per thousand for 1972 would correspond to a total fertility rate of approximately 3.7 births per woman, down from over 6 births per woman in the 1950's. This is a striking fertility decline to have been achieved by any province by 1972, and should be considered the lowest plausible birth rate for any province at that time outside the three province-level municipalities. If Liaoning's 1972 birth data were anywhere near correct, this would mean that the urban population had largely completed its demographic transition by 1972, that its suburban population had adopted substantial control of fertility during the 1960's, and that its rural population had achieved some real fertility decline by 1972. The Liaoning informant also reported, "Rough estimates indicate that of married women of childbearing age, 70 percent of such persons in urban areas practice birth control while 40 percent do so in the countryside."[64] Such widespread practice of birth control would be required to produce Liaoning's claimed 1972 birth rate.

Liaoning's family planning program achieved such success in 1973 in promoting late marriage and birth control that a sudden drop of 2.6 per thousand in the natural increase rate was reported in 1974.[65] Liaoning's reported natural increase rate fluctuated between 9 and 13 during 1977–81. This is a slightly higher range than reported for the three province-level municipalities in the same years, a relationship to be expected given that Liaoning is not an advanced municipality but a relatively urban and industrial province. Also reassuring is that local officials in Liaoning were willing to report rising natural increase rates in 1978 and again in 1981, in spite of heavy political pressure from provincial leaders to achieve a reduced rate every year. But the pressure may have taken a toll on statistical accuracy in the province. The 1982 census calculated a 1981 birth rate of 18.53, death rate of 5.32, and natural increase rate of 13.21, the latter figure being 2 per thousand higher than what Liaoning had officially reported for 1981.[66]

Liaoning had a surge of first births in 1981 and 1982, because the number of marriages in the first half of 1981 had been three times the number in the same period of 1980.[67] According to the annual reporting system, the province's natural population increase rate was 13.4 per thousand in 1982.[68] Success was reported in the control of fertility in Liaoning the following year. A broadcast in February 1984 claimed that the province had achieved a 1983 birth rate of 13.95, death rate of 4.93, and natural increase rate of 9.02 per thousand population. The Liaoning Government Work Report released in April 1984 claimed that the 1983 natural population growth rate had been only 8.4 per thousand.[69] By yearend 1983, according to another report, 91 percent of couples with one child had received a single-child certificate.[70]

Jilin

Like Liaoning, the relatively urbanized province of Jilin reported high rates of natural population growth during the PRC's first two decades: 37.76 per thousand population in 1954, 25.41 in 1957, and 30.78 in 1965.[71] For more than a decade after 1965, no statistics are available on Jilin's demographic trends. Finally for 1978 and 1979 the province reported natural increase rates of 14.3 and 13.89 respectively. After the one-child program began, a low natural growth rate of 9.65 was claimed for 1980.[72] Under the pressure to reduce fertility, some underreporting of births may have occurred in 1980. Jilin had a problem with underreporting of births of second or higher parity in 1981. Based on the annual reporting system, Jilin reported a 1981 natural increase rate of 9.79 per thousand population, and claimed that 76 percent of 1981 births were first births, 17 percent second births, and 7 percent third or higher order births.[73] But the 1982 census resulted in a 1981 natural increase rate of 12.35 for Jilin, 2.56 per thousand higher than earlier reported, and the parity distribution of 1981 births from census reporting was 60 percent first births, 25 percent second births, and 15 percent third births, as shown in Table 8.7.

Because Jilin's annual system of birth reporting appears weak, its claims for successes in 1982 and subsequent years based on that statistical system may be exaggerated. For 1982, the province reported a birth rate of only 16.76 and natural increase rate of 10.93.[74] These figures probably underestimate the actual fertility in the province. Jilin also claimed that 85 percent of births were first births and only 3 percent third and higher order births in 1982.[75] It is likely that second and higher order births are still being left out of the birth registration and reporting system. Nevertheless, Jilin already had the low total fertility rate of 1.8 births per woman in 1981, and the province's fertility probably declined further in 1983 and afterwards under the national program of required sterilization, abortion, and IUD insertion.

Heilongjiang

For the decades since 1949, and over a century before that, Heilongjiang has been a frontier province in the far northeast regularly receiving new in-migrants. Its population of 32.7 million as counted in 1982 is comparatively highly urbanized, and many of the workers outside cities are employed by vast state farms, the forestry industry, and the oil industry. This province, like the other two northeastern provinces, reported unusually high natural population increase rates in the first two PRC decades: 31.97 per thousand population in 1954, 26.05 in 1957, and 32.38 in 1965.[76]

Heilongjiang claimed a steep fertility decline sometime between 1965 and 1975, to a 1975 birth rate of only 21.9 and natural increase rate of 16.7 per thousand population, approximately half the reported 1965 rate of natural population growth.[77] Little or no information is available on the province's family planning program or fertility changes during that decade. Heilongjiang reported further decline in its natural increase rate to 12.1 in 1978, to 10.14 in 1979, and to 8.64 in 1980.[78] By late 1980 the province reported that 86 percent of the persons who got married that year adhered to the late marriage guidelines, that 88 percent of women "capable of childbirth" were practicing birth control, and that 79 percent of couples with one child had received a single-child certificate.[79]

Though Heilongjiang residents do indeed have very low fertility, a total fertility rate of only 2.06 births per woman in 1981, the vital registration system that produced the low birth rates and natural increase rates reported above for the 1970's and 1980 is so faulty that the figures cannot be believed. For instance, the province claimed a natural population increase rate of only 8.24 per thousand population for 1981 and reported that firstborn children constituted 70 percent of all 1981 births.[80] But the census achieved more complete birth reporting for 1981. As shown in Table 8.7, the province had a natural increase rate of 14.8 based on the census, and 54 percent of the 1981 births were first births. This suggests that Heilongjiang's vital registration system missed a third of all 1981 births, especially births above first parity.

For 1982, the province claimed a birth rate of 15.50, death rate of 4.90, and natural increase rate of 10.60 apparently based on vital registration.[81] Other sources reported a 1982 birth rate of 16.07 and 16.27, the latter figure alongside a natural increase rate of 10.85 for that year.[82] These numbers may represent adjustments based on late registrations of 1982 births and deaths. But none of these figures can be trusted because the birth reporting system is so incomplete.

The government of the province released in March 1984 a natural population increase rate of only 7.76 per thousand population for 1983 based on vital registration.[83] But the leaders seem to have subsequently realized that this figure was useless, because one month later the Heilongjiang Statistical Bureau issued this report: "According to a sample survey, the birth rate of the province in 1983 was 17.54 per thousand, a decline of 0.91 per thousand. The mortality rate was 5.5 per thousand, up 0.62 per thousand. The natural growth rate was 12.04 per thousand, a decline of 1.53 per thousand."[84] The implied figures for 1982, then, are a birth rate of 18.45, a death rate of 4.88, and a natural increase rate of 13.57. No information has been released about this survey, so its validity is unknown. The 1982 birth and death rates both appear suspiciously low, but the 1983 estimates appear plausible. The natural increase rate estimate of 12.04 should be used in preference to the vital registration figure of 7.76.

It is likely that Heilongjiang's fertility is now below replacement level, as in the other two urbanized provinces of the northeast. But a temporary surge of marriages and first births swelled birth rates during 1981–83. In addition, the high fertility that these provinces had through 1965 ensures a bulge in the population age structure of young adults in their twenties until the mid-1990's. Even with very low fertility per woman, these age structure effects will tend to inflate their birth rates.

Zhejiang

Zhejiang, on the east coast, had a 1982 census population of 38.9 million, 26 percent of whom lived in urban areas. Based on census data, this province had a total fertility rate of only 1.98 births per woman in 1981. Of the births that year, 54 percent were first births, 27 percent were second births, and 19 percent third or higher order births, as shown in Table 8.7.

The history of Zhejiang's demographic transition is not yet well documented. The province reported a sharp drop in its natural increase rate from 18.6 per thousand population in 1977 to 12 in 1978, followed by a further decline to 10 or 11 in 1979. For 1980, Zhejiang reported five different official natural increase rates for the whole province ranging from 4.03 to 8.5 per thousand population, "setting an all-time low" or "the lowest since liberation" according to several sources.[85] There was a rise in the natural population increase rate in 1981. The figure from the census, 11.66 per thousand population, was 1 per thousand higher than the natural increase rate of 10.54 previously reported for 1981.[86]

Age structure data available for Zhejiang confirm that fertility has greatly declined. According to 1964 and 1982 census data, the proportion of the population age 0–14 declined from 41.23 percent in 1964 to 29.30 percent in 1982, indicating much lower fertility in the 15 years prior to 1982 than prior to 1964.[87] Single-year age data from the census suggest that the number of births declined yearly from 1969 through 1974, rose slightly during 1975–77, declined again in about 1978, and dropped sharply in 1980, confirming trends reported from vital registration data.[88] Using a demographic technique known as "reverse survival" on Zhejiang's 1982 census age structure suggests that the province's birth rate dropped from about 30 in 1970 to 20 during the period 1974–77, to 19 in the next two years, 16 in 1979–80, and 15 in 1980–81 (or slightly higher in recent years if there was any undercount of young children).

By 1981, Zhejiang reported, 40.7 percent of all couples with one child held single-child certificates; but in response to the production responsibility system in agriculture, a few counties had "basically lost control over their population growth."[89] Family planning work in Zhejiang continued to encounter "a lot of difficulties and a great deal of resistance."[90] In early 1982 provincial authorities mandated an "inspection" of women throughout the province to discover pregnancies not approved by the government. Localities were ordered to carry out required abortions and sterilizations: "When unplanned pregnancies are discovered, remedial measures are to be adopted promptly. Continue to mobilize with effort rural couples of childbearing age with two children to undergo sterilization in order to stop excessive numbers of births."[91] Later in the year, some parts of the province reported sharp increases in the numbers of abortions and sterilizations, and general success in their campaigns to minimize births outside the official plans.[92] The province's 1982 birth rate, based on vital registration, was 18.28 per thousand, and the natural increase rate 12.34, both slightly higher than the 1981 figures.[93]

In late 1983, Zhejiang reported that "a total of 920,000 sterilization operations were conducted in the first six months this year, bringing the rate of couples practicing birth control to 90.83 percent."[94] The birth rate that year reportedly dropped 3.29 per thousand (to 14.99) and the natural increase rate declined 3.67 per thousand (to 8.67). During "the second Zhejiang provincial family planning month" at the beginning of 1984, "1,090,000 people underwent various kinds of birth-control operations," including sterilizations, abortions, and IUD insertions.[95] Though refined fertility measures are not available for years after 1981, the government of Zhejiang appears to be succeeding in its drive to hold down its population's fertility.

Jiangsu

During the 1970's the two model provinces singled out for emulation in fertility control were Jiangsu and Sichuan. Jiangsu is an east coast province of 60.5 million persons, 16 percent of whom lived in urban areas according to the 1982 census. The rural population is more prosperous than that of most other provinces.[96] Jiangsu is flat, fertile, and very densely populated, especially on the Changjiang River delta in the southern half of the province.

Jiangsu's birth and death rates for 1954 appear underreported (see Table 8.11), but the errors offset one another to result in a plausible natural increase rate estimate for that year. Similarly, a natural increase rate of 25 or 27.5 per thousand reported for 1965 looks reasonable.

Jiangsu claimed a sharp fertility decline between 1970 and 1973, resulting in a drop in the province's official natural increase rate from 23.8 in 1970, to 15.09 in 1972, to 12 in 1973. In these years, Jiangsu was looked up to by the leaders of all the other provinces (except of course for

TABLE 8.11
Reported Crude Birth, Death, and Natural Increase Rates for Jiangsu Province, 1954–83
(Rates per 1,000 population)

	Cities		Counties		Provincial total		
Year	Crude birth rate	Rate of natural increase	Crude birth rate	Rate of natural increase	Crude birth rate	Crude death rate	Rate of natural increase
1954					(36.72)	12.06	24.66
1956					37.6		
1965							25
							27.5
1970							23.8
1972					(21.93)	6.84	15.09
1973							12
1974							10.73
1976							10.02
1977					15.99	(6.02)	9.97
1978	11.77		16.04				9.5
1979							8.4
							8.78
1980		6.61		6.21	12.15	5.90	6.25
1981					15.38	5.85	9.53
					18.47[a]	6.10[a]	12.37[a]
1982					16.43	5.75	10.68
1983	11.88	6.13	11.54	5.55	11.59	5.95	5.64

SOURCES: See Table 8.8.
[a]Based on 1982 census questions referring to calendar year 1981.

the three leading municipalities) as a marvel of birth planning success. This reputation appears to have been based primarily if not entirely on Jiangsu's natural increase rate as calculated from reported births and deaths: in 1972 it was 3 per thousand lower than the rate reported for Liaoning, and the claimed rate for 1973 was 5 per thousand lower than that of Liaoning. Independent information is needed to confirm or correct these figures, but very little is available. Some Jiangsu municipalities by 1972 reported high contraceptive use along with low birth rates and natural increase rates similar to those claimed for Shanghai. A few model communes and counties reported late marriage and contraceptive use to be universal practices among their populations in the reproductive ages. But the province has yet to document the stark changes in family planning policy and implementation, contraceptive use, and incidence of abortion and sterilization that could have lowered the provincial natural increase rate as reported for 1970–73.

After 1973 Jiangsu reported a slowly declining natural increase rate to a low of 6.25 in 1980. The fertility decline achieved in Jiangsu during the 1970's was largely a rural phenomenon as urban birth rates were already low early in the decade. By 1978 the recorded rural birth rate was still slightly higher than the urban rate. For 1980 Jiangsu's Family Planning Commission proudly reported that the rural natural increase rate had dropped below that in cities.[97] Another report said that between 1970 and 1980 the crude birth rate of rural Jiangsu dropped by 19.56 per thousand population.[98] Some underregistration of births and deaths was detected in the 1982 census, as seen in Table 8.11. Based on the vital registration system, the province reported a 1981 birth rate of 15.38, with first births 72 percent of all births and third and higher order births constituting 6 percent.[99] The census resulted in a 1981 birth rate of 18.47, with firstborn children 61 percent and third and higher order children 13 percent of reported births. The problem of underreporting of births was largely confined to second and higher order births. The 1981 natural increase rate was calculated as 12.37 from the census, 3 per thousand higher than the 9.53 previously reported. If underreporting of vital events is worse in rural than urban areas, then the actual rural natural increase rate may have remained higher than the urban rate in 1980 and perhaps thereafter.

Jiangsu's family planning program has reported steady success; the contraceptive use rate was given as 83.7 percent in 1977 and 88 percent at yearend 1980. By the end of 1981, of couples with one child in the province, 79 percent reportedly held single-child certificates.[100] During 1983 the provincial government further tightened its control over fertility in the province. By year's end the Provincial Family Planning Commission claimed a single-child certificate acceptance rate of 90 percent, and reported that 97 percent of the fecund couples in childbearing ages were practicing birth control.[101] For 1983, very low birth and natural increase rates were reported from cities and counties and for the whole province, as seen in Table 8.11. If the same proportion of births was unregistered in 1983 as in 1981, then the actual 1983 Jiangsu birth rate was about 14 per thousand population and natural increase rate was approximately 8, representing strikingly low fertility for any largely rural province.

Shandong

As of the 1982 census, Shandong was China's third most populous province with 74.4 million people, 19 percent of whom lived in urban areas. It is a densely populated province located on the east coast in the middle of the north China plain and jutting out into the Yellow Sea. No information is available on fertility, mortality, or natural increase for the whole province in the 1950's or 1960's. According to Table 8.12, by 1970 Shandong's birth rate was still 34 and natural increase rate was about 27 per thousand population. The province claimed a halving of the birth rate to 17 in 1977, with a natural increase rate of only 10. These figures stabilized through 1979 and further reductions were reported in 1980.

In February 1982 Shandong made the claim, based on registration data, that it had achieved a natural increase rate of 9 for the year 1981.[102] Shandong's vital rates as derived from the 1982 census were an improve-

TABLE 8.12

Reported Crude Birth, Death, and Natural Increase Rates for Shandong Province, 1970–83

(Rates per 1,000 population)

Year	Crude birth rate	Crude death rate	Rate of natural increase	Year	Crude birth rate	Crude death rate	Rate of natural increase
1970	(34.2)	(7.6)	26.55	[1980]			7.13
			26.60		(15.3)	(6.6)	8.67
			27.55				9
1972	(27.3)	(7.4)	19.94	1981	16.5		9
1975	(21.5)	(7.5)	14.03				10.07
1977	(17.0)	(7.3)	9.72		18.84[a]	6.26[a]	12.58[a]
1978	(16.7)	(6.4)	10.27	1982	17.05	6.10	10.95
1979	(17.0)	(6.2)	10.79				12.21
1980	13.90	6.40	7.50	1983	15.10	6.73	8.37

SOURCES: See Table 8.8. Most of the figures in this table were derived from data presented in Yang Xiaobing (1983): 25. Yang gives the rates of natural increase and the absolute figures for total births and population.

[a]Based on 1982 census questions referring to calendar year 1981.

ment over registration data. For 1981 the census reported a provincial birth rate of 18.84, death rate of 6.26, and natural increase rate of 12.58 per thousand population.[103] It was primarily second and higher order births that had not been registered in 1981. The claim that 76.9 percent of all Shandong's 1981 births were first births was an exaggeration based on faulty statistics.[104] As shown in Table 8.7, the census found that 61 percent of children born in 1981 were firstborn.

From local reports compiled upward, the province claimed that 85 percent of married women of reproductive age were practicing contraception in 1981.[105] As of early 1982 a vice governor of Shandong reported that there had been no relaxation of the constant pressure on couples to bear only one child and only at a time approved by the government.[106] By late 1982 it was claimed that 87 percent of couples with one child held single-child certificates.[107] The province reported a 1982 natural increase rate of 11 or 12 in different sources, corresponding to a birth rate of 17 or 18, and a decline in births during 1983 to a birth rate of 15 and natural increase rate of 8. (See Table 8.12.) The actual 1983 birth rate may have been about 17 if the proportion of births missed by the registration system was similar to 1981. This would imply an adjusted natural increase rate of about 10 per thousand. This populous province already had fertility around replacement level in 1981, and fertility apparently remained low in subsequent years.

Shanxi

Shanxi, a mostly hilly province in north central China, had 25.3 million people in 1982 of whom 21 percent lived in urban areas. Fertility data for Shanxi have been sparsely reported. The province claims to have achieved a natural increase rate of 22.9 in 1970, which if correct would imply considerable fertility control by then. But the statistical origin of this estimate is not clear, as parts of the province may have had no functioning system of birth and death registration during the early 1970's. For instance, as of 1972–74 Dazhai commune had to take some sort of survey in order to estimate its birth rate, death rate, and natural increase rate, and the survey appears to have underestimated all three rates.[108]

As shown in Table 8.13, Shanxi claimed rapid declines in its birth rate to 15.6 in 1978 and in its natural increase rate to 9.1. These vital rates stabilized for three years, according to the registration system. The census reported a 1981 birth rate of 20.31 and natural growth rate of 13.77, probably more complete figures than those (still unreported) derived from vital registration that year. By 1981, as shown in Table 8.7, Shanxi's

TABLE 8.13
Reported Crude Birth, Death, and Natural Increase Rates for Shanxi Province, 1970–83
(Rates per 1,000 population)

Year	Crude birth rate	Crude death rate	Rate of natural increase	Year	Crude birth rate	Crude death rate	Rate of natural increase
1970			22.9	1980			9.11
1974	25.9	7.7	18.2		15.69	6.49	9.2
1975	23.0	7.8	15.2	1981	20.31[a]	6.54[a]	13.77[a]
1976	19.5	7.2	12.4	1982	18.38	6.46	11.92
1977	17.5	7.1	10.4		21.07	6.64	14.43
1978	15.6	6.5	9.1	1983	17.32	6.6	10.7
1979	15.5	6.4	9.1				

SOURCES: See Table 8.8. Most of the figures in this table are from Ni Jianglin, "Shanxisheng weilai renkou de yuce" (A projection of the population of Shanxi province), in *Tongji yanjiu* (Statistical research, vol. 5), Beijing, 1982: 106.
[a]Based on 1982 census questions referring to calendar year 1981.

population had a total fertility rate of 2.4 births per woman, and 48 percent of births reported in the census were first births.

Two different sets of official vital rates were reported for 1982. The birth rate of 18.38 and natural increase rate of 11.92 probably came from vital registration.[109] Data that appear more plausible, a provincial birth rate of 21.07 and natural increase rate of 14.43, might have come from the January 1983 vital rate survey, but the source of the statistics was not given.[110] A reduction in the birth and natural increase rates was reported for 1983, again without reference to the origin of the figures.

Shaanxi

The province of Shaanxi, west and south of Shanxi, had a 1982 census population of 28.9 million of whom 19 percent were urban. These two provinces have reported similar fertility levels and trends. Shaanxi estimated a natural increase rate of 23.2 per thousand population for 1971, dropping to only 10–11 for the years 1977 through 1979.[111] A 1979 survey of the whole province found that women married on average at age 23, and that of the ever-married women of reproductive age, 1 percent were widowed or divorced, 4 percent had been unable to conceive or could no longer conceive, 13 percent had been sterilized, 56 percent were using other forms of contraception, and 26 percent were not using contraception.[112] Of the last group, some were pregnant, trying to conceive, or breastfeeding. The survey resulted in a 1978 Shaanxi total fertility rate of 2.13 births per woman, composed of 2.19 in rural areas and 1.49 in cities. It was estimated that 36 percent of births in 1978 were first, 33 percent were second, and 32 percent were third and higher order births. The survey gave a provincial birth rate of 17, composed of a rural birth rate of 18 and city birth rate of 11. The 1978 natural increase rate was estimated at 10.36 per thousand population, very close to the officially reported rate of 10.32. One weakness of this demographic survey was that the survey design assumed that marriage registration, population registration, birth reporting, and death reporting in Shaanxi were essentially complete. Most of the tabular information was compiled from written records. Interviewers went to the homes of women whose births had been recorded but did not try to detect unregistered marriages and unreported births by interviewing all households or all women in the reproductive ages.[113] It is, therefore, no surprise that the survey data completely confirmed the registration data: the former could not serve as a check on the validity of the latter.

For 1980 Shaanxi claimed great success in fertility control, including a contraceptive use rate of 86 percent, a birth rate of 14.0, and a natural increase rate of 7.19 per thousand population.[114] Partly as a result of the 1981 Marriage Law, the recorded natural increase rate for 1981 rose to 9.65.[115] But, as Table 8.7 shows, the census achieved more complete birth reporting for 1981, a birth rate of 20.4 and natural increase rate of 13.3. Shaanxi's birth registration system had missed almost 20 percent of 1981 births.

In early 1982 a vice governor of Shaanxi reported that "current problems are the drastic increase in the number of marriages, the decline of the deferred marriage rate, the decline in the number of persons practicing contraception, and the decline of the one-child rate."[116] He blamed these problems on the production responsibility system in agriculture and on the reluctance of leadership cadres to do the required family planning work. In late 1982 Shaanxi issued regulations ordering all couples to stop at one child (with minor exceptions), encouraging severe economic penalties against farmers who have more than one child, and requiring abortion: "Those who become pregnant in excess of the plan should adopt remedial measures at the earliest possible stage during pregnancy. Whoever objects to this must be severely punished."[117] The province reported a 1982 natural increase rate of 12.34, dropping to 9.42 in 1983, the latter figure from a 1983 birth rate of 16.01 and death rate of 6.59.[118] If these data were from vital registration, and completeness of reporting was constant from 1981, then the actual 1983 birth rate was about 20 and natural increase rate about 13.

Sichuan

Sichuan is China's most populous province, with a 1982 census count of 99.7 million, only 14 percent urban. The province is situated near China's geographical center and consists of rugged mountains both in the western half and surrounding the rich agricultural basin in the eastern half where almost the entire population of the province lives. During the last half of the 1970's the model province in birth planning was Sichuan, yet planned parenthood work did not even begin there until 1971.[119] Reported vital rates for Sichuan are shown in Table 8.14. A 1980 report estimated that in 1965 Sichuan had had a birth rate of 42.39, death rate of 11.46, and natural increase rate of 30.93 per thousand population, reasonable estimates for a population without birth control.[120] Contradictory figures have been given for 1970. One analysis reported a birth rate of 52.7 and natural increase rate of 40.1, implying a 1970 death rate of 12.6 per thousand.[121] Given the chaos known to have occurred in Sichuan during and immediately after the Cultural Revolution, a death rate that high is possible. Birth rates that high are seen elsewhere in the developing world and therefore are possible for Sichuan before its family planning program began. But an alternate plausible explanation is delayed registration of births and deaths that had occurred in previous years. The other official estimate of Sichuan's 1970 birth rate, 40.72, and natural increase rate, 31.21 per thousand population, also indicate the continuation of traditional high fertility.

According to Table 8.14 Sichuan's natural increase rate stayed high through 1973, then began dropping sharply from 27 per thousand in 1973 to 23 in 1974 and 20 in 1975. A fertility decline this fast, if true, would already be extraordinary. But the most striking assertion made by officials of this populous province is that the natural population increase rate dropped even more steeply from 20 in 1975 to 12 in 1976. No supporting evidence or explanation for this drop is yet available. Continuing decline was reported, until the province claimed an all-time low natural increase rate of 4 or 5 for 1980, the lowest in China. Sichuan reported a rise in the natural increase rate to 9.17 per thousand in 1981, but the 1982 census indicated a 1981 rate of 10.94. If Sichuan's 1981 birth rate of 17.96 from the census represented complete birth reporting, then the birth registration system had missed around 11 percent of that year's births.

The sources and validity of Sichuan's estimated vital rates for the 1970's and previous decades are not apparent. But throughout the 1950's and 1960's Sichuan's leadership seems to have had great difficulty gathering adequate statistical data for the province. One problem was occasional

TABLE 8.14
Reported Total Fertility Rates and Crude Birth, Death, and Natural Increase Rates for Sichuan Province, 1954–83
(Rates per 1,000 population)

Year	Total fertility rate	Crude birth rate	Crude death rate	Rate of natural increase
1954				24.43
1965		42.39	11.46	30.93
1970		40.72	(9.51)	31.21
		52.7	(12.6)	40.1
1971	5.3			28.98
1972				27.32
1973				26.92
1974				22.91
1975				20
1976		20.7	(8.4)	12.25
1977				8.67
1978		13.08	(7.02)	6.06
1979		13.58	6.88	6.70
1980				4.45
				5.12
1981	2.434[a]	15.92	6.75	9.17
		17.96[a]	7.02[a]	10.94[a]
1982		15.83	(6.87)	8.96
1983	1.73	11.61		
		13.13	7.08	6.05

SOURCES: See Table 8.8.
[a]Based on 1982 census questions referring to calendar year 1981.

submission of invented numbers, as recounted in a 1952 article: "The term 'fairy figure' is very popular in the conversation of district and *hsiang* cadres of Chien-yang. Figures which are not obtained through statistical investigations conscientiously carried out, but are based on subjective estimation or are falsified, are all referred to as 'fairy figures.' These figures are used especially for the purpose of meeting assignments and coping with the higher levels."[122]

Another problem has been the simple enormity of Sichuan. To gather accurate data on a province of 100 million persons is a herculean operation. Sichuan's statistical apparatus appeared unequal to the task at least until the mid-1970's. During 1974 a "provincial inspection group on birth control and the patriotic sanitation campaign" traveled around the province trying to assess the demographic situation.[123] The inspection team pinpointed Chengdu and Chongqing Municipalities and one prefecture as "progressive typical examples" in birth control work as of 1974.

Demographic data reported from Sichuan ought not inspire unquestioned confidence as the adequacy of the statistical system has been in doubt for decades. It is possible that the steep decline in Sichuan's natural increase rate in the mid-1970's, for instance, was partly due to a shift in the sources of vital rate data or in the estimation procedures between 1975 and 1976. Another possibility is that as demands from the higher levels became more stringent, local cadres began refusing to report "excess" births or began substituting "fairy figures" for collected statistics.

In spite of any problems with the statistics, it is clear that Sichuan's population underwent a remarkable fertility decline in only one decade. In 1981 one report claimed that there had been 10 million sterilizations performed in Sichuan.[124] By then 1.8 million of the 2.3 million couples with one child, 80 percent, had reportedly taken a single-child certificate.[125] Provincial leaders detected some loosening of controls on fertility during 1981 after the production responsibility system in agriculture was put in place: "As a result, there were declines last year in most parts of the province in the percentages of couples marrying late, having only one child and taking out single-child certificates. The natural population growth rate rose from a decline. We must therefore be resolved to take resolute and appropriate measures to change this situation as soon as possible, strive to improve the quality of planned parenthood work and focus the work on the rural areas."[126] The provincial government ordered cadres to carry out regular pregnancy inspections and to require couples to sign contracts promising no childbirth during the agricultural production year.[127]

Sichuan reported fairly steady fertility for 1982 and then a drop to a total fertility rate of 1.73 births per woman in 1983 compared to 2.43 in 1981. By yearend 1983 it was reported that 89 percent of women in reproductive ages were practicing contraception and that of couples with one child, 89 percent held single-child certificates.[128] The claimed 1983 birth rate of 13.13 and natural increase rate of 6.05 were reportedly based on "sample census figures." The same radio broadcast said that 76 percent of 1983 births in Sichuan were first births.[129] All of this success was attributed to Sichuan's "relentless persistence in family planning work" during 1983.[130]

Hubei

According to Table 8.7 the province of Hubei had low fertility by 1981, a total fertility rate of 2.4 births per woman with first births constituting half of all births. Yet very little information is available on the fertility transition in this populous province located east of Sichuan on the middle basin of the Changjiang River. Hubei's 1982 census count was 47.8 million, of whom 17 percent lived in urban areas. The province claimed low natural increase rates of 10.5 in 1978, 11.34 in 1979, and 8.58 in 1980.[131] The census recorded a 1981 birth rate of 20.17, death rate of 7.33, and natural increase rate of 12.84 per thousand population. Probably based on the vital registration system, Hubei claimed that its natural increase rate dropped to 10.06 in 1982 and 6.96 in 1983, and that third and higher order births constituted only 7 percent of 1983 births, down from 22 percent in 1981.[132]

Nei Mongol

Statistics for the Inner Mongolian Autonomous Region during the 1970's are complicated by the fact that a large proportion of its territory was taken away in July 1969 and redistributed to five adjacent provinces, and in July 1979 all this lost territory was returned to Inner Mongolia.[133] Presumably all vital rates reported for 1970–78 refer to the population of the truncated region, and data for 1979 and beyond apply to the population within the restored larger boundaries of Nei Mongol. Inner Mongolia had a 1982 census population of 19.3 million, of whom 15.6 percent were members of minority groups. The province's population at that time was 29 percent urban.[134]

Inner Mongolia reported a natural increase rate of 26.1 in 1970, dropping to 24.1 in 1971, to 22.1 in 1972, and to 21 in 1973. For 1972 the natural increase rate was derived from an official birth rate of 28.66 and death rate of 6.55.[135] No figures are available for 1974 through 1976, when further fertility decline was apparently taking place because Nei Mongol then announced natural increase rates of 12.4 in 1977 and 12.0 in 1978.[136] After restoration of its former boundaries, the province reported a 1979 natural population growth rate of 13.2, dropping to 11.05 or 11.53 in 1980.[137]

The 1982 census estimated a 1981 birth rate of 23.11, death rate of 5.77, and natural increase rate of 17.34. Inner Mongolia's total fertility rate was calculated to be 2.6 births per woman, as shown in Table 8.7, and 29 percent of the births were third or higher order. Fertility and mortality data from the census appear more completely reported than birth and death rates based on vital registration for the years before and after 1981. The census-based 1981 death rate of 5.77 deaths per thousand population is probably underreported but not nearly so badly as the 1980 death rate of 4.95 or the 1982 death rate of 4.78 apparently calculated from death registration. Similarly, the official birth rates of 16.48 for 1980 and 18.40 for 1982 look much less complete than the 1981 birth rate of 23.11 from the census.[138]

Hebei

Hebei province surrounds the province-level municipalities of Beijing and Tianjin in north China. Hebei includes a densely inhabited plain south of these municipalities and a semicircle of mountains and hills to the north. The 1982 census counted 53.0 million people in the province, of whom 14 percent lived in urban areas. Hebei claimed considerable fertility decline by 1970 with an official birth rate of 26.73 and with a natural increase rate of 20.24, down from 25 in 1965. A rapid drop in fertility was reported by the mid-1970's. Hebei's official natural growth rate dropped to 14 in 1973 and further to 8.75 in 1977. On the strength of these possibly underreported natural increase rates, Hebei was considered one of China's leading provinces in birth planning.[139]

Hebei's natural population growth rate reportedly stabilized through 1980, when it was 9.2 per thousand population. For 1981 the province reported an "upswing" in its natural population increase rate that was attributed to "failure to adjust to the new economic situation," but the vital rates from the registers were not revealed.[140] The 1982 census achieved more complete reporting of births in Hebei than the registration system seems to have managed before or since. As shown in Table 8.7, the province had a 1981 total fertility rate of 2.65 births per woman, and just over half the births were first births. From census data Hebei's 1981 birth rate was 23.99 and natural increase rate was 17.94, almost double the claimed 1980 increase rate from vital registration. Though the annual statistics have been faulty, the province's 1982 census age structure reveals that the birth rate was particularly low during 1974–77 as Hebei had claimed and rose during 1978–82, probably because of large numbers of people reaching childbearing ages.[141] The use of reverse survival on the age structure produces estimates of a birth rate of 30 or 31 in 1970 dropping sharply to 18 in 1974–75; the birth rate rose slowly to about 21 in 1978–79 and stabilized at 20 through 1980–81. The vital registration system missed about a quarter of the births by then.

Based on birth registration, Hebei reported a 1982 birth rate of 19.35 and natural increase rate of 13.41; the actual rates were probably higher because Hebei had a surge of marriages in 1981 that was surely followed by unusually large numbers of first births during 1981–83.[142] From January through August 1983, there were 2 million sterilization operations in Hebei plus a million other birth control operations (abortions or IUD insertions).[143] For 1983 the province reported a birth rate of 14.86 per thousand and a natural increase rate of 9.13, noting that "the momentum of population growth has been checked."[144] It must be assumed, however, that birth registration remained incomplete.

Henan

By the time of the 1982 census, Henan had edged past Shandong to become China's second most populous province with 74.4 million people, a fact Henan authorities found an embarrassment rather than a source of pride.[145] This densely populated inland province on the north China plain was 14 percent urban in 1982. Table 8.15 shows Henan's official vital rates as reported for 1954 through 1983. After high birth rates of 40 and 39 in the late Cultural Revolution years 1969–70, perhaps swollen by delayed registrations of earlier births, the province recorded a puzzling drop to a birth rate of only 31 in 1971. Henan's official birth rate was steady through 1973, dropped steeply to 19 in 1976, and stabilized through 1979. In 1979 the province claimed great success in birth control work: during the first half of the year there were 1.4 million sterilizations performed, and the number of induced abortions greatly increased.[146] Henan then reported a drop in its birth rate from 19 in 1979 to 16 in 1980. It claimed continued success in holding down the natural increase rate in 1981 and reported that the number of couples having only one child had increased. But the production responsibility system in agricul-

TABLE 8.15
Reported Crude Birth, Death, and Natural Increase Rates for Henan Province, 1954–83
(Rates per 1,000 population)

Year	Crude birth rate	Crude death rate	Rate of natural increase	Year	Crude birth rate	Crude death rate	Rate of natural increase
1954	37.0	13.3	23.7	1973	30.6	7.3	23.4
1955	30.8	11.7	19.0	1974	26.6	7.4	19.2
1956	35.8	14.0	21.8	1975	22.8	7.7	15.1
1957	33.7	11.8	21.9	1976	19.4	7.2	12.2
1958	33.1	12.7	20.4	1977	19.7	7.0	12.7
1959	28.0	14.1	13.9	1978	19.7	6.3	13.4
1960	14.0	39.6	−25.59	1979	19.2	6.3	12.9
1961	15.3	10.1	5.1		19.23	6.34	12.88
1962	37.5	8.0	29.4	1980	15.8	6.3	9.5
1963	45.0	9.4	35.6		15.9	6.39	
1964	36.0	10.6	25.4		15.87	(6.32)	9.55
1965	36.0	8.5	27.6		15.84	6.31	9.53
1966	35.6	8.5	27.1	1981			10.39
1967	30.4	8.5	21.9		17.35	6.57	10.78
1968	35.7	7.9	27.8		20.64	6.01	14.63
1969	40.2	7.7	32.5	1982			9.8
1970	39.0	7.5	31.5		18.07	6.21	11.86
1971	31.3	7.5	23.8	1983	14.31	6.32	7.99
1972	31.1	7.1	23.9				

SOURCES: See Table 8.8. Most of the figures in this table were reported in Lin Furui & Chen (1983): 115.

ture had resulted in a strong desire for more children on the part of the peasants.[147]

There are some problems with the data in Table 8.15 that dictate caution in using Henan's figures without adjustment. The census recorded a 1981 birth rate of 20.64 compared to a birth rate of 17.35 from vital registration, suggesting that about 84 percent of the births that year were registered. Incomplete birth reporting may have been a problem throughout the 1970's. Henan's 1982 census age structure, for instance, indicates an approximately constant number of births in the province each year during 1970–73. The steep drop in the official birth rate from 1970 to 1971 is not visible in the age structure of surviving children. A decline in births after 1973 and stabilization after 1975 is clear in the age distribution, but no significant drop in the birth rate is seen for 1980.[148] Using the reverse survival technique, one can estimate from the age structure that Henan's birth rate was still about 35 in 1970–71, then dropped to 33 during 1971–73 and further to 31 in 1973–74. The birth rate dropped sharply to 26 in 1974–75 and to 22 in 1975–76, the level at which it stabilized through 1977–78. Henan's birth rate apparently stayed at 20–23 from mid-1978 to the 1982 census and did not drop to the low levels reported by vital registration. Underreporting of births was significant in 1980 and 1981. It is probable that unreported births are primarily those that are forbidden, namely births above the first parity. For example, Table 8.7 shows that 28 percent of all 1981 births detected in Henan by the census were third and higher order births, but only 17 percent of registered 1981 births had belonged to this category.[149]

Given this history of problematic birth registration, fertility after 1981 is difficult to estimate. Henan's official 1982 birth rate of 18 may represent an actual birth rate of 21 or 22, little or no change from 1981. The census had found that 45 percent of 1981 births were first births; the province claimed that firstborn children were 61 percent of all births in 1982 and 69 percent in 1983, but the latter figures are probably too high because unregistered births tend to be higher order births.[150] The census had estimated a 1981 total fertility rate of 2.65, and the province reported a decline to 2.1 in 1982, but the latter figure may be an underestimate.[151] Similarly, the natural increase rate of 8 shown in Table 8.15 for 1983 is very likely too low. Nevertheless, this populous province already had low fertility in 1981 and probably has reduced its population's fertility in subsequent years.

Fujian

Fujian, a hilly province on China's southeast coast, had a 1982 census count of 25.9 million, 21 percent in urban areas. Apparently because Fujian recorded comparatively high birth and natural increase rates during the 1970's, these figures were never released until a high 1978 rate could be contrasted with a lower one the next year.

Statistics showing a sudden decline in the natural increase rate from 17.86 in 1978 to 13.02 in 1979 were derived from the annual reporting system.[152] This claim followed insistent demands for success publicized in September 1978:

> Planned parenthood work is the task of the whole party. It is a major matter. . . . Our province has scored some success in planned parenthood. However, we are very far from meeting the demands of the party Central Committee. We must absolutely not be complacent or slack. Next year's plan must be tightly grasped now, otherwise work next year will be passive. . . . The conference noted: The progress of the work in Fukien [Fujian] has been uneven and the restrictions on population growth are very far from hitting the targets laid down by the state. In order to reduce the rate of population growth to below 1 percent in three years, the province must now start to achieve a great decline in its rate of population growth.[153]

> The decline in the rate of population growth in the province is rather slow and we lag far behind the majority of fraternal provinces and municipalities. . . . This situation in planned parenthood work must be rapidly transformed. The whole province must effectively control the rate of natural population growth and strive to greatly reduce it within a short period, grasping this as an important strategic task.[154]

Fujian's leaders clearly found it unacceptable that other provinces were reporting low natural increase rates while Fujian was not. The possibility that many other provinces were actually underreporting their rates may not have occurred to them. In China an apparent success, whether real or not, obliges other provinces to match the claimed accomplishment or the implication is that their leaders are inadequate. Poor demographic statistics from some provinces may cause politically inspired deterioration of data from other provinces.

After claiming a sharp drop in its natural increase rate for 1979, Fujian followed up with another remarkable claim for 1980, a natural increase rate of only 9.33 per thousand population, ostensibly meeting the national target.[155] Fujian reported that in 1981 its natural increase rate rose to 12.47 because of the impact of the production responsibility system in agriculture.[156] The census elicited much better reports of births for 1981 and derived a natural increase rate of 16.20 for that year. The registration system had missed about 17 percent of 1981 births.

For the year 1982 Fujian reported one of the highest provincial natural increase rates, 17.55 per thousand population, and then claimed a sharp drop to 11.35 for 1983. After the census estimated that 41 percent of 1981 births had been first births, the province reported that firstborn children comprised 45 percent of 1982 births and 50 percent of births in 1983.[157]

Gansu

Gansu is a hilly and somewhat arid province in north central China whose 1982 census count was 19.6 million, mostly Han Chinese with 8 percent of the population belonging to minority groups, and with 15 percent of the total population living in urban areas.[158] Gansu is one of China's poorest provinces as measured by average household income and per capita income in rural areas.[159] Table 8.16 shows Gansu's official vital rates since 1949. The province reported high birth rates in the 1960's that declined somewhat to 35 per thousand population in 1973. A sharp drop in the birth rate was reported between 1973 and 1974, and an even steeper decline was claimed between 1975 and 1976, to a low birth rate of

TABLE 8.16
Reported Crude Birth, Death, and Natural Increase Rates for Gansu Province, 1949–83
(Rates per 1,000 population)

Year	Crude birth rate	Crude death rate	Rate of natural increase	Year	Crude birth rate	Crude death rate	Rate of natural increase
1949	30	11	(19)	1972	—	—	28.9[b]
1950	32	11	(21)		37.8	8.1	(29.7)
1952	33	11	(22)	1973	35.3	8.1	(27.2)
1953	34	11	(23)	1974	27.4	7.1	(20.3)
1955	29	12	(17)	1975	29.0	7.9	(21.1)
1956	28	11	(17)	1976	17.7	6.7	(11.0)
1958	31	21	(10)	1977	17.4	6.0	(11.4)
1962	41	8	(33)	1978	17.7	5.9	(11.8)
1964	47	16	(31)		—	—	12.2[c]
1965	45	12	(33)	1979	16.5	5.7	(10.8)
1966	43	12	(31)	1980	14.03[d]	5.15[d]	8.88[d]
1967	44	8	(36)	1981	—	—	11.97[f]
1968	42	8	(34)		20.12[e]	5.72[e]	14.40[e]
1969	42	9	(33)	1982	17.07[g]	5.60[g]	11.47[g]
1970	39.5	7.9	(31.6)	1983	—	—	9.16[b]
1971	37.1	7.9	29.1[a]				

SOURCES: 1949–79, World Bank (1983): Vol. 3, Annex H, 92, and also as noted below.
[a] "Population: Gansu," SWB-WER, no. W1177 (24 Mar. 1982): 1.
[b] Gansu Family Planning Commission. "Gansu jihua shengyu gongzuo chengji xiren" (Gansu's achievements in family planning work are heartening), JHSYB, 28 Sept. 1984: 2.
[c] Released by the Family Planning Office, PRC, to the Library of the U.N. Fund for Population Activities, U.N. Development Program in China, Beijing.
[d] Sun Jingzhi & Li (n.d.): 185.
[e] Tongji Data Office (1984): 23.
[f] "Renzhen guanche qieshi zhixing" (It takes serious implementation and concrete execution), GSRB, 2 Apr. 1982: 1.
[g] Encyclopedic Yearbook of China 1983 (1983): 107.

18 per thousand. The official birth rate stabilized through 1979, then dropped to an all-time low of 14 with an official natural increase rate of 9 in 1980.

Gansu reported a resurgence in the birth and natural increase rates in 1981 because of the production responsibility system in rural areas and an increase in marriages.[160] The vital registration system showed a 1981 natural increase rate of 11.97 but the census got improved birth reporting. Tables 8.7 and 8.16 show that Gansu had the low total fertility rate of 2.73 births per woman in 1981, which produced a birth rate of 20.12 and a natural increase rate of 14.40. The system of birth registration had not reported about 12 percent of 1981 births. For 1982 Gansu got apparently from the vital registration system a birth and natural increase rate about the same level as had been derived from vital registration in 1981, indicating essentially no change in the province's birth rate from 1981 to 1982. For 1983, Gansu reported that the proportion of married couples in reproductive ages practicing contraception rose to 85 percent and the natural increase rate dropped to 9 per thousand.[161] It is likely that under-registration of births, and probably also deaths, continued in 1983. The province's population practiced essentially no contraception in the late 1960's; just over a decade later Gansu's fertility was low and the birth rate was half what it had been so recently.

Jiangxi

Jiangxi is a hilly province in southeast China with a 1982 census population of 33.2 million, 19 percent of whom lived in urban areas. Jiangxi reported that its birth rate was over 30 per thousand in 1976, and the birth rate dropped to 27.01 in 1978. With a recorded death rate of 7.39, this gave an official natural increase rate of 19.62 per thousand for 1978.[162] Jiangxi then reported a steep decline in its natural increase rate to 13.74 in 1979. This achievement followed several frustrating years in which Jiangxi had been unable to reduce its natural increase rate, according to an August 1978 broadcast which demanded success in planned parenthood work.[163] The natural increase rate was reported to have plummeted again from 13.74 in 1979 to 9.11 in 1980.[164]

The 1982 census estimated that Jiangxi's total fertility rate had been reduced to 2.79 births per woman as of 1981, that the birth rate was 20.42, and that the natural increase rate was 13.88 that year. These data indicate that Jiangxi's population had already experienced considerable fertility decline by 1981. But the registration system had estimated a natural increase rate of only 9.38 per thousand for 1981.[165] This suggests that about 80 percent of Jiangxi's births were registered that year. For

1982, apparently based on vital registration, Jiangxi reported a birth rate of 16.48 and natural increase rate of 10.41.[166] Given the weak registration system, these figures indicate that the actual birth and natural increase rates for 1982 were probably higher than they had been in 1981.

Anhui

Anhui province on the north China plain had a 1982 census population of 49.7 million people, 14 percent urban. As shown in Table 8.17, Anhui has released its official vital rates for 1949 through 1981 except for the famine years. Anhui is thought to have been one of the provinces worst hit by the famine. Beginning in 1962 and throughout the decade, Anhui recorded unusually high birth rates and natural increase rates. Then there was a slow decline in the official birth rate to 35 in 1972.

A 1981 report stated that "the family planning programme was begun in the province of Anhui at the end of 1971. Extensive education and organizational work was undertaken in 1972 and practical results began to be obtained in the following year."[167] Official data show a precipitous decline in Anhui's birth rate, from 35 in 1972 to 18 in 1976, with the birth

TABLE 8.17
Reported Crude Birth, Death, and Natural Increase Rates for Anhui Province, 1949–83
(Rates per 1,000 population)

Year	Crude birth rate	Crude death rate	Rate of natural increase	Year	Crude birth rate	Crude death rate	Rate of natural increase
1949	18.09	6.97	11.12	1969	39.29	6.76	32.53
1950	18.30	7.05	11.25	1970	37.18	6.45	30.73
1951	18.31	7.05	11.26	1971	35.90	5.91	29.99
1952	18.26	7.03	11.23	1972	35.17	6.58	28.59
1953	18.65	7.18	11.47	1973	29.70	5.94	23.76
1954	43.30	16.60	26.70	1974	24.27	5.71	18.55
1955	27.67	11.80	15.87	1975	22.13	5.68	16.45
1956	33.17	14.25	18.92	1976	18.34	5.51	12.83
1957	29.75	9.10	20.65	1977	17.88	5.52	12.36
1958	23.83	12.36	11.47	1978	18.56	4.78	13.78
1962	53.26	8.23	45.03	1979	18.43	4.69	13.74
1963	50.69	7.92	42.77	1980	14.33	(4.65)	9.68
1964	39.85	8.60	31.25				9.9
1965	41.79	7.24	34.55		15.16	4.62	10.54
1966	41.08	7.12	33.96	1981	18.73[a]	5.20[a]	13.53[a]
1967	40.61	6.99	33.62	1983	16.76	5.83	10.93
1968	39.94	6.87	33.07				

SOURCES: See Table 8.8.

[a]Based on 1982 census questions referring to calendar year 1981.

rate leveling out thereafter. The 1982 census estimated for Anhui a 1981 total fertility rate of 2.80 births per woman and vital rates similar to those being reported from the vital registration system. For 1983, as shown in Table 8.17, death reporting may have been more complete than in earlier years, and the birth rate was reported to be slightly reduced compared to 1981.

Hunan

Information is sparsely reported on demographic trends in Hunan, a province of 54 million persons in south central China, 14 percent of whom lived in urban areas based on the 1982 census. Hunan did release a series of absolute birth totals, which can help to chart its fertility transition.[168] Though births were clearly underreported during the late 1950's, by 1964 Hunan reported 1.6 million births, which meant a crude birth rate of 43, reasonable for that year. The number of reported births stayed high through 1969, for which 1.6 million births were still reported, resulting in a birth rate of about 36 per thousand population. But suddenly and so far without explanation, the reported number of births dropped to 1.36 million in 1970, corresponding to a birth rate of about 30. One hypothesis would be that there was strong demand for birth control in rural Hunan that was met during 1969 with the initial deployment of barefoot doctors. But 1970 was unusually early for such a sharp fertility decline, so birth data for 1970 and years immediately after should be treated with caution until supporting information is made available.

For all the years 1970–75, Hunan reported 1.3–1.4 million births annually. By 1975 this corresponded to a birth rate of about 27 per thousand population. Suddenly in 1976 the number of reported births dropped to 1.0 million, for a birth rate of approximately 20. Hunan officials have not clarified how such a steep birth rate decline took place. Widespread adoption of family planning methods during 1975, after moderate levels of use in 1974, would have been required.

Recorded births declined slowly after 1976. The 946,000 births reported for 1977 would correspond to a birth rate of about 18.6, and the 893,900 births reported for 1978 means a birth rate of 17.4. Hunan's recorded birth rate for 1978 came from a birth rate of 17.66 for rural areas and 13.43 for cities.[169] The province reported a slowly declining natural increase rate from 10.82 in 1977 to 8.93 in 1980.[170] The census estimated that Hunan had a total fertility rate of 2.8 births per woman in 1981, resulting in a birth rate of 21.11 and natural increase rate of 14.08. A provincial report stated that 86.5 percent of eligible couples were practicing birth control in 1981.[171] Essentially no change was reported in

Hunan's crude vital rates for 1982, but a big drop in fertility was reported during 1983. The official birth rate dropped to 16.51 and natural increase rate to 9.72.[172] This was attributed to the performing of almost a million sterilization operations during family planning propaganda month at the beginning of 1983 and 140,000 abortions throughout the year.[173]

Guangdong

Guangdong is a province on the southern coast with a population of 59.3 million at midyear 1982, of whom 19 percent lived in urban areas. Reported vital rates for Guangdong are given in Table 8.18. Official birth rate data reported for 1962, 1965, and 1970 indicate that Guangdong achieved a substantial drop in fertility by 1970. Guangdong reported a slowly declining birth rate through 1973, then steep drops of 3 per thousand population in 1974 and again in 1975, and 2 per thousand in 1976. A drop in the birth rate in the early 1970's seems to have resulted from a vigorous drive to raise ages of marriage and limit births. It was claimed that in 1974 "the rates of birth control and late marriage [age 23 for women, 25 for men] both exceeded 60 percent and the rate of natural population growth was 3.66/1,000 lower than in 1973."[174]

It is believable that Guangdong's lowest birth rates came in 1976 and 1977. This implies that the large cohorts born in the 1950's married late

TABLE 8.18
Reported Crude Birth, Death, and Natural Increase Rates for Guangdong Province, 1962–83
(Rates per 1,000 population)

Date	Crude birth rate	Crude death rate	Rate of natural increase	Date	Crude birth rate	Crude death rate	Rate of natural increase
1962	43.3	6.5	36.8	1978	20.7	(5.9)	14.75
1965	36.28	6.68	29.60	1979			16.78
			29.46				16.96
1970	29.24	5.78	23.46	1980	20.2	(5.7)	14.5
1971	29.02	5.52	23.50		20.34	5.36	14.99
			23.52				15.91
1972	28.55	5.97	22.58	1981			15.4
1973	27.21	5.95	21.26		24.99[a]	5.54[a]	19.45[a]
1974	23.91	6.30	17.61	1982	19.76	5.33	14.43
1975	21.01	6.06	14.95		21.33		
			14.97		23.2	5.9	17.3
1976	18.85	6.25	12.60	1983	19.24		
1977	18.58	5.97	12.61		21.15	6.32	14.83

SOURCES: See Table 8.8. Most of these data were released to Chen Pi-chao by the Guangdong Provincial Planned Birth Staff Office on 27 July 1978.

[a]Based on 1982 census questions referring to calendar year 1981.

enough that they, for the most part, postponed their first births until 1978 or thereafter. A 1978 report confirms the impression that by then marriage ages were fairly high and birth control use was widespread in the province: "At present, of the some 6 million married couples of child-bearing age in Kwangtung [Guangdong], 4.6 million couples have carried out measures to prevent conception, with the total rate of prevention of conception reaching 76.5 percent. The rate of late marriage is 75 percent."[175]

For a province with an approximately steady death rate during the late 1970's, and where high marriage ages and high rates of contraceptive use had already been achieved, one would expect a rising birth rate and natural increase rate as those born in the 1950's reached marriage age. In 1977, some localities in Guangdong began reporting rising natural population increase rates. For example, Hainan Island reported that its natural increase rate reached a low of 15.22 per thousand in 1976 and then began rising.[176] The subsequent reported increases in Guangdong's overall natural increase rate in 1978 and 1979 were probably genuine. The fact that local and provincial officials in Guangdong reported them despite criticism inspires confidence in their vital registration and reporting system during those years.

During the early and mid-1970's the people of Guangdong had adjusted to government demands that they marry later, minimize higher order births, and practice birth control. But in the late 1970's and early 1980's the population proved unwilling to further reduce their average family size below two or three children per couple. The government tried to persuade or force the people to stop at two, then at one child, and popular resistance to the family planning program rose. By 1981 it appears that one by-product of this struggle was deterioration in the completeness of birth reporting. Couples defiantly had babies but did not report them, or cadres caught in the middle falsified the number of births in their unit. For 1980 and 1981 the province reported lower natural increase rates than for 1979, as shown in Table 8.18, yet underreporting of births was serious. Some of those missing births were reported by respondents in the 1982 census. The census reported a Guangdong birth rate of 24.99 per thousand population, death rate of 5.54, and natural increase rate of 19.45, which was 4 per thousand higher than the natural increase rate of 15.4 derived from the regular reporting system. But not all 1981 births were accounted for in the census. The sex ratio of the reported births was 110.5, suggesting that female births were selectively underreported.[177] Adjusting the number of female births upward to get a plausible sex ratio at birth gives an estimated 1981 birth rate of 25.6 per thousand population, implying a slightly higher total fertility rate than estimated from census data (see Table 8.7).

Guangdong is the best example so far of a popular backlash against China's increasingly restrictive family planning program. If a similar backlash has taken place anywhere else in China, it is not as well documented.

Conflicting statistics reported for 1982 all suggested some decline in the birth rate from 1981, and a sample survey was used to derive a 1983 birth rate of 21.15 and death rate of 6.32.[178] The birth rate appears more completely reported than the figure of 19.24 probably based on vital registration, and the death rate seems more completely reported than in other data sources. Therefore, Guangdong's government may have had some success in requiring its population to limit their fertility further after 1981, and the provincial natural increase rate apparently declined from 19 per thousand population in 1981 to about 15 in 1983.

Yunnan

The rugged southwestern province of Yunnan counted 32.6 million people in the 1982 census, of whom 32 percent belonged to more than 24 different minority nationalities.[179] Only 13 percent of the province's population lived in urban areas. As shown in Table 8.19, Yunnan reported high natural increase rates in the 1960's such as 31 per thousand popula-

TABLE 8.19
Reported Crude Birth, Death, and Natural Increase Rates for Yunnan Province, 1957–83
(Rates per 1,000 population)

Year	Crude birth rate	Crude death rate	Rate of natural increase	Year	Crude birth rate	Crude death rate	Rate of natural increase
1957			20.16	1978	17.96[a]		19.23
1962			28.86		26.72[b]		
1965			31.04	1979			14.60
			31.09	1980			10.25
1971			24.70		17.76	7.36	10.40
1972			23.97				10.93
1973	35	(9)	26.41	1981			12.93
1974			23.36		25.36[c]	8.60[c]	16.76[c]
1975			20.86	1982			14.04
1976			21.12	1983	17.37	7.42	9.95
1977			21.79				14.38

SOURCES: See Table 8.8.
[a]Urban. [b]Rural.
[c]Based on 1982 census questions referring to calendar year 1981.

tion in 1965. By 1973 Yunnan claimed that its birth rate had dropped to 35 and natural increase rate to 26. Further fertility decline reduced the official natural growth rate to 21, at which it stabilized from 1975 through 1977.

As of 1978 Yunnan reported higher fertility and natural increase than most provinces. A low birth rate of 18 had reportedly been brought about in urban areas, and rural areas claimed their birth rate had declined to 27. The reported provincial natural increase rate of 19 per thousand was unacceptably high to provincial officials who in November and December 1978 broadcast the following demands:

> The remnant influences of Lin Piao and the gang of four have not been eliminated. Besides, we have not firmly grasped this work. Our province's planned parenthood work has progressed slowly. This situation must be quickly changed. . . . All units must work out their plans early and carry them out. They must conduct regular inspections, assessments, and comparisons. Cadres at all levels and party and CYL [Communist Youth League] members must play exemplary and forward roles.[180]

> The Yunnan Provincial CCP [Chinese Communist Party] Committee recently held a conference in Kunming on planned parenthood. The participants . . . revised the plan for and requirements of planned parenthood work in the province. . . . The participants held: "There are many reasons for the poor work of planned parenthood in our province. Apart from not eliminating the pernicious influence of Lin Piao and the gang of four the main reason is that we have not grasped the work firmly and well and have not included it in the agenda of the party committees as an overall major task. . . . The collectives and individuals who have done well in planned parenthood work should be commended and rewarded in a timely fashion. Units and individuals who have not attached importance to planned parenthood work should be criticized and disciplinary action should be taken in serious cases.[181]

Given this threat of criticism and disciplinary action, it would not be surprising if some officials during 1979 minimized the recording of births or invented low birth figures to please their superiors. Yunnan reported a steep drop in its natural increase rate to 15 in 1979 and again to 10 or 11 in 1980. It is unlikely that Yunnan's natural increase rate actually went from 19 in 1978 to 10–11 in 1980, especially considering that the minority groups would still have much higher fertility than the Han majority. Perhaps Yunnan's data from 1979–81 referred only to the Han and did not include minority areas. Whatever the reason, the regular vital reporting system greatly underestimated Yunnan's 1981 natural increase rate, officially reported as 12.93 per thousand. The 1982 census resulted in a 1981 natural increase rate of 16.76 in Yunnan, 4 per thousand higher than the previous report. The province's birth rate was reported as 25.36

and the death rate as 8.60, which means that the census got much more complete reporting of births and deaths than had vital registration. Year-end reporting had missed about 14 percent of deaths and nearly 20 percent of births. In 1981 Yunnan still had a total fertility rate of 3.8 births per woman, and almost half were third or higher order (Table 8.7), not surprising given the large minority group population.

Yunnan has promoted family planning among the minorities for some years.[182] During 1984, it was announced that members of minority groups in high and frigid mountainous areas where the population was small were allowed a third child at most, and no limits were set for fertility in "frontier regions," but persistent family planning propaganda and education were to be carried out there. Otherwise, minorities were to be treated approximately the same as the Han.[183]

The province announced that third and higher order births were 29 percent of all births in 1983, but if this was based on birth registration it was probably an underestimate. For 1981, this category was 37 percent of registered births compared to 48 percent of births detected by the census, which suggests that higher order births tend to be underreported by vital registration.[184]

Based on the vital registration system, Yunnan claimed that its natural population growth rate was 14.04 in 1982 and only 9.95 per thousand population in 1983. But a sample survey resulted in a 1983 natural increase rate of 14.38, probably more realistic than that from vital registration.[185] Therefore, the most usable data so far available indicate that Yunnan's natural increase rate dropped from 17 in 1981 to 14 in 1983, based on the census and a survey.

Xinjiang

Xinjiang province in the far northwest had a 1982 census count of 13.1 million people, 28 percent of whom lived in cities and towns. It is an arid province; 75 percent of its territory is virtually uninhabited desert, drifting sand, or mountains. The census showed that minorities constituted 60 percent of the province's population in 1982.[186]

A high natural increase rate of 30.6 per thousand population was reported for 1965 and 1972, a reasonable estimate for a province whose health system was functioning adequately but three-fifths of whose population married early and did not practice contraception.[187] The next usable information on Xinjiang's vital rates and fertility comes from the 1982 census and is given in Table 8.7. As of 1981, the total fertility rate of the province's population was 3.9 births per woman based on responses to census questions. This implies that a significant proportion of the province's population had begun to practice family planning. The provincial 1981 birth rate was calculated as 29.08 and the natural increase rate 20.67, down 10 per thousand from the 1972 estimate.

Some information was reported for intervening years, but users of Xinjiang demographic data should be cautious about believing the reported numbers. The main problems with the figures are underregistration of births and confusion about whether data are for the urban Han population, the total Han population, or the whole province's population. It is clear that China's family planning program was applied to the Han people of Xinjiang during the 1970's and caused real fertility decline. A 1979 report described this trend:

> The population growth rate of the Han people in the Xinjiang Uygur (Uighur) Autonomous Region, northwest China, has dropped from 24.26 per thousand in 1975 to 14.86 per thousand, while the rate in cities and farms densely populated by Han people has been reduced to under 10 per thousand. . . . The region has a population of 11 million, about half of whom are people of Han nationality. . . . Wang Feng stressed that Xinjiang's family planning work is mainly to be done among the Han people. "Family planning is not emphasized among the minority nationalities," he pointed out, "but technical guidance should be made available for those who have too many children, who have given birth to children at very short intervals or who wish to practice birth control."[188]

The natural population increase rate of 14.86 for 1978, attributed above to the Han population of Xinjiang, was reported in other sources as the whole province's natural growth rate.[189] The fertility of Xinjiang's minority people has not been reported except for 1979, and data for that year appear to underestimate their births. For the minority peoples of the province, a 1979 birth rate of 26.9, death rate of 12.3, and natural increase rate of 14.6 per thousand population was given.[190] The actual birth rate among the minorities was probably considerably higher.

Problems continued with Xinjiang's data reports. For 1980, one broadcast claimed that the province's Han population had a natural increase rate of 12.3 per thousand, while another report also broadcast from Xinjiang stated that the whole province had a natural growth rate of 12 while the natural increase rate among the people of Han nationality was only 8.4 per thousand.[191] A third source reported that the whole province had a birth rate of 20.87, death rate of 7.46, and natural increase rate of 13.41 for 1980.[192] Comparing these figures with vital rates for the following year from the census (birth rate: 29.08, death rate: 8.41, natural increase rate: 20.67) suggests that births, deaths, and natural increase were all underreported in 1980 because of an inadequate vital registration system. Unfortunately official figures for 1982 appear to be based on this system and therefore inaccurate. Xinjiang reported the low birth rate of 21.16, low death rate of 6.65, and low natural increase rate of 14.51 for 1982, all of which seem underestimated in comparison to the more complete census reports for 1981.[193] Great success has been claimed for fertility control among Xinjiang's Han population. Broadcasts from Urumqi, the province's capital, reported Han natural increase rates of 10.21 per thousand in 1982 and under 8 in 1983.[194] The quality of these statistics, probably based on vital registration, is unknown.

Qinghai

Qinghai province is primarily a vast, cold, arid plateau that is barely inhabited. The province had only 3.9 million people as of the 1982 census, of whom about 73 percent lived in an eastern agricultural zone around Xining City and nearby towns that covers only 4 percent of the province's land area.[195] Based on the census count, 20 percent of Qinghai's total population lived in urban areas and 39 percent of the total belonged to minority groups.[196]

Qinghai reported the high natural population increase rate of 32.4 per thousand for 1971.[197] Significant fertility decline was claimed by the late 1970's, to a natural increase rate of 19.5 in 1978 with further decline to 15.53 in 1980, derived from a birth rate of 21.14 and death rate of 5.61.[198] But there was a problem of underreporting of births, deaths, and natural increase by this time. From vital registration, Qinghai reported a 1981 natural increase rate of only 15.16 per thousand population, but census questions derived a rate of 19.17, or 4 per thousand higher.[199] The census got a 1981 death rate of 7.48 per thousand for Qinghai, suggesting that the province was failing to register at least one-fourth of all deaths. Similarly, the census-based 1981 birth rate of 26.65 indicates that over 20 percent of births had been missed by the birth registration system. By 1981, according to Table 8.7, Qinghai's fertility had been reduced to 3.9 births per woman, and 54 percent of births were still third or higher order.

The provincial government pushed family planning very hard during 1982. In June provincial regulations were issued severely penalizing couples and families who bore a second or higher order child: "Difficulties in living caused by having many children will not be subsidized. Children who are not only-children will not be distributed farmland under the responsibility system and will not be given private plots. When distributing houses and residential lands, they will not be considered."[200] The province claimed that of couples with one child, 35 percent had been issued a single-child certificate.[201] Family planning was required in minority as well as Han areas, and there was a great increase in contraceptive surgery, especially tubal ligations, during the two family planning propaganda months held in Qinghai during 1983.[202]

Fertility in Qinghai has probably fallen since 1981, based on reports of increased practice of family planning, but the claimed vital rates appear to be based on the vital registration system and therefore cannot be believed. For 1982 the province reported a birth rate of 19.40, death rate of 5.10, and natural increase rate of 14.30.[203] Given the extent of underreporting detected for 1981 by comparison with census data, these 1982 figures imply little change from 1981 in the birth rate and natural increase rate, perhaps a drop of 1 per thousand in each. Similarly, the report that Qinghai's 1983 natural increase rate declined to "below 14" per thousand suggests only a slight birth rate decline between 1982 and 1983.[204] If vital registration remained as poor in 1982 and 1983 as it was in 1981, the provincial natural increase rate may have actually been 17 per thousand or higher during those years.

Guangxi

The south China province of Guangxi counted 36.4 million people in 1982, of whom 62 percent were Han Chinese, 34 percent were members of the Zhuang minority group (China's largest minority nationality), and 4 percent belonged to other minorities. The province was very rural, with only 12 percent of its population in urban areas. Table 8.20 shows the official vital rates reported for Guangxi. A significant drop in the province's natural increase rate was claimed between 1965 and 1972. Gradual decline was reported in Guangxi's rate of natural population growth from 1972 to 1981, when the province claimed a rate of 16 per thousand based on the vital registration system. But the census detected far more 1981 births, for a birth rate of 27.25 and natural increase rate of 21.64, implying that the birth registration system had missed about 20 percent of births that year. As shown in Table 8.7, Guangxi's total fertility rate had declined to 4.1 births per woman by 1981.

Since the province's 1982 official vital rates were based on the faulty registration system and got about the same vital rates as the system produced for 1981, one should assume essentially no change in Guangxi's actual crude vital rates from 1981 to 1982. This means the 1982 birth rate was probably about 27 per thousand and the natural increase rate still 21 or 22. Guangxi claimed a decline in its birth rate to 19 and natural growth rate to 13 for 1983, but these figures appear to be from the vital registration system. Assuming the same extent of underreporting as 1981 gives a 1983 estimated birth rate of 24 and natural increase rate of 18.

TABLE 8.20
Reported Crude Birth, Death, and Natural Increase Rates for Guangxi Province, 1965–83
(Rates per 1,000 population)

Year	Crude birth rate	Crude death rate	Rate of natural increase	Year	Crude birth rate	Crude death rate	Rate of natural increase
1965			33.37	1981			16
1972			23.14		27.25[c]	5.61[c]	21.64[c]
1975			20.76	1982	21.20	5.60	15.60
1978	16.84[a]		18.27	1983	18.69	5.60	13.09
	24.48[b]						
1980	22.30	5.80	16.50				

SOURCES: See Table 8.8.
[a]Urban. [b]Rural.
[c]Based on 1982 census questions referring to calendar year 1981.

Apparently based on birth registration data, Guangxi claimed its total fertility rate dropped to 2.8 births per woman in 1983, far lower than the 4.1 derived from 1982 census data.[205] The province also reported that 32 percent of 1982 births and 28 percent of 1983 births were third and higher order births, much lower than the 45 percent of 1981 births in this category as estimated from the census.[206] But because births are significantly underreported in Guangxi and higher order births are probably selectively omitted since they are forbidden, these statistics on fertility are likely to be very much in error.

The province reported that 68 percent of couples in childbearing ages were practicing birth control by yearend 1983 and that 26 percent of couples with an only child had received a single-child certificate.[207] In 1984 the Guangxi Family Planning Commission expressed its determination "to take effective measures to enforce strict control of population growth and to put an end to the backwardness of the region's family planning work."[208]

Ningxia

The small population of Ningxia, 3.9 million counted in the 1982 census, is concentrated along the Yellow River in the northern part of an otherwise arid province, 22 percent of the total population living in urban areas. Han people constitute 68 percent of Ningxia's population and the Muslim Hui nationality 32 percent. As of 1972, Ningxia reported the high birth rate of 40 and natural increase rate of 33.[209] Family planning reportedly reduced the natural increase rate to 24 in 1977, gradually declining to 20 in 1980.[210] But the 1980 birth rate of 24 and death rate of 4 were both underreported. For 1981, the vital registration system recorded a natural increase rate of 19.56, but the census derived a rate of 23.57.[211] The census-based 1981 death rate of 6.08 implied that the province's death registration system missed about a third of the deaths. The census derived a 1981 birth rate of 29.65, suggesting that about 20 percent of births had been missed by birth registration that year. Table 8.7 shows that Ningxia had a total fertility rate of 4.1 births per woman in 1981, and almost half the births were of third or higher order.

For 1982 the province reported a birth rate of 24.92, death rate of 4.39, and natural increase rate of 20.53, all based on the faulty vital registration system.[212] However, a sample survey resulted in a natural increase rate of 23.05, almost as high as the 1981 rate based on the census.[213] This means that Ningxia's birth, death, and natural increase rates should be assumed essentially the same in 1982 as 1981. The province claimed that 70 percent of married couples of childbearing age practiced birth control in 1982.[214]

At the end of 1982, in preparation for the first family planning propaganda month, provincial leaders emphasized that they were going to carry out strict family planning policies in minority nationality areas. In the middle of 1983 the province reported "gratifying achievements" in family planning work, especially the high proportion of married women in reproductive ages who had had a tubal ligation during the propaganda month.[215]

Guizhou

Guizhou province in the southwest counted 28.6 million people in 1982, of whom 20 percent lived in urban areas. A variety of small minority groups add up to 26 percent of the provincial population. Before launching its family planning program in 1975, Guizhou had the high natural increase rates of 30 per thousand population in 1971 and 29 in 1974 according to official data. The province claimed a precipitous drop in its natural increase rate to 19 in 1977, to 16 in 1978, and to 13 in 1980.[216] Because the minorities were not required to practice family planning, one would suppose their birth rate was still high and was considerably higher than that of the Han population by 1980. But one report said the Guizhou minorities had a birth rate of 20.79 per thousand in 1980 compared to the provincial birth rate of 19.97.[217] A reasonable hypothesis would be that births among the minorities were seriously underreported.

Guizhou's registration system recorded a rise in the natural increase rate to 14.95 in 1981, but the census was able to get more complete recording of 1981 births and natural increase.[218] According to the census, Guizhou had a total fertility rate of 4.4 births per woman, birth rate of 27.89, and natural increase rate of 19.41 that year. Vital registration had missed 15 or 20 percent of 1981 births.

During 1982 the province carried out record numbers of abortions and emphasized sterilization.[219] Guizhou then recorded a drop in the birth rate to 20.41 and natural increase rate to 12.81 in 1982.[220] But these figures appear to be from vital registration. Assuming the same degree of omission as 1981 suggests an actual birth rate of 24–26 and natural increase rate of 16 or 17.

The next year there was an escalation of the sterilization program following national policy: "In 1983, all localities paid close attention to various sterilization measures. As a result, the birth control rate was 85.88 percent, rising 5.66 percent over the previous year. Of this figure those undergoing ligation operations accounted for 51.68 percent of the total number of people taking birth control measures." The province claimed the 1983 birth rate dropped to 15.04 and natural increase rate to 8.09, apparently from vital registration, which might translate to an actual 1983 birth rate of 18–19 and natural increase rate around 10 or 11.[221] No matter how the official data are adjusted, this province, one-quarter of whose population consists of minority nationals, seems to have experienced steep fertility decline in 1983.

Tibet

The far western province of Tibet (Xizang) consists of the world's highest mountains and frigid, arid plateaus that can barely provide subsistence for the small resident population, counted in 1982 as 1.9 million, 9 percent of whom lived in Lhasa or a small town. Of the total population excluding military personnel, 94 percent were Tibetan, 1 percent other minority groups, and only 5 percent Han Chinese.[222] The minorities in Tibet were exempt from family planning until the early 1980's, and it appears that demographic data about them were poorly collected, if at all, until the 1982 census. Before the census, vital rates reported for Tibet appeared to reflect the use of Han statistics to represent the whole province. Natural increase rates of 14.2 per thousand population in 1978 and 14.78 in 1980 are just plausible for the tiny Han minority.[223] These figures are not reasonable for the entire population of the region. The Tibetan people of Xizang since the early 1970's have benefited from a national effort focused on improving health and mortality in the province, which would be expected to reduce the death rate and raise the natural increase rate.[224]

The census questions on fertility and mortality resulted in an estimated 1981 birth rate of 31.05, death rate of 9.92, and natural increase rate of 21.13 for Tibet. Official data for 1982 also seem to refer to the province's whole civilian population rather than the Han portion. Tibet reported a 1982 birth rate of 30.40, death rate of 9.70, and natural increase rate of 20.70, while another source said the 1982 natural growth rate was 23 per thousand.[225] The birth rates for 1981 and 1982 indicate that some fertility control was already taking place among Tibet's population.

A journalist visiting Tibet in early 1983 noted: "The Tibetans are allowed up to three children, as against the single child permitted Han couples under the state's tough birth-control policies, though even this seems widely ignored in rural areas."[226] At midyear Tibet's Family Planning Office reported that the natural increase rate in Tibet during early 1983 was "even higher than that in the same period of last year," and resolved to become more effective in family planning work.[227] In October, however, it was claimed that 80 percent of peasants and herdsmen in Tibet were already practicing family planning. New rules were publicized limiting peasants, herdsmen, and urban workers of Tibetan nationality to two children per couple unless they lived in sparsely populated border or outlying areas.[228]

Conclusion

The foregoing analysis has shown that there was still great variation in levels of fertility from province to province by 1981, and that provinces have differed enormously in the quality and accuracy of the vital rate statistics they have reported both before and after the 1982 census. In spite of these differences, all provinces have experienced considerable fertility decline in comparison to their fertility levels in earlier decades, and the leaders of all provinces continue to try to reduce the fertility of their populations. Fertility also differs between urban and rural areas, and especially between Han Chinese and minority groups, but considerable convergence is expected in the future as rural people and minority nationalities reduce their fertility further under government pressure.

9

Population Distribution, Internal Migration, and Ethnic Groups

China covers a huge land mass, but its population is unevenly distributed throughout that area. The northern and western sections consist of steep mountains, vast deserts, high plateaus, and arid grasslands, none of which can easily support a dense population; about half of China is inhospitable and very thinly populated. In contrast the eastern, central, and southeastern parts are densely populated. The densest settlements are in cities and on alluvial plains extending inland from the coast, river valleys, the North China Plain, and the Red Basin in the center of China. As of yearend 1979 the PRC reported that 84 percent of its civilian population, or 814 million persons, were classified as agricultural.[1] These people live near the land cultivated by their families, in most cases outside urban agglomerations, but that cultivated land takes up only 10.3 percent of China's area.

Population Density

Systematic data are not yet available on population densities in small areas such as the county, which would give us a much better idea of the geographical distribution of the population. Such data may become available following the computer tabulation of 1982 census data; meanwhile, we can see some crude variations in population density at the province level.[2] Table 9.1 lists the provinces with their 1982 overall population density and their numbers of people per unit area of cultivated land.

There are enormous variations in these figures. Xizang (Tibet) reports only 2 persons per square kilometer, Qinghai 5, Xinjiang 8, and Nei Mongol 16 persons. These four provinces alone contain 50 percent of the PRC's land area but only 4 percent of its population. Four other prov-

TABLE 9.1

Population Density of the PRC by Province, 1982

Province	Population, midyear 1982 (thousands)	Total land		Cultivated land		
		Area in km²	Population per km²	Area in km²	Area as percent of total	Population per km²
North						
Beijing	9,231	16,807	549	4,260	25.3%	2,167
Tianjin	7,764	11,305	687	4,667	41.3	1,664
Hebei	53,006	187,700	282	66,414	35.4	798
Shanxi	25,291	156,300	162	38,800	24.8	652
Nei Mongol	19,274	1,183,000	16	51,095	4.3	377
Northeast						
Liaoning	35,722	145,700	245	36,667	25.2	974
Jilin	22,560	187,400	120	40,494	21.6	557
Heilong-jiang	32,666	453,300	72	86,667	19.1	377
East						
Shanghai	11,860	6,186	1,917	3,528	57.0	3,362
Jiangsu	60,521	102,600	590	46,481	45.3	1,302
Zhejiang	38,885	101,800	382	18,212	17.9	2,135
Anhui	49,666	139,900	355	44,519	31.8	1,116
Fujian	25,873	123,100	210	12,840	10.4	2,015
Jiangxi	33,185	166,600	199	25,310	15.2	1,311
Shandong	74,419	153,300	485	72,367	47.2	1,028

Central and South						
Henan	74,423	167,000	446	71,055	42.5	1,047
Hubei	47,804	185,900	257	37,247	20.0	1,283
Hunan	54,009	204,000	265	34,228	16.8	1,578
Guangdong	59,299	212,000	280	31,818	15.0	1,864
Guangxi	36,421	236,200	154	26,389	11.2	1,380
Southwest						
Sichuan	99,713	569,000	175	65,801	11.6	1,515
Guizhou	28,553	176,300	162	19,024	10.8	1,501
Yunnan	32,554	394,000	83	28,377	7.2	1,147
Xizang	1,892	1,228,400	2	2,255	0.2	839
Northwest						
Shaanxi	28,904	205,600	141	37,824	18.4	764
Gansu	19,569	454,000	43	35,436	7.8	552
Qinghai	3,896	721,500	5	5,872	0.8	663
Ningxia	3,896	60,000	65	8,835	14.7	441
Xinjiang	13,082	1,646,800	8	31,693	1.9	413
TOTAL	1,008,175[a]	9,596,000	105	988,175	10.3%	1,020

SOURCES: For *population*, Communique on 1982 Census (1982): K4. For *land*, the table totals are simply the sums of the provincial areas. The figure for total land area in the table is close to the 9,597,000 km² reported in *Chung-hua jen-min kung-ho-kuo ti-t'u chi* (Atlas of the People's Republic of China), 1st ed., Beijing?, 1957: Plate 5-6. A total cultivated area of 987,468 km² is reported in *Zhongguo nongye nianjian, 1982* (Agricultural yearbook of China, 1982), Beijing, 1983: 33, which was the source of most of the provincial figures in the table.

NOTE: The slight discrepancy between the Agricultural Yearbook's total cultivated area and the total shown in the table reflects the fact that the yearbook's data pertained to sown area and were given in units of 10,000 *mu*. These units were first converted to square kilometers, and the total was then divided by the reported multiple cropping index to get the cultivated area figure by province. Numerous sources were consulted for the total area and cultivated area of each province, and the least rounded data and those most likely to be applicable to 1982 were selected from the often conflicting figures. In addition to the Agricultural Yearbook, these sources were compared: Encyclopedic Yearbook of China 1982 (1982): 63–103; Encyclopedic Yearbook of China 1983 (1983): 67–113; Sun Jingzhi & Li (n.d.): 174–75, 182–83; Ministry of Internal Affairs, *Chung-hua jen-min kung-ho-kuo hsing-cheng ch'ü-hua chien-ts'e* (A simplified handbook of the administrative divisions of the People's Republic of China), Beijing, 1958: 5; and China Handbook Editorial Committee, comp. *Geography*, tr. Liang Liangxing, Beijing, 1983.

[a] Includes 4,238,000 members of the armed forces whose geographical location has not been reported.

inces—Gansu, Ningxia, Yunnan, and Heilongjiang—have fewer than 100 persons per square kilometer. Fifteen provinces have an overall population density of 100–400 persons per square kilometer. A few are even more densely populated. The three province-level municipalities are of course more crowded, but so are Henan with 446, Shandong with 485, and Jiangsu with 590 persons per square kilometer. These provinces are far more densely populated than most countries of the world with the exception of some islands and city-states and the country of Bangladesh, which had 650 persons per square kilometer in 1982. The eight provinces with over 300 persons per square kilometer are all situated on the fertile low-lying alluvial plains of east China formed by the Yellow, Huai, and Changjiang Rivers and associated tributaries.

When data on current population and geographical area become available for smaller areas than whole provinces, it will become possible to document the extraordinary population density of many rural areas. The closest approximation available now is the figures in Table 9.1 of the total population per square kilometer of cultivated land. These are only rough estimates because the amount of cultivated land is grossly underreported in some localities. Beijing, Shanghai, and Tianjin of course have very large populations per unit of cultivated land within the municipality, but what is striking is that so do many of the predominantly rural provinces. Along the southeast coast Zhejiang and Fujian are the most densely populated provinces by this measure, with 2,135 and 2,015 persons per square kilometer of cultivated land respectively; Guangdong, on the south coast next to Fujian, has 1,864. The provinces with 1,200 to 1,600 persons per unit area of cultivated land—Jiangsu, Jiangxi, Hubei, Hunan, Guangxi, Sichuan, and Guizhou—are all clustered in central and south China, primarily along the Changjiang River and its tributaries. This is because there is flat and fertile land in some deltas and basins of this region, the growing season is longest in that part of China, rainfall is heaviest, and water supply is most predictable there.[3] In most of this area, two or three crops can be grown on the same land each year.

To the north and northwest the climate is colder, the growing season shorter, the annual rainfall less, and precipitation less predictable. This change is reflected in the steady decline toward the north and northwest in population density per unit area of cultivated land. The provinces with fewer than 400 persons per unit area of cultivated land, Nei Mongol and Heilongjiang, are both on the northern border. Those provinces with 400 to 900 persons per square kilometer of cultivated land are all in northern and western China.

China's overall population density has increased markedly since 1953, from 61 to 105 persons per square kilometer in 1982. The rising population density has been destructive to the land. As the population has grown and the economy developed, much farmland has become sites for homes, factories, roads, and other uses. Between 1957 and 1977 some 291,000 square kilometers of arable land was taken out of cultivation, mostly in densely populated areas, while 171,000 square kilometers of more marginal land was reclaimed for farming. The net result was that the area of cultivated land declined from 1,113,000 square kilometers to 993,000 in twenty years.[4] Farms were started on forested land, grasslands, marshes, and steep hillsides. The tilling of inappropriate lands contributed to erosion, flooding, desertification, and a sharp decline in fish yield from freshwater sources.

Provincial Population Sizes and Interprovincial Migration

Few statistics have been reported on migration between provinces and regions of China since 1949. Part of the problem is that such data were not systematically collected.* Results from the 1982 census will not be helpful because no question was asked on place of birth or recent migration. However, some provinces have collected and reported migration data, and this information can be supplemented by analyzing variation in the population growth rates of the different provinces.

Table 9.2 lists the population size and growth rate of China's provinces from the three censuses and from administrative reports at yearend 1957, adjusted to correspond to today's boundaries. Despite errors and uncertainties in these data, and although natural population increase rates vary from province to province, it is possible to compare the growth rates in Table 9.2 to derive some tentative hypotheses about the patterns of interprovincial migration since 1953.

For the three decades 1953–82 some provinces appear to be net recipients of in-migrants because their long-term population growth rates are higher than would be expected from natural increase alone. Similarly, some provinces have lower population growth rates than would be expected from natural increase. Net recipients appear to be Beijing, Nei Mongol, Heilongjiang, Qinghai, Ningxia, and Xinjiang. Qinghai, for example, reported large influxes of people during 1954–60, 1964–73, and 1979–81.[5] Shanghai Municipality is the only province that clearly had a long-term net loss through out-migration, judging from its very low rate

* One source said, "Statistics on mechanical changes in the population are actually not being compiled." Wang Weizhi (1982a): 41. But the head of the State Statistical Bureau implied that for 1980 and 1981 localities reported their total in-migrants and out-migrants: added up for the whole country, an excess of local in-migrants was reported over the number of reported out-migrants. Li Chengrui (1982b): 37.

TABLE 9.2

Population Growth by Province, 1953–82, Adjusted to 1982 Boundaries

Province	Population (thousands)				Annual growth net of boundary changes (percent)			
	Midyear 1953	Yearend 1957	Midyear 1964	Midyear 1982	1953–57	1957–64	1964–82	1953–82
North								
Beijing	4,130	5,470	7,597	9,231	6.24%	5.05%	1.08%	2.77%
Tianjin	4,530	5,220	6,249	7,764	3.15	2.77	1.21	1.86
Hebei	33,740	36,960	39,417	53,006	2.03	0.99	1.65	1.56
Shanxi	14,314	15,960	18,015	25,291	2.42	1.86	1.88	1.96
Nei Mongol	7,338	9,200	12,334	19,274	5.03	4.51	2.48	3.33
Northeast								
Liaoning	20,566	24,090	26,946	35,722	3.51	1.72	1.57	1.90
Jilin	11,290	12,550	15,669	22,560	2.35	3.41	2.02	2.39
Heilong-jiang	11,897	14,860	20,133	32,666	4.94	4.67	2.69	3.48
East								
Shanghai	9,427	10,460	10,816	11,860	2.31	0.51	0.51	0.79
Jiangsu	37,710	41,670	44,522	60,521	2.22	1.02	1.71	1.63
Zhejiang	22,866	25,280	28,319	38,885	2.23	1.75	1.76	1.83
Anhui	30,663	33,560	31,241	49,666	2.01	−1.10	2.58	1.66
Fujian	13,143	14,650	16,757	25,873	2.41	2.07	2.41	2.34
Jiangxi	16,773	18,610	21,068	33,185	2.31	1.91	2.52	2.35
Shandong	50,130	55,440	55,496	74,419	2.24	0.02	1.63	1.36

Central and South								
Henan	43,910	48,340	50,324	74,423	2.14	0.62	2.17	1.82
Hubei	27,790	30,790	33,709	47,804	2.28	1.39	1.94	1.87
Hunan	33,227	36,220	37,182	54,009	1.92	0.40	2.07	1.68
Guangdong	34,770	37,960	40,448	59,299	1.95	0.98	2.13	1.84
Guangxi	19,561	19,390	23,198	36,421	−0.20	2.76	2.51	2.14
Southwest								
Sichuan	65,685	72,160	68,013	99,713	2.09	−0.91	2.13	1.44
Guizhou	15,037	16,890	17,141	28,553	2.58	0.23	2.84	2.21
Yunnan	17,473	19,100	20,453	32,554	1.98	1.05	2.58	2.15
Xizang	1,274	1,270	1,251	1,892	−0.07	−0.23	2.30	1.36
Northwest								
Shaanxi	15,881	18,130	20,767	28,904	2.94	2.09	1.84	2.07
Gansu	11,286	12,750	12,631	19,569	2.71	−0.14	2.43	1.90
Qinghai	1,676	2,050	2,146	3,896	4.48	0.70	3.31	2.91
Ningxia	1,642	1,860	2,107	3,896	2.77	1.92	3.41	2.98
Xinjiang	4,874	5,640	7,270	13,082	3.24	3.91	3.26	3.40
National total	582,603	646,530	694,582[a]	1,008,175[b]	2.31%	1.10%	2.07%	1.89%

SOURCES: *1953*, Communique on 1953 Census (1954): 2. *Yearend 1957*, Ten Great Years (1960): 11. *1964 and 1982*, State Council Population Office (1982): 8–9.

NOTE: The 1964 and 1982 totals were adjusted to 1982 boundaries in the source. Most of the adjustments of the 1953 and 1957 figures to today's boundaries were made by John S. Aird.

[a]Includes 3,362,000 members of the armed forces.

[b]Includes 4,238,000 members of the armed forces.

of population growth. A 1982 report gave these figures: "The total of Shanghai people who took on jobs in the hinterland and border regions amounts to 1.3 million. Among them, 950,000 left Shanghai in the period from 1953 to 1963, and 200,000 after 1964."[6] (The discrepancy in the totals is not explained, but may arise because some out-migrants returned.) Other provinces that appear to have had sizable net out-migration since 1953 are Shandong, Sichuan, and Xizang. Hebei, Jiangsu, Anhui, Henan and Hunan are also reported to have had long-term net out-migration.[7] The major long-term pattern thus seems to have been migration from provinces in populous areas of northern and central China to the northern tier of sparsely populated provinces. This information suggests that interprovincial migrants have not moved in great numbers from the provinces of the south and southeast farthest from the most common destinations in the north. As migrants to the northwest, north, and northeast appear to have come from northern and central China, perhaps the cost of moving was an important factor in the choice of migrants.

The movement of migrants northward and northwestward has not been a steady flow for all years since 1953; rather, different provinces were recipients of migrants in different periods, and sometimes the migration toward a province stopped or started suddenly.[8] During the period 1953–57 interprovincial movement appears to have been relatively great. Recipients of net in-migration during those years were Beijing and Tianjin Municipalities and the northern provinces of Nei Mongol, Liaoning, Heilongjiang, Qinghai, and Xinjiang, judging from their high annual population growth rates shown in Table 9.2. Though less certain, it also appears that Shaanxi, Gansu, and Ningxia in the north, and possibly Guizhou in the south, experienced net in-migration. Because most provinces reported 1953–57 population growth of roughly the same magnitude, it is difficult to detect the sources of the out-migrants. Perhaps the lack of variation is because out-migrants came from most of the populous provinces during the 1950's. Those provinces that probably achieved mortality improvements similar to the national average, yet reported lower 1953–57 population growth—Hebei, Anhui, Hunan, Guangdong, and Sichuan—may have provided a disproportionate share of out-migrants.

The migration picture for the 1950's is clouded by poor data on the total population size of some provinces; therefore, these hypothesized patterns of migration can only be suggestive rather than conclusive. The extreme example of poor data is Tibet (Xizang), for which there was no actual field count of the population until the 1982 census.[9] The estimated lack of population growth in the 1950's probably reflects in part a lack of data. In addition, Tibet continued to have high mortality and low natural population increase, and emigration to India resulted in substantial population loss.

The period 1957–64 included the famine of the Great Leap Forward and its aftermath. Figures on provincial populations at the beginning and end of this period may mask enormous temporary migrations in the interim. The data from the endpoints (Table 9.2) indicate that at least five provinces had significant net in-migration during 1957–64: Beijing, Nei Mongol, Jilin, Heilongjiang, and Xinjiang. Four provinces apparently ceased to receive so many annual in-migrants as they had during the mid-1950's: Liaoning, Guizhou, Gansu, and Qinghai. In the case of Qinghai the endpoint figures are misleading, because people fled from the famine into Qinghai during 1958–60 only to be sent back before 1964.[10] In four provinces either the famine was not particularly severe or in-migration made up for some of the famine losses: Tianjin, Shaanxi, Fujian, and Ningxia.

It can be assumed that any province that recorded a population loss from 1957 to 1964, after adjustments for boundary changes, either severely undercounted its population in the count of 1964 or was very hard hit by the famine, which may then have triggered out-migration. Anhui and Sichuan recorded the most extreme rates of population decline during 1957–64. In Xizang the estimates may be meaningless because there was no count in either year. Loss of population during the period is likely, not only because of a probable famine but also because of the 1959 Tibetan uprising and the flight of refugees to India.

Many other provinces recorded a population gain from 1957 to 1964, but the annual rate of growth was so low that there must have been enormous loss of life plus a net out-migration. Shandong was severely affected, as were Guizhou and Hunan. In sum, the provinces with the greatest population losses due to famine and out-migration during this period were predominantly in central China away from the coast. Shandong was the most strongly affected coastal province.

By 1964 famine-inspired migration had diminished or ceased. In the period 1964–82 six provinces appear to have received net in-migration: Heilongjiang, Qinghai, Ningxia, and Xinjiang in the north, and possibly Guangxi and Guizhou in the south. Jilin and Nei Mongol seem to have ceased receiving much net in-migration, because their population growth rates in 1964–82 could have been due to natural increase alone. The three province-level municipalities Beijing, Tianjin, and Shanghai were sources of interprovincial migrants during that period. Beyond this the data do not show where the migrants originated, because the variations in provincial population growth rates could easily reflect different natural increase rates.

The data in Table 9.2 show that the only provinces that received in-migrants throughout the period 1953–82 were Heilongjiang and Xinjiang, in the far northeast and northwest respectively. Only Shanghai can be documented from these data as a steady source of out-migrants for the entire period.

These interprovincial migrants, particularly in the 1950's, were predominantly male. For example, as a result of male migration into Ningxia, the reported sex ratio there rose from 110 in 1949 to 118 males per hundred females in 1960. A similar trend occurred in Qinghai, where the reported sex ratio rose from 100 in 1949 to 112 in 1956 to 123 in 1958.[11] None of these figures should be taken at face value as neither province had any good basis for estimating population sex ratios in 1949, but an increasing sex ratio during the 1950's is believable.

Much interprovincial migration has been initiated and paid for by the government. Many migrants are military personnel. As these are not included in the provincial population totals, the population movements described here did not include shifts of military personnel. But it is clear that the People's Liberation Army has moved huge numbers of people to guard the borders, especially the borders with the Soviet Union, India, Nepal, Vietnam, Hong Kong, and along the Taiwan Strait. This sort of migration is of course age and sex selective, emphasizing young men.

Another important interprovincial movement is the migration of Communist Party and government cadres to areas that the government wishes to bring under tighter political control from Beijing. Rather than recruiting local leaders to fill high political positions in border areas, minority group areas, or places that have been resisting central government directives, the national government tends to send its own trusted cadres. These migrants are probably mostly middle-aged and older men.

Another common kind of interprovincial migration is the government-sponsored movement of technically skilled personnel, sometimes for short assignments but often for many years or permanently. Skilled medical workers have been sent in great numbers to Xizang, Xinjiang, and other remote and minority group areas all over the country. Petroleum workers and oil industry managers have been assigned, commonly for a permanent move with their families, to open up and staff new oilfields. Skilled workers from established factories begin and run new factories elsewhere, and transport workers build railroads and roads. When possible the government moves only the skilled personnel without any dependents, to minimize the costs. The New China News Agency described one such government campaign in 1979:

> More than 3,000 cadres and professionals have come to Tibet to participate in local socialist construction. They are from Shandong, Shanxi, Liaoning, Jiangsu,

Anhui, Hunan, Hubei, Henan, Hebei, Shanghai, Tianjin, Beijing, Zhejiang, Sichuan, Yunnan, Guizhou, Jilin, Heilongjiang, and Shaanxi provinces and cities as well as from central departments. Most of them are 30 to 40 years old. About half are professionals from various fields such as light industry, science, education, medicine, telecommunications, transportation, television, radio, agricultural machinery, and so on. After a period of adjusting to the thin air of the highlands, many of them have begun work in their new posts.[12]

Note that in this case the government moved cadres and professionals from nineteen provinces to a single targeted province, and that half of this large group were cadres, presumably sent to help run Tibet's government along the lines of Beijing's policies. It is doubtful that the government would go to such expense to send these people for less than a year, yet it is unlikely that they were accompanied by their families.

The government has also sponsored the migration of political prisoners, intellectuals, leaders out of favor, and various persons considered politically or morally or economically suspect. These unwilling migrants have been moved away from their families, friends, and work as punishment, sometimes for a year or two and sometimes for decades. At their destinations they have been assigned physical labor rather than the work for which they were trained. Since the arrest of the "gang of four" the government has slowly been "reversing the verdicts" against many thousands of these persons. A persecuted person, even after being cleared of all wrongdoing, may not be immediately returned home but remain far from home and family, petitioning for redress or permission to return. The bottleneck seems to be that local, provincial, and national bureaucracies are unwilling to grant petitions until the potential returnees have guaranteed jobs, but in many cases their jobs were long ago taken over by someone else or the position ceased to exist.

The most highly publicized group of interprovincial migrants has been "educated youth," city-born middle-school graduates sent most often to rural parts of their own province but sometimes to sparsely populated or border provinces.[13] Hardly ever mentioned in the press, but possibly significant in number, are young adults from rural areas of more crowded provinces who move from their own villages where opportunity is limited to frontier areas where work is available. While rural youth may move voluntarily to another province, the movement of urban youth to undeveloped areas has been unpopular. The Chinese press for decades described "comfort groups" sent to a border or backward province to bring greetings to the educated youth, encourage their revolutionary enthusiasm in the face of unaccustomed hardships, and persuade them that they served themselves and their country best by working hard in their assigned location. This migration was government-directed, the migrants having little or no choice of destination and, in the case of urban youth, having essentially no choice as to whether they migrated. As far as can be determined, educated young men and women from their mid-teens to mid-twenties were sent in approximately equal numbers to remote and border provinces. They were almost always unmarried and were frequently sent as groups of classmates to one destination, where they could assist one another.

Some data have been released on the numbers involved in these transfers, referring mostly to the period from 1968 to about 1975. The following cities were most often mentioned as the sources of urban youth sent to other provinces: Shanghai, Beijing, Tianjin, Nanjing (in Jiangsu), Hangzhou (in Zhejiang), Wuhan (in Hubei), and Chengdu and Chongqing (in Sichuan). The provinces that received them were Shanxi (50,000 by midyear 1976), Nei Mongol (over 110,000 by September 1975), Heilongjiang (490,000 as of the end of 1974), Yunnan (300,000 by midyear 1976), Shaanxi (over 26,000 by early 1976), and Xinjiang (over 100,000 by the end of 1975). In general, this pattern conformed to the long-term migration pattern suggested by provincial totals for 1953 and 1982: mostly from northern and central, not southern and southeastern China, and mostly to the northernmost provinces.

Regarding the destinations of these different categories of government-directed migrants, some of them went to newly developed industrial, mining, or oil-producing complexes in the receiving provinces. Some were sent to expanding cities to help govern the province or provincial subunit, staff new industries, train technical personnel, or expand the work of hospitals. Many have been sent to huge state farms, where they opened up new agricultural lands or developed timber or fishery production. The migrants often moved into enclaves with other migrants rather than integrating with the existing communities.

During the Cultural Revolution of the late 1960's and early 1970's, however, the apparent emphasis of interprovincial migration was on sending small groups of migrants to live in established villages. The migrants were clearly outsiders, often speaking a different dialect of Chinese, and were much more privileged and better educated than those in the village to which they were sent. Sometimes the in-migrants were appreciated, particularly if they had some valuable skill to offer like medical expertise or the ability and willingness to teach in the local school. But the transfer of large numbers of untrained city youth to remote villages was bound to cause resentment. The villagers complained about the transferees, who at first had large resettlement costs and ate more food than they could produce. The government paid the villages for expenses connected with feeding and housing the youth for about the first six months of their stay; after 1973 the subsidy was increased to cover most of a year's expenses.

The foregoing forms of interprovincial migration are government-sponsored, but not all interprovincial movements are approved or paid for by the government. Most rural-to-rural population flows between provinces have been spontaneous:

> According to data from Xinjiang, the influx of migrants from other provinces (or regions) through automatic [spontaneous] population flow accounted for two-thirds of the net population influx for the entire autonomous region, and in other provinces (or regions) where population influx was fairly heavy, the same situation obtained. Population migration is attributable primarily to economic factors. People from poor places want to migrate to places where living is good, and people from disaster-stricken areas seek even more to make a living elsewhere. In eastern China, population is large relative to arable land and the work force is abundant. In the northwest and north, land is vast and population scant; the work force is inadequate. Before Liberation, the poverty-stricken peasants and the disaster-stricken peasants from the east who had been exploited and oppressed, had a historical tradition of migration to the north and west. After Liberation, peasants from some low-yield areas and from disaster areas continued spontaneous migration to the aforementioned regions.[14]

In the last three decades spontaneous population movement probably peaked during the Great Leap Forward and its aftermath as peasants fled from famine in eastern and central China. But migration from disaster areas has not ceased. The press occasionally refers obliquely to the likelihood of unplanned migrations by urging officials to do disaster relief work well so people will not have to move. For example, Hunan provincial authorities responded to 1981 floods and crop failures with the following instructions:

> A recent provincial conference on disaster relief through production, held in Changsha, laid stress on studying and making arrangements for this work during spring and summer this year. The meeting conveyed the central authorities' intentions on disaster relief work. The meeting demanded that leadership departments in the province's disaster areas, especially heavily stricken areas, do a good job in arranging the livelihood of the local people, and organizing the civil affairs, grain, banking, finance, and other departments concerned to go into the disaster areas to investigate the situation and issue and use relief funds and materials in a rational way. . . . The meeting also demanded that leaders of basic-level districts and communes strengthen ideological and political work for the people in disaster areas, make proper arrangements for their production and livelihood, and prevent a population outflow.[15]

It is not only natural disasters that cause population outflows but also human-made disasters from misguided policies, local mismanagement, conflict, or alienation between government and the governed. The calamity of the Great Leap Forward and subsequent years was as much a government policy disaster as a natural disaster. The Cultural Revolution also sparked "fairly substantial" interprovincial migrations.[16] Political upheaval in Sichuan during 1970–75 caused heavy out-migration and the 1976 food shortages in Sichuan may have been caused in part by counterproductive agricultural policies in the previous decade.[17] The reported population movements resulting from lack of food may have been for short distances, but some were probably forced to leave the province altogether. Another example of migration caused by mismanagement was reported from 1976:

> In 1976, a county in our Jilin province exaggerated its grain output by more than 42 million catties [23,000 tons], and hogs by 2,000 head. They obtained by cheating the honor of "having fulfilled the target set by the national program" for grain and hogs. At the end of the year, they were unable to supply the state the required number, and had to force the masses to kill their piglets, or to sell their pork to meet their quota. Due to falsification of food grain output, state purchase exceeded the norm. By July of the next year, 70 percent of the households were short of grain. More than 16 million catties of grain [9,000 tons] had to be bought from the state. More than 600,000 catties [300 tons] of wheat bran was used as food. The members were more than 600,000 yuan short of funds for purchasing food grain. A large number of the population of some communes left for other places.[18]

Another major type of unauthorized movement appears to be return migration from government assignment in another province back to one's home province. Some return migration is officially permitted, for example by professionals, cadres, or skilled workers who have completed a temporary assignment, and in the 1970's by some "sent-down" urban youth who became seriously ill or emotionally disturbed. But for the most part the government refuses assigned migrants the right to move back home. For example, a 1981 report revealed that about 3,000 people who tried to return to Shanghai from Xinjiang had been sent back to the northwest. Some had returned home in secret, "while others had permission from the Xinjiang authorities. But Shanghai refused to take them back and recent months have seen street demonstrations in the city by young people claiming jobs and food coupons."[19]

Unwilling migrants pose many problems for the government. For instance, a necessary part of the routine assignment of persons far from their homes is the provision that the migrants may return home at government expense once a year or at least once every several years for the spring festival (lunar new year). Unwilling migrants sometimes use the occasion to prolong their stay, try to wangle permission to stay, or simply refuse to board the train back to their assigned jobs in another province. This annual attempt to remain home has been characteristic of those urban young adults bitter about their assignments. Because unauthorized returnees are likely to evade the police and therefore avoid formally registering their presence beyond a temporary stay, the registration data are probably inadequate for estimating the extent of return migration. The data, such as they are, would be expected to record the government-sponsored migrations but miss those movements that run counter to the government policy stipulating that one must stay where one is unless explicitly authorized to move. Therefore, China's own collected data on interprovincial migration may exaggerate the net movement of persons to the targeted provinces and away from the source provinces.

What have been the dominant effects of interprovincial migration from the early 1950's to the present? One result has been to slightly ameliorate the growth in the population size and density of provinces that have been the main sources of migrants. In the case of Shanghai Municipality before 1978, the net out-migration was large enough to practically stabilize the provincial population at its 1957 size.

A second result has been to greatly increase the population size and density of target provinces. For example, Xinjiang might have had a 1982 population of about 10 million rather than 13 million if it had received no net in-migration. The massive in-migration has also affected Xinjiang's age structure, because the migrants tend to be in or approaching the most fertile age groups. In addition, the migration pattern favoring young adults of both sexes tends to lower the subsequent crude birth rate of the sending provinces, at least until the migrants return, and tends to increase the birth rate of the receiving provinces to the extent that the migrants marry and settle there. Therefore, the migration programs have had the intended effect of shifting some of China's surplus population to lightly populated areas.

A third important effect has been to modulate the disastrous consequences of regionalized famine or economic collapse. When all else fails, the option of moving away from a disaster area provides a crucial safety valve, given the marginal economic conditions of many of China's people. Until the late 1970's the media suppressed information on the occurrence of food shortages and the flight of migrants from hunger, so it is still difficult to document what may have been a numerically important flow of people over time.

A fourth consequence has been much publicized, that is, the contribution of migrants to the economic and social development of the sparsely populated and border regions.[20] The migrants have assisted in medical advances, agricultural modernization, energy development, industrialization, surveying and mining for mineral resources, and popularizing elementary education. They have encouraged and personified relatively modern attitudes and practices regarding the role of women, the control of fertility, literacy, male-female and family relationships, hygiene, and the treatment of illness. In essence, the contribution of the directed interprovincial migrants to China's development has been to diffuse modern techniques and ideas. While more backward regions might eventually develop on their own, the migrants speed and direct the process. On the negative side, some migrants and groups of migrants may so antagonize the natives in the target province that they set back the progress of development there. Because China's media publicize the positive contributions and are silent on the negative impacts of the interprovincial migrants, a balanced assessment is hard to make.

Migration, mostly of military personnel but also of civilians, has been used to strengthen border defenses. Since 1949 China's borders have been defined more closely than in previous centuries. The government has tried to seal the borders in most years, and traditional customary movements of traders and nomadic herders have been circumscribed or stopped. Emigration from China has for most people been forbidden, and border military patrols arrest those who attempt to leave. The militarization and the populating of the border areas has been spurred on by border hostilities, with India over Tibet, with the United States in Vietnam and now with Vietnam itself, and most seriously with the Soviet Union since the Sino-Soviet split in 1960. Huge population movements are required to defend China's 7,000-kilometer (4,400-mile) border with the Soviet Union and additional 3,800-kilometer (2,400-mile) boundary with Mongolia, a Soviet ally. China's special emphasis on rapidly developing areas in northern Xinjiang or northern Heilongjiang thus has strategic as well as economic importance.

Ethnic Diversity and Distribution

Perhaps one of the most far-reaching effects of interprovincial population movements in recent decades has been to Sinicize China's separate minority groups and integrate them and their previously isolated territory into the Chinese economy and society. As of the 1953 census 94 percent of the country's population was counted as the Han ethnic group. For millennia this numerically dominant population had moved into areas thinly settled by smaller groups, either intermarrying with and assimilating them or pushing them into mountainous and other marginal agricultural areas. Intermittently since at least the first millennium B.C. much of the Han migration into minority group areas has been organized and aided by China's government, with the settlers accompanied by army units and acting as soldier-households for border defense.[21] By 1949 successive waves of Han migration had ensured their numerical dominance throughout most of central, southern, and eastern China, but their domination never took hold in the far north and northwest because the land could not support settled agriculture using traditional techniques. The vast grasslands, the deserts, the northern forests, and the mountains were mostly left to minority groups who moved with their herds or traded on their camels or lived in remote isolated villages.

Since 1949, however, the government's aggressive sponsorship and encouragement of Han migration has shifted political power in minority group regions to the Han. The interprovincial migrants to the remote and border provinces are, as in the past, almost all of the Han ethnic group. At some of their destinations they simply outnumber the small minority groups. But elsewhere the Han migrants, backed by the power of the national government and military, make their influence and power felt far beyond their numbers because they are placed in positions of political and economic control over the minority groups. This process has been assisted by gerrymandering the borders of some minority group provinces, known as Autonomous Regions, and some minority group prefectures (Autonomous *Zhou*) and counties, to ensure a Han majority. For example, the reasons for drawing the boundaries of the Inner Mongolian Autonomous Region to include the Han province of Suiyuan, which left the autonomous region with over six times as many Han as Mongolians, were given as follows: "On the basis of the historical national relationships in the Inner Mongolia region and its historical conditions, and in order to promote national solidarity and in consideration of the needs of economic and cultural development of the Mongolian and other national minorities in the autonomous region, a large number of Han people, who form the majority of the total population of the autonomous region, is also included in the region."[22] When the Guangxi Zhuang Autonomous Region was being planned in 1957 it was decided not to divide Guangxi province into two parts, with the western half of the province a separate autonomous region that would have had an overwhelming majority of Zhuang people. In that instance the rationale given was less patronizing and more illuminating:

> From the consideration of socialist construction, particularly the industrial construction of Kwangsi [Guangxi], division is undesirable. The areas inhabited by the Han nationality have better conditions for agricultural production, but from the viewpoint of future industrial mining development, the conditions are not as good as those in the areas inhabited by the Chuang [Zhuang] nationality. The industrial resources of Kwangsi, according to existing data, are mainly distributed in the western part inhabited by the Chuang and other minority nationalities. The Han nationality has a larger population, with higher cultural and technical levels. These conditions precisely call for the Han, Chuang and other nationalities to contribute their respective talent for the common cause of socialist construction within a single local administrative unit. This situation in Kwangsi is a miniature

of the whole country. The total population of all minority nationalities in the whole country is less than 40,000,000, but the area inhabited by them occupies 60 percent of the total area of the country. In the Han areas, there is a large population. In the minority areas there are expansive territory and rich resources. This calls for close cooperation among all, mutual assistance to build the motherland into a powerful socialist industrial country.[23]

The perspective of the government on minority group affairs is that all the territory of the PRC belongs to China's whole population, to be used for the benefit of all. It does not matter whether the Tibetan people, for example, have controlled Tibet for millennia, or whether the steppes belonged to the Mongols or most of what is now Xinjiang belonged to the Uygurs. China has taken over that territory for China. If oil is discovered in Xinjiang or some mineral in Xizang, it is inconceivable to Beijing that the resource belongs to the Uygurs or Tibetans, and that the government should buy it from the local people or give them royalties for it. But the minority groups might argue with some justification that their continuing poverty relative to the Han is due to the expropriation of their lands and resources without fair and continuing compensation. China's wholesale absorption of minority lands is the basic condition that has caused friction between the Han and minority groups since 1949; friction will continue until the minority groups become fully integrated and interspersed with the Han, or until the government drastically changes its policy. This long-standing situation was recognized in late 1980 by members of the Standing Committee of the Guangxi Zhuang Autonomous Region People's Congress:

The committee members held: The most fundamental thing in instituting the autonomy of nationality areas is to have full autonomy rights; and the right of autonomy must first be expressed in insuring that the cadres of the autonomy organs are themselves of minority nationality. However, this has not yet been accomplished very well.

The committee members expressed strong views on the lack of economic autonomy rights. They cited abundant evidence to show that the autonomous counties do not possess any economic autonomy rights. The life of some minority nationality masses is still rather poor. Due to the fact that the county's autonomy rights have not been put on a sound basis, leadership over production in Jinxiu Yao Autonomous County cannot be carried out in the light of local conditions and large tracts of forest have been indiscriminately cut down, seriously damaging the forest resources of this minority nationality area. Although minority nationality areas have developed some industrial and mining enterprises, the local masses have not benefited much from them because they have no autonomy rights over the exploitation and management of resources.[24]

China's minority groups, many of which were formerly protected by geography from complete domination by the Han, have seen the barriers broken by new roads, railroads, and telephones. Using these new transportation links Han cadres, armies, and civilians have in-migrated in droves, setting up or taking over the government that controls the minority areas. Understandably the minority groups resent the rapid and permanent loss of their former partial independence. Exacerbating their bitterness is the all-too-frequent Han attitude of superiority and condescension known as "Great Han chauvinism." The Han migrants have frequently found minority group customs abhorrent and labeled them backward. While some customs of some groups were backward by almost any definition, other customs were merely different.

The government's tolerance for minority groups has been greatest during periods of practicality and moderation. But during the Great Leap Forward and the Cultural Revolution Beijing's impatient, radical line would tolerate no deviation. The government during those periods tried to force minority group customs out of existence and immediately wipe out all vestiges of economic, political, and social differences between Han and minority. Expressions of minority group distinctiveness were vilified as "local nationalism," at those times equivalent in the leadership's eyes to treason against New China. This attitude led to suppression of the minorities and the arrest and maltreatment of many of their leaders. But since about 1979 the government has been reassessing its national minorities policy. A 1980 scholarly report from Beijing described the last quarter century of Han-minority affairs as follows:

> In our struggle against local nationalism in 1957, we magnified class struggle, accused some minority national cadres of attacking the party because they explained the true conditions in their regions and expressed the complaints and wishes of their people, and labeled them as local nationalists. We criticized proper national feelings, national desires, and demands as bourgeois nationalism. In 1958, we again departed from the reality of minority nationality regions, ran counter to objective laws, advocated the so-called "reaching the sky in a single bound," . . . undermined the economy of the minority nationality regions, and created tension among the minority nationality regions. In 1962, the national conference on the work among the minority nationalities correctly summed up our experience and lessons drawn, and pointed out profoundly that [we must understand fully] the protracted nature of the existing national differences. . . . But later in 1964, under the domination of "left" deviation, we again vigorously criticized the so-called "Right capitulationism" and "revisionism" in the national united front work, and refuted many of our good experiences. . . . During the Great Cultural Revolution, Lin Biao and the "gang of four" . . . artificially created large numbers of horrible, unjust, false, and wrong cases, and used the big stick of class struggle to attack and persecute many minority national cadres and the masses. They slandered minority national customs and habits and spoken and written languages as "four old things," . . . undermined very seriously the party's policy towards the minority nationalities and the economic and cultural recon-

struction in their regions, and caused serious calamities. This is an extremely bitter experience from which we learned a lesson.[25]

Han-minority relations during the last three decades, then, have been anything but smooth; nevertheless, there have been positive aspects to the interaction. Continuing annexation of minority lands and integration with the economy and polity of China has caused, it is fair to say, mixed feelings among the minority peoples. On the one hand they appear to have welcomed the medical advances, the intermittent economic benefits directed specifically at them, and perhaps some aspects of increasing literacy and education.[26] Some may indeed be proud to identify with the great nation of China, a world power, rather than more narrowly with their own nationality, which has little weight in the world. But on the other hand resentment of the Han appears to lie just below the surface most of the time, to emerge frequently in the form of complaints of Han dominance and on occasion to explode in reaction to Han insensitivity and oppression. Those groups that in recent centuries were most assimilated by the Han have apparently accommodated themselves to the treatment they have received, but those that fended off assimilation have been more likely to resist actively. They have slaughtered animals rather than hand them over to the government, engaged in armed revolt, or fled across the border to join fellow members of their nationality in a neighboring country. Probably most of the episodes of resistance are not known outside of China, because the media tend to suppress information about them. So far as can be documented, the groups that have resisted control by the PRC most consistently are the Tibetans, Uygurs, Kazaks, and Hui.

Tibetan dissatisfaction has been caused by the loss since 1950 of Tibet's semi-independent status, by the Chinese attempt to wipe out Tibet's lamaist religion, by Han intolerance for Tibetan customs, and by hunger resulting at times from economic mismanagement. Tibetans in western Sichuan rebelled in 1956, Tibetans in Gansu and Qinghai revolted in 1958, and opposition to control by China spread throughout Tibetan areas in 1958 and culminated in armed revolt in 1959, which was suppressed by the People's Liberation Army.[27] Relations between Han and Tibetan have remained uneasy since then.

Muslim groups have remained most resistant to assimilation. They have reacted with fury to violations of their customs and religious beliefs, such as the requirement in some localities during the Cultural Revolution that Muslims raise pigs. China's Muslim minorities include the Hui, Uygur, Kazak, Dongxiang, Kirgiz, Salar, Tajik, Uzbek, Tatar, and Baoan. The Hui group, distinct from the Han only in their religion, are scattered over much of China. Some Hui staged sporadic anti-Han revolts after 1949 in what later became the Ningxia Hui Autonomous Region, and rose up again during the Great Leap Forward. A Hui group in Henan proclaimed an "independent Islamic kingdom" in 1953, and Hui in Beijing organized and rebelled during the Cultural Revolution. There was a Hui rebellion in Yunnan in 1975; the army reportedly killed hundreds while putting it down.[28]

Xinjiang, the home of most of the Muslim minorities, has been particularly characterized by armed revolts against Han domination. The largest Muslim groups there, the Uygurs and Kazaks, were restive during the Great Leap Forward; they staged demonstrations and armed rebellions in 1957–58 and sporadically during 1959–62, culminating in a major revolt in 1962.[29] During the Cultural Revolution in 1967 the Uygurs took part in another rebellion against the Han, and again in 1980–81, violent conflict erupted in Xinjiang, accompanied by Uygur demands for self-rule.[30] The protests centered on treatment of the minorities by the army, which in Xinjiang appears to be a fully Han security force.[31] China's government is struggling to deflect the smoldering resentments felt by the Muslim minorities of Xinjiang and elsewhere, according to one visitor to China who interviewed specialists on minority affairs: "Acutely aware of the failures of Chinese nationality policy in the past several decades, specialists in Urumqi and Beijing are seeking solutions to the most pressing minority complaints among China's substantial Muslim population."[32]

Revolts against the Han have not been confined to northern and northwestern China; during the 1950's there were outbreaks among the minority groups of the south and southwest. The incidents included assassinations of government officials in Yunnan in 1955, an uprising on Hainan Island in Guangdong in 1956–57, "nationalistic surges" among the Dong and Miao of Guizhou in 1957–58, and a rebellion of the Yi minority during the Great Leap Forward.[33]

Because armed revolt is sure to be violently suppressed, minority groups must take this action only in desperation. During a rebellion and especially after its failure, minority group members sometimes flee en masse to a neighboring country. For example, in 1959 when the Tibetan rebellion was put down, the Dalai Lama and an estimated 60,000 Tibetans fled to Nepal and India, and during the Cultural Revolution there was further flight of Tibetans.[34] During 1962, after years of uprisings in Xinjiang, "several tens of thousands" of minority nationals migrated to the Soviet Union; by 1963 it was estimated that about 70,000 persons had left Xinjiang for the Soviet Central Asian republics.[35] In 1963 another 60,000 refugees reportedly fled from famine in Xinjiang to the Soviet Union.[36] Some minorities have emigrated in lieu of staging a violent revolt. For instance, a sizable group of Dai people from Yunnan reportedly fled to Burma, Laos, and Thailand in 1957 because of their opposition to land reform and the anti-rightist campaign of that year.[37]

In the 1980's China's government is trying to make up for some of its catastrophic policies toward the minority groups in previous decades. The government is restoring the 1950's policy of encouraging the use of minority languages, and books are once again being published in several minority languages, especially Korean, Mongolian, Uygur, Kazak, and Tibetan. Greater local economic autonomy is being discussed and possibly implemented. Since 1981 minorities have in theory been allowed to choose their preferred arrangements for ownership and management, to design their own production plans, and to keep herds as large as they can handle.[38] The distinctive dress, customs, food preferences, dances, and songs of minority groups are being accorded more tolerance.

Tentative steps have been taken to allow a modicum of religious expression among minority groups. Some religious practices and organizations that had been effectively banned have been weakly revived. For example, in Tibet by midyear 1979 only ten of the previous 2,464 monasteries had been allowed to remain, and most of the Tibetan Buddhist monks had fled China, shifted to lay work, or been imprisoned, with the result that there were 2,000 lamas left from the previous 120,000.[39] Therefore Tibetan Buddhism has been basically destroyed as an institution in China; yet since the early 1970's some forms of religious observance have been tolerated, such as the celebration of a religious holiday, some monks have been released from prison, and intermittent negotiations with the Dalai Lama have explored the possibility of his return.[40] Small concessions have also been made to Muslim beliefs: the Koran was republished in 1979 for the first time in decades, and local governments were instructed no longer to force Muslims to raise swine.[41]

Slowly, minority leaders who had been jailed or mistreated are being released and in some cases reinstated. There is renewed emphasis on training cadres from minority groups and even apparently some determination to place them in positions of real political power in minority areas. It remains to be seen how far the government will go in giving genuine authority to the minority groups and their representatives.

Since the arrest of the "gang of four," improvement of Han-minority relations and constructive response to minority grievances has been slow. As late as November 1979 a *People's Daily* article gave the following assessment:

> Since the smashing of the "gang of four," the party Central Committee has turned chaos into order, implemented the policy toward nationalities, and healed the wounds so that conditions have greatly improved. However, in quite a few areas, the nationalities and religious policies have not been seriously implemented, some miscarriages of justice have not been corrected, institutions for nationalities work and other measures that serve the production and livelihood of the national mi-

> norities have not been completely restored, the difficulties in production and livelihood among certain masses of national minorities have not been notably improved, and the phenomenon of lacking respect for the national characteristics and customs and habits still exists.[42]

In the long run, because of the numerical superiority of the Han along with the lack of tolerance for individual human differences characteristic of the PRC, the minority groups are likely to lose much of their distinctiveness. Many groups were greatly assimilated before 1949, speaking a dialect of Chinese, engaging in intensive settled agriculture, with dress and customs indistinguishable from the Han, and often intermarrying with them. Many minority persons during the last 30 years have surely found it expedient or necessary to blend in with and adapt to Han culture. Especially susceptible are the estimated 10 million members of minority groups who live in densely settled areas scattered among the Han.[43]

Intermarriage between Han and minority was officially promoted starting in 1958 as a step toward the complete assimilation of the minority groups, but its actual prevalence in the last several decades has not been reported.[44] A visitor to Nei Mongol in 1979 was told that mixed marriages between Han and non-Han are technically not forbidden, but that they are rarely if ever allowed to occur: "'Even if both sets of parents agree,' said a Mongol soldier on the train to Huhehot, 'you never get permission.'"[45] But current policy seems to be the promotion of interracial marriage to speed the historical process of the merging of China's ethnic groups and the blurring of distinctions between them. A 1978 policy statement traced the history of interracial marriage over the centuries in China and concluded: "This serves as historical evidence of the fact that 'interracial marriage' adds to unity among nationalities. . . . The 'gang of four' totally negated 'interracial marriage.' . . . In fact, 'interracial marriage' expands and strengthens economic and cultural exchanges among fraternal nationalities in our country. It is conducive to social development and pushes history forward."[46]

The Chinese government is not dedicated to preserving cultural, social, or economic differences among the country's ethnic groups. Those minorities that are most assimilated have given the government the least trouble, so it is understandable if government leaders see assimilation as the long-term solution to national minority problems. In the short run the government may show more tolerance and give the minorities greater local autonomy, partly to stop the continuing problems of minority group complaints, restiveness, rebellions, and flights across the border. But it is reasonable to predict that no rights will be allowed minority groups that would give them full control over the rich resources of their former territories, and their political self-determination will be severely limited by the continued dominance of the military and the Communist Party in minority areas.

The future role of government-directed migration of Han into minority areas is less certain. The minority groups appear to have profound distaste for the policy, and at the same time the Han migrants themselves often do not choose to go to minority areas. It is possible that Han reluctance on one side and minority resistance on the other could slow down or even stop the Han tide, but the weight of the evidence to date points to continuation of the government's policy.[47]

For example, in 1980 the Beijing government agreed to limit the number of Han cadres in Tibet, and began transferring large numbers of them back home. This policy sparked a demand from Uygurs in Xinjiang that the Han cadres there also leave, and the Han were impatient to go home.[48] But after some confusion, the Communist Party Committee of Xinjiang in 1982 reaffirmed the policy of keeping the Han cadres there: "Through study, all Han cadres should firmly establish the notions of working in Xinjiang for a long time and wholeheartedly serving the people of all nationalities in the region. The cadres of all nationalities should firmly establish the notion of the inseparability of the nationalities."[49] In 1983 and 1984, policy statements strongly reaffirmed the national policy of promoting continued Han migration to sparsely populated and border areas, where many minorities live, with pronouncements such as: "Planned and organized in-migration for land reclamation is the necessary strategy for the future development of Qinghai,"[50] and:

> Comrade Hu Yaobang and Comrade Zhao Ziyang visited Qinghai and Xinjiang successively in July and August of this year [1983]. Afterwards a formal announcement was made that: "the opening up of Xinjiang and the entire northwest region to enable it to become a most important Chinese base in the 21st century is a major strategic idea proposed by the Party Central for China." . . . In order to develop agricultural and livestock production and to open up mining resources, a large number of laborers, especially workers with skills, is needed from the interior provinces and municipalities where the population density is high. . . . What a great role the large-scale movement and redistribution of population will play toward the building of the four modernizations![51]

China counted its minority groups in the 1953, 1964, and 1982 censuses. Minority figures for 1978 were also compiled, probably based on the permanent population registers as of yearend 1978. The available data from these counts are reported in Table 9.3. The number of recognized minority groups shifted as new ones were identified and others were merged under a different ethnic designation.

According to the first two censuses the minority population slowly increased from 35 million in 1953 to 40 million in 1964, thereby declining from 6.1 percent of China's total population in 1953 to 5.8 percent in 1964. This decline in percentage may have taken place for several reasons. First and perhaps most important, the natural population increase among minority groups as a whole may have been lower than among the Han due to both worse mortality conditions and lower fertility among minorities from disease. Second, emigration of minority people from China slowed population growth. Third, as assimilation of minority groups continued many of minority or mixed blood began to call themselves Han. Also, if the count or designation of minority persons in 1964 was less accurate and thorough than in 1953, the apparent proportional decline of minorities in China's population could be partly spurious. Undercounting of minorities was clearly a problem in 1978; population registration in minority areas must have been especially poor.

In preparation for the 1982 census care was taken to reinstate the minority nationality status of those who had come to list themselves as Han.[52] A minority population of 67 million was counted, constituting 6.7 percent of China's total. The more rapid increase of the minorities than the Han during 1964–82 was due primarily to higher fertility and faster natural increase in minority communities, though part of the increase may be spurious if the minorities were badly underreported in 1964.

Particular groups have been affected differently by these various trends. Several minority nationalities reported far lower population totals in 1978 registration figures than in the 1982 census. The Miao, Manchu, Mongol, Bouyei, and Dong minorities were probably becoming assimilated and redefining themselves as Han by 1978, but they quickly reverted to minority status when given the opportunity or when required to do so in preparation for the census. As these groups live interspersed among the Han, their ethnic identification may be in flux. The relatively slow growth recorded for the Korean minority from 1964 to 1982 may also be due in part to assimilation.

The willingness of individuals from many minority groups to "reaffirm their origins" in 1982 is attributed by the government to its enlightened policies toward minority groups since the death of Mao Zedong:

> Another reason [for more rapid population growth of minorities than Han] is that some minority nationality people previously registered as Han nationality and reported their real nationality during this census. Moreover, the offspring of intermarrying parents were previously registered as Han nationality and also changed back to their respective minority nationalities. This phenomenon is especially conspicuous among the Manchu, Tujia, and Dong nationalities . . . the experts said: "The fact that minority nationality people are willing to report their real nationalities shows that after correcting the 'Left' mistakes, the Party's nationality policy has won their confidence."[53]

TABLE 9.3

Population Growth by Ethnic Group, 1953–82

Ethnic group	Population				Approximate annual average growth (percent)		
	Midyear 1953	Midyear 1964	1978 estimates	Midyear 1982	1953–64	1964–82	1953–82
Zhuang	6,611,455	8,386,140	12,090,000	13,378,162	1.9%	2.6%	2.3%
Nung	196,000	—[a]	—[a]	—[a]			
Hui	3,559,350	4,473,147	6,490,000	7,219,352	2.1	2.7	2.4
Uygur	3,640,125	3,996,311	5,480,000	5,957,112	0.8	2.2	1.7
Yi	3,254,269	3,380,960	4,850,000	5,453,448	0.3	2.7	1.8
Miao	2,511,339	2,782,088	3,920,000	5,030,897	0.9	3.3	2.4
Manchu	2,418,931	2,695,675	2,650,000	4,299,159	1.0	2.6	2.0
Tibetan	2,775,622	2,501,174	3,450,000	3,870,068	−1.0	2.4	1.2
Monba	—[b]	3,809	40,000	6,248	—	—	—
Loba	—[b]	—[b]	200,000	2,065	—	—	—
Mongolian	1,462,956	1,965,766	2,660,000	3,411,657	2.7	3.1	2.9
Tujia	590,000	524,755	770,000	2,832,743	−1.1	9.4	5.4
Bouyei	1,247,883	1,348,055	1,720,000	2,120,469	0.7	2.5	1.8
Korean	1,120,405	1,339,569	1,680,000	1,763,870	1.6	1.5	1.6
Dong	713,000	836,123	1,110,000	1,425,100	1.4	3.0	2.4
Yao	666,000	857,265	1,240,000	1,402,676	2.3	2.7	2.6
Bai	567,000	706,623	1,050,000	1,131,124	2.0	2.6	2.4
Hani	481,000	628,727	960,000	1,058,836	2.4	2.9	2.7
Kazak	509,000	491,637	800,000	907,582	−0.3	3.4	2.0
Dai	479,000	535,389	760,000	839,797	1.0	2.5	1.9
Li	361,000	438,813	680,000	817,562	1.8	3.5	2.8
Lisu	317,000	270,628	470,000	480,960	−1.4	3.2	1.4
She	219,000	234,167	330,000	368,832	0.6	2.5	1.8
Lahu	139,000	191,241	270,000	304,174	2.9	2.6	2.7
Va	286,000	200,272	260,000	298,591	−3.2	2.2	0.1
Shui	134,000	156,099	230,000	286,487	1.4	3.4	2.6
Dongxiang	156,000	147,443	190,000	279,397	−0.5	3.6	2.0
Naxi	143,000	156,796	230,000	245,154	0.8	2.5	1.9
Tu	53,200	77,349	120,000	159,426	3.4	4.0	3.8
Kirgiz	70,900	70,151	97,000	113,999	−0.1	2.7	1.6
Qiang	35,600	49,105	85,000	102,768	2.9	4.1	3.7
Daur	44,100	63,394	78,000	94,014	3.3	2.2	2.6

Jingpo	101,000	57,762	83,000	93,008	−5.1	2.6	−0.3
Mulao	43,100	52,819	73,000	90,426	1.8	3.0	2.6
Xibe	19,000	33,438	44,000	83,629	5.1	5.1	5.1
Salar	30,600	34,664	56,000	69,102	1.1	3.8	2.8
Bulang	35,000	39,411	52,000	58,476	1.1	2.2	1.8
Gelao	20,400	26,852	26,000	53,802	2.5	3.9	3.3
Maonan	18,400	22,382	31,000	38,135	1.8	3.0	2.5
Tajik	14,400	16,236	22,000	26,503	1.1	2.7	2.1
Pumi	12,000	14,298	22,000	24,237	1.6	2.9	2.4
Nu	12,700	15,047	19,000	23,166	1.5	2.4	2.1
Achang	17,700	12,032	18,000	20,441	−3.5	2.9	0.5
Ewenki	6,200	9,681	13,000	19,343	4.1	3.8	3.9
Uzbek	13,600	7,717	7,500	12,453	−5.2	2.7	−0.3
Benglong	2,900	7,261	10,000	12,295	8.3	2.9	5.0
Jing	4,300	4,293	5,400	11,995	−0.0	5.7	3.5
Jinuo	—	—	10,000	11,974	—	—	—
Yugur	3,800	5,717	8,800	10,569	3.7	3.4	3.5
Baoan	4,900	5,125	6,800	9,027	0.4	3.1	2.1
Drung	2,400	3,090	4,100	4,682	2.3	2.3	2.3
Oroqen	2,200	2,709	3,200	4,132	1.9	2.3	2.2
Tatar	6,900	2,294	2,900	4,127	−10.0	3.3	−1.8
Russian	22,600	1,326	600	2,935	−25.8	4.4	−7.0
Gaoshan	—	366	—	1,549	—	8.0	—
Hezhe	450	718	800	1,476	4.2	4.0	4.1
Unknown	—	32,411	—	879,201	—	—	—
All minorities	35,320,360	39,923,736	55,800,000	67,233,254	1.1%	2.9%	2.2%
Han Chinese	547,283,057	651,296,368	—	936,703,824	1.6	2.0	1.9
Naturalized citizens	—	7,416	—	4,842	—	—	—
Military personnel[c]	—	3,361,655	—	4,238,210	—	—	—

SOURCES: *1953*, Han total and totals for all minority groups over 1 million, Communique on 1953 Census (1954): 2; other minority groups (given in the highly rounded figures shown), "Wo-kuo yu na-hsieh shao-shu min-tsu" (What minority nationalities does China have?), *Shih-shih shou-ts'e* (Handbook on current events), no. 17 (10 Sept. 1956): 21–23. Minority totals from the 1953 census are also reported in Bruk (1974): 633; Fang Jen, "Wo-kuo shao-shu min-tsu te jen-k'ou yü fen-pu" (The population sizes and distribution of minority nationalities in China), *Ti-li chih-shih* (Geographical knowledge), no. 6 (14 June 1958): 258–59; Zhang Tianlu (1980): 29; and Zhou Qing & Xiong (1982): 76. *1978*, Estimates of individual minority groups in BR 23, no. 9 (3 Mar. 1980): 17; Zhou Qing & Xiong (1982): 76; Zhang Tianlu (1980): 29; *China Handbook* (Hong Kong, 1980): 320–23. *1964 and 1982*, State Council Population Office (1982): 2, 23–24.

NOTE: The 1953 census included the military in its breakdown of ethnic groups; in that year minorities were 6.1% of the total population. Thereafter, only the ethnic composition of the civilian population was recorded. The minorities' share of that population was 5.8% in 1964 and 6.7% in 1982. The growth rates shown are thus only approximate, based on the easiest assumption—that the military was 100% Han from 1964 to 1982. The 1978 total for minorities is not a reported figure but merely a sum of the figures in the column.

[a]Redefined as Zhuang. [b]Included under Tibetan. [c]Ethnic composition not reported.

Another significant incentive for reporting minority group membership is that minority couples are allowed to bear more children than Han couples.

Higher mortality than among the Han has been an element restraining the natural increase rates of minority groups, especially before 1964 and particularly among the least assimilated groups living in economically backward areas. In addition, the violent rebellions of some minorities and the repressions that followed have cost the lives of at least tens of thousands, and perhaps hundreds of thousands of minority persons, especially Tibetans, Uygurs, Kazaks, Yi, and Hui.*

Certain minority groups have grown in size more slowly than their natural increase would have allowed as people emigrated from China. Almost all Russians in China appear to have emigrated, as shown in Table 9.3. The slow growth of the Tibetan and Uygur minorities during 1953–82 can be attributed in part to net emigration. An estimated 90,000 Tibetans have emigrated since the early 1950's, and few apparently have returned.[54] The number of Uygur emigrants is unknown, but it is possible to see their effect in the Soviet Union. Between the 1959 and 1970 Soviet censuses the enumerated Uygur population grew from 95,208 to 173,276, far faster than could be accounted for by natural increase alone.[55] Assuming that during this period Soviet Uygurs had a high natural increase rate of 30–35 per thousand population, the excess population growth attributable to immigrants was 33,000 to 41,000. Table 9.3 lists other Muslim peoples of China whose population decline or slow growth could have been caused by net emigration: the Kazak, Uzbek, Tatar, Dongxiang, and Kirgiz groups, whose numbers in China declined between 1953 and 1964, and the Baoan minority, which registered slow growth at the same time.

The study of the demography, economy, and culture of Chinese minority groups has been neglected since 1949. Only in the early 1980's was nationalities research resumed with some urgency.[56] China today still knows little about its own minority peoples, and of the information that has been gathered, much has been suppressed or distorted by ideological blinders. The figures shown in Table 9.3 leave many unanswered questions. Why, for example, did the Mongolian, Yao, Hani, and some smaller minority groups increase greatly in size during both 1953–64 and 1964–82, when most other minorities showed different trends? What changing definitions have been used to determine membership in certain minority nationalities, such as the Zhuang, Tibetan, and Tujia, and by

* The Dalai Lama made the following claim: "The Chinese themselves admit to killing 87,000 Tibetans then [in 1959]. We estimate that starvation, labor camps, and later Cultural Revolution oppression raised that to 200,000 deaths." Ward (1980): 228.

what criteria are new minority groups listed separately? The available anecdotal information about individual minority groups, coupled with the figures compiled in Table 9.3, do indicate that there has been a great range of demographic experience among China's minorities since 1953.

Province-level data on the growth of minority group populations have rarely been released. After the 1982 census some provincial census communiques gave the 1964 and 1982 minority totals in the province. Many provinces have small minority populations compared to the Han, a legacy of historical geographical patterns of migration and settlement. In Guangdong, for example, only 1.8 percent of the 1982 population consisted of minority individuals, up from 1.4 percent in 1964. The minority proportion in Sichuan increased from 2.6 percent in 1964 to 3.7 percent in 1982. In many other provinces the minority proportion remained under 1 percent in 1982, for instance, Shaanxi, Shanxi, Shandong, Anhui, Shanghai, Jiangsu, Zhejiang, and Fujian.

For those provinces where the minority proportion of the population was 15 percent or more in the 1950's, Han in-migration has tended to lower the minority proportion but higher natural increase rates among minorities since the mid-1960's have tended to increase it. In 1958 Nei Mongol had a population about 15 percent minority; the largest minority group, the Mongols, made up about 13.4 percent of the provincial population.[57] Partly because of the Han influx, by 1964 Mongols constituted 11.2 percent of Nei Mongol's population, but because of rapid natural increase they recovered to 12.9 percent by 1982. All the minority groups together were 15.6 percent of Nei Mongol's 1982 population, slightly up from the 1958 percentage.

Yunnan had 5.7 million minority people in 1958, or 30 percent of its population.[58] In spite of some reported Han in-migration, no major shift in the minority proportion has occurred. In 1964 Yunnan's population was 31.3 percent minority, and in 1982 it was 31.7 percent. In 1958 Ningxia was about one-third Hui and almost two-thirds Han, with small numbers of other nationalities.[59] The minority proportion was 30.9 percent in 1964, perhaps slightly down from 1958, and 31.9 percent in 1982. Guangxi was 41.6 percent minority in 1957, and 38.5 percent in 1982.[60] Guizhou's minority population constituted 25.9 percent of the province's 1953 census count and 24.1 percent in 1982.[61]

In some provinces Han in-migration may have resulted in a declining proportion of minority people during the 1950's or early 1960's but not thereafter. This seems to have been the case in Qinghai. A report on Qinghai stated, "Because of the influx of population of Han race and their rapid growth, the ratio of the Han population to total population increased from 48 percent in 1959 to 62.2 percent in 1979."[62] But this whole shift had taken place by 1964. According to the 1964 census 38.7 percent of Qinghai's population was minority, and this changed only slightly to 39.4 percent in 1982. Much Han in-migration was reported after 1964, but it must have been balanced by faster natural increase among minorities.

There are only two provinces where the Han remain in the minority, Xinjiang and Xizang.[63] In 1953 Xinjiang had about 3.64 million Uygurs, 75 percent of its population, around 475,000 Kazaks, 10 percent of the population, many other minority groups, and about 300,000 to 500,000 Han, or 6 to 10 percent of Xinjiang's population.[64] By 1982 due to Han in-migration the number of Han was 5.29 million and the province was 40.4 percent Han.

The Han population of Tibet was probably negligible before the Red Army took over in 1950. After three decades the 1982 census of Xizang counted 91,660 Han, who made up 4.8 percent of the population. But this figure may be conservative if it excludes large numbers of Han in-migrants on "temporary" assignment. The Han of Xizang are concentrated in Lhasa and other towns, governing the province and managing its industries, while the Tibetans were excluded from positions of economic and political power at least until the late 1970's. The small number given for the Han in Xizang is also misleading because it excludes the People's Liberation Army garrisons dotting the landscape, variously estimated at 150,000 to 300,000 soldiers.[65] If these are almost all Han, then the Han population residing in and controlling Tibet is about 250,000–400,000, most of them military.

The areas where minority groups live have been strongly incorporated into the PRC since 1949, first by the entrance of the Red Army and later by military occupation of border provinces. Where possible, the borders of the autonomous regions were gerrymandered as they were being established in the 1950's in order to create a Han majority. Han migration into minority provinces helped ensure their domination even where it did not greatly change their proportions in the population, because the Han took over provincial governments and developed the modern economic sectors in minority provinces. Tight economic links have been forged between minority areas and the rest of China through the building of transport and communication systems and the reorientation of minority economies along socialist lines.

Urbanization

China's government has exercised an unusual degree of control over interprovincial migration, compared to the governments of most developing countries. Even more remarkable, the flow of migrants from rural to

TABLE 9.4
Population of the Largest Cities, 1982

City	Population	City	Population
Shanghai city proper	6,320,872	Xian, Shaanxi	2,185,040
Shanghai total urban	6,975,179	Liupanshui, Guizhou	2,107,100
Beijing city proper	5,597,972	Nanjing, Jiangsu	2,091,400
Beijing total urban	5,970,227	Changchun, Jilin	1,747,410
Tianjin city proper	5,142,565	Taiyuan, Shanxi	1,745,820
Tianjin total urban	5,333,622	Dalian, Liaoning	1,480,240
Shenyang, Liaoning	3,944,240	Kunming, Yunnan	1,418,640
Wuhan, Hubei	3,287,720	Tangshan, Hebei	1,407,840
Guangzhou, Guangdong	3,181,510	Zhengzhou, Henan	1,404,050
Chongqing, Sichuan	2,673,170	Lanzhou, Gansu	1,364,480
Harbin, Heilongjiang	2,519,120	Guiyang, Guizhou	1,350,190
Chengdu, Sichuan	2,499,000	Taian, Shandong	1,274,770
Zibo, Shandong	2,197,660	Zaozhuang, Shandong	1,244,020

SOURCES: State Council Population Office (1982): 16–17; State Council Population Office (1983): 28–211.

NOTE: The Shanghai, Beijing, and Tianjin figures are exact counts. The city proper populations of the other cities are extrapolations based on a 10% sample of census questionnaires.

urban areas has been restrained and in some periods reversed by China's mechanisms of political and economic control. If no attempts had been made to affect rural-to-urban migration during the last three decades, China's urban population could be at least twice its current size. In particular, the urbanized populations of the primary cities would have mushroomed to several times their current number, producing the phenomenon of over-urbanization so common in developing countries today. For instance, by now Shanghai could easily have 15 or 20 million urban residents living in sprawling slums without amenities, mostly underemployed or unemployed. As shown in Table 9.4, even China's largest cities had urban populations of fewer than 7 million according to the 1982 census. The urban population of Shanghai, for instance, is modest in size compared to the urban populations of Calcutta (10 million), Seoul (14 million), São Paulo (15 million), or Mexico City (17 million).[66]

There have been just a few years when migration into urban areas was allowed or even encouraged, based on the idea that very rapid industrialization was taking place in urban areas and would continue indefinitely, thus requiring a constant influx of workers from the countryside. The first such period of unbridled optimism was in the first years after the establishment of the PRC, 1949–51, and the second was during the Great Leap Forward, 1958–60. In all other years, however, China's policy has been to stabilize the size of the leading cities, or allow very slow population growth if laborers were required to staff growing industries in particular cities. Meanwhile restrictions have been slightly less rigid over migration into small and medium-sized cities, especially those located away from the already developed coastal areas. As such cities industrialized, controlled recruitment of workers from rural areas has been allowed; nevertheless, workers have often been forbidden to bring their families.

China's unusually tight restrictions on urban population growth have been based on practical considerations reinforced by ideological biases. In the PRC's economic system urban areas are essentially owned and administered by the state, and their residents are the state's direct responsibility. The state budget must supply urban areas with employment, housing, food, water, sewage disposal, transportation, medical facilities, police protection, schools, and other essentials and amenities of life. In 1957 the State Construction Commission calculated that a total of 558–695 yuan in construction costs was required for each additional person in the urban population, and a 1979 report put the figure at over 700 yuan.[67] In rural areas, however, the collective or family economy is responsible for supplying these needs, and the government rarely concerns itself with budgeting for the basic needs of rural residents. Therefore the government has a powerful fiscal incentive to keep urban population to an absolute minimum. Reinforcing this practical consideration is a profound, sometimes irrational anti-urban bias in Maoist thought, which sees city people as leeches corrupted by material comforts and peasants as hardworking, productive, rugged, virtuous people. Partly as a result of this government policy, China's population remains highly rural.

The State Statistical Bureau in 1983 published a compilation of urban population totals for 1949–82 that included adjustments of the originally collected official data for some years. These are shown in Table 9.5. There are some problems with this series as a description of China's urbanization trends, in part because the definition of "urban" has shifted over time.[68] It appears that rather traditional and ad hoc notions of what was an urban or a rural place were used for the 1953 census, and only after definitional problems arose in the census did a debate ensue over the question. The 1954 Constitution stated that a place had to have an established political and administrative structure to be classified urban. Additional criteria were issued in 1955. The following places were to be called urban: those with a population of 1,000–2,000 of whom 75 percent or more were nonagricultural, and those with 2,000 or more people at least 50 percent of whom were nonagricultural. A revision of these criteria was issued at the end of 1963, requiring a larger population size and higher proportion nonagricultural before a locality was called urban: places with a population of 2,500–3,000 of whom 85 percent or more were nonagricultural and larger places whose populations were 70 percent or more nonagricultural were to be considered urban places. But these new definitions meant disqualifying many places formerly called towns. The

TABLE 9.5
Official Urban Population Totals, 1949–83
(Thousands)

Year	Census midyear	State Statistical Bureau reconstruction, yearend: As reported	As percent of total	Year	Census midyear	State Statistical Bureau reconstruction, yearend: As reported	As percent of total
1949		57,650	10.6%	1967		135,480	17.7%
1950		61,690	11.2	1968		138,380	17.6
1951		66,320	11.8	1969		141,170	17.5
1952		71,630	12.5	1970		144,240	17.4
1953	77,257	78,260	13.3	1971		147,110	17.3
1954		82,490	13.7	1972		149,350	17.1
1955		82,850	13.5	1973		153,450	17.2
1956		91,850	14.6	1974		155,950	17.2
1957		99,490	15.4	1975		160,300	17.3
1958		107,210	16.2	1976		163,410	17.4
1959		123,710	18.4	1977		166,690	17.6
1960		130,730	19.7	1978		172,450	17.9
1961		127,070	19.3	1979		184,950	19.0
1962		116,590	17.3	1980		191,400	19.4
1963		116,460	16.8	1981		201,710	20.2
1964	127,103	129,500	18.4	1982	206,589	211,540	20.8
1965		130,450	18.0	1983		241,280	23.5
1966		133,130	17.9				

SOURCES: The State Statistical Bureau's reconstruction of yearend urban population totals and its estimates of annual percent urban are from Statistical Yearbook of China 1983 (1983): 103–4. The 1953 census urban figure is from Communique on 1953 Census (1954): 2. Urban totals from the 1964 and 1982 censuses are from State Council Population Office (1982): 3. The yearend 1983 urban figure is from Statistical Abstract of China 1984 (1984): 15.

1963 restrictions were implemented slowly during the 1960's and 1970's, so that many localities not meeting the criteria remained on the lists of towns until they were deleted in preparation for the census of 1982. Because the definition of urban places became more restrictive over time, and explosive urban growth did not take place, the number of places defined as urban declined from 5,402 in the 1953 census to about 3,600 in 1979 to 2,900 in the 1982 census.[69] The series in Table 9.5 repeats without adjustment the official urban figures from the 1950's that included large numbers of small towns; these figures are not fully comparable with recent urban data based on a much smaller number of urban places.

There was another definitional problem that caused confusion about China's urban population size until after the 1982 census and that may still be affecting the adjusted series in Table 9.5. During the period 1964–81, a highly restrictive concept of "urban population" was utilized in the officially collected urban data from the 1964 census and from the annual yearend reporting system. Persons living within the boundaries of urban areas but categorized as agricultural because they were not receiving commercial grain rations were lumped together with the rural population, by definition lowering the urban proportion of China's total population.[70] In those years, official figures further underestimated the urban population by excluding urban residents who did not have permanent residence status in the city or town. For the 1982 census, a much more realistic and internationally comparable definition of the urban population was adopted. All residents of officially designated urban places were considered the urban population, including any "agricultural" people living within the urban boundaries and all "temporary" residents or contract employees who had lived there for more than a year.[71] After 1982, the State Statistical Bureau used what information it had to reconstruct urban figures for 1964–81 based on a definition somewhat comparable to that of the 1982 census, but the information required for an accurate adjustment may not be available.

The 1953 census counted 77.3 million urban persons, constituting 13.3 percent of China's population. Extrapolating backward from the census the government estimated that at yearend 1949 China had 57.7 million urban persons, or 10.6 percent of the estimated total population.[72] The apparent speed of urbanization during 1949–53 may be partly spurious, because population statistics before 1953 were weak or nonexistent. The government simply extrapolated from estimated population trends in some urban areas to all urban areas of China, a questionable procedure. It is best to use 1953 census data, not the 1949 figures, as benchmark statistics for tracing subsequent urbanization trends.

Beginning in 1954, population registration and rationing were instituted in some cities, and estimates of urban population size began to be based partly on registration data. Urbanization was rapid during the 1950's, according to the available information. The urban population rose from 77.3 million in 1953 to 99.5 million at yearend 1957, or 13.3 percent to 15.4 percent of China's total population.[73]

The Great Leap Forward witnessed a surge in China's urban population. Because statistics were especially poor for that period, estimates of urban population as in this report should be taken as rough approximations: "In the three years from 1958 through 1960, more than 19 million people from rural areas were recruited as workers. Together with their family members, the number of urban population increased from more than 99 million in 1957 to over 130 million in 1960, a sharp increase of more than 31 million persons."[74] Urban figures for the Great Leap period were presumably based on application of the 1954 and 1955 definitions of urban places, definitions more restrictive than the 1953 census procedures. Therefore, the sharp urbanization trend of the 1953–60 period shown in the available statistics may even underestimate the actual shift.

The swelling of the urban population during 1958–60 resulted from several things. After the euphoric beginning of the Great Leap Forward in 1958 controls on rural-to-urban migration were relaxed, and urban industries, confident of expansion, recruited rural labor. In addition, serious economic dislocations and discouragement caused by the rural communization movement pushed peasants toward the cities. A 1959 account stated that as a result of the compulsory formation of agricultural communes, "Work enthusiasm on the farms immediately fell, and there was an unchecked flight of farm population from the land."[75] It is also likely that as the famine spread people streamed toward urban areas in hopes of begging for food or finding ways to earn it.

In the early 1960's some of the new urban in-migrants were forcibly relocated in the countryside, perhaps many back to their home villages. For example, during the last quarter of 1960 and the first quarter of 1961 the government reportedly attempted to expel more than 10 million peasants from the cities; this continued at least into 1962.[76] The urban population data given in Table 9.5 for the years 1961–63 should be used with caution or not at all. The government may have attempted to expel former peasants and others from the cities by taking away their official right to be there, but millions may have stayed on illegally or returned quickly to urban areas after being forced to leave. The sharp increase of 11 million from the yearend 1963 registration figure to the adjusted midyear 1964 census figure for China's urban population appears to constitute a correction of faulty registration data.

Table 9.6 shows the urban population of China from the 1964 and 1982 censuses, nationwide and for some provinces. The State Statistical Bureau tried to use the same definition of urban in presenting these data from the two censuses, that is, the 1982 definition that includes the "agricultural" population living inside city and town boundaries. Using these criteria, by 1964 China had an urban population of 127.1 million, constituting 18.4 percent of the enumerated civilian population.

Of the provinces that have released data on their 1964 urban population, those with the strongest urbanization trend up to that time were primarily those receiving in-migration. For example, Nei Mongol increased from about 10.7 percent urban in 1953 to 24.4 percent in 1964.* Heilongjiang progressed from approximately 31.1 percent urban in 1953 to 40.0 percent in 1964. Qinghai, only 7.0 percent urban in 1953, grew to 16.6 percent urban in 1964. Provinces whose populations did not grow

* Data on the urban proportion of each province's population from the 1953 census were never reported, but provincial urban estimates were derived from other reported census data by Ni (1960). The actual 1953–64 urbanization trend in these provinces was probably stronger than implied by these figures, because the category of urban place was more inclusive in 1953 than 1964.

TABLE 9.6

Official Urban Population by Province, 1964 and 1982

Province	Midyear 1964 urban population		Midyear 1982 urban population	
	Number	As percent of total	Number	As percent of total
North				
Beijing	—	—	5,970,227	64.7%
Tianjin	(3,450,580)	(55.2%)	5,333,622	68.7
Hebei	(4,435,394)	11.3	7,272,130	13.7
Shanxi	(3,172,890)	17.6	5,314,528	21.0
Nei Mongol	(3,003,984)	(24.4)	5,561,306	28.9
Northeast				
Liaoning	(10,979,256)	(40.7)	15,132,303	42.4
Jilin	—	—	8,941,108	39.6
Heilong-jiang	8,044,181	(40.0)	13,241,697	40.5
East				
Shanghai	—	—	6,975,179	58.8
Jiangsu	(6,617,000)	(14.9)	9,572,186	15.8
Zhejiang	—	—	9,996,952	25.7
Anhui	—	—	7,082,496	14.3
Fujian	(3,416,280)	(20.4)	5,480,708	21.2
Jiangxi	—	—	6,452,413	19.4
Shandong	(7,176,000)	12.9	14,190,511	19.1
Central and South				
Henan	—	—	10,509,111	14.1
Hubei	—	—	8,275,865	17.3
Hunan	—	—	7,766,220	14.4
Guangdong	(7,185,344)	17.8	11,081,573	18.7
Guangxi	—	—	4,306,961	11.8
Southwest				
Sichuan	(9,482,494)	13.9	14,251,131	14.3
Guizhou	—	—	5,631,434	19.7
Yunnan	—	—	4,187,276	12.9
Xizang	—	—	179,450	9.5
Northwest				
Shaanxi	(3,192,149)	15.4	5,490,608	19.0
Gansu	(1,785,000)	14.1	3,002,499	15.3
Qinghai	(355,670)	16.6	797,931	20.5
Ningxia	(390,939)	(18.5)	875,940	22.5
Xinjiang	—	—	3,715,217	28.4
National total	127,103,041[a]	18.4%[a]	206,588,582	20.6%

SOURCES: National urban data and 1982 provincial data, State Council Population Office (1982): 3, 16–17.

NOTE: The provincial figures for both years were released in each province's separate census communique, on file at the China Branch, Center for International Research, U.S. Bureau of the Census. Figures in parentheses were derived from other figures in the communiques. "Urban" in this table pertains to the civilian population only.

[a]Includes the provinces whose 1964 urban populations have not been reported.

through in-migration generally had more moderate urbanization. The simplest explanation is that much of the interprovincial migration stream before 1964 went to urban areas in the targeted provinces.

Throughout the 1960's and most of the 1970's the government attempted to block most rural-to-urban population flows and continued forcing people out of China's cities. The net result was that in the 18-year period 1964–82 China's population "urbanized" only slightly from 18.4 percent to 20.6 percent urban. Most provinces reporting for both these years recorded a similar trend. During these two decades, however, the urbanization trend was not smooth. According to Table 9.5 the proportion of Chinese living in urban areas declined after 1964, reaching the lowest point in 1972, and rose slowly thereafter. If there had been no migration in this period, the urban proportion of the population would have declined every year because natural increase was slower in urban than in rural areas. The rising urban proportion in the years after 1976 was caused by increased net rural-to-urban migration in the post-Mao era despite government attempts to minimize it.

The fact that the Chinese population was only 20.6 percent urban by 1982 can be attributed to the government's anti-urbanization policies for most of the previous three decades but particularly since the Great Leap Forward. Was it wise for the government to block continuing urbanization after 1960? In favor of this strategy one could point out that uncontrolled urban growth was stopped, over-urbanization with its attendant human misery was prevented, urban unemployment was kept to a minimum, and rural areas benefited economically by retaining their relatively creative, hardworking, and educated young adults who might otherwise have headed for the city if given a chance. In opposition one might emphasize that blocking urban population growth worsened some of the existing distortions in China's economy. During two decades of rapid population growth the PRC forced its rural areas to accommodate the entire surplus population. This policy's effect was to maintain or widen the differences between urban and rural living standards. Rural communes had to provide work and sustenance for their rapidly growing populations with negligible investment from outside and with few outlets for their surplus people. This situation made the problem of rural underemployment worse than it would otherwise have been and held down per capita incomes in the villages because everyone had to be provided for even if some could not add much to local production. Meanwhile urban governments had the luxury of exporting their unemployed. Capital-intensive heavy industry was emphasized in China's modern sector, while more labor-intensive light industry and services were de-emphasized or forbidden. The rapidly growing urban industrial sector did not provide the number of jobs that would have been consistent with its increasing importance in the economy. Therefore, the policy of controlling urban population growth was beneficial in avoiding over-urbanization but was overdone because of Maoist ideological blinders. Urban areas should have been required to share in the task of providing more employment and other essentials for the growing population, rather than laying so much of the burden on the countryside.

The geographical distribution of China's urban areas has apparently remained surprisingly constant since 1949.[77] China has a long history of the development of cities and towns as administrative, trading, and production centers. Since 1949 the government has retained the traditional administrative structure of provincial capitals, prefectural cities, and county towns but enhanced the functions of these old administrative centers by locating new industries in them. Cities that already had an industrial and supporting infrastructure in 1949 have continued to receive industrial investment, and cities and towns not previously industrialized have now been industrialized. In addition, new cities and towns have been built where appropriate: at new railroad and highway junctions, mining centers, and oilfields. Traditional market towns were turned into the administrative centers of rural people's communes and became sites for new commune-owned industries in the commune center. The result has been the retention of the pre-1949 distribution of urban areas, with the addition of some new urban centers.

A national conference of urban planners held in October 1980 reaffirmed existing urban policy as follows:

> On 15th October in Peking a national conference of town planners closed, having called for more small towns to be built throughout China, and for strict control of the growth of population in big cities. . . . Delegates agreed that three categories of small towns should be developed but limited to 200,000 people, with a balance of men and women and a mixed industrial base. The three categories are: Existing towns already with some industries, which are to be developed into local economic, political, and cultural centers (there are more than 3,200 of these throughout China, about half of them with populations of more than 10,000), towns to be built in new industrial and construction areas like mines, power stations, resource projects, railways, harbors, and [areas of] tourism; and satellite towns which will accommodate factories to be moved out of nearby cities. A number of satellites have already been built around Peking, Shanghai, Tianjin, Wuhan, and Shenyang.
>
> The conference called for the development of other small towns into regional political, economic, and cultural centers. These are the central towns in China's 53,000 people's communes, many of which have a flourishing industrial and commercial life.[78]

Rather than allow people to migrate from rural areas to cities, China's leaders expressed their intention to keep the population dispersed and "urbanize the villages," employing surplus agricultural labor in small enterprises and service trades located in the commune, township, or brigade centers.[79]

The maintenance of the traditional dispersed urban pattern has been reinforced by the hugeness of China's population and geographical area and the continuing weakness of its transportation system. Without a modern transport system the PRC can hardly move the people or goods necessary in a more modern economy. Today the mileage of paved roads and railroads, and especially the number of trucks and railroad cars, are inadequate to move enough fuel, food, building materials, industrial raw materials, and industrial products around the country. The creation of a largely self-contained economy within each province has been mandated by the lack of transport. This system is inefficient because many localities have been forced to produce what they cannot produce best while diverting their resources from making those products in which they enjoy a natural advantage. But China still has no alternative unless it greatly develops its transportation system.

The severe restriction of city population growth has also followed naturally from the slow development of the transportation system. Cities have great difficulty getting enough food if it has to be carried in by mule-drawn carts, as is still the case. The rural areas right next to cities cannot grow enough grain for them, yet grain is so bulky that great quantities cannot be transported long distances in China. Nor can the contiguous rural areas grow enough perishable foods, yet the lack of refrigerated trucks and railroad cars means that perishables cannot be transported long distances. When a city's population increases rapidly its food supply often becomes so strained that the city government tends to react in desperation and start rounding up people to send immediately to rural areas. Keeping the vast majority of Chinese down on the farm minimizes the need for transporting essentials from rural to urban areas.

Rural-to-Urban and Urban-to-Rural Migration

China has been unusual in its policy of controlling urbanization and in its ability to do so. There has been an ongoing struggle between people trying to move to urban areas and their government trying to stop them. In China as in most developing countries, the natural flow of migration in the absence of controls would be to the city, because the countryside is in general economically depressed while urban incomes are higher and urban life is more varied and interesting.

To prevent this natural movement, migration controls were set up in the 1950's and have functioned in most years. Each person in China is supposed to be permanently registered somewhere as part of a household. Moving one's registration location from an undesirable to a desirable place has normally been difficult or impossible. There are at least three categories of registration: city, town, and rural. City registration carries with it more privileges than the other categories; it is extremely hard to get unless one is born in the city, and it can easily be taken away by the authorities even from city-born persons. Town registration is not nearly as desirable as wages are lower, food rations are smaller, educational benefits are less, and extra allowances are fewer, but it is far preferable to rural registration in terms of benefits received.[80] Town registration has been difficult to obtain if one was born in the countryside, unless that rural area was in the environs of a city and became urbanized and administratively transformed into a town. The great majority of Chinese are born into rural households and registered there.

Anyone wishing to leave a rural area must overcome a number of hurdles. First, the would-be migrant must have permission from the village leaders, who may be cautious about handing out such permissions at the risk of being censured. The higher-ups take a dim view of village leaders who give their residents letters of introduction that get them into urban areas "without convincing grounds."[81]

Second, the migrant must have written proof of a job in the intended destination and permission from the authorities there to move into the area. Periodically, during the 1950's and since, urban enterprises have recruited workers directly from rural areas without involving the city authorities. City governments tried to make the industries recruit through the urban labor bureaus. The national and provincial governments periodically censured officials who allowed rural-to-urban migration to remind all officials that this population movement was not permitted. For example, in 1978 a recently fired provincial official was criticized for having "arbitrarily transferred agricultural manpower so that manpower on the front line of agriculture was weakened. He did not control the population in cities, so that the number of people consuming marketable grain in our province increased unduly, more than that of fraternal provinces."[82]

The policy of keeping rural people out of urban areas had such high official priority that cadres who loosely administered the migration controls risked losing their jobs. The following case from early 1980 was placed on the front page of China's leading newspaper the *People's Daily* to underscore its seriousness:

On 15 January, the Henan provincial party committee issued a "circular concerning Wugang District's violation of policy on population transfer." The circular pointed out: A handful of leading cadres in Wugang District disregarded party discipline and state law, violated the policy on population transfer, and moved a number of rural families into non-agricultural population areas where they were not qualified to live. The Henan provincial party committee endorsed a report by Xuchang prefectural party committee on the "handling of the case of Wugang District's severe violation of policy on population transfer" and approved the dismissal of Comrade Xin Yanhui from his post as first party secretary of Wugang district party committee and the dismissal of Comrade Zhou Dongzhao from his posts as member of the Standing Committee of Wugang district party committee and director of Wugang District Public Security Bureau.[83]

The singling out of the head of the Public Security Bureau was important because it is the responsibility of the urban police to keep out migrants from rural areas.

Even if all the above permissions to migrate are obtained, migrants from a rural area to a town or city may be granted only a temporary registration in order to maintain the fiction that they have not really moved and to allow urban authorities to ship them back to their place of origin any time there is unemployment in the urban area. Persons of rural origin may be hired as contract or temporary urban laborers.[84] These marginally employed urban workers, to judge from the local age structures, usually are men from rural areas of the municipality or of the surrounding province.[85] The vulnerability of their position in the urban area is suggested by the following report, which urged urban areas to solve their acute unemployment problems in 1979 by firing migrants and hiring urban-born youth in their place:

Qianshan County has strengthened labor management, sorted out and dismissed unplanned and surplus laborers from their posts, and paid special attention to sorting out and dismissing those unplanned surplus laborers who are experienced rural laborers. This is worth drawing the great attention of all levels of party committees and all departments. Sorting out and reducing the number of unplanned surplus laborers is an important way of solving current urban labor employment problems. Due to the interference and sabotage of Lin Biao and the gang of four, an extremely irrational situation has emerged. On the one hand, unemployed people in urban areas cannot be fully employed; on the other hand, a large number of rural laborers have been employed in urban areas.[86]

Rural-to-urban migrants, therefore, are used as a surplus labor force in urban areas. For political and economic reasons they may never be granted permanent resident status but remain "temporary residents" in cities for years. Their families cannot join them; if a man goes to work in an urban area his wife, children, and parents must remain in his home village, and the whole family retains legal permanent residence in the rural area. By this means urban areas block in-migration of dependents who would require housing, schooling, and other necessities, but they benefit from the labor of rural adults without having to pay for their upbringing or education. Urban workers recruited from rural areas are given the minimum dormitory housing and sustenance. They are not entitled to the full regular wage or to fringe benefits. When they are fired or retire they are sent back to the village where their family resides. No retirement pension would be paid.

Even with these elaborate controls there have been times when people streamed into cities and towns. In 1957 urban police were authorized to set up a system of roadblocks on the major arteries and checkpoints in railroad stations and forcibly turn back anyone coming into the city without authorization.[87]

As a result of the nationwide blockages to human movement, China's population appears to be unusually immobile geographically. Though national data are not available, some information from Guangdong lends support to this impression. William Parish and Martin Whyte took household "censuses" of four Guangdong production teams based on interviews with refugees in 1973–74 and also derived information on other teams. From these data they estimated that at the time of their study, 90 percent of the young men in these parts of the Guangdong countryside were still in their home villages, frequently living with or next door to their parents.[88] Elizabeth and Graham Johnson got a similar impression from their interviews with county leaders in the Guangzhou delta of Guangdong:

> The great majority of rural village people are still living in their ancestral villages. There appears to have been very little movement of population. According to our informants, there is at present very little migration, and that which exists conforms to certain patterns. Some commune members, especially younger people, may take employment on state farms or other enterprises particularly in the developing frontier areas. During the past two years, more than 400 people left Lokang Commune (population 53,000) to take up residence elsewhere. At Loktong Brigade (population 1,700) we were told that a few dozen people had left to work elsewhere. Some moved permanently with their families, while others left their families behind and return to visit them every year at the Spring Festival. There is little migration of rural families either to cities or to other rural areas.[89]

But this situation of extreme rural immobility may have eased somewhat beginning in 1979. Though data are lacking, there might be increased movement of villagers from their home villages for short or long periods of time in response to the new agricultural policy supporting rural trade and sideline occupations. For example, a November 1979 report from Hunan lamented: "The labor force is scattered. Some production teams have allowed large numbers of laborers to leave in order to increase their income. At this busy production season, some peasants have abandoned collective production and are building houses instead. Others have left to do business."[90]

It appears that the government has largely succeeded in its attempts to prevent movement out of the country's rural areas. Even so, the government has not been able to block all rural-to-urban migration. During periods of political upheaval, for example, people take advantage of the confused administrative situation to go to urban areas and attempt to find work and a place to live. The only way that the government has been able to drastically limit urbanization of the population has been through forced counterstreams of population from urban to rural areas. For instance, in 1980 Beijing Municipality reported, "In the past 30 years, a total of 5.37 million persons moved into Beijing, and 4.33 million moved out, resulting in a net in-migration of 1.04 million persons."[91]

This example illustrates that Beijing Municipality might have had a 1980 population of 13 million instead of the actual population of 9 million, even given all the barriers blocking rural-to-urban migration, had it not been for substantial urban-to-rural population movement. The total population would probably be even larger because these reported data may include only those persons who got registered in Beijing Municipality and those whose Beijing registration was canceled. Missing from the statistics may be all the people who were expelled from Beijing without ever being recorded as living there. It is likely that most other cities have also experienced significant in-migration countered by substantial out-migration, which combined have produced China's modest urbanization of the last three decades.

The rural-to-urban and urban-to-rural streams of population are age- and sex-specific. As with interprovincial migrants, these migrants ever since the early 1950's seem to have been mostly unaccompanied men. For example, the municipality of Chengdu in Sichuan has released data on the age-sex structure of its population from the 1964 census.[92] The sex ratio of the municipal population was 110 males per hundred females, suggesting previous in-migration of males. The sex ratios were particularly high in all the age groups 20–54, and there were over 120 males per hundred females in every five-year age group 25–29 through 45–49. There seems to have been a dramatic influx of working-age men from outside the municipal boundaries before 1964.

During the 1970's this pattern of male rural-to-urban migration appears to have continued. Data from rural production brigades and a rural people's commune in Chengdu Municipality show that many of the males are missing in the adult ages. At the end of 1971, for instance, Yinmenkou commune in Chengdu Municipality reported only 83.3 males per hundred females.[93] The male deficit was all in the age groups 20–49 and was very pronounced at ages 20–24 and 25–29, which retained only half as many males as females in the commune. We can presume that most of the missing men were living and working in the urban area of Chengdu. Similarly, in three rural production brigades of Chengdu Municipality as of 1979, there were very low sex ratios especially in the age groups 25–29 through 45–49, suggesting male movement to the city. Men move to urban areas primarily to work in industry, probably with an emphasis on heavy industry, and their incomes help to support their families in the villages.

Statistics available for two cities of heavy industry newly built in the 1950's suggest that in this type of city especially, the original in-migrants were overwhelmingly working men.[94] The municipality of Maanshan in Anhui was 67 percent male in 1959; in the young working ages 21–30 the population was 78 percent male, for a sex ratio of 359 males per hundred females. Zhuzhou Municipality in Hunan had 147 males per hundred females in 1961; in the ages 21–30 the sex ratio was 216. In municipalities such as these, young men have a very difficult time finding marriage partners, both because so few women live within the municipal boundaries and because the men are not allowed to find wives elsewhere and bring them to the city.

Who were the urban-to-rural migrants? Some were men who first had come legally or illegally to cities from rural areas. In the 1950's and early 1960's most of the forced migration out of urban areas probably involved persons like these. But by the late 1960's it appears that the bulk of out-migration from urban areas consisted of persons born and raised there. For instance, the government assigned adult professional workers of both sexes to move from urban to rural areas, in order to contribute their specialized abilities where needed and to train rural workers in their urban-based skills. But during the Cultural Revolution urban professionals were sent to the countryside simply as punishment for being intellectuals. They usually were forbidden to work in their fields of specialization but instead were ordered to participate in labor-intensive agriculture where there was already a labor surplus. A decade of progress in most technical, educational, and scholarly fields was lost because of this political attack on intellectual workers. Their out-migration from cities helped slow urban population growth, but during the late 1970's some of them were allowed to return to urban areas, contributing to the increasing urban proportion of China's population after 1975.

The main urban-to-rural migration flow between 1966 and about 1978 was the systematic assignment of urban youth to rural areas. Upon completion of junior or senior middle school young adults just entering the labor force were allocated jobs by urban employment bureaus. Some of the graduates got urban jobs while the rest were assigned to move to rural areas; in this way cities and towns exported their unemployed youth. Both males and females of ages 15–20 or so were sent in small groups to live in the villages. The available information suggests that these people were by and large sent to villages within their home province, probably for logistic reasons because it was so expensive to move them long distances and then pay for their spring festival visits to their families. Often they were sent to the more prosperous villages in their own province, or to nearby suburban truck-garden communes, because villages with some surplus were the only ones that could afford to house them and provide for any of their needs not covered by their government stipends.[95]

By December 1978 a total of 17 million urban-raised young adults had "been to the countryside," some for a few years but some for over a decade. Of the 17 million only "more than 900,000" had married and thereby, from the government's perspective, accepted their move to the countryside as permanent; the rest had not yet married, partly because marriage would make them ineligible for most forms of transfer out of the area to which they had been assigned, and they continued to hope that they would be reassigned to an urban area.[96] As of January 1978 nearly 10 million of the sent-down young adults were still working in rural areas and frontier regions.[97] The rest had apparently been allowed to return to an urban area, though not necessarily the city or town of their origin. The flow of urban youth from one urban area to another via a stint in a rural area was one way to transfer people from overcrowded cities to growing urban areas in need of workers.

One of the main purposes of sending urban young adults out of their home towns was to solve the problem of youth unemployment, although paradoxically the employment regulations and practices of the two decades before 1979 gave many of the available urban jobs to migrants from rural areas rather than to youth born in the cities. For example, during the same period that 17 million urban youth were sent out of urban areas, 14 million urban jobs went to workers reportedly recruited from rural areas.[98] Given that urban policies created far too few jobs for both these rural-to-urban migrants and the city-born population, expelling unemployed urban youth temporarily solved the most visible urban unemployment problems. Different cities and towns sent out very different proportions of their urban populations, depending on the perceived need for labor. Shanghai sent out of its city districts the equivalent of about 18 percent of the city proper's population. Eleven other cities for which data are available sent out between 7 and 13 percent of their city district populations. Other cities expelled less than 5 percent of their populations, and many growing urban areas probably sent out few or no urban youth.[99]

This attempt to "ruralize" the population was so counter to the needs and preferences of the affected people that it finally failed. The price of minimizing urban youth unemployment had been very high: The great majority of the sent-down youth were disaffected if not bitter, their parents struggled to get them back home, and peasants in areas where the youth were sent complained about the burdens of supporting them. After the demise of the "gang of four," universal hostility to this policy was expressed to the newly dominant leadership in ways they could not ignore. Their first response was to try to ameliorate the problems of the sent-down youth by assigning them to separate rural accounting units and giving them state aid to take the financial burden off the villages where they had been sent, but such palliatives did not solve the basic faults of the underlying policy or change the disaffection.

Finally in November and December 1978 a national conference met to deal with the whole problem. While attempting to affirm that the program had been good and necessary, the conference tried to radically restructure living conditions of the sent-down youth and gradually cut down the number to be sent out each year. Policies adopted at the conference were explained by an official:

> Vice-Premier Chen Yung-kuei said here recently that China would continue encouraging middle school [graduates] to settle in the country for a number of years to come. But, he added, the policy would be modified and methods of organization changed and, as the modernization program develops, the number would gradually be reduced. The rapid progress made since the overthrow of the gang of four was providing more opportunities for educated young people to continue study and find jobs.[100]

The national policy stated at this conference remained in force at least until early 1980. The government, to judge from its public statements, continued to retain the option of forcing urban-born youth to move to rural areas. During 1979 there were large contingents assigned to leave cities in Liaoning and Tianjin that summer and Shandong that fall, and in August 1979 another national meeting announced that about 800,000 newly graduated middle-school students would go to the countryside that year.[101]

In a similar vein, leaders of Heilongjiang and Jilin stated as late as June-July 1980 that it was still the policy to ameliorate urban unemployment problems by sending middle-school graduates to rural areas.[102] But since then mention of the practice has disappeared from China's media. Though the PRC never formally and publicly rescinded it, this unpopular policy was quietly abandoned.

The available information suggests that national, provincial, and urban leaders backed down reluctantly as a result of effective popular resistance. While the government continued trying to impose this hated policy on urban youth and their families, the youth themselves rebelled against it. There is some doubt that the 800,000 sent-down youth mentioned above ever actually went to the countryside. In 1978 and 1979 after graduating in the spring, some of the graduates assigned to go to rural areas refused to go, or procrastinated, or actively resisted their orders. There were oblique references to these problems in the media, such as this July 1979 report from Anshan in Liaoning:

> We should earnestly . . . press on to mobilize educated youth to go to the countryside and make proper arrangements for their placement so that they will live a stable life. This year our task of mobilizing educated youth to go to the countryside and settling them there is very arduous. Party committees at all levels must pay great attention to this task and devote several times more effort to it than in previous years. . . . The provincial party committee has made the decision that those educated youth who should go to the countryside but refuse to do so cannot apply for jobs or for admission to schools, nor should they be hired on a temporary basis. . . . With regard to the work of sending educated youth to the countryside, we must no longer waver, wait and see, or hesitate. It is necessary for the whole party to pitch in and grasp the work to the finish. We must make every effort to see that all educated youth to be rusticated have gone to the countryside before the end of this coming September.[103]

Shandong also reported on the new difficulties being encountered in the rustication program and urged leaders to strengthen control over the work.[104] Because of the level of resistance to this policy, the government escalated the level of coercion. Yet there must have been enough ambivalence among the leaders and empathy with the youth that this degree of force could not be sustained after 1979, and the government had to give up its plans to send new middle-school graduates to the countryside.

In an associated development, many persons who had been sent out in the 1960's and 1970's began insisting on returning to their homes, or at least to some city. Their patience had worn thin, and they tried various ways to get the government to rescind their assignments and let them come back. During 1978 and 1979 and possibly before and after, large numbers of sent-down youth began "abandoning their posts" without authorization and returning home. In 1979 the press included articles and broadcasts urging young adults absent from their assigned locations to return to their rural posts and in particular to return to the state farms in Heilongjiang and Yunnan, which could not carry on spring planting without the missing workers.[105] This mass movement, dubbed the "wind of returning to the city," became acute after the spring festival of January-February 1979 when many sent-down youth returned to their homes in Shanghai, Tianjin, and other cities in northern and central China and then refused to leave again.[106]

Many rusticated youth formally petitioned for permission to return to their homes. When permission was refused or action on the request was delayed for too long, many of the unwilling migrants resorted to militant action. There is an unconfirmed American press report that 50,000 city youths working on state farms in Yunnan staged a strike in late 1978, but China's news agency mentioned in February 1979 only that "work stoppages, troublemaking, and visits en masse to higher levels" had taken place among rusticated youth in Yunnan.[107] The broadcast stated that "the turbulent situation in some state farms is stabilizing" and that unsatisfactory conditions at state farms in Yunnan were being remedied. But the youth apparently did not obtain permission to return to the cities. During January of that year 31 young adults who had been working in rural Shaanxi for twelve years went on a hunger strike in an attempt to get permission to move back to Xian. Their parents put up posters in a "Save Our Children" campaign in support of the strikers' petition. Demonstrations by youths illegally returning to Shanghai began in December 1978 and culminated in the blocking of trains and traffic in the city during February 1979.[108] Other demonstrations took place in Hangzhou, Nanchang, and other cities.[109]

The national, provincial, and municipal governments responded to this popular movement in a variety of ways. While arresting or otherwise cracking down on the "troublemakers" they also tried to quickly create more jobs in the cities so that those who had been away from home for many years could be assigned an urban job. During 1979 some 9 million jobs were made available primarily to returned rusticated youth and newly graduated urban youth.[110] In succeeding years city governments continued to rapidly expand the number of urban jobs in an attempt to erase the unemployment backlog. This was accomplished by a radical shift in China's urban economy: For the first time in decades city residents were allowed to set up their own businesses and be self-employed; they were encouraged to engage in service occupations previously forbidden but much needed by the urban populace; more collective enterprises were set up; and state employees were allowed to retire early and let their son or daughter take a guaranteed job in the same factory. In 1979 and succeeding years, as previously rusticated youth returned to the cities and more middle-school students graduated, China's municipalities attempted to institute some minimum unemployment benefits and expand educational and training programs in order to keep the unemployed meaningfully occupied and fed while diverting them from any engagement in criminal activity.[111]

Gradually, several provinces announced a policy of bringing back those sent-down youth who had been rusticated many years before. In January

1979 Shanxi announced its intention to "make proper arrangements as soon as possible" for those sent out before 1975. Shaanxi announced the following month that educated youths who had been in the countryside for a long time had priority in educational enrollments. And in a striking reversal of previous policies, Beijing Municipality announced in November 1980 that any youths from Beijing who had spent more than two years in the countryside could return to the municipality and wait for employment; they were to be given priority in employment and for admission to vocational schools.[112]

Simultaneously during 1979 urban areas had difficulty persuading newly assigned youth to go to the countryside and at the same time experienced the "wind of returning to the city." Therefore the number of sent-down youth remaining in rural areas rapidly diminished. In November 1979 the official news agency reported that there were 5 million city youth working in the countryside.[113] If this figure is defined the same as the "nearly 10 million" sent-down youths working in rural and frontier areas just two years earlier, then the period January 1978 to November 1979 witnessed a net flow of around 5 million back to urban areas. Data from Yunnan and Beijing bear out this observation. Yunnan reported in November 1979 that "there are now 48,000 educated young people in the countryside throughout Yunnan," a small proportion of the 800,000 who had "settled down" in rural Yunnan during 1969–76.[114] Similarly, as of November 1980 Beijing Municipality announced that since 1968 some 620,000 of its educated youth had been sent to the countryside and that only some 10,000 remained there. It also announced the following policy shift: "Secondary school students who graduate in the municipality this year will not be required to go to the countryside in accordance with past regulations and policies. However, Beijing Municipality has decided to readjust the policy and improve work so as to attract educated youths to volunteer to go to the countryside."[115] Thereafter, educated youths leaving Beijing to work elsewhere would have written contracts with a stipulated period of service and salary, and they would retain their Beijing household registration and grain ration while they were gone. Upon completion of their contract they were to be free to return to Beijing.

It appears that in about 1980 the rustication of newly graduated middle-school students ceased in China. By the end of that year, most of those previously sent out of the cities had been reassigned to an urban area or allowed to return to their home city to "await employment." The exception to this trend is that some city-born Han youth sent to border provinces during the 1960's and 1970's have been required to remain there, or forced to return there if they came unauthorized to their home cities. For example, Beijing prohibits the return of those forced to leave the municipality but who have since married and acquired a job elsewhere. Shanghai authorities have also refused to accept former residents who had been sent to Xinjiang, married there, and had children there.[116] It appears that Shanghai forbids former citizens who have acquired dependents from returning because it is still trying to limit the number of people for whom its economy is responsible. Besides, as the PRC has not rescinded its policy supporting Han colonization of minority and border areas, the government would be expected to discourage those Han sent to the frontier from returning home.

Reports from 1981 and 1982 made clear that the "wind of returning to the city" continued. For instance, though Shanghai's government struggled to "strictly control" the return of those who had been sent out, between 1979 and midyear 1981 more than 400,000 educated youths came back.[117] A September 1981 report from Shanghai conceded that "for a number of years to come the net number of in-migrants will remain high," and by April 1982 half a million educated youth had returned to the city.[118] Other cities also adjusted to the need to take back the young adults they had sent out. For example, a Communist Party leader in Hangzhou, Zhejiang, predicted in 1982, "In the next few years, there will be more than 30,000 educated youths returning to Hangzhou."[119]

China's policy of forced rustication of urban youth was abandoned in the early 1980's. But why did this not happen before? The policy was thoroughly unpopular among all concerned from its inception, yet the government pursued it with dogged determination and some success from 1968 to 1978.

Official acquiescence to the reversal of this policy in the face of popular discontent may have been encouraged by an important demographic change, the transition to low fertility in the cities. Shanghai city proper, for instance, recorded low fertility by 1963 after having had very high fertility in the 1950's. The years when Shanghai sent out over a million graduating middle-school students, 1968 through the mid-1970's, were the years when enormous cohorts of children born in the 1950's were graduating. But the cohort of 1963 was around half the size of 1957's in the city of Shanghai. The small 1963 cohort graduated from senior middle school in about 1980, and subsequent cohorts were smaller still, so the task of fully employing Shanghai city's graduating classes of 1980 and beyond was much more manageable than before.

Beijing and many other cities recorded their first year of low fertility in 1965; those cohorts began graduating in about 1982. But cities in Sichuan apparently did not reach low fertility until the early 1970's; thus graduating cohorts were large until after 1985. The radical fertility shifts in the cities were bound to make the rustication program obsolete by about the mid-1980's. Policy statements in the late 1970's occasionally indicated that the rustication program would be necessary for only a few more years, and could be gradually phased out.[120] National as well as provincial policy statements during 1978–80 confirmed the official intent to continue the rustication program even against determined popular resistance, yet the program apparently ceased some time in 1980. This sequence of events suggests that the grassroots movement against rustication brought about its cessation earlier, in some places years earlier, than the government had planned. In acceding to popular demands, however, the leadership may have been influenced by expected shifts in urban age structures that would ameliorate the youth employment problem.

The other important shift that allowed the mass anti-rustication movement to succeed began with the deaths of Mao Zedong, Zhou Enlai, and many other top revolutionary leaders in the late 1970's. The unquestioned legitimacy of their leadership had enabled them to sustain an unpopular policy against great resistance. The subsequent leaders, in reversing policies of the Cultural Revolution period, raised people's hopes that wrongs perpetrated against them in the previous decade would be righted. Those who saw themselves as victims were not easily quieted by a new untested regime, and they prevailed.

China's government was alarmed by the urbanization trend of the late 1970's and early 1980's. Because it was unable to block the return of the rusticated youth or force new graduates to leave, it once again shifted emphasis to blocking the in-migrants. In early 1982 the State Council issued a circular demanding that urban units cease hiring rural workers and discharge those already hired.[121]

In 1984, a member of China's State Planning Commission admitted in an article on migration policy that urban educated youth had returned en masse to the cities and that national policy makers were not in agreement in their evaluations of the past ruralization policy or regarding what to do next. He praised the effects of the rustication policy in spite of its reversal and proposed to renew the movement of urban youth to border areas:

> Facts show that the sending of youths to the mountains and rural areas had many shortcomings, side effects, and bad results, but the problem was mainly a matter of party guidelines and policy and a matter of management and education. The broad masses of youth are by nature good, and we definitely cannot deny their activism. In the future, although we should not promote nationwide large-scale movements, since there are a large number of surplus laborers of young and adult age, it is inevitable that educated youths will be called to volunteer to support the border areas in their great undertakings, in a planned way with preparation and step by step while giving emphasis to key points. Furthermore, it is still true that before mobilization the first thing that needs to be done is to strengthen political and ideological education of the youths.[122]

Just how voluntary this might be is not clear. On the one hand, the author suggested that any necessary guarantees be implemented, such as the retention of the migrants' household registration in their home city and a signed contract for 5–10 years service in the border area. But he was confident that after economic and cultural improvements are made in border provinces, the educated youth "will not insist on returning to the interior anymore." If many volunteers to leave the cities are not forthcoming, or if those who migrate decide to return home for good and this policy of "planned dispersement of the population" does not succeed, one possible outcome is another attempt at compulsory migration to the targeted border provinces.

Rural-to-Rural, Seasonal, and Nomadic Migration

In a country where rural-to-urban migration has been so obstructed by official policy, one of the few outlets for the surplus population of a poor rural area has been migration to another rural area. In addition to the interprovincial migration of peasants described earlier, there is surely some movement within provinces. For example, on a visit to China in 1971 my delegation was shown some land planted in corn, newly reclaimed from a riverbed in Shanxi. A new village was being built next to the fields, and surplus laborers from nearby villages were planning to move there to till the new land.

Probably the most common type of rural-to-rural migration in the PRC is at marriage. Usually the bride moves from her village to that of her husband. Men in more well-to-do villages have had an easier time finding mates than men in poor villages, because women are less willing to move permanently to a poor village. But China's new emphasis on encouraging the groom to move into the household of his new wife, especially if she has no brothers, could provide an avenue of escape for men raised in poor villages. Now it is at least theoretically possible for both men and women to marry out of poor villages and into wealthier ones. For example, the wealthy Evergreen commune in a suburban county of Beijing Municipality received many in-migrants through marriage:

> The population of the commune has increased a great deal in recent years, and this creates pressure on housing and labor utilization. The crude birth rate by year 1970 through 1980 has been: 23.4, 21.7, 21.6, 20.1, 14.1, 17.6, 12.7, 12.6, 18.3, 16.1, and 20.2. Birth rates are relatively high because of the large number of marriages—800 in 1979, 1,057 in 1980, and 480 January–March 1981. This is partly a function of the age structure and partly a function of prosperity in the commune, with young men from elsewhere marrying young women in the commune and moving into the commune.[123]

Some rural residents move seasonally rather than permanently. They migrate to where there is work for part or most of the year, returning home for peak agricultural seasons or just for the spring festival. Jiangxi regularly employs surplus workers from other areas for construction jobs: "surplus laborers from Fujian, Zhejiang, Anhui, Jiangsu, and Hubei provinces regularly come to Jiangxi to work and return to their native province during festival time. Most of them are skilled in construction, transport, carpentry, and other specialties. Their labor productivity is comparatively high, and they are well liked by the pertinent departments of the province."[124]

In some of China's more rugged areas such as the Himalayas, the high plateaus of Qinghai and Tibet, the steppes of Nei Mongol, and the deserts of Xinjiang, nomadic minority populations historically moved their herds across the grasslands to find fodder, or carried goods on overland trade routes. The PRC's policy since 1949 has been to urge or require the nomads and traders to settle down in one primary location, even if it was still necessary for them to migrate during part of the year. The stated purpose of the policy was to increase the prosperity of the former nomads by developing diversified production, including agriculture as well as more advanced animal husbandry. Indeed, settled pastoralism in the PRC has been accompanied by the expansion of water supplies from wells and irrigation, the planting of forage crops, increases in the size of herds, introduction of improved animal breeds, veterinary advances, more adequate winter feed and winter shelter for the animals, and other sources of food and income in addition to the herds.[125] An ancillary purpose of settled pastoralism may have been to better control the lives of the nomads, who tended to be independent of Han domination in the past. As a result of the application of this policy for over 35 years, it is likely that a far smaller proportion of the population today engages in nomadic migrations.

Conclusions

China's uneven population distribution reflects the enormous differences in water supply, climate, and topography found throughout the country. Because differences in population density are due primarily to geographical factors, policies directed toward evening out the population distribution have changed the pattern only marginally. China's minority groups continue to be concentrated in their historical homelands in the mountainous and the arid parts of the country. After 1949 the drawing of provincial boundaries to give minority provinces a Han majority along with the in-migration of Han cadres, workers, youth, and military personnel have strengthened Han control in minority areas.

Since the 1950's China's population seems to have been relatively immobile geographically, due in part to the country's tight controls on movement. The degree of urbanization that would otherwise have occurred has been moderated considerably. Some rural-to-urban migration that continued in spite of the controls was balanced by massive forced out-migration from urban areas until the late 1970's. Though popular resistance and demographic changes have combined to stop the expulsion of city-born youths from their urban homes, municipal governments continue pressuring rural-to-urban migrants to leave the cities. Because forced urban-to-rural population flows have counteracted much of the cityward movement, and because urban natural increase since the mid-1960's has been lower than that of rural areas, the PRC's population urbanized only slightly from 18.4 percent in 1964 to 20.6 percent urban in 1982.

10

Review and Prospect

WE HAVE SEEN how the PRC achieved a remarkable mortality decline and, two decades later, an unusually sharp fertility decline as well. Let us distill what we can deduce about China's population trends into a single list of numbers. Table 10.1 presents a computer reconstruction of the demographic events in China from 1953 through 1984, with estimates back to 1949. Annual fertility levels in the reconstruction for the years 1949 through 1981 come from birth histories in the 1982 nationwide fertility survey. Age-specific and total fertility rates by year are as reported and have not been adjusted. The mortality estimates used here were described in some detail in Chapter 4. This reconstruction begins with the 1953 census age structure slightly adjusted and comes close to matching the 1964 and 1982 census age distributions. Figure 10.1 graphs the birth and death rates from the table, the difference between the two lines representing natural population increase.

The reconstruction models the sharp drop in mortality that took place in the 1950's and resumed after the setback of the Great Leap Forward period. A high life expectancy of 65 years is estimated to have been achieved by 1977. Thereafter, further mortality improvement for males and for females at most ages has been assumed, but a sharp rise in the female infant mortality rate is modeled in order to reconstruct the somewhat high sex ratios at ages 0–3 in the 1982 census age structure. This has the effect of stabilizing the estimated expectation of life at birth. While it is likely that infanticide has added to the infant mortality rate for girls, the extent of its effect is still unknown, so these infant mortality estimates remain highly speculative. This reconstruction assumes that underreporting of deaths, clearly a problem in both the 1953–64 and 1964–82 intercensal periods, is still going on. Therefore the estimated crude death rates are higher than officially reported death rates for recent years as well as earlier years.

TABLE 10.1

Computer Reconstruction of the Population Dynamics of the PRC, 1949–84

Year	Midyear population (thousands)	Crude birth rate	Crude death rate	Rate of natural increase	Total fertility rate	Life expectancy at birth	Infant mortality rate
1949	559,545	44	38	6	6.14	—	—
1950	563,253	42	35	7	5.81	—	—
1951	567,659	41	32	9	5.70	—	—
1952	574,991	46	29	17	6.47	—	—
1953	584,191	42.24	25.77	16.47	6.05	40.25	175
1954	594,725	43.44	24.20	19.24	6.28	42.36	164
1955	606,730	43.04	22.33	20.71	6.26	44.60	154
1956	619,136	39.89	20.11	19.78	5.86	46.99	143
1957	633,215	43.25	18.12	25.13	6.40	49.54	132
1958	646,703	37.76	20.65	17.11	5.68	45.82	146
1959	654,349	28.53	22.06	6.47	4.31	42.46	160
1960	650,661	26.76	44.60	−17.84	4.02	24.56	284
1961	644,670	22.43	23.01	−0.58	3.29	38.44	183
1962	653,302	41.02	14.02	27.00	6.03	53.00	89
1963	674,249	49.79	13.81	35.98	7.51	54.91	87
1964	696,065	40.29	12.45	27.84	6.18	57.08	86
1965	715,546	38.98	11.61	27.37	6.07	57.81	84
1966	735,904	39.83	11.12	28.71	6.26	58.59	83
1967	755,320	33.91	10.47	23.44	5.32	59.41	82
1968	776,153	40.96	10.08	30.88	6.45	60.29	81
1969	798,641	36.22	9.91	26.31	5.73	60.84	76
1970	820,403	36.98	9.54	27.44	5.82	61.41	70
1971	842,456	34.87	9.24	25.63	5.45	61.98	65
1972	863,439	32.45	8.85	23.60	4.99	62.55	60
1973	883,020	29.85	8.58	21.27	4.54	62.96	56
1974	901,318	28.08	8.32	19.76	4.17	63.37	52
1975	917,899	24.79	8.07	16.72	3.58	63.79	49
1976	932,671	23.05	7.84	15.21	3.23	64.21	45
1977	946,100	21.04	7.65	13.39	2.85	64.63	41
1978	958,766	20.73	7.52	13.21	2.72	65.06	37
1979	971,786	21.37	7.61	13.76	2.75	64.98	39
1980	983,379	17.63	7.65	9.98	2.24	64.89	42
1981	994,905	21.04	7.73	13.31	2.69	64.80	44
1982	1,008,175	21.09	7.89	13.20	2.71	64.72	46
1983	1,020,461	19.01	7.97	11.04	2.35	64.63	48
1984	1,031,278	18.05	8.00	10.05	2.16	64.55	50

SOURCE: Reconstructed by author at the China Branch, Center for International Research, U.S. Bureau of the Census.

NOTE: This reconstruction does not reflect the official vital rates for 1983 and 1984, which were unreported at the time the work was done. The birth, death, and natural increase rates are per 1,000 population; the total fertility rate is births per woman; life expectancy is in years; and the infant mortality rate is per 1,000 live births.

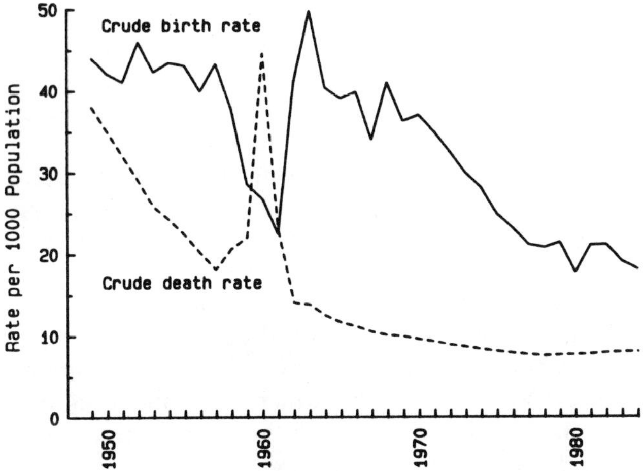

Fig. 10.1. Estimated Birth and Death Rates, 1949–84. Data from Table 10.1.

Given the age structure as it evolves from census to census, the reported age-specific and total fertility rates from the fertility survey imply the crude birth rates given in Table 10.1. Birth rates were moderately high during the 1950's, 40 births per thousand population or higher each year until fertility was depressed in 1958–61 by disruption of family life and by famine. The birth rate rebounded and stayed in the range 39–41 in the early 1960's, except for 1963 whose very high birth rate could have been caused by simultaneous resumption of fecundity in many couples as food supplies recovered, or by couples trying to replace children lost during the famine years. The fertility level was rather high during the Cultural Revolution of the late 1960's, as seen in Figure 10.1.

The national total fertility rate dropped swiftly from 5.82 births per woman in 1970 to 2.85 in 1977, reflecting the effectiveness of the intensive family planning program, the importance of the barefoot doctors and cooperative medical system in making birth control available, and a great deal of latent willingness on the part of married couples to limit their fertility. The birth rate therefore declined from 37 to 21 in only seven years. Though compulsion and coercion in the family planning program have spread geographically and steadily intensified since 1977, subsequent declines in the total fertility rate and the birth rate have been slow for several reasons. First, mean age at marriage for women ceased rising and then declined slightly in response to the new Marriage Law. Second, huge cohorts born in the 1950's reached their peak childbearing ages. Third, couples seem more resistant to dropping from three births to one birth than they had been to dropping from six births to three. The birth rate has declined to 18 or 19 per thousand population, very low for a developing country, and the Chinese population is at or below a replacement level of fertility which would be just over two births per woman.

Table 10.1 reconstructs the apparent trends in China's rate of natural population increase since 1949. Because the volume of international migration is thought to be negligible in comparison to China's huge population size, the natural increase rate is assumed to approximately equal the population growth rate. China's rate of population growth probably rose rapidly in the early 1950's as modeled in Table 10.1. It appears to have leveled out at about 2 percent in the mid-1950's and peaked at approximately 2.5 percent in 1957. During the famine the death rate rose and birth rate fell, resulting in population decline for a short period. The post-famine years were characterized by high population growth rates of 2.7–2.9 percent a year, with a peak in 1963 of about 3.6 percent. The population continued its rapid growth throughout the Cultural Revolution, then the population growth rate declined steeply from 2.7 percent in 1970 to 1.3 percent in 1977. The available information suggests that the rate of population growth stabilized through 1979, dropped suddenly in 1980 as the one-child program was implemented, rose in 1981 and 1982 because a surge of first births followed the surge of marriages, and declined to about 1.0 percent by 1984.

The rapid population growth of the last several decades was surpassed by China's overall economic growth, with the result that the real per capita gross national product grew by 2.5–3.0 percent per year on average during the period from 1957 to 1979.[1] The industrial sector has had such high priority that 1978 industrial production was about 6.5 times that of 1957. But because agriculture was neglected relative to industry, it barely kept up with population growth. Agricultural production in 1978 was about 1.5 times as great as in 1957 (both were years of good harvests), but the 1978 population was also 1.5 times that of 1957.[2] Per capita agricultural production, then, was no higher in 1978 than it had been two decades earlier.

It also appears that the quantity of food produced per capita and the quality of the Chinese diet did not improve between 1957 and the late 1970's. Because most alternative foods remained in short supply, grain still provided almost all the calories and protein in the diet. But annual per capita grain production through 1977 was about the same as in the late 1950's: it averaged 301 kilograms in 1955–57 and 305 kilograms in 1975–77.[3] After use of some grain for seed, feed, and export, much of the rest was rationed in order to allocate available grain with some fairness. A scholarly article from China in 1980 commented: "For nearly all of the twenty years from the Second Five-Year Plan period (1958–62) to the downfall of the Gang of Four in 1976 there was little or no rise in living standards. Each peasant's annual grain ration remained for a long time at around 400 *jin* or 200 kilograms of unprocessed grain . . . and the consumption of vegetable oils, eggs, and aquatic products, according to our estimates, has not returned to the 1957 level."[4]

Although the absolute increases in total grain production and total agricultural production from the late 1950's to the late 1970's were substantial, population growth ate up all the increase. Stagnant per capita food production was caused both by rapid natural population increase and by agricultural policies that suppressed the incentives of peasants to produce beyond subsistence. Beginning in 1978, per capita grain production improved, because of the introduction of the production responsibility system in agriculture, great increases in chemical fertilizer use, and a population growth rate much reduced from the peak levels of the 1960's.[5] Per capita grain output grew to 318 kilograms in 1978, rose to 342 kilograms with the bumper crop of 1979, and held at 326 or 327 kilograms in 1980 and 1981. In 1982 per capita grain production escalated to 351 kilograms. The same years saw impressive increases in per capita production of vegetable oils and meat.[6] National grain production jumped significantly in 1983; per capita output was 380 kilograms.[7] China's modest population growth rate, less than 1.5 percent annually during 1978–83, was matched or surpassed in most years by improved production of grain and some other important foods.

From the 1950's until the late 1970's, rapid population growth made it very difficult for China's population to raise their living standards and especially their food intake. But counterproductive and periodically disastrous economic policies were partly to blame for China's failure to increase food and overall agricultural production ahead of population growth in those decades. Now much slower natural population increase and much faster rise in agricultural output are combining to raise rural and national living standards.

Future Population Trends

Predicting the future anywhere is hazardous. It is especially so for China, mainly because of uncertainties about trends in the political system during the next few decades. Will the government be relatively stable and continue to promote steady economic development, as it has only in the last few years, or will a radical line emerge triumphant once again as in the Great Leap Forward or the Cultural Revolution? Sharp political or economic change might contribute to a partial breakdown of the government's unpopular controls on fertility. Will the government continue its compulsory fertility control policy backed up by coercive methods, or will the successors to the current leadership repudiate it? In future years will the people of China quietly acquiesce to compulsory family planning, or grumble against it but obey, or conduct an effective political backlash? The answers to these closely intertwined questions will determine fertility trends during the next few decades.

General mortality conditions can be expected to improve slowly, barring some major catastrophe such as international war, civil war, or several years in a row of extensive drought or flooding. China will probably continue to attack endemic and epidemic diseases along with today's major causes of death, all with good effect. But current and likely trends in China's economy may have a mixed effect on health and mortality. For example, the production responsibility system in agriculture may allow people to earn higher incomes resulting in better nutrition, clothing, and housing, which in turn contribute to better health and longer life. At the same time, the production responsibility system is weakening the collective organizations—the production brigade and the people's commune—which have heretofore channeled funds to the commune clinic, the cooperative medical system, the barefoot doctors, public health work, and minimal welfare payments for persons in distress. As discussed more fully in Chapter 3, in some localities the assignment of full production responsibility to households has been followed by the breakdown of cooperative medical service.[8] If rural public health work and the delivery of primary medical care are disrupted for very long, deteriorating health and rising mortality can result. The PRC is vulnerable to such a reversal if it neglects the public health system that brought about the mortality decline in the first place.

The future population projections to be discussed here all assume the same slow mortality improvements, slow both because rather low mortality has already been achieved and because the production responsibility system has weakened primary and preventive health care and such economic changes are accelerating. All projections assume that the low mortality reported in the 1982 census was not achieved in 1981 as reported, but rather will be attained at most ages by 1990, and that excess female infant and early childhood mortality will continue in the next century but will not be as severe as they were modeled to be in the early years after the introduction of the one-child policy. Presumably some changes will come about in the economy, law, and social norms to mitigate the perceived need for a son, and people may get accustomed to low fertility and its implications. It is assumed for all the projections that the expectation of life at birth will rise to 73 years for males and 75 for females by the year 2025 and further to 78 and 80 years respectively in 2050.

Although overall mortality in China is likely to improve, the crude death rate will paradoxically remain steady or rise. This is because fertility and mortality are already relatively low, producing a progressively older age structure, and old people are more likely than children to die in a given year. Therefore, the death rate is projected to remain about 7–8 per thousand population at least through the year 2000 and possibly to 2020. Depending on trends in fertility, which has the greatest effect on the age structure, China's crude death rate is projected to rise to at least 11 per thousand population in 2050, and could be as high as 26 by then if extremely low fertility prevails.

The most important unknown factor is future fertility. Three different projections of China's population for the future illustrate the range of possibilities.[9] These are simplifications that of course do not encompass all the complexities of reality, but they do capture the tenor of the changes that may take place.

The first projection is the "one-child" projection, which proceeds from the sweeping assumption that the government's policy of promoting the one-child family will be completely effective. This projection implicitly assumes that popular resistance will have little effect and that the national and provincial governments will prevail in persuading or forcing almost all couples to stop at one child. This could mean a total fertility rate as low as 1.0 birth per woman, which is far below the lowest previous national total fertility rate of 1.4 births per woman, if those women whose first children die or are defective are the only ones who have a second child, and assuming that some women do not marry and that some couples are infertile.

This one-child projection assumes that the total fertility rate will drop rapidly during the 1980's down to 1.0 birth per woman in 1990 and hold steady at that level to the year 2050. The government might decide to continue the one-child policy indefinitely as projected here, if the leaders agree that China long ago exceeded its optimum population size and is now badly overpopulated in relation to its land and resource base. Some of the mathematicians-turned-demographers strongly influencing Chinese population policy believe that the optimum population is far smaller than 1 billion people and that China should first reach zero population growth, then reduce its population to an optimum size of about 650–700 million.[10] The one-child projection follows this unprecedented scenario. The PRC population would increase from 1.01 billion at midyear 1982 until it peaked at about 1.11 billion in the years 2003–2007. The population would then begin to decrease until it dropped below 1 billion in 2028, then decrease rapidly to just over 700 million by 2050.

Is this projection completely unrealistic? No population in the world has yet been satisfied to keep its fertility so low for so long, and even the Chinese government has set somewhat more modest goals and expectations, such as the current "strategic target" of preventing the population from surpassing 1.2 billion by the turn of the century.[11] But as China has achieved a record fertility decline for a large population in only one decade, we would be unwise to underestimate its capabilities. The government continues to report success in controlling the birth rate, expanding enforcement of the one-child limit, and reducing the proportion of births that are second and higher order.[12] If, in spite of popular desires for more children, China's compulsory program continues to maintain tight control over fertility, it is possible to visualize a shift in popular expectations and feelings about the value of children. The people might gradually internalize the notion that one child is ideal. Though this one-child projection appears extreme today, in a decade or two hindsight may reveal that such low fertility was achievable in the Chinese context. In any case, the one-child projection should be seen as the low end of a plausible range for future population size, fertility, and population growth.

The second projection is the "two-child" projection, which assumes that the one-child program will not succeed in lowering the total fertility rate far below replacement level. Rather, couples stopping at one child would be balanced by couples having more than two, and people would continue to average two children per couple from now on. In this projection, popular insistence that two children is the minimum acceptable number, especially in rural areas, would overcome the government's insistence that everybody stop at one. The government would be forced to save face and raise the limit to two children, at least for rural couples or those not on pension. This policy change could also come about through a change in leadership. Some couples would get away with exceeding the two-child limit, while urban couples in particular would often be satisfied with one child, the net result being an average of around two children per couple. This projection assumes that the total fertility rate drops to 2.0 births per woman in 1985 and remains at that level until 2050. Based on this simplified assumption, the PRC's population would increase from 1.01 billion at midyear 1982 to 1.23 billion in 2000 and peak at 1.45 billion in 2038. It would begin declining slowly thereafter.

This projection is also plausible, though fertility might temporarily dip below replacement level in the mid-1980's before political events brought about a two-child policy. The projection assumes that the government has great influence on the nation's fertility but that its power is not infinite against widespread popular distaste. There is much evidence that a two-child family is far more palatable to Chinese couples than a one-child family. For example, a 1981 survey in one of the model communes of Shanghai Municipality asked women ages 15–55 how many children they wanted to have; 84 percent wished to have two children.[13] In most rural areas, the desire for two children is particularly strong among those couples with a firstborn daughter, as suggested in the following 1981 report: "Many of the people who have only a daughter are unwilling to accept the single-child certificate. They are hoping to have a second child after a few years. At a discussion meeting held by us at the Jieshi Brigade, all those who have two sons or one son and one daughter are comparatively happy and are willing to forgo having a third child. Those who have two daughters are still hoping for a son."[14] The desire for a son continued to sabotage the one-child program. Population scholars at a 1983 meeting of the Population Association of China emphasized that: "The wish of the peasants to have sons is an acute problem today."[15]

During the 1980's under the one-child policy, a large proportion of the couples who already have one child have tried or may try for a second. Some fail at first, or even repeatedly, because the government forces them to abort the pregnancy, but many succeed. Many couples are taking advantage of any opportunity to have a second child, as a 1981 report hints:

> The masses are unhappy with the policy of having only one child. Since the policy has changed frequently, they hope that the policy will one day be relaxed so that they will be able to achieve their purpose of having more children. Some of the masses appreciate very much the speeches made by some of the delegates to the third session of the Fifth People's Congress and use them as reasons for having additional children. In some areas, some of the masses even take advantage of the weakness and confusion in our policy to rush into having a second child.[16]

Couples determined to have another child sometimes leave their work units temporarily in order to avoid abortion.[17] Women sometimes visit relatives or hide long enough to complete a pregnancy. How frequently they resort to this solution is suggested by the proud report of one model brigade referring to the first half of 1982: "There was not one woman who left the area to hide in order to have a child."[18] In those localities where forced abortion is not routine, couples may try to stay at home for their second pregnancy and birth, in which case they must contend with an onslaught of "persuasion" from cadres and family planning workers. A 1981 survey of couples in Shaanxi province who bore a second child outside the local government birth plan revealed that they had been aware of the obstacles they would face, gave the matter a great deal of thought before choosing to attempt a second birth, and most did not regret having the second child even though they had to pay financial penalties.[19] Hebei province reported in 1984 that: "The promotion of one child per couple is not yet accepted by a considerable number of people."[20]

Not only do those couples who did not sign the one-child pledge try for a second child, so also do millions of those who were compelled to sign the pledge, and perhaps millions more who willingly signed in anticipation of promised rewards that never materialized. China's press has reported cases of couples who signed the pledge and then saved the rewards to pay them back when the second child is born, and couples who signed the pledge and have been "wavering" ever since in their commitment to it. A 1981 scholarly report from Wuhan assessed the national situation as follows:

> It is necessary to carry out concrete analyses of those people holding the single-child certificates. Those who are resolute and have a comparatively higher sense of awareness are not in the majority. Most of them have made the pledge under the stress of circumstances. Therefore, a considerable number of those who have received the certificate and the award have put aside their award for safekeeping. They do not dare to spend it because they mean to return it in the future when they give birth to a second child. As to those who have not made the pledge, their thinking is even more complicated. They are always waiting for a chance to have a second child.[21]

The nationwide fertility survey of September 1982 estimated the proportion of couples who had borne a second child after receiving a single-child certificate. The certificates had been in existence only three years, so these figures underestimate the percent of couples in the childbearing ages as of 1982 who eventually bore a second child. Of women in urban non-agricultural households who held a single-child certificate, almost none had a second child by the time of the survey, but 10.7 percent of rural women with a single-child certificate had already borne their second child.[22]

During the 1980's resistance to the one-child limit is expected to continue on a couple-by-couple basis, but it may also gradually build into a general public outcry, especially in many rural areas. The government may succeed in squelching such an outcry, as it apparently has so far, or it may back down. The two-child projection assumes that the government would retreat only as far as a two-child limit and that compulsory family planning would still be intact. This outcome is plausible because while all factions of the top government hierarchy are united in their policy of compulsory fertility control, the government is divided over the wisdom of the one-child policy. Some military leaders worry that parents of an only child will not let their son risk his life in military service, some demographers advise the government to allow couples with a firstborn daughter to have another child, and many local cadres are sympathetic with people's desire for two children.[23] Those who must carry out the family planning program in the villages may ask for a national policy of allowing two-child families to make their work less onerous. They could also argue convincingly that allowing all couples to have two children would help alleviate the alarming rise in female infanticide. Although the national government continues to rebuff all suggestions that it relax the limit to two children per couple, there is evidence that the message is being heard. For example, a 1982 article in China's leading official newspaper, the *People's Daily*, reported: "As peasants will not conscientiously restrain themselves in childbearing under the objective conditions in rural areas at present, it is very difficult to push forward birth control work. Under these circumstances, some comrades think that the birth control task can easily be fulfilled if we relax the regulations and allow peasants to have two children."[24] The article recommended expanding the conditions for allowing two children.

The official response to the above considerations was to retain the policy of preventing all unauthorized second births while increasing the categories of couples for whom a second birth would be approved. In early 1984 the Central Committee of the Chinese Communist Party issued the still-classified "Document Number 7" which, according to press reports, stated that "family planning policies must be built on a foundation that is fair and reasonable, supported by the masses, and easy for the cadres to carry out."[25] Press commentary indicated that the one-child limit is unpopular and must be modified if it is to become a foundation with these characteristics. To this end, peasants in certain poor areas, peasants in "real difficulties," or those with particular family situations in which two children seemed to be needed were to receive approval to bear a second child.[26] At the International Population Conference in Mexico City in August 1984, the spokesman for the Chinese government noted that the policy of one child per couple had been promoted since 1979 but added: "However, this is only a policy of a specific historical period and does not mean one child only in every case. In carrying out the family planning program, the government sets different requirements and offers specific guidelines to the people of various localities with different economic, cultural and demographic conditions."[27]

Government leaders were aware that the desire for a second child is very widespread, so statements explaining the official policy emphasized that this "reasonable" policy did not mean permission for every couple to have two children. The loosening of the strict one-child limit was hedged with qualifications: "To understand and implement fully the guideline of the party directives means that based on extensive promotion of one child per couple, the scope of permission for a second child in a planned and controlled way in rural areas may be widened a little. For those rural masses who have real difficulty and request a second child, arrangements may be made to let them have one in a planned way after obtaining approval. At the same time strict control must be applied to unplanned second births and to excessive births."[28] But in response to Document Number 7, some local leaders "overly relaxed the restrictions on the birth of a second child," and rumors spread that in urban as well as rural areas, "the family planning policy has been changed. A second child is now universally permissible."[29] Provincial leaders moved to curb this illusion as quickly as possible. For example, in June 1984 a radio broadcast from Inner Mongolia stated: "It is sheer rumor that the family planning policy will change, the restrictions on birth control will be relaxed, and one couple will be allowed to bear two children. This rumor must be clarified immediately."[30]

Popular reactions like this show that pressure on the government to revert to a two-child limit is strong. In addition to the accommodations mentioned above, more adjustments in the direction of allowing two children have been announced. In 1983 pilot projects began in preparation for the drawing up of regional population plans.[31] From about 1984 provinces were to carry out population projections to figure out the annual fertility levels they could have and still attain the target population size assigned to them by the national government for the year 2000. The provincial targets add to a national target of 1.2 billion people, which would allow a national total fertility rate not far below two births per woman in the interim. China's State Family Planning Commission made this important announcement in late September 1984:

> Based on the population target for the year 2000, all areas throughout China are carrying out experiments on scheduling the birth of a second child by means of computing in detail the population growth year by year. Following a decrease in the rate of excessive births, the proportion of permitted second births will gradually be increased. Following progress in experimental work, family planning policy will become more and more reasonable and will be supported more and more by a majority of the masses.[32]

This directive means that as third and higher order births are effectively blocked, provincial governments may allow more women, eventually most women, to have a second birth.

Another adjustment toward allowing two children was also announced in 1984. The government promised that whenever a man and woman marry, each of whom was an only child, the new couple will be allowed two children: "Particularly worth noting is the policy that couples of only children can have two children. Because only children will become the majority of people at child-bearing age 20 years from now, the practice of one child per couple prevails only for a single generation."[33] These various accommodations toward the overwhelming preference of the Chinese people to bear no fewer than two children mean that the two-child projection is very plausible in the coming decades and on into the next century.

A third future projection, the "voluntary family planning" alternative, makes the bold assumption that the days of compulsory family planning are numbered in China, and that at some point the government will find it politically necessary to shift completely and rather abruptly to a voluntary family planning program. If this sounds farfetched, it is well to caution that the post-Mao government has already made some rapid major shifts toward voluntarism and away from compulsion in other policy spheres. For instance, unemployment in the cities persuaded the government to allow people to go into business for themselves for the first time in several decades. The passive resistance of the peasants hampered collectivized farming so much that the government introduced the "production responsibility system" to give peasants more control over their production and their incomes, thus more incentive to produce. In some demographic as well as economic realms, the triumph of voluntarism is apparent in recent years. For example, this book has documented two examples of population policies doggedly and stubbornly pursued by the government, both before and after the arrest of the "gang of four," against popular resistance. They are the forced late marriage policy of the 1960's and 1970's, and the policy of forced migration to the countryside of urban-born persons. In the case of the late marriage policy, the government found it necessary in 1981 to greatly reduce the mandated minimum marriage ages. Since then, all levels of government have struggled to reintroduce marriage as late as age 23 rather than continue to allow women to marry at 20 and men at 22 as stipulated in the 1981 Marriage Law. The outcome of this ongoing battle between the government and young betrothed couples is unknown. In the case of the policy of forced out-migration of city youths, the popular will appears to have prevailed after a decade of at least partial government success. As late as 1977, hardly anyone would have predicted the radical policy shifts allowing earlier marriage, the return of sent-down youth to the cities, and the cessation of forced out-migration of educated youth. There may be a parallel between the about-face of the government on these population policies and a future reversal of the current single-mindedly pursued policy of compulsory fertility control. Just as the people of China care very much about when they marry and where they live, they also care greatly about how many children they have. The preference for several children continues in rural and mountainous areas, as documented in a 1981 fertility survey of rural areas in Hubei province: "Among 728 [peasants] questioned, only 5 percent want to have only one child, but 51 percent wish to have two, 28 percent wish to have three, and 15 percent wish to have four children. In the mountainous areas where traditional ideology is strong, 27 percent want two and 72 percent wish to have three or four."[34]

A political reaction against the family planning program escalated during the early 1980's. Some areas reported a weakening of cadre control and resulting "freedom of childbearing."[35] An article in the authoritative *People's Daily* in early 1982 lamented that if this "tendency toward liberalization" could not be checked, "the overall plan for population control in the country will surely fail."[36] Leaders were puzzled, according to one article, when heightened coercion in family planning bred heightened resistance:

> Some of the problems caused us to have deep thoughts: Regardless of the measures we have taken and the effort we have devoted to our work, why is there still so much resistance to family planning on the part of the masses: Why is it that when the system of penalty and reward is becoming stricter, unplanned pregnancies and excessive births continuously occur? Why do some cadres in charge of family planning, even cadres who are Party members, talk tough when in reality they are soft at heart and unwilling to take up the work? . . . In recent years we have emphasized administrative decrees and awards and penalties while failing to see the new contradictions and new problems created by them. Some of the cadres and the masses did not continue to voluntarily practice family planning through understanding of the Party's policy, but rather were forced by certain pressure to adopt birth control measures. Thus, their resistance grew.[37]

Bitterness against those carrying out family planning has risen. In the late 1970's and early 1980's China's media began vaguely referring to sporadic acts of violence against family planning workers and urged workers to courageously persevere and not to be afraid of being beaten. There followed reports of verbal harassment of family planning workers; sabotage of their private plots, contract plots, and personal possessions; and physical violence against them. A sampling of these reports from 1982 and 1983 follows:

> Lin Xiuqun . . . is very active in carrying out family planning work, but she has been subjected to a great deal of ridicule and sarcastic remarks. She has suffered many wrongs by being the object of abusive language from backward masses, mothers-in-law, husbands, and children. Because of this, a strong basic-level cadre . . . gets tears in her eyes whenever the subject of family planning is brought up.

> Cases in which family planning workers were abused must be handled seriously.

> Those who . . . insult, beat, and frame family planning workers and activists . . . must be handled seriously.

> It is necessary to curb erroneous acts that discriminate against or attack people doing planned parenthood work.

Those who attack or frame planned parenthood personnel should be strictly dealt with.

On January 8 the deputy county head of Dengta county, Fan Rongkai, visited Party member Cheng Shuyan whose house and property were smashed due to her active promotion of family planning.

They [government and Party leaders in a township] have made a decision that it is necessary to strictly investigate the sabotaged private plots and the sabotaged plots whose fixed output is stated in a contract, of cadres and the masses who are engaged in family planning.[38]

A Hong Kong journal reported that birth control activists in Sichuan were so unpopular that their private plots and even their persons had to be protected from angry peasants. In 1983 the authorities began giving them special protection.[39] Under such unpleasant working conditions, many local cadres and family planning workers have periodically let up on the degree of coercion they were willing to implement in the villages. The national leadership responded with the "cadre job responsibility system" that punishes cadres who do not stop unauthorized births in their jurisdiction.

Mass intimidation of family planning workers is one of the few ways that peasants can express their antagonism toward the family planning program. The people cannot vote out of office the national leaders responsible for the policy. There is, however, a limited system of local democracy that gives villagers a chance to express their displeasure. For example, in 1981 five commune and brigade cadres in a county of Anhui province lost local elections for positions such as county people's delegate because they offended many people through their family planning work.[40] The political role of women in China is being crippled because female cadres are usually required to engage in family planning work at the local level, and then they are despised for it. In a speech to a national family planning conference in late 1982, Vice-Premier Bo Yibo remarked: "During the experimental period for direct voting for county magistrates, I asked Comrade Cheng Zihua how many women were voted to be county magistrates since we have promoted equality of the sexes for so many years. He said that almost none of the women candidates were elected. Why? Many of the women candidates were good and qualified, but because they had offended people in family planning work, they were not elected."[41]

The political reaction against the family planning program is sporadic and uncoordinated, but it may not remain so. Its ineffectiveness thus far is demonstrated by the inability of the people to stop the implementation of the required sterilization program to which they began to be subjected in early 1983. Yet in 1984 cadres continued to fear that required fertility control will be reversed in the future as have so many other unpopular programs. At a Guangxi province conference of directors of county and municipal family planning commissions held in summer 1984, the First Secretary of the province's Party committee reassured the activists that their fears were groundless:

> Comrade Qiao Xiaoguang pointed out that in order to control population growth, we should emphasize dispelling thoughts such as fear that those who carry out family planning work are making [what will later be characterized as] a mistake. Some said that the "Cultural Revolution" happened years ago, yet today thorough repudiation is still required. In the future, will family planning also be repudiated? This way of thinking confuses family planning with "cultural revolution" and it is wrong. They are fundamentally different in nature. The way to differentiate between right and wrong is to judge whether the policy benefits or harms the interests of the state and the people. Whatever corresponds to the interests of the state and the people is correct and otherwise is wrong. Based on this reasoning, repudiation does not occur. Thus, there is no reason to repudiate family planning.[42]

If China's people eventually find politically effective ways to overcome the compulsory qualities of the program, then the country will shift to a voluntary program, either under the present leading faction, which would be forced to adjust to the political realities, or under a different faction part of whose program would be denunciation of coercive family planning. The "voluntary family planning" projection used here arbitrarily assumes that 1989 would be the first year of full voluntarism in birth planning, but such a shift could come in some earlier or later year. The voluntary projection should therefore be used only to illustrate what would be likely to happen if and when China's family planning program became a voluntary one.

The first year of full voluntarism would see a jump in the number of pregnancies as millions of couples add to their previously restricted families, but the hopes of many couples for more children would be doomed by subfecundity or previous sterilization. By then perhaps almost all couples with two children would have one partner sterilized as the government requires. The inability of so many couples to have further children would modulate the rise in fertility under voluntary family planning, and would lead to numerous cases of estrangement and remarriage by the still-fecund partners determined to have another child. Gradually, as the sterilized couples aged and new couples started bearing their desired number of children, the national fertility level would increase.

To illustrate what might happen under voluntary family planning, this model assumes that by 1989, the year of the hypothesized political shift,

China's fertility level will have declined to a total fertility rate of 1.5 births per woman, and the next year it would increase to 2.0. As unsterilized couples replaced sterilized couples in the reproductive ages, the total fertility rate is assumed to increase to 3.0 in the year 2000, but to go no higher even under a voluntary program. This scenario implicitly assumes that China's government would continue its family planning publicity and persuasion work with some effect, and that many couples by that time would have grown accustomed to the idea that small families of two or three children are large enough. Thereafter, this projection assumes that China's people would slowly reduce their fertility of their own accord, as over the decades the economy modernizes and attitudes toward the need for children change. In this model, a total fertility rate of 2.0 births per woman is reached through voluntary birth control by 2020 and held at that level through 2050.

In the voluntary projection the population of the PRC would increase from 1.01 billion at midyear 1982 to 1.27 billion in 2000 and 1.53 billion in 2020. With two births per woman after that, the population would continue growing at less than 1 percent a year and would reach 1.72 billion by the year 2050. Of course, there is no reason to assume that women will average two births apiece into the indefinite future. During the first half of the twenty-first century China's economy and society may change enough to alter patterns of universal marriage, universal fertility, and the multi-child family, with the possible result of fertility below replacement level in a voluntary family planning context, as has already

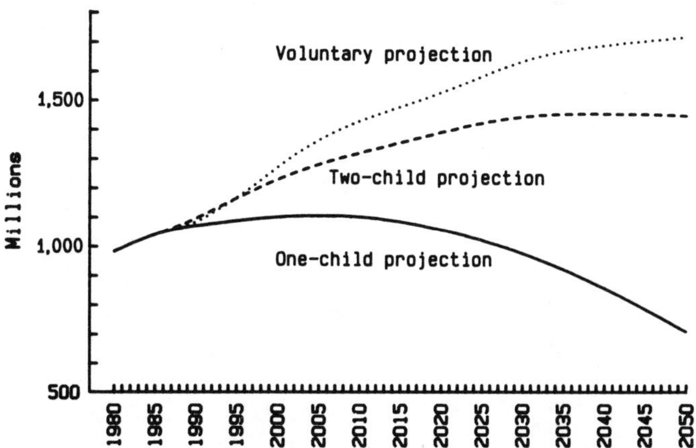

Fig. 10.2. Population Size of the PRC Under Three Projections, 1980–2050. Data projected at the Center for International Research, U.S. Bureau of the Census.

happened in many developed countries. Should this be the outcome, then China's population might be smaller than that projected here for 2050.

Figure 10.2 displays the population size under the three alternative projections. Clearly, the lower the fertility of the population as a whole, the sooner will China reach its peak population size and stop growing, and the smaller will be that peak population. Among these three projections the peak population size could range from 1.11 billion persons as early as 2005, assuming complete success of the one-child drive, or as late as the second half of the twenty-first century at over 1.72 billion, assuming voluntary family planning.

Future Age Structure

Table 10.2 shows the growth in size of China's future population in the working ages 15–64 under the three projections, and the proportion of the total population that working-age people represent. Because the working-age population through the year 1999 is already born, changes in fertility will not change the absolute size of the working-age population until after that date. The population of working age will increase from 677 million in 1985 to 841 million in 1999, a 24 percent increase. At present, by international standards, an unusually large proportion of

TABLE 10.2
Projected Population of the PRC in the Working Ages 15–64, 1985–2050

	Working-age population, one-child projection		Working-age population, two-child projection		Working-age population, voluntary projection	
Year	Thousands	As percent of total population	Thousands	As percent of total population	Thousands	As percent of total population
1985	677,382	65%	677,382	65%	677,382	65%
1990	758,542	71	758,542	69	758,542	70
1995	807,186	74	807,186	69	807,186	69
2000	846,231	77	846,350	69	846,352	67
2005	859,164	78	882,361	69	871,206	64
2010	855,623	78	930,301	70	932,524	65
2015	839,026	77	965,313	71	1,006,626	68
2020	799,662	76	972,861	70	1,055,353	69
2025	755,597	74	973,692	69	1,081,153	68
2030	686,070	70	955,797	66	1,077,091	66
2035	594,320	65	926,101	64	1,061,325	64
2040	505,169	59	903,680	62	1,062,811	63
2045	438,909	56	902,384	62	1,091,687	64
2050	374,424	53	899,857	62	1,114,282	65

SOURCE: Projected by the author at the China Branch, Center for International Research, U.S. Bureau of the Census.

China's working-age population is employed, but primarily at labor-intensive jobs with very low productivity. Based on 1982 census data, about 4.7 percent of the labor force was unemployed.[43] The serious current problems of underemployment and unemployment in China are in danger of worsening as the number of people in the working ages increases. It will be a challenge during the next 15 years to expand the number of available useful jobs for the huge and growing potential labor pool.

After the turn of the century the size of the working-age population would diverge radically from one of these projections to another as shown in Table 10.2. In the one-child projection, the population 15–64 would peak at 859 million in 2005 and then begin to shrink, which would help ease the employment problem.[44] The diminution of the labor pool would not be a serious problem for decades, because the long-overdue popularization of labor-saving machinery could offset it. Shortages of available labor might begin to be worrisome after around 2040 if fertility remained very low early in the next century. Therefore, if China does succeed in reducing fertility to about one birth per woman during the next several decades, the government might need to ease up considerably on the one-child limit after about 2020 to ensure an adequate supply of labor during the middle decades of the next century.

Under the two-child assumption, the population of working ages would continue increasing from 846 million in 2000 to a maximum of 978 million in 2026 and slowly decline thereafter. The problem of finding productive jobs for the population of working ages would be a burden throughout the first half of the next century. Under the voluntary family planning scenario, the employment problem would be even more serious. By 2050 China's working-age population would be about 64 percent larger than in 1985. Between now and then, the structure of the economy would have to remain geared to providing the maximum number of jobs possible, while mechanization of agriculture and automation in industry would have to proceed very slowly.

China's population of school age is expected to continue decreasing as a proportion of the total population throughout the 1980's owing to the fertility decline that has already taken place. Table 10.3 shows the total population in the ages of potential mass education, ages 5–14, which would include kindergarten, elementary, and junior secondary education.[45] The absolute number of children in that group will decline from 219 million in 1985 to 185 million in 1990. Because educational attendance among that age group is currently not universal, this imminent decline will allow China to emphasize the provision of education to the remaining children who do not now go to school.[46] In localities where

TABLE 10.3
Projected Population in the School Ages 5–14, 1985–2050

	School-age population, one-child projection		School-age population, two-child projection		School-age population, voluntary projection	
Year	Thousands	As percent of total population	Thousands	As percent of total population	Thousands	As percent of total population
1985	218,562	21%	218,562	21%	218,562	21%
1990	185,358	17	185,479	17	185,481	17
1995	156,114	14	179,484	15	168,246	14
2000	118,676	11	193,720	16	195,952	15
2005	105,769	10	209,622	16	262,295	19
2010	100,014	9	199,509	15	280,148	20
2015	88,294	8	181,222	13	247,809	17
2020	74,414	7	172,244	12	211,507	14
2025	61,183	6	176,521	12	204,796	13
2030	52,657	5	183,703	13	222,153	14
2035	47,470	5	182,410	13	237,277	14
2040	42,502	5	174,341	12	230,756	14
2045	36,890	5	168,160	12	213,071	13
2050	31,366	4	168,241	12	204,644	12

SOURCE: Projected by the author at the China Branch, Center for International Research, U.S. Bureau of the Census.

elementary and junior middle school education are already provided to almost every child, China will have the option of expanding the availability of education beyond the age range currently served or enhancing its quality after decades of attention to simply increasing the number of places for students in school. One prefecture that reported fertility decline in the 1960's and 1970's described the educational effects as follows: "Due to the in-depth promotion of family planning, the number of elementary school admissions has declined markedly. The number of middle school students is increasing. Family planning has begun to play a role in making middle school education universal, in raising the quality of education, and in training and supplying quality students to the higher educational institutes."[47] But there is no guarantee that policy makers will choose to improve educational opportunity and quality as the school-age population shrinks. In some other countries, education budgets have been slashed as the number of children in school ages declined.[48]

In China after 1990, the number of children 5–14 differs greatly from one projection to another. Under the one-child assumption, the school-age population would keep declining in absolute size from 219 million in 1985 to 119 million in 2000, to 74 million in 2020, and, if the one-child policy continues, to only 31 million in 2050. The one-child per couple limit, if successful, would require a massive ongoing shift of resources away from the education of children toward other purposes. The number of teachers and classrooms needed would keep declining, and teaching would be a doomed occupation. This would mean that talented people might avoid the profession of teaching the young, and even if ordered to be teachers, they would have to prepare a second career while they were teaching, which would suggest that the quality of education might suffer. The brighter side of this picture is that China could in the future divert resources now being used to educate a quarter of its population toward more directly productive uses.

The two-child projection demonstrates a future path in which the absolute size of the school-age population would not change much from decade to decade. In many ways, this trend would be beneficial to the provision of universal and high-quality education for China's children. The relative constancy in the number of students moving through school would require maintenance of school buildings, libraries, teacher training schools, and other basic educational facilities, and would make it worthwhile to steadily improve them. Teachers could dedicate themselves to their career, knowing that their profession was not rapidly becoming obsolete.

The voluntary family planning projection shows some fluctuations in the number of children ages 5–14, peaking in the first decade of the next century. After 2015 the absolute number of children 5–14 would fluctuate around the size it had been in 1985, but would constitute around 14 percent rather than 21 percent of the total population. No matter which of these three projections turns out to be closest to reality, the proportion of China's population of school ages is destined to become smaller than it is now, which means that the burden of educating the children will be lighter on a per capita basis. The government, if it chooses, will be able to shift its emphasis toward quality education, increasing the "human capital" invested in its people, which in turn should be beneficial to the country's long-term economic development.

Meanwhile, the elderly population is destined to become much larger, both in absolute size and in its proportion of the population, than it is today. As shown in Table 10.4, as of 1985 the population age 65 and above was 53 million persons, which constituted only 5 percent of the population. All three projections reveal that the aged population will increase to 84 million by the year 2000, then jump to 153 million in 2020 and further to 295 million in 2045. This will occur no matter what happens to fertility between now and 2045, because the aged of that date are already born. Only a rise in mortality or slower mortality improvement than assumed in these projections would reduce the elderly population of 2045. Therefore, China should prepare itself at the beginning of the

TABLE 10.4

Projected Elderly Population (Ages 65 and Above) and Dependency Ratios, 1985–2050

Year	One-child projection			Two-child projection			Voluntary projection		
	Elderly (thousands)	Elderly as percent of total	Dependency ratio[a]	Elderly (thousands)	Elderly as percent of total	Dependency ratio[a]	Elderly (thousands)	Elderly as percent of total	Dependency ratio[a]
1985	53,063	5%	54	53,063	5%	54	53,063	5%	54
1990	61,579	6	41	61,579	6	44	61,579	6	43
1995	71,768	7	35	71,768	6	44	71,768	6	45
2000	83,744	8	30	83,744	7	45	83,744	7	50
2005	93,538	8	29	93,538	7	45	93,538	7	57
2010	103,469	9	29	103,469	8	42	103,469	7	53
2015	122,030	11	29	122,030	9	40	122,030	8	47
2020	153,320	15	32	153,320	11	43	153,320	10	45
2025	177,743	17	35	177,743	13	46	177,743	11	46
2030	213,385	22	42	213,385	15	51	213,385	13	52
2035	258,054	28	55	258,054	18	57	258,054	15	57
2040	290,966	34	69	290,966	20	61	290,966	17	59
2045	294,808	38	79	294,808	20	61	294,808	17	56
2050	289,425	41	89	289,529	20	60	289,531	17	54

SOURCE: Projected by the author at the China Branch, Center for International Research, U.S. Bureau of the Census.

[a]The population in the dependent ages (under 15 and 65 and above) per 100 people in the working ages (15–64).

twenty-first century to provide for the huge number of persons about to age to the status of elderly dependents.

Although the absolute population age 65 and above in the middle of the next century is already predictable, the proportion of the population that group will constitute will depend on population growth between now and then. For example, if the PRC has a two-child or a voluntary family planning record between now and the middle of the next century, these projections indicate that the population age 65 and above will constitute 17–20 percent of the total population by 2040. Such a proportion is much higher than the 5 percent of 1985, but nowhere near the percentages under the long-term one-child projection: 22 percent in 2030, 34 percent in 2040, and 41 percent in 2050. To have 20 percent of the population in the older ages would probably be just barely manageable. So far at least two countries, Sweden and East Germany, have experienced an "old" population with 16 percent of the population age 65 and above.[49] Demographers and policy makers in Japan are concerned that 14 percent of Japan's population will be age 65 and above in the year 2000.[50] The United States had 12 percent of its population in these elderly ages as of 1982 and is experiencing political conflict over the costs of their care.[51] By the time China has 17–20 percent of its population age 65 and above, many countries will have had some experience with the same phenomenon. China can try to learn from them. By 2040, for instance, the PRC will surely have found it necessary to provide a far more comprehensive social security system than now exists, so that millions of elderly persons do not experience serious deprivation in old age. But in addition, Chinese and foreign observers have suggested that China should try to maintain family and local community responsibility for the aged as the primary sources of their care during the next century.[52]

Because China's government is so dedicated to the policy of limiting most couples to one child and carefully controlling the number of second births, the future extreme aging of the population implied by that policy is rarely addressed by officials. The few available statements on the matter show that the leaders are aware of this problem but are trying to persuade the people that it is nothing to worry about, and some scholars echo this official line:

> [Vice Premier] Chen Muhua said that people put forward many arguments over "having only one child." Some people said that encouraging a married couple to have "only one child" would result in too high a "proportion of old people." She admitted that a decline in the population growth rate would indeed result in a rather high proportion of old people after several generations, but this was nothing to worry about. Other people worried that . . . the increase in support for old people would increase our society's burdens. This problem would be

solved with satisfactory results after production developed, people's living standards improved, and social welfare was developed.

Some comrades are worried about whether or not the population will become "old" if each couple has only one child. With the reduction of population growth, in a certain number of years, the number of old people will indeed rise. However, we need not worry about the problem of the population "becoming old" for a fairly long period.

Even by the year 2080, the percentage of elderly would be only 50 percent [sic]. . . . Those who are concerned about the population growing old need not worry.

[Director of the State Family Planning Commission] Qian Xinzhong points out that the promotion of one child per couple by the state at the present is based on the realities of China's economic and population conditions. . . . Its fundamental purpose is to . . . accelerate the construction of socialist modernization. Upon achieving the above task, the population policy of our country will be adjusted according to the new realities. It is without any foundation to worry about the danger of population aging in the promotion of one child per couple.

Of course, in the next century, the problem of an able-bodied couple supporting four old people and one child will probably become more serious. By then, however, our productivity will be greatly developed, and material and cultural standards as well as labor insurance will be greatly improved. It will be completely possible for society to handle the problem of looking after the old. The burden will be taken off the sons and daughters.[53]

Those young couples in China who cannot expect pension coverage are concerned that if they have only one child, they will not receive adequate support in old age. This fear is well founded. Chinese sources describe this concern with the model of two couples today each having one child, those children growing up and marrying one another, and thereafter that one couple being burdened with raising one child and caring for four aging parents.[54] The future willingness and ability of this adult couple to care for its five hypothetical dependents are in doubt. At the societal and personal levels, the elderly might be shunted aside as too great a burden to contend with. The comparatively small number of people of working age would resent diverting much of their incomes to support the aged. This is especially so since, under the one-child projection, China would have experienced several decades with a relatively small aged population and also a small population of children. For example, as shown in Table 10.4, under the one-child scenario China's "dependency ratio"—the number of persons under 15 and age 65 and over per hundred persons in the working ages—would be around 29–32 between 2000 and 2020, meaning that each dependent would have on average three people in the working ages to support him or her. After twenty years of having so few dependents to provide for, the rapid increase in the aged dependent population would come as an unaccustomed shock to the society.[55] Under the two-child and the voluntary projections there is more long-term continuity in the dependency ratio, with the dependent population slowly shifting from mostly children to a smaller proportion of children and an increased proportion of elderly. No matter what happens, Chinese society will have to shift its institutions and values away from caring for young dependents toward increasing emphasis on caring for the old.[56]

It appears that China's government is going to persist in requiring a one-child limit for most couples in the near future, in spite of the considerable pressures to allow two children. In 1984 it seemed that the Central Committee of the Communist Party meant to loosen up and allow more second children, but an article in October of that year claimed that "Document Number 7" instructed local leaders to only "open a small gap" and allow about 10 percent of couples to have a second birth while preventing all other second births.[57] If this goal were achieved and held, then early in the next century the government would need to allow increased fertility in order to help alleviate the future aging problem.[58] Several of China's population scholars in 1983 and 1984 began emphasizing that the aging problem is serious under a one-child projection and that the government should allow higher fertility at some time. One scholar in August 1983 cautioned: "In order to avoid a serious population aging problem in the next 100 years, we are now only promoting and implementing one child per couple for the next 20 to 30 years and 30 to 40 years at the most."[59] But soon thereafter, two of China's most respected demographers began gently suggesting that the aging crisis must be avoided by reconsidering the one-child policy in the near future. In December 1983 the following analysis appeared:

> However, we should see that the rate of population aging in our country will be the fastest in the history of mankind. According to forecasts, population aging will reach its peak around 2040, and at that time, people over the age of 65 will number as many as 250 to 270 million. In other words, for a considerable period in the 21st century, people over the age of 65 will account for about 20 percent of the entire population. This is a serious problem. From now on, we should strategically take this into consideration and get prepared. On the one hand, we must, in ideology, social custom, and especially social welfare, prepare for the problem of supporting the old people. On the other hand, we must promptly and appropriately make certain adjustments in the childbearing policy to not let the aging problem become too serious.[60]

Another demographer in late 1983 advised the use of long-term population projections to help set fertility goals and cautioned: "Based on studies of foreign demographers, the proportion of the elderly age 65 and above should not be more than 20 percent of the total population. Otherwise, serious social problems would arise."[61] He then carried out some population projections and published an article in March 1984 urging the avoidance of "very low fertility rates causing serious aging of the population." He devised what he called his "medium projection" that allowed slow reduction of the total fertility rate to no lower than 1.5 births per woman in 2000 and then allowed fertility to slowly rise in the next century to two births per woman, estimating that this would prevent the elderly population from exceeding 20 percent of the population.[62] Subsequent official statements that the one-child policy is only for one generation were probably strongly influenced by these scholarly analyses. Other PRC demographers are also becoming sophisticated in their use of future population projections to devise optimum fertility paths toward the dual goals of controlling population growth and avoiding severe aging of the population.[63]

If by 1990 the Chinese government totally succeeds in allowing only 10 percent of couples to have a second birth and none to have more, can severe aging of the population be avoided in the future? To answer this question, a population projection was carried out on the assumptions that a total fertility rate of 1.1 births per woman was achieved in 1990 and held through 2000, but then the government allowed two births per woman from 2001 to 2050 in line with its claim that the one-child policy applies to only one generation. Such a fertility path would keep China's total population from exceeding 1.23 billion, but the proportion of the population age 65 and above would reach 25 percent during 2042–50. Therefore it is necessary to modify the strict one-child program before the year 2000 to avoid this severe an aging problem.

Conclusions

From a demographic perspective, the PRC has come a long way since 1949. A sweeping mortality decline took place in the 1950's, and after a temporary but jolting setback, slower improvement in mortality occurred during the 1960's and 1970's. Even allowing for considerable underreporting of deaths, China has attained relatively high life expectancy and relatively low infant mortality for a developing country, at least until the rise in female infanticide caused by the compulsory one-child limit. Health conditions have improved markedly, primarily because of control of infectious diseases and the provision of simple preventive and curative health services. Mortality decline was accompanied by an apparent increase in fertility compared to the pre-1949 period, possibly due to the longer life of both members of married couples, better nutrition, the prevention and cure of sterility-inducing diseases, and a more secure economic base for the peasants after land reform.

The combination of steep mortality decline and some increase in fertility set in motion two decades of rapid natural population increase, which raised China's official population size from 583 million as counted in the midyear 1953 census to 830 million at yearend 1970 as based on permanent registration reports. The 1970's saw a most extraordinary fertility decline, resulting not only from the accumulated social and economic changes in Chinese society, the supply of free birth control techniques by barefoot doctors, and effective educational and motivational work promoting low fertility, but also from the government's growing use of compulsory family planning and coercive fertility control tactics. The policy of trying to enforce a limit of one child per couple through punitive and sometimes brutal measures is the culmination of this trend. The fact that this limit is imposed from the central government and is unpopular with great numbers of citizens as well as opposed by important elements of the power hierarchy lends uncertainty to predictions about future fertility. The fate of the one-child limit will have important repercussions for future population growth, population size, and age structure.

After thirty-five years of socialism, in some ways the people of China are not particularly well off compared to the people of many other developing countries. Many aspects of China's economic experiments in recent decades are being repudiated, and the economy is in great flux once again. Per capita income is still low. Food supplies, though they are improving, remain tight, and the variety and nutritional adequacy of the diet are marginal. Population density in urban areas and on the arable land is extremely high and getting higher. Underemployment and unemployment are serious problems with no end in sight until possibly in the next century. The Cultural Revolution decade left higher education and professional training in a shambles. China's intellectuals and other people of independent thought are still an embattled species.

But in other ways the people of China are well off today compared to those in most other developing countries. Their health is relatively good, and mortality is comparatively low—important determinants of the quality of life for the general population. They have been through the rapid population growth phase of their demographic transition and now are likely to experience annual population growth rates well under the 3 percent a year they would be enduring if fertility had not declined considerably. Over the decades, China has achieved high growth rates in its industrial sector, and the country is unusually independent in energy and mineral resources. It does not have a crushing burden of international or national debt. It has avoided the over-urbanization characteristic of many developing countries today. It has thrown off many of the shackles of the past that are best eliminated, such as footbinding, autocratic control within the family by its head, ownership of the land by a small elite, and its national weakness of the previous century in the face of foreign incursions. Elementary education today is not far from universal, though still lacking in quality. Women in particular have experienced many positive changes and some revolutionary changes in their own lives, although some of their hard-won gains are being fast eroded by the compulsory family planning program, whose detrimental effects are felt most by young girls and women in reproductive ages. Last but not least, in several important examples of recent years, the citizens have shown their capacity to turn around government policies they do not like, a small positive sign to those who hope for a more democratic future for the Chinese people.

In the future, can the Chinese achieve significant improvement in their quality of life and general level of prosperity under a two-child limit or with a voluntary family planning program? Propaganda from China emphatically answers no, that without the success of the one-child limit, the future is grim. Indeed, certain important aspects of the quality of life would deteriorate if China's population rose to 1.5 billion or 1.7 billion people. Per capita arable land would obviously be less than if the population size never exceeded 1.2 billion. Problems of feeding the population and problems of providing employment would be much greater under the two-child or voluntary projections. These difficulties would not be unsolvable, assuming that the world further improves its agricultural production techniques and the understanding of how to successfully engineer balanced economic growth. These problems would, however, strain the economy and ecology of China and would require enlightened, creative government leadership for their solution. No matter how the population grows in the coming half-century, beyond that time China's people and government may well choose to gradually reduce the country's population in order to ease its pressure on the environment.

Nevertheless, the attitude that China is doomed if fertility is not tightly controlled at one child per couple is an exaggeration founded on a narrow definition of the quality of life. In some ways, a two-child or voluntary family planning alternative would enhance the quality of life and a one-child limit would continue to harm the quality of life and cause further deterioration. For instance, love and devotion between generations in a family are important values in Chinese culture. If China's people were given a choice, they might choose to have two or three children per couple in each generation and accept a lower level of per capita consumption over the alternative of one child with higher per capita consumption. A two-child or voluntary family planning future would enhance the quality of life by helping to preserve the Chinese family. In contrast, the one-child limit threatens to destroy the family as a close and mutually supportive group. Siblings, aunts, and uncles would become extinct, families would continue to be divided and embittered over the sex of the only child, female family members would still be victims of the recent intensification of discrimination, and doting families would each raise a single child many of whom would be self-centered and might later ignore their aging parents' needs as too burdensome.

A two-child or voluntary family planning future would also improve the quality of life by reducing or eliminating the current strong incentive for female infanticide. China's women would see a dramatic improvement in the quality of their lives with the restoration of reproductive freedom. No longer under attack by the medical system, they could receive prenatal care and a safe birth setting for pregnancies of any parity, get an intrauterine device safely removed when desired, and see medical personnel when needed without fear of a forced abortion or sterilization. Personal safety and improved health are, after all, important aspects of the quality of life.

Government statements imply that if the one-child policy succeeds, a bright future is assured for China's people. On the contrary, a one-child limit is neither necessary nor sufficient to guarantee future prosperity. No matter what the future population size, the Chinese government needs to continue its recently adopted policy of greatly improving its management of the economy and further direct the country's output toward meeting human needs. It would be a sad irony if China's people were forced to severely limit the reproduction of their families, on which they depend for their welfare and happiness, only to discover that per capita living standards remained depressed well into the twenty-first century anyhow.

Apologists for the one-child limit argue that the situation is so desperate that China has no choice. In fact it has a range of choices. The government would be far more popular with the people if it chose to allow them to have more than one child while at the same time giving them full access to all forms of birth control and continuing to teach people the importance of limiting population growth. By emphasizing pragmatic policies to promote agricultural and industrial production, the leadership could bring about a gradual rise in per capita consumption while keeping the strong family as a safety net to provide care for those who are elderly, disabled, or without adequate income. Each of the three future demographic alternatives outlined here is a genuine choice with considerable strengths and weaknesses. It is important that China's government and people find the demographic solution most consistent with their hopes and their values.

Appendixes

Appendix A

SUPPLEMENTARY DATA

The following pages contain supplementary data for males and females by age: intercensal survival ratios, 1964–82; corrected life tables, 1973–75; corrected and adjusted life tables, 1973–75; and unadjusted life tables, 1981.

TABLE A.1
Intercensal Survival Ratios for Females by Single Years of Age, 1964–82

1964		1982		18-year survival ratio
Age	Total	Age	Total	
0	13,974,327	18	12,396,270	.88707
1	14,732,717	19	13,723,740	.93151
2	7,544,061	20	7,907,350	1.04816
3	5,573,791	21	5,363,780	.96232
4	6,855,169	22	6,975,870	1.01761
5	7,125,623	23	6,892,520	.96729
6	9,696,907	24	9,317,300	.96085
7	9,374,110	25	9,097,730	.97052
8	8,906,221	26	8,688,870	.97560
9	9,791,224	27	9,499,600	.97022
10	9,211,052	28	9,024,370	.97973
11	8,808,110	29	8,499,010	.96491
12	8,582,340	30	8,447,470	.98429
13	7,356,421	31	7,089,830	.96376
14	7,388,463	32	7,270,880	.98409
15	6,369,672	33	6,274,790	.98510
16	6,159,124	34	5,968,370	.96903
17	6,132,437	35	5,904,640	.96285
18	5,811,427	36	5,392,380	.92789
19	5,286,479	37	5,002,890	.94636
20	5,032,393	38	4,819,540	.95770
21	4,796,616	39	4,537,940	.94607
22	5,092,190	40	4,720,060	.92692
23	4,798,844	41	4,658,270	.97071
24	4,617,663	42	4,379,100	.94834
25	4,672,045	43	4,384,600	.93848
26	4,729,056	44	4,446,640	.94028
27	4,722,869	45	4,486,910	.95004
28	4,805,961	46	4,547,880	.94630
29	4,667,027	47	4,416,060	.94623
30	4,739,930	48	4,459,400	.94082
31	4,584,935	49	4,406,760	.96114
32	4,227,840	50	4,041,310	.95588
33	4,223,047	51	3,809,230	.90201
34	4,210,540	52	3,979,190	.94505
35	4,085,782	53	3,705,360	.90689
36	4,140,729	54	3,754,700	.90677
37	3,719,508	55	3,377,620	.90808
38	3,745,427	56	3,324,130	.88752
39	3,887,242	57	3,413,310	.87808

TABLE A.1 (continued)

1964 Age	1964 Total	1982 Age	1982 Total	18-year survival ratio
40	3,783,661	58	3,322,070	.87800
41	3,372,465	59	2,972,470	.88139
42	3,355,651	60	3,038,830	.90559
43	3,341,478	61	2,855,120	.85445
44	3,353,612	62	2,824,340	.84218
45	3,088,814	63	2,514,170	.81396
46	3,014,455	64	2,435,440	.80792
47	3,047,834	65	2,485,250	.81542
48	3,042,757	66	2,325,510	.76428
49	2,948,295	67	2,160,640	.73284
50	3,034,128	68	2,226,470	.73381
51	2,636,374	69	1,894,260	.71851
52	2,507,860	70	1,742,680	.69489
53	2,446,581	71	1,662,650	.67958
54	2,588,306	72	1,605,370	.62024
55	2,576,191	73	1,554,310	.60334
56	2,349,037	74	1,344,890	.57253
57	2,285,008	75	1,220,360	.53407
58	2,378,603	76	1,173,190	.49323
59	2,230,213	77	1,003,520	.44997
60	2,181,739	78	909,580	.41691
61	2,064,394	79	804,260	.38959
62	1,876,626	80	694,390	.37002
63	1,836,832	81	579,180	.31531
64	1,586,133	82	446,630	.28158
65	1,413,502	83	340,720	.24105
66	1,417,684	84	295,970	.20877
67	1,282,003	85	234,090	.18260
68	1,239,651	86	183,860	.14832
69	1,173,062	87	144,030	.12278
70	1,069,224	88	105,350	.09853
71	984,694	89	77,390	.07859
72	877,214	90	61,810	.07046
73	751,498	91	38,430	.05114
74	693,276	92	27,660	.03990
75	627,977	93	18,430	.02935
76	551,605	94	11,700	.02121
77	468,223	95	9,840	.02102
78	403,318	96	5,730	.01421
79	328,554	97	3,980	.01211
80±	1,245,972	98±	8,040	.00645

SOURCES: State Council Population Office (1982): 40–42; State Council Population Office (1983): 264–73.

TABLE A.2
Intercensal Survival Ratios for Males by Single Years of Age, 1964–82

1964		1982		18-year survival ratio
Age	Total	Age	Total	
0	14,509,500	18	12,710,940	.87604
1	15,515,387	19	13,653,690	.88001
2	8,025,093	20	7,689,790	.95822
3	5,961,473	21	5,312,940	.89121
4	7,450,438	22	7,326,100	.98331
5	7,758,234	23	7,397,730	.95353
6	10,699,407	24	10,128,730	.94666
7	10,342,156	25	9,792,210	.94682
8	9,771,901	26	9,232,860	.94484
9	10,711,651	27	10,173,660	.94978
10	10,001,128	28	9,593,370	.95923
11	9,530,651	29	8,989,340	.94320
12	9,257,381	30	8,908,890	.96236
13	8,026,136	31	7,540,560	.93950
14	8,189,963	32	8,006,090	.97755
15	7,099,181	33	6,884,960	.96982
16	6,885,212	34	6,565,930	.95363
17	6,674,639	35	6,508,270	.97507
18	6,070,530	36	5,901,470	.97215
19	5,626,787	37	5,560,660	.98825
20	5,475,825	38	5,421,410	.99006
21	5,200,977	39	5,154,170	.99100
22	5,498,218	40	5,328,790	.96918
23	5,231,306	41	5,333,170	1.01947
24	5,076,719	42	4,987,080	.98234
25	5,278,678	43	5,002,090	.94760
26	5,452,581	44	5,141,230	.94290
27	5,386,660	45	5,104,680	.94765
28	5,443,913	46	5,105,030	.93775
29	5,236,618	47	4,879,030	.93171
30	5,369,854	48	4,995,490	.93028
31	5,152,650	49	4,962,760	.96315
32	4,772,857	50	4,529,310	.94897
33	4,755,864	51	4,342,140	.91301
34	4,668,573	52	4,467,370	.95690
35	4,514,180	53	4,076,950	.90314
36	4,560,395	54	4,145,220	.90896
37	4,153,654	55	3,704,760	.89193
38	4,115,241	56	3,592,970	.87309
39	4,247,754	57	3,643,490	.85775

TABLE A.2 (continued)

1964		1982		18-year survival ratio
Age	Total	Age	Total	
40	4,073,212	58	3,476,510	.85351
41	3,632,453	59	3,081,980	.84846
42	3,612,806	60	3,122,190	.86420
43	3,570,690	61	2,908,090	.81443
44	3,549,187	62	2,857,750	.80518
45	3,232,655	63	2,459,400	.76080
46	3,154,761	64	2,367,200	.75036
47	3,203,405	65	2,328,200	.72679
48	3,094,701	66	2,158,880	.69761
49	3,025,159	67	1,991,150	.65820
50	3,113,758	68	2,018,680	.64831
51	2,694,842	69	1,678,090	.62270
52	2,557,780	70	1,510,130	.59041
53	2,435,503	71	1,406,080	.57733
54	2,490,250	72	1,303,820	.52357
55	2,413,645	73	1,200,600	.49742
56	2,173,241	74	1,018,420	.46862
57	2,089,385	75	889,220	.42559
58	2,105,149	76	816,620	.38792
59	1,967,775	77	687,280	.34927
60	1,902,039	78	598,500	.31466
61	1,794,586	79	506,010	.28196
62	1,596,500	80	423,530	.26529
63	1,536,154	81	338,390	.22028
64	1,296,451	82	250,300	.19307
65	1,147,094	83	184,300	.16067
66	1,132,111	84	153,150	.13528
67	1,011,676	85	118,800	.11743
68	940,409	86	85,280	.09068
69	877,924	87	63,790	.07266
70	765,713	88	45,340	.05921
71	698,304	89	30,700	.04396
72	597,579	90	24,830	.04155
73	498,494	91	13,670	.02742
74	442,253	92	9,920	.02243
75	388,493	93	5,950	.01532
76	325,301	94	4,360	.01340
77	269,574	95	3,690	.01369
78	221,288	96	2,340	.01057
79	173,033	97	1,760	.01017
80±	566,631	98±	3,620	.00639

SOURCES: Same as Table A.1.

TABLE A.3
Corrected Life Tables for Males and Females, 1973–75, from the Cancer Epidemiology Survey

Age group	Probability of dying during age interval q_x	Age-specific death rate m_x	Survivors entering age interval l_x	Person-years lived during age interval L_x	Life expectancy (years) e_x
		MALES			
0	0.06290	0.06613	100,000	95,115	63.46
1–4	0.02103	0.00533	93,710	369,839	66.71
5–9	0.01147	0.00231	91,739	456,063	64.11
10–14	0.00504	0.00101	90,687	452,290	59.83
15–19	0.00548	0.00110	90,229	449,910	55.12
20–24	0.00738	0.00148	89,735	447,018	50.41
25–29	0.00784	0.00157	89,073	443,616	45.76
30–34	0.00994	0.00200	88,374	439,674	41.11
35–39	0.01419	0.00286	87,496	434,374	36.49
40–44	0.02035	0.00411	86,254	426,881	31.98
45–49	0.03063	0.00622	84,499	416,023	27.59
50–54	0.04806	0.00985	81,911	399,711	23.39
55–59	0.07408	0.01539	77,974	375,427	19.44
60–64	0.11908	0.02532	72,197	339,492	15.80
65–69	0.17199	0.03763	63,600	290,652	12.60
70–74	0.26329	0.06064	52,661	228,643	9.69
75–79	0.38313	0.09478	38,796	156,821	7.26
80±	1.00000	0.19154	23,932	124,945	5.22
		FEMALES			
0	0.05582	0.05837	100,000	95,632	65.94
1–4	0.02294	0.00582	94,418	372,112	68.83
5–9	0.01051	0.00211	92,252	458,835	66.41
10–14	0.00423	0.00085	91,282	455,446	62.09
15–19	0.00478	0.00096	90,896	453,395	57.34
20–24	0.00726	0.00146	90,462	450,667	52.61
25–29	0.00851	0.00171	89,805	447,115	47.97
30–34	0.01038	0.00209	89,041	442,895	43.36
35–39	0.01390	0.00280	88,117	437,523	38.79
40–44	0.01853	0.00374	86,892	430,435	34.30
45–49	0.02529	0.00512	85,282	421,018	29.90
50–54	0.03805	0.00776	83,125	407,719	25.61
55–59	0.05602	0.01153	79,963	388,613	21.53
60–64	0.09140	0.01916	75,483	360,165	17.66
65–69	0.13459	0.02886	68,583	319,840	14.18
70–74	0.20738	0.04627	59,353	265,991	11.00
75–79	0.30717	0.07258	47,044	199,094	8.22
80±	1.00000	0.17355	32,594	187,807	5.76

SOURCE: Rong et al. (1981): 25–26.

NOTE: These life tables are as published in the source, except that the 80± entry has been completed by computer, to replace unreliable death data at the upper ages, and an apparent error in age groups 0 and 1–4 has been corrected to account for the traditional way of reporting ages whereby infants below the age of 1 are said to be age 1 or 2. This error was corrected by using the relation between infant deaths and deaths age 1–4 in West model life tables Levels 18 and 19 (Coale & Demeny 1966: 19–20). In generating these corrected life tables, computer assistance was provided by Jack Gibson and Peter Johnson. For a discussion of the column heads, see the note to Table 4.6.

TABLE A.4
Corrected and Adjusted Life Tables for Males and Females, 1973–75, from the Cancer Epidemiology Survey

Age group	Probability of dying during age interval q_x	Age-specific death rate m_x	Survivors entering age interval l_x	Person-years lived during age interval L_x	Life expectancy (years) e_x
		MALES			
0	0.07353	0.07780	100,000	94,514	60.79
1–4	0.02469	0.00627	92,647	364,713	64.59
5–9	0.01350	0.00272	90,360	448,749	62.19
10–14	0.00592	0.00119	89,140	444,380	58.01
15–19	0.00645	0.00129	88,612	441,631	53.34
20–24	0.00867	0.00174	88,041	438,295	48.67
25–29	0.00919	0.00185	87,277	434,381	44.07
30–34	0.01170	0.00235	86,475	429,847	39.46
35–39	0.01668	0.00336	85,464	423,753	34.90
40–44	0.02389	0.00483	84,038	415,170	30.45
45–49	0.03593	0.00732	82,030	402,783	26.13
50–54	0.05631	0.01159	79,083	384,281	22.01
55–59	0.08661	0.01811	74,630	356,989	18.18
60–64	0.13862	0.02979	68,166	317,208	14.66
65–69	0.19930	0.04427	58,717	264,330	11.62
70–74	0.30271	0.07134	47,015	199,494	8.89
75–79	0.43599	0.11151	32,783	128,181	6.66
80±	1.00000	0.20489	18,490	90,241	4.88
		FEMALES			
0	0.06529	0.06867	100,000	95,076	63.30
1–4	0.02691	0.00685	93,471	367,388	66.70
5–9	0.01233	0.00248	90,955	451,973	64.51
10–14	0.00499	0.00100	89,834	448,048	60.28
15–19	0.00563	0.00113	89,386	445,670	55.57
20–24	0.00855	0.00172	88,882	442,511	50.87
25–29	0.01001	0.00201	88,122	438,405	46.29
30–34	0.01222	0.00246	87,240	433,535	41.74
35–39	0.01634	0.00329	86,174	427,350	37.22
40–44	0.02176	0.00440	84,766	419,220	32.80
45–49	0.02967	0.00602	82,922	408,457	28.47
50–54	0.04463	0.00913	80,461	393,328	24.27
55–59	0.06560	0.01356	76,870	371,745	20.28
60–64	0.10669	0.02254	71,828	339,979	16.53
65–69	0.15648	0.03395	64,164	295,719	13.21
70–74	0.23957	0.05443	54,124	238,201	10.19
75–79	0.35183	0.08539	41,157	169,584	7.62
80±	1.00000	0.18545	26,677	143,848	5.39

SOURCE: Same as Table A.3.
NOTE: These life tables have been adjusted on the assumption that deaths were 85% reported at all ages in the Cancer Epidemiology Survey.

TABLE A.5

Unadjusted Life Tables for Males and Females, 1981

Age group	Probability of dying during age interval q_x	Age-specific death rate m_x	Survivors entering age interval l_x	Person-years lived during age interval L_x	Life expectancy (years) e_x
		MALES			
0	0.035561	0.036468	100,000	97,511	66.43
1–4	0.015999	0.004032	96,444	381,966	67.87
5–9	0.006502	0.001305	94,901	472,759	64.94
10–14	0.003935	0.000789	94,284	470,482	60.36
15–19	0.005409	0.001085	93,913	468,405	55.58
20–24	0.007077	0.001420	93,405	465,383	50.87
25–29	0.007289	0.001463	92,744	462,037	46.22
30–34	0.008809	0.001770	92,068	458,385	41.54
35–39	0.012152	0.002445	91,257	453,651	36.88
40–44	0.017427	0.003516	90,148	447,027	32.30
45–49	0.026531	0.005377	88,577	437,390	27.83
50–54	0.043107	0.008811	86,227	422,435	23.52
55–59	0.069907	0.014488	82,510	399,096	19.46
60–64	0.116481	0.024737	76,742	362,504	15.72
65–69	0.177205	0.038886	67,803	310,346	12.44
70–74	0.277138	0.064344	55,788	240,996	9.56
75–79	0.390904	0.097174	40,327	161,828	7.25
80–84	0.558238	0.154877	24,563	86,315	5.32
85–89	0.687218	0.209393	10,851	32,971	4.08
90±	1.000000	0.300727	3,394	11,286	3.33
		FEMALES			
0	0.033724	0.034535	100,000	97,640	69.35
1–4	0.017780	0.004485	96,628	382,257	70.75
5–9	0.005374	0.001078	94,910	473,048	68.01
10–14	0.003294	0.000660	94,400	471,239	63.36
15–19	0.004655	0.000933	94,089	469,452	58.57
20–24	0.006674	0.001339	93,651	466,724	53.83
25–29	0.007374	0.001480	93,026	463,415	49.17
30–34	0.008425	0.001692	92,340	459,802	44.52
35–39	0.010812	0.002174	91,562	455,405	39.87
40–44	0.014453	0.002912	90,572	449,746	35.28
45–49	0.020972	0.004239	89,263	441,931	30.76
50–54	0.032658	0.006640	87,391	430,209	26.36
55–59	0.050049	0.010267	84,537	412,789	22.16
60–64	0.082858	0.017288	80,306	385,783	18.19
65–69	0.127532	0.027244	73,652	346,133	14.60
70–74	0.207566	0.046321	64,259	289,064	11.34
75–79	0.303765	0.071633	50,921	216,655	8.64
80–84	0.468197	0.122260	35,453	134,649	6.30
85–89	0.609738	0.175431	18,854	62,912	4.70
90±	1.000000	0.286471	7,358	25,685	3.49

SOURCE: Jiang et al. (1984): 15–17.

NOTE: These life tables were calculated from the 1982 census question on deaths in the household in calendar year 1981, supplemented by locally compiled data on the ages of those reported deaths. The population age structure is the 1982 census age structure backdated to midyear 1981 through an iterative computer procedure.

TABLE A.6
Unadjusted Life Table for Both Sexes, 1981

Age group	Probability of dying during age interval q_x	Age-specific death rate m_x	Survivors entering age interval l_x	Person-years lived during age interval L_x	Life expectancy (years) e_x
0	0.034679	0.035543	100,000	97,572	67.88
1–4	0.016865	0.004252	96,532	382,103	69.30
5–9	0.005943	0.001192	94,904	472,897	66.47
10–14	0.003604	0.000722	94,340	470,852	61.85
15–19	0.005043	0.001011	94,000	468,920	57.07
20–24	0.006875	0.001380	93,526	466,043	52.34
25–29	0.007343	0.001474	92,883	462,713	47.69
30–34	0.008633	0.001734	92,201	459,075	43.02
35–39	0.011520	0.002317	91,405	454,498	38.37
40–44	0.016048	0.003236	90,352	448,324	33.79
45–49	0.023925	0.004843	88,902	439,533	29.30
50–54	0.038179	0.007784	86,775	426,087	24.95
55–59	0.060303	0.012436	83,462	405,552	20.84
60–64	0.099734	0.020994	78,429	373,592	17.00
65–69	0.151557	0.032797	70,607	327,633	13.59
70–74	0.239091	0.054311	59,906	264,595	10.55
75–79	0.340105	0.081958	45,583	189,337	8.06
80–84	0.502493	0.134221	30,080	110,992	5.93
85–89	0.635550	0.186317	14,965	48,450	4.49
90±	1.000000	0.290384	5,454	18,782	3.44

SOURCE: See source and note to Table A.5.

Appendix B

GLOSSARY OF DEMOGRAPHIC TERMS

Age structure, age-sex structure. The composition of a population as determined by the proportion of the total population, or of males and females, in each age category. The age-sex structure of a population is the cumulative result of past trends in fertility, mortality, and migration.

Age-sex-specific undercount. The proportion of the true number of males or females in a particular age group who are missed in a census or survey.

Age-specific marital fertility pattern. The average annual number of births to married women in each reproductive age group during a specified period of time per thousand married women in the same age group, based on the mid-period population.

Barefoot doctor. In China beginning in 1968, a paramedic trained in first aid, treatment of common complaints, and birth control techniques who provides primary medical care to a rural area.

BCG immunization. Bacillus Calmette-Guérin vaccine, a vaccine prepared from a living attenuated strain of tubercle bacilli, used to immunize humans against tuberculosis.

Census. A canvass of a given area, resulting in an enumeration of the entire population and the compilation of demographic, social, and economic information pertaining to that population at a specified time.

Cohort. A group of people who experience the same event in the same time period, such as birth or marriage in the same year.

Contraceptive use rate, contraceptive prevalence rate. Of the total number of currently married women in the reproductive ages 15–44 or 15–49, the number of women currently practicing contraception or contraceptively sterilized, or whose husbands are contraceptively sterilized.

Crude birth rate (CBR). The average annual number of births during a specified period per thousand persons in the mid-period total population.

Crude death rate (CDR). The average annual number of deaths during a specified period per thousand persons in the mid-period total population.

De facto population count. A population count in which persons are attributed to the geographical area where they are physically located at census time, no matter where they normally reside.

De jure population count. A population count in which persons are attributed to a geographical area by virtue of their usual place of residence, whether or not they were actually located in that area at the time of the enumeration.

Demographic momentum. The tendency of a population to continue past demographic trends into the future, owing to the time it takes for major demographic changes to occur and to transform the current size, distribution, and age-sex structure of the population.

Demographic transition. The shift from a traditional pattern of relatively high mortality and fertility to a modern pattern of relatively low mortality and fertility. Because the decline in mortality usually leads the decline in fertility, there is an interim period of rapid natural population increase during the transition period.

Demography. The scientific study of human populations, including their size, composition, distribution, density, and growth, along with the relationships between population processes and other socioeconomic characteristics of the population.

Dependency ratio. The total number of dependents at ages 14 and younger and 65 and older per 100 persons in the working ages 15–64.

Endemic disease. A disease that is native to a particular place and constantly present in it.

Expectation of life at birth (e_o). The average number of years a person could expect to live after being born alive, if mortality conditions stayed the same as those found at each age in a given year.

Family planning program. An organized attempt by a country's government or by a non-governmental organization to provide birth control methods to a population, often associated with efforts to motivate birth control use and often accompanied by an explicit goal of reducing the population's fertility.

Fecundity. The physiological capacity to produce a live child, including the capacity of a man or a woman to contribute to conception, the capacity of a couple to conceive, and the capacity of a woman to carry a fetus to a live birth once conceived.

Fertility. Actual reproductive performance of individuals, couples, or populations, as measured by the production of live births.

General fertility rate. The annual number of births per 1,000 women of childbearing age.

Incidence of a disease. The number of persons contracting a disease during a given time period per population at risk.

Infant mortality rate (IMR). A measure of the frequency of deaths experienced during a specified period by infants between the moment of their live birth and the attainment of exact age one. Usually calculated as the number of deaths to infants under one year of age per thousand live births occurring during the same calendar year.

Internal migration. The movement of a person from one residence to set up a new residence across a specified boundary but within the same country. See also *Migrant.*

Life expectancy, see *Expectation of life at birth.*

Life table. A tabular display of the expectation of life at each age and the probability of dying at each age for a given population, according to the age-specific death rates prevailing at one particular time. The life table gives an organized, complete picture of a population's mortality by age.

Malthusian theory of population. Part of the doctrines of the English economist Thomas Malthus (1766–1834), the theory that population tends to increase at a faster rate than its means of subsistence, and that widespread poverty and degradation of the lower classes inevitably result unless the population growth is checked by sexual abstinence or by disease, famine, or war.

Married women of reproductive age. Females in the age group 15–49 (or within other specified age boundaries) who are currently married.

Migrant. A person who moves across a specified boundary and sets up a new permanent or temporary residence for a long enough period to be classified a resident at the destination.

Morbidity. The frequency of disease and illness in a population.

Mortality. Deaths as a component of population change.

Natural fertility. The average level and pattern of fertility experienced by couples not practicing any form of birth control, which may vary with the ecological and cultural setting.

Natural population increase rate. The increase rate per thousand population that results solely from an excess of births over deaths and does not take migration into account. Crude birth rate minus crude death rate equals crude rate of natural increase.

Neonatal mortality rate. The number of deaths in the first month of life per thousand live births in a specified time period.

Permanent population registration system. An administrative system that attempts to register people at their permanent residence, adding promptly to the registers those who are born or who move in and deleting those who die or move out.

Population growth rate. The average annual percent change in the size of a population, resulting from a surplus (or deficit) of births over deaths and the balance of migrants entering and leaving the country.

Post-enumeration survey or check. A survey for checking the coverage and accuracy of a population census by independently re-enumerating a sample of the population after the census.

Postneonatal mortality rate. The number of infant deaths between ages one month and one year per thousand live births.

Prevalence of a disease. The number of persons who have a particular disease at a given time per population at risk; includes new cases and continuing cases.

Replacement level fertility. The fertility level at which women on average have only enough daughters to replace themselves in the population over time.

Representative sample. A sample that is a relatively faithful reflection of the population with respect to the characteristics studied. In probability sampling, chance methods are used to obtain a representative sample.

Reverse survival technique. The estimation of births in the years prior to a census by means of the backward reconstruction of birth cohorts from the census count at each age and an assumed mortality level between birth and enumeration.

Sample survey. A canvass of selected persons or households in a population, used to infer characteristics of or trends for a larger segment or for all of the population.

Sex ratio. The number of males per hundred females, at birth, in a whole population, or in particular age groups of a population.

Singulate mean age at marriage (SMAM). A measure of average age at first marriage, derived from a set of proportions of men or women who are still single at different ages, and not derived directly from records of the ages of brides and bridegrooms.

Stable population. A population with an unchanging rate of growth and an unchanging age structure, because age-specific fertility and mortality rates have remained constant and there has been no migration over a long period of time.

Survival ratio. The proportion of persons in a given age group who are still alive a specified number of years later.

Total fertility rate (TFR). The average number of children who would be born alive to a woman during her lifetime if she lived through all her childbearing years and conformed to all the age-specific fertility rates of a given year.

Urbanization. An increase in the proportion of a country's total population who are residing in urban areas.

Vital rates. Measures of the frequency of births, deaths, marriages, and divorces in a population.

Vital registration system. A government-run system that attempts to record all the births, deaths, marriages, and divorces in a population as they occur.

Zero population growth. The condition of stationary population size resulting from a balance between additions to the population through births and immigration and losses to the population through deaths and emigration.

Reference Matter

Abbreviations

The following abbreviations are used in the Notes and Bibliography:

AR	The Asia Record
AS	Asian Survey
BJRB	Beijing ribao (Beijing Daily)
BR	Beijing Review, from 1 Jan. 1979
CB	Current Background
CBR	China Business Review
CD	China Daily, Beijing
CJP	Chinese Journal of Pediatrics
CJWTYJ	Caijing wenti yanjiu (Studies on Financial and Economic Problems)
CMJ	Chinese Medical Journal
CNA	China News Analysis
CQ	China Quarterly
CR	China Reconstructs
CS	Current Scene
DZRB	Dazhong ribao (Popular Daily, Jinan)
ECMM	Extracts from China Mainland Magazines
FBIS	Foreign Broadcast Information Service Daily Report—People's Republic of China, Vol. 1
FEER	Far Eastern Economic Review
FJRB	Fujian ribao (Fujian Daily, Fuzhou)
GMRB	Guangming ribao (Bright Daily, Beijing)
GPO	U.S. Government Printing Office
GRRB	Gongren ribao (Workers Daily, Beijing)
GSRB	Gansu ribao (Gansu Daily)
GWYGB	Zhonghua renmin gongheguo guowuyuan gongbao (PRC State Council Bulletin)
HLJRB	Heilongjiang ribao (Heilongjiang Daily)
IFPP	International Family Planning Perspectives

JFRB	Jiefang ribao (Liberation Daily, Shanghai)
JHSYB	Jiankang bao jihua shengyu ban (Health Gazette, Family Planning Edition)
JJGL	Jingji guanli (Economic Management)
JJKX	Jingji kexue (Economic Science)
JJYJ	Jingji yanjiu (Economic Research)
JKB	Jiankang bao (Health Gazette, Beijing)
JMJP	Jen-min jih-pao (People's Daily, Peking, to l Jan. 1979)
JPE	Journal of Political Economy
JPRS	U.S. Joint Publications Research Service
LNRB	Liaoning ribao (Liaoning Daily, Shenyang)
MMFQ	Milbank Memorial Fund Quarterly
NFRB	Nanfang ribao (Southern Daily, Guangzhou)
NXRB	Ningxia ribao (Ningxia Daily)
NYT	New York Times
PDR	Population and Development Review
PI	Population Index
PR	Peking Review, to l Jan. 1979
PS	Population Studies
RKJJ	Renkou yu jingji (Journal of Population and Economics)
RKYJ	Renkou yanjiu (Population Research)
RMRB	Renmin ribao (People's Daily, Beijing, from l Jan. 1979)
RPFP	Reports on Population/Family Planning
SCMP	Survey of China Mainland Press
SCRB	Sichuan ribao (Sichuan Daily)
SFP	Studies in Family Planning
SH	Shehui (Society)
SPRCP	Survey of People's Republic of China Press
SWB	Summary of World Broadcasts, Part 3: The Far East, Second Series
SWB-WER	Summary of World Broadcasts, Part 3: The Far East, Weekly Economic Report, Second Series
TJ	Tongji (Statistics)
TJRB	Tianjin ribao (Tianjin Daily)
TKP	Ta kung pao (The Impartial Paper, Beijing and Hong Kong)
WHB	Wenhui bao (Cultural Paper, Shanghai)
WP	Washington Post
XHRB	Xinhua ribao (New China Daily, Nanjing)
YNRB	Yunnan ribao (Yunnan Daily, Kunming)
ZGFN	Zhongguo funü (Women of China)
ZGQN	Zhongguo qingnian (Chinese Youth)
ZGQNB	Zhongguo qingnian bao (Chinese Youth Gazette)
ZGSHKX	Zhongguo shehui kexue (Social Sciences in China)
ZJRB	Zhejiang ribao (Zhejiang Daily, Hangzhou)
ZMRB	Zhengming ribao (Contending Daily, Hong Kong)

Notes

For the works cited here in short form, complete authors' names and publication data are given in the Bibliography, pp. 449–71. In the Notes and Bibliography, Chinese characters are transliterated according to the Wade-Giles system for all sources up to 1 January 1979. Thereafter, PRC publications converted to the Pinyin system, and so does this book for subsequent citations.

Chapter 1

1. "Country News: Bangladesh," *Population Headliners* (ESCAP, Bangkok), no. 81 (Dec. 1981): 1.

2. For fuller explanation of each population estimate in Table 1.1, and a discussion of the determinants of population growth and decline throughout the last two millennia, contact the author for a copy of her paper "China's Population Growth through History."

3. For further information see Perkins (1969), especially pp. 18–78, 183–91, 240.

4. Buck (1937).

5. Barclay et al. (1976).

6. Japanese data from Taeuber & Taeuber (1959); Jiangsu data from Chiao et al. (1938): 40–48.

7. Fertility Survey (1984).

8. For details on the intensity of Chinese traditional agriculture, see Buck (1937).

9. Perkins (1969): 15.

10. Detailed data on mortality declines prior to 1963 are analyzed in U.N. Population Bulletin no. 6 (1963). The reasons for this unprecedented mortality trend are succinctly explained in U.N. Concise Report (1974): 1.

11. Demographic Yearbook 1966 (1967): 1.

12. These estimates refer to the 1960–66 period. Demographic Yearbook 1966 (1967): 95.

13. Crude birth rate minus crude death rate equals natural population increase rate. Crude death rates declined in all developing regions between 1960–66 and

1965–74, while the crude birth rate for Asia and Latin America declined slightly, and Africa's crude birth rate increased slightly. United Nations estimates for 1965–74 population growth rates were 2.1 percent for Asia, 2.7 percent for Africa, and 2.7 percent for Latin America. Demographic Yearbook 1974 (1975): 105.

14. Demographic Yearbook 1974 (1975): 105; Demographic Yearbook 1966 (1967): 95; Frejka (1973): 84.

15. UNFAO (1975).

16. Details on the World Population Conference can be found in Teitelbaum (1974); Mauldin et al. (1974); and World Population Conference Special Issue (1974).

17. Nortman (1982): 41.

18. Vital rate estimates for Indonesia and India were made at the U.S. Bureau of the Census. Estimates of Indonesia's total fertility rates were provided by the Central Bureau of Statistics, Jakarta, based on the own-children method of fertility estimation from successive censuses.

19. World Population 1983 (1984).

Chapter 2

1. On the development of the PRC statistical system to the early 1960's, see Li Choh-ming (1962); and Emerson (1965): 11–39.

2. Emerson (1980): 4.

3. Sun Yefang (1981): L4-L5.

4. For details see Chen Xian, "Dangqian tongji gongzuo xuyao jiaqiang de jige fangmian" (The areas that need to be strengthened in current statistical work), TJ, 17 Oct. 1983: 3–4.

5. "Zhonghua renmin gongheguo tongjifa" (The Statistics Law of the People's Republic of China), RMRB, 10 Dec. 1983: 2.

6. Aird (1961).

7. Ibid.: 7, for a brief description of inherited Marxist population theory.

8. The relevant texts were translated and published in Meek (1971).

9. "Economist Ma Yinchu Rehabilitated," BR 22, no. 31 (3 Aug. 1979): 3–4.

10. Hu Huanyong (1981): 65.

11. "China's Production Increases Faster than Population," FBIS 185 (24 Sept. 1973): B1.

12. Report of an interview with Li Xiannian in *Yomiuri Shimbun*, Tokyo, in Japanese, 5 Mar. 1979: 3.

13. Communique on 1953 Census (1954): 1.

14. Barclay et al. (1976).

15. Goldman (1980).

16. Communique on 1953 Census (1954): 1.

17. Aird (1961): 74–78.

18. Barclay et al. (1976): 620.

19. Communique on 1982 Census (1982): K2. For more detailed analysis of the reasons for China's high population sex ratio of 1982, see Banister (1984d).

20. Wang Lihua, "Tianjin jihua shengyu bumen renwei sheng yitai buhui zaocheng nannü xingbie bili shitiao" (The Tianjin Family Planning Department

believes that one child per couple will not cause an imbalance in the sex ratio), GMRB, 27 Sept. 1980: 1.

21. Demographic Yearbook 1963 (1964): 196–97, 200–201; Demographic Yearbook 1975 (1976): 204–9, 448–51; Taiwan Demographic Fact Book 1973 (1974): 64.

22. Zhu Yilin, "Benshi xingsheng yinger zhong nanhai do yu nühai" (Among newborns in Beijing, males are more numerous than females), BJRB, 7 July 1980: 2.

23. This system of compiling annual yearend population totals is described in Li Chengrui (1981): 17.

24. These overcount estimates are reported in Li Chengrui (1981): 18, and in State Council Population Census Office, "Guanyu Wuxi renkou pucha shidian diaocha dengji he shougong huizong jieduan gongzuo de zongjie" (A summary of the Wuxi population census pretest and the hand tabulation work) (abstract), TJ, no. 2 (10 June 1981): 16–21.

25. Li Chengrui (1981): 17.

26. Nee (1981): 33.

27. "Caiqu youli cuoshi gaohao jihua shengyu" (Adopt effective measures and do well in family planning), *Hebei ribao* (Hebei Daily), 29 Oct. 1981: 2.

28. Liu Yan, "Gai haizi luo hu jing yao gai shisange gongzhang" (It takes thirteen official seals to register my child), GMRB, 4 Feb. 1982: 1.

29. For example, see "Pingnanxian renkou pucha shidian zhong de er san shi" (A few anecdotes concerning the census pretest in Pingnan county), FJRB, 19 June 1982: 2.

30. Zhou Qichang, "Problems of population composition in new cities discussed," JPRS 77764 (7 Apr. 1981): 88.

31. Fujian Provincial Population Census Office, "Sheng renkou pucha bangongshi zhuren huiyi yanjiu bushu zhuajing jinxing renkou pucha gongzuo" (Meeting of the directors of population census offices in Fujian province studies and makes arrangements for undertaking population census work), FJRB, 18 May 1981: 1.

32. As pointed out in Aird (1982a). See also Li Chengrui (1981): 18–21.

33. See, for example, Li Chengrui (1981); Aird (1982a); and Kannisto & Yu (1981).

34. These census rules were described in Li Chengrui (1981): 18–20; and Kannisto & Yu (1981): 4–5.

Chapter 3

1. Ho Ch'eng (1950).

2. Lampton (1977): 13, 25.

3. Lampton (1977): 33.

4. Po I-po (1952).

5. Chang Kai (1957).

6. Chien & Kochergin (1959): 39.

7. Narcotics Report (1953).

8. Horn (1969): 81–93. Another source states that during the 1940's, 5–10 percent of the total outpatients seen by hospitals in large cities were suffering from syphilis. Hu Ch'uan-k'uei et al. (1959).

9. Hu Ch'uan-k'uei et al. (1959).

10. Horn (1969): 85.

11. Hu Ch'uan-k'uei (1951): 1, 4.

12. Horn (1969): 86.

13. This campaign was described in Hu Ch'uan-k'uei et al. (1959); and Horn (1969): 87–93.

14. Details in this paragraph are from Hu Ch'uan-k'uei et al. (1959); and Horn (1969): 81–93.

15. Personal communication from Arthur Wolf.

16. Yu Chia-chün (1953): 24–26.

17. Details on leprosy in China are from Hu Ch'uan-k'uei et al. (1959).

18. Huang (1973): 242–44.

19. "No Need for Leprosy Villages—A Proposal by Noted Doctor Ma Haide," BR 24, no. 13 (30 Mar. 1981): 26–27.

20. "Quanguo dierci mafeng fangzhi gongzuo huiyi tichu zhengqu zai benshi jimo jiben xiaomie mafengbing" (The Second National Leprosy Prevention and Treatment Work Conference proposes to basically eliminate leprosy by the end of the century), JKB, 3 Dec. 1981: 1.

21. Chien & Kochergin (1959): 36.

22. Chu Fu-t'ang (1959).

23. Foege (1980): 97.

24. Chu Fu-t'ang (1959): 368.

25. Wei et al. (1958).

26. Horn (1969): 125.

27. Hu Ch'uan-k'uei (1951): 4.

28. Chu Fu-t'ang (1959); Wei et al. (1958).

29. Chu Fu-t'ang (1959); Chien & Kochergin (1959): 43.

30. Jung Ch'in (1958): 17.

31. Jung Ch'in (1958): 16.

32. Chinese Journal of Tuberculosis (1958): 273.

33. Chang Kai (1957).

34. These disease-specific mortality comparisons are from Chien & Kochergin (1959): 36.

35. Chien & Kochergin (1959): 41–42.

36. Most information in this paragraph is from Ho Ch'i (1965) and Huang (1973): 249–51.

37. Hou et al. (1959), cited in Huang (1973): 249.

38. Information in this paragraph is from King & Locke (1983): 404; Tropical Medicine Delegation Report (1979): 31–32; Chien & Kochergin (1959): 41; and Wang Chao-tsung, "Ending the Scourge of Kala-azar," CR 14, no. 1 (Jan. 1965): 27–29.

39. Details on China's policy and programs for eradicating schistosomiasis are found in Lampton (1977): 64–65.

40. Snail Fever Report (1976): 167.

41. Chang Kai (1957).

42. Su Tsu-fei (1959): 424.

43. Chu Fu-t'ang (1959); Fan P'ei-lu et al. (1959); Liu Hsiang-yün (1959); Ch'en Chien-hung & Yung (1959).

44. Xue Xinbing (1979): 194.

45. Chu Fu-t'ang (1959): 367.

46. Cheng Chu-yuan (1973): 151.

47. Details on the skewed distribution of the meager national budget for health work are found in Lampton (1977).

48. People's Handbook (1957): 608.

49. Peng Dehuai, "Peng Dehuai Notes on Lushan Plenum Published," JPRS 77668 (25 Mar. 1981): 8.

50. Zhang Qingwu (1979): 3.

51. Lampton (1977): 108, 112, 118, 137.

52. Ho Ch'i (1965): 495.

53. For some evidence on health effects of the Great Leap Forward, see Worth (1963).

54. "AFP: Cholera Reported in Kwangtung," FBIS 50 (13 Mar. 1962): DDD1; "Reuters: Anticholera Drive Stepped Up," FBIS 65 (3 Apr. 1962): DDD1; "Cholera Said Spreading in South China," FBIS 115 (13 June 1962): DDD6.

55. Pediatrics Proposal (1965).

56. Ho Ch'i (1965).

57. Pediatrics Proposal (1965).

58. Lampton (1977): 185–87; Sidel & Sidel (1973): 29–30; Mao Tse-tung, "June 26 'Directive' (June 26, 1965)," SCMP, supplement no. 198 (1967): 30.

59. Lythcott (1973). On the provincial distribution of tuberculosis, see "Conference on Preventing, Treating Tuberculosis Held in Tsinghai," FBIS 206 (26 Oct. 1977): E15-E16.

60. "Well Known Tuberculosis Expert, Qiu Zuyuan, Points Out that Prevention and Treatment of Tuberculosis Must Not be Neglected," GMRB, 9 Nov. 1980: 1.

61. "Health Ministry Reports Drop in Tuberculosis Rate," FBIS 118 (19 June 1981): K20; "Drop in TB Incidence," BR 24, no. 34 (24 Aug. 1981): 9.

62. Qian Xinzhong (1979): 2. For further details on infectious disease control, see Foege (1980).

63. "Facts and Figures," BR 24, no. 33 (17 Aug. 1981): 7.

64. "Public Health, Kwangtung," SWB-WER, no. W969 (1 Mar. 1978): 1.

65. "Health Minister Qian Outlines 1982 Tasks," FBIS 24 (4 Feb. 1982): K19.

66. Lampton (1977): 15.

67. Felsenfeld (1972); cited in Akhtar (1975): 34.

68. Tropical Medicine Delegation Report (1979): 44; WHO Health Statistics Report (1979): 36.

69. "Zai changdao chuanranbing fangzhi gongzuo huiyi shang Qian Xinzhong tongzhi zhichu hezuo yiliao yao shi ying nongcun xin xingshi linghuo duoyang" (At the Conference on Infectious Intestinal Disease Prevention and Treatment Work, Comrade Qian Xinzhong pointed out that cooperative medicine must be flexible and suited to new developments in rural areas), JKB, 20 Aug. 1981: 1.

70. "Chengdu shi renzhen yufang changdao chuanranbing" (Chengdu Municipality conscientiously prevents infectious intestinal diseases), JKB, 6 Aug. 1981: 2; "Shi renda changweihui renzhen taolun weisheng gongzuo haozhao kaizhan aiguo weisheng yundong jinkuai gaibian weisheng mianmao" (The Standing Committee of the Municipal People's Congress conscientiously discusses public health work and calls for the carrying out of the patriotic public health movement in order to change public health conditions as soon as possible), BJRB, 8 Aug. 1981: 1.

71. "Qieshi jiaqiang yinshi weisheng guanli yanfang changdao chuanranbing liuxing" (Earnestly strengthen food and drink sanitation in order to strictly control the prevalence of infectious intestinal disease), JKB, 9 Aug. 1981: 1.

72. "National Sanitation Standards Committee Set Up," FBIS 34 (20 Feb. 1981): L5; "Circular on Food Sanitation Law Issued," FBIS 80 (25 Apr. 1983): K18-K19.

73. Tropical Medicine Delegation Report (1979): 46–48.

74. Weisskopf (1981): A17.

75. Tropical Medicine Delegation Report (1979): 59–60.

76. T'ang et al. (1958); cited in Huang (1973): 244–46.

77. This conclusion is from Huang (1973): 246; based on Hsin-hua Hospital Ophthalmology Report (1970).

78. Weisskopf (1981): A17.

79. "Official Discusses Child Care," JPRS 76672 (22 Oct. 1980): 65.

80. "Canjia quanguo gouloubing fangzhi keyan xiezuo huiyi de zhuanjia tichu yao zhongshi xiaoer gouloubing de fangzhi keyan gongzuo" (Participants attending the National Rickets Prevention, Treatment, and Research Conference point out the importance of the work of research and of preventing and treating rickets in children), GMRB, 12 Oct. 1980: 1.

81. "North China Goiter Prevention," FBIS 213 (31 Oct. 1980): R3.

82. "Deputies' Speeches—Tianjin Deputy Zhu Xianyi on Prevention and Treatment of Local Diseases," FBIS 191 (30 Sept. 1980): L12.

83. "Li Desheng, Guo Feng at Liaoning Health Meeting," FBIS 227 (25 Nov. 1981): S3-S4; "Bixu jiaqiang difangbing de fangzhi" (The prevention and treatment of endemic diseases must be strengthened), JKB, 22 Nov. 1981: 1.

84. Ibid. See also, "Difangbingqu shiqiwanren chishang zilaishui" (In endemic disease districts, 170,000 persons are supplied with piped water), HLJRB, 24 Jan. 1982: 1.

85. Environment and Endemic Disease Group, "Woguo Keshanbing fenbu he yi liangshi di xi wei biaozheng de dili huanjing de guanxi" (The relationship between the distribution of Keshan disease and the selenium content of food grains as a factor in the chemical geographical environment), *Dili xuebao* (Acta Geographica Sinica) 36, no. 4 (Dec. 1981): 376.

86. "Fighting Keshan Disease," CR 30, no. 5 (May 1981): 20; "Heilongjiang Keshanbing fabingshu xianzhu xiajiang" (The incidence of Keshan disease in Heilongjiang province has declined markedly), JKB, 11 June 1981: 1; "Pin xi shi Keshanbing bingyin zhi yi" (Selenium deficiency is one of the causes of Keshan disease), RMRB, 18 July 1981: 1.

87. "China Conducts Massive Diabetes Survey," JPRS 77740 (2 Apr. 1981): 14.

88. Tropical Medicine Delegation Report (1979): 30–43; Huang (1973): 246–57; King & Locke (1983): 398–403; Qian Xinzhong (1979): 2; "Shishi xiangzhe haizimen de jiankang" (All the time keep in mind the children's health), RMRB, 9 June 1981: 3.

89. Tropical Medicine Delegation Report (1979): 33–34; "Woguo sichongbing fangzhi gongzuo chengji xianzhu" (Prevention and treatment of filariasis in China has obtained marked results), JKB, 1 Nov. 1981: 1.

90. "For Early and Complete Elimination of Snail Fever," PR 21, no. 44 (3 Nov. 1978): 6. For further information, see Schistosomiasis Delegation Report (1977). Progress during 1979–82 is reported in "Decrease in Incidence of Parasitic, Communicable Diseases," JPRS 81712 (7 Sept. 1982): 35.

91. Details on malaria in China are from Kung & Huang (1976); and Tropical Medicine Delegation Report (1979): 13, 30–31.

92. Lampton (1977): 15; "Shanghai Malaria Prevention," FBIS 166 (24 Aug. 1979): O9.

93. WHO Health Statistics Report (1979): 36.

94. "Wosheng nueji fabinglü liannian xiajiang" (Zhejiang province's malaria incidence rate is declining year after year), ZJRB, 2 Apr. 1981: 1; "Guowuyuan bangongting fachu tongzhi yaoqiu gedi kaizhan kangnue miewen gongzuo" (State Council office issues notice demanding that all areas carry out anti-malaria and mosquito elimination work), ZJRB, 31 Aug. 1981: 1.

95. Maternity and Child Care (1975): 61.

96. "Official Discusses Child Care," JPRS 76672 (22 Oct. 1980): 65-66; "Shishi xiangzhe haizimen de jiankang" (All the time keep in mind the children's health), RMRB, 9 June 1981: 3.

97. For example, see Chalmers (1977): 88–89 on lack of eye protection in an iron and steel complex; Gingras & Geekie (1973): N, on factory noise levels and accidents; and Lindbeck (1975): 11, on lack of safety glasses, protective clothing, and adequate lighting in a machine tool factory.

98. "Forum on Health and Safety at Work," SWB-WER, no. W1033 (30 May 1979): 3.

99. "Need for Measures to Prevent Occupational Diseases," SWB-WER, no. W1033 (30 May 1979): 3.

100. "Industrial Health Standards," SWB-WER, no. W1069 (13 Feb. 1980): 1.

101. "Heilongjiang Oilfield Pollution Control," FBIS 51 (13 Mar. 1980): S2.

102. "Shenyang Meeting on Pollution in Coastal Waters," SWB, no. 6202 (24 Aug. 1979): 17.

103. "First National Meeting on Air Pollution Control Held," FBIS 135 (12 July 1979): L17.

104. E. M. Reingold, "The Lure of a China Experience," *Washington Star*, 19 July 1981: C–3.

105. See, for example, "Wuhan Pollution," CD, 6 Aug. 1981: 4.

106. "Anhui Environmental Pollution," JPRS 74643 (27 Nov. 1979): 49.

107. "PLA Unit Combats Radioactive Pollution from Uranium Mining," FBIS 224 (19 Nov. 1979): L16.

108. "Guangzhou Oil Spillage," FBIS 226 (21 Nov. 1979): P11.

109. M. G. Bloche, "China Discovers Health Perils Accompany Modernization," WP, 19 Aug. 1979: A21.

110. Jay Mathews, "Epidemics Follow Peking's Political Turmoil," WP, 17 May 1977.

111. Data in this paragraph are from Communique on 1980 Economic Plan (1981): K14. Another description of China's health care system is found in Chen Pi-chao (1981): 13–33.

112. Communique on 1979 Economic Plan (1980): 23.

113. K. K. Jain (1972); abstracted in Akhtar (1975): 78. Blakeslee (1973); abstracted in Akhtar (1975): 60.

114. "Health Minister Interviewed on Barefoot Doctors," FBIS 57 (25 Mar. 1981): L18.

115. SSB Indicators (1980): 10; "Medical and Health Work: Convincing Statistics," BR 24, no. 47 (23 Nov. 1981): 8.

116. Maternity and Child Care (1975): 61.

117. "Medical Services," SWB-WER, no. W1053 (17 Oct. 1979): 1. For more detail on the barefoot doctors, see Rogers (1980).

118. Chen Wen-chieh & Ha (1971); abstracted in Akhtar (1975): 109.

119. "Cooperative Medical Service, Barefoot Doctors Service Expanded," JPRS 73272 (23 Apr. 1979): 29.

120. Chen Hai-feng (1979).

121. For more detail see Tsui (1979); Tsui (1980); and Mechanic & Kleinman (1980).

122. Lampton (1977): 238.

123. For a critique of the very low technical level of China's medical and public health system, and discussion of how to raise its quality, see "Ba weisheng shiye jianshe zhongdian fangzai xianyou yiliao jigou shang" (Put the emphasis on existing medical organizations in constructing our public health undertaking), RMRB, 24 Mar. 1981: 3.

124. "Guangdong Cooperative Medical Services," FBIS 202 (17 Oct. 1979): P6.

125. "Health Minister Qian Xinzhong Inspects Rural Guangdong," FBIS 204 (20 Oct. 1980): P1.

126. "Barefoot Doctors Want to be Integral Part of National Health Services," JPRS 76401 (10 Sept. 1980): 2–7.

127. "Yunxu duozhong yiliao xingshi cunzai Pingguoxian xunsu huifu nongcun yiliao weishengwang" (Pingguo county quickly revived its rural medical and public health network after having allowed a variety of forms for medical work), JKB, 22 Oct. 1981: 1.

128. "Reporter Talks with Cui Yueli, Minister of Public Health," JPRS 82049 (21 Oct. 1982): 16–17.

129. For example, see "Rural Doctors," ZGFN, no. 10 (Oct. 1983): 25.

130. "Renzhen zuohao gongshe, dadui liangji weisheng jigou de gaike gongzuo" (Conscientiously carry out the structural reform of the commune and brigade public health organizations), JKB, 4 Sept. 1983: 1.

131. "Renmin Ribao Calls for Stronger Leadership Over City Hygiene," FBIS 143 (24 July 1979): L11.

132. Lardy (1980).

133. Fei (1979): 59.

134. "Relief Work in Tibet," SWB, no. 6316 (11 Jan. 1980): 17.

135. "Large Decrease in Agricultural Production in Tibet in 1979," SWB, no. 6331 (29 Jan. 1980): 12.

136. "Meeting on Relief Work Held in Xinjiang Recently," FBIS 25 (6 Feb. 1981): T3.

137. Details on the food shortages of 1980 in flood and drought areas are from Weisskopf (1981): A17; and Sterba (1981): 1.

138. Sterba (1981): 1.

139. "Death Toll for 1976 Tangshan Earthquake Announced," FBIS 236 (6 Dec. 1979): L16.

Chapter 4

1. "Science, Politics Cannot Be Divorced," FBIS 194 (7 Oct. 1957): BBB3.

2. Barclay et al. (1976): 617–21.

3. Balfour et al. (1950): 73–79; Bowers (1973): 44–45; Croizier (1975): 25–28; Lampton (1977): 13.

4. Zhu Zhengzhi (1980); Liu Zheng (1981a): 5.

5. Sources of PRC population data during the 1950's were exhaustively analyzed in Aird (1961).

6. Infant mortality data for localities prior to 1949 are shown in Table 4.2. See also Li Te Chuan (1957): BBB4. Chu Fu-t'ang (1959): 367. "Science, Politics Cannnot Be Divorced," FBIS 194 (7 Oct. 1957): BBB3.

7. Burnashev (1958): 39; Tsin Hsin-chung (1958): 14.

8. Li Te Chuan (1957): BBB4; Chu Fu-t'ang (1959): 367.

9. Lin Fude (1981): 4.

10. Barclay et al. (1976): 617–18.

11. Chu Fu-t'ang (1959): 371; Teng Chin-hsi (1959): 21.

12. This quotation and all data in this paragraph on infant mortality were reported by Chandrasekhar (1959): 52–54. The use of "key points," which are usually advanced localities with relatively developed statistical systems, to estimate infant mortality rates in the 1950's was described in Liu Changxin & Cang (1980).

13. Confidential data source.

14. Ku et al. (1965).

15. Li Chengrui (1981): 4; Wang Xinfa (1980).

16. Fox Butterfield, "Peking Indictment Accuses Radicals of Killing 34,000," NYT, 17 Nov. 1980: A3; "Anhui Military District Hails Lin-Jiang Verdict," FBIS 21 (2 Feb. 1981): O5; Georges Biannic, "AFP Reports 400,000 Persons Killed in Cultural Revolution," FBIS 25 (5 Feb. 1979): E2; Francis Deron, "Poster Cites 67,400 Killed in Guangxi During Cultural Revolution," JPRS 74099 (20 Aug. 1979): 51; "Guangdong Provincial Delegation Visits Macao," FBIS 113 (10 June 1980): U1.

17. Most of the analysis in this section was first published in Banister & Preston (1981a).

18. Interview with Li Junyao, 13 May 1981, in Bethesda, Md.

19. Li Bing & Li Junyao (1980): 1; Cancer Investigation Report (1980).

20. Frederick P. Li (1980): 3; King & Locke (1983): 385.

21. Coale & Demeny (1966): 20.

22. For further details, see Banister & Preston (1981a); Banister & Preston (1981b); Brass (1975); Martin (1980); and Preston et al. (1980).

23. Song Jian & Li (1980): 62–63.

24. Ling (1981): Table 3.

25. "Improvements in Living Standards Since the Founding of the People's Republic," CR 30, no. 11 (Nov. 1981): 57.

26. For more detail on health and mortality in Tibet, see Banister (1977b): 449–53.

27. Barclay et al. (1976): 620.

28. "Beijingren de shouming duo chang?" (What is the length of life of Beijing's population?), BJRB, 2 May 1980: 1; "Hangzhoushi renmin pingjun shouming chaoguo qishisui" (The life expectancy of the people of Hangzhou exceeds 70 years), GMRB, 3 Feb. 1980: 1; "Wuhan Life Expectancy," JPRS 74829 (27 Dec. 1979): 103; "Shanghai ren yuelai yue changshou" (The people of Shanghai are living longer), WHB, 29 Dec. 1979: 1.

29. Banister & Preston (1981a): 105–7.

30. Preston found that the level of respiratory tuberculosis is a critical determinant of the relationship between mortality at ages 5–40 and mortality at other ages. Preston (1976): Chapter 5.

31. Rural and urban male and female infant mortality rates are calculated from Ling's (1981): Table 3 data using the formula

$$ {}_1q_o = \frac{{}_1m_o}{1 + (1 - {}_1\alpha_o){}_1m_o} $$

where ${}_1\alpha_o = 0.33$.

32. Demographic Yearbook 1976 (1977): 309–10. But Japan may underreport deaths of infants under one day old.

33. Demographic Yearbook 1976 (1977): 320–21.

34. Dong Hengde et al., "Shanghai shiqu kongzhi yinger siwang loubao de cuoshi yu xiaoguo" (Measures for overcoming omissions in the reporting of infant deaths in the Shanghai metropolitan areas and their effectiveness), RKYJ no. 4 (29 July 1982): 49–50.

35. For further details, see Banister (1977b): 451–52.

36. See Banister & Thapa (1981): 41; Thapa & Retherford (1982): 77.

37. Demographic Yearbook 1978 (1979): 290–92.

38. "Sex Ratio of China's Newborns Normal," BR 26, no. 18 (2 May 1983): 9.

39. State Family Planning Commission, *Chart for One-per-thousand-population Fertility Sampling Survey in China*, Beijing, 1984: 100–101.

40. WHO Health Statistics Report (1979): 36.

41. Wu Yingkai (1979): 13–22.

42. Wu Yingkai (1979): 20–22.

43. Atlas of Cancer Mortality (1979); Cancer Investigation Report (1980).

44. For further detail on the reasons for the prevalence of stomach cancer in China, see "New Insight into Stomach Cancer," BR 24, no. 12 (23 Mar. 1981): 30.

45. Tropical Medicine Delegation Report (1979): 49.

46. Atlas of Cancer Mortality (1979).

47. Preston (1976): 93.

Chapter 5

1. This generalization refers to one measure of fertility called the "total fertility rate." For further details, see Chapter 8.

2. Liu Chenlie, "How a Farm Family Gets Its Income," CR 28, no. 11 (Nov. 1979): 40–41.

3. For comparison with Taiwan, see Coombs & Sun (1978) on the relationships between strong son preference and fertility in Taiwan.

4. The analysis in this paragraph and all the information on which it is based come from Parish & Whyte (1978): 180–92. See also Tan Manni (1981): 19.

5. Ibid. Further details on bride price and dowry are found in Wolf & Huang (1980): 75–76 and 266–69; and in Croll (1981): 43–47, 50–54, and 113–17.

6. "Women's Leader Encourages Change in Marriage Customs," FBIS 4 (5 Jan. 1979): E23; "Marriage—The New Way," BR 22, no. 5 (2 Feb. 1979): 4–6; Cao Shunqin, "Love and Marriage," BR 22, no. 10 (9 Mar. 1979): 22.

7. L. L. Chu (1977): 131–35.

8. "Hopei County Lauches Effective Birth Control Campaign," FBIS 29 (11 Feb. 1975): K1-K2. Also in SWB, no. 4831 (15 Feb. 1975): 10–11.

9. Wolf & Huang argue that uxorilocal marriage was not rare in some parts of China in the past, though it was despised as an inferior form of marriage. Wolf & Huang (1980): 94–107, 124–25.

10. L. Liu (1981): 15. For a description of the plight of "five guarantee" elderly persons in one village, see Nee (1981): 8–9.

11. A village study in India suggests that male respondents do not expect to live long enough to retire and depend on their sons, thus the desire for old-age support does not seem to be a major cause of their high fertility (Vlassoff & Vlassoff, 1980). But applying their conclusions to China is doubtful because Chinese villagers may now expect to live longer and because of crucial differences regarding landholding patterns and out-migration of sons. Also, women may feel more need than men for support from their sons. Similar research is needed in Chinese villages to determine how much this concern motivates childbearing there. See also Holm (1975) for evidence that social security programs have a measurable negative effect on fertility.

12. "Shanghai Commune Members Receive Retirement Allowance," FBIS 223 (16 Nov. 1979): O12.

13. For example, a prosperous commune in the suburbs of Beijing. Liu Zheng (1981a): 23.

14. "National Forum on Population Growth Opens in Peking," FBIS 231 (30 Nov. 1978): E20.

15. For further information on social security for the elderly in China, see L. Liu (1981).

16. Hou Wenruo (1981): 73; Wang Ziying et al. (1981): 71–72.

17. "Beijing Ribao Explains Average Per Capita GNP," FBIS 223 (17 Nov. 1980): L24.

18. Central Educational Research Institute, "Investment Out of Proportion: It is Difficult to Develop Education," WHB, 18 Nov. 1980: 3. China's 1983 national

income was reported to be 467.3 billion yuan in 1983 prices, equivalent to 458 yuan per capita, or U.S. $232 at the 1983 official exchange rate. Communique on 1983 Economic Plan (1984): K2.

19. Knodel & van de Walle (1979).

20. State Council Population Office (1983): 338, 350–53.

21. See Caldwell (1978) on reproductive decision-making in the traditional peasant family.

22. Croll (1981): 140, 159–64.

23. Tian Xueyuan (1981): 53.

24. The complex workings of the grain distribution system and its pronatalist effects in one village are described in detail in Nee (1981): 12, 28–31.

25. Parish & Whyte (1978): 65–71, 139–40.

26. Parish & Whyte (1978): 142.

27. "National Forum on Population Growth Opens in Peking," FBIS 231 (30 Nov. 1978): E20.

28. "Hunan Announces Planned Parenthood Regulations," FBIS 124 (26 June 1979): P2.

29. "Anhui Report on Planned Parenthood Policies," FBIS printout, 18 Apr. 1979, mimeo.

30. "New Planned Parenthood Policy for Guangdong Established," JPRS 72770 (6 Feb. 1979): 30; "Coverage of Guizhou Planned Parenthood Meeting," FBIS 225 (23 Nov. 1981): Q1. See also CNA, no. 1163 (14 Sept. 1979): 7.

31. Linda Mathews, "China Offers Bonuses, Extra Food to Parents Who Stop at Only One Child," *Los Angeles Times*, 2 Apr. 1979: 2.

32. Knodel & van de Walle (1979); Acharya (1981): 12–13; Dixon (1975).

33. For details on historical precedents for the 1950 Marriage Law, details of the law, judicial interpretations of stipulations in the law, and attempts to implement the law, see Meijer (1971).

34. Chou En-lai, "Government Administration Council Directive on the Investigation of Conditions Relating to the Implementation of the Marriage Law," CB, no. 136 (10 Nov. 1951): 13–15.

35. National Committee for the Thorough Implementation of the Marriage Law, "Outline of Propaganda on the Thorough Implementation of the Marriage Law," CB, no. 236 (10 Mar. 1953): 22–29.

36. Parish & Whyte (1978): 135. On cases of men taking concubines in 1980, see "Guangdong Marriage Law," FBIS 60 (30 Mar. 1981): P5.

37. The evolution of new mixed models of mate choice in China is documented in Croll (1981): 24–40. Further information on mate choice is found in Parish & Whyte (1978): 169–80; and Tan Manni (1981): 17–19.

38. "Marriage Law Adopted by Fifth National People's Congress," FBIS 184 (19 Sept. 1980): L24. The continuing problem of family violence against women is described in the following sources: "'Jilin Daily' on Arranged Marriage, Old Customs," JPRS 72653 (18 Jan. 1979): 14; "Anhui Ribao Discusses Marriage, Family Relations," FBIS 79 (23 Apr. 1979): O1.

39. Birdsall (1974): 4–5.

40. State Council Population Office (1983): 350–53. See Emerson (1980): 15–21 for an analysis of PRC women in nonagricultural employment.

41. State Council Population Office (1983): 353. See Birdsall (1974): 3–4 on relationships between female employment and fertility in developing countries, and see the other sources abstracted in her bibliography for the argument that only incompatibility between work and home activities lowers fertility. Further theoretical elaboration of the women's role incompatibility explanation for fertility decline is found in Mason & Palan (1981): 551–54, 566–73.

42. See Thorborg (1978): 540–55 for documentation of this problem.

43. See Thorborg (1978): 555–67 on women and overwork in agriculture. See also CCAS (1972): 282–84; Nee (1981): 34–35; and Parish (1984): 227, 234 on women's double burden.

44. Parish notes that women in China complain that raising children is a great burden to them, even when they have a large extended family to help out with child care. Parish (1984): 227.

45. Dernberger & Fasenfest (1978): 8, 12, 33.

46. Data in this paragraph are from Emerson (1980): Table 1.

47. Sun Keliang, "Funü jiuye yu kongzhi renkou" (The employment of women and population control), ZGFN, no. 11 (15 Nov. 1980): 28.

48. Chen Muhua (1979): 2.

49. "Guanxin qunzhong shenghuo jiakuai zhuzhai jianshe" (Be concerned about the livelihood of the masses; accelerate the construction of residential housing), RMRB, 6 Oct. 1979: 3.

50. R. Chang (1979): 6.

51. According to interviews with refugees from PRC urban areas in 1977–78, less than one-fifth of housing was privately owned in big cities such as Shanghai and Beijing, while one-half to two-thirds was privately owned in small towns and county seats. Parish (1984): note 31.

52. Banister (1977a): 268.

53. Banister (1977b): 125–32, 174–80, 229–31, 235–49, 263–65, 291, 305–6, 356–60, and 417.

54. See the theory and evidence presented in Janowitz (1976) and Caldwell (1979): 413.

55. See, for example, Birdsall (1974): 2–3 and sources abstracted in her article; Caldwell & Caldwell (1978): 7–8; Janowitz (1976); and Bagozzi & Van Loo (1978).

56. Germain (1975): 193.

57. A. K. Jain (1981).

58. Freedman et al. (1977): 14–18.

59. Parish & Whyte (1978): 83.

60. Communique on 1982 Census (1982): K3.

61. Most primary source data on enrollments are compiled in Pepper (1980): 6. See also Tso (1978b): 15; Emerson (1973): 94–97; SSB Indicators (1980): 9; Communique on 1980 Economic Plan (1981): K14; and Liu Zheng (1981a): 10.

62. "Secondary and Primary Schools," CNA, no. 868 (21 Jan. 1972): 7. Also Price (1970): 214.

63. Yu Wang & Xiao (1984): 7.

64. "Special Feature/Education: Facts and Figures," BR 23, no. 1 (7 Jan. 1980): 18.

65. See Becker & Lewis (1973) and Willis (1973).

66. Parish & Whyte (1978): 54.

67. Parish & Whyte (1978): 151–52.

68. "Mianxian cong shiji chufa zuohao jihua shengyu" (Mian county does well in family planning work by starting from reality), RMRB, 16 Aug. 1981: 1.

Chapter 6

1. For a thorough analysis of fertility policy in China from 1949 through 1971, see Aird (1972).

2. From sources in Warsaw, quoted in "Communist China—the Population Problem," *Current Notes on International Affairs* (Canberra) 29, no. 11 (Nov. 1958): 717. Discussed in Aird (1972).

3. Details in this paragraph are from Aird (1972): 253–61. See also Hou Wenruo (1981): 60.

4. "Chia-ch'iang pi-yün yao-chü kung-ying kung-tso" (Strengthen the work of supplying contraceptives), TKP Beijing, 5 Feb. 1958.

5. "Reports on Birth Control Work Submitted to Ministry of Public Health," SCMP, no. 1758 (25 Apr. 1958): 17–18.

6. K. T. Ts'ai, Y. T. Wu, and H. C. Wu, "Suction Curettage for Induced Abortion; Preliminary Report of 30 Cases; Preliminary Report of 300 Cases," *Chung-hua fu-ch'an-k'e tsa-chih* (Chinese Journal of Obstetrics and Gynecology) 6, no. 5 (Oct. 1958): 445–49.

7. For details of Chinese press and radio commentary on fertility policy during the Great Leap Forward, see Aird (1972): 275–86; and L. L. Chu (1977): 13–16.

8. For details of press coverage during the second campaign, see Aird (1972): 287–304.

9. Orleans (1973).

10. Cui (1982): 4; Hou Wenruo (1981): 63.

11. Cui (1982): 4.

12. Worth (n.d.), cited in Parish (1976): 7.

13. Orleans (1981): 10.

14. Meijer (1971): 164.

15. Aird (1972): 301.

16. "Minzhengju zhaokai huiyi xuexi zhengce jiaoliu jingyan wei mingnian shishi xin hunyin dengji banfa zuo zhunbei" (The Civil Affairs Bureau held a meeting to study the policy and to exchange experiences in preparation for implementing the registration method under the new Marriage Law next year), TJRB, 16 Dec. 1980: 1.

17. Whyte (1979): 50.

18. "Xizang Drafts National Marriage Law Modifications," FBIS 84 (1 May 1981): Q5; Tan Manni (1981): 20.

19. Wang Deyi (1980): 42–43.

20. Chen Pi-chao (1980a): Table 5; Chen Pi-chao (1980b): 108–12; Chen Pi-chao (1981): Table 6; Chen Pi-chao & Kols (1982): Table 7; Chen Pi-chao (1982): 211; Wu Banglan (1981a): 18.

21. Barclay et al. (1976): 609.

22. For a compilation and analysis of long-term refugee data on ages at marriage, see Parish & Whyte (1978): 163. For a compilation of survey data on age at marriage in China throughout this century, see Croll (1981): 66–71.

23. He Mi (1981): 32.

24. "Marriage Law Adopted by Fifth National People's Congress," FBIS 184 (19 Sept. 1980): L22. Translation corrected with reference to the Chinese version of the Marriage Law as published in GMRB, 16 Sept. 1980: 2.

25. "State Council Issues Circular on Marriage Law," FBIS 244 (17 Dec. 1980): L15-L16.

26. "Sharp Population Increase Anticipated," Beijing Xinhua news release, 12 Jan. 1981, item no. 011224: p-19.

27. Wang Daohan, "Government Work Report at the Third Session of the Seventh Shanghai Municipal People's Congress, 10 Apr. 1981," WHB, 18 Apr. 1981: 2.

28. Tan Manni (1981): 17, 20.

29. "Excerpts of Speeches by NPC Deputies at Panel Discussions," FBIS 179 (12 Sept. 1980): L20.

30. "Peng Zhen's NPC Standing Committee Work Report," FBIS 186, Supplement 76 (23 Sept. 1980): 39.

31. See, for example, "Li Xiuzhen Talks on Family Planning," JPRS 77401 (17 Feb. 1981): 49–50; "Beijing Sets Up Premarital Counseling Service," FBIS 32 (18 Feb. 1981): R3.

32. "Bixu jianjue kongzhi renkou de zengzhang" (Population growth must be resolutely controlled), LNRB, 24 Sept. 1981: 1.

33. "Woguo renkou de jing, xi, you" (The shocking, heartening, and worrying aspects of China's population), ZGQN, no. 6 (11 June 1982): 56.

34. Fertility Survey (1984): 174–82.

35. "Renmin Ribao Editorial Praises New Marriage Law," FBIS 187 (24 Sept. 1980): L3.

36. "Marriage Law Adopted by Fifth National People's Congress," FBIS 184 (19 Sept. 1980): L22; "Kang Keqing Urges Implementation of Marriage Law," FBIS 183 (18 Sept. 1980): L14; "Renmin Ribao, Zhongguo Qingnian Bao Extol Marriage Law," FBIS 182 (17 Sept. 1980): L33.

37. "Sharp Population Increase Anticipated," Beijing Xinhua news release, 12 Jan. 1981, item no. 011224: p-19.

38. "Minzhengju zhaokai huiyi xuexi zhengce jiaoliu jingyan wei mingnian shishi xin hunyin dengji banfa zuo zhunbei" (The Civil Affairs Bureau held a meeting to study the policy and to exchange experiences in preparation for implementing the registration method under the new Marriage Law next year), TJRB, 16 Dec. 1980: 1.

39. Wang Deyi (1980): 42–43.

40. "Wanhun zengjia hunjia wanyu zengjia chanjia" (Those who marry late receive additional leave, and those who begin childbearing late receive additional maternity leave), RMRB, 27 Aug. 1981: 3; "Yunchengxian dui jihua shengyu zuochu buchong guiding" (Yuncheng county formulates supplemental regulations on family planning), *Shanxi ribao* (Shanxi Daily), 22 Sept. 1981: 3.

41. Wu Banglan (1981a): 17.

42. "Hunyin dengji gongzuo ying zhuyi shenme" (What should marriage registration work emphasize?), ZGQNB, 12 Sept. 1981: 2.

43. Wu Banglan (1981b): 2; "Guangan pupian jianli jihua shengyu zerenzhi"

(Guangan county establishes the family planning responsibility system throughout the county), SCRB, 12 Feb. 1982: 1; "Wei shixian wosheng jinnian jihua shengyu renwu zuochu xin gongxian" (Make new contributions to accomplish the family planning task of Shandong province this year), DZRB, 15 Feb. 1982: 1, 4.

44. See, for example, Wu Banglan (1981a): 17; Cui (1982): 6.

45. H. Y. Tien (1983). Based on Li Ruo and Hang Ping, "Jiangsu sheng sandai ren shengyu qingkuang diaocha" (The fertility of three generations in Jiangsu province: an investigation), *Nanjing Daxue xuebao* (Nanjing University journal), special edition on population (1981): 35–43; and Sun Xinyuan, "Woguo shengyu de jijie guilu he jianshao renkou shu tongji wucha de guanxi" (Seasonality of births in China and the reduction of error in population statistics), *Nanjing Daxue xuebao* (Nanjing University journal), special edition on population (1981): 56–71.

46. "U.N. World Population Conference: China's Views on Major Issues of World Population," PR 17, no. 35 (30 Aug. 1974): 6–9.

47. "China Figures Withheld," *People* 1, no. 5 (1974): 39. (Special issue on the World Population Conference.)

48. There is confusion on the date of this decision. Hou Wenruo (1981): 66, stated that in 1974 a national circular was issued to the effect that contraceptives were to be supplied free of charge.

49. Chen Pi-chao (1980b): 107.

50. Chen Pi-chao (1981): 2; Hou Wenruo (1981): 65; Kirin Medical College Revolutionary Committee (1971): 352.

51. Wang Nairong (1981); Chen Pi-chao & Miller (1975): 354; Y. C. Yu (1979): 128.

52. This quotation was attributed to Premier Zhou Enlai. See Cheng Du (1981): 3.

53. For details on the practical applications of the slogan "wan, xi, shao," see H. Y. Tien (1980a) and Chen Pi-Chao (1980b).

54. Chen Pi-chao (1981): 3. The policy being popularized in early 1978 was "one couple, two children." See "Anhwei County Successfully Promotes Birth Control," FBIS 20 (30 Jan. 1978): G2; Tso (1978a): 20.

55. On the organization of the family planning program, see Wang Nairong (1981) and Chen Pi-chao (1981): 34–41.

56. See, for example, Liu Jo-ching, "Planned Control of Population Growth," JPRS 71627 (7 Aug. 1978): 112; "Fukien Establishes New Planned Parenthood Leadership Group," FBIS 152 (7 Aug. 1978): G3; Chen Pi-chao (1981): 41.

57. See L. L. Chu (1977): 61–63 on group discussions and home visits to promote family planning.

58. Zhejiang Regulations (1982): 3.

59. The use of rural maternal and child health workers to insert and remove IUD's was described in "How Woman and Child Health Work is Promoted in Our County," CMJ, new series 2, no. 3 (May 1976): 174.

60. "Sinkiang County Medical Education," FBIS 60 (28 Mar. 1973): H4; "Peking Hails Barefoot Doctors in Kiangsi," FBIS 128 (1 July 1976): G3.

61. "Gansu Planned Parenthood," JPRS 80550 (12 Apr. 1982): 68.

62. Li Xiuzhen (1980).

63. Most details on steroid contraceptives in China come from Djerassi (1974a) and Djerassi (1974b).

64. On local problems with the supply of birth control pills and other contraceptives, see "Biyun yaoju huoyuan buzu xiwang youguan bumen jiayi jiejue" (Contraceptives are in short supply; we hope the pertinent departments will solve the problem), TJRB, 23 Oct. 1980: 2; and "Qing ge yaodian huifu biyun yaoju zhuangui" (All pharmacies please restore a contraceptive distribution counter), JKB, 14 Mar. 1982: 1.

65. Djerassi (1974a); Djerassi (1974b); PIACT (1980): 4–5; Communique on the Fertility Survey (1983): 15.

66. PIACT (1980): 5. This organization, based in Seattle, is responsible for carrying out the UN Fund for Population Activities' five contraceptive production projects in China.

67. PIACT (1980): 3.

68. Faundes & Luukkainen (1972): 175; "One-man Technique of Ligation of Fallopian Tubes Described," JPRS 65903 (10 Oct. 1975): 22-26.

69. "Simon Trust in China," International Planned Parenthood Federation Open File for the two weeks ending 11 July 1980: 11; "Hunan Birth Control Meeting," JPRS 79765 (30 Dec. 1981): 152.

70. For an analysis of the demographic impact of sterilization and the importance of the age of the woman being sterilized in assessing the operation's impact in reducing her completed fertility, see Nortman (1980).

71. All these data are from H. Y. Tien (1980a): 71.

72. Lyle (1980): 559.

73. Chen Pi-chao (1980c): Table V–4. Both figures are for 1977.

74. "Sichuan shinian zuo nanzha shoushu yiqianwanli" (Sichuan performed ten million vasectomies in ten years), JKB, 16 Jan. 1983: 1.

75. Ibid., and "Male Sterilization," FBIS 171 (31 Aug. 1979): Q2.

76. H. Y. Tien (1980a): 72.

77. Chen Pi-chao (1981): Table 3.

78. Lyle (1980): 558.

79. See, for example, "Dingyuanxian geji lingdao tong zhua tong guan jihua shengyu gongzuo" (The leadership at all levels in Dingyuan county takes total control of planned birth work), RMRB, 17 Sept. 1981: 3.

80. Faundes & Luukkainen (1972): 173–74.

81. PIACT (1980): 3.

82. Cunningham (1980): 16.

83. Data on IUD use by age and parity in four locations were reported by H. Y. Tien (1980a): 69.

84. Analyzed by Banister (1977a): 285; and Banister (1977b): 149–50. Shanghai 1972 abortion data were reported in Han Suyin (1973): 12. The number of births recorded in Shanghai Municipality for 1972 was reported in Djerassi (1974a): 28. Tianjin data from Lyle (1980): 559; Chengdu data from H. Y. Tien (1980a): 73.

85. Chen Pi-chao (1980b): 111; Chen Pi-chao (1981): 50–53. For example, in

1977 Xinhui county, Guangdong, reported 3,700 abortions and 15,600 births; Taoyuan county, Hunan, reported 3,800 abortions and 12,500 births. Guangdong province reported declining births, from 1.4 million in 1973 to 1 million in 1977, while abortions numbered 250,000–300,000 per year during that time.

86. Personal communication from Siri Melchior.

87. Communique on the Fertility Survey (1983): 15.

88. Ibid.

89. On the use of contraceptive sterilization throughout the world, see Stepan et al. (1981).

90. "Quanguo jihua shengyu xuanchuanyue chengji da xiaoguo hao" (The nationwide family planning propaganda month obtained great success and good results), JKB, 27 Feb. 1983: 1; "Qian Xinzhong on Family Size," FBIS 43 (3 Mar. 1983): K11; "Qian Xinzhong zai jihua shengyu keyan gongzuo zuotanhui shang qiangdiao jihua shengyu keyan yao tong weisheng bumen xiezuo" (At the Family Planning Research Work Symposium, Qian Xinzhong stressed that scientific research on family planning must be conducted in collaboration with public health departments), JKB, 14 Aug. 1983: 1.

91. PIACT (1980): 5; Communique on the Fertility Survey (1983): 15.

92. Larson (1981): 8–9.

93. "Quanguo qianfenzhiyi renkou shengyulü chouyang diaocha xunwen tigang" (Questions for interviews in the nationwide one per thousand population sample fertility survey), Nationwide Sample Fertility Survey Material no. 3, 1 Sept. 1982. See also Caldwell & Srinivasan (1984): 76–77.

94. Communique on the Fertility Survey (1983): 15.

95. Larson (1981): 4; and U.S. Bureau of the Census unpublished tabulations (1984). The contraceptive use rate for China is available only for married women ages 15–49, which is not strictly comparable with the proportion of married women ages 15–44 using contraception. Hong Kong, 1977, reported a contraceptive use rate of 76.7 percent of married women 15–44 and 71.9 percent of married women 15–49. Assuming the same relationship for the other countries gives the following estimated contraceptive use rates for married women ages 15–49: South Korea 1979, 51 percent; Japan 1968, 64 percent; Taiwan 1981, 66 percent; Singapore 1978, 67 percent; China 1982, 69 percent; and Hong Kong 1977, 72 percent.

96. One source claims that "A few unmarried women get pregnant in the urban areas but they are also given a free abortion at a hospital. Since there are no private practitioners in China, induced abortions at a high price are out of the question." Yan Renying, "Family Planning," BR, no. 10 (9 Mar. 1979): 24.

97. For details see Murray Feshbach, "The Soviet Union: Population Trends and Dilemmas," *Population Bulletin* 37, no. 3 (Aug. 1982): 25; Tomas Frejka, "Induced Abortion and Fertility: A Quarter Century of Experience in Eastern Europe," PDR 9, no. 3 (Sept. 1983): 494–520; and "Women Who Average Six Abortions," *London Times*, 11 May 1981: 7.

98. Qian Lingjuan, Xu Bing, and Huang Shuyuan, "Beijingshi de renkou fazhan qingkuang he dangqian de renwu" (The population growth of Beijing and our present tasks), RKYJ, no. 1 (Apr. 1980): 39–44.

99. "Beijing Sets Up Premarital Counseling Service," FBIS 32 (18 Feb. 1981): R3.
100. Qiu et al. (1984): 143.
101. Lyle (1980): 560.
102. This important shift was described in L. L. Chu (1977): 85.
103. For example, see Banister (1977b): 241; Kane (1975): 79-83; Chin (1975): 71; supra note 99.

Chapter 7

1. "'Tianjin Daily' on Planned Parenthood," SWB, no. 6334 (1 Feb. 1980): 7.
2. "Discussion on Family Planning," BR 22, no. 28 (13 July 1979): 22–23.
3. Discussed in Chen Pi-chao (1981): 2.
4. "Beijing Radio Urges Strict Population Control," FBIS 31 (16 Feb. 1982): K14.
5. "Population," CNA, no. 1163 (14 Sept. 1979): 5–6.
6. "Jinyibu kongzhi renkou zengzhang sudu" (Further control the population growth rate), RMRB, 27 Jan. 1979: 1.
7. "Renda daibiao fayan yaoqiu jihua shengyu ying lifa" (Deputies to the National People's Congress demand that a family planning law be enacted), JKB, 13 Dec. 1981: 1.
8. "Hua Guofeng, 26 February Report," FBIS 52, Supp. 1 (16 Mar. 1978): 27.
9. On the various "single-child rates" and their definitions, see Qie Jianwei (1981): 59–60.
10. Li Xiuzhen (1980): 3–5, 47.
11. "Chen Muhua, Bo Yibo Speak at Family Planning Meeting," FBIS 24 (4 Feb. 1980): L2.
12. Chen Muhua (1981): 2; "Guojia jihua shengyu weiyuanhui shouci quanti huiyi zai jing zhaokai jixu tichang yidui fufu zhi shengyu yige haizi" (The State Family Planning Commission held its first plenary meeting in Beijing; one child per couple continues to be promoted), JKB, 7 June 1981: 1.
13. Li Jieping & Shao (1984): 145.
14. "Quanguo jihua shengyu xuanchuanyue chengji da xiaoguo hao" (The nationwide family planning propaganda month obtained great success and good results), JKB, 27 Feb. 1983: 1; State Family Planning Commission, "Do Family Planning Work in a Chinese Way," *China Population Newsletter* 2, no. 1 (Mar. 1985): 1.
15. "Shanghai Regulations on Family Planning," SWB, no. 6228 (25 Sept. 1979): 14.
16. "Renmin Ribao Discusses Dazhai as Agricultural Model," FBIS 197 (10 Oct. 1979): L17; "Guizhou Instructions on Relaxing Rural Policies," FBIS 142 (22 July 1980): Q3; "Adieu Communes?" CNA, no. 1192 (24 Oct. 1980): 2–7; "Obstructing Implementation of Policy on Private Plots Criticized," JPRS 74800 (20 Dec. 1979): 51–53.
17. On the variety of production responsibility systems in agriculture, see "Renmin Ribao on Fixing Output Quotas on Household Basis," FBIS 218 (7 Nov. 1980): L21.
18. USDA (1981): 3. A survey of 10,282 households in 23 provinces indicated

that in 1979, private sector activities accounted for 36 percent of the peasants' total income, up considerably from 1978. Xinhua, 2 Jan. 1981. Discussed in Dernberger (1984): 120–22.

19. Zhongguo nongcun fazhan wenti yanjiuzu (China Rural Development Research Group), "Anhui Chuxian diqu 'shuang bao dao hu' hou de fazhan qushi" (Development trends in Chuxian prefecture of Anhui province after implementation of the system of "fixing farm output quotas for each household and assigning households full responsibility for task completion"), in *Zhongguo nongye nianjian 1982* (Agricultural yearbook of China, 1982), Beijing, 1983: 262.

20. "Guizhou Instructions on Relaxing Rural Policies," FBIS 142 (22 July 1980): Q1-Q2; "Renmin Ribao on Fixing Output Quotas on Household Basis," FBIS 218 (7 Nov. 1980): L21-L29.

21. "Hunan Radio Commentary on Responsibility Systems," FBIS 90 (11 May 1981): P6.

22. "Adieu Communes?" CNA, no. 1192 (24 Oct. 1980): 6.

23. See, for example, Zheng Guizhen (1983): 26; and Zhao Liren & Zhu (1983): 39.

24. "Jilin Telephone Conference on Family Planning," FBIS 193 (3 Oct. 1979): S1-S2; "Tianjin Issues Decision on Family Planning," FBIS 89 (8 May 1981): R2-R3.

25. Liu Zheng (1981b): 5–6.

26. Gui Feng (1982): 2.

27. "Fujian Scotches Family Planning Policy Rumors," FBIS 244 (21 Dec. 1981): O2.

28. PRC delegation to the 29th session, Economic Commission for Asia and the Far East, Tokyo, 16 Apr. 1973, reported in "PRC Representative on Population Issue," FBIS 74 (17 Apr. 1973): A9.

29. PRC delegation to 1974 World Population Conference, Bucharest, reported in "China's Views on Major Issues of World Population," PR 17, no. 35 (30 Aug. 1974): 9.

30. "K'ang K'o-ch'ing Delivers Report to PRC Women's Congress," JPRS 72292 (22 Nov. 1978): 57.

31. "Hua Guofeng's Speech at the Third Session of the Fifth National People's Congress, September 7, 1980," BR 23, no. 38 (22 Sept. 1980): 18.

32. "Excerpts of Speeches by NPC Deputies at Panel Discussions: Shanghai Deputy Qian Xinzhong: Control the Size of the Population," FBIS 184 (19 Sept. 1980): L13.

33. "Dui wosheng jihua shengyu gongzuo de jidian xiwang" (A few expectations concerning planned parenthood work in Guangdong), editorial, NFRB, 6 Oct. 1980: 1.

34. Speech to the International Conference on Family Planning in the 1980's, Jakarta, May 1981, "China Takes Steps to Limit Growth of Its Population," *Popline* 3, no. 5 (May 1981): 4.

35. "Spokesman on Family Planning Work Policy," FBIS 151 (4 Aug. 1983): K8.

36. Muñoz-Paraiso (1978): 13.

37. Epstein (1980): 22.

38. Chen Pi-chao (1981): 41.

39. H. Y. Tien, 20 Apr. 1982, letter to the editor of the *New York Times*, published 2 May 1982.

40. "Shanghai Holds Planned Parenthood Meeting," FBIS 187 (26 Sept. 1978): G4; "Yunnan Daily Urges Further Work in Planned Parenthood," FBIS 239 (12 Dec. 1978): J3; "People's Daily Editorial Stresses Planned Parenthood Work," FBIS 135 (13 July 1978): E10.

41. "Gongzuo zuode heqing heli jiu neng dedao qunzhong zhichi" (When work is done reasonably, it will gain the support of the masses), JHSYB, 13 Apr. 1984: 1.

42. "Hunan Family Planning Congress Concludes 28 Oct., Commentary Stresses One-Child Policy," FBIS 212 (1 Nov. 1983): P3.

43. "Guangdong Family Planning Drive Set for May, June," FBIS 91 (9 May 1984): P1.

44. Joint Investigation Team (1983): 2.

45. See, for example, "Guizhou Couple Punished for Having Third Child," SWB, no. 6406 (28 Apr. 1980): 3; "Worker Sacked for Third Child," CD, no. 469 (28 Jan. 1983): 3; and "Party Cadre Punished for Having Third Child," JPRS 84590 (24 Oct. 1983): 49.

46. "Shaanxi Holds Conference on Family Planning Work," FBIS 16 (24 Jan. 1984): T2.

47. "Shanxi Promulgates Planned Parenthood Regulations," JPRS 82678 (19 Jan. 1983): 64.

48. State Family Planning Commission Investigation Team, "Gongzuo zuo xi nongmin huanying" (Meticulous work is welcomed by the peasants), RMRB, 19 July 1981: 3; Song Youtian (1982): 3.

49. "Shenyang Brigade Ties Birth Control to Economics," FBIS 213 (4 Nov. 1981): S4.

50. "Qidingshan gongshe jianli jihua shengyu zherenzhi" (Qidingshan Commune establishes the family planning responsibility system), LNRB, 3 Jan. 1983: 1.

51. Peng Zhiliang and Xin Dan, "Sichuansheng Pengxian shixing jieyu jishu zherenzhi de jingyan" (Experiences of Peng County, Sichuan province, in carrying out the birth control operations responsibility system), RKYJ, no. 6 (29 Nov. 1982): 29–31.

52. "Marriage Law Adopted by Fifth National People's Congress," FBIS 184 (19 Sept. 1980): L22-L23.

53. Zhu Zhuo (1980): 15–16; Xu Xuehan (1981): 3; Hou Wenruo (1981): 76; Lei Xueyuan (1982): 84–85; "Sheng zhengfu zhaokai quansheng jihua shengyu gongzuo huiyi" (The Yunnan provincial government held a provincial family planning work conference), YNRB, 14 Mar. 1982: 1; "Sichuan Discusses Planned Parenthood Work," FBIS 100 (24 May 1982): Q1; "Qinghai Issues Provision on Birth Control," FBIS 115 (15 June 1982): T4.

54. "Zhonghua renmin gongheguo xianfa" (The Constitution of the PRC), GWYGB, no. 394 (7 Feb. 1983): 860.

55. "Guangming Daily on Current Problems in Drafting Laws," FBIS 3 (4 Jan. 1979): E7.

56. "Kiangsi Meetings Discuss Questions of Planned Parenthood," FBIS 152 (7 Aug. 1978): G4.

57. See analysis in L. L. Chu (1977): 64–71.

58. Yuan Zongjie, "Jihua shengyu gongzuo buneng songxie sixiang jiaoyu gongzuo bixu jianchi" (Family planning work cannot slacken and ideological education must persist), NXRB, 18 Mar. 1983: 2.

59. "Quanguo jihua shengyu xuanchuanyue chengji da xiaoguo hao" (The nationwide family planning propaganda month achieved great success and good results), JKB, 27 Feb. 1983: 1.

60. Shen Xiaozeng, "Zai quanqu jihua shengyu xuanchuanyue guangbo dongyuan dahui shang de jianghua" (Speech at the Ningxia Regional Family Planning Propaganda Month Broadcasting and Mobilization Meeting), NXRB, 29 Dec. 1982: 1; "National Planned Parenthood Month Begins," FBIS 3 (5 Jan. 1983): K22; "'Yunnan Ribao' on Importance of Family Planning," JPRS 82886 (16 Feb. 1983): 39–41.

61. Bai Rubing, "Quan dang dongyuan dali xuanchuan he shixing jihua shengyu" (Let the entire party be mobilized to publicize and carry out planned birth with great effort), DZRB, 26 Dec. 1982: 1.

62. "Sichuan Compiles Regulations on Planned Parenthood," JPRS 84176 (23 Aug. 1983): 31.

63. The often-used phrase "technical measures" is defined here: "Measures to control births should be carried out while the publicity work to encourage family planning is under way. On the basis of widespread publicity work and the mobilization drive, technical measures, such as installing intrauterine devices, performing ligation surgery and taking remedial measures for unplanned pregnancies must be firmly carried out, so that there will be more one-child families and more families will pledge to bear only one child." Source: "Zhejiang Begins Family Planning Propaganda Drive," FBIS 222 (16 Nov. 1983): O5–O6.

64. "Hebei Provincial Telephone Meeting on Family Planning," JPRS 83105 (21 Mar. 1983): 119. These words were also attributed to a "leading central comrade" in "Shanxi's Huo Shilian Stresses Family Planning," JPRS 82880 (16 Feb. 1983): 43.

65. "Guangdong Radio on County's Family Planning Work," FBIS 157 (12 Aug. 1983): P2.

66. "Shandong: Need for Family Planning Emphasized," JPRS 83105 (21 Mar. 1983): 121.

67. "Sheng jihua shengyu ban fuzeren dui jizhe shuo zhi yunxu liuzhongren shengyu diertai" (The responsible person of the provincial family planning office told this reporter that only six categories of persons may have a second child), NFRB, 5 Jan. 1983: 1.

68. "'Text' of Zhao Work Report at Sixth NPC," FBIS 122 (23 June 1983): K11.

69. For example, see "Tianjin's Penalties for Unplanned Births," SWB, no. 6208 (1 Sept. 1979): 13; and "Jilin Telephone Conference on Family Planning," FBIS 193 (3 Oct. 1979): S1-S2.

70. Mathews (1980): A-23.

71. Liu Yan, "Gei haizi luo hu jing yao gai shisange gongzhang" (It took thirteen official seals to register my child), GMRB, 4 Feb. 1982: 1.

72. "Fujian Stresses Importance of Family Planning," JPRS 82880 (16 Feb. 1983): 36.

73. "Yutun dadui qianding hetong jianli zerenzhi wuge baogandui meiyou jihua wai shengyu" (Yutun brigade signs contracts and establishes a responsibility system; five teams that fix output for each household have no unplanned birth), LNRB, 8 Jan. 1983: 1; "Hebei Family Planning Issues Discussed," FBIS 124 (27 June 1983): R1.

74. Li Xiuzhen (1980): 3–5, 47.

75. "Obstructing Implementation of Policy on Private Plots Criticized," JPRS 74800 (20 Dec. 1979): 51–53.

76. For more detail, see Aird (1978): 243–45.

77. For further details see Banister (1984a) and Banister (1984c). See also "Jining diqu dali tuixing jihua shengyu zerenzhi" (Jining prefecture promotes planned parenthood responsibility systems with great effort), DZRB, 12 Sept. 1981: 3; "Tansuo xin jingyan jiejue xin wenti" (Explore new experiences and solve new problems), YNRB, 12 Oct. 1981: 3; and "Wosheng jinnian de jingji gongzuo yingdang zenyang zhua?" (How should Zhejiang carry out this year's economic work?), ZJRB, 31 Jan. 1982: 3.

78. "Jiu youguan nongcun jihua shengyu wenti da duzhe wen" (Questions and answers on the problems of rural family planning), LNRB, 6 Jan. 1983: 3.

79. Yang Xiaobing (1983): 25–26.

80. Qian Xinzhong, "Xie zai jihua shengyu xuanchuanyue qianmian" (Some words written prior to the family planning propaganda month), JKB, 19 Dec. 1982: 1.

81. "Minzhengju zhaokai huiyi xuexi zhengce jiaoliu jingyan wei mingnian shishi xin hunyin dengji banfa zuo zhunbei" (The Civil Affairs Bureau held a meeting to study the policy and exchange experiences in preparation for implementing the registration method under the New Marriage Law next year), TJRB, 16 Dec. 1980: 1.

82. Population Research Delegation (1981): 47–48.

83. "Population: Jiangxi," SWB, no. 6228 (25 Sept. 1979): 16.

84. "Sifabu fachu wenjian yansu zhichu feifa wei funü qu huan pohuai jihua shengyu qingjie elie houguo yanzhongche yifa yancheng" (The Ministry of Justice issued a document which emphasized that those who illegally remove IUD's for women to sabotage family planning with vile and serious consequences will be severely punished according to law), GMRB, 27 Aug. 1981: 2; "Yushan gongshe shixing zerenzhi hou tichu jihua shengyu gongzuo xinbanfa" (Yushan commune proposed new methods for family planning work after the implementation of the responsibility system), GMRB, 22 Oct. 1981: 2; "Baoningzhen qunian yitailü dadao 91% yishang" (One-child rate reached over 91 percent last year in the town of Baoning), SCRB, 12 Feb. 1982: 1.

85. Song Qixia, "Yifeng buzheng yu duotai shengyu" (Improper conduct by doctors and excessive numbers of births), JKB, 6 Feb. 1983: 2; and Liu Xun (1983): 74.

86. See, for example, "Xijiaoqu Zhangwo gongshe ganbu Zang Yongfen wei sheng ertai nongxu zuojia shou chufen" (Cadre Zang Yongfen of Zhangwo com-

mune in Xijiao district received punishment for employing trickery in having a second child), TJRB, 13 June 1981: 1.

87. "The Maos of Shaoshan Refuse Family Planning," SWB, no. 6302 (20 Dec. 1979): 18.

88. "Guangdong Family Planning Conference: Concern at Rising Population Growth," SWB, no. 6165 (12 July 1979): 15.

89. "Guangdong Holds Conference on Planned Parenthood," FBIS 223 (16 Nov. 1979): P15.

90. Mark Baker, "Population Still Booming Despite Harsh Measures," *Financial Times*, 19 Oct. 1983.

91. "Hainan Prefecture Family Planning Work Commended," FBIS 224 (18 Nov. 1983): P1.

92. "Shandong Paper on Population and Living Problems," SWB, no. 6195 (16 Aug. 1979): 13.

93. "Jiangxi Conference Discusses Population Control Program," FBIS 99 (20 May 1980): O1; "Sheng jihua shengyu bangongshi zhaokai zuotanhui yanjiu xin qingkuang jin yibu gaohao jihua shengyu" (Yunnan Provincial Family Planning Office convenes symposium to study the new conditions and do better in family planning), YNRB, 6 Sept. 1981: 1; Fujian Provincial Family Planning Office Information Team, "Sheng jihua shengyu gongzuo huiyi zai Fuzhou zhaokai" (The Fujian Provincial Family Planning Work Conference was held in Fuzhou), FJRB, 4 May 1982: 1.

94. Lo Ming, "'Zuo' xing weigai huaiyun youzui" ("Leftist" nature has not changed; it is a crime to be pregnant), ZMRB, 27 July 1981: 1; "Cong jihua shengyu kan zuozai" (A view of the calamity from the Left as shown in family planning), ZMRB, 27 July 1981: 1; Lo Ming, "Xiaohua guaishi wuqibuyou" (Laughable and queer events; nothing is too strange), ZMRB, 28 July 1981: 1; "Problems in Guangdong Planned Parenthood Work," JPRS 78901 (3 Sept. 1981): 68–70; "Xuexi Huiyang diqu jingyan zhuahao jihua shengyu gongzuo" (Learn from the experiences of Huiyang prefecture and do family planning work well), NFRB, 29 Aug. 1981: 1. Further analysis of the Huiyang case is in Aird (1985a).

95. Rongcheng County People's Government, "Jianchi 'san wei zhu' de gongzuo fangfa shi jihua shengyu gongzuo shenru fazhan" (Persevere in the working method of "taking three things as the main emphasis" to enable family planning work to develop in depth), RKYJ, no. 6 (29 Nov. 1982): 24.

96. "Sichuan to Further Strengthen Population Control," JPRS 83568 (27 May 1983): 30; "Jilin quansheng kaizhan cang wu duotai shengyu wu jihua wai huaiyun wu dayuefen yinchan danwei huodong" (Jilin promotes provincewide activities to create units without an excessive number of births, without unplanned pregnancies, and without abortions in the later months of pregnancy), JKB, 28 Apr. 1983: 1; "Ningxia Holds Family Planning Conference," FBIS 145 (27 July 1983): T2.

97. "Benxi kongzhi renkou zengzhang chengji tuchu" (Benxi Municipality obtains outstanding results in controlling population growth), LNRB, 4 Jan. 1983: 1.

98. "Jiu youguan jieyu jishu zhengce, shengyu zhengce deng wenti Wang

Pingshan fushengzhang da jizhe wen" (Vice Governor Wang Pingshan answers a reporter's questions concerning policies on birth control techniques and childbearing), NFRB, 15 May 1983: 2.

99. Ibid., and "Hebei Provincial Telephone Meeting on Family Planning," JPRS 83105 (21 Mar. 1983): 119.

100. "Planned Parenthood Encouraged in Hebei," JPRS 84590 (24 Oct. 1983): 40. See also Ju Genhua (1983): 2.

101. Ju Genhua (1983): 2; Liu Xun (1983): 77.

102. "Hainan 'Second Phase' in Family Planning Begins," FBIS 182 (19 Sept. 1983): P5.

103. "Guizhou Couple Punished for Having Third Child," SWB, no. 6406 (28 Apr. 1980): 3.

104. "Shengfu zhaokai jihua shengyu gongzuo huiyi yanjiu jinhou gongzuo" (The Guangdong provincial government holds a family planning work meeting to study plans for the coming year), NFRB, 2 Dec. 1981: 1. See also Mathews (1980): A-23.

105. Liu Xun (1983): 77.

106. "Hunan Letter Complains of Evasion of Birth Control Measures," FBIS 188 (26 Sept. 1979): P2.

107. See also "Guizhou Begins Family Planning Propaganda," FBIS 245 (20 Dec. 1983): Q2.

108. Mathews (1980): A-23.

109. "Birth Control Program Abuses," JPRS 76310 (27 Aug. 1980): 32–34. See also "Yin-ren-zhi-yi luoshi jieyu zuoshi" (Apply the birth control measure to fit the person), FJRB, 5 Sept. 1981: 2.

110. "Kweichow Planned Parenthood," FBIS 242 (15 Dec. 1978): J5.

111. "Yunnan Holds Conference on Planned Parenthood," FBIS 224 (20 Nov. 1978): J3.

112. "Jiu youguan jieyu jishu zhengce, shengyu zhengce deng wenti Wang Pingshan fushengzhang da jizhe wen" (Vice Governor Wang Pingshan answers a reporter's questions concerning policies on birth control techniques and childbearing), NFRB, 15 May 1983: 2. See also Michael Weisskopf, "China Orders Sterilization for Parents," WP, 28 May 1983: A1; and Ju Genhua (1983): 2.

113. "Guanyu kaizhan quanguo jihua shengyu xuanchuanyue huodong de tongzhi" (Circular on carrying out the activities of the nationwide family planning propaganda month), GWYGB, no. 21 (12 Feb. 1983): 1063–70. (State Family Planning Commission Document, 1982, no. 207.)

114. "Sheng jihua shengyu xuanchuan gongzuo huiyi bushu xuanchuan yue huodong zhuyao lingdao yao qingzi zhua jihua shengyu" (The Shaanxi Provincial Family Planning Propaganda Work Meeting has made arrangements for propaganda month activities. The principal leadership must personally take charge of family planning), *Shaanxi ribao* (Shaanxi daily), 30 Nov. 1982: 1. See also "Hebei Provincial Telephone Meeting on Family Planning," JPRS 83105 (21 Mar. 1983): 118–19.

115. Liu Xun (1983): 74.

116. "Wosheng jihua shengyu xuanchuanyue chengji xianzhu" (Marked re-

sults were obtained in Hebei province during family planning propaganda month), *Hebei ribao* (Hebei daily), 5 Apr. 1983: 1.

117. "Guangdong Official Reviews Birth Control Policy," FBIS 112 (9 June 1983): P1.

118. "Henan Family Planning Conference Concludes," FBIS 229 (28 Nov. 1983): P5; "Ningxia Meeting Discusses Family Planning," FBIS 235 (6 Dec. 1983): T4.

119. "Guangzhou Planned Parenthood Meeting Reports Results," JPRS 84045 (28 June 1984): 86.

120. "Tianjin Holds Planned Parenthood Conference," JPRS 82678 (19 Jan. 1983): 58.

121. Song Qixia and Zhang Zhiqiang, "Shaanxi nongcun pai she siqianduo jieyu shoushudian" (More than 4,000 birth control surgical field stations have been established in the rural areas of Shaanxi province), JKB, 27 Jan. 1983: 1.

122. "Sheng weishengting fachu tongzhi yaoqiu geji weisheng bumen zuohao jihua shengyu jishu gongzuo" (The Provincial Public Health Department issued a circular requesting that public health units at all levels do well in technical planned birth work), NFRB, 10 May 1983: 1; "Guangdong Conference Sums Up Family Planning Work," FBIS 197 (11 Oct. 1983): P1.

123. "Wosheng jihua shengyu xuanchuanyue chengji xianzhu" (Marked results were obtained in Hebei province during family planning propaganda month), *Hebei ribao* (Hebei daily), 5 Apr. 1983: 1.

124. "Hebei Family Planning Issues Discussed," FBIS 124 (27 June 1983): R2.

125. "Chengsheng qianjin" (Advance on the crest of victory), JKB, 27 Feb. 1983: 1.

126. "Weishengbu he guojia jihua shengyu weiyuanhui lianhe fachu tongzhi yaoqiu gedi guance zhongyang zhishi jingshen zuohao jihua shengyu jishu zhidao gongzuo" (The Ministry of Public Health and the State Family Planning Commission issued a joint circular requesting that all areas carry out the Central Committee guidelines by doing well in the work of giving guidance on family planning techniques), JHSYB, 8 June 1984: 1.

127. "Lanchow Planned Parenthood Rally," FBIS 4 (5 Jan. 1979): M2.

128. "Wangdaicun dangzhibu . . . dingli xianggui baohu dunühu hefa quanyi" (The party branch of Wangdai village . . . formulated village regulations to protect the legal rights of households with only a daughter), JKB, 1 Nov. 1983: 1.

129. "Excerpts of Speeches by NPC Deputies at Panel Discussions: Control the Size of the Population, Jiangxi Deputy Jiang Weiqing Points Out the Need to Strengthen Propaganda and Education in Family Planning," FBIS 184 (19 Sept. 1980): L14.

130. Xing Peng, "Shifangxian 1981-nian yi wu duotai shengyu" (Shifang county by 1981 had no excess births), RKYJ, no. 6 (29 Nov. 1982): 31.

131. "Hebei Family Planning Issues Discussed," FBIS 124 (27 June 1983): R2.

132. "World Population Plan of Action," SFP 5, no. 12 (Dec. 1974): 385.

133. "Symposium on Population and Human Rights," *Population Newsletter*, no. 32 (Dec. 1981): 13; "Integral Part of Development," *Popline* 4, no. 1 (Jan. 1982): 4.

134. For other analyses of the coercive elements in China's family planning program, see Davies (1977): 21; Orleans (1981): 12–19; Aird (1982b); Banister (1984c); Aird (1985a); and Wong Siu-lun, "Consequences of China's New Population Policy," CQ, no. 98 (June 1984): 220–40. For discussion of the ethical dilemmas facing foreigners who deal with China in the population field, see Aird (1981a). For further discussion of the responses of international donor and family planning organizations to China's family planning program, see Aird (1985a).

135. On the denial of medical benefits for third and higher order children, see for example "'Nanfang Daily' Publishes Guangdong Province Planned Parenthood Regulations," SWB, no. 6356 (27 Feb. 1980): 4; and Fraser (1979): 62.

136. "Buyao shanghai feidusheng zinü de xinling" (Do not hurt the feelings of those children who are not an only child) and "Guli dusheng buyao yingxiang haizi" (Encourage having a single child, but do not let it affect the children), GRRB, 8 Aug. 1981: 1.

137. "Female Infanticide Evokes Danger of Sexes Imbalance," CD 2, no. 530 (9 Apr. 1983): 3; "Ji Zongquan Speaks on Planned Parenthood," FBIS 78 (21 Apr. 1983): K7.

138. "Kongzhi woguo renkou zengzhang de xuanchuan yaodian" (An outline of propaganda for controlling China's population growth), RKYJ, no. 2 (Apr. 1981): 2. The rise in infanticide is also traced to the one-child policy in "Hongqi Commentator Scores 'Sex Discrimination'," FBIS 43 (3 Mar. 1983): K11; and "Why Female Infanticide Still Exists in Socialist China," ZGFN, no. 5 (May 1983): 1.

139. See Chapter 8 for further details and sources.

140. Su Zhongheng and Zhang Bowen, "Yanjin nibi nüying" (Strictly prohibit the killing of baby girls), NFRB, 7 Feb. 1983: 2; "Paper Urges End to 'Preferring Boys to Girls'," FBIS 35 (18 Feb. 1983): K11; Li Yuchang, "Heisi yinger shi fanzui xingwei" (Infanticide is a criminal act), ZGFN, no. 7 (1 July 1983): 41.

141. Zhang Wansong et al., "Yinger xingbili shitiao yao qieshi jiuzheng" (Effective steps must be taken against the disproportionate sex ratio at birth), SH, no. 2 (20 Apr. 1983): 29.

142. See, for example, Zhuang Bingjin and Huang Xinmei, "Dui Zhejiang sheng sange xian de renkou yuce" (A projection of the population of three counties in Zhejiang province), RKYJ, no. 3 (July 1981): 32; Li Shaowen, "Yao zhongshi renkou chusheng de xingbie pingheng" (Pay attention to the sexual equilibrium of the population), SH, no. 4 (Nov. 1982): 21; and "Female Infanticide Evokes Danger of Sexes Imbalance," CD 2, no. 530 (9 Apr. 1983): 3.

143. "Further Coverage of Fifth Session of Fifth NPC," FBIS 240 (14 Dec. 1982): K11; "Gaoqiao gongshe caiqu qixiang cuoshi cong duo fangmian guanxin dushengnühu" (Gaoqiao commune adopts seven measures to care for the households with only one daughter), JKB, 1 Nov. 1983: 1.

144. Medical Experts (1980): L15.

145. Sun Dongsheng (1981): 41.

146. "Relationship Between Ecology, Population Described," JPRS 77668 (25 Mar. 1981): 91.

147. Qian Lingjuan, Xu Bing, and Huang Shuyuan, "Beijingshi de renkou

fazhan qingkuang he dangqian de renwu" (Population growth in Beijing and our present tasks), RKYJ, no. 1 (Apr. 1980): 39–44.

148. Medical Experts (1980): L14.

149. See, for example, Su Xiufang (1982): 3.

150. Parish & Whyte (1978): 169–72.

151. Medical Experts (1980): L15.

152. Medical Experts (1980): L15; Zhang Peizhu (1981): 117.

153. "Marriage Law Adopted by Fifth National People's Congress," FBIS 184 (19 Sept. 1980): L22.

154. "Beijing Sets Up Premarital Counseling Service," FBIS 32 (18 Feb. 1981): R3.

155. Medical Experts (1980): L15; "Yousheng de yixiang zhongyao cuoshi" (An important measure for quality birth), JKB, 11 Dec. 1983: 1.

156. Ye Qiwen (1981): 30–31.

157. Zhang Peizhu (1981): 117–18; "Chen Muhua Speaks at Population Science Meeting," FBIS 40 (2 Mar. 1981): L12-L13.

158. Ye Qiwen (1981): 31; "Genetic Counseling Outpatient Service," BR 23, no. 7 (18 Feb. 1980): 27–28.

159. Jay Mathews, "Chinese Said to Determine Sex of Fetus, Abort Females," WP, 1 Mar. 1977: 11.

Chapter 8

1. See, for example, Banister (1977b), Aird (1978), Banister (1981), Aird (1981b), Aird (1982a), Aird (1982b), and Banister (1984a).

2. For details on the survey design and sampling technique, see Xiao Zhenyu (1984).

3. These consistency tests and results were reported in Coale (1984): 20–22, 31–32.

4. Bongaarts (1980); based on Stein et al. (1975).

5. See Groen & Kilpatrick (1978): 649, for China's annual grain production, per capita grain production, and per capita grain availability from both production and imports. On demographic trends during the famine, see Ashton et al. (1984).

6. Groen & Kilpatrick (1978): 649.

7. Coale (1984): 27–29.

8. Ibid.

9. Aird (1961): 4–42.

10. Liu Zheng (1980b): 6.

11. Personal communication from John S. Aird.

12. Personal communication from Arthur P. Wolf.

13. For an analysis of the problem of falsification of data in China during the 1970's and 1980's see Aird (1982a): 202–13.

14. Zhu Zhengzhi (1980): 58.

15. Liu Shuyi (1980): 3.

16. Details of these sanctions are found in Parish & Whyte (1978): 142.

17. The Civil Affairs Office of Dahe commune, Huolu county, Shijiazhuang prefecture, in Hebei province as of 1980 would not enter a newborn in the popu-

lation registration book until it was 100 days old. Personal communication from Steven Butler.

18. "Caiqu youli cuoshi gaohao jihua shengyu" (Adopt effective measures in order to do well in family planning), *Hebei ribao* (Hebei daily), 29 Oct. 1981: 2.

19. "Banjiang xiang nongxu zuojia manbao chusheng renkou" (Banjiang township resorted to deception to conceal the number of births), JHSYB, 10 Aug. 1984: 3.

20. Song Yuanjie, Shi Yulin, and Zhang Guihao, "Birth Parities of Females," in China Population Information Centre, *Analysis on China's National One-per-Thousand-Population Fertility Sampling Survey*, Beijing, 1984: 62.

21. State Council Population Office (1983): 440–41.

22. "Pingnanxian renkou pucha shidian zhong de er san shi" (A few anecdotes from the census pretest in Pingnan county), FJRB, 19 June 1982: 2.

23. The temptation for cadres to manipulate 1982 census data in order to mask previously unreported births and children is discussed in Banister (1981): 42–44; and Banister (1984a).

24. Shen Yimin (1982): 4.

25. Data reported in Liu Chunmei and Li Zhu, "Sex Structure of Population in China," in China Population Information Centre, *Analysis on China's National One-per-Thousand-Population Fertility Sampling Survey*, Beijing, 1984: 158. Also discussed in Coale (1984): 25–26.

26. Circular on Sample Vital Rate Survey (1983): 822.

27. Communique on 1982 Economic Plan (1983): K16.

28. Communique on 1983 Economic Plan (1984): K14.

29. "Wo canjia guoji renkou huiyi de daibiaotuan yi zhucheng" (The Chinese delegation to the International Population Conference has already been organized), JHSYB, 6 July 1984: 1. For further assessment of China's official population data, see Aird (1985b).

30. Xiao Zhenyu (1984): 22; Li Baohua (1984): 24; Banister (1984b): 264–65.

31. See also the analysis of these data in Coale (1984): 58–62.

32. State Council Population Office (1983): 276–79, 284–87, 294–97.

33. These details on Han and minority fertility and marriage were calculated from data presented in Li Hechang, Song Tingyou, and Li Cheng, "Current Fertility Status of Women of the Han and Minority Nationalities in Rural Areas," and in Shen Biguang and Ma Qingping, "Recent Nuptiality of Rural Women of Han and Minority Nationalities," in China Population Information Centre, *Analysis on China's National One-per-Thousand-Population Fertility Sampling Survey*, Beijing, 1984: 100–105 and 131–34 respectively.

34. "Family Planning Becomes Popular in Xizang," FBIS 210 (28 Oct. 1983): Q2.

35. "Dali tichang yidui fufu zhi sheng yige haizi bushi zuo de biaoxian" (To vigorously promote one child per couple is not a leftist manifestation), FJRB, 30 Aug. 1981: 4.

36. "Fewer Mouths to Feed," FEER 118, no. 46 (12 Nov. 1982): 11; "Xinjiang

Planned Parenthood Telephone Conference," JPRS 82678 (19 Jan. 1983): 70–71; "Jiji xingdong qilai, wei jinyibu kongzhi renkou zengzhang zuochu xin gongxian" (Take positive action and make new contributions toward further controlling population growth), NXRB, 29 Dec. 1982: 1; Clare Hollingworth, "Letter from Kashgar," FEER 121, no. 33 (18 Aug. 1983): 93.

37. "Resurgence of Birthrate in Northwestern Cities Viewed," JPRS 83478 (16 May 1983): 162.

38. "Flexible Population Policies Needed for Minorities," CD, 15 Apr. 1983: 4; Dong Zijian and Yang Yucai. "Yunnan shaoshu minzu diqu jingji shehui fazhan zhanlue wenti qianjian" (My views on the strategic problem of economic and social development of the minority nationality areas in Yunnan), *Jingji wenti tansuo* (Inquiry into economic problems), no. 4 (1983): 34.

39. "Text of Sixth Five-year Plan," JPRS 84005 (25 Jan. 1984): 107.

40. "Family Planning Becomes Popular in Xizang," FBIS 210 (28 Oct. 1983): Q1-Q2.

41. "Qinghai Conference on Family Planning Propaganda," FBIS 199 (13 Oct. 1983): T2.

42. Christopher S. Wren, "China's Policy on Size of Families Is Extended to Include Minorities," NYT, 10 Feb. 1983; "Hainan Issues Minority Family Planning Regulations," FBIS 199 (13 Oct. 1983): P1.

43. "Hainan Minority Family Planning Reported," FBIS 222 (16 Nov. 1983): P3.

44. For a detailed analysis of Shanghai's population data as reported by 1977, see Banister (1977a).

45. Zhang Changgen, Liu Minghao, and Hu Yanzhao, "Shanghai: Population Developments Since 1949," in Liu Zheng et al., *China's Population: Problems and Prospects*, Beijing, 1981: 134. See Ivory & Lavely (1977) for details on the rustication of Shanghai-educated youth.

46. Gu Xingyuan et al. (1981): 140–42.

47. Gui Shixun (1982): 4.

48. Municipal Statistical Bureau of Shanghai, *Communique on Fulfilment of Shanghai's 1983 Economic and Social Development Plan, Issued on April 28, 1984*, Shanghai, 1984.

49. Demographic data from Beijing Municipality were extensively analyzed in Banister (1977b): 165–210.

50. "Population Peking," SWB-WER, no. W1103 (8 Oct. 1980): 1.

51. Calculated from data given in Zhang Lizhong (1981): 116. The total fertility rates may be slightly underestimated here because age-specific fertility rates are missing for women over age 40, under age 23 in the counties, and under age 25 in the city. A contradictory set of data was released in Liu Zheng (1981c): 58, giving a total fertility rate of 2.2 births per woman, ostensibly applicable to the whole municipality.

52. "Population Peking," SWB-WER, no. W1103 (8 Oct. 1980): 1.

53. "Shoudu jihua shengyu gongzuo qude jiaohao chengji" (Family planning work in the capital has obtained comparatively good results), RMRB, 26 Oct. 1982: 3.

54. "Benshi shangbannian dusheng zinülü da baifen zhi bashisan" (In the first half of this year, Beijing's single-child rate reached 83 percent), BJRB, 1 Oct. 1981: 3.

55. "Benshi qunian xinshenger bi yuce shao liangwan" (The number of births in 1982 was lower by 20,000 than the expected figure), BJRB, 4 Mar. 1983: 1; "Beijing's Birthrate Goes Down," CD 3, no. 801 (20 Feb. 1984): 3.

56. "Benshi jihua shengyu chuxian hao shitou" (Family planning work in Beijing shows favorable momentum), BJRB, 30 Apr. 1983: 1.

57. Lyle (1980): 566–67.

58. Lyle (1980): 556, 562.

59. "Tianjin shi jiben gaibian renkou mangmu fazhan zhuangkuang" (Tianjin Municipality basically changed the situation of blind population growth), JHSYB, 10 Aug. 1984: 1.

60. "Population: Tianjin," SWB-WER, no. W1217 (5 Jan. 1983): 3.

61. Estimates for 1953 from Ni (1960); 1982 data from State Council Population Office (1982): 16.

62. Li Yijun (1983): 125.

63. V. H. Li (1973): 350–54. Detailed analysis of Liaoning's population data is found in Banister (1977b): 315–28.

64. V. H. Li (1973): 352.

65. "Liaoning Holds Meeting on Planned Parenthood, Child Care," FBIS 236 (6 Dec. 1974): L5-L6.

66. "Population: Liaoning," SWB-WER, no. W1177 (24 Mar. 1982): 1.

67. "Bixu jianjue kongzhi renkou de zengzhang" (Population growth must be resolutely controlled), LNRB, 24 Sept. 1981: 1.

68. "Liaoning Government Work Report," SWB, no. 7638 (9 May 1984): 5.

69. Ibid.; and "Liaoning Planned Parenthood," JPRS 84020 (7 Mar. 1984): 99.

70. "Liaoning Holds Family Planning Meeting 11–12 May," FBIS 95 (15 May 1984): S1.

71. Li Yijun (1983): 125.

72. The 1978 figure was released by China's Family Planning Office to the Library of the United Nations Fund for Population Activities, Beijing. For 1979 and 1980 see "Jilin Population Growth," FBIS 52 (18 Mar. 1981): S1.

73. "Jilin Birth Control," JPRS 81785 (16 Sept. 1982): 68.

74. Encyclopedic Yearbook of China 1983 (1983): 76.

75. "Jilinsheng jihua shengyu jishu gongzuo zhuo you chengxiao" (Family planning technical work in Jilin province has achieved fruitful results), JKB, 22 Nov. 1983: 1.

76. Li Yijun (1983): 125.

77. "Heilongjiang Family Planning Conference," FBIS 164 (23 Aug. 1983): S2.

78. Figure for 1978 released to UNFPA library, Beijing. Other rates reported in "Heilongjiang Population Reduction," FBIS 60 (30 Mar. 1981): S1.

79. Wu Banglan (1981a): 18, 22.

80. "Heilongjiang Population Growth," FBIS 72 (14 Apr. 1982): S2.

81. Encyclopedic Yearbook of China 1983 (1983): 78.

82. "Heilongjiang Family Planning Conference," FBIS 164 (23 Aug. 1983): S2;

"Heilongjiang tichu xue Dedu" (Heilongjiang province proposes to learn from Dedu county), JKB, 13 Sept. 1983: 3.

83. "Heilongjiang Government Work Report," SWB, no. 7629 (28 Apr. 1984): 2.

84. "Communique on Heilongjiang 1983 Development," JPRS 84041 (4 June 1984): 16.

85. "Zhejiang Population Growth," SWB, no. 6341 (9 Feb. 1980): 15; "Family Planning Targets in Zhejiang Province," SWB, no. 6356 (27 Feb. 1980): 6; "Population: Zhejiang," SWB-WER, no. W1081 (7 May 1980): 1; "Zhejiang Birth Rate," FBIS 57 (17 Mar. 1981): O1; "Population Growth Rate Drops," BR 24, no. 12 (23 Mar. 1981): 8; "Population," SWB-WER, no. W1126 (25 Mar. 1981): 1, 3; "Zhengfu gongzuo baogao" (Government work report), ZJRB, 23 May 1981: 2.

86. Li Fengping (1982): 2.

87. Li Chengrui (1982b): 30.

88. State Council Population Office (1982): 33.

89. Li Fengping (1982): 1–3.

90. Zho Yinchai, "Kongzhi renkou shi guoce yao zhuajing zhuahao" (The control of population growth is state policy and must be firmly carried out), ZJRB, 20 June 1982: 2.

91. "Quansheng jihua shengyu gongzuo huiyi tichu caiqu youli cuoshi kongzhi renkou zengzhang" (The Zhejiang Provincial Family Planning Work Conference proposes effective measures for controlling population growth), ZJRB, 24 Mar. 1982: 1.

92. "Jiangshanxian kaizhan jihua shengyu jiancha" (Jiangshan county carries out the family planning inspection), ZJRB, 9 May 1982: 1; "Juzhoushi kongzhile renkou zengzhang huisheng qushi" (Juzhou Municipality controlled the upswing in population growth), ZJRB, 23 June 1982: 4; "Birth Control Increasing in Zhejiang," JPRS 82440 (10 Dec. 1982): 55.

93. "Zhejiang Communique on 1982 Plan Fulfillment," JPRS 83836 (7 July 1983): 130.

94. "Birth Control: Zhejiang," SWB-WER, no. W1256 (5 Oct. 1983): 1.

95. "Family Planning in Zhejiang," SWB-WER, no. W1279 (21 Mar. 1984): 1.

96. Statistical Yearbook of China 1981 (1982): 202, 445. For further detail on the demographic transition in Jiangsu, see Banister (1977b): 213–58.

97. Zhang Xiluo (1981): 1.

98. "Jiangsu qunian renkou chushenglu nongcun di yu chengshi" (Jiangsu's 1980 rural birth rate was lower than the city rate), RMRB, 11 June 1981: 5.

99. "Qunian wosheng jihua shengyu gongzuo qude hao chengji" (In 1981 Jiangsu province obtained good results in family planning work), XHRB, 3 May 1982: 1.

100. Ibid.; Chen Pi-chao & Kols (1982): 598 (for 1977); Zhang Xiluo (1981): 1 (for 1980).

101. Jiangsu Provincial Family Planning Commission, "Jiangsu sheng 1983-nian renkou dongtai" (Population dynamics of Jiangsu province in 1983), RKJJ, no. 4 (25 Aug. 1984): 63.

102. "Shandong Family Planning," JPRS 80318 (15 Mar. 1982): 107.

103. "Shandong Releases Census Figures 28 Oct," JPRS 82204 (9 Nov. 1982): 115.

104. Jin Qi (1982): 3.

105. "Quansheng jihua shengyu xianjin daibiao huiyi kaimu" (Shandong holds a meeting of advanced units and individuals in family planning work), DZRB, 13 Feb. 1982: 1.

106. Wang Zhongyin, "Wei shixian wosheng jinnian jihua shengyu renwu zuochu xin gongxian" (Make new contributions toward accomplishing Shandong's family planning task this year), DZRB, 15 Feb. 1982: 1, 4.

107. "Population: Shandong," SWB-WER, no. W1205 (6 Oct. 1982): 1.

108. Rural Small-Scale Industries Delegation (1975): 55; Perkins (1974); Banister (1977b): 298–300.

109. Encyclopedic Yearbook of China 1983 (1983): 71.

110. "Shanxi Communique on Fulfillment of 1982 Economic Plan," JPRS 84244 (1 Sept. 1983): 18.

111. Song Youtian (1982): 3; "Shaanxi Holds Planned Parenthood Telephone Conference," FBIS 33 (15 Feb. 1979): M3; "Governor Notes Province's Progress," FBIS 252 (30 Dec. 1980): T10.

112. Feng Zhonghui (1982).

113. This information is from an interview with Dr. Feng Zhonghui in Washington, D.C., on 28 Dec. 1982.

114. Chen Pi-chao & Kols (1982): 598; "Population," SWB-WER, no. W1126 (25 Mar. 1981): 1–2.

115. "Shaanxi: Ma Wenrui on Planned Parenthood Problem," FBIS 39 (26 Feb. 1982): T4.

116. Song Youtian (1982): 3.

117. "'Shaanxisheng jihua shengyu zanxing tiaoli' buchong guiding" (Supplement to the "Provisional Regulations on Family Planning in Shaanxi Province"), *Shaanxi ribao* (Shaanxi daily), 1 Nov. 1982: 2.

118. Encyclopedic Yearbook of China 1983 (1983): 105; "Shaanxi Ribao Carries 1983 Provincial Statistics," JPRS 84045 (11 June 1984): 53.

119. "Sichuan, Tianjin renkou ziran zengzhanglü xiajiang" (The natural population increase rates of Sichuan and Tianjin have declined), GMRB, 15 Mar. 1981: 1. For information on Sichuan's demographic situation during the early 1970's see Banister (1977b): 397–406.

120. Yang Xuetong (1980): 59.

121. Fan Jinchun (1981): 79.

122. "Ts'ung i-ko tiao-ch'a t'ung-chi k'an-tao te wen-t'i" (Problems revealed from a statistical investigation), *Hsin Chung-kuo fu-nü* (Women of new China), no. 12 (5 Dec. 1952): 29–31.

123. "Birth Control Practiced Poorly in Szechwan," SWB, no. 4792 (31 Dec. 1974): 5–6.

124. Liu Yunbo, "NPC Deputy on Family Planning in Rural Areas," JPRS 79686 (18 Dec. 1981): 31–32. There is confusion on this statistic. The Ministry of Public Health attributed 10 million vasectomies to Sichuan, as discussed in Chapter 6.

125. Fraser (1981): 77; "Sichuan Population Growth Rate Shows Drop in 1980," JPRS 78012 (6 May 1981): 65.

126. "Sichuan Ribao Comment," FBIS 100 (24 May 1982): Q2.

127. "Sichuan Discusses Planned Parenthood Work," FBIS 100 (24 May 1982): Q1-Q2; "Shangwei Shengzhengfu zhaokai dianhua huiyi dongyuan bushu zai quansheng jizhong jinxing yici jihua shengyu xuanchuan huodong" (The Sichuan Party Committee and the Provincial Government called a telephone conference to arrange concentrated family planning propaganda activities throughout the province), SCRB, 11 July 1982: 1.

128. Hou Wenfang, "Sichuan ziran zengzhanglü jiang dao 6.05" (Sichuan's natural increase rate declined to 6.05), JHSYB, 28 Sept. 1984: 2.

129. "Sichuan Province Reports Decline in Birthrate," FBIS 101 (23 May 1984): Q2.

130. "Sichuansheng jihua shengyu gongzuo chengji xianzhu" (Family planning work in Sichuan province obtained marked results), RMRB, 17 Dec. 1983: 3.

131. Figure for 1978 released by the PRC Family Planning Office to the UNFPA library, Beijing. Data for 1979 and 1980 from "Hubei sheng renkou xuehui chengli" (Hubei province establishes a population association), RKYJ, no. 3 (July 1981): 62.

132. Encyclopedic Yearbook of China 1983 (1983): 92; Ye Caisheng, "Hubei jihua shengyu mianmao bianhua da" (The status of family planning in Hubei has undergone great change), JHSYB, 28 Sept. 1984: 2.

133. "Administrative Division Changes in China," SWB, no. 6193 (14 Aug. 1979): 1.

134. "Nei Monggol Issues Census Figures," JPRS 82402 (7 Dec. 1982): 107–8.

135. "Population: Inner Mongolia," SWB-WER, no. W1172 (17 Feb. 1982): 1; "Nei Monggol Population Growth," FBIS 238 (9 Dec. 1980): R2; Chen Lihsin (1973): 234; "China on the Population Question," CR 23, no. 11 (Nov. 1974): 13. See Banister (1977b): 422–28 on the demography of Inner Mongolia.

136. "Population: Inner Mongolia," SWB-WER, no. W991 (2 Aug. 1978): 1. Figure for 1978 released to the UNFPA library, Beijing.

137. "Nei Monggol Population Growth," FBIS 238 (9 Dec. 1980): R2; "Population: Inner Mongolia," SWB-WER, no. W1172 (17 Feb. 1982): 1; Sun Jingzhi & Li (n.d.): 184–85.

138. Ibid.; and Encyclopedic Yearbook of China 1983 (1983): 73.

139. "China on the Population Question," CR 23, no. 11 (Nov. 1974): 13; "Family Planning," PR 20, no. 13 (25 Mar. 1977): 29; "Liu Tzu-hou Addresses Hopei Meeting on Planned Parenthood," FBIS 202 (18 Oct. 1978): K1. For further information see Banister (1977b): 268–82.

140. "Sheng jihua shengyu xianjin daibiaohui kaimu" (The Hebei Provincial Conference of Delegates from Advanced Family Planning Units opens), *Hebei ribao* (Hebei daily), 10 Mar. 1982: 1.

141. State Council Population Office (1982): 31–32.

142. Encyclopedic Yearbook of China 1983 (1983): 70.

143. "Hebeisheng jiaqiang jieyu jishu gongzuo" (Hebei province strengthens birth control technical work), JKB, 25 Oct. 1983: 1.

144. Hebei Family Planning Commission, "Hebei renkou ziran zengzhanglü xiajiang xianzhu" (A marked decline in Hebei's natural population increase rate), JHSYB, 28 Sept. 1984: 2.

145. "Henan qunian renkou zengzhanglü jiangdao 9.8" (Henan's population growth rate dropped to 9.8 in 1982), RMRB, 21 Jan. 1983: 4.

146. "Henan Holds Meeting on Planned Parenthood Work," FBIS 169 (29 Aug. 1979): P1.

147. "Henan Radio Airs Planned Parenthood Problems," FBIS 35 (22 Feb. 1982): P3.

148. State Council Population Office (1982): 35. A problem in this analysis is that reconstructing births from a midyear census age structure gives estimates of the number of births from one midyear point to the next, so the estimates do not correspond to calendar year registered births.

149. Lin Furui & Chen (1983): 112.

150. "Population: Henan," SWB-WER, no. W1276 (29 Feb. 1984): 1.

151. Ma Luxia, "Henan zonghe shengyulü jiang wei 2.1" (Henan's total fertility rate dropped to 2.1), JHSYB, 28 Sept. 1984: 2.

152. "Liao Zhigao, Others Attend Planned Parenthood Conference," FBIS 36 (21 Feb. 1980): O3.

153. "Fukien Holds Meeting on Planned Parenthood," FBIS 174 (7 Sept. 1978): G3-G4.

154. "*Fukien Daily* Editorial," FBIS 174 (7 Sept. 1978): G4.

155. "Fujian Population Growth," FBIS 53 (19 Mar. 1981): O4.

156. Hu Ping, "Guanyu 1981-nian guomin jingji jihua zhixing qingkuang" (Report on the implementation of the 1981 national economic plan), FJRB, 14 Mar. 1982: 2.

157. "Ba wosheng jihua shengyu gongzuo zai tigao yibu" (Family planning work in our province should be raised a step further), FJRB, 14 May 1984: 1.

158. "1982 Population Statistics," JPRS 82402 (7 Dec. 1982): 133.

159. Statistical Yearbook of China 1981 (1982): 202, 445.

160. "Renzhen guanche qieshi zhixing" (It takes serious implementation and concrete execution), GSRB, 2 Apr. 1982: 1.

161. Gansu Family Planning Commission, "Gansu jihua shengyu gongzuo chengji xiren" (Gansu's achievements in family planning work are heartening), JHSYB, 28 Sept. 1984: 2.

162. Liu Junde, "Shilun Jiangxisheng renkou de yanbian ji qi fazhan qushi" (Changes in the population of Jiangxi province and its future development), in *Renkou yanjiu lunwenji* (Collection of papers on population research), Shanghai, 1981: 65, 81.

163. "Kiangsi Meetings Discuss Questions of Planned Parenthood," FBIS 152 (7 Aug. 1978): G3-G4.

164. "Jiangxi Population Growth," FBIS 51 (17 Mar. 1981): O1.

165. "Jiangxi Urges Strengthening Family Planning," JPRS 80293 (10 Mar. 1982): 69.

166. Encyclopedic Yearbook of China 1983 (1983): 87.

167. Zhao Yugui (1981): 155.

168. Chen Pi-chao (1981): 82.

169. Yuan Fang et al. (1980): 22.

170. "Hunan Population Growth," FBIS 230 (29 Nov. 1978): H6; Sun Jingzhi & Li (n.d.): 185.

171. "Population: Hunan," SWB-WER, no. W1182 (28 Apr. 1982): 1.

172. "Fall in Birth Rates in Hunan and Jiangsu," SWB-WER, no. W1281 (4 Apr. 1984): 1.

173. "Hunan Family Planning," JPRS 83259 (14 Apr. 1983): 177–78.

174. "Population: Kwangtung," SWB-WER, no. W824 (30 Apr. 1975): 1. Error in original translation corrected in "Population: Kwangtung," SWB-WER, no. W825 (7 May 1975): 1.

175. "Kwangtung Urges Tightening Planned Parenthood," FBIS 234 (5 Dec. 1978): H4.

176. "Population: Kwangtung," SWB-WER, no. W1015 (24 Jan. 1979): 1.

177. State Council Population Office (1982): 20–21.

178. "Nanfang Ribao Carries 1983 Guangdong Statistics," JPRS 84045 (11 June 1984): 35.

179. "Yunnan Population Statistics," JPRS 82402 (7 Dec. 1982): 135.

180. "Yunnan Holds Conference on Planned Parenthood," FBIS 224 (20 Nov. 1978): J3.

181. "Yunnan Holds Conference on Planned Parenthood in Kunming," FBIS 234 (7 Dec. 1978): J1-J2.

182. See, for instance, "Wosheng jihua shengyu gongzuo qude kexi chengji" (Family planning work in Yunnan obtained gratifying results), YNRB, 30 Sept. 1982: 1.

183. Yang Ming, "Yunnan cong shiji chufa shixing fenlei zhidao" (Yunnan starts out from reality and implements the program of giving guidance by category), JHSYB, 24 Aug. 1984: 1.

184. Ibid.; and "Kongzhi duotai shi wosheng nongcun jihua shengyu gongzuo de zhongdian" (Controlling excess births is the focal point of family planning work in Yunnan villages), YNRB, 4 Nov. 1982: 1.

185. Ibid.; and "Yunnan Makes Achievements in Family Planning," FBIS 73 (13 Apr. 1984): Q7.

186. "Xinjiang Releases Population Census Results," JPRS 82402 (7 Dec. 1982): 111–12.

187. Zhu Zhuo (1980): 16.

188. "Wang Feng on Family Planning," FBIS 178 (12 Sept. 1979): T5.

189. Released to the UNFPA library, Beijing, by the National Family Planning Office; Zhu Zhuo (1980): 16.

190. Hu Huanyong, "Xinjiang renkou de guoqu, xianzai he weilai" (The past, present, and future of Xinjiang's population). In *Renkou yanjiu lunwenji (di er ji)* (Collection of papers on population research, vol. 2). Shanghai, 1983: 28.

191. "Xinjiang Family Planning," FBIS 51 (17 Mar. 1981): T2; "Population Xinjiang," SWB-WER, no. W1137 (10 June 1981): 1.

192. Sun Jingzhi & Li (n.d.): 185.

193. Encyclopedic Yearbook of China 1983 (1983): 112.

194. "Population: Xinjiang," SWB-WER, no. W1241 (22 June 1983): 1; "Xinjiang Meeting Discusses Planned Parenthood," FBIS 59 (26 Mar. 1984): T3.

195. Yu Ruihou & Li (1982): 72.

196. "Qinghai Releases Population Census Statistics," JPRS 82402 (7 Dec. 1982): 109.

197. "Xining Reports Family Planning Work Achievements," JPRS 83946 (21 July 1983): 101.

198. Figure for 1978 released to the UNFPA library, Beijing. Figures for 1980 from Sun Jingzhi & Li (n.d.): 185.

199. "Population: Qinghai," SWB-WER, no. W1190 (23 June 1982): 1.

200. "Qinghai Issues Provision on Birth Control," FBIS 115 (15 June 1982): T3-T4.

201. "Xining Reports Family Planning Work Achievements," JPRS 83946 (21 July 1983): 101.

202. "Qinghai Reports Success in Family Planning," FBIS 44 (5 Mar. 1984): T3.

203. Encyclopedic Yearbook of China 1983 (1983): 108.

204. "Qinghai Reports Success in Family Planning," FBIS 44 (5 Mar. 1984): T3.

205. Guangxi Family Planning Commission, "Guangxi shixing fenlei zhidao xiaoguo hao" (The implementation of giving guidance by categories has brought good results in Guangxi), JHSYB, 28 Sept. 1984: 2.

206. Guangxi Family Planning Commission, "Guangxi Zhuangzu zizhiqu 1983-nian renkou dongtai" (Population dynamics of Guangxi Zhuang Nationality Autonomous Region in 1983), RKJJ, no. 4 (Aug. 1984): 64.

207. Ibid.

208. "Guangxi Forum Calls for Population Growth Control," FBIS 86 (2 May 1984): P1.

209. "Kongzhi renkou zengzhang tigao renkou suzhi" (Control the growth and improve the quality of the population), NXRB, 29 Apr. 1982: 1; Chen Xinhui, "Jihua shengyu gongzuo qianwan buneng fangsong" (Never relax family planning work), NXRB, 5 Jan. 1983: 3.

210. Xiao Heng, "Yao liangzhong shengchan yiqizhua" (We must simultaneously grasp the two kinds of production), NXRB, 22 Oct. 1981: 3.

211. "Ningxia Holds Planned Parenthood Meeting," FBIS 89 (7 May 1982): T1.

212. Encyclopedic Yearbook of China 1983 (1983): 110.

213. "Ningxia: 1982 Economic, Social Development Plan Report," JPRS 83836 (7 July 1983): 94.

214. "Ningxia Holds Family Planning Conference," FBIS 145 (27 July 1983): T1.

215. Ibid.; and "Jiji xingdong qilai, wei jinyibu kongzhi renkou zengzhang zuochu xin gongxian" (Take positive action in order to make new contributions toward further controlling population growth), NXRB, 29 Dec. 1982: 1.

216. "Kweichow Holds Planned Parenthood Conference," FBIS 230 (29 Nov. 1978): J1; figure for 1978 released to UNFPA library, Beijing; "Guizhou Planned Parenthood," FBIS 61 (31 Mar. 1981): Q8; Sun Jingzhi & Li (n.d.): 185; Guizhou Family Planning Commission, "Guizhou lianxu liannian wancheng renkou jihua" (Guizhou fulfilled its population plan for two consecutive years), JHSYB, 28 Sept. 1984: 2.

217. Zhang Tianlu & Chen (1983): 21.

218. "Guizhou Issues Notice on Population Growth," FBIS 122 (24 June 1982): Q1.

219. "Guizhou Leader at Family Planning Conference," JPRS 82347 (30 Nov. 1982): 85–86.

220. Encyclopedic Yearbook of China 1983 (1983): 101.

221. "Guizhou Records New Successes in Family Planning," FBIS 67 (5 Apr. 1984): Q1.

222. "The Population of Tibet," SWB-WER, no. W1208 (27 Oct. 1982): 2.

223. Figure for 1978 released to UNFPA library, Beijing, by the National Family Planning Office. For 1980 see Sun Jingzhi & Li (n.d.): 185.

224. See Banister (1977b): 449–52 on the demography of Tibet.

225. Encyclopedic Yearbook of China 1983 (1983): 104; "Xizang Calls for Checking Population Growth," FBIS 126 (29 June 1983): Q1.

226. Christopher S. Wren, "Chinese Trying to Undo Damage in Tibet," NYT, 3 May 1983: A8.

227. "Xizang Calls for Checking Population Growth," FBIS 126 (29 June 1983): Q1.

228. "Family Planning Becomes Popular in Xizang," FBIS 210 (28 Oct. 1983): Q1-Q2.

Chapter 9

1. Zhu Zhuo (1980): 12.

2. For a discussion of population density across China based on 1953 census data see Zhu Zhuo (1980). Recent density data are discussed in Zhang Zehou & Chen (1981): 44–46; and in Sun Jingzhi & Li (n.d.).

3. Tregear (1980): 19–27.

4. "Renmin Ribao Urges Attention to Land Problems," FBIS 73 (15 Apr. 1982): K3-K6.

5. Yu Ruihou & Li (1982): 70.

6. "Shijie Jingji Daobao Cited on Population Control," FBIS 81 (27 Apr. 1982): Q3-Q4. The latter two figures appear to refer to net migration.

7. Chou (1982): 54.

8. For other analyses of interprovincial population trends during the last three decades see Chou (1982) and Aird (1982a): 196–200.

9. "While this census is the third national population census taken in China since liberation, it is actually the first taken in Tibet." From "Outline of Census Work, Results in Xizang," JPRS 82226 (12 Nov. 1982): 174.

10. Yu Ruihou & Li (1982): 70.

11. Yan Quanshan, "Ningxia renkou xingbie jiegou" (Ningxia's population by sex), NXRB, 7 Jan. 1982: 3. For Qinghai see Yu Ruihou & Li (1982): 70–71.

12. "Chinese Participate in Tibet's Construction," SWB, no. 6189 (9 Aug. 1979): 17.

13. Details in the next four paragraphs are from Bernstein (1977): 26–30 and 143–56.

14. Chou (1982): 56.

15. "Hunan Holds Disaster Relief Conference in Changsha," FBIS 25 (6 Feb. 1981): P3.

16. Chou (1982): 56.

17. Chou (1982): 58; Lardy (1980): 16.

18. Liu Shuyi (1980): 3. One million catties = 500 metric tons = 551.27 tons.

19. "AFP: Unemployed Young People Demonstrate in Shanghai," FBIS 56 (24 Mar. 1981): O6.

20. For details see Bernstein (1977): 172–241.

21. Lee (1978): 20–39.

22. Cha-leng-ku-ssu (1958).

23. "Some Views on the Question of the Establishment of the Chuang Nationality Autonomous Region," CB, no. 451 (22 May 1957): 25.

24. "Guangxi People's Congress Discusses Autonomy Problems," FBIS 201 (15 Oct. 1980): P3.

25. Ma Weiliang (1980): 78.

26. For example see Dreyer (1976): 101, on the popularity of medical work among the minorities. On the benefits of education and literacy for a minority group, see Ko Wa, "The Development of Education in Inner Mongolia Over the Past 15 Years," CB, no. 683 (1 June 1962): 16–21.

27. For details see Dreyer (1976): 164–69.

28. See Dreyer (1976): 154, 171, for Ningxia, and Pillsbury (1981): 113, for Henan and Beijing. The Yunnan revolt, now known as the Shajien incident, is discussed in "China: The Other 60 Million," *Asiaweek* 50, no. 50 (21 Dec. 1979): 35.

29. Tretiak (1963): 3, 8–10; Dreyer (1976): 169–70.

30. Dreyer (1976): 214–15, discusses the 1967 uprising. The 1980–81 conflict is reported in Michael Weisskopf, "Ethnic Conflict in Strategic Western Province Alarms Peking," WP, 12 Sept. 1981: 1, 25; and in Ma Zheng (1981).

31. David Bonavia, "Deng Holds the Line," FEER 114, no. 47 (13 Nov. 1981): 26; Tony Walker, "Xinjiang, China's Land of Promise, Waiting in the Far West," AR 3, no. 2 (May 1982): 19; Dreyer (1982).

32. Wimbush (1981): vi.

33. Compiled in Wetzel (1979): 22. Sources: "Mainland Minorities," FBIS, 10 Aug. 1955; "The National Minority Problem," CNA, no. 232 (13 June 1958): 1–7; N. N. Cheboksarov. "Basic Stages in the Development of Ethnography in China," JPRS 16431 (30 Nov. 1962): 108; Dreyer (1976): 171.

34. Dreyer (1976): 169, 219.

35. Dreyer (1976): 170, quoted from PR, 13 Sept. 1963; Zunun Taypov, "History of Uighur National Liberation Movement in China Reviewed," JPRS 75699 (14 May 1980): 44.

36. AFP Moscow, 12 Sept. 1963, cited in Tretiak (1963): 5.

37. Moseley (1973): 120–21; Dowdle (1980): 101.

38. "PRC Increases Publication of Minority-language Textbooks," FBIS 52 (15 Mar. 1979): E10; "Implementation of Party's Policy on Minorities Ordered," JPRS 77730 (1 Apr. 1981): 7–9.

39. Butterfield (1979).

40. "The Chinese May be Loosening their Grip on Tibet," *The Economist*, 6 Oct. 1973: 37–38; Ward (1980): 231.

41. "'Renmin Ribao' Notes Aid to Minority Nationalities," JPRS 74800 (20

Dec. 1979): 106; "China: The Other 60 Million," *Asiaweek* 50, no. 50 (21 Dec. 1979): 35; Ma Weiliang (1980): 78.

42. "'Renmin Ribao' Commentator on Minority Nationalities," JPRS 74829 (27 Dec. 1979): 69.

43. Ibid.: 68.

44. Dreyer (1976): 161.

45. "China: The Other 60 Million," *Asiaweek* 50, no. 50 (21 Dec. 1979): 36.

46. "Kwangming Daily on History of Interracial Marriage," FBIS 190 (29 Sept. 1978): E6.

47. Sun Jingzhi (1981): 82; Dreyer (1982).

48. Ma Zheng (1981): 24–25.

49. "Xinjiang Issues Circular on Nationality Policies," FBIS 102 (26 May 1982): T5.

50. Xie Shusen & Chen (1984): 57.

51. Tian Fang (1984): 8–9.

52. Bai Jianhua (1982): 17–18; "Liaoning Census Circular," FBIS 168 (31 Aug. 1981): S1.

53. "Results of China's Census: Minority Nationalities," SWB, no. 7174 (4 Nov. 1982): 1. See also Wang Ke, "Manchu People Reaffirm Their Origins," CR 32, no. 8 (Aug. 1983): 50–52.

54. Dalai Lama's estimate. Ward (1980): 228.

55. Rapawy (1980): Table 1.

56. For details see Wimbush (1981).

57. Cha-leng-ku-ssu (1958): 14.

58. Huang Chang-lo, "Minority Nationalities in Yunnan Freed from the Bondage of Old Customs," SCMP, no. 1859 (23 Sept. 1958): 11.

59. "The Ninghsia Hui Autonomous Region—Background," SCMP, no. 1884 (29 Oct. 1958): 11.

60. "Some Views on the Question of the Establishment of the Chuang Nationality Autonomous Region," CB, no. 451 (22 May 1957): 23.

61. Zhang Tianlu & Chen (1983): 19.

62. Yu Ruihou & Li (1982): 70.

63. "Nationalities Minister Discusses Policy at Press Conference," FBIS 187 (25 Sept. 1979): L13.

64. Data compiled by Tretiak (1963): 3, 12.

65. Ward (1980): 240; Butterfield (1979).

66. Estimated by the U.S. Bureau of the Census, Center for International Research, World Cities Project, from information on population size and density in and contiguous to these cities.

67. Yu Sheng-fang, "Cheng-ch'ueh pa-wo hsin-chien ho k'uo-chien ch'eng-shih jen-k'ou te fa-chan," *Chien-she yueh-k'an* (Construction monthly), no. 11 (1957). Discussed in Koshizawa (1978): 10. The 1979 figure is from Zhang Qingwu (1979).

68. For discussions of government definitions of urban see Ullman (1961): 6; Orleans (1972): 59–63; Chang Sen-dou (1976): 399–400; Orleans (1982): 270–77; Aird (1982b): 279–82; Li Chengrui (1982b): 31; and Zhang Qingwu (1983): 52–54.

69. Hsieh I-yuan, "Delineation of Administrative Regions of the People's Republic of China," JPRS 650-D (14 Apr. 1959): 29–30; Ullman (1961): 6–10; "Text of Renmin Ribao Commentator on Collective Enterprises," FBIS 165 (23 Aug. 1979): L14; Communique on 1982 Census (1982): K3.

70. K. C. Tan (1981): 15; Liu Changxin & Cang (1980): 47–49.

71. Li Chengrui (1982b): 31–32; Wang Jin, "Zuohao renkou pucha de xuanchuan gongzuo" (Population census propaganda work must be done well), RKYJ, no. 2 (29 Mar. 1982): 33–34.

72. The 1949 estimate is from "Data on China's Population from 1949 to 1956," ECMM, no. 91 (22 July 1957): 22–23. Discussed in Orleans (1972): 62.

73. Percent urban for 1957 given in Zhang Zehou & Chen (1981): 41. Absolute figure derived from Hsueh Cheng-hsiu. "Tentative Treatise on the Relationship between Increase of Urban Population in Socialist Cities and Development of Industrial and Agricultural Production," SCMP, no. 3093 (4 Nov. 1963): 2. Discussed in Emerson (1971): 187–88.

74. Zhang Qingwu (1979): 3.

75. "Peng Dehuai Notes on Lushan Plenum Published," JPRS 77668 (25 Mar. 1981): 9.

76. Sources compiled and analyzed in Emerson (1971): 192.

77. Information in this paragraph is derived from Chang Sen-dou (1976) and Koshizawa (1978).

78. "National Conference of Urban Planners," SWB-WER, no. W1110 (26 Nov. 1980): 8.

79. Chen Xuguang (1982): 50. In the early 1980's, the political functions of the communes were transferred to the governments of newly formed townships with the same boundaries and small town center as the communes had.

80. Bao Guangqian, "Expansion of Medium-, Small-Sized Towns Discussed," JPRS 74665 (28 Nov. 1979): 24.

81. "Joint Directive of CCP Central Committee and State Council on Prevention of Blind Exodus of Rural Population," SCMP, no. 1682 (2 Jan. 1958): 3.

82. "Kirin's Wang En-mao Reports to Agricultural Conference," FBIS 37 (23 Feb. 1978): L6.

83. "Henan Punishes Cadres Violating Policy on Population Transfer," FBIS 43 (3 Mar. 1980): P1.

84. For details see Emerson (1982): 251–53; and Emerson (1983).

85. For examples see H. Y. Tien (1980b): 656–62.

86. "Anhui Ribao on Reducing Surplus Labor Supply," FBIS 105 (30 May 1979): O1.

87. "Joint Directive of CCP Central Committee and State Council on Prevention of Blind Exodus of Rural Population," SCMP, no. 1682 (2 Jan. 1958): 3.

88. Parish & Whyte (1978): 5–11.

89. Johnson & Johnson (1977): Chapter 4.

90. "Hunan Radio Comments on Drought, Related Problems," FBIS 222 (15 Nov. 1979): P5.

91. "Shoudu renkou buyao chaoguo yiqianwan" (The population of Beijing must not exceed 10 million), BJRB, 6 Oct. 1980: 1.

92. H. Y. Tien (1980b): 656.

93. Ibid.: 657–61.

94. Zhou Qichang (1981): 88.

95. Bernstein (1977): 63–70; Fung (1981): 16.

96. Bernstein (1977): 161–66; Laurence J. C. Ma (1977): 8; number married from "Chen Yung-kuei Report," FBIS 242 (15 Dec. 1978): E5.

97. "National Meeting on Training Educated Youth in Countryside," FBIS 16 (24 Jan. 1978): E18.

98. Feng Lanrui and Zhao Lukuan, "Dangqian woguo chengzhen laodongzhe de jiuye wenti" (The current problem of employment of China's urban laborers), ZGSHKX, no. 6 (Nov. 1981): 191.

99. See analysis in Bernstein (1977): 29–44.

100. "Chen Yung-kuei Report," FBIS 242 (15 Dec. 1978): E4.

101. "Liaoning Issues 'Emergency Circular' on Rusticated Youth," FBIS 143 (24 July 1979): S1-S2; "Youth Farewell," JPRS 73881 (23 July 1979): 56; "Shandong Holds Work Conference on Settling Educated Youth," FBIS 171 (31 Aug. 1979): O8-O9. The 800,000 figure is from "National Meeting Examines Policy on Educated Youth," FBIS 163 (21 Aug. 1979): L4-L5.

102. "Heilongjiang Holds Conference on Settling Jobless Youths," FBIS 124 (25 June 1980): S1; "Jilin's Wang Enmao Attends Educated Youth Work Conference," FBIS 138 (16 July 1980): S3-S4.

103. "Liaoning Takes Steps to Send Youth to Countryside," FBIS 135 (12 July 1979): S2.

104. "Shandong Holds Work Conference on Settling Educated Youth," FBIS 171 (31 Aug. 1979): O8-O9.

105. See, for example, "'Heilongjiang Ribao' Urges Educated Youth to Return to Countryside," JPRS 73263 (20 Apr. 1979): 17–18; "Shanghai Youths Urged to Return to Distant Jobs," FBIS 60 (27 Mar. 1979): O11; "Shanghai CYL Meeting on Youth Returning to Countryside," FBIS 119 (19 June 1979): O4-O5.

106. See, for example, "Peng Chong Receives Youths in Shanghai," FBIS 39 (26 Feb. 1979): G6-G8; "'Jiefang Ribao' Carries Letter on Youths Remaining in Shanghai," JPRS 73292 (24 Apr. 1979): 35–36; "Tianjin Radio Cites Wang Zhen's Speech to Educated Youth," FBIS 85 (30 Apr. 1979): R3.

107. David Holley, "Lost Generation in China Lashes Out," *Los Angeles Times*, 4 Apr. 1979: 34; "Yunnan Educated Youths Study Wang Zhen's Talk," FBIS 30 (12 Feb. 1979): J3.

108. "AFP Reports Educated Youth on Hunger Strike in Shaanxi," FBIS 4 (5 Jan. 1979): M1-M2; Gold (1980); "Shanghai CYL Discusses Troublemaking Youth," FBIS 28 (8 Feb. 1979): G2; "Shanghai Workers Urged to Return to Construction Site," FBIS 28 (8 Feb. 1979): G3; "Jiefang Ribao Reports on Shanghai Railway Incident," FBIS 30 (12 Feb. 1979): G1-G4.

109. "Hangzhou Educated Youth Block Traffic, Hold Gatherings," FBIS 30 (12 Feb. 1979): G1; "Jiangxi Youth Agree to Return to Countryside," FBIS 31 (13 Feb. 1979): G4-G5.

110. "Fuller Utilization of Manpower Resources Discussed," JPRS 76528 (2 Oct. 1980): 1–6.

111. Ibid.: 3, 6–11; Gold (1980): 762–70; Emerson (1983); Liu Zheng

(1981a): 8; "Urban Unemployed only Three Million, Six Million Placed in '81," AR 3, no. 2 (May 1982): 18.

112. "Shanxi Holds Conference on Educated Youth," FBIS 9 (12 Jan. 1979): K6; "Shaanxi Conference on Rustification of Educated Youths," FBIS 32 (14 Feb. 1979): M1; "Beijing Implements New Policy on Educated Youths Going to Countryside," FBIS 229 (25 Nov. 1980): R2.

113. "Educated Youth to be Shifted from Communes to Collective Farms," FBIS 217 (7 Nov. 1979): L12.

114. Quote is from "Yunnan Rustification Conference," JPRS 74829 (27 Dec. 1979): 93; the 1969–76 figures are from "Millions of Educated Youth Go To Countryside," FBIS 132 (8 July 1976): E3, analyzed in Bernstein (1977): 27–29.

115. "Beijing Implements New Policy on Educated Youths Going to Countryside," FBIS 229 (25 Nov. 1980): R1-R2.

116. "Beijing Depot Implements Residence Policy," FBIS 93 (11 May 1979): R2; "Wen Hui Bao: Shanghai Youths Return to Xinjiang," FBIS 61 (31 Mar. 1981): T3-T4.

117. "Quanmian he chaoe wancheng benshi jinnian jingji jihua" (Comprehensively overfulfill this year's municipal economic plan), WHB, 19 Apr. 1981: 3; "Youer ru tuo ru yuan nan ruhe jiejue" (How to resolve the difficulties in enrolling young children in child care centers and kindergartens), WHB, 9 Aug. 1981: 2.

118. "Benshi jihua shengyu gongzuo qude xin jinzhan" (Family planning work in Shanghai has made new progress), JFRB, 24 Sept. 1981: 2; "Shijie Jingji Daobao Cited on Population Control," FBIS 81 (27 Apr. 1982): O4.

119. Gu Yaode, "Shilun Hangzhoushi de renkou kongzhi he chengshi fazhan fangxiang" (A tentative discussion on population control in Hangzhou and the orientation of its development), RKYJ, no. 4 (29 July 1982): 31.

120. For example, see "Shaanxi Conference on Rustication of Educated Youths," FBIS 32 (14 Feb. 1979): M1.

121. "Guowuyuan guanyu yange kongzhi nongcun laodongli jin cheng zuogong he nongye renkou zhuan wei fei nongye renkou de tongzhi" (State Council circular on the strict control of rural laborers working in cities and agricultural population becoming nonagricultural), GWYGB, no. 27 (10 Feb. 1982): 885–87.

122. Tian Fang (1984): 11.

123. Population Research Delegation (1981): 17.

124. Liu Junde, "Shilun Jiangxisheng renkou de yanbian ji qi fazhan qushi" (The changing population of Jiangxi province and its future development), in *Renkou yanjiu lunwenji* (Collection of papers on population research), Shanghai, 1981: 79–80.

125. Tregear (1980): 130–39.

Chapter 10

1. Ludlow (1981): 6.
2. CIA (1978): Table 1 for industry and agriculture figures.
3. Grain output reported in USDA (1984): 12.
4. Liu Guoguang and Wang Xianming, "Dui woguo guomin jingji fazhan sudu

he bili guanxi wenti de tantao" (An exploration into the problems of the rate and balance of China's national economic development), ZGSHKX, no. 4 (1980): 19; discussed in Dernberger (1984): 101–3.

5. See Statistical Yearbook of China 1981 (1982): 185 on the use of chemical fertilizer.

6. USDA (1984): 12, 15, and 28.

7. United States Department of Agriculture, *China, Outlook and Situation Report*, Washington, D.C., 1984: 24.

8. "Renmin Ribao on Rural Responsibility Systems," FBIS 174 (9 Sept. 1981): K9.

9. Readers interested in comparing my future projections with those of other scholars are referred to: Y. C. Yu (1980); Song Jian et al. (1980); Lin Fude (1980); Coale (1981); Lambert (1981); Chen Pi-chao (1981): 88–95; "China's 'One-Child' Population Future," *Intercom* 9, no. 8 (Aug. 1981): 1, 12–14; Charles Chen & Tyler (1982); Yu Jingyuan (1983); "Nation's Population Growth Discussed," JPRS 84693 (7 Nov. 1983): 51–63; Nathan Keyfitz, "The Population of China," *Scientific American* 250, no. 2 (Feb. 1984): 38–47; Aird (1984); Tian Xueyuan (1984); Han Jingqing et al. (1984); Yu Jingyuan et al. (1984); and the continually updated estimates and projections of the China Branch, Center for International Research, U.S. Bureau of the Census.

10. On China's future optimum population size, see Song Jian, "Population Development—Goals and Plans," in Liu Zheng et al., *China's Population: Problems and Prospects*, Beijing, 1981: 28; Wu Kailiu, "Wei huodai shuli yige renkou fazhan de lichengbei" (To set a population growth milestone for future generations), GMRB, 17 June 1981: 3; Takashi Oka, "Can China Cut Population by 30% in 100 Years?" *Christian Science Monitor*, 4 Nov. 1981: 1, 9; Song Jian and Sun Yiping, "Food Resources, Maximum Population Which Can Be Supported Studied," JPRS 79882 (18 Jan. 1982): 40; Yu Jingyuan (1983); and Han Jingqing et al. (1984).

11. This has been mentioned in many sources, including Xu Xuehan, "Tiaozheng woguo renkou zaishengchan de guanjianxing juece" (Key policy decisions in readjusting the reproduction of China's population), GMRB, 29 Aug. 1981: 3; and Ren Tao and Yue Bing, "Population and Employment," BR 26, no. 13 (28 Mar. 1983): 18.

12. See Chapters 7 and 8 in this book and Peng Zhiliang, "Ba jihua shengyu gongzuo tigao dao yige xin shuiping" (Raise family planning work to a new level), RKYJ, no. 6 (1982): 21.

13. Gao Ersheng et al., "Shanghaixian qiyi gongshe shengyulü de duili fenxi" (A cohort analysis of fertility in the July First People's Commune in Shanghai county), RKYJ, no. 3 (29 May 1982): 46.

14. Wang Ziying et al. (1981): 72.

15. Xiong (1983): 59.

16. Cheng Du (1981): 4.

17. "Worker Sacked for Third Child," CD, 28 Jan. 1983: 1.

18. Luo Qiong, "Zan yi jihua shengyu wei rong de xin fengshang" (In praise of

the new fashion of considering family planning an honorable practice), RMRB, 23 Jan. 1983: 4.

19. Zhao Liren & Zhu (1983): 36.

20. Wang Mingyuan, "Shi tan jihua shengyu gongzuo de jiben tedian" (The basic characteristics of family planning work), JHSYB, 16 Mar. 1984: 3.

21. Cheng Du (1981): 8. See also "Zhege jueding hao" (This decision is good), TJRB, 30 Apr. 1981: 1; "Xuduo duzhe lai xin tichu buyao fangsong jihua shengyu gongzuo" (Letters from many readers urge no relaxation of family planning work), DZRB, 7 Oct. 1981: 3; "Commentary Stresses One-Child Policy," FBIS 212 (1 Nov. 1983): P2-P3.

22. Li Jieping & Shao (1983): 148.

23. See Zhang Xiluo and Yang Chuanxin, "Qianjin zhong de xin wenti" (New problems in the forward march), GMRB, 29 Sept. 1981: 2; Song Youtian (1982): 3; Zuo Xiantang, "Lun woguo nongcun renkou wenti" (On China's rural population problem), *Jingji wenti tansuo* (Inquiry into economic problems), no. 5 (20 Sept. 1982): 41–42; Gui Shixun (1983): 65.

24. "Renmin Ribao on Rural Population Policy," FBIS 31 (16 Feb. 1982): K11-K12.

25. Peng Zhiliang, "Tan jihua shengyu zhengce yao heqing heli" (Family planning policy must be fair and reasonable), JHSYB, 29 June 1984: 3.

26. Ibid.; Shen Guoxiang (1984): 3–4; Liang Jimin & Peng (1984): 3; "Guojia jishengwei juban dishi jishengwei zhuren xuexi yantaohui" (The State Family Planning Commission convened a meeting of the directors of prefectural and municipal family planning commissions for training, research, and discussion), JHSYB, 18 May 1984: 1; "Woguo jinyibu wanshan jihua shengyu de juti zhengce" (China takes a further step to refine the concrete policies on family planning), RMRB, 4 July 1984: 3.

27. Shen Guoxiang (1984).

28. Liang Jimin & Peng (1984): 3.

29. Wu Xuping, "Buyi suiyi fangkuan ertai zhibiao" (It is inadvisable to soften the restrictions on a second child), JHSYB, 21 Sept. 1984: 3; "Rumor on Permission for Second Child Refuted," FBIS 85 (1 May 1984): P1; Hu Fuqiang, "Guangdong sheng, Guangzhou shi lianhe zhaokai jihua shengyu gongzuo dongyuan dahui" (A mobilization meeting on family planning work was jointly held by Guangdong province and Guangzhou Municipality), RKJJ, no. 4 (25 Aug. 1984): 63.

30. "Nei Monggol Denies Family Planning Policy Change," FBIS 112 (8 June 1984): R7-R8.

31. "National Population Conference Closes 28 March," FBIS 62 (30 Mar. 1983): K14-K15; "Yixiang jiaqiang woguo jihua shengyu gongzuo kexue guanli de zhongyao cuoshi" (An important measure for strengthening the scientific management of China's family planning work), RKJJ, no. 2 (25 Apr. 1983): 13–14; Xu Zugen, "Weishenme yao zhiding renkou quhua?" (Why is it necessary to delimit population zones?), *Banyuetan* (Semi-monthly tribune), no. 8 (25 Apr. 1983): 21–22; "Quanguo renkou fazhan quyu guihua jiang zhiding" (Regional

population growth plans will soon be drafted), RMRB, 6 Aug. 1983: 1; "Regional Population Growth Plans to be Prepared," CD 3, no. 634 (9 Aug. 1983): 3; Wang Lingling, "Quanguo wushi duo ge xian jinxing renkou quyu guihua shidian" (More than 50 counties throughout the country carried out experiments in regional population planning), JHSYB, 12 Oct. 1984: 1.

32. State Family Planning Commission, "Zou Zhongguoshi de jihua shengyu gongzuo daolu" (Take the Chinese road to family planning work), JHSYB, 28 Sept. 1984: 1.

33. Xin Lin, "A Realistic Population Policy," BR 27, no. 30 (23 July 1984): 4.

34. Cheng Du, "Hubeisheng nongcun shengyulü diaocha" (A fertility survey in rural areas of Hubei province), RKYJ, no. 5 (29 Sept. 1982): 31.

35. Zhu Qingfang, "Sanzhong quanhui yilai nongye shengchan fazhan qingkuang" (The development of agricultural production since the third central plenary session), TJ, no. 2 (17 Apr. 1982): 29.

36. "Renmin Ribao on Rural Population Policy," FBIS 31 (16 Feb. 1982): K11.

37. "Guangfan kaizhan 'san puji' jiaoyu, tigao qunzhong shixing jihua shengyu de zijuexing" (Extensively carry out education in the 'three popularizations' to raise the consciousness of the masses in practicing family planning), RKYJ, no. 6 (29 Nov. 1982): 27.

38. "Jihua shengyu yao zhenzheng dangcheng dashi lai zhua" (Family planning must be carried out as an important matter), FJRB, 6 Mar. 1982: 2; Song Youtian (1982): 3; "Qinghai Issues Provision on Birth Control," FBIS 115 (15 June 1982): T4; "Bo Yibo Stresses Propaganda on Population," FBIS 218 (10 Nov. 1982): K21; "Shanxi Promulgates Planned Parenthood Regulations," JPRS 82678 (19 Jan. 1983): 65; "Cheng Shuyan xuanchuan jihua shengyu jiazhong bei za" (Cheng Shuyan's home was smashed because she publicized family planning), LNRB, 11 Jan. 1983: 1; and "Family Planning Personnel Protected," JPRS 82842 (10 Feb. 1983): 178, respectively.

39. "Bodyguards Needed," FEER 119, no. 7 (17 Feb. 1983): 7.

40. Zhang Xiluo and Yan Chuanxin, "Tamen zai zhi nan er jin" (They know the difficulties and yet push forward), GMRB, 27 Sept. 1981: 2.

41. Bo Yibo, "Kongzhi renkou yao tong shixian fan liangfan de zhanlue mubiao tong bu jinxing" (Population control must march in step with the strategic target of quadrupling output), JKB, 28 Nov. 1982: 2.

42. "Guangxi zhuangzu zizhiqu dangwei diyi shuji Qiao Xiaoguang shuo bixu zhuozhong jiejue zhua jihua shengyu pa fan cuowu de sixiang" (Qiao Xiaoguang, First Secretary of the Party Committee of the Guangxi Zhuang Nationality Autonomous Region, says we should emphasize dispelling the thought of being afraid of making a mistake by carrying out family planning work), JHSYB, 17 Aug. 1984: 1.

43. Taylor (1985a); Taylor (1985b); Arriaga & Banister (1985).

44. Emerson (1982): 249, argues that the ability of China's agricultural sector to absorb more labor in the future is not good.

45. The age range selected is arbitrary. A narrower or broader range would lead to similar conclusions.

46. Chen Muhua, "Controlling Population Growth in a Planned Way," BR 22, no. 46 (16 Nov. 1979): 18; Tso (1978b): 15.

47. Zhao Changxin (1981): 64.

48. E. A. Hammel, "The Consequences of Diminished Fertility on Population Growth and of Diminished Growth on the Socioeconomic System," in E. A. Hammel, *The China Lectures*, Berkeley, Calif., 1983: 52–53, U. C. Berkeley Program in Population Research Working Paper no. 10.

49. Sweden, National Central Bureau of Statistics, *Statistical Abstract of Sweden 1979, vol. 66*. Stockholm, 1979: 41; Deutsche Demokratische Republik, Staatlichen Zentralverwaltung fur Statistik, *Statistisches Jahrbuch 1980 der Deutschen Demokratischen Republik*, Berlin, 1980: 350; United Nations Department of International Economic and Social Affairs, *Selected Demographic Indicators by Country, 1950–2000: Demographic Estimates and Projections as Assessed in 1978*, New York, 1980: 158, 168.

50. "Japan: Implications of the Aging Population," *Asian Pacific Population Programme News* 10, no. 4 (1981): 35.

51. "Elderly Americans Now 12 Percent of Population; Increased Income, Longevity Improve Life-Style," *Family Planning Perspectives* 16, no. 3 (May/June 1984): 143–44.

52. World Health Organization, "Fertility, Family and Health: Some Current Issues," in United Nations Department of International Economic and Social Affairs, *Fertility and Family; Proceedings of the Expert Group on Fertility and Family, New Delhi, 5–11 January 1983*, New York, 1984: 358; Zheng Guizhen, "Shanlao zunlao shi kongzhi nongcun renkou de zhanlue cuoshi" (To support and respect the elderly is a strategic measure for controlling rural population growth), SH 3, no. 2 (Apr. 1983): 26–29; Liu Junji, "Chutan nongmin yanglao xingshi dui shengyu de yingxiang" (The effects on childbearing of the form of care for the rural elderly), SH 3, no. 6 (Nov. 1983): 20–22; Alice Goldstein and Sidney Goldstein, "The Challenge of an Aging Population in the People's Republic of China," presented at the annual meeting of the Population Association of America, Minneapolis, May 1984.

53. "Birth Control Meeting in Chengdu Addressed by Chen Muhua," SWB, no. 6317 (12 Jan. 1980): 13; "'Tianjin Daily' on Planned Parenthood," SWB, no. 6334 (1 Feb. 1980): 7 (see also "Scientists Predict Various Rates of Future Population Growth," FBIS 33, 15 Feb. 1980: L12-L13); Lin Fude and Zhou Qing, "Shifang County: Family Planning," in Liu Zheng et al., *China's Population: Problems and Prospects*, Beijing, 1981: 168; "Qian Xinzhong jiu jihua shengyu zhanxian ruhe dizhi jingshen wuran wenti fabiao tanhua yao dui 'renkou jueding lun' de cuowu sixiang baochi jingti" (Qian Xinzhong talked about the problem of resisting spiritual pollution on the family planning front. Vigilance must be maintained against the erroneous thought of 'population determinism'), JKB, 1 Nov. 1983: 1; and Zhou Shujun, "Prospects for China's Population in 2000," BR 27, no. 14 (2 Apr. 1984): 22, respectively.

54. CCP Central Department of Propaganda and State Council Family Planning Leadership Group, "Kongzhi woguo renkou zengzhang de xuanchuan yao-

dian" (An outline of propaganda for controlling population growth in China), RKYJ, no. 2 (Apr. 1981): 2.

55. See also Tian Xueyuan (1984): 49–52 in the Chinese version and 203–6 in the English version.

56. For a more refined measure of the burden of elderly dependents in the future—China's parent:progeny ratio—see Arriaga & Banister (1985).

57. Long Guangrong, "Renzhen kai hao xiaokou qieshi duzhu dakou" (Earnestly do well in opening a small gap and effectively close the big gap), JHSYB, 19 Oct. 1984: 3.

58. A reevaluation of the one-child policy at the end of this century in order to avert severe aging of the future population was suggested in Liu Zheng, Wu Cangping, and Lin Fude, "Dui kongzhi woguo renkou zengzhang de wudian jianyi" (Five recommendations for controlling population growth in China), RKYJ, no. 3 (Oct. 1980): 4.

59. Gui Shixun (1983): 64.

60. Wu Cangping, "Shanghai Journal on Future Demographic Problems," FBIS 8 (12 Jan. 1984): K5.

61. Tian Xueyuan (1983): 3.

62. Tian Xueyuan (1984).

63. See, for example, Yu Jingyuan (1983); Han Jingqing et al. (1984); Yu Jingyuan et al. (1984).

Bibliography

The items in the Bibliography are arranged in strict alphabetical order according to the short form used in the Notes. Under each author, the listings are arranged by date. The primary sources whose complete citations are given in the Notes are not repeated here.

Acharya, Meena. "Time Use Data from Nepalese Villages: Policy Implications," presented at the annual meeting of the Population Association of America, Washington, D.C., Mar. 1981.

Aird, John S. *The Size, Composition, and Growth of the Population of Mainland China*. Washington, D.C., 1961. U.S. Bureau of the Census, International Population Statistics Reports, Series P-90, no. 15.

———. "Population Policy and Demographic Prospects in the People's Republic of China." In U.S. Congress, Joint Economic Committee, *People's Republic of China: An Economic Assessment*. Washington, D.C., 1972: 220–331.

———. *Population Estimates for the Provinces of the People's Republic of China: 1953 to 1974*. Washington, D.C., 1974. U.S. Department of Commerce, Bureau of Economic Analysis, International Population Reports, Series P-95, no. 73.

———. "Fertility Decline and Birth Control in the People's Republic of China," PDR 4, no. 2 (June 1978): 225–53.

———. 1981a. "Current Prospects for Demographic Research in the People's Republic of China." In Robert J. Lapham and Rodolfo A. Bulatao, eds., *Research on the Population of China: Proceedings of a Workshop*. Washington, D.C.: 5–17.

———. 1981b. "Fertility Decline in China." In Nick Eberstadt, ed., *Fertility Decline in the Less Developed Countries*. New York: 119–227.

———. 1982a. "Recent Demographic Data from China: Problems and Prospects." In U.S. Congress, Joint Economic Committee, *China under the Four Modernizations*. Washington, D.C.: 171–223.

———. 1982b. "Population Studies and Population Policy in China," PDR 8, no. 2 (June 1982): 267–97.

———. "Future Implications of Alternative Family Planning Policies," presented at the Workshop on China's 1982 Population Census, Honolulu, Dec. 1984.

———. 1985a. "Coercion in Family Planning: Causes, Methods, and Consequences." In U.S. Congress, Joint Economic Committee, *The Chinese Economy in the Eighties*. Washington, D.C., 1985.

———. 1985b. *Official Population Data of the People's Republic of China*. Washington, D.C., unpublished manuscript.

Akhtar, Shahid. *Health Care in the People's Republic of China, a Bibliography with Abstracts*. Ottawa, 1975.

Arena, Jay M. "China's Children," *Nutrition Today* 9, no. 5 (Sept.-Oct. 1974). 20–25.

Arriaga, Eduardo E., and Judith Banister. "The Implications of China's Rapid Fertility Decline," presented at the Twentieth General Conference of the International Union for the Scientific Study of Population, Florence, June 1985.

Ashton, Basil, Kenneth Hill, Alan Piazza, and Robin Zeitz. "Famine in China, 1958–61," PDR 10, no. 4 (Dec. 1984): 613–45.

Atlas of Cancer Mortality (1979). Editorial Committee for the Atlas of Cancer Mortality in the People's Republic of China, eds. *Atlas of Cancer Mortality in the People's Republic of China*. Shanghai.

Bagozzi, Richard P., and M. Frances Van Loo. "Toward a General Theory of Fertility: A Causal Modeling Approach," *Demography* 15, no. 3 (Aug. 1978): 301–20.

Bai Jianhua. "Tianxiehao renkou pucha biao shi tigao renkou pucha zhiliang de guanjian" (The key to raising census quality is to fill out census questionnaires well), TJ, no. 2 (17 Apr. 1982): 17–18.

Balfour, Marshall C., Roger F. Evans, Frank W. Notestein, and Irene B. Taeuber. "China (Excluding Taiwan)." In *Public Health and Demography in the Far East, Report of a Survey Trip, September 13-December 13, 1948*. New York, 1950: 71–87.

Banister, Judith. 1977a. "Mortality, Fertility and Contraceptive Use in Shanghai," CQ, no. 70 (June 1977): 255–95.

———. 1977b. "The Current Vital Rates and Population Size of the People's Republic of China and Its Provinces." Ph.D. dissertation, Stanford University. University Microfilms order no. 7808759.

———. "What is China's True Fertility Level?" Presented at the annual meeting of the Population Association of America, Washington, D.C., Mar. 1981.

———. 1984a. "China's Census and the Decade Beyond." In Norton Ginsburg and Bernard A. Lalor, eds., *China: The 80s Era*. Boulder, Colo.: 173–91.

———. 1984b. "An Analysis of Recent Data on the Population of China," PDR 10, no. 2 (June 1984): 241–71.

———. 1984c. "Population Policy and Trends in China, 1978–83," CQ, no. 100 (Dec. 1984): 717–41.

———. 1984d. "Implications of Sex Ratio Data from China's 1982 Census," presented at the Workshop on China's 1982 Population Census, Honolulu, Dec. 1984.

———, and Samuel H. Preston. 1981a. "Mortality in China," PDR 7, no. 1 (Mar. 1981): 98–110.

———, and Preston. 1981b. "Estimates of Completeness of Death Recording in the Chinese Sample Survey 1972–1975." In Robert J. Lapham and Rodolfo A. Bulatao, eds., *Research on the Population of China: Proceedings of a Workshop*. Washington, D.C.: 22–39.

———, and Shyam Thapa. *The Population Dynamics of Nepal*. Honolulu, 1981.

Bao Ruo-Wang (Jean Pasqualini) and Rudolph Chelminski. *Prisoner of Mao*. New York, 1973.

Barclay, George W., Ansley J. Coale, Michael A. Stoto, and T. James Trussell. "A Reassessment of the Demography of Traditional Rural China," PI 42, no. 4 (Oct. 1976): 606–35.

Becker, Gary, and H. G. Lewis. "On the Interaction Between Quantity and Quality of Children," JPE 82, no. 2, part 2 (Mar.-Apr. 1973): S279–88.

Bernstein, Thomas P. *Up to the Mountains and Down to the Villages; The Transfer of Youth from Urban to Rural China*. New Haven, Conn., 1977.

Birdsall, Nancy. "An Introduction to the Social Science Literature on 'Woman's Place' and Fertility in the Developing World," *Smithsonian Institution Interdisciplinary Communications Program Annotated Bibliography* 2, no. 1 (30 Sept. 1974): 1–39.

Blakeslee, A. "Chinese Medicine: A Truly Great Leap Forward," *Saturday Reviews* (N.Y.), no. 1 (23 Oct. 1973): 70–73.

Bongaarts, John. "Does Malnutrition Affect Fecundity? A Summary of Evidence," *Science* 208 (9 May 1980): 564–69.

Bowers, John Z. "The History of Public Health in China to 1937." In Myron E. Wegman, Tsung-yi Lin, and Elizabeth F. Purcell, eds., *Public Health in the People's Republic of China*. New York, 1973: 26–45.

Brass, William. *Methods for Estimating Fertility and Mortality from Limited and Defective Data*. Chapel Hill, N.C., 1975.

Bruk, S.I. "Distribution of National Minorities in the People's Republic of China." In Stephen P. Dunn and Ethel Dunn, eds., *Introduction to Soviet Ethnography, vol.* 2. Berkeley, Cal., 1974: 629–54.

Buck, John Lossing. *Land Utilization in China*. Nanjing, 1937.

Burnashev, E. Yu. "Public Health in People's China," *Zdravookhranenie rossiiskoi federatsii* (Public health in the Russian Federation), no. 11 (Nov. 1958): 35–41.

Butterfield, Fox. "Assignment Tibet—And Many Chinese Don't Like It," NYT, 29 July 1979.

Cai Shangzhong. *Renkou jichu zhishi* (Basic knowledge about population). Beijing, 1982.

Caldwell, John C. "A Theory of Fertility: From High Plateau to Destabilization," PDR 4, no. 4 (Dec. 1978): 553–77.

———. "Education as a Factor in Mortality Decline, an Examination of Nigerian Data," PS 33, no. 3 (Nov. 1979): 395-413.

———, and Pat Caldwell. "The Achieved Small Family: Early Fertility Transition in an African City," SFP 9, no. 1 (Jan. 1978): 2–18.

———, and K. Srinivasan. "New Data on Nuptiality and Fertility in China," PDR 10, no. 1 (Mar. 1984): 71–79.

Cancer Investigation Report (1980). PRC Ministry of Public Health, Cancer Prevention and Treatment Research Office. *Zhongguo exing zhongliu siwang diaocha yanjiu* (Cancer mortality investigation and research in China). Beijing.

CCAS (1972). Committee of Concerned Asian Scholars. *China! Inside the People's Republic.* New York.

Cha-leng-ku-ssu. "A Large Han Population is an Important Condition for Rapid Development of Inner Mongolia Autonomous Region," SCMP, no. 1725 (6 Mar. 1958): 14–19.

Chalmers, Iain. Unpublished travel notes of a visit to the PRC, 1977.

Chandrasekhar, Sripati. *China's Population: Census and Vital Statistics.* Hong Kong, 1959.

Chang Kai (1957). "Speech by Vice Minister of Public Health Chang Kai," Beijing Xinhua, 30 Mar. 1957.

Chang, Roberta. "Report on China." Unpublished travel notes of a visit to China, June 1979.

Chang Sen-dou. "The Changing System of Chinese Cities," *Annals of the Association of American Geographers* 66 (Sept. 1976): 398–415.

Chen, Charles H. C., and Carl W. Tyler. "Demographic Implications of Family Size Alternatives in the People's Republic of China," CQ, no. 89 (Mar. 1982): 65–73.

Ch'en Chien-hung and Yung Ch'eng-wen. "Hsin Chung-kuo fei-hsi-ch'ung-ping fang chih yen-chiu te chin-chan" (Progress in investigating the prevention and treatment of paragonimiasis in new China), CJP 10, no. 6 (3 Nov. 1959): 474–76.

Chen Hai-feng. Lecture on the public health agreement between the U.S. and China, Honolulu, 16 Nov. 1979.

Chen Lihsin. "Population Planning in China," *Pakistan Economic and Social Review* 11, no. 3 (Autumn 1973): 231–38.

Chen Muhua. "Shixian sige xiandaihua, bixu youjihuadi kongzhi renkou zengzhang" (Realization of the four modernizations hinges on planned control of population growth), RMRB, 11 Aug. 1979: 2.

———. "Fazhan renkou kexue wei kongzhi renkou zengzhang mubiao fuwu" (To develop population science in the service of controlling population growth), RKYJ, no. 3 (July 1981): 1–7.

Chen Pi-chao. 1980a. "Population Policy and the Rural Health System in China," mimeo.

———. 1980b. "Birth Planning." In *Rural Health in the People's Republic of China, Report of a Visit by the Rural Health Systems Delegation, June 1978.* Washington, D.C.: 105–26. National Institutes of Health Publication no. 81–2124.

———. 1980c. "The Birth Planning Program," presented at the China Population Analysis Conference, Honolulu, May 1980.

———. *Rural Health and Birth Planning in China.* Research Triangle Park, N.C., 1981.

———. "The Evolution of China's Birth Planning Policy." Appendix A in U.S. Congress, Office of Technology Assessment, *World Population and Fertility Planning Technologies: The Next Twenty Years.* Washington, D.C., 1982: 205–19.

———, and Adrienne Kols. "Population and Birth Planning in the People's Republic of China," *Population Reports* 10, no. 1 (Jan.-Feb. 1982): 577–618.

———, and Ann Elizabeth Miller. "Lessons from the Chinese Experience: China's Planned Birth Program and Its Transferability," SFP 6, no. 10 (Oct. 1975): 354–66.

Ch'en Ta. "New China's Population Census of 1953 and Its Relations to National Reconstruction and Demographic Research," prepared for the meeting of the International Statistical Institute, Stockholm, Aug. 1957.

Chen Wen-chieh and Ha Hsien-wen. "Medicine and Health Work in New China," mimeo. Montreal, 1971.

Chen Xuguang. "Population Control Seen as Vital for Economic Progress," JPRS 81393 (29 July 1982): 41–52.

Cheng Chu-yuan. "Health Manpower: Growth and Distribution." In Myron E. Wegman, Tsung-yi Lin, and Elizabeth F. Purcell, eds., *Public Health in the People's Republic of China*. New York, 1973: 139–57.

Cheng Du. "Woguo renkou zhengce de jige wenti ji qi jiejue tujing" (China's population policy: some problems and the prospects for their solution), *Wuhan daxue xuebao, shehui kexue ban* (Wuhan University journal, social sciences edition), no. 3 (28 May 1981): 3–9.

Cheng Hsiang. "Population Growth Reported Set to Rise," JPRS 79892 (19 Jan. 1982): 84.

Chiao Chi-ming, Warren S. Thompson, and D. T. Chen. *An Experiment in the Registration of Vital Statistics in China*. Oxford, Ohio, 1938.

Chien Hsin-chung and I. G. Kochergin. *Zdravookhranenie i meditsina v Kitaiskoi narodnoi respublike* (Public health and medicine in the People's Republic of China). Moscow, 1959.

Chin, Edwin, Jr. Unpublished group travel notes for PRC trip, 5–25 Mar. 1975.

Chinese Journal of Tuberculosis (1958). "Mu-ch'ien chieh-ho-ping te liu-hsing-ping-hsüeh tiao-ch'a kung-tso chung ts'un-tsai-che shen-me wen-t'i?" (What problems now exist in the epidemiological survey of tuberculosis?), editorial, *Chinese Journal of Tuberculosis* 6, no. 4 (11 July 1958): 273–74.

Chou Weizhi. "Past, Likely Future Trends in Migration Discussed," JPRS 79882 (18 Jan. 1982): 51–60.

Chu Fu-t'ang. "Chien-kuo shih-nien-lai erh-t'ung pao-chien shih-yeh te ch'eng-chiu" (Achievements in child health care in the ten years since liberation), CJP 10, no. 5 (3 Sept. 1959): 367–73.

Chu, Leonard L. *Planned Birth Campaigns in China 1949–1976*. Honolulu, 1977. East-West Communication Institute Case Study no. 5.

CIA (1978). Central Intelligence Agency, National Foreign Assessment Center. *China: Economic Indicators*. Washington, D.C.

Circular on Sample Vital Rate Survey (1983). "Guowuyuan bangongting zhuanfa guojia tongjiju, guojia jihua shengyu weiyuanhui, guowuyuan disanci renkou pucha lingdao xiaozu guanyu renzhen zuohao 1983-nian renkou biandong qingkuang chouyang diaocha gongzuo de yijian de tongzhi" (The Office of State Council Circulars transmits the opinions of the State Statistical Bureau, the State Family Planning Commission, and the State Council Leadership Group for the Third Population Census concerning conscientiously doing well in the sample survey of 1983 population changes), GWYGB, no. 18 (20 Sept. 1983): 822. (State Council Office issue no. 71, 31 Aug. 1983.)

Coale, Ansley J. "Population Trends, Population Policy, and Population Studies in China," PDR 7, no. 1 (Mar. 1981): 85–97.

———. *Rapid Population Change in China, 1952–1982*. Washington, D.C., 1984. National Academy of Sciences, Committee on Population and Demography, Report no. 27.

———, and Paul Demeny. *Regional Model Life Tables and Stable Populations*. Princeton, N.J., 1966.

Communique on 1953 Census (1954). State Statistical Bureau. "Communique of Results of Census and Registration of China's Population," CB, no. 301 (1 Nov. 1954): 1–2.

Communique on 1979 Economic Plan (1980). People's Republic of China, State Statistical Bureau. "Communique on Fulfillment of China's 1979 National Economic Plan," FBIS 85 (30 Apr. 1980): L1-L10. Also in PR 23, no. 19 (12 May 1980): 12–15; continued in PR 23, no. 20 (19 May 1980): 20–24.

Communique on 1980 Economic Plan (1981). People's Republic of China, State Statistical Bureau. "'Text' of Communique on 1980 Economic Plan," FBIS 82 (29 Apr. 1981): K7-K16. Also published as *Communique of the State Statistical Bureau of the People's Republic of China on Fulfillment of China's 1980 National Economic Plan*. Beijing.

"Communique on 1982 Census," FBIS 208 (27 Oct. 1982): K2-K5.

Communique on 1982 Economic Plan (1983). People's Republic of China, State Statistical Bureau. "'Text' of PRC 1982 Economic Plan Communique," FBIS 85 (2 May 1983): K1-K16.

Communique on the Fertility Survey (1983). State Family Planning Commission. "Quanguo qianfenzhiyi renkou shengyulü chouyang diaocha gongbao" (Communique on the 0.1 percent sample fertility survey of China's population), RKYJ, no. 3 (29 May 1983): 14–15.

Communique on 1983 Economic Plan (1984). People's Republic of China, State Statistical Bureau. "PRC Statistical Bureau Communique on 1983 Plan," FBIS 85 (1 May 1984): K2-K14.

Coombs, Lolagene C., and Te-hsiung Sun. "Family Composition Preferences in a Developing Culture: The Case of Taiwan, 1973," PS 32, no. 1 (Mar. 1978): 43–64.

Croizier, Ralph. "Medicine and Modernization in China: An Historical Overview." In Arthur Kleinman, Peter Kunstadter, E. Russell Alexander, and James L. Gale, eds., *Medicine in Chinese Cultures: Comparative Studies of Health Care in Chinese and Other Societies*. Washington, D.C., 1975: 21–35.

Croll, Elisabeth J. *The Politics of Marriage in Contemporary China*. Cambridge, England, 1981.

Cui Fengyuan. "Population Policy, Relation to Present Situation Outlined," JPRS 79882 (18 Jan. 1982): 1–9.

Cunningham, William J. "Report on the Visit to the People's Republic of China and Indonesia, by the Delegation from the United States Committee for UNICEF, 31 March to 15 April 1980," mimeo. New York, 1980.

Davies, Derek. "Traveller's Tales," FEER, 30 Sept. 1977: 21.
DeBakey, Michael E. *A Surgeon's Diary of a Visit to China*. Phoenix, Arizona, 1974.
Demographic Yearbook (annual). United Nations Department of Economic and Social Affairs, Statistical Office. *Demographic Yearbook*. New York.
Demographic Yearbook Historical Supplement (1979). United Nations Department of International Economic and Social Affairs. *Demographic Yearbook Historical Supplement*. New York.
Dernberger, Robert F. "China's New Economic Development: Problems and Prospects." In Norton Ginsburg and Bernard A. Lalor, eds., *China: The 80s Era*. Boulder, Colo., 1984: 99–143.
———, and David Fasenfest. "China's Post-Mao Economic Future." In U.S. Congress, Joint Economic Committee, *Chinese Economy Post-Mao, Vol. 1, Policy and Performance*. Washington, D.C., 1978: 3–47.
Dixon, Ruth B. "Women's Rights and Fertility," RPFP, no. 17 (Jan. 1975): 1–20.
Djerassi, Carl. 1974a. "Fertility Limitation Through Contraceptive Steroids in the People's Republic of China," SFP 5, no. 1 (Jan. 1974): 13–30.
———. 1974b. "Some Observations on Current Fertility Control in China," CQ, no. 57 (Jan.-Mar. 1974): 40–62.
Dowdle, Nancy. "The Dai People: A National Minority in the Chinese Revolution." M.A. thesis, University of Hawaii, 1980.
Dreyer, June Teufel. *China's Forty Millions*. Cambridge, Mass., 1976.
———. "The Role of the National Minorities in the Sino-Soviet Dispute," lecture at George Washington University, Washington, D.C., 25 Oct. 1982.
Durand, John D. "The Population Statistics of China, A.D. 2–1953," PS 13, no. 3 (Mar. 1960): 209–56.
Emerson, John Philip. *Nonagricultural Employment in Mainland China: 1949–1958*. Washington, D.C., 1965. U.S. Bureau of the Census, International Population Statistics Reports, Series P-90, No. 21.
———. "Manpower Training and Utilization of Specialized Cadres, 1949–68." In John W. Lewis, ed., *The City in Communist China*. Stanford, Calif., 1971: 183–214.
———. *Administrative and Technical Manpower in the People's Republic of China*. Washington, D.C., 1973. U.S. Department of Commerce, Bureau of Economic Analysis, International Population Reports, Series P-95, no. 72.
———. "Growth of Nonagricultural Employment in the People's Republic of China," presented at the China Population Analysis Conference, Honolulu, May 1980.
———. "The Labor Force of China, 1957–80." In U.S. Congress, Joint Economic Committee, *China under the Four Modernizations*. Washington, D.C., 1982: 224–67.
———. "Urban School-leavers and Unemployment in China," CQ, no. 93 (Mar. 1983): 1–16.
Encyclopedic Yearbook of China 1980 (1980). *Zhongguo baike nianjian, 1980* (Encyclopedic yearbook of China, 1980). Shanghai.

Encyclopedic Yearbook of China 1982 (1982). *Zhongguo baike nianjian, 1982* (Encyclopedic yearbook of China, 1982). Beijing.

Encyclopedic Yearbook of China 1983 (1983). *Zhongguo baike nianjian, 1983* (Encyclopedic yearbook of China, 1983). Beijing.

Enderton, Catherine Schurr. "Geographical Notes from a China Diary: March 1975," *The China Geographer*, no. 1 (Spring 1975): 39–47.

Epstein, Sarah G. "Family Values Study Group, May 1978," *Draper Fund Report*, no. 8 (Mar. 1980): 22.

Fan Jinchun. "Kongzhi renkou zengzhang gaohao sihua jianshe" (Control population growth and do well in building the four modernizations), *Shehui kexue yanjiu* (Social science research), no. 6 (15 Nov. 1981): 76–80.

Fan P'ei-lu, Yü Ting-hsin, and Su Tsu-fei. "Erh-t'ung kuo-ch'ung-ping hui-ch'ung-ping chi jao-ch'ung-ping fang chih kung-tso te ch'ing-k'uang" (Prevention and treatment of hookworm, ascariasis, and enterobiasis in childhood), CJP 10, no. 5 (3 Sept. 1959): 424–29. (Excerpts.)

Faundes, Anibal, and Tapani Luukkainen. "Health and Family Planning Services in the Chinese People's Republic," SFP 3, no. 7 (Supplement, July 1972): 165–76.

Fei Xiaotong. "Szechuan: Calamity and Recovery," CR 28, no. 1 (Jan. 1979): 59–63.

Felsenfeld, O. "Epidemiology of Infectious and Parasitic Diseases." In *Topics of Study Interest in Chinese Medicine and Public Health: Report of a Planning Meeting*. Washington, D.C., 1972. U.S. Department of Health, Education, and Welfare Publication no. 72–395.

Feng Zhonghui. "Shaanxisheng yuling funü hunyin yu shengyu zhuangkuang" (Marital status and fertility of women of childbearing age in Shaanxi province), RKYJ, no. 2 (29 Mar. 1982): 36–40.

Fertility Survey (1984). China Population Information Centre. *Analysis on China's National One-per-Thousand-Population Fertility Sampling Survey*. Beijing.

Foege, William. "Surveillance and Antiepidemic Work." In *Rural Health in the People's Republic of China, Report of a Visit by the Rural Health Systems Delegation, June 1978*. Washington, D.C., 1980: 93–104. National Institutes of Health Publication no. 81–2124.

Fraser, Stewart E. "One Is Fine, Two Is More than Adequate," FEER 106, no. 40 (5 Oct. 1979): 61–62.

———. "Make Posters, Not Babies," FEER 112, no. 27 (26 June 1981): 77.

Freedman, Ronald, Tze-Hwa Fan, Sou-Pen Wei, and Mary Beth Weinberger. "Trends in Fertility and in the Effects of Education on Fertility in Taiwan, 1961–74," SFP 8, no. 1 (Jan. 1977): 11–18.

Frejka, Tomas. *The Future of Population Growth, Alternative Paths to Equilibrium*. New York, 1973.

Fung, K. I. "China's City Regions: Agricultural Land Use Planning," presented at the annual meeting of the Canadian Association of Geographers, Corner Brook, Newfoundland, Canada, 1981.

Germain, Adrienne. "Status and Roles of Women as Factors in Fertility Behavior: A Policy Analysis," SFP 6, no. 7 (July 1975): 192–200.
Gingras, G., and D. A. Geekie. *China Report.* Ottawa, 1973.
Gold, Thomas B. "Back to the City: The Return of Shanghai's Educated Youth," CQ, no. 84 (Dec. 1980): 755–70.
Goldman, Noreen. "Far Eastern Patterns of Mortality," PS 34, no. 1 (Mar. 1980): 5–19.
Groen, Henry J., and James A. Kilpatrick. "China's Agricultural Production." In U.S. Congress, Joint Economic Committee, *Chinese Economy Post-Mao, Vol. 1, Policy and Performance.* Washington, D.C., 1978: 607–52.
Gu Xingyuan, Li Jieping, Shu Baogang, and Qi Xinju. "Shanghai: Family Planning." In Liu Zheng et al., *China's Population: Problems and Prospects.* Beijing, 1981: 136–52.
Gui Feng. "Yao ba sixiang jiaoyu gongzuo baizai shouwei" (Ideological education must be top priority), GMRB, 27 May 1982: 2.
Gui Shixun. "Bashi niandai Shanghai renkou tedian yu renkou pucha" (The distinguishing features of Shanghai's population in the 1980's and the population census), JFRB, 17 June 1982: 4.
———. "Diqijiang: Weilai renkou ziran biandong yao youli yu shehui de fazhan" (Lecture VII: The rate of natural population change must be favorable to social development), SH, no. 4 (Aug. 1983): 61–65.
Han Jingqing, Lee-Jay Cho, Griffith Feeney, and Zhao Qinghua. "Controlling the Population Transition," presented at the Workshop on China's 1982 Population Census, Honolulu, Dec. 1984.
Han Suyin. "Population Growth and Birth Control in China," *Eastern Horizon* 12, no. 5 (1973): 8–16.
He Mi. "Dali tichang he guli yidui fufu zhi sheng yige haizi" (Vigorously promote and encourage one child per couple), RKJJ, no. 1 (25 Feb. 1981): 32–34.
Ho Ch'eng. "Chung-hsi-i t'uan-chieh yü chung-i te chin-hsiu wen-t'i" (The problem of uniting doctors of Chinese and Western medicine and giving advanced training to doctors of Chinese traditional medicine), JMJP, 13 June 1950.
Ho Ch'i. "Studies on Malaria in New China," CMJ 84, no. 8 (Aug. 1965): 491–97.
Holm, Charles F. "Social Security and Fertility: An International Perspective," *Demography* 12, no. 4 (Nov. 1975): 629–44.
Horn, Joshua S. *Away with All Pests, an English Surgeon in People's China: 1954–1969.* New York, 1969.
Hou T. C., Chung H. L., Ho L. Y., and Weng H. C. "Achievements in the Fight Against Parasitic Diseases in New China," CMJ 79 (Dec. 1959): 493–520.
Hou Wenruo. "Population Policy." In Liu Zheng et al., *China's Population: Problems and Prospects.* Beijing, 1981: 55–76.
Hsin-hua Hospital Ophthalmology Report (1970). Hsin-hua Hospital Ophthalmology Department. *Prevention and Treatment of Common Ophthalmic Diseases.* Shanghai.
Hu Ch'uan-k'uei. "Medical Conditions in the Northwest," CB, no. 109 (20 Aug. 1951): 1–6.

——— et al. "Shih-nien lai p'i-fu hsing-ping hsüeh-k'o te ch'eng-chiu" (Achievements in dermatology and venerology in the past ten years), *Chung-hua p'i-fu-k'o tsa-chih* (Chinese journal of dermatology) 7, no. 5 (Oct. 1959): 290–94.

Hu Huanyong. "Nation's 'Serious' Population Problem Examined," JPRS 77764 (7 Apr. 1981): 65–71.

Huang Kun-Yen. "Infectious and Parasitic Diseases." In Joseph R. Quinn, ed., *Medicine and Public Health in the People's Republic of China*. Washington, D.C., 1973: 239–62.

Ivory, Paul E., and William R. Lavely. "Rustication, Demographic Change, and Development in Shanghai," AS 17, no. 5 (May 1977): 440–55.

Jain, Anrudh K. "The Effect of Female Education on Fertility: A Simple Explanation," *Demography* 18, no. 4 (Nov. 1981): 577–95.

Jain, K. K. "Glimpses of Chinese Medicine 1971: Changes with the Cultural Revolution," *Canadian Medical Association Journal*, no. 106 (Jan. 1972): 46–50.

Janowitz, Barbara S. "An Analysis of the Impact of Education on Family Size," *Demography* 13, no. 2 (May 1976): 189–98.

Jiang Zhenghua, Zhang Weimin, and Zhu Liwei. "A Preliminary Study of Life Expectancy at Birth for China's Population," presented at the International Seminar on China's 1982 Population Census, Beijing, Mar. 1984.

Jin Qi. "Rural Population," BR 25, no. 44 (1 Nov. 1982): 3.

Johnson, Elizabeth, and Graham Johnson. *Walking on Two Legs, Rural Development in South China*. Ottawa, 1977.

Joint Investigation Team (1983). "Nongcun jihua shengyu gongzuo de yixiang zhongda cuoshi" (An important step in rural family planning work), JKB, 3 Apr. 1983: 2.

Ju Genhua. "Tichang nongcun yi sheng liangtai de yuling fufu ziyuan zuo jiezha" (Encourage rural couples of childbearing age who already have two children to volunteer for sterilization), JKB, 16 Jan. 1983: 2.

Jung Ch'in. "Anti-tuberculosis Work in New China," SCMP, no. 1692 (16 Jan. 1958): 15–17.

Kane, Penny. Unpublished travel notes of a trip to China, 3–23 Nov. 1975.

Kannisto, Väinö, and Y. C. Yu. "Plans and Preparations for the 1982 Population Census of China," presented at the meeting of the International Union for the Scientific Study of Population, Manila, Dec. 1981.

King, Haitung, and Frances B. Locke. "Selected Indicators of Current Health Status and Major Causes of Death in the People's Republic of China: An Historical Perspective." In John L. Scherer, ed., *China Facts & Figures Annual, Vol. 6, 1983*. Gulf Breeze, Fla., 1983: 375–422.

Kirin Medical College Revolutionary Committee. "*Ch'ih-chiao i-sheng*" *p'ei-hsün chiao-ts'ai* (Teaching material for fostering and training "barefoot doctors"). Peking, 1971.

Knodel, J., and E. van de Walle. "Lessons from the Past: Policy Implications of Historical Fertility Studies," PDR 5, no. 2 (June 1979): 217–45; excerpted as "Development Without Family Planning Will Not Speed, and May Hinder, Fertility Decline," IFPP 5, no. 4 (Dec. 1979): 163–65.

Koshizawa, Akira. "China's Urban Planning: Toward Development Without Urbanization," *The Developing Economies* 16, no. 1 (Mar. 1978): 3–33.

Ku Yu-lin, Pao T'ung-min, Ch'ien Shao-chung, and Liu Li-kuei. "Nung-ts'un erh-t'ung pao-chien tsu-chih shih-tien yen-chiu" (A pilot study of rural child health organizations), CJP 14, no. 1 (10 Feb. 1965): 2–6.

Kung Chien-chang and Huang Shen-chi. "Malaria Control in China, with Special Reference to Bioenvironmental Methods of Control," CMJ, n.s. 2, no. 3 (May 1976): 195–202.

Lambert, André. *The Population of China*. Louvain, Belgium, 1981. Université Catholique de Louvain, Département de Démographie, Working Paper no. 105.

Lamm, Steven H., and Victor W. Sidel. "Appendix E: Analysis of Preliminary Public Health Data for Shanghai, 1972." In Victor W. Sidel and Ruth Sidel, *Serve the People: Observations on Medicine in the People's Republic of China*. New York, 1973: 238–66.

Lampton, David M. *The Politics of Medicine in China: The Policy Process, 1949–1977*. Boulder, Colo., 1977.

Lardy, Nicholas R. "Food Consumption in the People's Republic of China," unpublished 1980.

Larson, Ann. *Patterns of Contraceptive Use Around the World*. Washington, D.C., 1981.

Lee, James. "Migration and Expansion in Chinese History." In William H. McNeill and Ruth S. Adams, eds., *Human Migration, Patterns and Policies*. Bloomington, Ind., 1978: 20–47.

Lei Xueyuan. "Planned Parenthood for National Minorities," JPRS 79882 (18 Jan. 1982): 79–85.

Li Baohua. "Assessment of the Accuracy of a Sampling Survey." In China Population Information Centre, *Analysis on China's National One-per-Thousand-Population Fertility Sampling Survey*. Beijing, 1984: 24–32.

Li Bing and Li Junyao. "Zhongguo exing zhongliu de siwang qingkuang ho fenbu tedian" (Special aspects of cancer mortality and distribution in China), *Chinese Journal of Oncology* 2, no. 1 (22 Mar. 1980): 1–10.

Li Chengrui. *Population Censuses in China*. Beijing, 1981.

———. 1982a. "Zhongguo renkou chushenglü he siwanglü de fazhan qushi" (The trend in the birth rate and death rate of China's population), RKYJ, no. 1 (29 Jan. 1982): 15–16.

———. 1982b. "Cong renkou pucha gongbao kan Zhongguo renkou de xianzhuang—jian lun Zhongguo renkou tongji shuzi de zhunquexing" (China's population as shown by the population census communique, and some comments on the accuracy of the Chinese population statistics), JJYJ, no. 12 (20 Dec. 1982): 28–38.

Li Choh-ming. *The Statistical System of Communist China*. Berkeley, Cal., 1962.

Li Fengping. "Zhengfu gongzuo baogao" (Government work report), ZJRB, 25 June 1982: 1–3.

Li, Frederick P. "Cancer Incidence in China, 1975–2000: Implications for Cancer Control," mimeo. Bethesda, Md., 1980.

Li Jieping and Shao Wei. "Single Children and their Mothers." In China Population Information Centre, *Analysis on China's National One-per-Thousand-Population Fertility Sampling Survey*. Beijing, 1984: 144–48.

Li Muzhen, "Zhongguo renkou wenti zhongdian zai nongcun" (The focal point of China's population problem is in the rural areas), RKJJ, no. 6 (25 Dec. 1982): 3–7.

Li Te Chuan. "Speech by Health Minister Li," FBIS 177 (12 Sept. 1957): BBB4-BBB7.

Li, Victor H. "Field Notes for 1973 Trip," unpublished travel notes.

Li Xiuzhen. "Dangqian jihua shengyu gongzuo de xingshi he renwu" (The present situation and tasks concerning planned birth), RKYJ, no. 1 (Apr. 1980): 3–5, 47.

Li Yijun. "1953-1982-nian woguo renkou zhongxin yanjiu" (The center of gravity of China's population, 1953–1982), ZGSHKX, no. 6 (10 Nov. 1983): 122, 125–26.

Liang Jimin and Peng Zhiliang. "Ying quanmian lijie zhengque guanche jihua shengyu zhengce" (The implementation of family planning policy should be understood correctly and fully), JHSYB, 13 Apr. 1984: 3.

Liaoning Provincial Statistical System. "Dalianshi 1980-nian renkou zhuangkuang chubu fenxi" (A preliminary analysis of the 1980 population of Dalian), CJWTYJ, no. 1 (1982): 75–78.

Lin Fude. "Projections of China's Population Growth," RKYJ, no. 2 (1980): 16–22.

———. "The Status-quo and Prospect of China's Population," presented at the Nineteenth General Conference of the International Union for the Scientific Study of Population, Manila, Dec. 1981.

Lin Furui and Chen Daiguang. *Henan renkou dili* (Population geography of Henan). Zhengzhou, 1983.

Lindbeck, John R. Unpublished travel notes of a visit to the PRC, 5–24 Apr. 1975.

Ling Rui-Zhu. "A Brief Account of 30 Years' Mortality of Chinese Population," *World Health Statistics Quarterly* 34, no. 2 (1981): 127–34.

Liu Changxin and Cang Kaiji. *Renkou tongji* (Population statistics). Beijing, 1980.

Liu Hsiang-yün. "Hsin chung-kuo erh-t'ung szu-ch'ung-ping fang chih kung-tso te chin-chan" (Progress in the prevention and treatment of filariasis in children in new China), CJP 10, no. 5 (1959): 429–31.

Liu, Lillian. "Social Welfare for the Elderly in the People's Republic of China," presented at the Mid-Atlantic Regional Conference of the Association of Asian Studies, College Park, Md., 17–18 Oct. 1981.

Liu Shuyi. "Tongji yao zhunque; xu li tongjifa" (Statistics must be accurate; it is necessary to establish a statistics law), RMRB, 21 Dec. 1980: 3.

Liu Xun. "Birth Control Policy Continues in Sichuan," JPRS 84640 (28 Oct. 1983): 73–78.

Liu Zheng. 1980a. "Laogu shuli you jihua kongzhi renkou zengzhang de zhanlue sixiang" (Firmly establish the strategic ideology of planned control of population growth), RMRB, 25 Feb. 1980: 5.

———. 1980b. "The Present Situation and the Development of China's Population," presented at the Beijing International Round Table Conference on Demography, Oct. 1980.

———. 1981a. "Population Planning and Demographic Theory." In Liu Zheng et al., *China's Population: Problems and Prospects*. Beijing, 1981: 1–24.

———. 1981b. "Targets and Policy of Population Control in China," presented at the meeting of the International Union for the Scientific Study of Population, Manila, Dec. 1981.

———. 1981c. "Chushenglü, shengyulü, zaishengchanlü" (Birth rates, fertility rates, and reproduction rates), RKYJ, no. 2 (Apr. 1981): 56–60.

Ludlow, Nicholas H. "World Bank Report: China's Options in the 1980's Hinge on Saving Energy," CBR 8, no. 4 (July-Aug. 1981): 6–8.

Lyle, Katherine Ch'iu. "Planned Birth in Tianjin," CQ, no. 83 (Sept. 1980): 551–67.

———, Sheldon J. Segal, Chih-cheng Chang, and Li-chuan Ch'ien. "Perinatal Study in Tientsin: 1978," mimeo, n.d.

Lythcott, George I. "Pediatric Health Care in the People's Republic." In National Academy of Sciences, Institute of Medicine, *Report of the Medical Delegation to the People's Republic of China, June 15-July 6, 1973*. Washington, D.C., 1973: 139–63.

Ma, Laurence J. C. "Counterurbanization and Rural Development: The Strategy of Hsia-hsiang," CS 15, nos. 8 and 9 (Aug.-Sept. 1977): 1–12.

Ma Weiliang. "Various Aspects of Nationality Question, Situation Discussed," JPRS 76883 (25 Nov. 1980): 78.

Ma Zheng. "Trouble Between Han, Uygur Minority Reported in Xinjiang," JPRS 78873 (1 Sept. 1981): 22–25.

Martin, Linda G. "A Modification for Use in Destabilized Populations of Brass' Technique for Estimating Completeness of Death Registration," PS 34, no. 2 (July 1980): 381–96.

Mason, Karen Oppenheim, and V. T. Palan. "Female Employment and Fertility in Peninsular Malaysia: The Maternal Role Incompatibility Hypothesis Reconsidered," *Demography* 18, no. 4 (Nov. 1981): 549–75.

Maternity and Child Care (1975). "Maternity and Child Care in China," SPRCP, no. 5885 (1 July 1975): 60–62.

Mathews, Jay. "One-child Family Plan Pushed by Chinese," *Sunday Star-Bulletin and Advertiser* (Honolulu), 2 Mar. 1980: A-23. (Washington Post Service.)

Mauldin, W. Parker, Nazli Choucri, Frank W. Notestein, and Michael Teitelbaum. "A Report on Bucharest, the World Population Conference and the Population Tribune, August 1974," SFP 5, no. 12 (Dec. 1974): 357–95.

Mechanic, David, and Arthur Kleinman. "Financing of Medical Care." In *Rural Health in the People's Republic of China, Report of a Visit by the Rural Health Systems Delegation, June 1978*. Washington, D.C., 1980: 17–22. National Institutes of Health Publication no. 81–2124.

Medical Experts (1980). "Medical Experts Advocate Eugenics, Birth Control," FBIS 168 (27 Aug. 1980): L14-L15.

Meek, Ronald L., ed. *Marx and Engels on the Population Bomb*. Berkeley, Calif., 1971.

Meijer, Marinus J. *Marriage Law and Policy in the Chinese People's Republic*. Hong Kong, 1971.

Minkowski, Alexander. "Care of Mother and Child." In Myron E. Wegman,

Tsung-yi Lin, and Elizabeth F. Purcell, eds., *Public Health in the People's Republic of China*. New York, 1973: 218–32.

Moseley, George V. H., III. *The Consolidation of the South China Frontier*. Berkeley, Calif., 1973.

Muñoz-Paraiso, Norma. "Information, Education, Motivation: Persuasion, Not Coercion," *Initiatives in Population* (Manila) 4, no. 3 (Sept. 1978): 12–16.

Narcotics Report (1953). "Slanderous Narcotics 'Report' of U.S.-directed Remnant KMT Clique Denounced by Central People's Government Spokesman," SCMP, no. 542 (31 Mar. 1953): 6–8.

Nee, Victor. "Peasant Household Individualism, the Collective Economy and the State," presented at the Conference on Bureaucracy and Rural Development in China, Chicago, Ill., Aug. 1981.

Ni, Ernest. *Distribution of the Urban and Rural Population of Mainland China: 1953 and 1958*. Washington, D.C., 1960. U.S. Bureau of the Census, International Population Reports, Series P-95, no. 56.

Nortman, Dorothy. *Voluntary Sterilization: Its Demographic Impact in Relation to Other Contraceptive Methods*. Honolulu, 1980. Papers of the East-West Population Institute, no. 65.

———. *Population and Family Planning Programs, A Compendium of Data through 1981*. New York, 1982.

Notestein, Frank W., and Chi-ming Chiao. "Population." In John Lossing Buck, *Land Utilization in China*. Nanjing, 1937: 358–99.

Orleans, Leo A. *Every Fifth Child: The Population of China*. Stanford, Calif., 1972.

———. "Family Planning Developments in China, 1960–1966: Abstracts from Medical Journals," SFP 4, no. 8 (Aug. 1973): 197–215.

———. *China's Population Policies and Population Data: Review and Update*. Washington, D.C., 1981.

———. "China's Urban Population: Concepts, Conglomerations, and Concerns." In U.S. Congress, Joint Economic Committee, *China under the Four Modernizations*. Washington, D.C., 1982: 268–302.

Parish, William L. "Birth Planning in the Chinese Countryside," presented at the annual meeting of the American Sociological Association, New York, Aug. 1976.

———. "The Family and Economic Change." In Norton Ginsburg and Bernard A. Lalor, eds., *China: The 80s Era*. Boulder, Colo., 1984: 222–42.

———, and Martin King Whyte. *Village and Family in Contemporary China*. Chicago, 1978.

Pediatrics Proposal (1965). "Kuan-yu mu-ch'ien k'ai-chan ch'eng-hsiang erh-t'ung pao-chien kung-tso te chien-i" (Proposal concerning the present undertaking of urban and rural child health work), CJP 14, no. 1 (10 Feb. 1965): 52–53.

People's Handbook (1957). *Jen-min shou-ts'e* (People's handbook). Beijing.

Pepper, Suzanne. "Chinese Education after Mao: Two Steps Forward, Two Steps Back and Back Again?," CQ, no. 81 (Mar. 1980): 1–65.

Perkins, Dwight H. *Agricultural Development in China, 1368–1968*. Chicago, 1969.

———. Unpublished travel notes of a visit to the PRC, July 1974.
PIACT (1980). "Contraceptive Use in China," *PIACT (Program for the Introduction and Adaptation of Contraceptive Technology) Product News* 2, no. 1 (1980): 1–8.
Pillsbury, Barbara L. K. "Islam 'Even unto China.'" In Philip H. Stoddard, David C. Cuthell, and Margaret W. Sullivan, eds., *Change and the Muslim World*. Syracuse, N.Y., 1981: 106–14.
Po I-po. "Three Years of Achievement of the People's Republic of China," CB, no. 218 (5 Nov. 1952): 8.
Population Research Delegation (1981). "Report on the Population Research Delegation Visit to the People's Republic of China, 9–25 April, 1981," mimeo. Washington, D.C.
Preston, Samuel H. *Mortality Patterns in National Populations*. New York, 1976.
———, Ansley J. Coale, James Trussell, and Maxine Weinstein. "Estimating the Completeness of Reporting of Adult Deaths in Populations That Are Approximately Stable," PI 46, no. 2 (Summer 1980): 179–202.
———, Nathan Keyfitz, and Robert Schoen. *Causes of Death: Life Tables for National Populations*. New York, 1972.
Price, R. F. *Education in Communist China*. New York, 1970.
Public Health Yearbook of China 1983 (1984). *Zhongguo weisheng nianjian (1983)* (Public health yearbook of China 1983). Beijing.
Qian Xinzhong. "Health Minister on Child Care," SWB-WER, no. W1036 (20 June 1979): 2.
———. "Health Minister Discusses Life Expectancy, Birth, Death Rates," FBIS 86 (1 May 1980): L4-L5.
Qie Jianwei. "Guanyu 'dusheng zinü lü' zhibiao de jisuan fangfa" (On methods of measuring the 'single-child rate'), RKYJ, no. 4 (Oct. 1981): 59–60.
Qiu Shuhua, Wu Shutao, and Wang Meizeng. "A Survey of China's Birth Control among Women of Child-Bearing Age." In China Population Information Centre, *Analysis on China's National One-per-Thousand-Population Fertility Sampling Survey*. Beijing, 1984: 139–44.
Rapawy, Stephen. "Census Data on Nationality Composition and Language Characteristics of the Soviet Population: 1959, 1970, and 1979," unpublished manuscript. Washington, D.C., 1980.
Rogers, Everett M. "Barefoot Doctors." In *Rural Health in the People's Republic of China, Report of a Visit by the Rural Health Systems Delegation, June 1978*. Washington, D.C., 1980: 43–62. National Institutes of Health Publication no. 81–2124.
Rong Shoude, Li Junyao, Gao Runquan, Dai Xudong, Cao Dexian, Li Guangyi, and Zhou Youshang. "Woguo 1973–1975 nian jumin pingjun qiwang shouming de tongji fenxi" (A statistical analysis of life expectancy in China, 1973–1975), RKJJ, no. 1 (1981): 24–31.
Rural Small-Scale Industries Delegation. Unpublished group travel notes from a visit to the PRC, June-July 1975.
Schistosomiasis Delegation Report (1977). "Report of the American Schistosomiasis Delegation to the People's Republic of China," *American Journal of Tropical Medicine and Hygiene* 26, no. 3 (1977): 427–62.

Shen Guoxiang. "A Brief Introduction to China's Family Planning Programme," presented at the International Population Conference, Mexico City, Aug. 1984.

Shen Yimin. "China's Population: Why There are More Males," CD, 8 Nov. 1982: 4.

Sidel, Victor W., and Ruth Sidel. *Serve the People: Observations on Medicine in the People's Republic of China*. New York, 1973.

Snail Fever Report (1976). "China Makes Remarkable Progress in Controlling Snail Fever," SPRCP, no. 6033 (12 Feb. 1976): 167–69.

Song Jian and Li Guangyuan. "Renkou fazhan wenti de dingliang yanjiu" (Quantitative research on the problem of population growth), JJYJ, no. 2 (20 Feb. 1980): 60–67.

Song Jian, Tian Xueyuan, Li Guangyuan, and Yu Jingyuan. "Guanyu woguo renkou fazhan mubiao wenti" (On the problem of the targets for China's population growth), RMRB, 7 Mar. 1980: 5.

Song Youtian. "Guanyu jihua shengyu gongzuo qingkuang de baogao" (Report on family planning work), *Shaanxi ribao* (Shaanxi daily), 9 Mar. 1982: 3.

SSB Indicators (1980). People's Republic of China, State Statistical Bureau. "Main Indicators, Development of the National Economy of the People's Republic of China (1949–1979)," mimeo. Beijing.

State Council Population Office (1982). Population Census Office under the State Council and Department of Population Statistics, State Statistical Bureau. *The 1982 Population Census of China (Major Figures)*. Hong Kong.

State Council Population Office (1983). Population Census Office under the State Council and Department of Population Statistics, State Statistical Bureau. *Zhongguo 1982-nian renkou pucha 10% chouyang ziliao* (The 10 percent sample tabulation of the 1982 population census of China). Beijing.

Statistical Abstract of China 1983 (1983). State Statistical Bureau. *Zhongguo tongji zhaiyao 1983* (Statistical abstract of China 1983). Beijing.

Statistical Abstract of China 1984 (1984). State Statistical Bureau. *Zhongguo tongji zhaiyao 1984* (Statistical abstract of China 1984). Beijing.

Statistical Yearbook of China 1981 (1982). State Statistical Bureau, comp. *Statistical Yearbook of China 1981*. English edition. Hong Kong.

Statistical Yearbook of China 1983 (1983). State Statistical Bureau, comp. *Statistical Yearbook of China 1983*. English edition. Hong Kong.

Stein, Z., M. Susser, G. Saenger, and F. Marolla. *Famine and Human Development*. London, 1975.

Stepan, Jan, Edmund H. Kellogg, and Phyllis T. Piotrow. "Legal Trends and Issues in Voluntary Sterilization," *Population Reports* 9, no. 2 (Mar.-Apr. 1981): 73–102.

Sterba, James P. "China Is Said to Have Understated Scale of 1980 Drought and Floods," NYT, 25 Apr. 1981: 1, 5.

Su Tsu-fei. "Hsin Chung-kuo fang chih erh-t'ung hsüeh-hsi-ch'ung te ch'eng-chiu" (Achievements in the prevention and treatment of childhood schistosomiasis in new China), CJP 10, no. 5 (1959): 422–24.

Su Xiufang. "Tigao renkou zhiliang luoshi yousheng cuishi" (Raise the quality of the population and implement measures for optimal quality births), RMRB, 4 July 1982: 3.

Sun Dongsheng. "Puji yousheng zhishi jiji tichang yousheng" (Popularize the knowledge of eugenics and vigorously advocate optimal quality births), RKYJ, no. 4 (Oct. 1981): 37–41.

Sun Jingzhi. "Economic Development—A Major Solution to Population Problem." In Liu Zheng et al., *China's Population: Problems and Prospects*. Beijing, 1981: 77–85.

———, and Li Muzhen. "Zhongguo renkou fenbu yu renkou kongzhi wenti" (China's population distribution and the problem of population control). In Beijing Center for Communication and Education on Family Planning, comp., *Renkou lilun xuan jiang* (Selected lectures on population theory). Beijing, n.d.: 170–88.

Sun Yefang. "Economic Journal on State of Statistics Work," FBIS 58 (26 Mar. 1981): L4-L9.

Taeuber, Irene B. "Colonial Demography: Formosa," PI 10 (1944): 147–57.

———, and Karl E. Taeuber. "The Fertility of the Chinese in Northeast China." In *Proceedings of the International Population Conference, Vienna, 1959*. Vienna, 1959: 348–54.

Tai Shih-kuang. "1953 Population Census of China," presented at the meeting of the Indian Statistical Institute of Calcutta, Dec. 1956, Calcutta.

Taiwan Demographic Fact Book 1973 (1974). China, Republic of, Ministry of the Interior. *1973 Taiwan Demographic Fact Book, Republic of China*. Taipei.

Tan, K. C. "The Four Modernizations and Chinese Urban Geography," presented at the annual meeting of the Canadian Association of Geographers, Corner Brook, Newfoundland, Aug. 1981.

Tan Manni. "Why New Marriage Law Was Necessary," CR 30, no. 3 (Mar. 1981): 17–21.

T'ang, F. F., H. L. Chang, Y. T. Huang, Y. F. Li, K. C. Wang, and P. L. Lu. "Studies on the Morphology, Growth Characteristics and Biology of Trachoma Agent," *Chinese Journal of Ophthalmology* 8 (Jan. 1958): 7–10.

Taylor, Jeffrey R. 1985a. "Labor Force Developments in the People's Republic of China, 1952–1983." In U.S. Congress, Joint Economic Committee, *The Chinese Economy in the Eighties*. Washington, D.C., 1985.

———. 1985b. *Employment and Unemployment in China: Results from Ten-Percent Sample Tabulation of 1982 Population Census*. Washington, D.C. U.S. Bureau of the Census Foreign Economic Report no. 23.

Teitelbaum, Michael S. "Not Everyone Can Hear a Population Explosion," NYT, 18 Aug. 1974: 1.

Ten Great Years (1960). People's Republic of China, State Statistical Bureau. *Ten Great Years, Statistics of the Economic and Cultural Achievements of the People's Republic of China*. Beijing.

Teng Chin-hsi. "1958-nien tung tsai Pei-ching liu-hsing te ying-yu-erh fei-yen te yen-chiu" (Study on the 1958 epidemic of pneumonia in Peking among infants and children), CJP 10, no. 6 (3 Nov. 1959): 21.

Thapa, Shyam, and Robert D. Retherford. "Infant Mortality Estimates Based on the 1976 Nepal Fertility Survey," PS 36, no. 1 (Mar. 1982): 61–80.

Thorborg, Marina. "Chinese Employment Policy in 1949–78 with Special Emphasis on Women in Rural Production." In U.S. Congress, Joint Economic

Committee, *Chinese Economy Post-Mao, Vol. 1, Policy and Performance.* Washington, D.C., 1978: 535–604.

Tian Fang. "Lun renkou shudao zai guotu zhengzhi zhong de diwei" (On the role of population migration in national land management), *Jingji wenti tansuo* (Inquiry into economic problems), no. 3 (20 Mar. 1984): 7–11.

Tian Xueyuan. "A Survey of Population Growth Since 1949." In Liu Zheng et al., *China's Population: Problems and Prospects.* Beijing, 1981: 32–54.

———. "Queding renkou fazhan zhanlue yaoyi kongzhi shuliang wei zhongdian" (Decisions on population growth strategy must emphasize controlling the size of the population), GMRB, 13 Nov. 1983: 3.

———. "Lun renkou nianling goucheng biandong he renkou guihua fangan de xuanze" (Changes in the age composition of the population and the selection of programs for population planning), ZGSHKX, no. 2 (Mar. 1984): 39–52. Tr. as "On Changes in the Age Composition of the Population and Policy Options for Population Planning," *Social Sciences in China* 5, no. 3 (Autumn 1984): 191–206.

T'ien Feng-t'iao. "Wo-kuo chi-hua sheng-yü ho jen-k'ou tseng-chih wen-t'i" (The problem of planned births and population increase in China), *Jen-min pao-chien* (People's health) 1, no. 5 (May 1959).

Tien, H. Yuan. 1980a. "Wan, Xi, Shao: How China Meets Its Population Problem," IFPP 6, no. 2 (June 1980): 65–73.

———. 1980b. "Age-Sex Statistics for China: What Do Recent National Disclosures and Local Figures Reveal?" PDR 6, no. 4 (Dec. 1980): 651–62.

———. "Age at Marriage in the People's Republic of China," CQ, no. 93 (Mar. 1983): 90–107.

Tongji Data Office. "Woguo disanci renkou pucha 10% chouyang ziliao zhaiyao" (Abstract of data from the ten percent sample of China's third population census), TJ, no. 2 (17 Feb. 1984): 20–25.

Tregear, T. R. *China, a Geographical Survey.* New York, 1980.

Tretiak, Daniel. "Peking's Policy Towards Sinkiang: Trouble on the 'New Frontier,'" CS 2, no. 24 (15 Nov. 1963): 1–13.

Tropical Medicine Delegation Report (1979). American Tropical Medicine Delegation to the People's Republic of China. "Tropical Medicine and Hygiene in Modern China," *Tropical Medicine and Hygiene News* 28, no. 3 (June 1979): 1–62.

Tsin Hsin-chung. "Nekotorye problemy zdravookhraneniia Kitaiskoi narodnoi respubliki" (Some problems of health services in the People's Republic of China), *Sovetskoe zdravookhraneniia* (Soviet public health), no. 6 (June 1958): 11–17.

Tso An-hua. 1978a. "Declining Population Growth," PR 21, no. 14 (7 Apr. 1978): 18–20.

———. 1978b. "Ideological Education in a Primary School," PR 21, no. 36 (8 Sept. 1978): 14–18.

Tsui, Wai-ying. "Regionalization and Accessibility of Rural Health Services in the People's Republic of China—A Comparative Case Study of the Huancheng and Doushan Communes." M.A. thesis, Chinese University of Hong Kong, 1979.

———. "Equity and Disparity in Access to Health Care," presented at the China Population Analysis Conference, Honolulu, May 1980.

Ullman, Morris B. *Cities of Mainland China: 1953 and 1958*. Washington, D.C., 1961. U.S. Bureau of the Census, International Population Reports, Series P-95, no. 59.

U.N. Concise Report (1974). United Nations Department of Economic and Social Affairs. *Concise Report on the World Population Situation in 1970–1975 and Its Long-Range Implications*. New York.

UNFAO (1975). "World Food and Agricultural Situation—February 1975," *United Nations Food and Agriculture Organization Monthly Bulletin of Agricultural Economics and Statistics* 24, no. 4 (Apr. 1975): 1–19.

U.N. Population Bulletin No. 6 (1963). United Nations Department of Economic and Social Affairs. *Population Bulletin of the United Nations No. 6—1962, with Special Reference to the Situation and Recent Trends of Mortality in the World*. New York.

U.N. Population Division (1981). United Nations Population Division. *New Model Life Tables for Developing Countries*. New York.

USDA (1981). U.S. Department of Agriculture. *Agricultural Situation in the People's Republic of China, Review of 1980 and Outlook for 1981*. Washington, D.C.

USDA (1984). U.S. Department of Agriculture. *Agricultural Statistics of the People's Republic of China, 1949–82*. Washington, D.C. Statistical Bulletin no. 714.

Vlassoff, M., and Carol Vlassoff. "Old Age Security and the Utility of Children in Rural India," PS 34, no. 3 (Nov. 1980): 487–99.

Wang Deyi. "Xin hunyinfa yu jihua shengyu" (The new Marriage Law and family planning), ZGFN, no. 11 (15 Nov. 1980): 42–43.

Wang Nairong. "Solving China's Population Problem," CR, Apr. 1980: 5.

———. "Woguo kongzhi renkou zengzhang zhengce de jige wenti" (Several problems concerning the policy of controlling China's population growth), RKYJ, no. 2 (Apr. 1981): 51–55.

Wang Weizhi. 1982a. "Tongguo renkou pucha tigao renkou tongji ziliao de zhiliang" (To improve the quality of demographic statistics through the population census), RKYJ, no. 1 (29 Jan. 1982): 41–42.

———. 1982b. "Shehui zhuyi zhidu jiasule renkou xiandaihua de jincheng" (The socialist system accelerates the process of population modernization), CJWTYJ, no. 3 (July 1982): 19–22, 35.

Wang Xinfa. "1953, 1964-nian woguo renkou pucha gongzuo de jingyan" (Our experiences with population censuses in 1953 and 1964), RKYJ, no. 2 (1980): 9–15.

Wang Ziying, Li Xiuyu, Peng Lianhong, and Song Jingan. "Beijingshi Mentougouqu Qingbaikou gongshe renkou jingji diaocha baogao" (Report of an investigation on the population and economy of Qingbaikou Commune of Mentougou Ward, Beijing Municipality), JJKX, no. 4 (20 Nov. 1981): 71–73.

Ward, Fred. "In Long-Forbidden Tibet," *National Geographic* 157, no. 2 (Feb. 1980): 218–59.

Wegman, Myron E. "Public Health Policy and Practice in the People's Republic of China." In National Academy of Sciences, Institute of Medicine, *Report of the Medical Delegation to the People's Republic of China, June 15-July 6, 1973*. Washington, D.C., 1973.

Wei Hsi-hua, Wang Ch'ung-lin, and Li Te-hung. "Shang-hai shih 1950-1956-nien erh-t'ung chieh-ho-ping kan-jan-lü" (The rate of tuberculosis infection among children in Shanghai, 1950–56), *Chung-hua chieh-ho-ping-k'o tsa-chih* (Chinese Journal of Tuberculosis) 6, no. 4 (11 July 1958): 275–78.

Weisskopf, Michael. "Devastating Drought Forces Reluctant China to Seek Foreign Help," WP, 6 Apr. 1981: A17.

Wetzel, Hayden M. "Big and Little Brother: Majority-Minority Relations in China," unpublished manuscript, 1979.

WHO Health Statistics Report (1979). Uemura, K., K. Kupka, and M. Subramanian. *Report on the WHO Technical Visit to the People's Republic of China by the Health Statistics (HST) Group, 28 June to 9 July 1979*. Manila.

Whyte, Martin King. "Family Change in China," *Issues and Studies* 15, no. 7 (July 1979): 48–62.

Willis, R. "A New Approach to the Economic Theory of Fertility," JPE 82 (Apr.-May 1973).

Wimbush, S. Enders. *Nationality Research in the People's Republic of China: A Trip Report*. Santa Monica, Calif., 1981.

Wolf, Arthur P., and Chieh-shan Huang. *Marriage and Adoption in China, 1845–1945*. Stanford, Calif., 1980.

World Bank. *China, Socialist Economic Development*. Washington, D.C., 1983.

World Population 1977 (1978). U.S. Bureau of the Census. *World Population 1977—Recent Demographic Estimates for the Countries and Regions of the World*. Washington, D.C.

World Population 1983 (1984). U.S. Bureau of the Census, *World Population 1983—Recent Demographic Estimates for the Countries and Regions of the World*. Washington, D.C.

World Population Conference Special Issue (1974). *People* 1, no. 5 (1974): 1–38.

Worth, Robert M. "Health Trends in China since the 'Great Leap Forward,'" *American Journal of Hygiene* 78, no. 3 (Nov. 1963): 349–57. Reprinted in CQ, no. 22 (Apr.-June 1965): 181–89.

———. "Recent Demographic Patterns in Kwangtung Province Villages," unpublished, n.d.

Wray, Joe D. Unpublished travel notes from a visit to the PRC, Nov. 1973.

Wu Banglan. 1981a. "Xin hunyinfa yu jihua shengyu" (The new Marriage Law and family planning), RKYJ, no. 2 (Apr. 1981): 16–18, 22.

———. 1981b. "Dangqian jihua shengyu gongzuo de zhongdian shi zhuahao wanhun wanyu" (The current emphasis of family planning work is to do well in deferred marriage and late birth), HLJRB, 3 Nov. 1981: 2.

Wu Yingkai. "Epidemiology and Community Control of Hypertension, Stroke, and Coronary Heart Disease in China." In World Health Organization Cardiovascular Diseases Team, "Report on the Visit to the People's Republic of China, 24 June-8 July 1979," mimeo. Manila, 1979: 13–22.

Wu Zhongguan, Yang Zhiheng, and Wang Maoxiu. "Shilun woguo renkou zaishengchan" (On population reproduction in China), RKYJ, no. 1 (Apr. 1980): 25–31.

Xiao Wencheng, Li Menghua, and Wang Liyeng. "Changes in Total Fertility Rate Since 1950's." In China Population Information Centre, *Analysis on China's National One-per-Thousand-Population Fertility Sampling Survey*. Beijing, 1984: 58–62.

Xiao Zhenyu. "The Design of 1982's Fertility Sampling Survey in China." In China Population Information Centre, *Analysis on China's National One-per-Thousand-Population Fertility Sampling Survey*. Beijing, 1984: 11–23.

Xie Shusen and Chen Bing. "Qinghai de kaituo yu guonei yimin" (The opening of Qinghai and internal migration), JJYJ, no. 3 (1984): 54–58.

Xiong Yu. "Zhongguo renkou xuehui lishihui kuoda huiyi taolun woguo renkou yu shehui jingji wenti" (Population, social, and economic problems of China were discussed at the annual meeting of the Population Association of China), RKYJ, no. 2 (Mar. 1983): 59–60.

Xu Xuehan. "Tiaozheng woguo renkou zaishengchan de guanjianxing juece" (The key policy decision in the readjustment of China's population reproduction), GMRB, 29 Aug. 1981: 3.

Xue Xinbing. "Advances in Child Health Work in China," CJP 17, no. 4 (Nov. 1979): 193–96.

Yang Deqing. *Renkouxue gailun* (A general introduction to the study of population). Hebei, 1982.

Yang Xiaobing. "Planned Parenthood, Shandong Style," BR 26, no. 7 (14 Feb. 1983): 24–26.

Yang Xuetong. "Jihua shengyu shi woguo renkoushi fazhan de biran" (Birth planning is an inevitability in the history of China's population growth), RKYJ, no. 2 (1980): 51–60.

Ye Qiwen. "Influence of Heredity, Environment on Population," JPRS 78053 (12 May 1981): 30–31.

Yin Ming. *United and Equal, the Progress of China's Minority Nationalities*. Beijing, 1977.

Yü Chia-chün. *Ma-feng-ping-hsüeh kai-lun* (Introduction to leprosy). Shanghai, 1953.

Yu Jingyuan. "Theory of Population Control and Its Application to China," unpublished manuscript, 1983.

———, Tuan Chi-hsien, Xiao Zhenyu, Wang Yanzu, and Huang Ying. "Projecting the Trend of China's Population," presented at the Workshop on China's 1982 Population Census, Honolulu, Dec. 1984.

Yu Ruihou and Li Yanjun. "Some Solutions to Qinghai's Population Problems," JPRS 79882 (18 Jan. 1982): 69–75.

Yu Wang and Xiao Zhenyu. "A Brief Account of the National One-per-Thousand-Population Fertility Sampling Survey and Preliminary Analysis of Its Data." In China Population Information Centre, *Analysis on China's National One-per-Thousand-Population Fertility Sampling Survey*. Beijing, 1984: 3–11.

Yu, Y. C. "The Population Policy of China," PS 33, no. 1 (Mar. 1979): 125–42.

———. "A Projection of the Growth of Population for China, 1978–2028," presented at the China Population Analysis Conference, Honolulu, May 1980.

Yuan Fang, Cui Fengyuan, and Zhang Lizhong. *Xinzhongguo renkou de jihua shengyu he chushenglü jiangdi de chubu fenxi* (A preliminary analysis of planned births and the decline in the birth rate of new China's population). Beijing, 1980.

Zhang Huaiyu et al. *Renkou lilun gaishuo* (Introduction to population theory). Zhengzhou, 1981.

Zhang Lizhong. "Jieyu, wanhun yu renkou zengzhanglü de xiajiang" (Birth control, late marriage, and the decline in the rate of population increase), RKJJ, no. 1 (15 Sept. 1980): 35–39.

———. "Birth Control and Late Marriage." In Liu Zheng et al., *China's Population: Problems and Prospects*. Beijing, 1981: 111–18.

Zhang Peizhu. "WHO Specialist Stresses Need for Maternal, Child Care," JPRS 77179 (15 Jan. 1981): 117–18.

Zhang Qingwu. "Kongzhi chengshi renkou de zengzhang" (Control the growth of the urban population), RMRB, 21 Aug. 1979: 3.

———. *Hukou dengji changshi* (General information on household registration). Beijing, 1983.

Zhang Tianlu. "Youjihuadi fazhan woguo shaoshu minzu renkou cujin minzu fanrong" (Develop the population of China's minority nationalities in a planned way to promote their prosperity), RKJJ, no. 1 (1980): 27–34.

———, and Chen Xiuying. "Guizhou shaoshu minzu renkou fazhan he minzu fanrong wenti" (Population increase among the minority nationalities and the prosperity of the nationalities in Guizhou province), *Zhongyang minzu xueyuan xuebao* (Journal of the Central Nationalities Institute), no. 1 (15 Feb. 1983): 19–24.

Zhang Xiluo. "Jiangsu jihua shengyu gongzuo huo kexi chengji" (Jiangsu family planning work has achieved heartening results), GMRB, 8 Sept. 1981: 1.

Zhang Zehou and Chen Yuguang. "Shilun woguo renkou jiegou yu guomin jingji fazhan de guanxi" (On the relationship between population structure and economic development in China), ZGSHKX, no. 4 (10 July 1981): 29–46.

Zhao Beibei. "Woguo nongcun ertong baojian yanjiu jianxiao" (The child health project in rural China has achieved results), WHB, 16 May 1981: 1.

Zhao Changxin. "Yantai diqu kaizhan jihua shengyu gongzuo dailai de bianhua" (Changes brought about by launching the planned birth program in Yantai prefecture), RKYJ, no. 3 (July 1981): 41–42, 64.

Zhao Liren and Zhu Chuzhu. "Jihuawai ertai wenti chutan" (A preliminary inquiry into the problem of second births outside the plan), RKYJ, no. 3 (29 May 1983): 36–39.

Zhao Yugui. "Anhui Province: Population Growth and Planning." In Liu Zheng et al., *China's Population: Problems and Prospects*. Beijing, 1981: 153–58.

Zhejiang Regulations, 1982. "Zhejiangsheng jihua shengyu tiaoli (shixing caoan)" (Zhejiang province family planning regulations, tentative draft), ZJRB, 14 Mar. 1982: 3.

Zheng Guizhen. "Shanlao zunlao shi kongzhi nongcun renkou de zhanlue cuoshi"

(To support and respect the elderly is a strategic measure for controlling population growth), SH, no. 2 (Apr. 1983): 26–29.

Zhou Qichang. "Problems of Population Composition in New Cities Discussed," JPRS 77764 (7 Apr. 1981): 88.

Zhou Qing and Xiong Yu. "Some Perceptions on Minority Population Development," JPRS 81460 (5 Aug. 1982): 75–83.

Zhu Minzhi. "Chen Muhua tong Ruidian wanghou tan jihua shengyu" (Chen Muhua talked about planned birth with the queen of Sweden), *Banyuetan* (Semi-Monthly Tribune), no. 19 (10 Oct. 1981): 8–9.

Zhu Zhengzhi. "Dangqian woguo renkou wenti ji qi fazhan qushi" (China's present population problem and its trend of development), JJKX, no. 3 (1980): 54–58.

Zhu Zhuo. "Shilun woguo renkou heli fenbu wenti" (On the problem of the rational distribution of China's population), RKYJ, no. 3 (Oct. 1980): 11–17.

Index

Library of Congress Cataloging-in-Publication Data

Banister, Judith, 1943–
China's changing population.

Bibliography: p.
Includes index.
1. China—Population. 2. China—Population policy.
3. Birth control—Government policy—China. I. Title.
HB3654.A3B36 1987 304.6'0951 82-60105
ISBN 0-8047-1155-0 (alk. paper)